ANNIE ADAMS FIELDS

Annie Adams Fields

WOMAN OF LETTERS

Rita K. Gollin

University of Massachusetts Press

AMHERST AND BOSTON

Copyright © 2002 by University of Massachusetts Press
All rights reserved
Printed in the United States of America
LC 2001048091
ISBN 1-55849-313-1
Designed by Jack Harrison
Set in Monotype Dante with Deepdene display by Graphic Composition, Inc.
Printed and bound by Maple Vail Book Manufacturing Group

Library of Congress Cataloging-in-Publication Data

Gollin, Rita K., 1928–
    Annie Adams Fields : woman of letters / Rita K. Gollin.
        p. cm.
    Includes bibliographical references and index.
    ISBN 1-55849-313-1 (alk. paper)
    1. Fields, Annie, 1834–1915. 2. Authors, American—19th century—Biography.
3. Women and literature—Massachusetts—Boston—History—19th century. 4. Boston
(Mass.)—Intellectual life—19th century. 5. Boston (Mass.)—Biography. I. Title.

PS1669.F5 Z65
818'.409—dc21
[B]

                        2001048091

British Library Cataloguing in Publication data are available.

For my husband, our grandchildren,
and their parents

CONTENTS

Illustrations follow page 158.

PREFACE

At the time of her death, Annie Adams Fields (1834–1915) was primarily known as the widow of nineteenth-century Boston's major literary publisher, James T. Fields, and as the hostess of celebrated writers he had published—among them Nathaniel Hawthorne, Ralph Waldo Emerson, Harriet Beecher Stowe, and Charles Dickens. Seven years after she died, her literary executor Mark DeWolfe Howe perpetuated that identity in his *Memories of a Hostess: A Chronicle of Eminent Friendships Drawn Chiefly from the Diaries of Mrs. James T. Fields* (1922), from which she emerges as the publisher's charming wife, an animating presence in Boston's literary life during the 1860s and 1870s.

Though her interest and importance are hardly limited to those roles, it is useful to approach Annie Fields as an embodiment of genteel Boston. Born into privilege and raised in New England traditions of self-reliance and public service, she married into Boston's highest cultural echelon during a period of remarkable cultural efflorescence, and soon became known as a consummate hostess and a womanly woman—"one of the dearest little women in the world," as Dickens put it. The woman who from childhood on accepted period definitions of womanliness that required deference to men, and who revered literary genius, delighted in such praise even while lamenting that she never had enough time for projects of her own. Yet she was a fairly good poet, her celebrated friends leap to life from the pages of her journals, and she became an entrepreneurial philanthropist. Along the way, the genteel lady—who survived her husband by more than thirty years—exerted considerable power.

My book divides into two parts, the first covering the years of her marriage and the second her decades of widowhood, each focused on Annie Fields's personal relationships as they meshed with her personal, professional, and cultural goals and obligations. I follow her as she grew to authority without violating cultural norms that required womanly self-subordination. During her years of marriage with James T. Fields and her years of union with Sarah Orne Jewett, she struggled to reconcile her aspirations for self-fulfillment with service to others. Brilliant men and women were grateful for her hospitality and friendship, and other talented and ambitious women welcomed her help. She was also remarkably effective in the larger world, especially in her philanthropic work. Annie accepted conventional propriety yet stretched it. As Willa Cather put it, "she rose to meet a fine performance always—to the end." She also performed.

Through her journals, letters, poems, and memoirs, we can trace literary and cultural developments from the mid-nineteenth century to the transformed sensibility of the early modern period. We can also come to know Annie Fields; even her self-suppressions help define her. Through what she wrote and what others wrote to and about her, we can recuperate the enterprising Boston Lady who used what Cather recognized as her "great power to control and organize" in all her many roles and relationships.

I initially encountered Annie Fields through my interest in Nathaniel Hawthorne—through her *Nathaniel Hawthorne* (1899) and then through Sophia Hawthorne's letters of the early sixties to the much younger woman who was her beloved confidante. Willa Cather introduced me to her as a valorous survivor-custodian of America's cultural past. I then kept meeting her as a major source for biographers of writers she herself had memorialized (most of whom quoted Mark DeWolfe Howe's *Memories of a Hostess*). Reading Howe came next, followed by immersion in her journals and her voluminous correspondence.

I am indebted to the librarians of many archives for access to their holdings and for permission to quote from them. I have made extensive use of the journals of Annie Fields (from which all undocumented quotations are taken) and letters to and from her at the Massachusetts Historical Society, of the Fields Collection at the Huntington Library, San Marino, Calif., and of letters in the Boston Public Library Rare Books Department (Courtesy of the Trustees); and I have also used letters and other documents at the Schlesinger Library, Radcliffe Institute, Harvard University; the Boston Athenaeum; the Society for the Preservation of New England Antiquities; the Charles Dudley Warner Papers at the Watkinson Library, Trinity College Hartford, Conn.; the Robert Underwood Johnson Papers in the Rare Book and Manuscript Library of Columbia University; the Special Collections at Colby College, Waterville, Me.; the Richard Harding Davis Collection, Clifton Waller Barrett Library, the Albert H. Small Special Collections Library of the University of Virginia Library; the Cornell University Libraries; and the University of New Hampshire Library. For access to the papers of Annie Fields's brother Zabdiel Adams Jr., I am indebted to the librarians of the Countway Library at Harvard University.

For permission to quote from manuscripts in their care, I am also indebted to curators of The Henry W. and Albert A. Berg Collection of English and American Literature and the Manuscripts and Archives Division of The New York Public Library, Astor, Lenox and Tilden Foundations. And I owe a large debt of gratitude to the curators of the Houghton Library, Harvard University, for permission to quote seriatim from manuscripts bearing the shelf marks bMS Am 1844 (122) f.6, bMS Am 1844 (122) f.5, bMS Am 1784 (149), bMS Am 1784 (596), bMs Am 1648 (292), bMS Am 1743.1 (15), bMS Am 1743.1 (143), bMS Am 1524 (213), bMS Am 1587 (71), bMS Am 2016 (37), bMS Am 1854.1 (1293), bMS Am 1907.1 (444), bMS Am 1524 (457), bMS 1743 (344). bMS Am 1844 (122) f.1, bMS Am 1130.8 (1–144), bMS Am 1743 (255), bMS Am 1743 (71), bMS Am 1743.1 (103), bMS Am 1743.1 (117), MS Am 1745.2 (8), bMS Am 1743 (344), bMS Am 1844 (122), MS Am 1745.1 (17), MS Am 1743.25 (25), bMS Am 1844 (122) f.2, bMS Am 1844 (122) f.4, bMS Am 1844 (122) f.3, bMS Am 1844 (122) f.5, MS Am 1679, *AC85.F4604 872c, MS Am 1340.1, and bMS Am 1743 (255).

I owe a special debt to Mrs. Nancy Adams Bole (1909–1991), who showed me the many letters, paintings, photographs, furniture, and even dishes that once belonged to her great-aunt Annie Fields. And I thank Mitchell Adams—a cousin of Nancy Bole—for sharing his own collection of Fields letters and photographs.

My pursuit of Annie Fields also took me to the house in Manchester, Massachusetts, that she and her husband built, to the site of their Charles Street home, to Sarah Orne Jewett's house in South Berwick, Maine, and to Celia Thaxter's beloved Appledore Island. Of course, I also sought Annie Fields through her publications, her friends' recollections, and the portraits that display her enduring self-possession.

For the research, which has taken me more years than I care to count, I gratefully acknowledge the financial assistance of the National Endowment for the Humanities, the Huntington Library, the United University Professions, and the Geneseo Foundation. My deepest debt is to my husband, Richard Gollin, on whom I always depend for critical acumen and emotional sustenance—never more than while preparing this book.

RITA K. GOLLIN
Rochester, New York, and Mashpee, Massachusetts

ANNIE ADAMS FIELDS

INTRODUCTION

Life in the Great Garden

"Mrs. J. T. Fields Dies at Her Home; Widow of Former Boston Publisher," the *Boston Evening Transcript* announced on 5 January 1915, then elucidated:

> Mrs. Annie Adams Fields, the widow of James T. Fields, widely known more than a generation ago as a publisher in the firm of Ticknor & Fields, friend of Dickens and other leading people of the literary world both here and abroad, died this morning at her home, 148 Charles street, where she had lived for sixty years.[1]

The woman who had lived her own life for nearly thirty-four years after her husband's death would have been pleased to be identified primarily as his widow. The obituary goes on to list books by Annie Fields—four biographical volumes, two collections of poetry, and a charity manual—and it acknowledges her importance as a hostess.

Thirteen years earlier, another writer had seen something paradoxical in her life. "Gentle, quiet, and reserved as are the motions of her daily life, there is no power in Boston to-day like that of Mrs. Fields."[2]

Shortly before Annie died, a collection of essays appeared titled *Days and Ways in Old Boston,* edited by William S. Rossiter. One was unsigned—"Recollections of Old Boston, from a Conversation with a Boston Lady of the Period." As a local newspaper revealed, the lady was "none other than Mrs. James T. Fields."[3] Her recollections begin with the house on Pearl Street where Ann West Adams was born in 1834—"a delightful old house with a huge garden at the rear, which had been given to my father and mother at the time of their marriage." The garden was "generous" and "beautiful," an idyllic cultivated space. "I might almost say that my childhood was spent in a garden," the Boston Lady mused, "for the custom of leaving the city during all or parts of the summer months had not yet seized upon us."[4]

Her "childhood in the old mansion on Pearl Street and life in the great garden"

I

was protected but not confining. The garden received "the cooling breezes of the bay," school was nearby, and the whole world seemed within reach. By taking a few steps, the child could see the bay; and by crossing High Street, she could soon reach the harbor. There, lined up along the busy wharves, she could see the brigs and schooners that brought English and French fabrics for her annual "good dress of silk or satin or damask," household linen from Russia, and furs to be worn on sleighrides—perhaps to Quincy, home of her eminent Adams relatives.

"The decade from 1840 to 1850 looks dim and remote," the Boston Lady reflected after recalling her lost Eden, long since swallowed up by downtown Boston. She then quoted from the recent autobiography of a more famous survivor—Henry Cabot Lodge. His "Earliest Memories" also centered on a large house with an "ample garden," a "sunny and sheltered spot" where "it was possible to grasp one's little world" and "live contentedly within its limits." The passing of that little world seemed, Lodge wrote, a kind of slow continental drift: "The year 1850 stood on the edge of a new time, but the old time was still visible from it, still indeed prevailed upon it. The men and women of the elder time with the old feelings and habits were still numerous and for the most part quite unconscious that their world was slipping away from them. . . . But at all events it was entirely different from anything to be found today."[5] Characteristically, the "Boston Lady" ended her recollections by deferring to Lodge's. But by doing so, she appropriated them as her own.

For Annie Fields that "new time" began in 1854, when at the age of twenty she married James Thomas Fields, a man seventeen years her senior who had just become a partner in the thriving Boston bookselling and publishing firm of Ticknor and Fields. It might be argued that Annie did not even then leave the protected world of her girlhood: her bridegroom moved into her parents' house. It was more than a year before they found the house that seemed right for them, on a new landfill along the Charles River where "fine stately mansions were soon built, with a quiet street for a frontage and the river in the rear."[6]

The brownstone house first numbered 37 and later renumbered 148 Charles Street was not yet completed when James and Annie Fields first saw it, and its price seemed too high. But in May 1865, with the financial assistance of Ticknor and Fields, they moved in. Five years later they acquired the parcel behind it, which Annie soon turned into a flourishing garden with paths winding down to the river. The house was torn down after Annie died, and a garage now stands in its place, but she willed the garden to her neighbors whose land abutted it.[7]

During her lifetime but also afterward, friends rhapsodized about the domain that seemed as resistant to change as their hostess. To Sophia Hawthorne, it was an enchanted palace; to Willa Cather it was "a sanctuary from the noisy push of the present"; to Henry James it was "the little ark of the modern deluge." In her Charles Street house with its garden and the river beyond, as in her Manchester summer house with its garden sloping down to the sea, Annie did her best to reconstitute the Eden of her childhood.

Flowers were part of it. Gardening was a traditional "womanly" activity that fit into Annie's larger projects of creative self-extension and appreciation of natural beauty. She planted, tended, and exchanged seeds and slips with friends who were also gardening enthusiasts (including Celia Thaxter and Sarah Orne Jewett). Like them, she valued wild as well as cultivated flowers. Whittier sent her mayflowers each spring, Celia sent pussywillows, and Jamie marked birthdays and anniversaries with roses. Among the treasures preserved in her "Album of Fragrant Memories" in the 1860s are a rose from her husband, a violet leaf from Una Hawthorne, and a sprig of wild jasmine that Tennyson handed her. She always had fresh flowers in her house, and thought a dinner table without flowers was an abomination. She welcomed Charles Dickens to Boston in 1867 by filling his hotel room with flowers, and she marked the anniversaries of his death by bringing flowers to her working women's residence. Harriet Beecher Stowe and Oliver Wendell Holmes sometimes punningly addressed her as "Mrs. Meadows," but "Flower" was the nickname Celia Thaxter preferred. It seems wholly appropriate for the graceful woman who even in her seventies struck Willa Cather as "slight and fragile in figure, with a great play of animation in her face and a delicate flush of pink on her cheeks."[8]

Although she never blushed entirely unseen, Annie's unsigned "Recollections of Old Boston" reflects her lifelong reluctance to appear in a public spotlight. From childhood on, she had been taught that women should avoid publicity and that married women should appear in public only under cover of their husbands' names. Fittingly, Annie's early poems and essays and her novel appeared anonymously, other publications of the sixties were pseudonymous or signed "A.F.," and she signed four later books and several essays as "Mrs. James T. Fields" and a fifth as "Mrs. Fields."[9] In the sixties, when she most heavily veiled herself in anonymity, her vanity occasionally broke through. If a friend praised an unsigned poem, she admitted writing it. But when Julia Ward Howe publicly criticized Annie's anonymous "Ode" and when Sophia Hawthorne derided her anonymous novel *Asphodel,* she vented her outrage only in her diary. Anonymity accorded with period conventions of ladylike modesty and also served as a protective shield. Even at the end of her life, Annie worried about falling short of her own high standards and thereby exposing herself to public criticism. Rossiter elicited Annie's "Recollections of Old Boston" by promising that she would simply be an informant; he would take notes to "use without attribution." But when he submitted those notes for her approval and tried to cajole her into letting her name appear, she not only refused but urged him not to publish even the notes. They struck her as fragmentary and without lasting value.[10]

They are indeed fragmentary, but steeped in social history. Some illuminate nineteenth-century domestic life, as does her reference to the "one good dress" of imported material that seamstresses made each year for each Adams girl that "usually lasted for many years." Others point to larger period concerns, as does her anecdote of encountering a cotton mill manager on Boston Common during the Civil War and urging him to produce winter-weight dress fabric, so New England women could "patronize home industries." Rossiter had good reason to insist on publishing the piece, even without Annie's name.

He was the last of her many editors, and the last to realize how determined she was to protect her privacy. As she told her literary executor Mark DeWolfe Howe, she did not want her life to become "a subject of record—'unless . . . for some reason not altogether connected with myself,'" and her will enjoined him to extract from her diaries and letters only what was clearly of "public value." She did not want him to ransack her letters and journals to probe her private life, and he honored that wish. In his *Memories of a Hostess,* lengthy excerpts from Annie Fields's diaries and letters are arranged not as a biography but as a chronicle of the celebrated writers and artists for whom she had been "a central animating presence, a focus of sympathy and understanding."[11]

That is also the way she emerges from Henry James's memoir in the 1915 *Atlantic Monthly*—as a woman who retained the "personal beauty," "signal sweetness of temper," and benignity of her youth even at the age of eighty. Annie Fields would have cherished his praise and approved of his title: "Mr. and Mrs. James T. Fields." Her self-definition always included the husband who had died in 1881 and who had also "shone with the reflected light" of the eminent writers he published. Together they had made their Charles Street house a center of culture, and Henry James said with more truth than he knew that the Ticknor and Fields journal *Atlantic Monthly* "seemed very much edited from there." Holmes, Longfellow, Hawthorne, and Stowe were among the contributors who were regular guests, he noted. With only a tinge of irony, he then added that the childless Fieldses were "addicted to every hospitality and every benevolence, addicted to the cultivation of talk and wit and to the ingenious multiplication of such ties as could link the upper half of the title-page with the lower." James was at once witty and tender: Annie flourished "as a copious second volume," a "literary and social executor" of the ghostly past who nonetheless remained "insistently modern."[12]

For Howe and James as for Rossiter, Annie Fields represented the best of Old Boston, particularly of the good old days before the Civil War, industrialization, and slums. As John Singer Sargent portrayed her in 1890, she was a serene embodiment of the old genteel culture that still survived. For decades his portrait of her hung above the reception desk of the Boston Athenaeum; at once aloof and engaged, the woman in the high-necked white blouse seemed at home in that shrine of cultural achievement.

Through her, we enter bygone worlds. A study of Annie Fields could easily end up as a pastiche of Famous-Men-and-Women-She-Knew, on the order of Howe's *Memories of a Hostess.* But it is far more rewarding to explore the ways Annie Fields reconciled the contradictory demands put upon her. She struggled to combine ideals of self-fulfillment with Christian ideals of service to humanity, Republican goals of improving America with Arnoldian promotion of high culture, and nineteenth-century notions of True Womanhood with competing ideas about women's options and obligations. It is worth looking not only through her but at her.

As the wife of Boston's most important publisher, she was welcomed into the circle of great New England authors that included Ralph Waldo Emerson, Henry Wadsworth Longfellow, John Greenleaf Whittier, Nathaniel Hawthorne, and Oliver Wendell Holmes, and into the wider circles of English authors published by Ticknor and Fields—including Alfred Tennyson, Robert Browning, George Eliot, Leigh Hunt, Thomas De Quincey, Anthony Trollope, William Makepeace Thackeray, and Charles Dickens. With her husband, she befriended such "new" men as William Dean Howells, Henry James, Mark Twain, and Bret Harte. And the long list of eminent American women writers who were her friends includes Lydia Maria Child, Julia Ward Howe, Catharine Sedgwick, Harriet Beecher Stowe, Rebecca Harding Davis, Harriet Prescott Spofford, Lucy Larcom, Gail Hamilton, Elizabeth Stuart Phelps, Celia Thaxter, Rose Terry Cooke, Louise Imogen Guiney, Willa Cather, and Sarah Orne Jewett. Celebrated artists, musicians, and actors from this country and abroad who were her friends include Anne Whitney, William Morris Hunt, Ole Bull, Christine Nilsson, Adelaide Phillips, Ellen Terry, Mme. Modjeska, Mme. Ristori, Edwin Booth, and Charlotte Cushman; and her guests also included public figures ranging from the abolitionist William Lloyd Garrison to the inventor Alexander Graham Bell.

In her marriage, her lifelong goals of self-fulfillment and service to others sometimes conflicted. She shared her husband's friendships, his books, and even his editorial responsibilities. Yet the gratifications of such sharing made it difficult for her to establish her own priorities and her own voice. She kept her "Journal of literary events and interesting people" for his sake as much as hers, and later copied out long sections for "his" essays on Dickens and Hawthorne (and later still for her own memoirs). Yet many of her entries complain of insufficient time to make those entries, or to develop her own mind and talents.

Meantime, she assumed obligations beyond her inner circles of love and friendship, particularly after her husband retired from publishing. When she opened lodging houses for working women, or worked for women's admission to medical schools, or publicly advocated prison reform, she followed a categorical imperative: all individuals deserve decent living and working conditions and adequate opportunities to develop their powers and abilities. By her late thirties, Annie had become a conscientious public servant who repeatedly proved to be a remarkably effective innovator and organizer.

As an advocate of the examined life, she took inspiration from writers who fostered such examination. Her many intellectual fathers included Longfellow and Hawthorne, Tennyson and Dickens, Blake and Goethe; her intellectual mothers included George Sand and George Eliot; and in her last years she was struggling with Bergson and Ezra Pound and enjoying Rabelais. As one of her obituaries declared, she kept step with the times.

Though we can only guess what she repressed, we can assess Annie Fields through what she wrote. If her poems and biographies rarely reveal a distinctive voice or an original vision, they sometimes do, and they all meet period standards for literary excellence. Her letters and journals are a richer legacy. They enable us to appreciate the many ways in which this decorous and genteel lady augmented other lives, particularly the lives of women, while enlarging her own. Even the few individuals who resisted her charm acknowledged its power. Through her life and those who shared it—her husband and Sarah Orne Jewett, Hawthorne and Stowe, Whittier and Thaxter, and scores of others—we can expand and revise prevailing assumptions about American literature and American culture (including women's supposed subordination) from the mid-nineteenth century to the beginning of the First World War.[13]

Part One

MRS. JAMES T. FIELDS
(1854–1881)

SECTION I
Beyond the Garden
(1854–1868)

1

Marriage

"Just the Girl You Would Choose for Me"

"Have you room in your heart for one more American?" the Boston publisher James T. Fields asked the English novelist Mary Russell Mitford on 27 October 1854. He then gleefully explained, "after an engagement of a few weeks I am . . . to go to church with one of the best Yankee girls of my acquaintance. Indeed she is the best in any body's acquaintance. Just the girl you wd. choose for me." As Mitford knew, Fields's hopes for marriage had been dashed twice before. His first fiancée, Mary Willard, had died of tuberculosis in 1845. Then in March 1850 he married her sister Eliza, but in July 1851 she too died of tuberculosis. Aware that Mitford fondly regarded him as the son she never had, Fields assured her of the all-round healthiness of his future wife, who

> has never written books altho' she is capable of doing that some; never held an argument on Woman's Rights or Wrongs in her whole life, and so full of goodness of heart and beauty that you would say at once "that is the maid of all others for my friend Fields." Her name is Annie Adams, and I have known her from her childhood, and have held her on my knees many and many a time. Her father (and this must recommend her to your favor) is one of our leading Physicians & a great admirer of Miss Mitford, as well as his daughter. In short, Annie is a girl after your own heart and she told me to give her love to you and ask you to love her.[1]

Mitford promptly congratulated Fields on finding "so sweet a creature, . . . so lovely & so womanly," then said she had already heard about Annie's "beauty of mind as well as of body" from a friend who considered her "the most beautiful girl in New England." Though Mitford was then in her final illness and would die a few months later, she soon sent a smiling photograph that the newlyweds hung above their "choicest book shelf" to signal her inclusion in their happiness.[2]

Soon after telling Mitford about his engagement, Fields broadcast the news to friends closer to home. He had been accepted by "as pretty a little darkhaired goodhearted girl as one wd. wish to meet here below," he told the New York poet Bayard Taylor on 10 November; and that same day he told Henry Wadsworth Longfellow, "Nought of news other than that I go into King's Chapel next Wednesday with Miss Annie and bring her out as somebody else." In fact, Longfellow had already figured in his courtship. "The *Golden Legend* is a favorite of Miss Annie Adams the young lady of whom we spoke together on Saturday," Fields had written four days earlier, then made a request that simultaneously flattered the young lady, the poet, and (as the poet's publisher) himself: "May I ask you to put her name with yours on this copy and thus enhance the value of the beautiful vol. which I want her to own."[3] By making Annie "somebody else," Fields brought her into a world where authors she admired became her friends.[4]

The Fieldses were married in King's Chapel on the morning of 15 November, in a Unitarian service conducted by the Reverend Ezra Stiles Gannett of the Federal Street Church, the church Annie had attended as a child. Presumably Annie's parents, her three sisters, and her brother were there, and perhaps Fields's brother George.[5] If James T. Fields moved up the social ladder by marrying into one of Boston's long-established First Families, that was not the judgment of the literary community and certainly not the bride's. As evidence of their approval, her parents agreed to a short engagement and offered the newlyweds an apartment in their own house.

Despite her protected girlhood, the twenty-year-old Annie was ideally prepared to be the ambitious publisher's helpmeet. To begin with, her father was an exemplar of selfless service, and not only as a physician. An eighth-generation descendant of Henry Adams of Braintree, Zabdiel Boylston Adams had gone straight from Harvard College and Harvard Medical School to medical practice in Boston; and when he died of an "effusion of the brain" in January 1855—at the age of sixty-two, only two months after the Fieldses' marriage—newspapers identified him as a renowned physician who had taught at the Harvard Medical School, cofounded the Boston Society for Medical Improvement, been a councillor of the Boston Medical Society, served on the Boston School Commission, and belonged to the Bunker Hill Association and the Saturday Evening Club.[6]

Like her husband, Sarah May Holland Adams was a descendant of early Massachusetts settlers, and her family also included distinguished political figures, ministers, and merchants. The daughter of a sea captain who became a merchant on Boston's Long Wharf, she was admired for her "strong and beautiful character" and maintained a dignified independence through twenty-two years of widowhood.[7]

Ann West Adams—born on 6 June 1834—was the sixth of the Adamses' seven children and the fifth of their six daughters (two of whom died in infancy). As Mrs. James T. Fields she became the family celebrity. But both older sisters and her brother also attained distinction.

Her eldest sister, Sarah Holland Adams, eleven years older than Annie, was so lamed by childhood poliomyelitis that for the rest of her life she wore leg braces and used a cane. She was her widowed mother's companion until Mrs. Adams's death in 1877. Then a few months later—in July 1877—Sarah sailed for Europe, and her life began blossoming. By February 1878 Annie could report, "She has been 70 nights to the theatre there beside seeing and hearing Liszt in his own home and many other agreeable people."[8] Soon after settling in Germany, Sarah became the friend and translator of the popular biographer and cultural historian Hermann Grimm. In 1880 her translation of Grimm's *Life and Times of Goethe* won a medal from the kaiser (Germany's highest literary honor); and during the next eight years she published translations of four other German books, three of them by Grimm.[9] When she returned to Boston in 1892, her literary friendships overlapped Annie's; and when Grimm died in 1902, it was Sarah who wrote his obituary for the *Boston Transcript*. A photograph taken at about that time shows a white-haired, straight-backed and black-clad woman seated at a desk in a picture-hung room, holding a pen. The once-dependent invalid had long since become an autonomous woman of letters. Paradoxically, she would survive all of her siblings but the youngest.[10]

Elizabeth Adams, two years younger than Sarah, also attained professional success relatively late in life and also remained unmarried. Determined to be a painter from childhood on, she studied with private teachers and at the Boston Art School, though she was hobbled by Victorian proprieties that excluded women from life classes, and also by her own diffidence and frail health. Her professional options opened out when in 1860 at the age of thirty-four she accepted Annie's invitation to join her in Europe. She spent most of the next six years studying and painting in Florence and in Paris, where she gained admission to the French Salon. Returning to Boston in 1866, she spent nearly a year living with the Fieldses, working hard but by her own lights ineffectually. Next came another long period of study and painting in France and in Italy, then a final return to America. In 1874, she moved to Baltimore with her friend Frances Burnap. When Jamie lectured there the following year, he told Annie that "Every body speaks of Lizzy in Balt. with real feeling & admiration."[11]

By then she had won renown as a teacher as well as a painter. Her studio had become "a natural rallying point" and she herself had become "a stimulus and an example to other women." Following the Adams tradition of civic service, she helped found or develop Baltimore's Decorative Art Society, the Woman's Literary Club, and the Arundell Club. A contemporary photograph of her studio shows many portraits lined up for the camera—one of a man, several of women and children—and a few of what her biographer called "nature-poems in water-color or oil." She died in 1898.[12]

Zabdiel Boylston Adams Jr., five years older than Annie, followed his father's path by entering Harvard College, graduating from Harvard Medical school, and becoming a physician. But he lacked his father's steadiness. He was rusticated for pranks and academic mediocrity during his junior year at Harvard, eventually set up medical practice in Framingham rather than, as his father urged, in Boston, and then later still regretted it.[13]

His Civil War career might have been more distinguished had he been less of a malcontent. He enlisted as a lieutenant at the beginning of the war, and survived two serious wounds and months of Confederate imprisonment before being mustered out as a brevet major—by then with a limp, trembling hands, damaged eyesight, and debilitating self-doubt. The scores of letters he wrote home during the war include vivid descriptions of camp life, of wartime Washington, and of battles including Bull Run and Gettysburg. But they also include petulant criticisms of generals and politicians and self-righteous dismissals of formal charges against him that ranged from protesting military orders to stealing a pig. And though he often thanked the Fieldses for their letters and gifts, and once for a visit, he also once accused Annie of cruel indifference to him.[14]

After the war Boylston resumed an easy if not intimate relationship with Annie. He was married at Charles Street in 1870, many of the books in his library were gifts from Annie, and he and his two children were often guests at her summer cottage. He nonetheless continued to have personal problems. As his wife stated in her will, "inasmuch as he has never done anything for my support and his treatment has been most upsetting and that he has tried to desert his family entirely, I have no wish to leave him anything that belongs to my estate."[15]

Yet Boylston continued the Adams commitment to high culture in at least three ways: he established the Framingham library; he booked literary celebrities for the town's annual lecture series (James T. Fields among them); and he wrote short stories (among them a tale about three proud New England spinsters that won praise from his sister's friend Sarah Orne Jewett).[16] He also continued the Adams commitment to public service: when he died in 1902, his obituaries praised him as a conscientious doctor whose professional accomplishments included monographs on malaria and other medical problems. Another accomplishment was producing a son who became the third successive Zabdiel Boylston Adams, M.D., and Annie Fields's chief heir.

Annie's sister Louisa Jane, two years Annie's junior, was the only Adams daughter who passed her whole life within the domestic sphere. In 1862 at the relatively advanced age of twenty-six, she married Thomas P. Beal, a widowed banker with five children, and then spent the rest of her life as a Beacon Hill matron.[17] She soon had two sons of her own whom their doting Aunt Annie enjoyed babysitting. The Beals attended all of Annie's Christmas parties, the Fieldses regularly dined with them on Sundays, and Annie often helped Louisa open her summer house in Nahant. Though Louisa never shared Annie's literary interests or aspired to be her intellectual companion, she followed her older sister's lead as a Visitor in the Associated Charities of Boston, and when Annie grew frail Louisa put her automobile at Annie's disposal. According to Annie's will, her dear sister who had "always been kind and devoted" was to have "anything she wishes."[18]

The Rothwell portrait of Annie Fields at about the time of her wedding shows a wide-eyed sweet-faced young woman with dark wavy hair and what Henry James later called a "pensive Burne-Jones air."[19] She was the "Dear Love" of a solicitous and protective husband who sent her notes and gifts from his office almost daily, and their devotion was mutual from the start. Disappointments lay ahead: she never had children, housekeeping and hospitality often exhausted her, and she would never have enough time for study and writing. But marriage brought her the immediate and growing rewards of affection, security, and access to power in and beyond the world of high culture. She would wield that power all her life without abandoning genteel ideals of femininity.

She had been immersed in poetry from childhood on. As she told Longfellow in 1864, she had been so "bewitched" by his *Tales of a Wayside Inn* that she forgot she was reading, "as in my early school days when on Saturday afternoons I would sit in a high backed rocking chair of enormous dimensions and make the rockers keep time with the rhythms of your verses until I knew them, page after page, by heart."[20] That charming compliment was also a paradigm of limitation: her imagination preserved the small girl who rocked her chair while memorizing Longfellow's verses.

Meantime, she was absorbing Longfellow's moral messages along with his rhythms, as is evident from an autobiographical sketch she wrote for young readers in the mid-eighties. During her girlhood, Annie recalled, she was so distressed by her older sisters' frivolous prattle that she rebuked them by quoting Longfellow: "Lives of great men all remind us / We can make *our* lives sublime." Undaunted by their mockery, she gave Longfellow's lines a feminist spin by determining to model herself on exemplary women such as the abolitionist author Lydia Maria Child.[21] The sketch is vivified and its priggishness redeemed by the young girl's appropriation to her own purposes of a male mentor's lesson. The poem had empowered her to think and speak for herself.

A more poignant girlhood trauma is encapsulated in Annie Fields's 1895 memoir of Tennyson. Enchanted by "The Lady of Shalott," she had committed it to memory, expecting to unlock "a treasure-house" for her classmates on the next recitation day. But to her great dismay, "Not even her teacher could see what she saw, nor could feel what lay deep down in her own glowing heart." The sixty-year-old Annie Fields celebrated Tennyson by saying so, also vaunting her own precocious response to his genius.[22]

An idyllic memory of a slightly older self surfaces in a journal entry Annie made in the summer of 1872. Struck by the "pretty sight" of a young girl sitting beneath a tree and singing to herself, she recalled a moment in her own girlhood when she sat "under a tree I remember well, reading Italian and overcome by the music of nature." "What time is so sacred to noble idleness as youth and midsummer?" she then mused.

Her recollection reflects well upon her education at George B. Emerson's School for Young Ladies, Boston's best and most influential private secondary school for girls, where students were taught to read Italian, encouraged to read independently, and trained to appreciate nature. Only if they developed their minds and individual talents could they properly assume the responsibilities of womanhood, Emerson believed, more broadly insisting that learning and self-expression should be tributary to character development and an ethic of service.[23]

George Emerson had opened his School for Young Ladies in 1823, eleven years before Annie was born, and conducted it until 1855, the year after she married and a few years after the end of her formal schooling. After serving two years as the first headmaster of Boston's all-male English Classical School, then considered "the crowning achievement" of the city's public school system, Emerson had been persuaded by a group of eminent Bostonians including Josiah Quincy to assume the challenge of teaching their daughters. Beginning with a class of thirty-two, Emerson was determined "to give my pupils the best education possible, to teach them what it was most important for every one to know, and to form right habits of thought, and give such instruction as would lead to the formation of the highest character, to fit them to be good daughters and sisters, good neighbors, good wives, and good mothers."[24] From the start, he urged his pupils not to compete with one another but to "strive rather to surpass yourselves." That would ultimately "result in a worthy life here and a blessed immortality hereafter." A specific goal was to help them attain as complete a knowledge as possible "of our rich and beautiful English language." To that end, most of them took three years of Latin as well as French and Italian, reading such great writers as Virgil and Dante. An innovative pragmatist, Emerson taught Colburn's *Mental Arithmetic* to enable his students to calculate shopping costs more speedily than storekeepers; he taught history the "old way" through excellent texts but also urged his pupils to ask questions and required them to track historical events on maps; and he taught "natural philosophy" through the texts of such scientists as Galileo and Lavoisier but also with field trips and laboratory experiments. Meantime he also taught that the better we understand the world, the better we understand its Creator.[25]

Although he thought girls' minds were no different from boys', Emerson also thought a God who made girls more delicate than boys did not want them to enter the public arena. Therefore, although the curriculum at his School for Young Ladies was identical to the one he had offered male students at the English Classical School, he expected his Young Ladies to become accomplished yet modest wives who selflessly served their families and their communities.

The contradictions inherent in his precepts and expectations are clearly evident in the retirement address he gave in 1855. Taking the parable of the talents as his text, Emerson urged heroic self-development: "Whatever faculty you find within you, do not fear to use and cultivate it to the highest degree." Self-development was a religious obligation, he argued, since a perfect God wanted his creatures to perfect themselves. Thus Annie was following both her teacher and his cousin Ralph Waldo Emerson whenever she spurred herself to develop her own abilities. Evidently George Emerson saw no conflict between the idea that God wanted women to develop all their faculties and the idea that women should serve God by serving others, though the conflict would later trouble Annie.

Yet she had no such problem with Emerson's advice about ongoing education: to study nature, foreign languages, literature, history, travel books, and biography, and to cultivate one's "power of expression." Annie tried to do all of that. She also kept a diary, as he suggested, if not exactly the way he suggested. Though she usually kept her own feelings out of it, as Emerson advised, and sometimes recorded "good thoughts or beautiful images which are presented or suggested by your observation, by your reading, or by conversation," she concentrated on recording the table talk of her eminent guests. As that very fact suggests, she believed with her mentor that women should avoid self-display yet encourage conversation, which could be "the most delightful of all arts."

The fullest congruence of Emerson's advice to his students and Annie Fields's activities stems from his repeated insistence that "every good life is necessarily devoted, directly or indirectly, to the service of mankind." In his farewell address, he urged each listener "to prepare herself to . . . relieve or diminish the wants, the ignorance, the sufferings, and the sins of her poor fellow-creatures," first determining what poor people want and then "what ought to be and can be done by Christian women for them." That is what Annie did. "Will you not be willing to spend time in searching thoroughly into the wants, character, and condition of those whom you would relieve?" he asked his audience, virtually scripting Annie's later commitments as a philanthropist.[26]

Perhaps with Emerson in mind, Annie defined the ideal teacher in her novel *Asphodel* as "a fresh mind impelling the intellect through unwonted channels, and a fresh heart whose sympathies forerun the religious aspiration of the growing soul." It might be argued that Annie ignored Emerson's warning against overindulgence in fiction when she wrote that novel. But his warning was really against substituting frivolous pleasures for moral engagement, and *Asphodel* emphatically espouses moral engagement. Moreover, Emerson's belief that good literature embodies and promotes spiritual fulfillment is wholly consistent with Annie's respect for the work of Dickens, Hawthorne, and Stowe (among others), her translation of works she admired including Goethe's "Pandora," and her struggles to produce good literature of her own.

Of course, it would be foolish to give Emerson full credit for any of Annie's activities, or to blame him for her struggles to reconcile self-fulfillment and womanly subordination. But so pervasive was his influence on her in small matters and large that even decades after leaving school she could quote him, as when she began a lecture to charity workers with his cautionary yet upbeat admonition, "Take care girls what you wish for, because if you wish long enough and hard enough you are sure to get it."[27] As his published lectures and his *Reminiscences* make amply clear, he expected his girls to do a lot more than wish. On balance, George B. Emerson was a high-minded and articulate spokesman of Brahmin culture whose training enabled Ann West Adams to incorporate it, but as Mrs. James T. Fields to move beyond it.

In Annie's *James T. Fields: Biographical Notes and Personal Sketches,* she let her own name appear only once—in a quotation from her husband's 1854 letter to Mitford announcing his engagement to "Annie Adams." As she then tenderly recalled, "when at last the doors of home opened to him he entered reverently, and with a tenderness which grew only with years. What an exceptional experience, also, for a young girl, a younger member of a large family, with less reason for special consideration than any other person in the household, to be swept suddenly out upon a tide more swift and strong and all-enfolding than her imagination had foretold; a power imaging the divine life, the divine shelter, the divine peace. The winds of heaven might not visit her too roughly, and every shadow must pass first through the alembic of his smile before it fell on her."[28] We may resist Annie's floridity yet trust her testimony, including her use of the passive voice for her own experience (she was swept) and the active for her husband's (he entered). Trained to expect fulfillment through marriage, she had also been trained to remain subordinate to her husband.[29] When their goals and interests diverged, his came first. But meanwhile he did his best to support hers. As he had assured Mitford, his fiancée had never written a book but was capable of doing so. She was also capable of much more. Born into social and cultural privilege, she proved herself "just the girl" for America's most important publisher.

"The First Match in This Country"

In his letter congratulating James Thomas Fields on his impending marriage to Ann West Adams, the New York writer and editor Rufus Griswold declared, "I think my friend James is, as Mr. John Adams wrote of Josiah Quincy, when that old gentleman was young—'the first match in this country.'" As a corollary, Griswold said from no one else would he "more gladly have received an application for the hand of my own daughter."[30] Contemporary photographs display Fields as a consummate Victorian—bearded, buttoned up, and benign, as befitted one of the country's leading publishers.

Fields was then the junior partner in the flourishing Boston publishing firm of Ticknor and Fields, a position he had earned by over twenty years of hard work. If Annie was a kind of sleeping beauty in the garden of her childhood and he was the prince who wakened her, he was also a self-directed Poor Richard. Born in the seaport town of Portsmouth, New Hampshire, in December 1817, he was the son of a shipmaster and the "the kindest and the tenderest mother in the world." After his father's death at sea when Jamie was four, his mother reared her two sons in a small house in a working-class neighborhood crowded with other relatives and within "the straitest sect of the Unitarians of those days." A healthy and gregarious child, Jamie enjoyed writing poetry and read his way through the local library before finishing high school at the age of thirteen. With no hope of attending college, the thirteen-year-old boy became an apprentice to the Boston booksellers Carter and Hendee, located in the place already known as the Old Corner Bookstore, at a time when the city was on the way to becoming the publishing center of New England.[31]

He remained there after Carter and Hendee sold out to Allen and Ticknor in 1832, after William D. Ticknor took over in 1834, and after Ticknor made him a junior partner in 1843. By then he had become an urbane man of letters who belonged to the Mercantile Library Association and participated in its debates, who attended plays and invited friends to his rooms to discuss them, and who wrote poems and published a few of them. But what had primarily impressed Ticknor was Fields's sensitivity to literary taste and his shrewdness in marketing and publishing. He demonstrated all those qualities in 1840, when he persuaded Ticknor to publish De Quincey's *Confessions of an English Opium-Eater* and two other books, then edited and wrote prefaces for all three. They all sold well. Two years later he persuaded Ticknor to publish the first authorized American edition of Tennyson and pay the 10 percent royalty Tennyson requested, and the following year he persuaded Ticknor to publish John Greenleaf Whittier's *Lays of My Home, and Other Poems*. A month after its publication, Fields became a junior partner in the firm.

Although Ticknor's friend John Reed Jr. had become part of the company as a consequence of investing eight thousand dollars in it, Fields was expected to invest only himself. He negotiated genially and astutely with printers and bookbinders as well as authors and book reviewers, and in the process helped shape public taste. Ticknor & Company became the city's preeminent literary publisher. In 1854, the year Reed withdrew from the firm and James T. Fields married Ann West Adams, another new partnership was established: Ticknor & Fields. By then, the firm's list of eminent American authors included Longfellow, Holmes, and Hawthorne, and its English list included Browning and Thackeray as well as De Quincey and Tennyson. For English writers, a special incentive was receiving royalties, which were not then required by international copyright law. Moreover, Fields assiduously courted "his" writers, and not only those who lived in or near Boston. When he traveled to England in 1847 and 1850, for example, it was primarily to cultivate writers who were—or soon would be—on the firm's English list; and in 1850 he returned home with piles of new manuscripts after visiting and dining with literary celebrities and helping Thackeray plan his first American lecture tour. More important to everyone on his list, Fields hired Boston's best printers and bookbinders, maintained high standards of production, and vigorously promoted whatever he published. For reader and writer alike, the firm's imprint became a mark of excellence.

As a consequence, the Old Corner Bookstore became a lively center for literary exchange. Writers stopped by to see new books and old friends, Fields among them. He was "the literary partner of the house," as the New York editor and critic George William Curtis said years later, "the friend of the celebrated circle who have made . . . Boston . . . justly renowned." Writers who stepped behind the green curtain in the far corner to chat with Fields might be invited to dine with him at a nearby restaurant, and Curtis's trip to Boston in January 1854 was the occasion for the firm's first formal literary banquet.[32] But Fields's hospitality dramatically increased after 1856, when he and Annie moved into the house on Charles Street that they would occupy as long as they lived.

Martin Green does not exaggerate when he calls Ticknor and Fields "the great organ of the New England Renaissance, and a major instrument of New England's cultural ascendancy."[33] Fields was instrumental in Boston's emergence as a thriving cultural center. As the firm's chief editor and publicist, but also as the friend, host, and guest of the period's major writers, he enthusiastically served the firm, the writers, the region, and literature itself. He was the ideal Gentleman Publisher, as Susan Coultrap-McQuin defines him, a man who enjoyed close and trusting friendships with "his" authors and prided himself on serving the public by advancing high culture.[34] Because cultured Bostonians considered good literature one of life's essentials, he enjoyed unusual access to social power. Once he married, his wife shared that power. Once they acquired their own house, his wife was in the center of that center, in what Howells called a "friendly home of lettered refinement."

Whether or not Ann West Adams agreed with Griswold that James T. Fields was "the finest match in the country," his commitments to literature, self-development, friendship, and community complemented and augmented her own. It simply did not matter that he was seventeen years her senior, that he came from a poor family without social distinction, or that he had been engaged twice before and married once. In fact, as the accepted suitor of two of Annie's cousins and the husband of one of them, James T. Fields had entered her family long before he and Annie married.

Their marriage was remarkably happy, and "My Friend's Library," the title of Fields's 1861 *Atlantic* essay about their already legendary room, suggests a few reasons why. His wife was his friend, and their treasure-filled library (with its two desks in symmetrical alcoves) was hers as much as it was his. There he entertained friends and wrote essays, lectures, poems, and books. So did his wife.

37 Charles Street

"Next Spring, God willing, we intend to have a house somewhere. . . —and commence in earnest to live," Fields told Miss Mitford on 8 December 1854, soon after returning from his wedding trip to "apartments" in the Adams house. Whether or not the death of Annie's father in January interrupted the couple's search for a home of their own, they occupied those rooms for over a year. The house they finally chose was not finished when they found it, and it would be torn down after Annie died. But for sixty years, it was a "place of delight" and a "center of hospitality."[35]

The house stood on quiet Charles Street, in a new residential neighborhood

created on landfill, with a lot behind it bordering on the Charles River. None of
the houses on that street had "striking or attractive features," an early twentieth-
century guidebook declared, "yet at one time it was the abode of several Boston
worthies memorable in literature."[36] Oliver Wendell Holmes was the Fieldses'
neighbor for twelve years, Thomas Bailey Aldrich for ten, and at various times
both Henry James Sr. and Jr. lived nearby. Even at the end of the century when
Charles Street had become a busy thoroughfare (as readers of *Time and the Hour*
were told), "When you are admitted into Mrs. James T. Fields's home and, passing up the staircase, are seated in the drawing-room with its westward windows,
you look over a calm expanse of water beyond a quiet garden which might be the
neighbor of an outlying rural wilderness."[37] Like most Beacon Hill townhouses,
it was three stories high, with a kitchen in the basement, a reception room and
dining room on the first floor, a library (or drawing room) running the whole
length of the second floor, and three bedrooms on the third, with servants' quarters in the attic. But Annie Fields and her husband made their space unique, the
library in particular.

Everyone who wrote about that room overlooking the river at one end and
Charles Street at the other marveled at its treasures. Many of the books had previously belonged to famous English writers, including Southey's copy of a work
by Ben Jonson and a Boccaccio volume that Leigh Hunt had inscribed to his wife.
But they far were outnumbered by the books Fields had published, most of them
inscribed to him by their authors. The room's many paintings and sculptures, including a portrait of Dickens and a bust of Keats, sustained the literary atmosphere.

Harriet Prescott Spofford's chapter on Annie Fields in her *Little Book of Friends*
dramatizes the Fieldses' acquisition of the Charles Street house as the fulfillment
of a shared vision: "They climbed over heaps of building material and saw what
the place afforded; and they made it rarely individual." Spofford's attempt to re-
produce her own first impression of the house combines journalistic precision
with fairy-tale rhetoric:

> Entering the house you came into a reception room with dark blue velvet furnish-
> ings and gray rug, filled with flowers, every part of the walls hung with choice paint-
> ings; beyond you caught a glimpse of the dining room, whose windows, latticed with
> ivy, looked on a long, shady garden running down to the river. Upstairs the room of
> rooms, the library, ran the whole length of the house, with side alcoves at either end.
> It held unusual pictures and busts, but the greater part of the walls were covered with
> books to the ceiling. The moss-green carpet and draperies gave a subdued coloring,
> and the windows looked over wide water to distant hills . . . . I felt myself, in that
> first visit, in a new world, as if I had stepped inside a home in some enchanted wood
> and among a rarer race of beings; and although frequently sharing its beautiful hos-
> pitality since then, I never quite lost the sensation.[38]

For William Dean Howells, the house was also a place of enchantment, though
a particularly literary enchantment. As he recalled in *Literary Friends and Acquain-*

tance, when he arrived at the "house beside the Charles" in 1860, he was a diffident young midwesterner with a hankering for the literary life, and he was delighted to find "an odor and an air of books such as I fancied might belong to the famous literary houses of London." In that "friendly home of lettered refinement," he was served breakfast "in the pretty room whose windows look out through leaves and flowers upon the river's coming and going tides, and whose walls were covered with the faces and the autographs of all the contemporary poets and novelists." When her husband left for the office, "Mrs. Fields showed me from shelf to shelf in the library, and dazzled me with the sight of authors' copies, and volumes invaluable with the autographs and the pencilled notes of the men whose names were dear to me from my love of their work. Everywhere was some souvenir of the living celebrities my hosts had met."[39]

Henry James's celebration of the house in *The American Scene* is more sweepingly impressionistic and more subjective, while putting a mature writer's stamp on a young man's impression. It seemed the "one merciful refuge" where survivors from the past century "could breathe again, and with intensity, our own liberal air," he wrote after returning to America in 1904 following two decades abroad. Even more rhapsodically than Howells, he marveled. "Here, behind the effaced anonymous door, was the little ark of the modern deluge, here still the long drawing-room that looks over the water and towards the sunset, with a seat for every visiting shade, from far-away Thackeray down, and relics and tokens so thick on its walls as to make it positively, in all the town, the votive temple of memory."[40]

Four years after James said so, Willa Cather entered that drawing room and discovered two ladies at tea: "Mrs. Fields reclining on a green sofa, directly under the youthful portrait of Charles Dickens. . . , Miss Jewett seated, the low tea-table between them." In an essay appropriately titled "148 Charles Street," Cather recalled that "there was never an hour in the day when the order and calm of the drawing-room were not such that one might have sat down to write a sonnet or a sonata. The sweeping and dusting were done very early in the morning, the flowers arranged before the guests were awake." But like Henry James, she especially valued the house as "a place where the past lived on—where it was protected and cherished, had sanctuary from the noisy push of the present." After Annie Fields died, that sanctuary disappeared. "She died with her world (the world of 'letters' which mattered most to her) unchallenged," and it seemed only right that the "votive temple" itself was destroyed: "Only in memory exists the long, green-carpeted, softly lighted drawing-room, and the dining-table where Learning and Talent met, enjoying good food and good wit and rare vintages, looking confidently forward to the growth of their country in the finer amenities of life."[41]

But that house also lives on in other writers' celebrations of it, as in one of the eulogies published in the *Boston Evening Transcript* the day after Annie Fields died. "Her home on Charles Street with garden and shaded lawn running down to the edge of the lapping river, before the Embankment's day, was the keystone of the social prestige of that famous thoroughfare, even while Oliver Wendell Holmes, Governor Andrew, Josiah Quincy, . . . and other representative old Boston families lived there"; and the writer suggested that the "fine old house . . . might well be preserved as a memorial of the halcyon days of Boston as the literary centre of the New World, for it has entertained Dickens and Thackeray and many another of the great Victorians, and Mrs. Fields's 'salon' was habitually frequented by all the stars of the first magnitude . . . of the early Atlantic Monthly."[42] For nearly six decades, the house had been a literary landmark and a citadel of high culture, a place where writers and artists could meet and enjoy each other's conversation and perhaps also hear a lecture by Emerson or a violin recital by Ole Bull. Although such performances were relatively rare after Fields died, Annie Fields continued to entertain celebrities ranging from Matthew Arnold to Jane Addams and President Taft. Most of the paintings and books that dazzled them all had been acquired by Fields, but his wife had chosen almost everything else, from the bright pottery breakfast dishes to the Duke of Ormond dining chairs. "Doubtless there were other homes as interesting, as enviable, but with a difference," Harriet Spofford said. "The difference was Annie Fields."[43]

2

Grand Tour

The Fieldses moved into their new brownstone on Charles Street at a time of "large literary activity among our American authors," authors that Annie read, admired, and now also entertained.[1] Most of them were Ticknor and Fields authors who lived nearby. But Annie was also befriended by such literati as William Cullen Bryant and Washington Irving when she accompanied her husband to New York, and even the great English novelist William Makepeace Thackeray was eager to meet her when he came to Boston. Essentially a "fair little House-wife" during the early years of her marriage, she kept her identity almost entirely submerged in her husband's.[2]

Yet not entirely. "You have left your imagery here," the novelist Catharine Maria Sedgwick assured Annie after the Fieldses visited her in Lenox in June 1858, "and when I say *you* I have a fancy that you & your husband are blended in a sure unity." As she later explained, she refused to abide by propriety and "call you *Mrs* Fields for that I should say to any *Mrs* Fields, & you are very different & distinct in my mind from any other Mrs. Fields."[3]

A year later, the Fieldses embarked on a long and long-delayed trip abroad that was partly a business trip for Jamie and a Grand Tour for Annie. For the young woman who had just turned twenty-five, it would be an *annus mirabilis*. For nearly a full year, she would move easily among literary eminences and rejoice in the cultural wonders and scenic splendors of England and the Continent.

The Fieldses boarded the Cunard liner *Canada* with "books enough, 'to read on the voyage,'—to answer for three voyages" and laden with flowers from Long-fellow and other friends. To Annie's surprise, Longfellow's were "worshipfully" admired by the English passengers, and the year was off to a good start.[4] "Crazy with delight" when the ship finally reached Liverpool, Annie pinched herself to be sure she was awake, while Jamie was "so happy and so frisky he will not stop to pinch anybody." A few days later they could "resist London no longer," and the

"8 notes of invitation" awaiting them ushered in a month of privileged cultural encounters.[5]

At the annual Literary Fund Dinner where Gladstone presided, for example, Annie put faces to the names of England's leading publishers and writers; and at the Lord Mayor's lunch in the superb old Guildhall, "the past and myself had a private conference." Before long, even when Jamie went off to transact business with English authors and publishers or to attend a men-only dinner, Annie felt ensconced in a "world of friends" who were "as kind as they could be." Jamie nonetheless remained at the center of that world, as evident from an unusually personal diary entry: "I did not rise early. My darling did and came bringing me flowers before I arose. . . . while I lay still looking and loving him."

Given their crowded schedule, sleeping late was a rare luxury. As Jamie both bragged and complained to his brother-in-law Boylston, "Frequently we break-fasted out, dined out, & supped out, the same day, & Annie got used up with it."[6] Yet she also relished it. At a formal dinner given by the writer Barry Cornwall, for example, where Leigh Hunt and Nathaniel Hawthorne were among the guests, Annie was proud of being seated next to her host. Better still was visiting Leigh Hunt in his "very tiny cottage" and hearing the "dear old man" reminisce about Shelley, the kind of vicarious admission to the literary past that she would later offer visitors to Charles Street and readers of her memoirs (including one about Leigh Hunt). But perhaps her first stint as a literary witness came during a visit to Thackeray, when his daughters eagerly inquired about "our great men . . . whom I knew personally."

Vastly more gratifying was entering into friendship with three of the period's most celebrated writers and her own longtime favorites—Hawthorne, Dickens, and Tennyson. Hawthorne's first call at the Fieldses' hotel was such a momentous occasion for Annie that she recorded and pondered every detail of his appearance and every word he uttered. He had been in England when she married, and he had now returned after a year and a half in Italy. Awestruck at meeting America's most important novelist, Annie also savored her own role as a literary insider. "Hawthorne wishes us to take a villa near Florence where they lived," she wrote in her diary. "He dislikes all people of pretension but loves old friends in a way not often seen." As she also noted, he spoke of his new novel-in-process, *The Marble Faun*, "nervously with the muscles of his face twitching and lowered voice."[7]

"We have had Mr. Hawthorne and his little son to breakfast with us which is enough to make a dull morning sun-shiny," Annie complacently told her sister Louisa a few days later; "not that he talks much or is what the world calls gay but he is one of those gifted souls who sees clearly beyond this present . . . discovering, as it were, the meaning hid in all."[8] She also took pride in being privy to her husband's negotiations on Hawthorne's behalf. For the English rights to *The Marble Faun*, Smith and Elder offered the substantial sum of six hundred pounds, though (as Annie told her sister Sarah) Hawthorne had to be in England in October "in order to take out a copyright for his book." In fact, Smith and Elder's requirement of a three-volume novel and England's copyright requirements would keep Hawthorne in England until the Fieldses' return from the Continent. Excited by the possibility of renting the villa in Florence where he had begun his "new novel full of Italy," Annie marveled, "This wonderful world is so vast with its Hawthornes and villas on every side as it were that I feel quite lost when I sit down to write hoping to select at once from a list of impressions the best and most interesting effect."⁹ Taking Hawthorne as a role model, she resolved to observe her surroundings more attentively, to record her impressions more effectively, and to seek the meaning hid in all.

She was more emotionally drawn to Dickens, dazzled by "such kindliness as shows through the man's clay." Jamie was then marketing though not yet publishing Dickens's books, and he was already urging an American reading tour. From the moment she met him, Annie's respect for the charismatic writer bordered on reverence. When someone casually remarked that Dickens had no religion, the usually reticent young woman fervently protested, "Is it not religion to discover that within and around the meanest of God's children which can elevate them and give them a purpose in life?" Therefore she was elated by Dickens's invitation to spend a day at Gad's Hill in early July, and dejected when she felt too ill to go.

Annie's eagerness to meet Tennyson dated back to her schoolgirl worship of him as "a seer and a prophet." For nearly three decades, Tennyson's poetry had been refining the sensibilities of his readers, Annie among them; and for nearly two decades, Fields had been his American publisher. He was "the greatest magnet of our soul-world," Annie assured her sister Lissie in mid-July. The Fieldses traveled to the Isle of Wight as pilgrims, entered the "beautiful solitude" of Farringford as worshipers, then "lived on a higher plane" during their two-day visit.¹⁰ The first night, the Poet Laureate read them his new poem "Guinevere," seating his wife before him to block their view of him while his "thrilling voice went on for hours." Then, the next afternoon, Tennyson sat Annie to screen him as he read "Maud" to his listeners, a poem "full of pathos, full of Beauty." Grateful for her sojourn "beneath a roof sheltering Wisdom and Holiness," Annie fancifully declared that Tennyson's island "might have been Prospero's own."

In the afterglow of that visit, she made a vaguely Tennysonian exhortation about Salisbury Cathedral—"I would say to all lovers of architecture stay; stay before it at least until the beauty of the whole flashes over and floods the soul with light." Under the novelist Charles Reade's guidance, she also submitted to the enchantments of Oxford, where talking to the construction workers at the half-completed Ashmolean Museum (one of the "seeds of wisdom planted by John Ruskin") resulted in the surprising discovery that their social and aesthetic values matched her own. A visit to the aging poet Sidney Dobell and his wife brought a more private self-ratification: they had been engaged at fifteen, married at twenty, and were still "as one, bound in a most touching union."

Meantime, the admiring observer was observed and admired. "Old Mrs.

Robertson has fallen in love with Annie," Jamie told her brother Boylston after visiting the bereaved parents of the minister F. W. Robertson (whose sermons Ticknor and Fields would soon publish). In fact, as the proud husband summarily declared, "Annie has made a great strike among the English. They all wish her to stay here and make a home with them. Dickens told his daughter he had not met an American lady he admired so much & Mary Howitt writes to me she is most anxious A. shd. visit her in Dovedale as 'she hears so much of her.' Indeed we are having great times."[11]

Those great times continued during their eight months on the Continent. Though Annie's judgment was occasionally impaired by Brahmin prejudice, as when she said the nuns of the Ghent Beguinage exhibited "almost the only spark of true Christianity left in the Catholic Church," she was as fascinated by the battlefield of Waterloo as by Rubens's and Van Dyck's houses in Antwerp, and by riding down Frankfurt's Judengasse where Rothschild was born and Luther's house still stood. As dutiful tourists, the Fieldses visited Cologne Cathedral and journeyed up the Rhine, went from Heidelberg to Baden-Baden and Strasbourg, then "shook hands with Zurich" (where they were saddened by the news of Leigh Hunt's death) before heading for the Alps. Predictably, they were ecstatic at "the Alpine wonders all about us," and stood "breathless with clasped hands" before the beauty of Mont Blanc and the "apocalyptic glory" of the Jungfrau. But they also paid homage at houses where Mme. Necker and Voltaire had lived, and they enjoyed encountering the Unitarian minister O. B. Frothingham and other American travelers.

Next came two months in Paris, where on a typical day the Fieldses rambled through the streets, "saw Notre Dame the Palais des Tuileries bought a few things and returned to a cozy dinner and letters from home." They had ample time for the Louvre and side trips to Versailles and St. Cloud; they heard Mme. Viardot sing in Gluck's *Orphée* and attended St. Cecilia's Day services at St. Eustache; and they occasionally glimpsed the "majestic but sad-faced Empress" riding with the Emperor and their young son. During one "sadly eventful week," they mourned the deaths of Washington Irving and De Quincey, and news of John Brown's execution made Annie pray that America might "wipe out this national sin" of slavery and avert "the terrors of war." Meantime, Fields's business responsibilities were complicated by Ticknor's acquisition of the *Atlantic Monthly*.

Yet the couple's personal life remained remarkably serene. To mark their fifth wedding anniversary, "Dear Jamie" brought Annie flowers "and a sweet dear poem from the love that is always fresh"—a poem that concluded, "My home is where my Annie dwells." And a subsequent journal entry simply reported, "Walked out again as usual enjoying everything."

The "everything" included participation in Paris's lively expatriate colony which then included Thackeray, George Hillard, and the American ambassador (and Longfellow's close friend) George Washington Greene. For Annie, the Greenes' house was a domestic oasis where she could observe "family life in all its purity and simplicity" with Mrs. Greene at its center. On one occasion, her admiration of Mrs. Greene's clothing provoked a self-defining conflation of aesthetic judgment with moral imperative: "What a pleasant duty it is for those women who are able to do it to dress themselves gracefully and carefully!"[12]

Yet Annie was at least beginning to resist gender stereotypes. After a visit from the Countess de Montemora, a minor French writer, Annie granted that she "obtains good return for her fine energy," though neither the woman nor her work seemed particularly interesting. "Sometimes I think author-ship spoils women," she mused. Then after dismissing that thought as nonsense, she ventured another: "*small* authors, men or women, are apt to belong to a lower grade than the average remainder of *un*writing humans. Chiefly because their vanity overpowers in the end their fraction of common sense." It is easy to fault Annie's logic yet admire her effort at gender-free categorizing.

For Annie, the fact of the Countess's visit was more important than the visit itself. Ten days before, the celebrated poet Lamartine had honored the Fieldses by inviting them to a party, during which he called them aside for a private talk. Because of Jamie's minimal French, Annie did most of the conversing for them both, put at ease by Lamartine's "gentle magnetism." As an immediate consequence, the Fieldses were invited into literary circles that usually excluded foreigners. "It was truly a marked era for us," Annie exulted. "Doors everywhere now fly open to us."

Another pleasure of Annie's last days in Paris was her sister Lissie's arrival. Inviting Lissie to join her in Paris and proceed to Italy was Annie's first attempt to move another woman toward self-fulfillment, and the first time she invited another woman to share her life. Despite anxieties about Lissie's poor health, Mrs. Adams had at last withdrawn her objections. "Lissie came at midnight and we were thankful to get her here," Annie wrote in her diary on 22 December. Ten days later, the three travelers headed for Italy.

"Such warmth, such power of beauty as overspread us," Annie wrote soon after reaching Florence. The Fieldses' immediate priorities included visits to the city's most celebrated museums, churches, and palaces, and a pilgrimage to a private shrine—the tower where Hawthorne had written *The Marble Faun* and where the sunset was "a new miracle of beauty." Though she could only hope her "frail tenement of memory will stand bravely and retain what is best worth retaining for me," Annie was already confident about her own fused moral and aesthetic judgments, as when she admired a group of Roman portrait busts and then declared that "character had made the women and the marble expressed it as beauty."

Her social life within Florence's thriving expatriate community was more deeply gratifying. Whether at formal receptions or during calls upon or from such eminent literati as Thackeray, Landor, and Stowe, the Fieldses were treated like old friends. When they called on the courtly eighty-six-year-old Walter Savage Landor, for example, he moved from disparagement of Louis Napoleon and

Mrs. Browning's "faith in him" to complaints about his own "unnatural son" who had deprived him of his villa and his magnificent collection of paintings. Though "poor Lissie" usually felt too unwell to go along on such visits, she resolved to remain in Florence to continue painting and studying Italian after the Fieldses left for Rome.

There the doughty couple headed straight for St. Peter's, the Colosseum, and the Capitol, made a first quick pass at all the major museums and galleries, then revisited their favorite works of art and the studios of American expatriates including William Wetmore Story and Thomas Crawford. But as usual, people came first. A typical day might include breakfast with the great actress Charlotte Cushman and her sculptor-companion Emma Stebbins, dinner with Harriet Beecher Stowe, and an evening party attended by other denizens of Rome's expatriate community. "We have "engagements for breakfast, dinner, lunch, everyday," Annie noted in her diary, then complacently added, "We have been feted in Rome as few Americans have been."

A highlight of Annie's visit to Rome was meeting the two poets whose elopement had long since attained the status of myth. "We are to see the Brownings today and can think of nothing else," Annie wrote in her journal on 14 February; then, immediately afterward, she made fastidious word portraits of the ailing yet cordial Mrs. Browning, her strong but tender husband, and their beloved son. Awe did not impede her from registering each nuance of the couple's interchanges, as when Browning's remarks about his desire to finish *Sordello* prompted his wife to express doubts, and he turned to answer without "the least shadow of annoyance about him only a radiant expression of confidence in himself and belief in her." Yet because she was far more drawn to the frail yet forthright wife, Annie would feel disappointed by her *Poems Before Congress* a few months later, because "for the most part Poetry seems forgotten—in fire and ice—for Napoleon." A year later, Annie would take Mrs. Browning's death as a personal loss.

Although meeting Mrs. Browning stretched Annie's ideas about professional women's options, three otherwise very different American women that she met in Florence had already expanded them. Kate Field was the youngest, "a charming and intelligent" woman who was studying voice and supporting herself as a political journalist. She would soon return to America, where her contributions to the *Atlantic Monthly* and other interests she shared with Annie (including Charles Dickens and a new women's club) would eventuate in invitations to Charles Street and lively exchanges of letters, though never in intimacy.

The middle-aged actress Charlotte Cushman—a more complex and unconventional woman with a far more important career—would become a closer friend. The Fieldses had first encountered the "clear-hearted, clear-headed woman" and her companion Emma Stebbins in Genoa, where they all sat down for "a jubilant home-like talk"; and as Annie would recall over two decades later, "Many of the pleasantest days in Rome that winter were passed under her roof and at her table. Here was to be seen . . . everybody of interest either among the residents in Rome or the chance visitors to that city."[13] Related pleasures included visiting Stebbins's sculpture studio and taking excursions with the two women; and during the next decade, Annie relished each opportunity to watch Cushman perform and to entertain her at Charles Street.

The third of these friendships would be far more consequential—with Harriet Beecher Stowe. Their relationship began in Florence, continued in Rome, and then flourished after their return voyage from England to America together. Stowe anticipated "so much from the idea of making the voyage with you," she told Annie, not merely because James T. Fields was about to become her publisher.[14]

Returning to London after visits to Venice and Milan was a kind of homecoming. Immediately, the Fieldses found themselves "engaged in social activities every night for more than a week and still the invitations come in." Sometimes a social activity segued into a professional one, as when they visited the artist Joseph Severn and were so enthralled by his reminiscences of Keats that they persuaded him to write them out for publication in the *Atlantic*.

Annie had become so self-aware during her stay on the Continent that she could mock her own girlish delight when she finally dined with Dickens and his family. "I sat next to Dickens and tried to be as little awe-struck as possible at my position so that I might enjoy it to the full," she wrote in her diary, though what she primarily enjoyed was listening to Dickens himself. She now saw him as "rather the man of labor and of sorrowful thought than the soul of gaiety we find in all he writes."

Similarly, she now felt relatively at ease with Hawthorne and even proprietary about him. Writing to her family from Italy soon after *The Marble Faun* was published, she assumed they had already seen "Hawthorne's great novel" and urged them to "enjoy it enough for us also, because we cannot get it at present."[15] She started reading the "marvelous book" right after reaching England, and soon entertained Hawthorne himself. As she told her mother, "all the lion-hunters are upon his track, poor man! He seems to excite this particularly because he so seldom goes anywhere and the petitions from gentle & simple which flow in upon him must be very amusing I am sure."[16]

Yet he accepted her invitation to a breakfast party and displayed "a great deal of wit of his own kind in his talk." Surprised and amused by his discomfiture when an album was sent in for him to sign, and by his refusal to quote from his new book, "I gave him at his request for something Tennyson's song—'In love, if love be Love, if Love be ours.'" A new sense of parity with Hawthorne's family now colored her ambivalence about leaving England. "I fancy we are like a company of self convicted sufferers, the Hawthornes and ourselves," Annie told her mother, "because the latter do not want to leave exactly, at least they don't know *what* they want and we want to come home and see you all but it is hard breaking away from such a closely woven mesh of attractions."[17]

The Fieldses left London for Liverpool on 4 June, by way of York, the

Trossachs, Edinburgh, and the Lake Country. Ten days later, they returned to Mrs. Blodgett's boarding house, where they had spent their first nights in England. "Received 42 letters," Annie noted, and "answered the necessary ones." Hawthorne joined them the next day, "looking a melancholy silent grand genius as he is!" Almost exactly a year after arriving in England, the Fieldses were ready to depart, though "with a strange mixture of regrets and longings."

The voyage that had begun graced with flowers from Longfellow was ending even more triumphantly. Annie was now bound in friendship with both of America's most esteemed novelists, Hawthorne and Stowe. One had been published by Fields for a decade, the other was about to join his list, and both had promised to write for the *Atlantic Monthly*. Annie's introduction to the great sights of Europe and her entry into exclusive literary circles in England, France, and Italy had made her readier than ever to offer hospitality to celebrities whose professional and cultural ideals she admired. In that very readiness, she embodied period ideals of femininity. Yet with the approval and encouragement of the husband in whose work she would increasingly assist, her mind and emotions had already soared beyond period ideals. Even on shipboard, she was asking herself what one woman could do for and with another. Sitting on the deck of the boat in the company of Harriet Beecher Stowe and Sophia Hawthorne, Annie Fields felt herself to be more fully than before at the center of America's literary life.

3

Back Home

The Hostess

After a year of hotel living, zealous sightseeing, and easy intimacy with literary luminaries, Annie returned to Charles Street in June 1860 "unspeakably happy" to be back in her own "dear home" and ideally prepared for her burgeoning role as a literary hostess.

That role demanded well-honed social skills and adroit household management. As Willa Cather recognized, no one could have "blended so many strongly specialized and keenly sensitive people in her drawing-room, without having a great power to control and organize."[1] That control extended to the entire house and the garden beyond. Of course, Annie was hardly the only Boston matron who ran a three-story house with a basement kitchen, or the only one who hired, trained, and supervised a staff that included a cook, one or two maids, a handyman, and a laundress. But she had an unusual eye for good value, unusually sound taste, and an exceptional gift for hospitality.

Her housekeeping budget was flexible and generous. Among her husband's listings of personal disbursements such as "Teeth filled—$13" are such bi-monthly entries as "Gave A $100"—or perhaps $80, or $120, money that helped underwrite hospitality to Ticknor and Fields writers.[2] Annie was frugal and resourceful. She monogrammed her own linens, made her own flower arrangements, and used seasonal produce to prepare such tasty dishes that even veteran homemakers like Harriet Beecher Stowe requested her recipes. And her eight "ancient carved high-backed" chairs that once belonged to the Duke of Ormond's estate were bought in London "for a lower price than one gives in Boston for common chairs."[3]

Some of Annie's guests simply dropped by. Whittier often came for breakfast when he was in Boston, Holmes often crossed the street for a chat, and when Longfellow paid an afternoon call he often stayed for dinner. But most of Annie's hospitality was tightly scheduled. During a single week, a succession of overnight visitors might occupy both of her guest rooms; and the week's events might include a formal dinner for twelve followed by a violin recital in the library, a breakfast for ten, a tea party for twenty, and a reception for thirty-five. Two social events often framed a single cultural event, as when Ralph Waldo Emerson brought his wife and daughter Edith to tea before his public lecture on 3 December 1863, then afterward "they came home with us and about 20 friends." The *Harper's* editor Henry Alden joined them after his own Lowell lecture that same day, and he and his wife occupied one of Annie's guest rooms that night while "sunshiny Edith" had the other. The Aldens were still there when Nathaniel Hawthorne "passed the night with us" on 4 December, on his way to the funeral of Mrs. Franklin Pierce, though the second guest room was empty when he returned for another night two days later. As Annie once noted, an evening without guests was "really a novelty."

Most accounts of Annie's hospitality at least briefly mention such celebrities as Hawthorne and Emerson, ignoring such lesser lights as Henry Alden and also most of the women writers who became Annie's good friends. Even Mark De-Wolfe Howe says almost nothing about Celia Thaxter or Harriet Beecher Stowe in his *Memories of a Hostess,* and nothing at all about Rebecca Harding or Abby Diaz.[4] Admittedly, Annie gave many formal dinners to which only men were invited. But she also gave dinners and receptions honoring women writers, and a number of women writers were frequent houseguests. So were members of Annie's family. Her mother and sister Sarah came for days or even weeks at a time, her cousin Louisa May Alcott once stayed for several months, and Lissie Adams once stayed for nearly a year.

Still, most of Annie's guests during the sixties were writers, and entertaining them certainly served the business interests of Ticknor and Fields. Yet entertaining them was not primarily a matter of business. Annie and Jamie's ultimate purpose was to promote the culture of refined literary sensibility. But Annie's immediate purpose was to create "happy social occasions" for her guests, her husband, and herself.

The Editor's Assistant

Annie began what she called her "Journal of Literary Events and glimpses of interesting people" on 26 July 1863. The weather was warm, she wrote, but a lot of "literary labor" was going on and her husband was burdened by his editorial work. "What a strange history this literary life in America at the present day would make," she declared. "An editor and publisher at once stands at a confluence of tides where all humanity seems to surge up in little waves." She then took quick note of five of the country's major writers who were her good friends: Longfellow was vacationing at Nahant, his translation of Dante complete; Holmes had delivered a fine Fourth of July oration and written so much for the

Atlantic that he deserved a rest; Lowell was not well and was traveling; Hawthorne was completing *Our Old Home,* which he insisted on dedicating to Franklin Pierce; and Emerson had "written little of late" but was assembling a "volume containing his address upon Henry Thoreau."

Annie wrote as an insider, chronicling the "literary life in America" that she and her husband shared. She continued to do so in dozens of notebooks for the next fourteen years. Her own ideas, emotions, and accomplishments surfaced only intermittently, and she gave even less space to news of public concern such as Civil War battles. A self-appointed chronicler of literary life, she recorded her husband's accounts of events she had not witnessed—witty exchanges at the Old Corner Bookstore, for example, or at the monthly dinner meetings of Boston notables called the Saturday Club. "I enjoy myself privately in jotting down the strange things which have occurred within a day or two," she noted soon after beginning her journal, regretting only that she had let so many years pass without trying "to record something of the interesting events in literature which are constantly passing under my knowledge." She was proud of possessing that knowledge yet diffident about her ability to record it, and no one but her husband knew what she was up to. But she wrote with an eye to some future use of her material, and with a strong sense of noblesse oblige.

Her journal mentions the *Atlantic Monthly* at the outset, which her husband had been editing for the past two years. Blandly calling it "an interesting feature in America," Annie boasted that though "purely literary it has nevertheless a subscription list daily increasing of 32,000," and noted that "the editor's labors are not slight." But even in the privacy of her journal, she did not mention that he had help at home.

Ticknor had purchased the *Atlantic Monthly* on 20 October 1859 while the Fieldses were in Paris, "though of course not without correspondence and consultation."[5] The "Magazine of Literature, Art, and Politics" had then been in existence for two years, edited by James Russell Lowell and widely respected as a serious if essentially regional publication with high literary and moral standards. But its circulation had remained relatively low, the publishers Phillips, Sampson & Co. went bankrupt, and the bid Ticknor was cajoled into making turned out to be the only one. Even before returning to America, Fields as the firm's "literary partner" undertook to increase the magazine's circulation by soliciting lively manuscripts from well-established writers as well as neophytes. He urged Sophia and Nathaniel Hawthorne to submit manuscripts, for example, and welcomed Stowe's promise of a new story. By the time Fields replaced Lowell as editor in the summer of 1861, the *Atlantic* had become the country's most prestigious and most influential literary periodical.

That success was predictable. Fields was an efficient businessman with well-honed tastes, writers liked and respected him, and he worked hard. As editor of the *Atlantic,* he assumed responsibility for the entire magazine, deciding what to accept or reject, what to commission or cajole, what revisions to require, and how much to pay the authors. Until 1866 when William Dean Howells became his assistant, Fields composed every issue entirely on his own.

In doing so, the junior partner of Ticknor and Fields directly served the firm's wider interests—earning money for the firm while expanding its commitment to disseminate humane and genteel works of high literary quality. Obviously, he was also serving his contributors. For writers like Hawthorne whose books he had already published, though more crucially for new writers like Rebecca Harding, the *Atlantic* was a prestigious outlet, an incentive to productivity, and an important source of income. For the writers as well as the firm, that income multiplied whenever an *Atlantic* publication was reissued between Ticknor and Fields covers.

Meantime, Fields was serving but also controlling the reading public. Because one of his goals as *Atlantic* editor was to advance the liberal political beliefs he and Annie shared with most of their friends, he welcomed manuscripts that sympathetically presented the struggles of blacks, native Americans, and the urban poor. But he resisted radical political statements as firmly as he rejected eccentricities of style. In doing so, he retained the magazine's original identity as a product of genteel Boston with a multiple mission: to present "informing and stimulating" literature that would gratify "the imagination and a refined taste," while also serving as "a political, historical, and sociological review" and a "critical and scholarly journal" calculated to promote "the higher life of the nation."[6] Once Fields took over, the magazine became livelier, it began paying its own way, and its sphere of influence soon extended beyond New England to New York, with submissions and subscriptions flowing in from Ohio, California, and even London.

Yet there were no great differences between the last issue of the *Atlantic* edited by Lowell in June 1861 and Fields's July issue. In fact, each included a chapter of Stowe's *Agnes of Sorrento* and an installment of an article on Greek aesthetics, a short story, a few pages of poetry, and accounts of Civil War experiences. Lowell's practice of anonymous publication also continued, though in 1862 Fields began including a semi-annual key to authorship.[7] By then he was also making more substantive changes that steadily increased the magazine's circulation. Short and sprightly essays replaced the long and scholarly ones Lowell favored, and similar criteria guided his choices of poetry and fiction. A different kind of change involved the editor's wife. Lowell had also solicited submissions from new writers, many of them women. But Fields went further by offering personal friendship. In that enterprise (as in virtually every other nontechnical aspect of producing the *Atlantic*), his wife was his collaborator.

Though James T. Fields's role as editor was a matter of public knowledge as was Annie's role as his hostess, only a few friends knew that she was also his editorial assistant. "What excellence in the Atlantic generally!" Thomas Starr King wrote from California in 1863, then exclaimed, "No wonder when we remember the publisher & his wife!"[8] After visiting Charles Street the year before, Rebecca Harding had more broadly acknowledged their joint agency when she declared,

"I cannot separate you."[9] Whittier made a similar statement whenever he recommended a manuscript to both of the Fieldses (as he did for Charlotte Forten's "Life on the Sea Islands," her account of teaching former slaves in South Carolina), and whenever he sent a manuscript directly to Annie (he once asked her to read his friend Grace Greene's poem "with thy woman's heart, before James T. reads it with his critical eye"). Harriet Beecher Stowe was equally aware of the Fieldses' editorial partnership, as when she asked them both to read a "quaint" story by a Mrs. Ruggles "with care & see what can be done with it."[10]

Because Fields often enlisted his wife to correspond with *Atlantic* contributors, their friends in particular, many of them used Annie as a middleman to transmit or request information about their manuscripts. Anna Waterston once told Annie that she would complete an article the following week, for example, Harriet Beecher Stowe often told Annie that her submissions would be late, and Julia Ward Howe once asked her to "please tell Mr. Fields that I am waiting to hear from him about the poems I sent him." Occasionally, friends even used Annie as a production editor, as when Laura Johnson asked her to "see to" inserting the "corrections" she wanted before her poem "Picket Duty" was published.[11]

A complaint about the editor might also be transmitted through his wife, most dismayingly when a contributor whose name Annie entered in her journal but then decorously crossed out accused Fields of editorial "butchery."[12] Imperative requests were almost as dismaying. When Elizabeth Peabody asked Annie to attend a lecture on "the Gods of Verse," *'for a very particular reason'. . . . I went though I did not wish to, and discovered the reason to be that she wished it to be printed in the 'Atlantic.'"* Relieved to have "a good excuse" for turning Peabody down (a similar essay had already been scheduled), Annie complained, "as if it were not enough to pester my husband they prick him again through me."

Despite Annie's resentment of such pestering, she responded generously to women like Abby Morton Diaz who humbly requested advice (once meekly asking if some lines of a poem she hoped to submit had too many feet).[13] Out of the same dedication to serve deserving women as well as the magazine, when Eudora Clark sent her a "hospital manuscript" filled with "tearful truths," Annie painstakingly revised it to meet *Atlantic* standards.[14] Similarly, after receiving Louisa May Alcott's elegy "Thoreau's Flute" from Sophia Hawthorne, Annie suggested a few changes that Alcott made and thereby earned *Atlantic* publication.[15] Three of Alcott's wry domestic tales appeared in the *Atlantic* before "Thoreau's Flute" was published, and a Civil War story followed two months later (though Alcott's title "My Contraband" was changed to one Fields preferred—"The Brothers"). But Fields accepted nothing of Alcott's afterward, even though *Hospital Sketches* established her reputation for realistic reportage in August 1863 and *Little Women* brought her fame in 1868. Alcott complained to friends about Fields's rejections, delays in publication and payment, and lost manuscripts, claiming to be more interested in payment than in *Atlantic* prestige. In 1871, after repaying the forty dollars Fields had loaned her to furnish her kindergarten in 1862, Alcott reminded him that he had once advised her to stop writing and stick to teaching, where-upon he genially admitted his mistake (*Letters,* 160).

More surprisingly, Annie frequently served as critic and middleman for such established writers as Whittier and Stowe. After writing "a little ballad which I am quite doubtful of," for example, Whittier told Annie he wanted to "consult thee & James T. about it,"[16] and he often sent her a poem with the request that she pass it to "James T." if she thought it deserved publication. Stowe often wanted more than consultation, as when she sent Fields an essay urging Americans to buy na-tive products and wanted Annie to "look it over & if she & you think I have said too much of the Waltham watches make it right." Perhaps a paragraph about American glass should be added, Stowe wrote, but "If Annie thinks of any other thing that ought to be mentioned & will put it in for me she will serve both the cause & me."[17]

Meanwhile, Annie generously served the broad cause of humane letters by sharing her own personal experiences with *Atlantic* contributors, as when she provided Henry Alden with vignettes about Thackeray for an essay he was preparing. A related service was sharing her critical insights with *Atlantic* con-tributors, as when she discussed Goethe with David Atwood Wasson while he was preparing a long analysis of Goethe's *Wilhelm Meister.* As Wasson chivalrously told James T. Fields before completing the two-part study, "They belong, how-ever, to Mrs. Fields, the second in particular containing matters which she and I have talked over together."[18]

On at least one occasion, when she invited her friend Anna Waterston to write about Jane Austen, Annie corralled a new *Atlantic* contributor. "Had I been asked before reading your note, whether I could prepare an article immediately for a pe-riodical (a thing I never did in my life) I should have smiled at the absurdity of the question," Mrs. Waterston replied. But since Annie had "proposed a subject my heart cannot resist," she would write the essay "out of love for Miss Austen—and my dear Mrs. Fields."[19]

A more direct service to her editor husband stemmed from Annie's language skills—the knowledge of French she had attained at George B. Emerson's school, and the knowledge of German she pursued on her own. On several occasions she translated passages from George Sand and Goethe for the *Atlantic;* and Jamie also asked her to translate Victor Hugo's *Les Travailleurs de la Mer* for one of the an-thologies he edited.

But a more crucial service to her husband was judging submissions to the *At-lantic* and to Ticknor and Fields. "Dressmaking shopping & reading manuscripts," Annie once noted, and she once casually reported lying down after dinner to read a manuscript her husband wanted "to know of." Clearly, the editor trusted her judgments. "Jamie wants me to decide if he should print Miss Cary's book," An-nie wrote in the fall of 1865; and since no book by Alice Cary appeared under the Ticknor and Fields imprint (though eleven of her poems and two of her stories appeared in the *Atlantic*), presumably Annie decided against it. A more significant recommendation was advising the publication of Elizabeth Stuart Phelps's *Gates Ajar* three years later, a book that catapulted the author to fame. On at least one occasion, perhaps because her husband wanted "to know of" too many manuscripts, Annie herself enlisted a consultant—her friend Anna Waterston—who thought Caroline Chesebro's new stories fell short of her "Victor and Jacqueline."[20]

Especially rewarding was recommending a friend's manuscript to her husband, as Annie did for perhaps the last time in the summer of 1870 while vacationing at Manchester. Asked by Jamie to pass judgment on a manuscript submitted by Henry James, she read it, "finding the quality good (though the handwriting was execrable)," was moved to tears, then "invited my dear boy to a favorite nook in the pasture where we . . . lay down with our feet plunged into the cool, delicious grass while I read the pleasant tale of Italy to the close." "Compagnons de Voyage" appeared in the *Atlantic* in November and December, the last two issues edited by James T. Fields.

We can only guess about the Fieldses' agreements or disagreements about other *Atlantic* manuscripts, including the work of Annie herself. During her husband's editorship, nearly two dozen of her poems appeared in the *Atlantic* anonymously or pseudonymously. We have no way of knowing what editorial changes Fields recommended or required in those poems, how many others he may have rejected, or what payment (if any) she received. But undoubtedly both husband and wife exulted whenever a poem of Annie's met the editor's high standards.

The Ode and the Odist

Throughout the Civil War, Annie followed battle news and worried about Union soldiers, her brother among them, she grieved with friends whose sons and brothers were wounded or killed, and the war figured in many of her poems. A resolute abolitionist, she applauded Robert Shaw's "colored regiment, now 850 strong" when they marched in review on 30 April 1863, mourned their defeat at Fort Wagner, and participated in fund-raising fairs for the freedmen. Meantime her husband served the Union cause by publishing manuscripts in the *Atlantic* that supported it. Annie had begun writing poems during the preceding decade, and Jamie published several that dealt with the war, among them her *Ode Recited by Miss Charlotte Cushman, at the Inauguration of the Great Organ in Boston, November 2, 1863.*

Publication of that eleven-page ode was a momentous event for the anonymous author. The country's most distinguished actress declaimed it, the capacity audience at the Boston Music Hall applauded it, and the country's most important literary publisher had it printed and distributed. It was her longest and most ambitious poem, the only one written for oral delivery, and the only one she was commissioned to write—presumably through her husband's influence. For the many friends who received copies of that small book with its ponderous title gold-stamped on a white cover, it marked Annie's public debut as a poet.

The audience at the Music Hall on 2 November 1863 had assembled for a signal event: an inaugural concert on a German-built organ containing 5,474 pipes—"the largest and finest in existence."[21] As a prelude to that performance, the great actress Charlotte Cushman declaimed a patriotic poem written for the occasion. But there had been some uncertainty, because the organ's installation was incomplete until nearly the last moment. Cushman had returned to America for a series of benefit performances as Lady Macbeth, the role that had launched her career twenty-eight years before. Those sold-out appearances in four northern cities would net over eight thousand dollars for the Sanitary Commission.[22] She hoped to recite the ode on the eve of her return to Europe.

"There has been an ode written to be spoken at the organ opening," Annie wrote in her journal on 25 September, her comment curiously fusing modesty and vanity. "No one is to know who wrote it. Miss Cushman will speak it if they are speedy enough in their finishing. This is of interest to many." Annie, who had just seen Cushman's first benefit performance as Lady Macbeth, muted her own excitement at the prospect of having her ode delivered by America's most celebrated actress. As she scrupulously declared, Cushman was a "woman of effects [who] lives for effect. And yet doing always good things and possessed of the most admirable qualities." Declaiming Annie's patriotic ode would be one such good thing. On 6 October Annie cautiously reported that the organ was finally being tuned and "If no accident occurs Miss Cushman will read *the* ode."

There was no accident. The day before the reading, Cushman arrived at Charles Street "full of power and sweetness as usual"; and the two women sat up talking past midnight, then "scrambled to bed like naughty children." Hawthorne's daughter Una and the essayist Gail Hamilton joined them for dinner the next day, planning to stay overnight, and at seven they all left together for the Music Hall. After the performance, a few friends joined the group for supper at Charles Street, Julia Ward Howe among them, but were not told who had written the ode. "Charlotte read my ode in a most perfect manner," Annie complacently wrote in her journal that night. Although the actress seemed "nervous about it and skipped something . . . what she did read was perfect. Her dress & manner too were dignified and beautiful." All in all, "It was a night never to be forgotten."

The next day after Cushman set out for Liverpool, Annie "took a long delicious draught of talk" with Gail Hamilton and probably confided her authorship at that time. Sections of the ode appeared on the editorial page of the *Boston Daily Courier,* and several local newspapers praised both the poem and its delivery. Almost immediately, Annie's proud husband had the ode published and sent copies to friends, disclosing the author's name.

As Whittier hastened to tell "dear Mrs. Meadows," he was delighted "to find thee to be the author of the magnificent Ode to which fashion & beauty, manhood & . . . genius listened from the coal-touched lips of Charlotte Cushman. I supposed it to be Mrs. Howe's. Every body praised it. After all, I think I hear the juror of the Ticknor & Fields firm saying to the congratulating Public:— 'Have your way ladies & gentlemen. Take the poem & make the most of it: *I* have the writer, & I wouldn't swap the dear woman God bless her! for a new Divina Commedia or Paradise Lost!'"[23] Instead of exulting about that tribute in her journal, Annie wrote only that "JTF" thanked Whittier for his "heartfelt praise of a certain Ode."

Sophia Hawthorne's immediate praise was also heartfelt. As she told her "divine Cecilia," she had already read the poem six times to herself and twice aloud, finding it "better and better" each time; and she congratulated the poet's husband who could "look saucily at all the world, with such a Muse for his own better self."[24] A more professional tribute to Annie's "maiden white and gold" publication came from Edward Everett Hale, whose "The Man without a Country" was about to appear in the *Atlantic.* He welcomed her as a professional colleague and wondered if she wanted her anonymity preserved.[25] "I think you achieved a very difficult thing, in the production of such a poem, and have reason to be entirely satisfied with it," said Anna Waterston, who had recently published a moving eulogy for Robert Shaw and a well-received volume of poems. She had found "much in it that a *first* reading does not develop which is the true test of a *work* like this."[26]

But ten days after the reading, a bombshell fell. On the front page of the *Commonwealth* of 13 November appeared a review titled "How to Regard the Great Organ." It disparaged the newly remodeled Music Hall and the organ itself, declaring that no organ could be as satisfying as an orchestra, and then lambasted the *Ode Recited by Miss Charlotte Cushman.* The ode "had no characteristic of a poem other than phrase and rhyme" and "no stamp of originality," the author declared. "Surely, among the literary men and women of Boston, among those who really *could,* might have been found some one who *would* have spoken the word for the hour which, whether in prose or verse, was what the public wanted to hear."

For the Fieldses and their friends it was an open secret that the reviewer was one of their own—Julia Ward Howe, whose husband was then editing the *Commonwealth.* During Fields's two-and-a-half years as editor of the *Atlantic,* he had published two of Howe's essays and several of her poems including the "The Battle Hymn of the Republic," which had made her a national celebrity, and in 1853 he had published her first volume of poems. No doubt she counted herself among those who could have written a better poem than Annie's. Loftily, she declared that "in criticism, as well as in poetry, there are necessities of conviction which put far from us the conventional phrases of compliment, and force us to utter truths which are as unwelcome to us as they can be to those whom they arraign before the tribunal of opinion." She then blasted Annie's ode as poor work by "an unpractised hand."[27]

Fields spluttered with indignation. "Have you seen in the 'Commonwealth'

Mrs. Howe's notice of Annie's Ode?" he asked Sophia Hawthorne four days later. "That mistress of envy, scandal, and malice has cast the first stone at my wife's beautiful poem!" Attributing the attack wholly to jealousy, Fields assumed Howe "could not bear that the guild of Literature and Art should be wide enough to admit another of her own sex." He could not even entertain alternative hypotheses—that Howe genuinely disliked the ode, for example, or that she was revenging herself on the editor who had not only rejected several of her poems but was publishing others only at what seemed like random intervals. Fields simply wrote Howe off as a "false-hearted woman," assuming she had "hardly a real friend left."[28] Affecting disinterest, Annie vented the same conclusions in her journal: "Julia Ward Howe has said and sung her last as far as Boston goes. Her jealousy of the Odist got the better of her judgment and she has written out her gall for the 'Commonwealth.' Alas! Where was her good genius."[29]

Until then, Annie had admired Howe without feeling close to her. "Mrs. Howe witty as usual," she remarked after an evening at the Howes' in early October, during which her hostess "provoked and sustained a philosophic-scientific talk with the gentlemen which showed her cleverness and her knowledge of Comte, Spinoza, Kant, Hegel, and other writers of their class." A similar evening a few weeks later provoked a broader compliment: "Mrs. Howe always impresses us with her conversational skill. I am convinced that none of the French women were more clever at this." That conviction at least partly explains why Annie invited Howe to have supper at Charles Street after the ode's delivery. Given everyone else's praise, Annie could only conclude with her husband that Howe's later attack on the ode was fueled by jealousy.

Three weeks afterward, Howe sent a curiously unapologetic apology through their Minister friend Cyrus Bartol, asking the Fieldses to forget the article "which was an unpleasant business on her part." "Never mind Mrs. Howe's folly," Whittier advised James T. Fields on Christmas day, then offered a fresh bit of assurance: his friend Colonel Bogart "speaks high praise of the ode & its author & he is a man of true taste & scholarship."[30] But they could hardly forget it. It would be years before Annie could mention Howe's name without some expression of scorn.

A self-assertive woman of caustic wit who was fifteen years Annie's senior, Howe surely considered herself intellectually superior to the demure and charming woman she once referred to as a "fair little House-wife." Yet they were in many ways alike. They had both been reared in households of culture and privilege, they both read widely and wrote assiduously all their lives, and they had both married much older men who brought them into the exalted circle that included Emerson, Longfellow, and Holmes, and such liberal theologians as James Freeman Clarke.[31] Both then and thereafter, both women professed the same liberal social ideals and advocated the same causes. When the Sanitary Commission ran a National Sailors' Fair in November 1864 as a fund-raiser for a sailors' home, for example, Annie wrote a poem titled "An Appeal to the People for an American Seaman's Home" for the fair's newspaper, *The Boatswain's Whistle,* which was edited by Howe.[32] And in 1868 Annie was in on the start of the New England Woman's Club, which Howe cofounded and presided over.

Yet Annie continued to bridle at Howe's imperiousness, whether deploring the "vulgar salutatory" Howe delivered at a Ladies Club meeting in the fall of 1865 or complaining that her "little narrow personality" had disrupted an organizational meeting of the Society of Working Women in January 1870. That same month, however, Annie invited Howe to give a benefit reading for one of her charities, and Howe not only agreed but reported attending another "meeting in furtherance of your reform."[33] Nonetheless, the two women remained only coolly cordial until their decades of widowhood, the years when Sarah Orne Jewett and Howe's daughters Maud Elliot and Laura Richardson entered into their networks of affection and obligation. In her *Reminiscences* of 1899, Howe said she had drawn "comfort and instruction" from "the better acquaintance with my own sex [and] the experience of the power resulting from associated action in behalf of worthy objects."[34] Annie Fields might have said the same. But that could not have been predicted in November 1863, when Howe publicly attacked the ode.

Before then, and even then, almost nobody knew that Annie wrote poetry. For years she had carefully preserved fair copies of her poems, however, and between 1857 and 1864 she copied dozens into a notebook, dated and arranged in chronological order. Seven of them had already appeared in the *Atlantic,* and a few had been reprinted in Boston newspapers. Though they all appeared anonymously or pseudonymously, Annie's pleasure in seeing her work published is evident from a recurrent notation in her manuscript notebook: "(See Atlantic Mag.)."

But the ode was the longest and most serious of her efforts, written in a public voice for an important public occasion—a "night never to be forgotten." It is as easy to understand Annie's pleasure in her friends' praise as her resentment of Howe's attack.

The ode now seems to merit only moderate praise. It begins grandly enough:

> Listen to the invocation!
> Now awaking, praiseful breaking,
> It shall bear the heart of a nation,
> Swelling in vast convocation,
> Full of honor, full of song,
> Upward to the Source of Praise where harmonies belong.

It then unfolds logically in well-structured stanzas, until its six-part sequence reaches a stirring crescendo. Annie's resolutely high-minded expressions of pride in Boston and in her country's "hard-won glory," like her expressions of trust in "the Source of Praise where harmonies belong," rarely soar. The "city by the sea," for example, is prosperous, "laborious, brave, and free." Yet her poem develops a powerful momentum with its epic account of the organ's construction, and it resoundingly announces the Union's inevitable triumph in the Civil War: "the voice of Freedom rings / One choral chant, one song of praise,—A NATION'S VICTORY!"

Despite Howe's attack and the poem's conventional tropes, its spectacular de-livery, its rhetorical effects, and its subsequent publication established Annie Fields's credentials as a poet, and not only among such devoted friends as Whit-tier and Sophia Hawthorne. Perhaps because of pride in Annie's achievement, and also to honor their ninth wedding anniversary ("nine unsullied years," Annie mused in her journal), Fields commissioned the renowned artist Samuel Worces-ter Rowse to produce a black crayon portrait of his wife. "Sat for the 3 time to Mr. Rowse for portrait," Annie complacently wrote in her journal on 9 November, then remarked that the artist was "eccentric but true and interesting." After a week of "sitting to Rowse daily," Annie concluded with apparent detachment, "He has been successful in his work." Her husband agreed: he "pronounced it 'su-perb' to the profound satisfaction of all parties."

Those "parties" included Anna Waterston and her husband, who (at Annie's request) inspected the portrait in Rowse's studio and then praised it, especially the mouth—"that most difficult feature to draw in properly."[35] Soon afterward, Fields had the drawing reproduced and sent copies to friends. No one responded more enthusiastically than Whittier. As he told Annie, he and his sister Elizabeth "were perfectly delighted on breaking open the parcel last evening to meet the sweet face of dear Mrs. Meadows, (whom the Lord love and keep always!) admirable as a likeness and 'beautiful exceedingly.'" Poignant proof of Elizabeth's delight is the note she sent Annie from her sickbed in mid-March: "Last evening I had brought in from another room a *pictured* Lady as I often do, *for I love to see her.*"[36]

Only Sophia Hawthorne had reservations about the portrait. "At the first view of it, I did not like it—something about the expression—as if you were a little dis-gusted—troubled me," she told Annie. Then, fusing the artist's vision with the votary's, she admitted that "there is so much in it exactly like that it enchants me more than it disturbs with a certain shadow on the nose—It looks like a stag at bay somewhat—from the brilliant, intent look of the beautiful eyes"; and like the Waterstons, Sophia particularly admired the mouth. The portrait was "invalu-able," she said. Yet she wished she "could have the original picture, because in that there may not be this too pronounced shadow. I have touched it and tried to lessen it myself—but I do not quite erase it sufficiently." Annie soon sent another copy which Sophia greatly preferred; and at that point she exulted that she could tell Annie anything.[37]

Sophia's description of the portrait is precise, down to her complaint about the nose. Rowse's bust portrait of Annie Fields presents a contemplative young woman with a heart-shaped face, a sensitive mouth, and dark wavy hair parted in the center and covering her ears; she is facing half-left and wearing a high-collared white blouse. An art historian's description of an earlier Southworth and Hawes daguerreotype of Annie Fields applies equally well to the Rowse crayon: a young woman with a mild expression and undulating hair is seated "quietly wrapped in an atmosphere of her own, as if absorbed in private thought but capable at any moment of noticing another's presence and rising with a polite welcome."[38] Elizabeth Whittier's phrase *"pictured* Lady" would be an appropriate caption for both portraits.

"The Boston Woman" would be another. As Ednah Cheney described that paragon in *The Memorial History of Boston* (1881), she is "more intellectual than passionate, her impulses are under control," her "gentle purity inspires confidence," and "her morality is stern and exacting," but she has "great freedom of thought" and fulfills herself in "benevolent activity." Moreover, her "aesthetic nature" is serious and refined. Cheney might well have been describing Annie Adams Fields.[39]

4

The Conservative Feminist

"How Hard It Is for Women to Work in This World"

Even as a young woman, Annie Fields both accepted and challenged the prevailing assumption that women require marriage for fulfillment. She thought her sister Lissie would forfeit artistic success if she married, for example, and she feared that her own domestic responsibilities might destroy her "genius" for writing. That was all the more reason to admire happily married women who nevertheless pursued self-determined goals.

Maria Weston Chapman was one such paragon, a Boston Lady nearly thirty years older than Annie who was one of New England's most famous abolitionists. She had cofounded the Boston Female Anti-Slavery Society, written its annual reports, edited its periodicals, and run its annual fund-raising fairs. But her legendary fame dated from Boston's most notorious episode of anti-abolition violence. When thousands of rioters attacked the Anti-Slavery Society's annual meeting in 1835, Maria Chapman had denounced Boston's mayor for not dispersing the noisy mob, declared "If this is the last bulwark of freedom, we may as well die here as anywhere," then led the mixed-race abolitionist women in a two-by-two march to her own house.[1]

During one of Annie's calls on Maria Chapman in 1865, she felt drawn to the woman who talked "proudly of *our* people meaning the colored folk," a woman still in magnificent health who had been "one of the pioneers for their redemption when to espouse their cause was to be among the despised and rejected ones." In Mrs. Chapman's drawing room, two new portrait busts by the young black sculptor Edmonia Lewis were on display. One was of Colonel Robert Shaw, the young white Bostonian who had died while leading the all-black 54th Massachusetts Volunteers into battle. The other was of Mrs. Chapman.

After one of Mrs. Chapman's visits to Charles Street two years later, Annie entered a tribute in her journal that she copied out, perhaps with an eye toward publication. Mrs. Chapman was a remarkably beautiful older woman whose eyes would still "outshine those of ball-room belles," Annie wrote, a woman with loving children who had spent "much of the winter in New York playing with her grandchildren on the floor." More important, "her life has been an eventful one, as she was one of the first women to espouse the anti-slavery cause in this country. All her ability, which is great, all her spirit and heart were given to the cause." Though Annie had not yet found her own such cause, she surely saw something of herself in the woman who had started a salon in Paris in the late forties, "and became acquainted with M. Ampère and many of the most distinguished men and women of that period, and her career both at home and abroad has been that of a noble and able woman." She paid another kind of tribute to Mrs. Chapman when Harriet Beecher Stowe next came to Charles Street. She took Stowe to see Mrs. Chapman and prompted the latter to recall "some of the experiences of her anti-slavery career when her house was set on fire and then mobbed. 'What a queenly creature,' said Mrs. Stowe, as she waved to us from the door, 'who would think that woman came from old Puritan stock?'"[2]

Another "queenly creature" and dedicated abolitionist, James Russell Lowell's older sister Mary Lowell Putnam, was a less publicly visible role model. An accomplished linguist and a published poet, Mrs. Putnam was a large-souled, sweet-tempered woman whose home was "a model of hospitality and refinement," and her "sanctification by sorrow" when her last surviving son died during the Civil War inspired one of Annie's most moving poems.[3] "It is always most difficult to define the character of a woman like this," Annie once wrote; "It is like talking of the color of a crystal." She would teach Sunday school with Mrs. Putnam in James Freeman Clarke's Church of the Disciples and work with her on charity fairs and on the Centennial Committee to Preserve the Old South Church, and they regularly exchanged poems, books, flowers, and visits. But what Annie most enjoyed was their one-on-one talks. "A higher standard, a fuller life grows up from such intercourse," Annie wrote after one of their wide-ranging discussions of life and literature, then called her "the first lady of our time."

The Ladies Club that Annie attended during the sixties evidently provided few if any such gratifications, as suggested by Anna Waterston's report of "charades of large dimensions" at one of two successive meetings that Annie skipped in November 1863. Three years later, Annie planned to withdraw from the club to "keep as much at home evenings as possible." Though she later attended at least one more meeting, where Mrs. Silsbee presented a "good paper" on social life in Salem, Annie said nothing further about the paper itself or about anything else that occurred at the Ladies Club.[4]

Yet she often recorded even the trivial comments of her eminent male guests, on the grounds that it was stupid or derelict "not to bottle up any of the delicate effervescing fun" of their table talk. As her husband's surrogate, she also recorded his reports of the witticisms their male friends uttered at the Saturday Club, the Dante Club, and the Old Corner Bookstore. But the woman who had internalized period conceptions of cultural importance rarely quoted any women she knew and seldom recorded her own thoughts and feelings.

It is nonetheless clear that Annie Fields was an avid but discriminating reader who made the most of her access to the Boston Athenaeum as well as to every book her husband published or purchased. She kept up with the new and tried to master the great. Her pleasures in the new ranged from Whitman's poems to George Eliot's novels; she read George Sand in French, Dante in Italian, and Goethe in German; and she made her way through the classics in translation. As one way of appropriating what she read, she translated French and German poets. Another was preparing brief critical biographies of Blake and other writers she admired. She also determined to emulate Hawthorne's lively journal entries and eschew the boredom of Anne Bradstreet's.

As her enthusiasm for Whitman, George Eliot, and George Sand suggests, Annie Fields's intertwined personal and literary judgments were never wholly constrained by middle-class proprieties.[5] Thus she believed in the sanctity of marriage but condoned Dickens's adultery and did not worry about George Eliot's. And despite the period belief that women should avoid the limelight, she profoundly admired such great actresses as Charlotte Cushman and such noble-minded lecturers as Mary Livermore.

As a corollary of celebrating and supporting individual excellence, whether in a man or a woman, Annie tried to think the best of everyone in her overlapping circles. As a single representative example, when Cyrus Bartol sounded empty-headed, she made herself think about his generosity. A more paradoxical corollary was expecting everyone to think the best of her. Driven by lofty self-expectations, Annie feared falling short of her own goals and bristled at criticism. Julia Ward Howe's sneer at her anonymous *Ode on the Great Organ* was therefore as intolerable as her sister Lissie's complaint that she was overdemanding.

That complaint came near the end of Lissie's nearly year-long stay at Charles Street that began in September 1866. The year before, Lissie had exhibited in the French Salon and she had also received a proposal of marriage. "How hard it is for women to work in this world," Annie then mused; "they are made to love, to sympathize, to console, to labor for others, but only when their lives are cast on desert sands do they attain pre-eminence in art." If she was thinking about her own seemingly irreconcilable goals, her primary concern was with Lissie's: "With all her talent with her years of exile which have their fruit and given her a certain pre-eminence in art, now comes this man who wishes her for himself." Evidently Annie simply assumed that Lissie could not succeed as an artist if she married, but also assumed that Lissie would succeed if she remained single. To that end, Annie invited her to stay at Charles Street after she rejected her suitor, helped her find a studio when she arrived, often served as her model, recruited other sitters for her, and lined up potential purchasers. As a would-be muse, she also read Lissie two Hawthorne narratives that seemed appropriate for illustration—"Rappaccini's Daughter" on one occasion, and *The Dolliver Romance* on another.

But Lissie's professional success fell short of Annie's expectations. As their brother Boylston had once put it, Lissie set too low a value on her work and needed "that fearless self-confidence which alone she lacks."[6] As Annie saw it, Lissie drove herself hard but abandoned most of her projects before completing them; and her "diseased feelings" eventually made her accuse Annie of being too exacting. Lissie was at least partly right. But Annie thought her sister's unhappiness was "less my fault than an unreadiness and impossibility for enjoyment of life on her part at least while her work stands just where it is now." She even feared Lissie would "never accomplish much in art."

"Le Brun's motto for women is ever near my heart 'inspirez et n'écrivez pas,'" she once said, telling herself that she preferred "doing what I can for others" to pursuing her career. That preference was itself complicated by her belief that "'to inspire' one must take seasons of meditation and repose from the world and must live listening to the eternal harmony while the tempests of earth howl and sweep around our heads." Though such "listening" was of course crucial to writing, serving others continued to be her highest priority. "Heaven keep us from the narrowness of living only for ourselves," she once wrote in her journal. Thus she gave up a few "lovely days of retirement" with Jamie when her mother and sister Sarah wanted to come along, and she often reminded herself that time was "not my own to seize—housekeeping, entertaining visiting cannot be neglected or others would be uncomfortable." She could not even make adequate journal entries when visitors "succeeded each other too swiftly, not too swiftly for me to love and remember much but the writing appears impossible."

Despite such disappointments, Annie nonetheless rejoiced in her "strange full life" that included so many friends. "How good home is!" she once exclaimed. "How dear for the love that haunts it!" But no one and nothing was dearer than her husband. "Sunday on the rocks with my love," she exclaimed in July 1866, and a subsequent entry is even more blissful: "What a day! . . . My darling and I passed the morning on the rocks by the sea." Yet sometimes she wondered if she deserved such bliss. Thus one afternoon in the winter of 1867 when she did not feel up to writing or any other "close occupation," she read at the Athenaeum and visited Lissie's studio, then called on her "dear boy" at his office and walked home with him, but blamed herself for not accomplishing enough that day to deserve such a privilege. In that same spirit, she felt unworthy of Jamie's "sweetness and devotion" in an art gallery when he purchased the sketch she admired instead of the one he preferred. All in all, she was sure there was "neither end nor limit to his love," and equally sure there was none to hers. "We stand all to each in this world," she once reflected; and the sight of his footsteps on the Manchester beach after he had gone into Boston provoked her to declare, "We walk side by side in spirit."

"Fie! to My Genius"

"I am eager, eager to do something," Annie wrote in her journal in February 1868, then assured herself, "I *can* live the poem I *would* write." Sometimes her repeated resolve "to live more for those around me, to make them more happy, to leave deeper foundations" seemed "mere nonsense for the waves of time like those on the sea beach wash away the deepest imprints." Even so, she kept telling herself it was better to "live and use poetry than live for poetry." She vowed (in Dickens's words) "Never to put one hand to anything in which I could not throw my whole self, and never to effect depreciation of my work, whatever it was." But she often did both.

In the fall of 1868, Jamie casually remarked that she would never write anything better than her *Ode*. Wounded, Annie told herself she could "do something far more sustained and as truly lyrical," though not under her present circumstances, which required attention to "marketing and dresses—and so runs the day away." Provoked by a biography of Robert Burns she had just read, she then zigzaggingly interrogated her own restricted identity: "Burns was always a poet—surely we ought always to be ourselves, and yet I am too much a woman to be always a poet. Yet I know there is a heart of a singer hidden in me and I long sometimes to break loose—but on the whole I sincerely prefer to make others comfortable and happy as I can now do and say fie! to my genius if he does not sing to me from the sauce-pan all the same." A few months later when she felt a "poem stirring somewhere within me" but could not make time to develop it, she feared her poetic faculty might "die because the days pass thus." This time, she resorted to a pious platitude: "God knows best." "Nine for dinner," she once noted proudly but perhaps also wistfully in her journal, "all of them poets."

In her own mind she had become a poet by 1857, the earliest date she noted on any of the poems she preserved. She wrote for self-fulfillment but also hoping to attain parity with the many eminent poets she knew (many of whom would later praise her work).

Predictably, many of her early poems express love for her husband. "Come in thy strength and beauty, O my love, / And walk with me in this palace of the Soul," an 1857 sonnet begins; and in "Mary Shelley" (1859), the poet's poignant lament for the widow ends in terror "Lest he whom I revered o'er all the rest / Should vanish from the sight of his beloved." Devotion to her husband also informs two poems of marital advice addressed to Rebecca Harding Davis. "Espoused," written in January 1863 after Rebecca announced her imminent marriage, advises her to "Raise thy pure lamp for him to see / And love to one prove love to all"; and "To RH on her wedding day" urges her to "Look up and face the sunshine of thy bliss." Two years later, Annie wrote the first of what would be four "Canticles of Married Love" as an anniversary gift to her husband. The opening lines of the first poem in the 1865 Canticles are typical in their romantic urgency: "Quick, one long kiss, ere kisses be no more, / Though love endure." Not surprisingly, Annie reported in her journal that "Jamie was filled with happiness by the gift of 'Canticles.'"

Many of her other unpublished poems were also conceived as gifts, including ambitious birthday poems to Laura Johnson that figure Laura as a poet—for example, as a "bird / Who sings in the green top, while dark to dark complains. . . ." Several are elegies, including one for Annie's namesake Annie Adams Alden (Henry Alden's infant daughter who died in October 1863), another for the popular English novelist Elizabeth Sheppard (who died in 1862 at the age of thirty-two), and "The Traveller" (written "In memory of, and in love of, Nathaniel Hawthorne" a few weeks after his death). The elegy Annie later wrote for Sophia Hawthorne is unique in its self-righteousness: after accusing S. H. of wounding her, the speaker magnanimously forgives her.

Not surprisingly, the Civil War figures directly or indirectly in many of Annie's wartime poems. "Our President," written "for the Re-election in 1864," jauntily argues that since Lincoln "knows the ropes," we should bid him "Hold the rudder in this stormy sea." But most of the poems in this group explicitly present a woman's point of view. In "A Woman's Appeal for Volunteers," for example, the speaker resoundingly declares that "With him who makes a patriot's choice, / With him shall all the hours rejoice"; and the speaker of "A Picture in War-Time" sympathetically observes a woman mourning her heroic brother who "gave himself to death and freedom's cause."

Four of her eleven poems that appeared in the *Atlantic* during the war years were war poems—"The Wild Endive," "Waiting," "Give," and "The Future Summer." Each is a tightly structured and vividly detailed affirmation of life in the face of death, and she would republish all four in *The Singing Shepherd* (1895). But Annie's longest and most ambitious Civil War poem was also her first separate publication—the eleven-page *Ode*.

Unpublished narrative poems about admirable women constitute a separate subcategory of her sixties poems. "Alice of the Hills" (dated Campton, June 28, 1864) is a seven-page iambic pentameter narrative in which a blind girl makes her father's life happy and complete, a low-key Wordsworthian affirmation of heroic possibility within a limited pastoral existence. "The Lady Ursula—a tale of early New England" is a versified historical romance over twenty pages long which centers on a tender-hearted colonial aristocrat who acted heroically and "led the feet of men" until she was killed by Indians, a poem that melodramatically exhorts all Americans to remember our heritage and do "new deeds worthy of our past." The more tightly structured "In the Palace, Florence 1530" (a three-part poem in dactylic hexameter) centers on a noblewoman whose beloved husband is fighting against France and who refuses to sell her wedding bed to an emissary of King Francis. Conflating her own identity with her husband's and her city's, she heroically declares, "We who so love thee can suffer, can live or can die for thy freedom, / Stand while that stands, and when liberty falls, O my Florence, we fall!" Like Alice and Ursula, she is a courageous and self-confident womanly woman, a moral example. Like their author, each heroine accepts and yet transcends well-defined social bounds.[7]

Most of Annie's many poems of the sixties, published or unpublished, met or exceeded period standards for excellence. They are all tightly structured, passionately moral, confident, and humane; and their subjects include all the major ones: death, love, faith, and search for meaning.[8] Even the briefest—Annie's second published poem, "Compensation" (1862)—is of its period in offering a familiar Emersonian argument with tight metrical insistence: recompense is inherent "In the strength of the endeavor, / In the temper of the giver, / In the loving of the lover," and "In the fading of each hour." Two other *Atlantic* poems of the sixties manifest the period fondness for allegory: the brief dream poem "My Ship" ends by identifying a treasure-laden ship as the speaker's beloved; and the more conventionally moralizing two-and-a-half-page "My Palace" dramatizes the soul's progress from pleasure to sorrow to bliss.

Annie's first published poem, "The Wild Endive" (1861), is a four-quatrain meditation on what is "Only a weed to the passer-by, / Growing among the rest" whose "drop of the heaven's blue. . . . lodges in my breast." This Transcendental and even Blakean trope is implicitly given a Civil War context (the first passer-by is "a man with a soldier's load"), but its moral imperative goes beyond the war. As Annie's first *Atlantic* poem, as one she included in *The Singing Shepherd* thirty-four years later, as one of Sarah Orne Jewett's favorites, and as a quietly powerful affirmation, it warrants quotation in full:[9]

> Only the dusty common road,
>   The glaring weary heat;
> Only a man with a soldier's load,
>   And the sound of tired feet.
>
> Only the lonely creaking hum
>   Of the Cicada's song;
> Only a fence where tall weeds come
>   With spiked fingers strong.
>
> Only a drop of the heaven's blue
>   Left in a way-side cup;
> Only a joy for the plodding few
>   And eyes that look not up.
>
> Only a weed to the passer-by,
>   Growing among the rest,
> Yet something clear as the light of the sky
>   It lodges in my breast.[9]

Annie's most ambitious literary project of the sixties—her novel *Asphodel*—dramatizes the soul's progress. As in many of her sixties lyrics, a perceptive woman is at its moral center, and it draws on the Civil War. The central figure is a poet.

"Wrote a little to complete Asphodel," Annie noted in her journal on 9 November 1865, but said nothing more about what was to be her only novel. Six months later, Ticknor and Fields published *Asphodel* in its standard brown binding, with the title gold-stamped on the spine, but without naming the author. Annie sent copies to several of her friends without saying why. The reactions of two of them at least partly explain why her first novel was also her last.

"How very naughty you were not to tell me about Asphodel and to let me say that provoking thing," Laura Johnson wrote in June 1866 (though neither the letter containing the "provoking thing" nor Annie's response has survived). "I read it without any suspicion, though there were many things in it that made me think of you, and a poem in it seemed quite in your style," Laura continued. Straining to be complimentary, she said the novel was gracefully written and contained interesting thoughts. Then she attributed her initial disparagement to a hasty reading and promised to reread the book "many times." Clearly, she was paying tribute to the author rather than the book, most obviously when she exclaimed, "How charming it is to have a book of yours . . . in my hands."[10]

Sophia Hawthorne was so hard on the novel that Annie never told her who wrote it. "I began but *could not* read 'Asphodel' on account of its lack of nature, truth, simplicity, vraisemblance," Sophia declared, granting that she might not have been "in the mood, and perhaps it is better in the end," but doubting that she could ever finish it. Contrasting the novel with Annie's poem "In the Palace," Sophia said, "I would rather have your Florence mosaic (as I call it) than a library of such books as this." Then she dismissed the author of *Asphodel* as "no artist certainly."[11]

Sophia's criticism was not far from the mark. If *Asphodel* is not wholly devoid of "nature" and "truth," it would certainly profit from a tauter plot and more "vraisemblance." It can also be faulted for its thin characters and melodramatic subplot. Yet if only for its concerted anatomization of the genteel author's values and aspirations, the novel rewards attention.

Annie's lofty ambitions for her novel and herself are expressed through her epigraph—"Quinci si va chi vuole andar per pace"—from Dante's *Purgatorio* (24:141). The words "Here those who want peace ascend" are spoken to Dante and Virgil by the Angel of Temperance, affirming the need to curb excessive desire. The epigraph effectively displays the author's learning, hints at her knowledge of Italian, and announces her main theme: the need to subordinate earthly pleasures to spiritual ones.

The epigraph also implicitly asserts kinship with three eminent friends who were translators of Dante—T. W. Parsons and Charles Eliot Norton as well as Annie's beloved Longfellow. Of course she was excluded from the Dante Club, the group of men including her husband and Howells which convened to hear successive installments of Longfellow's *Divine Comedy*. But her epigraph suggests she was with them in spirit.

Annie's title more succinctly expresses her ambitions for her novel and for herself. The asphodel—traditionally associated with poetry and immortality—is identified by the novel's narrator as "the perfect lily of love, fadeless and perfected" and thus as a symbol of spiritual aspiration. The protagonist is a distinguished poet whose self-absorption indirectly destroys two women who love him, but who eventually attains spiritual insight. Unfortunately, the plot when not melodramatic is essentially a device allowing various characters to speak Annie's mind.

As the novel opens, Herbert Gregory has returned to Boston from Europe, convinced that "even the romance writer could find no better groundwork and material than New England affords" (8). This belief is shared by his happily married poet friend Russell. Later, we meet Herbert in "his own library-fireside" at his seashore home "The Cliff" with his wife Alice and their two children, all "held fast by the divine anchorage of home" (10).

The novel's center of consciousness then shifts to Alice, as she wakens on a spring morning in "the full strength of the morning of love." Happy in her marriage and in her children Ernest and Allegra, Alice is anxious only about her overworked husband, who is about to leave on a trip for his health. An idealized version of the childless Annie, Alice is a lover of poetry whose main concern is with "the well-being of others"; their happiness "was felt by none more deeply than herself" (34).

We next meet her old friend Erminia, whose "sweet simplicity of manner, . . . which is the soul of beauty, made her inexpressibly lovely to Alice" (21). Erminia's father has died, and she had feared that she had lost Alice to marriage. But she now agrees to keep Alice company and tutor her children in Herbert's absence.

When Russell's wife dies, Alice invites him and his young daughter Fanny to The Cliff. Partly out of undeclared love for Russell, "who had given much to her both from the inspiration of his books and from his visible presence" (47), Erminia takes charge of Fanny. When he hears Erminia sing a passionate song of longing that she herself had composed, Russell comes to believe she might "lead him to his better self." He falls in love with her, but never tells her so. Yet when he sails for California to secure an inheritance for his daughter, he leaves Fanny in Erminia's care.

Herbert returns home with his health restored, then departs to join the Union army "for the great cause." Alice remains at The Cliff with Erminia as her companion and the three children's tutor. At this stillpoint of the narrative, Annie focuses on the women's friendship, their self-sufficiency in the absence of men, and their lengthy philosophical exchanges on such issues as ideal teachers of children, the relative advantages of country over city living, and the difficulties of inculcating in the rich a sense of responsibility to the poor.

The novel then returns to Russell and veers into melodrama. On shipboard he is admired by the frail but flirtatious young Amy and her parents. He sends Erminia a ring "as a silent expression of what he knew not how to say." Erminia returns it. Soon afterward, Amy's parents invite Russell to attend what the other guests assume is an engagement party; and when Amy apologizes for that mistake, Russell impulsively kisses her. Assuming that he cannot win Erminia, Russell becomes engaged to Amy. At that point he receives a letter from Erminia explaining that she had returned the ring only because she was not sure what it meant, and insisting that she must speak to him. Erminia arrives with Fanny at the very moment of Russell's marriage to Amy, immediately goes mad, and then commits suicide. Amy dies shortly afterward, spiritually enriched by the love she had offered Russell and received from him. Now trebly bereaved, the agonized Russell blames himself for having yielded to adulation and returns to The Cliff.

There he becomes part of an extended family. Herbert has meantime been wounded in the war and then nursed back to health by Alice, and the three adults share the pleasure of overhearing young Ernest assure Fanny that he will love and protect her. The novel concludes by summarizing the spiritual progress intimated by its title and epigraph. Russell has started living for others and is attaining "new speech, deeper and more contained than the old," humbly aware that "the true lily of love waves forever to the faithful in those far, unfading gardens."

The novel is of its age in what it celebrates: love, friendship, and meditative poetry, but also patriotism, the spiritual refreshments of nature, and teachers who stress character development. In keeping with Emerson's belief in perfectibility, Annie created several flawed individuals but no villains. *Asphodel* is also of its age in being a roman à clef. Russell is partly based on James Russell Lowell, whose beloved wife Maria had died in 1853. His daughter Mabel was then placed under the care of a governess named Frances Dunlap who four years later became his second wife. Annie's tender portrayal of Russell's daughter reflects her own fondness for Mabel Lowell, and Erminia is partly a tribute to Frances Dunlap. Therefore Annie was probably not wholly surprised by what Thomas Bailey Aldrich reported while house-sitting for Lowell in 1872: he had discovered a well-worn copy of *Asphodel* in the study.

If one of James T. Fields's motives for publishing the novel was conjugal affection, he surely shared its values, welcomed its promise of healing love in the aftermath of the Civil War, and enjoyed seeing his own companionate marriage reflected in the marriage of Herbert and Alice. What Lucy Larcom particularly admired was Annie's dramatization of a deep friendship between two morally admirable women. The novel could hardly be called a critical success, even among the Fieldses' closest friends. Yet Annie had the satisfaction of writing a novel her husband thought worth publishing, a book that expressed her deepest beliefs and stretched her romantic wings.

5

"Grand as Ever"—Nathaniel Hawthorne

"Hawthorne is here, looking a melancholy silent grand genius as he is!" Annie Fields wrote in her diary at Mrs. Blodgett's Liverpool boarding house in June 1860, the day before all five Hawthornes and both of the Fieldses embarked for their return voyage to America. The admixture of familiarity with the melancholy man and awe at the grand genius would continue until Hawthorne's death four years later, years in which Annie's role as an informed participant in his life steadily expanded. Her friendship with Hawthorne certainly served her husband's business interests. But it also fostered her own moral and intellectual growth.[1]

Annie felt privileged whenever she saw him. During a brief visit to the Wayside in the summer of 1862, she reverently gathered a few wildflowers for a scrapbook of "Fragrant Memories" while walking with Sophia "on the path worn by Mr. Hawthorne's footsteps upon the hill back of his cottage 'The Wayside.'" They talked about "the genius of the place" and "the holy aspirations . . . held out to us through all beauty as well as by the hand of all-inspiring genius itself." The following July, alongside a clover pressed into that scrapbook, she noted that she had walked to the Old Manse with Hawthorne and her husband, watched a remarkable sunset, and walked home by moonlight. "He likes Concord," she wrote, then pondered his sad remark that "the moon rather lost something of its charm for him as he grew older. That was only his mood. Strange that he should not be exempt."[2]

Annie's account of that overnight visit in her newly begun "Journal of Literary Events and glimpses of interesting people" was entirely different. Paying tribute to the entire family, she called Sophia her husband's "mainstay" and praised her "artistic" decoration of the Wayside's woodwork and furniture, called Una an "exquisite maiden," and admired Julian's "illuminations" of Arthurian legends. But she stressed Hawthorne's "noble" insistence on dedicating his forthcoming "volume of English sketches" to Franklin Pierce, who had appointed him consul to

Liverpool. Because abolitionists abhorred Pierce's Confederate sympathies, and because Hawthorne needed "all that popularity can give him in a pecuniary way for the support of his family," her own husband had argued against that dedication. For Annie, however, it was "a beautiful incident in Hawthorne's life, the determination at all hazards to dedicate the book to his friend."

Annie's richest opportunities for observing Hawthorne occurred during his visits to Charles Street. He always came alone; and aware of his desire for privacy, she never invited anyone else to share his visits. During a typical visit in February 1863, he came "to pass Sunday" with the Fieldses in the course of "mining" his English notebooks for the *Atlantic* essays that eventuated in *Our Old Home.* As he told them, he found "'a good deal of intellectual lee mingled with this wine of memory.'" "'I never had a better time,'" he told Annie after breakfast the following morning. As Rose Hawthorne would remark years later, her father always enjoyed "the piquant flavors of merriment and luxury in this exquisite domicile of Heart's-Ease and Mrs. Meadows."[3]

But his health had already begun its irreversible decline. He looked "ill and more nervous than usual" when he spent the night at Charles Street in December before attending Mrs. Franklin Pierce's funeral. He had brought his long-promised opening section of the "Dolliver Romance" for the *Atlantic,* a work he despaired of completing. Yet "he was as courteous and as grand as ever, and as true," Annie wrote. "He does not lose that all-saddening smile, either."[4]

Hawthorne seemed much wearier when he returned to Charles Street two days later. The funeral itself had distressed him: "he could not generally look at such things, but he was obliged to look at the body of Mrs. Pierce"; and he had accompanied the grief-stricken widower all the way back to Concord, New Hampshire. Yet he had enjoyed talking to Annie's friend Harriet Prescott at the funeral, and he had been deeply touched by Pierce's "exquisite courtesy" as they stood at the graveside: he "drew up the collar of Hawthorne's coat to keep him from the cold."

The next morning, the Fieldses left Hawthorne to read in the library while they went out for a walk. The Boccaccio volume that Leigh Hunt had once owned was a "poor translation," he declared. But he had enjoyed reading *Dealings with the Dead,* a recent Ticknor and Fields publication whose self-deprecating narrator wittily discourses on funeral customs from ancient times to the present.[5] Switching the conversation to more immediate matters, Fields expressed "sincere admiration" for Hawthorne's "Dolliver," which gave him "better heart to go on with it." As author to editor, Hawthorne then tendered an unusual compliment: despite its "black Republican" politics, the *Atlantic* was "the most ably edited magazine in the world."

What he said "as the sunset deepened" was far more surprising. Hawthorne reminisced about "the happiest period" of his childhood, the two years when he lived "like a bird of the air" in the wilderness of Raymond, Maine, "so perfect was the freedom he enjoyed." Moving from one nostalgic recollection to another, he recalled skating on frozen Lake Sebago by moonlight, sometimes taking refuge in a log cabin and watching the stars through the chimney, then spoke of roaming through the woods "gun in hand" and learning "a nearness to Nature"—an edenic period that ended when he was sent back to Salem and "relatives who were all distasteful to him." That retrospection ended on a note of moody resignation: "How sad middle life looks to people of erratic temperaments. Everything is beautiful in youth—all things are allowed to it."

That renunciatory mood intensified when Oliver Wendell Holmes dropped by later on. After Holmes remarked that he would write a novel if Hawthorne were not in the field, Hawthorne sadly replied, "I am not and I wish you would." Then when Holmes urged Hawthorne to attend Saturday Club meetings, Hawthorne said he could no longer drink, eat, or talk. The doctor simply replied, "You can listen."[6]

But Hawthorne could also talk. After Holmes left, he argued that England was no longer a powerful empire, likening the country to a rambling squash vine which could be cut at the root and destroyed. Next he praised Boswell, "one of the most remarkable men who ever lived." More self-revealingly, Hawthorne confided that at Bowdoin College he had not "appreciated" Longfellow, who "was always finely dressed and was a tremendous student" while he himself was "careless in dress and no student, but always reading desultorily right and left." Annie was even more surprised when Hawthorne spoke about the Civil War, a subject he had previously avoided—"partly from his deep hatred of everything sad." He wanted the North to "beat now," because that seemed "the only way to save the country from destruction." Then taking stock of her own entry, Annie lamented, "He was intensely witty, but his wit is of so ethereal a texture that the fine essence has vanished and I can remember nothing now of his witty things!"

Yet Annie's record of Hawthorne's conversation on that December evening is important for its substance and particularly poignant as the last of its kind. In her biography of him, she would recall that occasion as the only time "during four years of intimate intercourse, when he really seemed to lay aside his own painful self-consciousness and speak because it was a pleasure to communicate what lay in him to be spoken."[7] Out of deeply affectionate respect, the Fieldses offered privacy when Hawthorne wanted it and sympathetic attention when he wanted to talk. It is easy to understand why Hawthorne told Annie that he "liked no house to stay in better than this."

When Hawthorne came to Charles Street on 28 March 1864, before heading south with Ticknor "on his journey for health," Annie was shocked "by his invalid appearance. He has become quite deaf, too. His limbs are shrunken but his great eyes still burn with their lambent fire," and he even "talked with something of his old wit at times." Though Annie heard him "walking in his room during a long portion of the night, heavily moving," he seemed good-humored at breakfast. He even gave a "singular account" of a visit from Bronson Alcott. When Alcott asked "if there was any difficulty" between their two families, Hawthorne said no, though he thought "it was not possible to live upon amicable terms with Mrs. Alcott." Alcott took it "like a saint."

Hawthorne traveled south with Ticknor the next day. But in Philadelphia, Ticknor became mortally ill, and only two weeks after leaving Charles Street, Hawthorne returned. Pale and exhausted, he confided that he had hardly eaten or slept since he left. He then retired earlier than usual. The following morning, the Fieldses had already started breakfast when Hawthorne "came gently in with the same pale solemn look and when we said, did you sleep well, has all been well with you since we parted, he answered 'Yes! all is well with me except life!'" He then told them about Ticknor's death. To Annie's surprise, he was often "overcome by the ludicrous." He recalled Ticknor's amused response to a servant's loud snore—"'Well done, Peter!'"; and he realized that he had left his slippers at their Philadelphia hotel because a friend was watching him so closely that he "forgot everything." The fastidious Hawthorne also said, "'there are some callings which no man ought to follow'": death would not "be so terrible if it were not for the undertakers. It was dreadful to think of being handled by those men."

"These are things I never can repeat to anybody," Annie repeated to her friend Laura Johnson, trusting her to "take them as we should take every thing from such a man, sacredly, to be held with judgment and reverence." Then speaking in her husband's name as well as her own, she delivered an extraordinary tribute: "[W]e regard Hawthorne as the greatest genius our country has produced and if he had never written a word, to watch a spirit more sensitive to every influence than a ripe wheatfield to passing breezes . . . is of greater value . . . than can be expressed." Next came a surprising comparison to the period's preeminent poet: "The solemnity of Hawthorne is something I have never met with except in Tennyson indeed they are more alike than either of them know."[8]

"Hawthorne is dead," Annie wrote in her journal on 19 May 1864, her sole entry for that day. She said nothing about the responsibilities she assumed for his funeral, which included making arrangements for the church service and the floral decorations. And because she knew Hawthorne hated undertakers and hated to be touched, and knew his widow was comforted "to think he was not touched," she did not let Sophia know that his body had been embalmed. "How can we tell the sadness of this day," she mused after his interment in Concord's Sleepy Hollow Cemetery. "Hawthorne's body was buried."

As she told Laura Johnson, "We made the little village church a shrine of white flowers. The day was radiant and we all felt the sacredness of it. It was truly a poet's burial. . . . I cannot tell you how beautiful—how sad it was."[9] Annie would later declare that "Hawthorne's passing was like losing a portion of our own household, so closely interwoven had become the interests and the affection of the two families."

The record bears her out, not only because her care and affection for the widow and her children continued. "It was Hawthorne's day," she wrote in her journal on 23 May 1865. "The anniversary of his burial." The Fieldses spent that day in Plymouth, New Hampshire, the town where he died, and Annie's elegiac mood was heightened by "the thought of Hawthorne's dying eyes looking out on the hills."

That thought was the germ of her solemn blank verse elegy "The Traveller," inscribed "In memory of, and in love of, Nathaniel Hawthorne":

> He rose upon an early dawn of May
> And looked upon the stream and meadow flowers
> Then on the face of his beloved, and went;
>
> And passing gazed upon the Wayside haunt,
> The homely budding gardens by the road,
> And harvest promise—Still he said, I go!
>
> Once more he mingled in the midday crowd
> And smiled a gentle smile, a sweet farewell,
> Then moved towards the hills and lay him down.
>
> Lying he looked beyond the pathless heights,
> Beyond the wooded steep and clouded peaks,
> And looking, questioned, then he loved and slept.
>
> And while he slept his spirit walked abroad,
> And wandered past the mountain, past the cloud
> Nor came again to rouse the form at peace.
>
> Though like some bird we strive to follow him,
> Fruitless we beat at the horizon's verge
> And fruitless seek the fathomless blue beyond.
>
> We work and wait and water with salt tears,—
> Learning to live that living we may sleep
> And sleeping cross the mountains to God's rest.[10]

It is easy to fault such epithets as "pathless heights," "wooded steep," and "clouded peak" as conventional and even cliché. Yet the poem successfully invokes the bounded yet boundless quality of the New Hampshire landscape, the analogue of a bird beating "at the horizon's verge" is moving, and Annie convincingly conveyed her own feelings of loss and yearning. Perhaps that was her main purpose. The poem exists only in manuscript, and there is no way to know if she ever showed it even to her husband.

Only weeks after Hawthorne's death, partly out of solicitude for Sophia and her children, the Fieldses undertook to expand the Hawthorne canon and thus increase Sophia's income. Arguing that everything Hawthorne wrote was important, they urged Sophia to prepare his notebooks for publication. She soon agreed to "copy out all that is possible—and I think there may be a good deal for the Atlantic and then we three will decide what to do."

Reading Hawthorne's notebooks as Sophia transcribed them deepened Annie's respect for his genius; and reading one of the fourteen original volumes in the summer of 1867 brought her even closer to him. "He seems always to be teaching himself to observe and to record with accuracy," Annie wrote after reading his descriptions of the Isles of Shoals, and of "the view from his back windows in the city" which became Coverdale's in *The Blithedale Romance.* The fact that he never made corrections provoked a more surprising tribute: "such marvelous accuracy of observation and such strange records of interesting people and places were perhaps never before made." Curiously, however, she attributed his empathetic description of the portrait painter Cephas Thompson to "a true charity in his composition for there is nothing especially congenial to Hawthorne in Mr. Thompson except a gentleness of temper." When *Passages from the American Note-Books of Nathaniel Hawthorne* was published in December 1868, she was awed: "What a picture of character laid bare such a book is! Such impatience under the discipline of days! He lacked the Jove-compelling power to drive his genius, so he was driven thereby. But there is great truthfulness in the passages and the man himself rises up as I read and sits again by our fireside." Annie Fields's appreciation of Nathaniel Hawthorne deepened after Sophia's death in 1871, when she read two posthumous publications: his *French and Italian Notebooks* and "'Septimius.'—the deathless man," a story Browning and "others who are judges" considered "one of his greatest productions." Annie concurred, then ventured an astute speculation: the "vast weird analysis" of Septimius, the restless seeker who tries to transcend the limits of mortality and ends up perhaps eternally alone, presents Hawthorne's "own character and motives under a slight viel [*sic*] of fiction." As she had come to realize, "the patience and microscopic power with which Hawthorne wrote his journals was a perpetual preparation for his books. Never a day elapsed that he did not work in this fashion."

During the years after Hawthorne's death, as a self-appointed custodian of his reputation, Annie preserved in her journals every bit of information and every judgment of him that came her way—recollections of the New Hampshire hotel manager who walked him upstairs the night he died, for example, or her own amused recollection that Hawthorne once refused to let her brush his coat for fear of wearing it out, or Bret Harte's "true" appreciation of Hawthorne's wit. So dense were Annie's accounts that when Jamie prepared his four-part "Hawthorne" for the *Atlantic* at the end of 1870 (later included in his *Yesterdays with Authors*), he borrowed freely and without acknowledgment from Annie's journals, and he also represented Sophia's letters to Annie as written to both of them.

When Thomas Wentworth Higginson was preparing to write about Hawthorne eighteen years later, he assumed that Annie was an authority: "Your good husband . . . told me that Hawthorne wrote some of the early Peter Parley books, & I have several times mentioned this as a fact, but am now asked to substantiate it. There is much internal evidence in their style; but can you help me to any external evidence? I don't think Goodrich mentions it in his Recollection; nor does Julian H. in his Biography. Also, do you know where 'The Hollow of the Three Hills' first appeared?" The following year when Moncure Conway was working on his own Hawthorne biography, he also wrote to Annie, "though to nobody else": he requested advice, possibly an anecdote, and perhaps a theory about Hawthorne's "supposed reserve, shyness, &c."[11] In 1900 when Houghton Mifflin was preparing a new edition of Hawthorne's work, Horace Scudder requested Annie's help with the Miscellany volume. The descriptions of Lincoln's uncouth appearance that Fields had asked Hawthorne to eliminate from "Chiefly About War Matters" because they seemed "injudicious in 1862 would be harmless and quite interesting in 1900," Scudder said, wondering "if Mr. Fields retained the manuscript of the article, and if so, if you wd allow the dropped passages to be restored."[12]

In 1899, Annie drew on her own private knowledge to prepare the Hawthorne volume for Small and Maynard's Beacon Biographies of Eminent Americans. Urged to do so by Mark DeWolfe Howe, she wrote her Nathaniel Hawthorne with remarkable dispatch, sympathetically testifying to his truthfulness, his generosity, and his wit. Ranging freely from such personal matters as his solitary habits and his reliance on Sophia to such professional matters as his painstakingly careful notebook records, she incorporated details that she alone knew, included a few passages from her predecessors Henry James and George Lathrop, and incidentally set a few records straight.[13]

Her account of his childhood draws from her own journal his recollection that in Maine he had lived "like a bird of the air, so perfect was the freedom I enjoyed" (5). And among her many insider's insights, she declares that "He could not be called idle" although he made that accusation against himself (13).

Bringing Hawthorne to life, she says he remained handsome even in decline, a "large, slow-moving, iron-gray man, with marvellous dreamful eyes [which]. . . . were soft and kind, but in-seeing." And she tells us that she never "had the impression of being looked at by Hawthorne," yet always had "a very keen sense of . . . being understood by him" (123).

She attributes Hawthorne's deteriorating health to his agitation about the Civil War, and offers unique details about his rapid decline. When he arrived at Charles Street in March 1864, two months before his death, she was "much shocked by the change in his appearance." She quotes from a letter she received immediately after his death, written by his friend and traveling companion Franklin Pierce, saying "he must have passed from natural slumber to that from which there is no waking." Since then, she says, whenever she has stood in the room where he died, "as I have frequently done since he passed out silently into the skies, it is easy to imagine the scene on that spring morning" (131).

A few of Annie's remarks allude to a controversy with Sophia Hawthorne over money after his death. "No temptation ever lured him into buying, or letting any member of his family buy, anything which he could not pay for at once," Annie says, then insists that Hawthorne never fancied "his books should bring more than the market for them warranted, and never mortgag[ed] his brains in advance" (13). She also unequivocally declares that Ticknor and Fields had earned

Hawthorne's trust. His publishers "were generous to him, though their wishes far outran anything they could do for him," she says. Not only did they constantly reprint his books, but—as Hawthorne himself had said—Fields "smote the rock of public sympathy on his behalf. Indeed, no author had a publisher he valued as much" (88–89).

As for two issues on which the author and publisher had differed, Annie sides with her husband. He had been right to persuade Hawthorne to eliminate unflattering descriptions of Lincoln from his "Chiefly About War Matters" in 1862, descriptions she still considered "petty." And in 1863 he had rightly though unsuccessfully tried to dissuade Hawthorne from dedicating *Our Old Home* to his old friend Pierce, the former president who was then reviled as a Confederate sympathizer. The woman who had praised Hawthorne's loyalty to Pierce in 1863 now asserted that he did not "know himself at that time," since he loved Pierce but "also loved his other friends and his country." As she astutely observes, Hawthorne usually looked "at every side of a question" (121–22).

Annie might well have offered her last pronouncements about Hawthorne in an undated and unpublished nineteen-page manuscript titled "American Literary Life." In it, she celebrates Lowell, Longfellow, and Holmes, but concentrates on Hawthorne and compares him with Emerson. America's literary life in the nineteenth century was chiefly associated with New England, she wrote, then launched her insider's comparison:[14]

> The habits of Hawthorne . . . were in entire contrast to those of Emerson. They long inhabited the same town yet they rarely met. His method of writing too was quite unlike, for whereas Emerson would bring home his poems from the field or wood and also doubtless many a noble sentence of prose, he found in his study a method of his own for putting his prose together and giving it such continuity as he could.

Next came a denser and more sympathetic account of Hawthorne's writing methods:

> Hawthorne made a footpath by frequent walking to & fro on the crest of a small hill behind the "Wayside" where he lived in Concord. There and in other walks and other places he wove the texture of his great romances so firmly together in his mind that when he came to write them down they sped on in one continuous flow scarcely needing a correction. Sometimes he would write the word he did not intend and blur it out speedily with his finger writing over it before the ink was dry; but once thought out in his great walks at Redcar in England at the Villa Montauto in Florence or at home on the little hill, there it lay clear in his mind and ready for the page. . . . In the pages of the "House of the Seven Gables" which is preserved entire, this method can easily be seen.

Her praise of Hawthorne's frugality incidentally pays tribute to her husband for maximizing his income:

> Hawthorne was a poor man as the world counts riches[.] He had no resources beyond his pen and his books never had very large sales, but his *publisher* made the most

of them and Hawthorne himself was a man of few wants. Sometimes he may have felt the need of money for his family but they also, the children being young, and Mrs. Hawthorne being a woman of small expenditure, were content with little. Hawthorne's probity in money matters and his real generosity were the traits of one of Nature's noblemen. He could never be induced to buy a thing which he could not pay for neither did he ever wear an air of poverty but bore himself with the dignity of one who had what he needed and otherwise spent no time in considering the question. I can believe that petty economies were seldom if ever a subject of discourse between husband and wife and whatever anxieties he suffered were borne in silence. Occasionally if it were proposed to buy something which he considered unnecessary he would say so and that was the end of it—

Far more penetrating is Annie's insight into what Sophia had called the "unviolated sanctuary" of his nature:

Hawthorne's inner life was largely his own: neither wife nor child nor friend shared freely in his experiences. His wife knew him more nearly than any other but although he rested on her and loved to hear her talk sometimes his whole heart seems to have unveiled to no living soul.

Returning to her central comparison, the woman who had loved and admired both Hawthorne and Emerson, and who had been their guest as well as their hostess, shrewdly celebrated their similarities:

In spite of the contrasted natures of the men I have spoken of, their ideals and general habits of life were not superficially very unlike. They loved simplicity of manner, dress and behavior and instilled these ideas into the minds of their children. They felt strong kinship with Wordsworth. His "plain living and high thinking" might have been said by one of themselves. Their highest pleasure was in their work and beyond that in the society of the men and women of their time. They were not generally frequenters of theatre nor seekers after entertainment. . . . Such is it to have had a habit of work, and love to others, and high aspirations, for one's country and oneself. In this spirit they lived and died leaving a legacy to their country which leavens it and lifts it up even when the mechinations [sic] of politicians take arms against its welfare[.]

Annie concluded by passionately praising Hawthorne and Emerson but also Lowell, Holmes, and other New Englanders as "teachers of America":

It is humanity and not a nation to which they address themselves. It is the human soul, the soul of their brother, they are calling, urging him to embrace the opportunities of life under the fresh conditions America has offered and to cherish these opportunities for the uplifting of the spirit into a larger and more indestructible happiness.

All in all, Annie Fields's Nathaniel Hawthorne is thinner than ours. She did not reckon with the probing psychologist, the ironic historian, the conflicted feminist, or the wily self-reflexive narrator. But she allows us to perceive and admire Hawthorne as she did: as an awesome genius yet a quirky individual; a reticent yet witty man who admired Boswell and could not bear to be touched; a man who enjoyed a good sunset yet thought the moon was losing its charm; a man whose loyalty to a friend made him risk poor sales on a book when his income was slim; a man who six months later could barely crank out the first chapter of a romance despite Fields's encouragement; a man who seemed shrunken and deaf the following month although his eyes still burned "with their lambent fire"; and a man who, with grotesque irony, witnessed the death of the traveling companion who had hoped to restore him to health.

Annie was an ideal witness of Nathaniel Hawthorne, a perceptive observer and careful recordkeeper who revered the writer even more than his work, a custodian of his reputation who also contributed to it. Even her unpublished writings about Hawthorne thicken our understanding of how he was judged by his famous and not-so-famous contemporaries, herself among them. When she read his journals after his death, Hawthorne himself seemed to rise up and sit by her fireside. What Annie wrote about him enables us to see him as she did, "grand as ever."

6

"Have Seen Mr. Dickens"

With Dickens in America

From the time Charles Dickens arrived in Boston in November 1867 until he left from New York the following April, Annie Fields basked in his approval and vicariously shared his triumphs. No literary lion was larger than Dickens, Americans were eager to see and hear him, and none was more eager than Annie.[1]

His five-month reading tour under the auspices of Ticknor and Fields was a calculated business venture that Fields had been proposing for years, pointing out that Dickens had not visited America since 1842. But the clincher was a large financial guarantee. Dickens's seventy-six readings netted $95,000, far more than even Fields had anticipated, as was Ticknor and Fields's 10 percent cut. Moreover, Fields's thousand-dollar expenditure for Dickens's three-part serial *George Silverman's Explanation* increased *Atlantic* sales; and the 10 percent royalty he promised on every book sold made Dickens designate Ticknor and Fields his sole authorized American publisher. Ticknor and Fields soon began issuing Dickens's fiction in de luxe, regular, and cheap editions, and sales were brisk. Dickens's readings spurred sales of his books, just as his books boosted attendance at those readings.

Annie Fields collected another kind of dividend. As her husband later boasted, "Steadily refusing all invitations to go out during the weeks he was reading, [Dickens] only went into one other house besides the Parker, habitually, during his stay in Boston."[2] Annie Fields's unusual exertions to entertain him at Charles Street assisted her husband and boosted her social prestige. But a deeper motive that she herself never fully understood was devotion to Dickens himself.

"Today the steamer is telegraphed with Dickens on board, and the tickets for his readings have been sold," Annie exulted on 18 November. "Such a rush! A long queue of people have been standing all day in the street—a good-humored crowd, but a weary one." The half-mile-long line had in fact started forming the night before, implicit proof of how prudent James T. Fields had been to reserve two hundred fifty tickets for friends. When "the Chief" arrived on the *Cuba* the next day, Jamie was there to greet him and escort him to the Parker House.[3] Excluded by gender from those rituals, Annie arranged her own vicarious welcome by filling his hotel suite with flowers and placing a few Ticknor and Fields books on his shelves.

She also arranged to give the first dinner in his honor two days later, though that meant requiring Longfellow to postpone his all-male welcoming party for a day. Hoping Longfellow would not be seriously inconvenienced, Annie told him that her husband had pledged to bring Dickens to Charles Street "on the first evening he should feel like going out." Politely but dauntlessly, she was asserting a prior claim. As Harriet Beecher Stowe wryly but presciently remarked to Fields, "Dickens has got possession of you. May he bring you back when he's done with you."[4] The *you* was plural.

When Longfellow, Emerson, Holmes, Louis Agassiz, Judge George Hoar, and the young scholar Charles Eliot Norton arrived at Charles Street on 21 November (wives were not invited), a new acquisition was on display: a portrait which the then-fashionable Francis Alexander had painted during Dickens's first American tour in 1842, and which the Fieldses had recently discovered in Alexander's studio.[5] Dickens himself "bubbled over with fun" from the moment he arrived, and even the usually solemn Agassiz followed suit. At the risk of shocking Annie's "New England sensibilities," he told a risqué anecdote that she considered worth recounting in her journal: when Mme. Helvetius asked Benjamin Franklin why he had not asked to sleep with her, he replied, "it is midsummer and so warm! If it were only winter when the nights are long!" But most of Annie's entry was about Dickens himself—who seemed to love no one more than Carlyle "and gave the most irresistible imitation of him"; who said he never smoked or drank when his readings "'set in'"; who confided that he had recently burned all his private letters; and whose witticisms repeatedly provoked "prodigious laughter." Her single example now seems at best only mildly funny. After Holmes recalled one of his country lectures where everyone but his landlady looked grim, Dickens unleashed "a tempest of laughter" by saying, "Probably because she saw money enough in the house to cover your expenses." Later that night, after resavoring the evening's pleasures, Annie recalled that only a few hours before she had been condoling with her sister-in-law Maria Fields on the death of her oldest son. "Ah me!" she concluded. "What a strange day for me."

For the next five months, Dickens remained constantly on Annie's mind. All that seemed worth reporting about her sister Louisa's Thanksgiving party, for example, was that "a sudden access of melancholy" kept Dickens from coming; and whenever Jamie returned from one of his long walks with Dickens and reported "the wonderful things" he said, Annie did her best to preserve them—for example, his remark that "Mr and Mrs Lewes" were both "exceedingly homely" but

George Eliot was "very interesting with her shy manner of saying brilliant things." Vastly better than such vicarious experience was hearing and seeing Dickens for herself, as when she and Jamie accompanied him to the Boston School Ship, an innovative reform school, on Sunday, 24 November. Though he had announced in advance that he would not address the boys, he proved "himself the Charles Dickens we have loved" by doing so: "The boys listened with their hearts in their faces as if they would treasure each word, forever. They manned the yards by way of salute on our departure as we steamed off slowly into the fog. We went afterwards to dine with the dear man." Better still was having the dear man under her own roof, as when she gave a "pretty supper" in his honor the following Wednesday (this time for a "pretty company" that included women), during which he regaled the group with ghost stories. As Annie gloated that night, "At nine oysters and fun began."

Five days later came the long awaited "first great reading" at the sold-out 2,000-seat Tremont Theater. Annie sent Dickens a bouquet beforehand and then surrendered her own sense of separate identity in "a world of . . . ardent admirers": "How we listened till we seemed turned into one eye-ball! How we all loved him! How we longed to tell him confidences! How he and Jamie did hug in the anteroom afterwards! What a teacher he seemed of humanity as he read out his own words which have enchanted us from childhood! And what a house it was!" According to his manager George Dolby, "Never before had anything called forth such enthusiasm as that night's reading"; and Dickens considered his reception "quite beyond description or exaggeration."[6]

The next night Sophia Hawthorne and Gail Hamilton dined with the Fieldses before accompanying them to the theater for another "remarkable" reading. Then afterward, "as usual" (as Annie curiously said), "we went to speak to him at his request after it was over. Found him in the best of spirits, but very tired."

By the end of that first series of four performances, Longfellow could assure his friend Charles Sumner that the "Readings, or rather Actings, have been immensely successful, according to our standard of success": the "proverbially cold" Bostonians had been "not Galvanized but Dickinized into great activity, very pleasant to behold."[7]

Annie and Jamie then accompanied Dickens to New York, where audiences were even more receptive. On Monday, 9 December, the first night of a two-week series, Dickens read "The Christmas Carol" even better than in Boston "because the applause was more ready and he felt stimulated by it." Summoned to his room afterward, the Fieldses basked in "the fine light of Charles Dickens's lovely soul" but "left early lest we should overfatigue him." That pattern was repeated throughout a week that also included socializing with such eminent friends as William Cullen Bryant and the violinist Ole Bull. On Wednesday, Dickens's day off, he and the Fieldses attended the long-run musical melodrama "The Black Crook," which they found enormously dull. Keeping his voice low to avoid insulting the performers, Dickens kept up a steady stream of talk on such topics as why "no ballet dancer could have pretty feet," talk that continued for hours after they returned to the hotel.[8]

A week after the Fieldses returned to Boston, Dickens returned to the Parker House and to rooms that Annie had festooned with flowers and traditional English Christmas decorations of red-berried holly and mosses.[9] In that same holiday spirit, because Dickens had contracted to perform in Boston on 23 and 24 December and in New York on Christmas Day, Annie prepared a traditional English Christmas dinner for him on 22 December—a meal that included goose, roast beef, and a blazing plum pudding. "It was really a beautiful Christmas festival, as we intended it to be for the love of this new apostle of Christmas," she wrote in her diary, complaining only about her own entry: "What a shame it is to write down anything respecting one's contact with Charles Dickens and have it so slight as my accounts are." In his letter to Georgina Hogarth that same night, Dickens told her about the dinner party and called Annie "one of the dearest little women in the world," a woman with an infectious laugh and a fine sense of humor.[10] After his "brilliant performance" of "A Christmas Carol" on Christmas Eve, Annie exulted "How the whole house rose and cheered!" For her husband, herself, and the entire audience, she declared, "we cannot help loving him."

She was marvelously surprised a few days later. Although Dickens had announced in advance that he never stayed with friends during a reading tour, he now asked if he could spend four days at Charles Street after returning from New York. "What a pleasure this will be to us!" Annie exclaimed. "We anticipate his coming with continued delight." Weathering a "crisis of servants," she had everything ready by the time he arrived on Saturday, 4 January, "in the best of good humor in spite of a cold which hangs about him and stuffs up head and throat, only leaving him for two hours at night when he reads." She gave a dinner in his honor the next day. Though a few guests were "kept away by accident when they would have given their eyes to come," Longfellow and his brother-in-law Tom Appleton helped the evening pass "brilliantly," and Celia Thaxter rejoiced to find her ideal of Dickens "so completely realised."

For the next few days, Annie closely monitored her houseguest and discreetly ministered to his preferences:

> We breakfast at half-past nine punctually, he on a rasher of bacon and an egg and a cup of tea, always preferring this same thing. Afterward we talk or play with the sewing-machine or anything else new and odd to him.[11] Then he sits down to write until one o'clock, when he likes a glass of wine and biscuit, and afterward goes to walk until nearly four, when we dine. After dinner, reading days, he will take a cup of strong coffee, a tiny glass of brandy, and a cigar, and likes to lie down for a short time to get his voice in order. His man then takes a portmanteau of clothes to the reading hall, where he dresses for the evening. Upon our return we always have supper and he brews a marvelous punch, which usually makes us all sleep like tops after the excitement.

A more lasting and more surprising result of their brief domestic intimacy was quasi-religious awe:

> The perfect kindliness and sympathy which radiates from the man is, after all, the secret never to be told, but always to be studied and to thank God for. His rapid eyes, which nothing can escape, eyes which, when he first appears upon the stage, seem to interrogate the lamps and all things below . . . are unlike anything before in our experience. There are no living eyes like them. . . . Such charity! Poor man! He must have learned great need for that.

She and Jamie agreed that no one "gave more pleasure during a little visit" than Dickens, and his remarkable kindliness now made Annie long to "help somebody" herself.

But the chief somebody continued to be Dickens, even during his month and a half on tour. "It is hard how prejudiced people have allowed themselves to become," Annie wrote, complaining about the backlash to America's Dickens mania. "I seldom make a call where his name is introduced that I do not feel the injustice done to him personally, as if mankind resented the fact that he had excited more love than most men." Each charge against him—of egotism, greed, and mistreatment of his estranged wife—seemed "almost as if said against myself. It is so hard to help this when you love a friend."

As one expression of that love, Annie celebrated his birthday on 7 February by having flowers placed on his breakfast table in his Washington, D.C., hotel room; and she and Jamie repeatedly found themselves "talking of him in a kind of unconscious way to each other." Meantime, they rejoiced in Dickens's letters, among them one saying Georgina Hogarth and his daughters asked if they could send Annie their love, and gallantly adding, "I may, I know—and do."[12] By 21 February, the Fieldses were so impatient for Dickens's return to what he now called his "native Boston" that they went to Providence to hear him read "Marigold." Though the audience was "stupid and unresponsive," Annie "lay awake from pure pleasure" after having supper and playing cards with "the dear great man." He had been "gentle kind and affectionate—indeed, something more," she mused, then surprisingly added, "—so much more that I have forgotten to be afraid of him."

On 24 February, Annie had the double pleasure of hearing "Marigold" again and watching Emerson's "stoicism" break down until "he laughed as if he must crumble to pieces at such unusual bodily agitation, and with a face on as if it hurt him dreadfully—to look at him was too much for me, already full of laughter myself." After they went backstage to shake hands with Dickens and returned to Charles Street without him, "Mr. Emerson asked me a great many questions about C.D. and pondered much. Finally he said, 'I am afraid he has too much talent for his genius; it is a fearful locomotive to which he is bound and can never be free from it nor set at rest. He is too consummate an artist to have a thread of nature left.'"

Perhaps hoping to modify that judgment, she invited Emerson as well as Dickens, Holmes, and Norton to celebrate Longfellow's sixty-first birthday three days later. As Longfellow remarked, having "a Dickens Reading and a Supper too, will make a great holiday."[13] Unfortunately, Dickens's troublesome cold kept him from attending the birthday celebration.

Increasingly worried about his health, Annie now had another reason for concern: a newspaper clipping Longfellow showed her that she hoped Dickens would never see. It was a copy of one of his private letters, "the saddest of letters, written at the time the separation from his wife took place. We could have cried as we read!" But she did not then—or ever—blame him for leaving a woman to whom he had been (in her words) "unfitly married," or for placing his wife's sister Georgina in charge of his household, or even for his liaison with Ellen Ternan.[14]

Two days later came one of the high points of Dickens's visit to Boston: the "Great International Walking Match" between his manager Dolby and Fields's junior partner James Osgood. A month earlier, Dickens had laid out the elaborate conditions "as if it were some fierce legal argument"; and on that snowy Saturday afternoon, he and Fields accompanied "their" men along the entire thirteen-mile course. At the halfway point, Annie drove up in her own carriage, gave "a cheer for America," then kept close to Osgood—the eventual winner—"administering brandy all the way in to town." That night at the Parker House, Annie was Dickens's guest of honor at an elegant dinner (to which he had also invited Lowell and his daughter Mabel, Longfellow and his daughter Alice, the Nortons, the Aldriches, the Holmeses, and the Howard Ticknors). "As she has done so much for me in the way of flowers, I thought I would show her a sight in that line at dinner," Dickens told his family, then explained that he himself had decorated the table with "exotics," violets, lilies, roses, and creeper, and provided "a rose for every buttonhole and a bouquet for every lady."[15] Never had she seen a dinner more beautiful or elegant, Annie wrote afterward, blissful about the flowers, the food, the guests, and Dickens's conversation, then concluded with unwitting self-revelation: "Jamie and I are truly penetrated with grateful love to C.D."

During the following week when Dickens's lectures were canceled because of the public ferment over Andrew Johnson's impeachment, he spent two "merry" evenings at Charles Street. On 5 March, the night before he left for Syracuse, Annie found it "very pleasant to have him leaning over me" while he helped her win a card game; and her guests' speculations about how far his manuscripts "would extend in a single line" left her with a "strange, weird sensation of the value of words over time and space." As her own way of trying to reach out over time and space, she had already asked the wife of Cornell University's president Andrew White to arrange for "a *sea-coal* fire" in Dickens's Syracuse hotel room and "a plain cloth on the table, with a few readable American books." As she explained, "I have such a strong desire to make his difficult work as easy to him as possible and to keep homesickness as far away that . . . I cannot forego the temptation of asking you to connive with me to make him most comfortable."[16] In her own mind, she was behaving "somehow like one of his daughters, and as if I could not take too great care of him."

Her desire to take care of him increased from the time that he returned for his final Boston performances two weeks later, debilitated by a persistent cold, insomnia, and "the use of soporifics, which at length became a necessity." As usual, he sounded vigorous during each of his readings, and his audiences were enthusiastic, especially during his "splendid" farewell. Even so, he seemed unable to "recover his vitality" afterward. Plans for a farewell banquet were scrapped, and Annie had good reason to fear that he would be "too ill and utterly fatigued to care much about anything but rest" when he reached New York.

But the trip down on Friday, 10 April, was remarkably pleasant, beginning with the moment when a smiling Dickens arrived at the railway station, wearing two roses in his lapel. It was Annie's first trip in a "compartment car," a luxuriously carpeted car with upholstered seats, and time passed quickly with card games and conversation. But Annie worried about Dickens's occasional lapses into languor; and thinking about his "massive brain" while observing "the rapid movements of those strong strong hands," she realized more fully than ever "how deeply we had learned to love him and how hard it would be for us to part." After they reached the Westminster Hotel, Dickens regaled the Fieldses with marvelous tales of his life as a newspaper reporter. The following day when they all went to the circus, Annie's pleasure was intensified by Dickens's extraordinary knowledge "of everything before him." Presumably with his heavy reading schedule also on her mind, she then praised his "martyr spirit," the spirit which makes "our work whatever it may be . . . more to us than our life."

He had ample opportunity to display that martyr spirit the following week as he delivered his final series of American readings. He read with his usual liveliness but ended up exhausted, then relaxed with the Fieldses. On Monday night, for example, he sang them old songs until they dissolved in laughter, certain "there is no living actor who could excel him in these things." Entering his room after the next night's performance, Annie was shocked by his prostration, "his head thrown back without support on the couch, the blood suffusing his throat and temples again where he had been very white a few minutes before." Yet he soon recovered and brewed one of his rum punches for himself and the Fieldses. A variation on the pattern occurred on Saturday, when he delivered a speech to the all-male New York Press Club at their dinner in his honor at Delmonico's. Although his foot was so painfully swollen that (as Annie learned) he had to lean on Dolby to reach the podium, he spoke splendidly to tremendous applause. Then he returned to the hotel, brewed one last rum punch for himself and the Fieldses, and delighted Annie even more by repeating his entire unscripted speech for her alone.

Two days later, she found an unusual way to return the favor. Although she could do nothing to ease the pain he still endured, she managed to relax him before his final reading—the thirtieth reading she attended—by delivering a burlesque version of a "Woman's League" meeting she had just attended.

He got through the evening "bravely" if not brilliantly, Annie noted, but this time ended up so totally exhausted that he went to bed right afterward and remained confined to his hotel room all the next day. Wednesday brought his "last embrace the look of pain" and Annie's "bitter bitter sobs" when she said goodbye. Remaining behind while Jamie accompanied him to the *Russia,* she wondered "what to him can be the tenderness of one woman like myself—I say this and then I remember how precious beyond all gifts is the gift of love." Still, she realized there could never again be "the old familiar intercourse, the care for him, his singleness of regard for us." When Jamie returned, "we put our arms about each other and then for the first time his grief gave vent to itself in tears."

They obsessed over Dickens afterward, mourning his departure as a kind of death: they prayed for him at night, woke up dreaming of him, and Annie could often "feel his parting kiss on my cheek and see my arms stretched out to hold him." One solace was her increased closeness to her beloved Jamie, and another was imagining the joy of Dickens's "beloved"—Ellen Ternan—when he returned. Venting her emotions in her journal was yet another, despite her complaint that it was hard "to tell straight things in a straight way." As Annie proudly reminded herself, no woman had spent more time with Dickens during the past five months than she had, or come to know him more intimately. In an effort to convert loss into gain, she resolved to take Dickens as a role model and "try to work for others and forget not *him* but myself." That resolve would have long-range consequences.

Season in England

When the Fieldses sailed for England on 28 April, 1869—almost exactly a year after Dickens's departure and on the very same ship—their chief purpose was to see their "best beloved C.D." It was also a way to take their minds off several dismaying events: Gail Hamilton had accused Fields of cheating her, Sophia Hawthorne had made a similar charge, and Fields had ousted Ticknor's son Howard from the firm for conducting an adulterous affair with one of their employees. Mabel Lowell sailed with the Fieldses, a favor to her and her father but also to Annie. The beautiful twenty-seven-year-old woman imbued with "the poetry of womanhood" was good company, and Annie enjoyed introducing her to people and places she had first encountered a decade earlier.[17]

Dickens reacted to the Fieldses' imminent arrival with a written shout—"Hurrah, Hurrah, Hurrah!"[18]—and he was the first to welcome them when they reached London on May 11. As Annie wrote in her journal, "Have seen Mr. Dickens! At last we can rest. I must confess the excitement was rather strong for all of us. He has been to our hotel 4 times today, beside a long walk with Jamie." His daughters and Georgina Hogarth had come with him so they could all "devote themselves to us"; and over the next few days, the man who "knows London better than anyone" took them to parks, theaters, and dining places of "fashionable London" but also to a children's hospital in a slum district, the London post office, and many other sites that had figured in his novels.[19]

While walking through the slums where Dickens had once lived, Annie felt deepened respect for his heroic submergence of private pain in hard work. The pain she herself felt that day would have an important impact on the rest of her life. "The sight of misery which cannot be relieved is too terrible to be sought after," she wrote, "—but it was best for us to go and we went." Dismayed by the sight of a woman who shared a small poorhouse room with her husband and seven children, Annie was sure she would "never forget the look in the eyes of that woman nor her patient manner." That night at the opera, Annie found herself "wandering away" from the fine performance of Christine Nilsson and "looking into that woman's eyes!" However indirectly, that powerful memory surely helped generate Annie's commitment to relieve the misery of Boston's slum-dwellers.

Though no one in London meant more to the Fieldses than Dickens, they also saw other English friends including Leslie Stephen and Charles Reade, and spent time with American friends including Charlotte Cushman and Longfellow. Determined to keep up with the latest cultural trends, they visited Rossetti's studio, where they admired his "Hamlet and Ophelia," his "Christ with the Magdalen," and his "weird and powerful" portraits of Jane Morris, and ventured into the then unfashionable district of Bloomsbury to visit another Pre-Raphaelite—William Morris, a man of striking health and integrity who made "painted glass windows & objects of medieval art. Poet, also." After meeting Swinburne, however, Annie wrote him off as "a half mad poet, a half baked man."

But meeting George Eliot was a stellar event. "This afternoon we have been to visit Mr and Mrs Lewes [sic], both as you know distinguished names in English literature," Annie told her sister Louisa, then made the sweeping judgment she would expand each time she read an Eliot novel: "She is a grand woman, one of the few women of genius I think we may say of the world now."[20] There would be other visits, the two couples would see a play together, and Fields would bring home two of Eliot's poems for the *Atlantic*. Yet what Annie treasured most was her first encounter with the "grand woman."

As Annie wrote in the *Century* thirty years later, she entered "a pleasant house somewhat retired from the road, with trees and shrubbery outside, and plenty of books inside," where she joined a small group of "ladies and gentlemen" who were deep in conversation. Soon her hostess "seated herself by my side for a more intimate acquaintance. I recall the glow which overspread her face when she discovered that we had a common friend in Harriet Beecher Stowe. . . . After this first visit to 'The Priory,' the doors were kindly open to us on Sundays during our stay in London." Eliot proved to be a woman after Annie's own heart: "I must always remember how the beauty of her voice impressed me. I also remarked the same quality I have mentioned in speaking of her letters,—a sense of perfectness in her presentation of any scene or subject." Before leaving, Lewes took the Fieldses into his study to show off Burton's portrait of George Eliot and the curtained shelves filled with bound manuscripts containing "touching dedications to him." "She was his chief topic of conversation, the pride and joy of his life," Annie recalled, "and it was quite evident that she returned his ardent devotion with a true love."[21] Thus Annie could ignore the question of whether Eliot and Lewes were legally married. It was enough that they shared her own deepest values.

By contrast, Annie felt repelled by an eminent writer she had once deeply admired, Robert Browning. His relationship with both of the Fieldses had been strained by disagreements about publishing *The Ring and the Book,* and he had two other strikes against him: his recent work was "unpoetic," Annie thought, and he had not supported the Union during the Civil War. After meeting him at "a London dinner-table of the first rank," where artfully arranged lights and colors made everything resemble "a French picture come to life," Annie wrote him off as "a piece of polished steel, receiving on his surface keen reflections of persons and giving back sharp points of light," a man who seemed at ease only with artifice. Years later when she recalled Emily Tennyson's lament that Browning no longer came to Farringford because she and her husband were "too quiet for him," she "remembered the fatuous talk at dinner-tables where I had sometimes met Browning," contrasting it with "Tennyson's great talk and the lofty serenity of his lady's presence."[22]

The Fieldses reveled in that talk and that serenity during their three-day excursion to Farringford at the end of May, where "things were conducted as in the old time but with somewhat more state." There was only one unpleasant moment. Before their first dinner, Annie put flowers in her hair and she and Mabel Lowell "did our best to look well" in an effort to please Tennyson. Yet he soon frightened Mabel by bitterly asking "if her father was a letter writer." By this, Annie understood, he expressed his unhappiness about the "unfortunate half private epistle" that Bayard Taylor wrote after visiting Farringford "which leaked unhappily, most unhappily into print."[23]

All went well the next day. The poet who was "full of rough play and banter in talk and hates a person to be thin-skinned" delighted in "the delight we took in his beautiful place, with the turf and the daisies and all his own flowers," and the renowned photographer Julia Margaret Cameron joined them for dinner. Because she wanted to photograph Jamie and Mabel—"the young, the fair, and the famous," Annie noted—the next morning they all trooped over to her seaside cottage. There Cameron took first Jamie and then Mabel into a darkened room, rearranged their clothes "to suit her artistic needs" and soon achieved "most satisfactory" results. Her "vision was as individual as it was keen," Annie concluded. Cameron would later send a package of her Tennyson portraits to Charles Street, saying the Fieldses were "worthy of the gift."[24] As they both agreed, their days in Farringford were "too few."

Far livelier and more varied was their week at Gad's Hill. Dickens awaited them outdoors on the afternoon of Wednesday, 2 June, showed them around his grounds before teatime, then presided over a splendid dinner and games that lasted until bedtime. The week's events included a glorious day-long expedition to Canterbury in two large carriages with red-jacketed postilions, and a splendid display of military exercises at Chatham. But best of all was simply standing beside "the dear man" on the battlements of Rochester's famous castle, "one of the happiest moments of my life." Meantime she felt increasingly close to Georgina Hogarth, who "told me about the family, showed me the house, the cellar etc. I have the deepest respect for her. She has been able to do everything for C.D. in his home."[25] Annie solemnly reflected after leaving Gad's Hill, "it is wonderful the flow of spirits C.D. has for he is a sad man. Sleepless nights come too often, oftener than they ever would to a free heart. . . . Mine has been an exceptional lot to have known this great man so well."

Though nothing in their five-week tour of England and Scotland or even their months on the Continent would match the satisfactions of sharing C.D.'s life, Annie was elated when her sister Lissie joined them in Paris and then traveled with them through France, Switzerland, Germany, Austria, and Italy. "Lissie paints, I read . . . , Mabel carves the head of her alpen stock," Annie wrote in a Swiss hotel, only mildly complaining about the rainy weather and uncomfortable beds. But a sad letter from Dickens made "the pain of the world . . . sting more bitterly than ever."

When the Fieldses returned to Gad's Hill for their final weekend in England, Dickens again presided over family games and lively dinners, during which Annie sat at his right "as usual." But as she lay awake at night in Dickens's own bedroom, she felt herself more deeply attuned to his sorrows than ever before. Dickens himself remained awake all Saturday night, then in the morning summoned "the Hon. J.T.F." to his study to hear the beginning of *The Mystery of Edwin Drood,* the dark novel he would not live to finish.

The Fieldses returned to London on Monday, and Dickens spent part of Tuesday with them. Then on the foggy morning of Friday, October 15, he saw them off at the railroad station. Annie wrote: "A crowd had collected to see him by the time we started but he did not seem to see it and the blood rushed all over his face as the tears came to ours, and we were off. He ran forward a few steps and all was over—except eternity." Dickens had been the first to greet the Fieldses when they reached England, and he was the last to bid them farewell.

After they returned to Boston, each of Dickens's "rather sad" letters and stories made the Fieldses recall the sorrow of their parting. Often Annie found herself reliving moments they had all spent together and then shared those recollections with Jamie. And whenever Dickens's actor-friend Charles Fechter came to Charles Street, they all shared their anxieties about him.

Dickens died the following June, and his death seemed almost unbearable to Annie. In a weak hand she wrote in her journal, "June 10. Friday—our dear friend, Charles Dickens died last night." Then she added in pencil, "June 9th at 6 o'clock." For two days, she made no further entries. Fechter soon came to mourn with the Fieldses, and friends from all over the country wrote to console them. The comfort Whittier offered was that they had "at least the satisfaction of knowing that his earthly life was made happier by your kindness & love."[26] Yet for two days, the Fieldses could do little more than weep, hug each other, and lament "What a change one year has made. These happy days, gone gone, and yet ours forever."

Then on June 13, the Fieldses produced a ten-page memorial of Dickens for the *Atlantic*. It was Annie's first unacknowledged collaboration with her husband, and the first of her many memoirs of celebrated writers. "We occupied ourselves during Sunday in making up a short paper for the A.M.," she wrote in her journal. "We knew some one must do it and I thought it better that we should." That it was written on Annie's initiative, not Jamie's, is significant. "Some Memories of Charles Dickens" appeared in the August *Atlantic;* it began with the Fieldses' week at Gad's Hill; and it was listed on the contents page as "by J. T. Fields."

A year later, Annie again culled her journals for an essay about Dickens that would be credited solely to her husband. She began by copying out "over 50 small mss. pages" about Gad's Hill "for J to use," and soon assembled about a third of the material that made up "his" long essay. It appeared first in the *Atlantic* and later in *Yesterdays with Authors*.

Annie also paid tribute to Dickens with a more private valediction—a four-quatrain elegy titled "The Holly-Tree by the door at Gad's Hill" that mythicized Dickens without naming him. The speaker begins by dispassionately urging the holly tree beside "his" grave to "Teach us to smile before we sleep," and dispassionately concludes that "wherever bends the Christmas bough / His blessing there is said." But the passionate protest in the third stanza seems to be in Annie's own voice: "He was ours! We may weep!"[27] She neither signed nor published the poem (as she had neither signed nor published her elegy for Hawthorne).

From then on, she ritualized her sorrow by marking three separate Dickens anniversaries—of his death, his birthday, and his last farewell to her. There was "none like him, none," she protested, and she once claimed that she thought about him every time she gave a dinner party. She nonetheless repeatedly reminded herself that death had ended his sufferings, and (without further specificity) told herself to forget "the dark side of his strange experience." Yet she and Jamie would continue to share their memories of him and even their dreams of him for the rest of their lives.

SECTION II
Befriending Women

7

Friendships of the Sixties

During the early sixties, Annie Fields entered into long-lasting friendships with dozens of talented, intelligent, yet conventionally womanly women. Whether they were married or not, her own age or older, and whether or not they lived in Boston, they all shared her commitments to high culture and hard work. Not so coincidentally, most of them wrote professionally and published in the *Atlantic*. By involving herself in their lives, the editor's wife served her husband's interests but also their interests and her own.

Given the strictures on women's speech in mixed company, Annie could speak her mind more freely with other women, whether about Longfellow's translation of Dante, the latest issue of the *Atlantic*, or the Battle of Bull Run. In a typical letter, she included social and domestic news but also raised philosophical issues and discoursed on women's needs and accomplishments—whether George Sand's, George Eliot's, Elizabeth Barrett Browning's, her friends', or (very rarely) her own. For most of the women she befriended in the sixties, Annie served as a confidante and a dispenser of social privilege; and a remarkable number of them regarded her as their closest friend. Through her, they entered into community with other women while also expanding their own status in and beyond the world of the *Atlantic*. Annie's rewards included their admiration, gratitude, and affection, vicarious entry into their lives, and knowing that she had served the deserving.

Rebecca Harding Davis (1831–1910)

In May 1861, as her husband's unofficial assistant, Annie Fields sent a letter to Rebecca Blaine Harding, a woman from Wheeling in what was then Virginia whose first story—"Life in the Iron-Mills"—had appeared in the April *Atlantic*. Several months earlier, struck by the strength and originality of a manuscript that touched all three bases of his "Magazine of Literature, Art, and Politics," James T. Fields had sent her a fifty dollar check and requested further submissions. Harding's stark story of dehumanized millworkers and middle-class indifference focused on an overworked and underpaid millhand whose skill as a sculptor indirectly led him to theft, imprisonment, and suicide. Such diverse readers as Nathaniel Hawthorne, Emily Dickinson, and a young Philadelphia lawyer named L. Clarke Davis were arrested by the narrator's demand: "Stop a moment, hide your disgust, take no heed of your clean clothes, and come right down with me— here, into the thickest of the fog and mud and foul effluvia," a place of despair and spiritual hunger where we may nonetheless find "some promise of the day that shall surely come."[1]

Annie's first letter to Rebecca Harding concerned what would turn out to be her second *Atlantic* publication and her first novel. Responding to her offer to complete a story then titled "The Deaf and the Dumb" for the *Atlantic,* James T. Fields had said it was too gloomy for readers who were coping with the onset of the Civil War. Harding had then posed three related questions: should she alter the story to "end in full sunshine" as she had originally intended, or should she "try again, or do you care to have me as a contributor?" At that point, the busy editor enlisted his wife to reply. In what Harding called a "courteous and womanly" letter, Annie evidently conveyed her husband's request for an altered manuscript that ended in "full sunshine," as the author herself had proposed. Harding said she would try to "meet his wishes by being more cheerful," but wryly remarked that "humor had need to be high and warm as God's sunshine to glow cheerily in Virginia soil just now." Then she prophetically signed herself "Very sincerely your friend."[2]

Three weeks later, again using Annie as an intermediary, Harding said her story would now "extend through three no's" and asked if she should submit the first installment for judgment. Presumably on Annie's instruction, she waited until she had drafted the entire narrative, now titled "A Story of To-Day." As in "Life in the Iron-Mills," Harding decried the moral failures of "this commonplace, this vulgar American life" through a bitter story set in a soot-stained factory town— but this time a new factory town in Indiana rather than Wheeling (which was at that point on the very "border of the battlefield"). Relieved by James T. Fields's acceptance of her manuscript in early August, Harding told him to "divide it as you please" and agreed to various minor changes he suggested. But she urged speedy publication and wanted to know where the first installment would end so she could improve the rest and "make it more truly a story of this day." Then a week later, after Fields told her that publication would begin the following month, she requested the editor's wife "to tell me if she likes the story when she reads it," stressing that she wanted "*criticism, not praise.*"[3]

Annie apparently liked the happy ending that Harding had contrived for her central couple. Instead of consigning the young bookkeeper Margret Howth to a solitary life as a social worker after her ambitious fiancé jilts her for a wealthy woman, Harding accorded her the traditional bliss of a self-subordinating marriage to her now spiritually reformed fiancé, and even the promise of imminent wealth. However facile that happy ending now seems, it satisfied contemporary readers. Evidently so did the book's depictions of industrial blight. In October, after the first of Harding's six installments appeared in the *Atlantic,* Fields signaled his satisfaction by offering book publication. *Margret Howth: A Story of To-day* went on sale in February 1862 and ran through three editions.[4]

Soon afterward, Fields asked Harding to write exclusively for the *Atlantic.* She agreed (though she would soon start breaking that promise without letting him know). Her next submission came in November—a denunciation of racism and the "filthy spewings" of the Civil War titled "John Lamar," about a slave owner imprisoned by Union soldiers who is violently murdered by his morally confused slave. Fields immediately accepted it; and Annie's separate signs of approval included a photograph of herself and an invitation to Charles Street.

Harding welcomed the invitation but repeatedly postponed the date of her arrival, variously pleading her father's illness, the problems of wartime travel, snowy weather, and her obligation to produce more manuscripts for the *Atlantic.* As she also poignantly admitted, she hoped the Fieldses were as eager to see her as she was to see them but feared that they might not like her. On the first Saturday in June 1862, that fear evaporated when Annie greeted her at the door of Charles Street in true "Virginia fashion."[5]

For the next ten days, the young woman from Wheeling had the time of her life. Sophia Hawthorne's stay at Charles Street overlapped hers, Oliver Wendell Holmes called almost immediately and took her out walking the next morning, and each day was crowded with outings that ranged from museum visits to a picnic at Nahant and a series of Charles Street parties. Eminent local abolitionists including Governor John Andrew, the Bartols, the Waterstons, the Whipples, and the Danas came to dinners and receptions, eager to meet the author of "John Lamar" and hear reports of the battlefront. As an overlapping category, so did many of the women whose work was then appearing in the *Atlantic,* including Celia Thaxter, Harriet Prescott, Kate Field, Elizabeth Peabody, and Louisa May Alcott. But for Rebecca Harding, the pleasures of meeting them were trumped by the satisfactions of discussing them with her hostess, who was no longer "Dear Mrs. Fields" but "beloved Annie."[6]

Rebecca Harding's New England interlude ended with two days in Concord, under the roof of the man whose stories had first helped her find "mystery and charm" in the commonplace, Nathaniel Hawthorne. "Miss Harding arrived at five," Sophia Hawthorne wrote in her diary on 17 June, then the next day recorded walks to the Old Manse, Sleepy Hollow cemetery, and Emerson's house, and a dinner that Emerson and the Alcotts attended. But what Rebecca Harding valued most was the chance to observe Hawthorne and converse with him, and she cherished his farewell: "I am sorry you are going away. It seems as if we had known you always." Her reverence for him now strengthened her bond with Annie

Fields; and two years later when Annie described his "going to rest" in Sleepy Hollow cemetery, Rebecca wistfully recalled sitting there beside him, "his hands clasped about his knees & the quaint smile with which he said 'Yes it *is* pleasant. The most beautiful pleasure grounds you will find in New England are our graveyards. *We* only begin to enjoy ourselves when we're dead.'"[7]

Two months after returning to Wheeling, Rebecca sent both of the Fieldses a remarkable letter which at once assumed and asserted her right to intimacy. She began by explaining why she omitted a salutation: "I don't know which to write to—I cannot separate you—and I do want a good talk to both of you this tropical morning. Such a long time since we looked out on the bay from that 'glorified' breakfast room!" Yearning to "see and touch you," she determined "to take up the old threads and feel as near to you all as I can." Although Wheeling was not pleasant at best and battles were raging nearby, she reminded them of their promise to visit, but meantime demanded "long gossipy letters" to help her feel she had "not left Boston altogether." To that same end, she asked Annie to "put Dr. Holmes in mind of me," to thank Elizabeth Peabody for the letters she had sent, to forward a note to Kate Field, and to tell her if anything had changed the Fieldses' minds about a scandalous person called "Foster." She did not send the photograph they had requested only because none seemed good enough. But she pleaded, *"don't* forget that time—so very happy for me." It was a plea she would often repeat.[8]

She would never again visit Charles Street. But in her letters to Annie, she repeatedly returned there, particularly to the sunlit breakfast room where the Fieldses sat facing each other every morning. They had become her icons of domestic bliss. She recalled particular dishes Annie had served, requested a few recipes, and introduced "Mrs. Fields's pudding" to her own family. Her pre-Boston years now seemed "wasted," she once told Annie, then tormented herself with a rhetorical question: "why did I not show more how happy I was? Make them love me more?"[9]

Meantime, she reported on her progress with manuscripts for the *Atlantic*, pronounced judgment on the publications of people she had met in Boston, and asked for gossip about them (including news of Harriet Prescott's wedding). But not until January 1863 did the thirty-two-year-old woman tell her "loving friend" Annie that for the past six months she had been engaged to L. Clarke Davis, the twenty-eight-year-old Philadelphia lawyer and reader for *Peterson's* magazine who had initiated their relationship in the spring of 1861 with a letter praising "Life in the Iron-Mills." "It isn't easy for me to tell you this I don't know why," Rebecca wrote, then told Annie she had stopped in Philadelphia on her way home from Massachusetts to see Clarke Davis, soon accepted his proposal of marriage, and was now about to marry him. "I would rather tell other women's stories than my own," she admitted. Yet now that she had told her own story, she exuberantly predicted, *"My* summer days are coming now." Next came an implicit request: "You, who are so happy in your married life will know how to ask for a blessing on mine." Responding to Annie's almost immediate reply, Rebecca rapturously described her fiancé, and reminded Annie to think about her on her wedding day "as you said—and pray for me."[10]

One way Annie did so was by writing an "Ode to R.H. on her Wedding Day," an epithalamion drenched in empathy. She never sent or published it, but the existence of two slightly different drafts suggests how seriously she took her self-imposed task. Although she was three years younger than R.H., Annie evidently felt entitled by her eight years of marriage to speak with authority. The woman she addresses is a typical nineteenth-century bride, a woman struggling to cope with what one scholar called "traumatic removal from her mother" and adjustment to a husband's different expectations.[11] After imagining the bride's grief at losing her maidenly identity and leaving her family, the speaker urges her to rejoice:

> Look up and face the sunshine of thy bliss.
> Such strength from this
> Shall stream
> That life no dream
> But fuller, stronger, mightier, ever more shall seem.

Annie Fields's "Ode to R.H." expresses her own deep commitment to marriage as the locus of a woman's fulfillment. Ignoring Rebecca's identity as a writer, Annie confidently predicted that marital bliss would dispel all her maidenly anxieties. Thinking of Rebecca "on that day" as she had promised, Annie solemnly noted on one copy of her ode that the wedding took place on a day of mixed sunshine and shadow, figuring "the broken circle of home."

Because Annie did not then (or ever) send the "Ode to R.H.," Rebecca had no reason to think of her beloved friend as a poet until the following November, when Annie sent a copy of her Ode for the inauguration of Boston's Great Organ and asked if that "utterance . . . in print" disappointed her. Avoiding a direct answer, Rebecca said she was not surprised that Annie's "full and varied life" had found poetic voice and wished she had been at the reading. But she also wished that Annie had more fully developed the organ's's "trial—pain—prophecy."[12] Perhaps vexed by that faint praise, Annie never again shared news about her own literary career.

Nonetheless, she continued to feel a proprietary interest in the diffident R.H. for whom she had prophesied marital bliss. Out of affection though surely also out of curiosity, Annie had urged Rebecca to make Charles Street a stop on her wedding trip. But there would be no such trip. The frugal newlyweds left Wheeling for Philadelphia right after their marriage, and began boarding with Clarke's sister.

Two months later, in early April, the Fieldses went down to see them. Back in Boston, Annie inserted a blossom just "like the flowers growing in Rebecca's little parlor" in her scrapbook of pressed flowers, then rapturously exclaimed, "What a life of happiness was this visit to Rebecca and her husband!" Rebecca was equally thrilled. It did her "true good" to know Annie cared "so much," she wrote. "We never really knew each other before."[13]

At that point Rebecca gave herself permission to consult Annie even on such matters as calling card etiquette, and to comment freely about Lucretia Mott and other eminent Philadelphians whose acquaintance Annie arranged for her. Rebecca also enlisted her help for Sarah Wallace, a recently widowed friend who hoped to support herself and her three children by running a circulating library in a nearby village. Through Annie's agency, Mrs. Wallace received several shipments of Ticknor and Fields books. Annie had meantime become a kind of muse for Rebecca. She looked at Annie's photograph when she sat down to write, Rebecca said, and her husband enjoyed displaying it to visitors.[14]

A few months later, Rebecca offered a few deeply painful confidences. During the summer of 1863 when the strains of boarding with Clarke's sister became exacerbated by illness—her husband's, her own, and her sister-in-law's—Rebecca became so depressed that she was forbidden to read or write. "If I get well we are going to live by ourselves," she told Annie in November; "*You* know all that means to me." Then after telling Annie "how dear you are to me," Rebecca said she had "never felt before how hard it was to justify my right to love as since I was sick." Out of fear that she might "become suddenly indifferent to you," she longed to say in person "what one cannot write without chilling it out of meaning." Meanwhile, she hoped to complete a story for the *Atlantic* which would also be a Christmas gift to her husband, and asked if "J.T.F." would "hold a place for it in the January number."[15] Never had she more poignantly appealed for Annie's sympathy and intervention.

One way that Annie and her husband responded to that appeal was by visiting the Davises in early February 1864, a visit recorded with unusual intensity in Annie's diary. Rebecca struck her as saintly, and Clarke also seemed so "brave in self-denial and self-discipline" that Annie felt moved to exclaim "What a sanctification such a marriage is!" Basking in mutual admiration, the Fieldses and the Davises talked from eleven in the morning until nine at night, their conversation ranging from the Civil War and urban poverty to such immediate problems as Rebecca's health and her professional future. They would never be closer. As Annie enigmatically noted after returning to Boston, Rebecca "has written a story and has some sketches planned, all of which she will set aside for the present."

What Annie did not say even in the privacy of her diary was that Rebecca was then seven months pregnant, and had "set aside" more than a few sketches. The long story she had originally planned as a Christmas gift for her husband—appropriately titled "The Wife's Story"—concerns a woman torn between professional fulfillment and family responsibilities, a tale of lightly veiled self-disclosure that ends when the heroine wakens from a bad dream of professional failure, determined to subordinate her career to her duties as a wife and mother. The story finally appeared in the *Atlantic* in July 1864.

By then the Davises were in their own quarters, and the future writer Richard

Harding Davis Jr.—the first of the couple's three children—was three months old. But instead of welcoming the visit Annie proposed at that point, Rebecca asked her to wait until the baby was fatter and happier. Perhaps Annie felt wounded. She never again proposed a visit and she declined all Rebecca's subsequent invitations for nearly a decade. Yet the women continued to share their lives through letters, and Rebecca continued to depend on Annie as a confidante and professional intermediary.

On a sticky professional matter, however, Rebecca kept silent. Among the sketches she had temporarily set aside during her first pregnancy were not only those she eventually completed for the *Atlantic* but several that she sold to *Peterson's Magazine*. In fact—yielding to the importunities of the *Peterson's* reader Clarke Davis even before meeting him—Rebecca had anonymously published in the better paying but less prestigious Philadelphia periodical since November 1861, even after promising Fields to write exclusively for the *Atlantic*. Then in July 1865 when her essay titled "Ellen" appeared in the *Atlantic,* she answered a charge of plagiarism by admitting authorship of the short story with the same title that had appeared in *Peterson's* two years before. She invited Fields to debit her account for what he had paid for her essay, nonetheless insisting that she had done nothing wrong. Fields did not debit her account, and he would subsequently publish four more of her manuscripts.

But whether as a delayed response to her tacit deception or as a judgment on her recent work, Fields did not put her name on the list of future *Atlantic* contributors which appeared in the magazine at the end of 1866. Aggrieved at being summarily "dismissed," Rebecca protested that she had taken a "pecuniary loss" by selling him manuscripts for half of what other magazines paid because she considered the *Atlantic* her "oldest friend": she liked its readers and thought they liked her. Putting her grievance aside, however, she continued to send manuscripts to the editor and affectionate letters to his wife.[16]

Just as before, she sent Annie news of what she was writing and publishing, interspersed with family news, comments about her reading, and pleas for letters and visits. After reading about Fields's imminent retirement at the end of 1870, she declared that Annie now had no excuse for not visiting her; and whenever a lecture by Fields was announced in the newspapers, she urged Annie to join him and offered to house them both. Annie could come and go in her house as freely as in a hotel, Rebecca once wrote, and "we can go back to the old friendship and begin a new one." Annie had never even seen any of her children, she later complained, signing herself "Your friend always."[17]

Perhaps moved by that appeal, Annie accompanied her husband to Philadelphia in the winter of 1873 (though she stayed in a hotel), and spent a few hours with "Rebecca Harding Davis whom I had not seen for ten years." Yet her account of that visit sounds remarkably detached. Rebecca "thought I had changed very little and said it honestly, an unexpected rebuke on her part as I had been feeling not quite well." Next came a distanced if admiring appraisal: "with her three children, she was a fine type of tender loving self forgetting motherhood." Perhaps Annie had never before realized how fully Rebecca had subordinated her professional identity to her family's needs.[18]

At the beginning of their friendship, Annie had regarded Rebecca as a woman after her own heart—conscientious and energetic, committed to social justice and literary excellence, dedicated to her family, and eager for affection. As a backwoods southerner with firsthand knowledge of both chattel slavery and wage slavery, Rebecca had the appeal of an exotic. She was also a valuable literary commodity. Fields would eventually publish sixteen of her manuscripts.

Annie had offered Rebecca encouragement even before meeting her, and her practical assistance during the sixties included transmitting information about when manuscripts were mailed or received, when they would be published, and when to expect payment. She also transmitted the praise of other readers, Dickens among them; and as an indirect consequence, "Blind Tom" appeared in Dickens's *All the Year Round* in November 1863, just before it appeared in the *Atlantic*.[19] As another kind of service, Annie overcame her husband's antipathy to one of Rebecca's manuscripts—the melodramatic story about a slum prostitute titled "The Promise of the Dawn"—by assuring him that it was drawn from life. Given the two women's lively exchanges about Elizabeth Barrett Browning, Annie may well have solicited Rebecca's review of one of Barrett Browning's books for the *Atlantic*. A more important service was criticizing Rebecca's manuscripts, though Rebecca often said that she did not feel bound to accept even Annie's advice. Thus Annie's praise of "Paul Blecker" helped alleviate Rebecca's doubts about it; but when a sentence was missing from the published text, she petulantly asked if Annie had deleted it.[20] Yet perhaps Annie's most consequential service to Rebecca was making her feel actively involved in New England's literary life, whether she was advising Harriet Beecher Stowe (through Annie) to write more "Chimney Corner" papers, or claiming credit for introducing Annie to Elizabeth Stuart Phelps, or producing manuscripts for the *Atlantic*.

Rebecca's single visit to Boston had brought her into community with the Fieldses and the world of the *Atlantic*. If she arrived as a shy Cinderella, Annie was her fairy godmother. Annie made no demands on Rebecca. But during the early sixties when Rebecca advanced swiftly into literary celebrity and then into marriage and motherhood, Annie valued her friendship almost as much as Rebecca valued hers.

During the seventies, Rebecca continued to send Annie detailed accounts of the domestic chores she juggled and the manuscripts she published, urged Annie to visit, and demanded long letters in return for short ones on the (mistaken) assumption that she was a writer and Annie was not. Without even trying to set her straight, Annie provided what Rebecca seemed to need and what she could easily supply: intellectual stimulus and temporary relief from deadlines and domesticity. In a sense, Rebecca paid off by continuing to produce high-minded manu-

scripts. But like the heroines of *Margret Howth* and "A Wife's Story," she had long
since given priority to her domestic responsibilities. That explains why she refused Annie's invitations to Charles Street, and (in August 1879, in her last surviving letter) to Manchester. Surely Annie saw no important role for herself in Rebecca's life after spending a few hours with her in the winter of 1873, when she
perceived her old friend as a "fine type of . . . motherhood."

Gail Hamilton (1833–1896)

One of Annie Fields's most exhilarating friendships of the 1860s was with Mary
Abigail Dodge, the popular essayist who published under the name of Gail
Hamilton. But for reasons that had nothing to do with Annie herself, it would last
for less than a decade.

Like Rebecca Harding when Annie first met her, Mary Dodge was an unmarried contributor to the *Atlantic* slightly older than Annie, a woman who had so
impressed the editor with her vigorous voice and fresh point of view that he
accepted her first submission and immediately requested more. But in almost
every other way, Mary was Rebecca's opposite. Mary Dodge—who would never
marry—was a feisty and fiercely independent New Englander, a woman as sharp
and witty in person as in her essays. Born and raised in the Massachusetts village
of Hamilton (the source of her pseudonym), she was the sole support of her
mother and sister. During the early and mid-sixties, she was often a guest at
Charles Street, where she enjoyed intimacy with Annie and friendship with the
Hawthornes and other literary notables. Fields was eager to publish her essays
and "get them up" as books. As Harriet Prescott Spofford wrote years later, "the
wind and the sunshine seemed to come in with her, so bright and breezy was her
presence, with a thought, an opinion, an epigram for everything, and sparkling
with sweet and wholesome wit, fearlessly frank and tenderly kind." Spofford's
metaphors are consistent with Annie's pronouncements about Mary Dodge during the sixties.[21]

When Mary's first humorously moralizing essay appeared in the 1860 *Atlantic,*
she had already published in the *National Era* and a few other periodicals. But that
essay launched her career. Fields would publish over two dozen additional submissions during the next seven years, as well as collections of her *Atlantic* essays
including the provocatively titled *Country Living and Country Thinking* (1862) and
Woman's Wrongs (1868). Fields also gave Mary's career another kind of boost in
1864 when he hired her to coedit his new children's magazine, *Our Young Folks.*

For Annie as for most readers of the *Atlantic,* the woman who signed herself
"Gail Hamilton" was a bracing source of irreverent good humor. In a typical essay titled "Happiest Days," for example, she argued that childhood is not the best
but the worst time of life. Yet many of her essays were far more serious, as when
she wrote in "A Spasm of Sense" that wives and mothers should not repress all

their personal desires, that mothers who "swamp themselves in a slough of self-sacrifice" harm their children and themselves, and that "the surest way to have high-minded children is to be high-minded yourself." More surprisingly, the unmarried and childless woman insisted on the mutual obligations of husbands and wives, and even recommended birth control.

Annie's unfinished essay on William Blake, written at the height of his rediscovery and presumably intended for the *Atlantic,* provides a curious gloss on her relationship with Mary. After reading Alexander Gilchrist's posthumous *Life of William Blake* (1863), Annie began writing a "short review" of it, perhaps at her husband's request. With her usual frugality, she began filling otherwise empty pages at the end of her 1863 journal. But nearly twelve pages in, this entry appears: "I have never copied corrected or finished this short review of Blake because when Gail Hamilton's article came, although it was too long for the assigned position it was too fine to set aside. Therefore I have done nothing with this." Annie must have felt disappointed. Possibly Jamie had said he wanted such a review in Mary's presence as well as Annie's, or perhaps it was simply a coincidence that Mary also wrote one. Annie's essay is painstaking, perceptive, and even elegant. But Gail Hamilton's "Pictor Ignotus" (which ran from pages 433 to 447 in the April 1864 *Atlantic*) is livelier and more captivating, as suggested by its very first sentence: "When William Blake flashed across the path of English polite society, society was confused."[22]

Annie probably never told Mary about her own Blake essay. In fact, with the possible exception of her Organ Ode, I find no evidence that Annie ever discussed her writings with Mary. But she closely followed Mary's work. After Mary took an unfinished essay to Charles Street in February 1863, for example, the editor read it and liked it, and Annie "came down and gave it a name and it comes out in the March number."[23]

But such interactions only begin to explain why Gail Hamilton's name frequently appears in Annie's journals and on her lists of dinner guests and overnight visitors. Her liveliness was enlivening. "Gail Hamilton has passed a day and night here this week. We went to hear the wonderful music at St. Paul's," Annie wrote in her scrapbook of "Fragrant Memories" in the spring of 1863, and a later journal entry reports a "long draught of talk" with Mary. Another entry is still more revealing: "She is the same affectionate sparkling lover as ever. It is good to see her." However startling the word *lover* may now seem, it simply pays tribute to Mary's exhilarating affection.

Annie's unusually long account of an unannounced visit to Mary's Hamilton home in August 1866 sounds affectionately proprietary. While Mary's sister went to fetch her from the garden, Annie complacently examined the tributes from admirers that crowded the plain little parlor. Then Mary came running in, looking "as fresh and bright as a girl of 20." Annie had brought a gift of peaches that Mary asked her to carry into her mother's sickroom; and as Annie noted with surprisingly intense sympathy, "the poor child's sorrow at the prospect of her mother's death had been a sorrow of our own." Almost as if scripting a play, Annie then sketched out the rest of the entire day's events—including the camp meeting they attended—and even included bits of dialogue.

After another visit to Hamilton the following spring, Annie described Mary to another close friend as an embodiment of rural wholesomeness, "with two little chickens one in each hand pressed up against her, the wind flinging about her fresh yellow hair and she herself laughing all over with pleasant excitement. She is such a good soul and so thoroughly healthy it is like being exposed to a fresh west wind to come near to her."[24] As that last metaphor suggests, Mary Dodge pierced Annie Fields's habitual reserve. That is what literally occurred on the September morning when she entered Annie's "chamber" at Charles Street without warning, bringing her sister and convalescent mother for a tour of the house. Welcoming rather than resenting that intrusion, Annie conducted the tour and served them all lunch. "I was truly delighted to see the old lady," Annie noted in her journal. "I dare say even the bit of a visit did her good." But she was more delighted to see Mary herself, "bright as ever full of sweetness and sincerity mingled with a tender amount of solicitude for her mother's health." A related pleasure was sharing Mary's company with other friends, as when Emerson and Harriet Beecher Stowe also came for breakfast and the three women then went out shopping. Annie's journal account of that day concludes with a few scraps of good-humored conversation and regret that she could not take time to record all the "good things" that were said.

But only three months later, in February 1868, Gail Hamilton abruptly terminated her friendship with the Fieldses, claiming that the publisher had cheated her. Although it was general knowledge that many periodicals paid better than the *Atlantic* and that many book publishers paid higher royalties than Ticknor and Fields, Mary was shocked to discover that Fields had paid some writers more than he paid her. She then accused him of bilking her by changing her royalty payments from a percentage rate to a unit amount. Independent arbiters cleared Fields of wrongdoing but recommended a cash settlement, which he paid.[25] Nonetheless, Gail Hamilton continued to feel so aggrieved that in 1870 she published a thinly disguised attack on Fields entitled *A Battle of the Books*.

Although Annie evidently destroyed all Mary Dodge's letters to her, she did not destroy the many references to Mary in her journals. "We had a real sorrow last night," Annie wrote in her journal on 12 February. "Mary Dodge whom we have known so well and sincerely loved has seen fit to withdraw her friendship—and without a word, only a little note refusing to explain," simply because she "thought she could make more money from her books, but instead of talking her affairs over in a gentle way with J. has thrown up the whole matter."

Even more testily, Annie said Mary Dodge seemed "forgetful of what she owes" to her true and steadfast friends. As the word *owes* suggests, however,

Annie was pitting one calculus of obligation against another. After reading Mary's curt "little note," Annie wrote a "farewell note of two pages" that Jamie persuaded her to delay sending. As Annie anticipated, however, the Fieldses' silence increased Mary's anger. After asking if her prior note had been received, she reported withdrawing the five thousand dollars in her Ticknor and Fields account—as if she "had been or expected to be robbed," Annie lamented.

Although at that point Annie's involvement with Dickens left her little time to brood, she made a curious diary entry a month later: "we do not forget to feel still the savagery . . . of Gail Hamilton." Not then or thereafter would Annie call her Mary Dodge. After professing pity "for what she has done," Annie vented her own dismay: "I really thought she cared for me! And now to find it was a pretense or a stepping-stone merely is something to shudder over. And all for a little of this world's poor money!!"

Annie's resentment peaked that June. Gail Hamilton had not only disseminated complaints about Fields all over the country, but during the meeting with Jamie that she herself had requested she was aggressive and "unwomanly," her temper was "shocking," and she had insultingly left Jamie alone for an hour and a half while she copied letters he had brought to support his "true position." Bewildered, Annie ventured a curious hypothesis: Gail resented exclusion from Annie's parties for Dickens. Perhaps she was partly right. Though she had taken both Gail Hamilton and Sophia Hawthorne to Dickens's second reading and then taken them backstage, she had not invited them to any of the parties she gave in his honor. Perhaps they felt relegated to a second tier of friendship. But Annie simply dismissed Gail's charge that Jamie had cheated her, and she would have the same reaction to Sophia Hawthorne's similar charge. "'Gail' and Mrs. Hawthorne are still implacable," Annie self-righteously wrote on 12 December 1868; "having conjured up a fancied wrong, they nurse it well."

"I can't help thinking you might have managed her more shrewdly," Whittier wrote Fields a year later, after reading Gail Hamilton's *Battle of the Books*. "If thee was an old bachelor like myself I should pity thee under such clapper-clawing, but haven't thee one of the dearest and best women to heal the scratches?" Then he soothingly predicted, "It won't amount to much anyway, and will cost more than will come to the writer."[26] Whittier was mistaken. The book sold well, as did everything else Gail Hamilton wrote until her death in 1896, and *A Battle of the Books* may well have influenced Fields's decision to retire in 1870.

Throughout Mary Dodge's years of intimacy with Annie, twenty-five of her essays appeared in the *Atlantic*, the collections Fields published increased her income and her fame, editing *Our Young Folks* brought her additional status and income, and she was comfortably ensconced in the Fields-centered literary establishment. A note from Whittier to Mary provides a curious gloss on the women's intimacy. Annie gave Mary a feathered hat in the spring of 1865 and suggested she should wear it to the Quakers' annual meeting in Newport, a joke that Mary shared with Whittier. "Annie Fields is a dear woman and I can't look her in her face and blame her for anything," Whittier replied, "but she has no right to make a 'great moral spectacle' of thee in such a head-gear."[27]

Mary Dodge had enlivened Annie's life, loosened her up, and enlarged her assumptions about acceptable womanly behavior. Losing her friendship was a wholly unanticipated blow.

8

The Author's Wife—Sophia Hawthorne
(1809–1871)

Annie Fields's friendship with Sophia Hawthorne began as an offshoot of their husbands' relationship, flourished while Hawthorne was alive, and lasted four years more. Their first meeting occurred in London in June 1859, when Sophia accompanied Hawthorne on his second visit to the Fieldses' hotel. "We all had lunch together and a delicious talk," Annie wrote in her diary, and she could soon write home that the parents and children were "quite after my own heart."[1] But the women's separate friendship did not begin until the following year, when the two families sailed for America together. She and Sophia enjoyed "delicious long talks," Annie wrote in her journal, and years later she called Sophia a "second Scheherezade," a "romancer in conversation [who] filled the evening hours by weaving magic webs of her fancies."[2] That description seems amply warranted by her letters to Annie Fields (letters that "*were* her talk," Annie once said).[3]

Often Sophia addressed the much younger Annie as her "dear Moonlight" or "dearest Lily," and even more often as a "Peri" (a Persian term for a fairy, or a beautiful woman). Annie's house was therefore "the Paradise of the Peri," Sophia once called Annie a "naughty little invisible Peri" for going on vacation without saying where, and she shared her grief at Hawthorne's death with "my dearest Peri—(who *never* at the Gate of Eden stood disconsolate)." She often fantasized visits to the "dark eyed Peri, who never left Paradise," yearning (as she once put it) "to lie upon the lounge in the bower of bowers, and do nothing and say nothing but watch you glide about or sit still, and listen to you when you spoke—or be silent with you. At all events to have you. You are in my heart and nothing can ever tear you out of it."[4] Sophia would sound many variations on that same romantic theme: she longed for her beloved Annie, who was nonetheless always in her heart.

Sophia's paeans to Annie's beauty were ways of saying so. She could be brief about it, as when she rejoiced that Annie was so "eminently beautiful" and then sighed, "Oh dear me—I really can't help saying it." But she often ran a surprising emotional gamut, as in a letter of August 1863 when Annie was at the seaside. She began by larding the language of fashion reportage with the hyperbole of lovestruck adoration: "I see you in a dear brown hat, swooping with lace and feathers, (not in your saucy white one—so espiègle with cherries and poppies—) looking forth over the sapphire waste of waters with those deep dark stars of eyes, so absorbent of light and rich with poetry—crowned with the untameable coronet of shadowy brown gold hair, gathered away from a brow and cheeks of the Egyptian Calla." Anticipating Annie's modest protestations, Sophia moved from petulant self-assertion to a rhetorical challenge: "I *will* say what I choose and you must bear it as you can. For how absurd for me to have these facts on the tip of my pen, and from a foolish conventional reticence, refrain from letting them crystallize on the paper when I wish to do so. When folk are beautiful, why should the mirror alone have the satisfaction of telling folk?" Her quasi-objective conclusion was seductively lofty: "In a large view of the matter, I think each one may look on one's own personal beauty as upon that of another as a work of Divine Art—upon which one's self has naught to do."[5]

An even more curious paean of praise begins by passing on another woman's tribute: "'Oh Mrs. Hawthorne! I saw Mrs Fields in the street—She looked so very handsome. She had on a *splendid* black velvet sack trimmed with sables—but I forget what her bonnet was. But oh she looked so very handsome.'" She envied "little Edith [Davidson] her vision," Sophia said, then imperiously declared, "This costume I intend to see you in myself sometime. Why have you not put it on for me? Do not you know I like to see you dressed in your bravest—though I love to see you just as well in undress. But beautiful attire so becomes you, though you can do without it."[6] However startling those demands and assertions may now seem, Sophia evidently saw nothing improper in them.

Meantime, she had no compunctions about requesting Annie's help with "the mundane affairs which perplex me." In the spring of 1862, for example, Sophia wondered if "a Peri were ever before asked to go shopping" and if her husband would "kill me for so employing you," then thanked Annie for a dress pattern; and she subsequently commissioned Annie to buy braid and ribbon, chintz for slipcovers, cloth for "saques," and vellum for Julian, and to help Una choose a hat. More important, she had come to depend on Annie's invitations to Charles Street—specific invitations for herself and the children and an open one for her husband. Annie's pamperings included gifts for the children, as when Julian returned to the Wayside in December 1862 sporting a waterpoof coat, new gloves, and a "cossack cap."[7] For Sophia, Charles Street was a place of enchanting release from "mundane affairs"; she arrived for a visit with Rose in September 1862 and rapturously told her husband that she had just "dined on nightingales tongues in the shape of pigeons, and ate ambrosia in the form of peaches and St Michael's pears and drank nectar in the disguise of claret," and said Annie was "as lovely as a rose and lily."[8]

Yet arguably Annie's most important role for Sophia was as her confidante. She could tell Annie almost anything, Sophia marveled, whether about her initiatives as "farmer and housekeeper, and housebuilder and so on," or about her children's illnesses, or about Julian's "illumination" of "Ring Out Wild Bells" for a Freedmen's Fair. In the summer of 1861, she agonized with Annie about the deaths of Mrs. Longfellow and of Elizabeth Barrett Browning, grieving for Longfellow and "those three young girls 'so much bereft'" and picturing Browning and his son "gazing at one another in wild dismay." And after Thoreau's death the following spring, Sophia defined him as "Concord itself in one man," then solemnly celebrated "his Alpine purity, his diamond truth, his stainless sincerity, his closeness to nature and faithful rendering."[9]

Other Concord neighbors enter Sophia's letters to Annie as they entered her life. Emerson stopped by and tried "badgering Mr. Hawthorne into dining with him," she told Annie on one occasion.[10] Her nearest neighbors the Alcotts are mentioned more frequently, often as nuisances. Annie's cousin Abba Alcott was an "appalling sensationalist" who spread "blood-curdling" rumors of Civil War debacles, Sophia complained: her report of General Banks's rout turned out to be "nearly all an exaggeration and I suffered for nothing."[11] More surprising is a comical and incidentally self-mocking anecdote about Bronson Alcott. As Sophia reported, she had climbed the hill behind the Wayside "to erect a temple to the god Pan (who is *not* dead)" when Alcott suddenly showed up. "With no regard to physics and their laws, the philosopher immediately took up a long board of a low semicircular shape and set it upon some columns not yet fixedly adjusted," whereupon the board fell on her head. But she was now recovering, and would not have told Annie the story "if I had not loved you immensely."[12]

That same letter of June 1863 includes a request on behalf of the Alcotts' daughter Louisa. The previous winter Louisa had returned home "almost sick with death" after nursing Union soldiers in Washington, and Sophia had helped the Alcotts tend her.[13] Now came an easier beneficence. After hearing Bronson read a "majestic" elegy for Thoreau that Louisa had written, Sophia read it to herself and copied it out for Annie. "I wish you would read it to yourself, and then to your husband aloud," she wrote, " . . . so that the full beauty of it may strike him. I *am sure* you will both agree with me that it is worthy [of] the best place it can be put into, and so I hope Mr. Fields will let it go into the Atlantic—that Louisa may have the honor as well as the pecuniary benefit." "Thoreau's Flute" appeared in the September *Atlantic*.[14]

But Sophia's most important confidences to Annie concern her beloved husband. Through Sophia's adoring eyes, we see the great writer just as she did, as when he returned from Washington in April 1862:

> We cannot tell how glad we are, but we are all taller and handsomer and wittier since our great sun shone again upon us. . . . [H]e arrived wrapt in royal garments of purple and gold, like the King he is—(I know you will forgive my heroics on this subject). I was in the Tower, giving the last touch to his couch in the study, when I heard

a scream of joy. And I was so contented, that I did not hasten down, but remained aloft till he ascended out of the welcome below to the welcome above.[15]

Yet she could also laugh at "my Lord," as when she described him patiently untying each knot on a package of books from the Fieldses because "it was such a very nice cord he must not cut it."[16]

Even in her more humorous account of Hawthorne's appearance at Una's eighteenth birthday party the following June, Sophia's groundnote was reverence:

> You will be glad to hear that my lord came down from his high estate in the Tower, and looked in [on] the gay throng, like a grand olympian, descended to a 'Paradise of children' in a golden age. Many of them had never seen him, and were glad enough, and greatly surprised—and at the end, they tried to get up courage to go and bid him good night. My neice [*sic*] told me that she heard one young lady say 'oh how I want to shake hands with Mr. Hawthorne but I am afraid.' Judge Hoar's son said 'oh don't be afraid—I am going to. It is proper and he is not a bear. He will not bite—' So Sam Hoar came in and did his duty, and then a piquante, vivid looking girl followed, and several took courage as well—and they all got hospitable smiles, and seemed hugely pleased.[17]

But before long, Sophia's letters to Annie confided concern about her husband's health. In July 1863 Sophia said he was planning to refuse tickets he had been offered for a trip to the White Mountains because he thought the related expenses would be too high, then confessed, "I do not know what I shall do with him unless I can find an Aladdins lamp and begin to rub. He needs change immensely." Her anxieties intensified in October. "I do not find Mr Hawthorne very well," she wrote: Concord was bad for his health, and he seemed to be "singing swan songs." She could share her "sacredest emotions" about her husband only with Annie, Sophia declared. "How I love you in the great spaces, and how all I wish to say to you is lost in the silences—and how I could not be consoled, if it were not that all eternity is before us."[18]

A crisis came at the end of November, which Sophia reported the next day. Hawthorne suddenly became "very ill, more ill than ever in his life, and being alone, with no adequate medical assistance possible, you can fancy my alarm. But upon these great emergencies, one has a marvelous power of concentration and efficiency," and within an hour the crisis had passed. At that very moment, after spending the morning on the couch, he was walking on the hill behind the Wayside and planning to spend the next day on the romance he was writing for the *Atlantic*—a sad chapter, she predicted. Less than a week later, Hawthorne spent a night at Charles Street en route to Mrs. Franklin Pierce's funeral; and when he did not return to the Wayside the next night, Sophia concluded that Annie had again "put him up in lavender and roses" at Charles Street.[19]

For the next six months, all Sophia's domestic news and protestations of love for Annie intertwine with increasingly plaintive reports of Hawthorne's failing health. In January, he decided against going to Boston because he caught cold so easily. But in March when Ticknor arranged to travel south with him, Sophia accompanied him to Boston, where he would spend the night at Charles Street before setting out, then returned home immediately "because of his fears to leave the children alone." She could soon report Ticknor's news that Hawthorne seemed tired but slept well. Understandably, the shocking news of Ticknor's death made her worry about her husband's reactions. Annie's news of Hawthorne's safe return to Charles Street on 13 April brought a measure of relief. But five days later Sophia poignantly reported what happened when he returned to Concord. After walking home from the station in the rain, he was frighteningly pale and "scored with pain and fatigue"; and he broke down a bit as he talked about Ticknor's death. In despair, Sophia wished the cold weather would pass or that he could go somewhere warm; but he was too weak to travel, and she could do nothing but sit with him: "The wheels of my small ménage are all stopped. He is my world and all the business of it." Though she managed to make him "laugh with Thackeray's humor," even then his eyes were dull: "an infinite weariness films them quite."[20]

Soon afterward, Sophia reported on Hawthorne's final rally of health. Despite his abhorrence of trains and his reluctance to leave the children alone, he considered going with Sophia to the Isles of Shoals. Instead, he accepted Franklin Pierce's offer of a bachelor jaunt to New Hampshire. Although Hawthorne could no longer walk for even ten minutes, he now anticipated a "serene jog-trot in a private carriage into country places, by trout streams and to old farm houses away from care and news." The following week, Sophia wondered why Pierce was delaying.[21] A few days later, just before Hawthorne left to meet Pierce in Boston, she made an unusual request through the Fieldses: her husband had refused to see a doctor, but she wanted Oliver Wendell Holmes to make an informal diagnosis. As Annie wrote in her journal afterward, Holmes told her "the shark's tooth is upon him." Hawthorne left Boston on 12 May. A week later he died in his sleep in Plymouth, New Hampshire.

The following day, 20 May, Sophia penciled a long letter to her beloved Annie—who later wrote on its envelope, "The original of a precious and extraordinary letter written by Mrs. Nathaniel Hawthorne while her husband lay dead." "I wish to speak to you Annie," Sophia began, then paid tribute to Hawthorne's "uniform majesty": "Such an unviolated sanctuary as was his nature, I, his inmost wife, never conceived nor knew. . . . Even to me who was himself in unity—he was to the last the holy of holies behind the cherubim."[22] In the more subdued letter she sent Annie five days later, Sophia found spiritual consolation: her husband still remained part of her. She also enclosed a memento for Annie, "a small fairy-like pearl scimitar—a symbol of his own fine nature—with which he cut the leaves and marked his place in books he read. It pleased his fancy from its delicate beauty—and is just fit for your use. I gave it to him and so I can give it to you."[23] This delicate token now linked all three of them.

During the next four years, Sophia told Annie how she marked the anniversaries of her marriage, of her husband's birth, and (most emotionally) of his death and burial. As she wrote during the first winter after his death, she wept whenever she recalled "that divine breezy, songful, blooming day when I followed my sacred form to the moment of vision, wreathed about with noble, loving friends," and thought of "you sitting with me in the chapel." After the first anniversary of his death, she urged a visit to "his lovely domain" while the hawthorn trees were in bloom, to walk on "his" path. But after the second anniversary of his death, she thought Annie might find the Wayside too "desolate without the Adam that made the perfect Paradise."[24]

Sophia's most remarkable expression of tender concern for Annie is a letter written within weeks of Hawthorne's death, after hearing that Annie's brother Boylston had been wounded in battle and taken prisoner: "My beloved Annie, and all this while you have been suffering such a pain and I was ignorant of it while you were doing everything for me. . . . I wish I could bear your sorrow for you—but here the tenderest friendship is at fault. I wish the blow always would fall first on me. . . . I wish my arms were round you." She praised Boylston's vitality, honored him for rushing to the front, and urged Annie not to believe rumors about how Confederates mistreated prisoners. Then from her own podium of sorrow, she offered the consolation which was helping her bear her own loss: there really is no Death.[25]

Only about her religious faith, her love for her husband, her devotion to her children, and her love for Annie did Sophia speak with such absolute confidence. But firm convictions also underlay the amateur artist's judgments of art, whether of Lissie Adams's paintings or a portrait of Annie. A corollary was pride in her own artistry; her New Year's gift in 1866 was her own drawing of the Archangel Raphael, intended for Annie's bedroom.

Sophia's connoisseurship also extended to literature, as when she called Tennyson "my poet," or said she wanted to read Plato's *Phaedo* with Annie, or pronounced judgment on books Annie loaned her. She praised *Les Misérables, Cloister on the Hearth,* and Elizabeth Sheppard's short stories, but dismissed *The Woman in White* as "an elaborated insanity." She also disliked an *Atlantic* writer who was Annie's friend: Harriet Prescott was "so sultry, so unrefined in her way of describing outright what never should be more than delicately hinted at—so inclined to portray and blazon unlawful relations and sinful affections, that I blush to read, and cannot bear to have Una and Julian read." A related pleasure came from passing on her husband's literary pronouncements. He praised Gail Hamilton's *Country Living and Country Thinking,* she said. "Mr. Hawthorne and Julian think she is the only good lady-author in America." She was "all right . . . pure, fresh, sensible, penetrative." By contrast, Hawthorne could no longer read Rebecca Harding's stories because her style was so bad, Sophia said, singling out the word "pulsing" for special contempt.[26]

She nonetheless continued to read both Harding and Prescott, though with increasing irritation. "I do wish that Miss Harding, who is now Mrs Davis, would cease to write about disgusting flabby men and 'dried up old women,' and present truth in a rather more Greek style," Sophia told Annie in the spring of 1866, then complained, "She makes me seasick—Why will she be so 'mouldy' as my husband told her she was—Why does she love squalor oh why? There is enough mire in the streets, without smearing the pages of books with it. Tell me—do you not hate this manner of the gifted Rebecca?" But Harriet Prescott repelled her even more. "I hate 'Azarian' and every other story that lady has written—(without denying her ability and rich fancy)," Sophia wrote in October, "and so I must return the book to you."[27]

Sophia knew that Annie wrote poetry at least as early as April 1863, when she asked who wrote a poem in the *Atlantic* titled "My Ship," and Annie confessed that it was hers. When Una Hawthorne attended Charlotte Cushman's reading of Annie's *Ode on the Great Organ* and brought home a copy, Sophia told Annie she had read it aloud six times and enjoyed it more with each reading. Even more characteristically, when Annie's "The Future Summer" appeared in the October 1864 *Atlantic,* Sophia called it "indescribably lovely" and rhapsodized that Annie was "not only a poem in yourself, but a poet too!" Two years later she would have even stronger praise for Annie's unpublished ten-page hexameter narrative, "In the Palace, Florence 1530," which Annie copied out for her and folded in a sheet inscribed "To S.H."[28]

Presumably Annie also expected Sophia to praise her anonymous novel *Asphodel* (which she sent in September 1866), perhaps especially the central friendship between two women—one happily married, stable, and loving, the other solitary, oversensitive, and eventually unbalanced by grief over lost love. Sophia returned the novel without even suspecting that Annie had written it: "I began but *could not* read 'Asphodel' on account of its lack of nature, truth, simplicity, vraisemblance—perhaps I was not in the mood, and perhaps it is better in the end. But I think I could not ever read it, and I hope you do not like it yourself well enough to care whether I like it or not. Is it some new young authoress, whom you are trying to befriend and bring forward? She is no artist certainly—I would rather have your Florentine mosaic (as I call it) than a library of such books as this. But you ought not to be mentioned on the same page as this one."[29] Surely Sophia's response distressed Annie. She would never tell Sophia who the "young authoress" was.

A few days after Sophia returned *Asphodel,* she wrote that she yearned to see Annie and hoped to visit Lissie's studio on her next trip to Boston. She also inquired about Annie's mother's health and reported meeting Annie's sister "Mrs. Beal at Hovey's. She looked beaming and said that Baby stood on his feet by a chain. I think also I met your sister Sarah; but was not sure enough to speak to her till she had rapidly passed me." Annie's failure to respond to these ingratiating overtures puzzled Sophia; and six weeks later, she plaintively asked,

> Oh Annie Fields—are you lost? Mr Fields wrote me that you were "full of mothers and sisters," and when I have been in town, he has turned me off you, every time, saying you were out, or busy or something, and that it would be of no use to go to see

you. But it is getting to be too hard to bear. . . . I am faithful unto death, and I can endure great silences, and long absences, but there seems no need of this endless separation, weeks on weeks of non intercourse of all kinds. . . . I have a thousand things to tell you, and I miss you mightily out of my daily life. . . . Why cannot I read my Bhagavad Gita, and Rig Veda with you—my Madame Guyon, my Lord Bacon, my Plato—all of whom and which my soul loveth and feedeth upon.[30]

Annie then invited Sophia to Charles Street, but only for a short visit.

Sophia's puzzlement and distress at Annie's continuing coolness generated a remarkably explicit dream in the fall of 1867:

I dreamed I went to see you, and, I suppose, on account of Mr. Fields' having said you were having great alterations or additions made to your house, when you took me upstairs, the rooms suddenly increased, till it seemed as if there were a city of chambers, all fair and orderly, spreading out and opening into one another. You then ascended another flight, and still the same unending chambers. But none of these were for me. A third flight of stairs led up to another suite. But here one vast apartment seemed to extend over the whole piano. It sloped on one side, but was very inviting and inhabitable. For there was a glorious fire on the hearth, and on a table the most radiant flowers. You, "a fairer flower," took up a vase full to show me particularly. There was evergreen in it, enclosing lovely gems—but, by some accident, a jarring caused the flowers to fall out, and we were shocked to find the water very offensive. And then, according to the nature of dreams, I found myself with enormous, muddy shoes on, and no headdress for my head—and I said to you, that this was a charming chamber, and that I would like it to be appropriated to me as long as I had breath enough to come up so many thousand stairs, but I feared that would not be long. Was there ever any thing so ridiculous? But I saw you, and you were in perfect beauty, and I was very much refreshed.

At least dimly, Sophia must have suspected that "according to the nature of dreams," she was not only venting discontent with her appearance and expressing a fear of dying, but acknowledging her anxiety about exclusion from Annie's Paradise. The dream language even seems overdetermined: it is all too easy to interpret the "radiant flowers" that fell out of a vase and left "offensive" water behind.[31]

In that same letter, Sophia asked Annie to return an opera cloak she had loaned her. Annoyed by seeing it in Lissie Adams's studio, Sophia said she had offered it to Annie only for her own use, and she now wanted to redye it for Rose. Clearly, Sophia now felt slighted, even betrayed.

Three years earlier, just after Hawthorne's death, Annie had wholeheartedly offered his widow practical and emotional sustenance. Both of the Fieldses urged Sophia to prepare a book about him, a project that she resisted. As she told her Dear Annie, "I can neither write a book, nor would I, if able, so entirely act in opposition to my husband's express wish and opinion as to do so. . . . My instinct is the same as his was. I feel no call—I am conscious of no faculty for it. If I felt the call and had the faculty, it would be totally impossible for me to accept such a task for a very long time. I have as much as I can do now to keep quiet and preserve a mood of cheer for the children." But as Sophia later told her "darling Annie," she was beginning to sort through her husband's manuscripts. Certain that Annie "would not wish to do anything with the papers against my wish," Sophia nonetheless promised to "copy out all that is possible—and I think there may be a good deal for the Atlantic—I shall copy all on separate sheets so as to have any part that is fitting available for the printers—and then we three will decide what to do."[32] Soon "we three" decided to publish all Sophia's transcriptions of Hawthorne's many-volumed notebooks, his letters, and his unfinished romances.

In fact, Sophia started sorting through her husband's letters with an eye to posterity in the immediate aftermath of his death, marveling at his "passionate sensibility" and "the restlessness of Pegasus in the pound." Within two weeks, she had read through hundreds of his letters "with mixed joy and grief," destroying some and copying others. "Have I done well?" she asked James T. Fields, calling him "the soul of honor and liberality," a man after her husband's heart who had earned his "entire trust" and who deserved thanks "for his sake and mine"; and she asked him to "Tell all this to beloved Annie."[33]

From then on, she herself directly told Annie about her transcriptions of Hawthorne's notebooks, and incidentally bragged about a few other commemorative enterprises. In March 1865, for example, she said she felt flustered that "publishers have got an idea of engraving" her recent portrait of her brother-in-law Horace Mann (who had died six years before): "Oh dear me!" she coyly exclaimed. A few weeks later, she told Annie that she had consoled a bereaved friend with a drawing of her dead daughter, but also sadly reported that she was unable to acquire the "sacred chair" her husband had sat in at the Old Manse during their early years of marriage when he wrote the *Mosses from an Old Manse* and read poetry to her.[34]

Sophia would continue to send such personal news until she left for Europe in the fall of 1868, often interjecting complaints of insufficient attention from her beloved Annie. "Writing seems now no part of your programme," she testily wrote in the fall of 1867, and Charles Dickens's arrival seemed to make matters worse. Though she gratefully accepted Annie's invitation to Dickens's second reading and enjoyed meeting him afterward, surely she felt jealous of Annie's absorption with him: "just one evening of him has made me live so fast that I am tired away into the future."[35] Even Sophia's exuberant praise of Dickens the following May while she was convalescing from an illness seems suspect. She was grateful for Annie's gift basket and Jamie's sympathy, rejoiced that Annie had found a "true, noble friend" in Dickens, anticipated hearing Annie read some of his letters, and then exclaimed, "O what is there worth anything but love and friendship through all their degrees." Surely Sophia realized the disparity of "degrees" between her love of Annie, Annie's fondness for her, and Annie's adoration of Dickens.[36]

Sophia Hawthorne's letters to Annie Fields reveal her as the passionately worshipful admirer of a beautiful young woman and the self-deprecating wife of an idealized husband, though also as a doting mother, a pragmatic homebody, a skillful amateur artist, a self-confident critic of art and literature, but sometimes also a bit of a bore. The woman who disliked novels that were not "Greek" enough and made outline drawings in the style of John Flaxman had been Hawthorne's chief model for Hilda, the idealistic copyist of *The Marble Faun* who virtually obliterated her own identity in worship of the Great Masters, sustained by her lofty conception of ideal beauty. Sophia was proud of her role as editor of her husband's notebooks, and she would subsequently publish her own travel journals. But in merging her own identity with that of her noble lord, though also in her worship of Annie Fields as a "perfect beauty," Hawthorne's Dove evaded her own self-fulfillment.

From Annie Fields's perspective, the trajectory of her friendship with Sophia Hawthorne looks much different. From the time they sailed for America together in June 1860, Annie admired Sophia's exuberant imagination and her devotion to her family, and she enjoyed cosseting them all. In July 1862, after an overnight visit to the Wayside, James T. Fields thanked Hawthorne for "such happy thrills as you gave me and mine of real delight" and said Annie was in love with Sophia.[37] He was not exaggerating. When Sophia showed Annie the vases she had painted with Greek figures for a Freedmen's Fair, Annie was impressed by more than her artistic skill. "What sunlight and joy it was to see her. How the day grew warmer and more beautiful," Annie declared.[38] Even so, Annie loved Sophia primarily as Hawthorne's "mainstay"; and during that July visit she preferred taking a walk with Hawthorne to remaining at the Wayside with his wife.

Annie's tenderness for Sophia was most intense in the aftermath of Hawthorne's death: his "passing was like losing a portion of our own household, so closely interwoven had become the interest and affection of the two families," she later recalled.[39] She helped arrange the funeral, attended it "with Hawthorne's other self his wife," and spent the rest of that day with Sophia. "How can we tell the sadness of this day," she wrote in her scrapbook of pressed flowers. In lieu of a flower, she inserted a penciled note from Sophia: "Annie—I see why you could not find a lily for the wreath that must fade. I have told your husband that it is because you are my lily of the wreath—and you are a lily that will never fade!"[40]

For nearly a year, Annie sentimentalized Sophia as an icon of bereavement. "Returning home we found Mrs. Hawthorne lying on the couch where she might watch the sunset and moonrise always the same, watched over by the eternal face of peace," she wrote in her diary in April 1865. But after visiting Sophia and her children at the Wayside that June—"the first real visit since that glorious presence has departed"—, Annie exclaimed in dismay, "What an altered household! She feels very lonely, and is like a reed. I fear the children will find small restraint from her." She would often say so again. Nonetheless sympathizing with the fifty-seven-year-old "poor child," Annie piously wondered "Will God spare her further trial, . . . and take her to his rest?"

When Annie attended Edith Emerson's wedding in Concord that August, she was glad to see that "Poor Mrs. Hawthorne laden with her many sorrows threw off her black robe for that day that she might rejoice with others." Better still, Sophia was "spending these long lovely days with her husband. She is copying passages from his journals beginning with the year 1836 the first which exist. Much within there is beautiful and ready for publication." Without even mentioning her own role in persuading Sophia to copy Hawthorne's notebooks, Annie happily reported that Sophia was "perfectly happy over them, happy too in our sympathy."

Soon afterward, perhaps as a sign of approval, Annie sent Sophia her hexameter poem "In the Palace," set in sixteenth-century Florence and focused on a "resplendent" woman who was her husband's regent during his war with France, a "fit queen of the house Borgherini." At the poem's center, King Francis attempts to buy her beautifully carved marriage bed while her husband is away, but the majestic heroine spurns his agent. Annie copied out the poem on ten half-sheets, initialed it, and laid it in a wrapper on which she wrote "To S.H."

Yet to Annie's increasing dismay, Sophia was less and less a "fit queen" of her house and increasingly dependent on the Fieldses. "I have omitted an account of a night and day from Mrs Hawthorne and Rose last week," Annie wrote in her journal on November 2, 1865: "She said she would like to stay over Sunday; but I knew that would imply many more hours broken in upon by talk and as Jamie needed rest and it was not essential for Mrs Hawthorne to stay I pleaded engagements, as indeed Louisa expected us especially at night." She was glad that Sophia left and "glad I found courage to speak." A week later, Annie issued a carefully limited invitation "to dine and spend the night" and solicitously took Sophia to a painting exhibition, "her love of Art making her forget the people she must encounter." But Annie said nothing about Sophia's visit the following July except that "SH brought lilies," little about her October visit except that she stayed for two nights, and nothing about her rejection of *Asphodel*. A year later when Sophia complained about Rowse's engraving of a Hawthorne photograph, Annie ruefully remarked, "I wish it were not always so. The poor woman is in a sad quandary." Pity mixed with contempt and emerged as metaphor: "Poor woman! She is a poor rudderless craft. Her husband was her compass and rudder; now she drives before the wind helplessly, except when she will take a friend on board as pilot for a time." Sophia was "daily more powerless over the children," Annie concluded. "How glad I am to do what I can for them!" she exclaimed after an overnight visit from all three Hawthorne children. "But they need a directing hand stronger than their mother's. Home and America are bad for them—too much ease—too great temptations to spend money." Their visits had become burdensome. Una seemed miserably "nervous," Rose was vain and superficial, and Julian seemed egocentric and even dishonest.

In April 1867, however, Annie's old feelings of tenderness for Sophia revived when she "made me her confidante" about Una's sudden engagement. "Una loves and is beloved!" Annie exulted, then recorded the poignant confession that Una had made to her mother: "I am so glad to feel my heart again, I was almost afraid it was dead, for since Papa died it has been like a lump of lead; and our very grief has been a barrier between us two, so I could not come to you—but now I feel again that I have a heart." Annie then invited Una to visit and confide "the particulars of her engagement."

But that summer, when the Fieldses were at Marblehead, Annie made an unusually specific complaint about Sophia's persistent requests for money. Jamie had "already given her 700 dollars above what he owes her and she has debts in Concord to the same amount," Annie wrote, "yet Julian lives at the Parker House and in spite of his mother's assertions to the contrary spends a good deal of money." It was sad to think "that in three years Hawthorne's family should be virtually beggars. He was so just and careful himself, never spending a cent he could not afford." Yet Sophia complained that "we do not come forward and do still more," even though the "just" and "generous" Jamie could "do no more."

Sophia briefly returned to favor when she brought fourteen volumes of Hawthorne's journals to show Jamie and said there were "piles on piles of romances begun but never finished." When Jamie returned to Marblehead for the weekend, he brought along Julian Hawthorne as well as a volume of those journals. "It was really good to watch his muscular figure swimming across the rocks with such perfect ease," Annie wrote. A "wanderer by nature and constitution" and not a prospective clergyman as his mother had absurdly contended, he was "blunt in speech but a noble manly fellow." As one consequence of that judgment, Annie included Julian and Rose in Sophia's overnight visit to Charles Street in December 1867.

Over the next few months, Annie's journal included a few eruptions of pain about Gail Hamilton's disaffection but no mention of Sophia. Sophia continued to report on her activities and the children's, and Annie solicitously sent a basket of flowers, fruit, and wine during Sophia's illness in May 1868. Her final gift a few months later was smaller and less personal: a copy of the poem Holmes had written for Longfellow's sixtieth birthday.

Sophia was then still signing her letters to Annie "Your affectionate friend." But spurred by Gail Hamilton, she had begun to suspect that James T. Fields was cheating her, and the accounting she eventually requested seemed to confirm those suspicions. She had assumed that Fields paid all the costs of Hawthorne's funeral, but discovered that she had been charged for half. She had assumed that Hawthorne's books earned a 15 percent royalty, but discovered that Fields had switched to a flat-rate compensation that eventually brought in less. And she could not understand why her royalty for editing *Passages from the American Note-Books* was only 12 percent, and why Fields had negotiated only a hundred pounds for the English copyright.

In August 1868 Fields responded to Sophia's "considerable dissatisfaction" with an unusually impersonal letter signed "Ticknor & Fields," assuring her that she had been fairly paid, and that her "administrator" (Hawthorne's old friend, the lawyer George Hillard) had accepted the flat royalty of twelve cents a volume for all Hawthorne's works. He also invited her to have a disinterested party investigate. Sophia's sister Elizabeth performed that task and concluded that Fields had been just but not generous. At that point Annie incredulously concluded that Sophia "listens to Gail Hamilton and allows herself to be persuaded that we have treated her dishonestly. But so it is. . . . All this towards *us* too, whom she has ever esteemed her best and truest. She clean forgets her husband's faith and her husband's wish and with the first wind of doctrine is turned aside. . . . Most strange of all people Mrs. Hawthorne should have proved disloyal." Next came some self-righteous stock-taking: "I know she has felt discontent for a year or two because we no longer asked the children and herself to stay in our house for long periods, but they were most fatiguing and ungrateful guests, the only redeeming pleasure being Mrs. Hawthorne's real talent and apparent happiness in our friendship. I could never do anything, but was obliged to relinquish every moment while either of them was in the house to finding congenial occupation and change of occupation for them." The entry concludes with dispassionate praise of Sophia's "expression" but not of the woman herself: "Mrs. Hawthorne is full of talent. Her expression is peculiar for exquisiteness of choice and fluency; more especially perhaps she may be distinguished by a power of transmuting the atmosphere of common things and presenting them in a new and sublimated light; her own childish earnestness always preventing this from the charge of affectation."

This entry is virtually an obituary for their friendship. It exonerates herself and her husband, but severely criticizes the woman who "found herself unequal to educate her children or take care of her affairs," and who resented "what she supposed to be too little payment made in return for her best service to literature." Sophia, who knew little about her husband's finances, naively assumed that funds from Ticknor and Fields would continue to cover her expenses after his death, and naively assumed that she knew the fair market value of her own "best service to literature"—her transcriptions of Hawthorne's American notebooks. In a single sentence in her diary in mid-December, Annie scornfully wrote her off: "'Gail' and Mrs. Hawthorne are still implacable, having conjured up a fancied wrong, they nurse it well."

Sophia Hawthorne and her children had by then sailed for Germany; and although Sophia would correspond with James T. Fields about publishing her husband's English notebooks and then his French and Italian notebooks, she gave her own travel book to another publisher. She died in February 1871.

That August, Annie noted in her journal that she had "read a touching article on Mrs. Hawthorne by G. W. Curtis." The following March, Annie told Celia Thaxter about Sophia's love for her, and read Celia several of Sophia's letters. "They gave her great delight," she noted, "although we both marvelled over the inconsistencies of such a character. One formed of the highest delicacy and yet capable of printing Hawthorne's private journal containing the entire history of

Mr. Thaxter and herself, names given in full as if they no longer inhabited the planet." Sophia had been posthumously restored as a loving if not a beloved friend.

Perhaps inspired by Curtis's tribute, Annie wrote a sonnet "To S. H."—dated September 1871, Manchester. It begins with regret: "No more these eyes shall see, nor fleshly hands / Embrace thy form, for thou art fled this shore." But the poet assumes S. H. is reunited with her husband in eternity, and makes a generous if self-justifying wish: "May thy home be sweet / Freed from the narrow grasp of earthly hands." Annie's last six lines are peculiarly self-righteous. She hopes S. H. is not

> touched by any memory of that grief,
> Which thou with mortal insight dealt to me,
> Leaving a gaping wound without relief,
> While yet we drifted on life's misty sea.
> But now thou knowst thy wrong, I pray that brief
> May be thy tears. Love hath forgiven thee.[41]

Years later, Annie compiled a lengthy memoir of Sophia that she never published. She began by praising Nathaniel Hawthorne, then focused on Sophia's "exquisite gift of expression which it was her life and delight to exercise." Sophia was "reluctant to come before the public" but "overflowed to her friends on paper in a manner peculiar to herself," a statement Annie substantiates through excerpts from over a hundred of Sophia's letters to her. In one, Sophia deprecates her own appearance and worries about Hawthorne's health, then rhapsodically describes "this summer Sunday just at the advent of winter"; in another, she recalls "how delicious it was in flowery Florence to stand and burn in those streets of Dante, while an angelic breeze from the Apennines came to freshen the soul." Annie Fields displayed Sophia Hawthorne as a sensitive idealist with an "exuberance of expression and sentiment" whose "life was bound up in that of her husband." She did not even hint that she too had been a focus of that sentiment.[42]

9

The Sixties and Beyond—Close Friends

Lucy Larcom (1824–1893)

Lucy Larcom's lifelong friendship with Annie Fields began when she was invited to Charles Street in the spring of 1861, shortly before making her *Atlantic* debut with a long and lofty poem titled "The Rose Enthroned." An unmarried, plain-faced woman ten years older than her hostess with almost none of her social graces or domestic interests, Lucy nonetheless shared Annie's commitments to Emersonian ideals of self-examination and self-fulfillment and her Arnoldian belief in the moral mission of literature. Though that could also be said of dozens of other women writers who first met Annie in the early sixties, no one was more enthralled by Charles Street or more grateful for Annie's friendship.

"I didn't know it was fairy-land at 37 Charles Street, nor did I dream of meeting so many of the Genii," Lucy told the *Atlantic* editor after her first few hours "among the treasures of your home-grotto," then protested, "you shouldn't have shown me so many curious and beautiful things. I am not used to them." The rhapsodic humility of her letter conveyed her desire to return, as did the extravagant figures and learned allusions of the poem she enclosed:

> Was it a dream
> Or waking vision of the gracious night?
> Did I on that enchanted isle alight,
> Aye blossoming in Shakespeare's line,
> With forms and melodies divine,—
>   Where all things seem
> Ancient yet ever new beneath the hand
> Of Prospero and his aerial band?
>   At every turn a change
>   To something rich and strange,—

106

. . . .
And when the lady of the grotto spoke,
'Twas like Miranda, when at first she woke
To Love, lighting the wild sea with her smile
Star of her beautiful and haunted isle;
   And the magician, who
Such harmony and beauty round him drew,—
He was her Ariel and Ferdinand
   Blended in one
And heir to Prosper's wonder-working wand.
. . . .[1]

When she first entered that home-grotto, Lucy Larcom was thirty-seven, a teacher at Wheaton Academy who had published dozens of poems and yearned to support herself by her pen. The ninth of ten children of a retired shipmaster who died when she was eight, Lucy became a wage-earner at the age of eleven, when her mother opened a boardinghouse in the new milltown of Lowell and she herself became a millworker. By her mid teens (as Annie later wrote), Lucy was "probably the best contributor to the 'Lowell Offering,' a magazine conducted by mill girls which attracted much attention in this country and in Europe."[2] The most consequential attention came from John Greenleaf Whittier, who was then editing a local newspaper. In 1846, Lucy accompanied her married sister Emeline to the western prairies, where over the next six years she supported herself as a schoolteacher, completed a rigorous course of study at Monticello Seminary, published a few poems, and became engaged to Emeline's brother-in-law Frank Spaulding. But she then returned to Massachusetts, resumed schoolteaching, continued to write and publish poems, and eventually dissolved her engagement. As he had first done over a decade earlier, Whittier offered her friendship and professional support. After 1861, so did the Fieldses. "I am very glad thee know Fields and his lovely wife," Whittier complacently wrote after Lucy reported on her first visit to Charles Street. "Of course, thee like them, and I know, for I had it from them, that they were delighted with thee."[3]

A new stage in the women's friendship began a year and a half later, when Annie addressed Lucy by her first name, asked her to reciprocate, and invited deeper intimacy by theorizing "that women reach the maturity of their spiritual life later than men." That overture prompted Lucy to a searching self-assessment:

I don't know how it would have been with me, had I been occupied otherwise than in teaching the greater part of my life; but my impression is that if I had been a washer-woman, I should have had more freedom of thought, and I should have written what would have been worth reading, whether of permanent value or not. When I have written at all, during these many years, it has been from an irrepressible desire, which yet conscience insisted must be repressed, in order to be faithful to the work allotted me as a teacher. Teaching to me is great; it implies study, constant development of one's own mind and life; and it does not allow of of [*sic*] dreaming flights and easy saunterings of thought that I always slide into when the writing-demon possesses me. I have religiously striven to make myself fit for the work I was in, with the hope that thus I was also ripening for something . . . more congenial. . . . My head feels like a worn-out machine most of the time; and now I struggle between the same old longing to write which would keep me within doors, and the necessity of being out in the free air and sunshine, which my languid brain is always reminding me of.

After apologizing for her "tiresome note," Lucy urged Annie to "write better things to me."[4] As an indirect consequence of that stocktaking, she left Wheaton (and full-time teaching) that spring.

Soon afterward, Lucy accepted Annie's invitation to spend a week in New Hampshire, which Whittier assured her "would be pleasant and profitable to thee and dear Mrs. Fields, even if I cannot be with you."[5] As an almost immediate form of profit, Lucy felt free to show Annie her new poem, "Hilary," an elegiac tribute to a beloved brother-in-law. Annie recommended it to her husband, who agreed to give it "an Atlantic voyage." Lucy then sent the editor a slightly revised "Hilary," whimsically stipulating that if Annie "doesn't like the new patches, nor you either, he can go in his original suit, or be sent home again."[6] The poem appeared in the August *Atlantic*.

The following month, Lucy solicited Annie's judgment of "A Loyal Woman's No," whose speaker refuses to marry her anti-abolitionist lover and abandon her "bleak ridge" of integrity for a low (if flowery) valley. When Lucy asked Annie to "look at the enclosed, as you have glanced at other verses of mine" to determine if it was "the thing" for the *Atlantic,* Annie assured her it was. When Lucy then asked whether her "No" might seem too polemical, too unwomanly, and too autobiographical, Annie offered reassurance but also suggested anonymous publication. Gratefully, Lucy thanked Annie "for thinking with me about that poem," saying she trusted her friend's "real womanishness" more than her own. "A Loyal Woman's No" appeared anonymously in the December *Atlantic.*[7]

By then, Lucy had an additional reason for trusting Annie's professional judgment: the *Ode Recited by Miss Charlotte Cushman, at the Inauguration of the Great Organ in Boston, November 2, 1863.* "Ah! that Ode!" Lucy rapturously exclaimed after reading it. "How I wish I felt at liberty to praise it!" A few weeks later, she allowed herself the mild liberty of reporting Elizabeth Whittier's note saying that "Annie Fields ought not to be so gifted, because she is so beautiful."[8]

As the phrase "at liberty" barely hints, however, Lucy was then struggling to mend a rift in their friendship. Evidently after some kind of plea for more private time with Annie, Lucy abjectly said she had "no right to a monopoly of what I greatly enjoy" and promised "not to be as foolish as before." Annie then invited her to attend an exhibition of Doré's Dante illustrations and "pass the night" at Charles Street. A subsequent invitation was to collect "at Mr. Fields' office, a package containing a certain photograph which you will please accept" (presumably the Rowse portrait that had been copied for distribution to friends), and have a "few words" at Charles Street before returning to Beverly. Shortly afterward,

Lucy asked if she could see Annie when she next came to town, and said her own "*need* of solitude" would keep her from feeling "neglected or hurt" if not. She understood that Annie's self-protectiveness "with regard to guests at your own house is the only one for a woman to take, who has a life of her own to live."[9]

The crisis had passed. Lucy "thinks of going South to teach the Freedmen, but her coming to town about it was my suggestion," Annie wrote in her journal two weeks later. Lucy was an experienced teacher, and working with the Freedmen might revive her "flagging" imagination. Optimistically, Annie accompanied Lucy to the job interview and then took her to a painting exhibition at the Athenaeum—a benefit for the Sanitary Commission. But for whatever reason, Lucy never did go south.[10]

In the fall of 1864, Annie became more intimately involved in Lucy's professional life. When the editor of the *Atlantic Monthly* thought of establishing an illustrated monthly magazine for children, both Annie and Lucy helped plan it. *Our Young Folks* was launched in January 1865 with Lucy as one of its three editors and the only one on salary. The fifty dollars a month she earned was enough to live on, frugally; any manuscripts she produced for *Our Young Folks* boosted that payment; and in 1868 Jamie increased her responsibilities and doubled her salary.[11]

Lucy's collected *Poems* appeared that same year. "Hilary" and "A Loyal Woman's No" were among the selections she made in consultation with the Fieldses and Whittier, and James T. Fields was the publisher. As Annie noted in her journal, Lucy was finally enjoying the success she deserved.[12]

Annie's nurturance had helped her attain it. "You have made the last two years so fragrant to me," Lucy wrote in May 1864, and two years later she more sweepingly declared, "I bring such refreshment from you always! I wonder if you do not feel the ether is gone out from you,—or are you like the flowers . . . ?" Still another visit prompted an even more passionate outburst: "If I could only make you feel the difference in myself going home through the apple-blooms last night, . . . I think you would know that you had not lived in vain." Gratefully and gracefully, she then likened Annie to "the flowers, that find an infinite sweetness in their hearts, replacing constantly what they give away." And after receiving a picture that she had often admired at Charles Street, Lucy offered a characteristic protest: "I don't deserve it. You are too good to me. But the lovely gift will always speak to me of you."[13]

She found her own ways to reciprocate. Alongside many of the pressed flowers in Annie's albums are such notations as "Lucy Larcom sent me a bouquet." She also sent such modest gifts as a photograph of herself to be kept "only if you like it"; a Christmas "bauble" as "a poor little effort to please the loveliest of women"; and a book she had enjoyed, because "You have already made my cup run over, and I shall not often be able to pass on a draught which I have tasted first."[14] Another kind of gift was the story of her life, as on the night when she told Annie about her prairie years. Reminded of Caroline Kirkland's account of life on the

Michigan frontier, *A New Home—Who'll Follow?* (1839), Annie was impressed that Lucy had also lived on roadless terrains where hardships were the norm, and that she too had coped heroically with illness and death.

Meantime, Whittier continued to relish the women's friendship, as when in February 1866 he jestingly told Lucy to explain why he had not stopped at Charles Street during his last trip to Boston: Gail Hamilton had told him about "Mrs. F's brusque rough way, and Mr. F's exacting and tyrannical behavior." In a variant jest, he later told Gail Hamilton that the Fieldses had joined the Shakers during an overnight visit: "Lucy Larcom saw them shut up in separate dormitories." The pun-laden poem-letter letter he sent Lucy in March 1866 is a witty and affectionate insider's tribute to Annie but also to the women's relationship. Though illness prevented him from accompanying Lucy to a Pre-Raphaelite exhibit that Annie's sister Lissie had arranged, Whittier rejoiced that

> at your head goes
> That flower of Christian womanhood, our dear good Anna Meadows.
> She'll be discreet, I'm sure, although once in a freak romantic
> She flung the Doge's bridal ring and married "The Atlantic."
> And, spite of all appearances, like the woman in a shoe
> She's got so many "Young Folks" now, she don't know what to do.[15]

When *Asphodel* appeared soon afterward, Lucy had new reasons for admiring Annie. "I took up 'Asphodel' just now and was drawn into a re-reading before I was aware," Lucy wrote, then moved from quasi-objective praise to an intensely personal tribute: "The womanly tenderness and insight in it are very remarkable. They do not often make themselves the soul of a book in the perfectly simple and natural manner of this. It is *fascinating* to me, as I told you once,—but as if attracted to one whom I would willingly let read any heart's secrets, if I had any. It seems to bring me into a sort of *rapport* that only women . . . can understand." Reading the published correspondence of two nineteenth-century German women of letters intensified that feeling. "Bettine and Gunderode I am with now," Lucy exclaimed. "How beautiful women-friendships can be!"[16]

That autumn, Lucy urged Annie to visit her in Beverly. The foliage was beautiful, she said, and Hawthorne's sister Elizabeth had "called several times to see if you were coming," particularly because Lucy had "taken the liberty" of lending her Annie's copy of *Silas Marner,* "she admiring it as I do." It was an admiration that she knew Annie shared. Though she was grateful for all the "treasures of the book world" that Annie had recently sent her, "Mill on Liberty" and "Thoreau's books" among them, Lucy had not found "so vigorous a hand as 'George Eliot,' anywhere."[17]

Yet despite their many shared values, Lucy resisted Annie's efforts to involve her in settlement house work. As she explained when canceling a promise to meet Annie at the North End Mission, her *Young Folks* responsibilities left her too tired to "get so much interested, as one must, in those poor people"; and she responded to Annie's unusual admission of weariness from settlement house work by wryly advising her to "let the world take care of itself a little while."[18] More broadly, Lucy had profound doubts about what any women could accomplish on their own. That is why she declined Annie's invitation to accompany her to an organizational meeting of the Woman's League in the spring of 1868. "Woman cuts herself aloof from her truest friend and helper, when she tries to work apart, and to live apart from man," Lucy argued; she herself could "never be one of the talking women" or make her pen "a javelin to fling at the heads of the brethren," or "go before the public in any way."[19]

Even so, she promised to keep an open mind about the Woman's League, and Annie continued to raise feminist issues with her. During one of Lucy's visits to Charles Street in the winter of 1870, for example, Annie made a strong case for woman's suffrage; and although Lucy remained unconvinced, she did accompany Annie to an organizational meeting of the Society for Working Women. She never joined that society or any other women's club. But the woman who was still best known for her early poem about a working woman titled "Hannah Binding Shoes," and who had been a wage-earner since the age of eleven, did write a hymn to celebrate the inauguration of Annie's Lincoln Street Home for working women.[20]

The professional tables were turned at least once, when Lucy asked Annie to contribute to one of her own enterprises—the 1873 anthology *Child-Life in Prose* (coedited with Whittier). All four of Annie's submissions were "good and beautiful," Lucy said, though she returned one and recommended a title change for another. When Annie organized a club of women writers to discuss one another's manuscripts four years later, Lucy was among them. More important to their separate and overlapping professional identities, in 1880 they each published a collection of poems: Annie's *Under the Olive* and Lucy's *Wild Roses of Cape Ann and Other Poems*. Annie's poems were "classically beautiful," Lucy said, and she was merely stating the facts when she said that her own poems about the "homely life of New England" lacked their "Greek atmosphere." But whether or not Jamie had already brought home a copy of her *Wild Roses*, Lucy wanted Annie to have "one of your own directly from myself." Then she concluded with her usual modesty, "I must write of what I love best, and extract from it such poetry as I can find."[21]

From the time they met, Lucy admired Annie Fields as a cynosure of fulfilled womanhood. When her sister Louisa died in 1863, Lucy sadly told Annie, "my pleasant dreams of home dissolve; it was she who said she would make a home for me, wherever I would choose. The earthly outlook is lonelier than before."[22] Annie made that outlook less lonely, whether by lending Lucy books, taking her to art exhibitions, sending her tickets for a Dickens reading, criticizing her poems, inviting her to "pass the night" at Charles Street, or (much more rarely) visiting her in Beverly. As Lucy confided to Annie in the fall of 1871, she had not felt "quite right" about leaving Beverly while Annie was staying in nearby Manchester, though "it never even occurred to me that you would miss me when I was away."[23]

Not surprisingly, when the Fieldses' Manchester cottage was completed in 1874, Lucy solicited an invitation by saying how eager she was to "quiet my busy brain with your grand ocean view, and with your own calm presence."[24]

Nor is it surprising that Lucy Larcom was the one person Annie invited to Manchester seven years later, when she began trying to pull her life together after Jamie's death. Lucy accepted immediately, though it meant canceling plans to join Whittier in New Hampshire. "I feel it is right and good for me to be with Mrs. Fields in her bereavement, if she wants me," she told Whittier, expressing the self-deprecating yet self-reliant adulation that was her major contribution to their "beautiful women-friendship" from the start.[25]

Lucy Larcom was a minor poet when she and Annie met, and she never became a major one. But Annie spurred her personal and professional growth, helped get her work published, and felt a vested interest in her professional achievements. She could identify with Lucy not only as a poet but as a high-minded individual who took literature seriously, a sensitive woman who responded as deeply to a "grand ocean view" as to a great painting, and a womanly woman who subordinated her own needs to those of her family and friends.

Therefore when Lucy became seriously ill in the fall of 1883 and Whittier proposed establishing an annuity for her, Annie was a major (though anonymous) contributor. As she explained, Lucy "was to have a part of our property after I have done with it, [but] in the course of nature this will not be likely to do her any good."[26] Their intimacy had dwindled by then—possibly because Sarah Orne Jewett had become such a large presence in Annie's life, and possibly also because the Reverend Phillips Brooks had become so important to Lucy. Yet Annie continued to invite Lucy to Charles Street—often to meet such new American writers as Edith Thomas or such established British writers as George Macdonald, and occasionally to spend the night. And she continued to share Whittier's pride in Lucy's career, as when in December 1886 she thanked him "for telling me of our Lucy's book"—presumably the *Beckonings for Every Day: A Calendar of Thought*— then said it "has been such a perfect Christmas card for several friends."[27]

Yet not even Whittier saw the tribute Annie paid to Lucy Larcom a year later, a brief unpublished sketch of the woman a decade older than herself with whom she had first discussed women's spiritual maturity twenty-five years before. Lucy's 1853 book of inspirational "parables, or prose poems" titled *Similitudes* was "gracefully written and picturesque in description," Annie said, "evincing that loving observation of outward nature and its moral and spiritual symbolism, which is so marked a feature of her later writings." She listed those writings, generously commenting on two, and mentioned Lucy's teaching positions, her editorial work, and the three anthologies she produced "associated with Whittier." Next she supported her own judgments by citing a male authority—Longfellow, who so admired Lucy Larcom's fresh and beautiful descriptions that she was "one of the three or four American authors most frequently quoted" in his anthology *Poems of Places*. But Annie gave herself the last word about Lucy's poetry, a high if limited compliment: "The moral tone and purity of her writings cannot be too much commended."[28]

Celia Thaxter (1835–1894)

In August 1852, when Nathaniel Hawthorne was vacationing at a hotel on Appledore Island—one of the nine picturesquely barren Isles of Shoals a few miles off the coast of New Hampshire—he met the hotel owner's Harvard-educated son-in-law Levi Thaxter and the seventeen-year-old girl he had married the year before. For Hawthorne, it was "a romantic incident to find such a young man on this lonely island; his marriage with this pretty little Miranda is true romance, only too much in the beaten track of romance," and the veteran romancer assumed the couple would later "look back to this rocky ledge, with its handful of soil, as to a Paradise."[29] Although he had no way of guessing it, nearly nine years later the "little Miranda" would make her *Atlantic* debut with "Land-Locked," the first of the poems that would popularize the rugged landscape and wild legends of the rock-ledged Isles of Shoals and make Celia Thaxter one of the best-known woman poets of her day. During his decade as editor of the *Atlantic*, James T. Fields published fifteen of her poems and her best known prose work, *Among the Isles of Shoals*. Until Celia Thaxter's death in 1894, Annie Fields served as her closest confidante and her most solicitous (and most professionally helpful) friend.

Born in Portsmouth in 1835, Celia moved to the Shoals at the age of four when her enterprising father, Thomas Laighton, became keeper of the White Island light. He soon bought four of the neighboring islands and helped revive the area's fishing industry. Meantime, he supervised the education of Celia and her two younger brothers and began planning a resort hotel on Appledore, the largest of his islands.

The year Celia was twelve, Levi Thaxter entered her life. An indolent twenty-three-year-old Harvard graduate who had studied law and acting but would never practice either, he came to White Island as a paying guest and soon became Laighton's partner in the Appledore venture, but quit after a year. During that year he lived with the Laightons, tutored Celia and her brothers, introduced her to the poetic cadences and moral idealism of Longfellow and Browning, and became an accepted suitor. Persuaded by Celia's parents to wait until she was sixteen, the couple married on Appledore in 1851, had their first child within the year, and moved to the mainland a few years later. In Newtonville, Massachusetts, where Levi's father bought them a house, Celia felt like an exile and longed for her summer return to the Shoals. After 1855, when Levi nearly drowned in a squall, he refused to accompany her. Their marriage was no longer a "true romance," and it continued to deteriorate, with Celia in sole charge of their retarded oldest son and in almost sole charge of the two who followed. The appearance of "Land-Locked" in the March 1861 *Atlantic* inaugurated her career as a poet. The wistful and often moving poem expressed her yearning for the "solemn sea" and

"The sad, caressing murmur of the wave / That breaks in tender music on the shore."[30]

Thomas Wentworth Higginson, a minister and major *Atlantic* contributor who had been Levi's Harvard roommate, was astonished that Celia had written it. He had been in on the start of Levi's romance with the "raw overgrown" girl whose father seemed "rough as a boatsman" and whose mother was "a plump goodnatured *frau*." As he also told Annie after Celia's death, Levi had responded coldly to his praise of "Land-Locked," claiming that he had not read it and complaining that "everybody was flattering & spoiling [Celia] & taking her away from her unfortunate boy." The poet herself had meantime "entered with the zest of a fishermaiden into the life opened to her among her Boston admirers." Nonetheless, she needed "tender & generous sympathy."[31]

Annie soon provided that sympathy, attracted by what Higginson called Celia's "loud-voiced roughnesses." "She was wild as a sea-bird," Annie exclaimed early in their friendship, struck by the picturesque beauty of the young woman adorned with seashells, "a gray poplin dress defining her lovely form," who overflowed with "noisy laughter."[32] Annie was also attracted by the poet's modesty. "The only merit of my small productions lies in their straightforward simplicity," Celia told Fields in September 1861 while resisting his editorial suggestions, "and when that bloom is rubbed off by the effort to better them, they lose what little good they originally possessed."[33] But she accepted professional advice from both of the Fieldses, her friendship with them certainly expanded her cultural horizons, and her loving friendship with Annie grew even stronger after James Fields's death.

They first met in May 1862, when the Fieldses called on the Thaxters and "brought home a carriage full of flowers and the sweet fragrance of a new friendship."[34] Two weeks later, Annie invited both Thaxters to one of her parties for Rebecca Harding. Charmed by the lovely young poet, Rebecca requested a photograph through Annie. Celia had none to send, but hoped that Annie would soon pay her another visit.

That September, after Celia returned from her summer on the Shoals, Annie invited her to meet another young *Atlantic* writer, Harriet Prescott. Though Celia refused because her husband and children were "under the weather," she assured Annie that her own attractions were "quite sufficient to draw me at any time without any foreign assistance." Then in October, after Celia mournfully wrote that she dreaded the onset of winter, Annie sent a remarkably solicitous gift: tickets for Emerson's new series of lectures. Two days later, Celia sent Jamie "some verses which have evolved among the pots and kettles," wryly remarking that "the rhymes in my head are all that keep me alive, I do believe, lifting me in a half unconscious condition over the ashes heap, so that I don't half realize how dry & dusty it is." She also sent a message for "A": "I have had such infinite satisfaction and refreshment out of her tickets to the Emerson lectures already, and forgot all weariness and perplexity on the crest of a breaker of earthly bliss."[35] Among the other refreshments Annie provided was an introduction to Emerson himself.

In November 1865, when Celia arrived at Charles Street so exhausted that she feared she might never write again, she inaugurated a new stage of intimacy by telling Annie a "strange story." Levi made her do all the family's cooking, clotheswashing, ironing, and even the heaviest housework, forbidding her to hire help even with the money she earned from the *Atlantic,* while he did "no business and pretends to be a philanthropist, a radical, all that is good." Annie could now more fully understand why Celia fled to Appledore every summer.

The Fieldses made their first trip there the following July, accompanied by the Aldriches and greeted by other friends when they arrived. As they soon discovered, Laighton's Hotel was large and comfortable, the food was excellent, and the scenery was spectacular.[36] That first evening as Annie sat in the flower-filled picture-hung parlor of Celia's cottage, she was impressed by Celia's loving attention to her mother. She enjoyed Celia's ghost stories as well, and admired her paintings (though she also noticed her friend's flash of envy when Jamie bought a painting from another guest).

Richer pleasures came the next morning when Celia rowed the Fieldses from one island to another, accompanied by her youngest son and once again "her own sweet childlike singing self." She sang snatches of sea chanteys, identified wildflowers and shorebirds for the Fieldses, told them about the history and geography of each island, and also told thrilling tales of storms, shipwrecks, and even a murder. As the Fieldses had discovered, Celia's storytelling could be even more captivating than her poems. In fact, Annie once became so absorbed in her account of watching her husband and brother nearly drown in a squall that she could "hardly judge" Celia's ballad about it.

Fascinated by everything they saw and heard that first morning, the Fieldses urged Celia to write about the Shoals for the *Atlantic.* It would take three years and considerable prodding from Annie and other friends before Celia completed the long project that would be her only prose contribution to the *Atlantic. Among the Isles of Shoals* ran in four issues—in August 1869 and January, February, and May 1870—winning high praise and attracting scores of new visitors to Appledore. Three years later, Celia prepared the series for publication by Fields's successor Osgood, consulting both Annie and Jamie about her revisions. It was so enormously successful that Osgood reprinted it twenty-eight times.[37]

Annie's first trip to Appledore would be followed by many others. Celia was a major attraction, Appledore's stark beauty was another, and she could also look forward to recitals by eminent musicians, encounters with such well-known artists as Childe Hassam and William Morris Hunt, and conversations with such old friends as the minister John Weiss, the reformer Mary Hemenway, and (best of all) Whittier.

Whittier entered into Annie's friendship with Celia at least by 1866, when he asked Celia if she saw Annie often. "It always does me good to meet her," he then remarked. "She is so thoroughly good and charming." As he told Annie herself in July 1872, he was enormously disappointed when she broke their tentative date for a trip to Appledore. Dramatizing his dismay, he said he had urged the captain to wait "some minutes after the time of leaving Portsmouth; &, after we swung off, a hack made its appearance tearing over the Street, & the captain put back for it. I was quite sure you were there, but much to my disgust, quite another lady than thyself stepped on board." Celia had filled his room with wild roses and morning glories and the weather was perfect, but they had both missed Annie. He and Celia also missed Annie "exceedingly" in July 1875, as Whittier wrote, particularly when they sat on the rocks to watch a sunset or to tell ghost stories.[38] The year before, however, both of the Fieldses had managed to join Whittier for a celebration of Celia's birthday at the Shoals, although they had to weather a storm before reaching the "seductive place."[39]

But Annie and Celia would never feel closer to Whittier than in July 1873, when they all spent an entire week on Appledore together. During one typical afternoon when their talk ranged from Emerson's use of Jesus' name to Mrs. Gaskell's biography of Charlotte Brontë and their own ideas about "future existence," Celia rapturously exclaimed, "how good it has been with the little song-sparrow putting in his oar over it all!" She spoke for them all. By the end of the week, the women felt more united than ever in their affectionate concern for the nearly deaf Whittier, who repeatedly took their hands "as if trying to say what words would never allow him to express."[40]

From the time of her first visit to Appledore, Annie could empathize with Celia's feelings of entrapment on the mainland. As she once mused, the Thaxters' home was only the shell of a house and a fitting emblem of their marriage, though there would be no divorce "except the divorce which death may bring." That explains why Annie sometimes invited both of the Thaxters to Charles Street (even to one of her dinners for Charles Dickens), sometimes sent concert tickets for them both, and at least once entertained the husband without the wife.[41] Yet as Annie well knew, Levi spent most of his time away from his wife. Ostensibly on grounds of health, he went north in the summer and south in the winter, often accompanied by one or both of his "normal" sons though never by Karl; and his usual behavior when he rejoined Celia is suggested by her amazed remark to Annie in the early seventies that "he really looks and speaks to me! instead of coming in like a deadly cold still vapor."[42]

Particularly amazing to Annie was that Celia's laughter continued to be "the most healthy, hearty, natural, enlivening thing possible." But after hearing her life story, Annie redefined the woman herself as "all youth with something of the tenderness of age grafted upon it." She had been "a woman" at eleven, engaged at twelve, married at sixteen, and at seventeen the mother of a son who was "alas! devoid of wits." Nothing could be "more horrible," Annie thought.

A year later at Charles Street, while Emerson was polishing a lecture in another room, Celia confided that Levi's family "had all died of ossification of the heart and the disease was now coming on him," and Annie marveled at the "external correspondence to the fact" that his heart had "been undergoing a real ossification toward his wife for many many years." Celia then told Annie about the strain of insanity in Levi's family that had emerged in their son Karl, a huge young man with "half awakened" senses and a "wavering" mind who seldom spoke and obeyed no one but his mother. Again Annie was amazed, though primarily because Celia's sympathy for her firstborn son was "so deep down, so tender."[43]

Perhaps as a kind of quid pro quo for Celia's revelations, Annie read her three loving letters from Sophia Hawthorne which "gave her great delight although we both marvelled over the inconsistencies of such a character," capable of "the highest delicacy" and yet also of revealing the intimate details about the Thaxters' relationships that Hawthorne had entered in his private journal. Annie did not even hint at her own role in persuading Sophia to publish Hawthorne's journals.

Next came tea and talk with Emerson and the dozens of friends who had come to hear his lecture about his aunt Mary Moody Emerson, "Amita." It was such an "extraordinary picture of a strange stoical noble character" that it provoked lively discussion which ended long past midnight. Emerson was in high spirits at breakfast the next morning, and so were Annie and Celia. When he left Charles Street to lecture on "Manners" to the Young Ladies' Saturday Morning Club—a club Julia Ward Howe had started primarily for her daughters and their friends, which many of the Fieldses' friends and Annie herself would subsequently address—Annie and Celia accompanied him, feeling "very happy in our friendship and in our 'privileges.'" They had never been closer, though they would grow closer still.

Annie now felt free to send Celia some of her own poems and to vent a few minor frustrations. Celia's replies were always sympathetic and admiring. In a single letter of November 1873, for example, she wrote of the "many threads in that delicate hand of yours," commiserated with Annie that young Esther Albee had not yet arrived for her promised long stay, regretted with Annie that an older protégée—"Poor Imogen"—had no way to support herself, and urged Annie, "Dear, dont you wear yourself out with 'troublous business'—you are so self-sacrificing, you won't spare yourself."[44]

But her comments about Annie's poems were sometimes guarded. Whittier once admitted that he could not criticize a poem of Celia's "any more than I could its author," and Celia evidently felt the same about Annie's.[45] Selective praise was the closest she came, as when she said the first four verses of a poem Annie had just sent were "sweet, simple, and full of feeling." As usual, whatever Celia said about Annie's poetry also applied to Annie herself. As an even clearer example, she said that *Persephone*—Annie's tribute to her mother—was "altogether lovely, . . . melodious and beautiful all through."[46]

Yet throughout the seventies, the decade of Celia's greatest professional success and her greatest professional dependency on Annie, the woman who could never disparage Annie's work continually disparaged her own. Annie responded with encouragement and practical counsel about where to "hawk my wares" and about the wares themselves. Celia usually followed her advice, as when in February 1872 she sent Annie the verses "you said 'Finish!'" although they now seemed

"so didactic and commonplace that I have a kind of loathing of them." Yet because she needed money, she hoped Howells would accept them for the *Atlantic*.
Annie had in fact already told Howells that Celia needed "all the kindness out-
siders can give, not to speak of the filthy lucre!!" He accepted the poem, sent Celia
a check for forty dollars, and accepted others in quick succession.[47]

But the following year when Howells accepted one of the two poems Celia
submitted, his rejection of the other dejected her. "Everything I do is feeble and
futile, fatuous and quite uncalled for," she once complained. Despite her enormous popularity, Celia could not overcome the diffidence she expressed only to
Annie. In the fall of 1872, she wistfully wrote, "You don't like my sonnets you
beautiful darling, but my heart is in them." Then two months later, she sent Annie a poem that "came when the winds howled" in which "all unconsciously I
drew your portrait for my heroine of romance," though she was not at all sure "if
it is worth anything."[48]

By contrast, Celia never questioned her judgments of other writers. After reading *Thoreau, The Poet Naturalist,* for example, the woman who was herself a poet
naturalist concluded that William Ellery Channing was not worthy of his subject
but merely "a drivelling idiot" who "aped" Emerson. Sometimes she simply
agreed with Annie, as when she said "I read the Bronte book all the way down: it
is all you say." Never a sycophant, she felt free to criticize the work of Annie's
friends—Bret Harte's coarse style, for example.[49] But she was both harder and
softer on another new novel by a closer friend of Annie's—Elizabeth Stuart
Phelps's *Story of Avis:*

> I have a great reverence for the work & the author, but I cannot help wishing through
> the first half of the book, that Avis did not so often "fling out her elbows," that the air
> didn't "throb like a topaz," that the oak shrubs didn't "throb dizzily," that the sea didn't
> throb & everything generally would stop "throbbing," & "flinging," & "thrusting,"
> & "tearing," & "sending," & "palpitating" & c. . . . There is a lack of simplicity &
> straightforwardness in the style. But these are small shortcomings. The story holds
> one, I am sure it would always hold *women,* with a breathless interest—men I know
> can never begin to care as much for it as women do! Yet I cannot forgive Avis for
> "flinging out her elbows."

Diplomatically, Celia blamed Avis for her behavior instead of the author, then
told Annie she hoped "to see Miss Phelps again & hope I may do so when she
comes to you."[50]

Meantime, Celia assumed Annie was interested in everything she did. Thus in
the fall of 1869 she reported setting aside her Shoals manuscript to nurse a con-
sumptive young girl whose parents had brought her to Appledore, performing
"every office for her until she at last died in her arms!"[51] She also sent detailed reports about nursing her terminally ill mother on Appledore in the winter of 1877,
both bragging and complaining that she had earned money by painting flowers
on cups and saucers, tiles, bowls, jugs, and vases—"one hundred and fourteen
pieces for different people."[52] And in September 1879 when she discovered the

drowned body of their dear friend William Morris Hunt, it was to Annie that she lamented, "It was reserved for me, who loved him truly, that bitterness!"[53] Celia was equally quick to report good news, however, and her longest and most exuberant letters during her one trip abroad in 1880 were to Annie.

Throughout their relationship, Celia addressed Annie as "My dear delicate Annie, you twilight full of stars" (for example), or called her "a dear heavenly thing and too good to everybody." And after a visit to Charles Street, she told Annie she should always wear white and "put your hair up in that enchanting way," then rhapsodized about Annie's "grand-ducal hospitality" in "that sumptuously beautiful room, so rich with thought & heavenly common-sense & lovely taste & comfort without limit—I'm talking of the library at 148, not Chardon St., & I'm *not* a lunatic, tho' I do appear to be. How the fairy lights sparkle across the Back Bay to its windows & how warm & sweet & pleasant it is inside! I wonder if there's any such nice place in Heaven—Don't believe there is."[54]

Though such tributes continued after Annie was widowed, the women's relationship changed when James T. Fields became seriously ill and for the first time Celia felt needed. Surprisingly, she even volunteered her husband's assistance, saying that Levi was "beautiful in sickness, gentle as a woman, with a born genius for the nurse's work, & if you wanted any one to sit up with dear J., to rest you, some one who would be *so* faithful,—he would be glad, Annie to help you—."[55] Annie never called on him. But Celia was at Charles Street when Jamie died, and she stayed there until after the funeral.

No one was tenderer or more solicitous during the following months. "Love can save us," Celia insisted in October, urging Annie not to "shut it out because you have lost the greatest love on earth, poor child, poor darling—Of all things on earth don't shut yourself away." She also drew on her own experience for another kind of advice: "Do not give up your work—what will become of you without it?" Longing to "get to you & put my arms round you & comfort you," Celia said she loved Annie "better than ever before, my precious one, my darling"; then after entreating Annie to write her every day, she fondly asserted, "I shall call you beautiful till my life's end, for you are, in body & in soul." A few days later came a poignant celebration of a marriage utterly unlike her own: "Ah, I know what twenty-six years were yours! Indeed, they were enough to unfit anyone to live in this tough world at all—a bit of heaven come down to earth—Few women ever had the like—what shelter!"[56]

Less than two months later, with no hint of jealousy and no sense of displacement, Celia gratefully acknowledged Sarah Orne Jewett's new role as Annie's companion. In fact, by entering into Annie's friendship with Celia, Sarah enlarged it. The nicknames Celia used for herself and the two others signal her delight in that widened intimacy, as when she used the signature "Sandpiper" or drew a picture of the bird, or called Annie her "Dearest Flower," or called Sarah "Owl." "I am glad the dear owl is with you & I wish she would stay forever," Celia wrote Annie in December 1881; "—happy is the creature who has her near—." The following week, Celia asked Annie to ask "the little owl if she has been asked to write a love poem for the new Illustrated Weekly in Philadelphia," and from then on she consulted Sarah as well as Annie about marketing her work.[57] During the winter of 1882, Celia also resumed her old practice of sending Annie detailed reports of her interests and activities, including her visits to a medium, and Annie and Sarah briefly followed suit.[58]

When Annie and Sarah sailed to Europe that May, Celia rhetorically embraced them both, lamented that she could not "stand on the wharf & wave to you & owlet to the last glimmering speck," and sent letters to greet them when they docked. Seven years later, Celia told Sarah about the serious illness she wanted no one else to know about "except of course Flower, as you two are kind of one." And after receiving one of Whittier's characteristically sad letters, Celia told Annie how she wished he lived closer so they could "run in & cheer him up now & then! You or Pinny, or 'some of us.'" Annie and Sarah were "kind of one," and the three together constituted "us."[59] It seems fitting and only slightly surprising that the delicate Annie—once chided by Celia for being too self-sacrificing—nursed Celia at Charles Street after both of her operations for skin cancer in 1893.

"I hear from our dear Annie Fields constantly; saw her not long since," Celia told the naturalist Bradford Torrey in July 1894, then commented, "Age has touched her dark hair with gray, but she is quite the same."[60] No one could say the same about Celia, whose hair turned white as her body grew stout, and who was then terminally ill. She died in August. Annie Fields then wrote her obituary for the *Boston Transcript* and a memoir for the *Atlantic,* which she soon included in *Authors and Friends* and in the *Letters of Celia Thaxter.*

She prepared the *Letters* on her own initiative, though with the approval and cooperation of Celia's two brothers and the assistance of Rose Lamb.[61] After Henry Alden rejected the project on behalf of Harper's, she offered it to Henry Houghton of Houghton Mifflin. "The family would like to have me undertake the labor," she assured him, pragmatically urging a quick decision "because it is important to make the announcement in season to prevent anything else being attempted." She began compiling Celia's letters right after Houghton agreed to publish them. Nearly three dozen were addressed to her, the last of them wistfully asking, "Dear Annie, has not Death been busy? Everybody gone. Bryant, Longfellow, Lowell, Whittier, Browning, Tennyson!"[62]

In the memoir which opens the book (and which first appeared in the *Atlantic* in February 1895), Annie took a generous overview of her friend's life, as she did for many of the others Celia listed in that last letter. She paid affectionate tribute to the perceptive child raised on "a desolate island in the deep sea" who became a large-souled child-woman, retaining a child's enthusiasms while bearing a woman's burdens, her work inspired by rocky Appledore and the sea and sky beyond. Celia Thaxter emerges from Annie Fields's pages as a talented and enterprising woman whose unique background and life-affirming enthusiasms generated six volumes of poetry, the lively prose sketches titled *Among the Isles of Shoals,* and the lovingly meticulous account of her garden on Appledore simply titled *An Island Garden*. But as a decorous biographer, Annie merely hinted at Celia's heaviest burdens—her unsympathetic husband and "daft" son. She concluded by describing Celia's beautiful funeral on Appledore—"a poet's burial" that celebrated "the passing of a large and beneficent soul."[63]

With Celia Thaxter, Annie Fields realized her highest ideals of friendship: each woman honored and encouraged what was best in the other. Annie encouraged Celia to write, criticized her manuscripts, offered shrewd advice about marketing them, and provided thoughtful gifts that ranged from concert and lecture tickets to jams and cordials for her ailing mother. Annie was never as emotionally open as Celia, and she knew relatively little about wildflowers and seabirds. Among the many other differences between them, Celia had neither the time nor the inclination to join Annie in her philanthropic enterprises or even to talk about them. But she expanded Annie's conventional assumptions about how married women should behave.

Although Celia preferred running the family hotel to cooking for her husband, she managed to do both. She even upholstered her own furniture and made her own dresses. In many of Childe Hassam's brilliant paintings of Appledore in the early 1890s, Celia Thaxter stands in her luxuriant garden overlooking the sea, her white hair pulled back from a now round and placid face, wearing a white dress she made herself, as picturesque as in her youth and more serenely beautiful. Her last few years included the pleasures of grandparenthood, though also the pains of cancer. But until the end, Celia Thaxter cultivated her own space and controlled her own self-display. Annie's memoir praises her for that, and more.

10

The Sixties and Beyond—Occasional Friends

Harriet Prescott Spofford (1835–1921)

In 1897, Harriet Prescott Spofford inscribed her new novel *An Inheritance* to "Dearest Annie with the love of her Hally."[1] Beyond that inscription is a mutual affection that began in the early sixties and lasted as long as they lived.

When Harriet Prescott was sixteen and a student at the Newburyport high school, she won a writing contest sponsored by Thomas Wentworth Higginson with what he called a "very daring and original essay on Hamlet." He encouraged her to pursue a literary career, and continued to be a trusted mentor.[2] But because of her father's financial and physical collapse in the mid-fifties, Hally concentrated on writing sensational tales for the omnivorous Boston "story papers." Though they paid five dollars apiece at most, she produced over six hundred within a few years.[3]

Her first taste of fame came in 1859, when she sold a story to the prestigious and far better paying *Atlantic Monthly*—"In a Cellar," a sardonic and sophisticated detective story narrated by an English diplomat in Paris. The story "dazzled us all," the veteran *Atlantic* writer Rose Terry Cooke later said, and readers were amazed to discover that the author was a proper New England girl.[4] They were even more dazzled by the more exotic story that appeared in the first two issues of the 1860 *Atlantic*—"The Amber Gods," narrated by a cruel and voluptuous self-adoring "golden blonde" with "thick, riotous curls" who ensnares her virtuous cousin's fiancé and whose final line is "I must have died at ten minutes past one." Even readers who (like Henry James) disdained the writer's "morbid unhealthy tone" were caught up by her story. A simpler and less exotic yet equally haunting narrative appeared in the May issue—"Circumstance," about a pioneer woman who manages to keep a ferocious animal at bay by singing to him. Therefore when William Dean Howells made his literary pilgrimage to New England the following month, he "thought it would be no less an event to meet Harriet Prescott" than Longfellow, Emerson, or Hawthorne.[5]

The new *Atlantic* star became part of Annie's life at about the same time, perhaps during one of the Fieldses' visits to Newburyport. Whatever Annie thought of Hally's eroticized Gothic fiction, she was immediately attracted to the vivacious and well-educated woman of good family who was almost exactly her own age. She was on Annie's guest list when Rebecca Harding came to Boston, and Celia Thaxter was once specifically invited to meet Harriet Spofford. Hally would soon form separate relationships with women she met at Charles Street, Gail Hamilton and the sculptor Anne Whitney among them.

Often Hally was the only other woman when such eminences as Longfellow and Emerson came to dine, and one of the earliest vignettes in Annie's journals suggests why. At Newburyport in the summer of 1863, just as Annie and a group of friends had agreed to define beauty as "a positive glorious power," a dog leaped into their midst followed immediately by its owner Harriet Prescott and her fiancé Richard Spofford. As in a charade, the radiant young woman seemed to embody that definition. Hally saw Annie in much the same way. Half a century later, she recalled first seeing Annie in Newburyport as "a vision of youth and beauty, . . . of exceeding feminine grace withal, a tall regnant young being."[6]

Annie's initial involvement in Hally's life was inseparable from Jamie's involvement in her career. Kindness, Hally called it, though it was also good business. At least once, Jamie commissioned an essay from her—a memorial tribute to the young English novelist Elizabeth Sheppard, who died in March 1862 and whose effusively romantic style was not unlike Hally's. Hally quickly prepared it for the June *Atlantic,* where (as Annie later said) it drew public attention to the "fine quality" of her mind.[7] Aware of the Fieldses' interest in local color fiction, Hally produced a story about a New England fisherman titled "The South Breaker" that featured storms, shipwrecks, and stormy passions. It appeared in the May and June *Atlantic.* Jamie would publish twenty-three of her submissions as well as her first collection of short fiction—*The Amber Gods and Other Stories* (1863), and her second novel—*Azarian: An Episode* (1864).

But presumably both author and publisher were surprised by the heavy attacks on *Azarian* in *Atlantic* circles and even in the magazine itself. In his *Atlantic* review, Hally's mentor Higginson criticized its loose plot, "morbid" characters, and "overdone" descriptions. Henry James was harder on the book in another Ticknor and Fields publication—the more conservative *North American Review.* And Sophia Hawthorne spoke for her husband as well as herself when she condemned Harriet Prescott's "sultry" and "unrefined" blazoning of "sinful affections." Even Annie faulted Hally's "love of expression." Nonetheless, there was no interruption in the Fieldses' friendship with Hally or in her appearances in the *Atlantic.*

In 1865 when Harriet Prescott married Richard Spofford, by then an established lawyer and politician, Annie had new grounds for admiration. When Annie called on the bride in Newburyport, she admired her wedding gifts but admired even more her "endeavors and her love": "a light came from her to me which made the day peaceful." When Hally confided that she was pregnant the following year, she also wryly remarked that she was "learning patience," and no longer considered herself a genius. Then in the fall of 1867 when the Spoffords' infant son died, Annie marveled that Hally still loved life and still loved her husband. The Spoffords' marriage had become like the Fieldses'—a loving but childless partnership.

Because the Spoffords were by then dividing their time between Newburyport and Washington and rarely came to Boston, their visit to Charles Street in October 1871 was their first in several years. Annie put them in what she called "Hawthorne's room," and the next morning Hally declared that "his restless ghost kept sleep away." But perhaps the most curious event of the visit was Richard Spofford's offer to have Jamie appointed minister to Spain, an offer that Annie noted without comment.

Three years later, the Spoffords bought a five-acre island near Newburyport and remodeled a large house that had once been an inn, where Hally began establishing a reputation for hospitality that nearly matched Annie's. "What a lovely home Harriet Spofford has," Annie told Whittier after visiting Deer Island in 1885, and urged him to see it for himself.[8] The two women literally grew closer after their husbands died and Hally began spending winters in Boston. She often simply dropped by, on one occasion accompanied by their mutual friend Mrs. Hopkins, the superintendent of Boston schools. She also shared in Annie's friendship with Sarah Orne Jewett. "Annie and I were delighted with the coming of your book of exquisite poetry on her birthday," Sarah wrote Hally in June 1897 (*In Titian's Garden and Other Poems,* which would be her best-known volume of poetry). In Annie's name, Sarah invited her to visit Manchester "when my dear French friend Madame Blanc and I get back."[9]

One of Annie's unpublished and undated essays takes brief stock of Harriet Prescott Spofford's long career. She began with a fanfare: "In the year 1859 a new writer was revealed in New England." As she then argued, the writer's strong characters and bold style were "in sympathy with the strong wave of feeling and color which arose at this period." More surprising is her statement that Emerson, the "great master" who had welcomed Whitman, "prepared the way for such writer as Harriet Prescott Spofford"; and when the young woman "nourished on sunsets, born out of flowers, daring as the wind and with as little self-consciousness, danced before the eyes of palefaced critics, dazzling their vision, no one smiled with a truer face of hopefulness than New England's master."

A single sentence leaps from 1859 to the unspecified present: "Harriet Prescott made herself immediately known to a circle of enthusiastic admirers by the publication of her first story called 'In a Cellar,' and from the date of its appearance in 1859 until now, she has continued to publish with a fertility prognosticated by her exuberant imagination." Still echoing Hally's own melodramatic style, Annie then acknowledged her limitations: "Haste, necessity, love of expression were ever at the door with their fatal temptations." Even so, she was a dependable worker who met her deadlines, her "continual labor" did not destroy her "natural gifts," and Annie thought a few of her poems "will cause her name to be remembered." In a graceful conclusion, Annie identified the writer with the Maine coast where she was raised: its "wild loveliness seemed to be her own."[10] Annie worked hard on the essay, crossing out many phrases and overwriting others. That makes it seem all the more curious that she gave few biographical facts, no private glimpses, and few specific comments about Hally's work.

Of all the woman writers who entered Annie Fields's orbit in the sixties, Harriet Prescott Spofford was the only one who survived her and the only one who memorialized her. Her essay on Annie Fields—fittingly the first of the five chapters in her *Little Book of Friends*—is a prolonged paean.[11] It begins by describing the young Annie Fields with a "gleam in her brown eyes, with a luxuriance of jacinth-colored hair whose innumerable dark waves broke full of glancing golden lights,—of exceeding feminine grace withal." It then describes her as equally beautiful in old age, "the smile as irradiating, the grace of movement as perfect." Next comes Spofford's extravagant description of the house on Charles Street and its "room of rooms," the library, followed by a rhapsodic tribute: "Everything moved in such responsive harmony under the hand of its young mistress . . . that it was always the house beautiful" and "a place of delight."

In her assessment of Annie's literary accomplishments, Hally stressed the nobility and refinement of her poetry (identifying her great Ode as the "first public evidence of her literary power"), then remarked that her biographies, her charity manual, and her "life work among the poor and suffering" all displayed the same deep commitment to humanity. Hally celebrated Annie's marriage and her subsequent friendship with Sarah Orne Jewett, and she presented Annie's final years as a series of mornings driving in her sister Louisa Beal's car and of afternoons spent enjoying books, music, and the company of her "brilliant" ninety-year-old sister Sarah Adams. The chapter concludes with a bravura description of Annie's Manchester home, "where the steep avenue leads up to a wonderful outlook of beauty set in the midst of flaming flowers, three sides overlooking the wide shield of the sea, but the fourth side so precipitous that the broad piazza there is only a turret chamber above the tops of the deep woods and orchards below, with the birds flying under it and looking far over winding river, ripening meadow, and stretching sea again." The site was fit for—and emblematic of—a majestic woman.

Harriet Spofford's Annie Fields is a paragon of womanhood: remarkably beautiful, a consummate hostess, a fine poet, a good samaritan, a beloved and loving wife, friend, and sister. Annie would certainly have welcomed more stylistic restraint. But as Hally put it in the book's epigraph,

> What are friends for, but to divine
> Fairest and finest that we are,
> And think in all our glances shine
> The morning and the evening star!

The tender intimacy of Annie's final bequest to her old friend seems wholly appropriate. In a codicil to her will, Annie Fields left Harriet Prescott Spofford her black camel's hair shawl and a piece of old lace.

Kate Field (1838–1896)

Kate Field was the youngest and most mercurial of the women writers who entered Annie's life in the sixties. She was twenty-two when the Fieldses met her in Florence, an ebullient young woman with blue eyes and chestnut curls who had already spent a year there studying voice and cinquecento art. She is now known, if at all, as the lively American girl who captivated Anthony Trollope, and as a leader in the women's club movement. But she also merits attention as a remarkably enterprising career woman—a freelance journalist, astute literary critic, and dynamic lyceum lecturer, a trained singer who also became an actress, playwright, and theatrical producer, the founder of a cooperative dressmaking association and a weekly Washington newsletter, a woman with no permanent address who repeatedly moved from America to Europe and from Boston to New York, then finally from Washington to Honolulu, where she died, still unmarried, at the age of fifty-seven.

During the sixties, Annie helped advance Kate Field's career as a writer and lecturer, for reasons that include their shared devotion to Dickens, their shared interest in groundbreaking women's clubs, and Annie's own commitment to cultivating *Atlantic* contributors. She was also attracted by the younger woman's charm, talent, and dedication to her mother. Yet by the early seventies, Kate began to seem too pleased with herself.

Kate Field was the only daughter of a man Jamie had often encountered during his bachelor years—the journalist, actor, playwright, and theatrical producer Joseph Field. After he died in 1856, leaving his wife in charge of their struggling theatrical company, a millionaire uncle offered to "finish" Kate's education and took her to Italy. Dismayed by her radical abolitionist ideas and more radical independence, he soon withdrew his patronage. But Kate had already become a lively participant in the social life of Florence, and managed to support herself as a correspondent for two American newspapers. As she told her doting Aunt Corda, Fields admired her journalism and considered her *the* person to write for the *Boston Transcript;* and his wife was "very pretty and has been more than kind."[12]

Both of the Fieldses continued to be more than kind when Kate returned to America at the end of 1861. When they were entertaining Rebecca Harding in June 1862, for example, they invited Kate to meet her. Kate's memorial tribute to Elizabeth Barrett Browning had already appeared in the *Atlantic*, the first of six essays that Jamie would publish. Except for the one titled "Conventions of the Stage," they are all grounded in her own bold feminism. While discussing George Eliot's novels in "English Authors in Florence" (1864), for example, Kate argued that "women are quite as capable of drawing male portraits as men are of draw-ing female." Far more important to the *Atlantic* editor, Kate's essays offered priv-ileged entrée into the private lives of cultural celebrities.

Annie therefore encouraged Kate to complete what became a three-part study of a poet who had treated them both with remarkable gallantry, Walter Savage Landor. She eagerly awaited a manuscript that was bound to "please the lovers of all good things," Annie wrote in February 1866, then commented on a new book by a woman they had both known in Florence: "In spite of inaccuracies of style," the book "fascinated me by bringing all Italy to my wintry fireside."[13] Kate rose to the implied challenge. Because her long manuscript turned out even better than the Fieldses had hoped, Kate received an unexpected "check for 88.50, mak-ing in all now 300, for the three articles."[14]

The following year, Kate's friendship with the great Italian tragedienne Ade-laide Ristori eventuated in another *Atlantic* publication. When Mme. Ristori came to Boston during her 1866 tour, the Fieldses were so moved by her "dignity and pathos" that they attended all her performances; and when she called at Charles Street bearing letters from mutual friends, Annie asked her to give a ben-efit reading for the Freedmen. Aware that Kate Field was not only Ristori's friend but one of the newspaper correspondents covering her American tour, Annie in-vited Kate and her mother to dinner in mid-November, pleased that Kate "really looked lovely with her beautiful head and eyes full of sweetness and enthusiasm." Perhaps at that point she encouraged Kate to write an essay on Ristori for the *At-lantic*. A month later, Annie thanked Kate for sending an autograph of Ristori and praised her "for the good book you have begun so ably."[15] Kate's long essay on Ris-tori appeared in the *Atlantic* in April 1867. It was then issued as a book, Kate's first.

Annie's regard for her increased during Charles Dickens's American tour, when Kate covered his readings for the *Springfield Republican* as well as the *New York Tri-bune*. In December 1867 when Annie was in New York to attend Dickens's read-ings, she visited Kate and her mother in their little room on 27th Street, "K. work-ing away on articles for the newspapers," both of them enthusiastic about Dickens. Kate showed Annie a note from Dickens thanking her father for a "most ingenious compliment" in 1842—"The Masque Phrenologic, Boz." Her father had compiled the masque from Dickens's novels, he and his wife had performed it for Dickens, and her father had then sent the manuscript to Dickens. The cher-ished note was the result.

A few weeks later, Kate acquired a Dickens note of her own. "Possessed with the idea to present the Great Charles with a New Year's offering in the shape of a bouquet," she bought a basket of violets, tied red, white, and blue ribbons on the handle, attached a note wishing Dickens "A Happy New Year in America," and had it placed on his reading desk on New Year's Eve. After his reading, Dickens wished the audience a Happy New Year—in response to her tribute, Kate chose to believe—then sent her a note of thanks that made her feel "one inch taller."[16] When Dickens told Annie about it, she felt "glad for Kate, because he wrote her a little note." Her own generous response was a note to Kate that praised her newspaper stories and said Dickens had told her about "the pretty basket of flowers on his desk," which made her feel "almost as much pleasure as you in the sending."[17]

Soon Kate found an ingenious way to capitalize further on Dickens's readings. During each performance, she took meticulous notes on his appearance and vocal delivery, using a scheme of her own to record his inflections and emphases. "Pen Photographs" she called them, "the hardest task I ever set myself." At the end of January 1868, a Boston publisher named Loring issued them as a thirty-eight-page pamphlet, priced at twenty-five cents, and Kate soon produced twenty more pages for an expanded version. Sales were so brisk that she regretted accepting ten dollars a page, wished she had "fought for a percentage of sales," and complained, "He will make money, and I not a cent. Alas!"[18] Presumably she arranged more advantageous terms for the book-length version that Osgood issued in 1871.

"Mrs. Fields asks me to visit her in Boston. Ay, Ay!" Kate gleefully wrote in her diary in March 1868, shortly before Dickens's last series of Boston lectures, hoping he would dine at Charles Street while she was staying there. She arrived in Boston on Wednesday, 1 April, and moved to Charles Street on Saturday. But as she told her mother a few days later, "Here I've been ever since Saturday evening, but there was no Charles Dickens to dinner. [He] has a serious attack of catarrh and is obliged to reserve all his strength for reading. Perhaps I may meet him, but now I doubt."[19]

Her stay nonetheless provided material for her newspaper articles: the Fieldses gladly shared reminiscences of Dickens, and the books by and about him in their library were a useful resource. Then after Tuesday's reading, the penultimate one, "the Great Charles" invited Kate backstage and exchanged courtly compliments with her. On the wave of that shared pleasure, both Annie and Kate sent Dickens floral tributes the next day—Annie "a palm leaf inlaid with flowers" and Kate a basket of pansies.[20] When Dickens left for New York on Friday, the Fieldses accompanied him and Kate returned on her own.

While Kate was at Charles Street, she and Annie pursued a new mutual interest. "Kate Field starting a Woman's League in New York which may ripen into something," Annie wrote in her diary on Sunday, 5 April. Earlier that day she had taken Kate to tea at Louisa Beal's and then to Josiah Quincy's house, where (as Kate wrote in her diary) "all receive my idea of Women's Club most cordially. Mrs. Fields will support it. Am to meet the Boston Women's Club just started in idea."[21]

Despite Kate's phrase "my idea," the idea of a women's club had in fact originated with the New York writer Jane Croly, with Dickens as the unwitting catalyst. The all-male New York Press Club announced a dinner honoring Dickens at Delmonico's Restaurant at the end of his American tour but refused to sell her a ticket. Croly then invited a number of literary women including Alice and Phoebe Cary, Fanny Fern, and Anne Botta as well as Kate to plan a club of their own. According to the constitution they soon drafted, their purpose was "to promote agreeable and useful relations among women of literary and artistic tastes," and so make "a kind of freemasonry among women of similar pursuits" which would not interfere with their traditional domestic obligations. But the name the founding members adopted while Kate was in Boston—"Sorosis," meaning an aggregation of fruit-bearing flowers—infuriated her. "I won't have the name," she immediately told Jane Croly. No one would understand what it meant, and "You will be laughed at." The *you* rather than *we* was proleptic.[22]

On 20 April, two days after the Press Club dinner at Delmonico's (and a day after Annie and Kate attended a Philharmonic concert together), twenty-four Sorosis members held their first open meeting in the same place. Annie and Kate were among them. "Attended a meeting of a new 'institution' just on foot, first called 'Sorosis' and afterwards 'Woman's League' for the benefit and mutual support of women," Annie reported in her diary. But though she shared those objectives, she was dismayed at how "intensely hot and vehement" the discussions became, particularly over such petty issues as the name change that Kate finally pushed through. "Miss Kate Field was accompanied by Mrs. James T. Field [*sic*] of Boston," Jane Croly wrote in her history of women's clubs thirty years later, "and in the weak and somewhat vague condition of the club membership managed to carry so much weight that the name Sorosis was set aside and her substitute, 'The Woman's League,' adopted."[23] To help Dickens relax before his final reading, Annie burlesqued the heated discussions until he exploded with laughter, then said "if anything could make him feel better for the evening that account of the Woman's League would."

But the name "Woman's League" did not last. "What are those foolish women thinking of?" Annie testily asked Kate a few weeks later after the issue was reraised. "Squandering time and opportunity over 'Sorosis!' But I respect your patience and endeavor and can only say 'hold on.'"[24] When the group renamed itself "Sorosis" during the next meeting, however, Kate left in a huff and planned to start a new club.

Annie then urged her to "forget the slander" and insist on high standards for membership in her new club. No organization could survive if its members were childish and "ill-regulated," Annie declared, then told Kate to remove her name from the Sorosis list "and transfer it, if it is wanted, to the one on a true foundation." As to her own recent activities, she reported attending a few concerts and a Freedmen's Fair and entertaining a mutual friend—the "good whole-souled Mr. Trollope," who "always seems the soul of honesty." There would be no further exchange about the club on a "true foundation" (which evidently never got off the ground).[25]

At the end of May, Annie attended the first public meeting of the New England

Woman's Club, then the weekly meetings that began in November. Including the Fieldses, there were a hundred eighteen women and seventeen men at that first meeting, a proportion that would continue. The very casualness of a November diary entry—"to Woman's Club meeting last night"—rightly suggests that the meetings quickly became a regular part of Annie's life. By then Kate was living in Boston, often attended those meetings, and often discoursed on cultural and social issues, but without becoming engaged in any reform activities. By contrast, Annie disliked the limelight but often addressed the club on reform projects that she advocated (on one occasion on "Homes for the Poor"). And unlike Kate, she worked actively to effect such reforms.

Moreover, Kate advocated woman suffrage only at the end of her life, but Annie did so from the start. "My heart is wholly with the movement," she declared after spending two days at the Boston Woman's Rights Convention in November 1868. Not surprisingly, however, she was repelled by many of the movers—hard-faced women "full of forthputting-ness . . . who love to un-sex themselves and crave audience from the rostrum."

At that point, the Fieldses were still offering Kate professional and personal sustenance. In the fall of 1868, for example, Jamie suggested that she might write an essay about Fields, Osgood and Company for the *Springfield Republican,* then provided the materials for what became one of her best-received articles.[26] Annie dined with Kate and her mother soon afterward, and Kate's mother reminisced about her experiences as an actress, including her encounters with Mrs. Scott-Siddons and Charles Dickens; and Kate read three treasured letters aloud—one from Poe to her father, another from Ruskin to Browning, and a third from Browning to her.

As one consequence of that nostalgic euphoria, Annie invited both Kate and her mother to celebrate New Year's at Charles Street. "At five o'clock Mrs. Fields sent a carriage for us, [and] after dinner there was conversation such as Mr. and Mrs. Fields know how to lead and inspire," Kate wrote in her diary. To her enormous disappointment, however, the Ouija board she demonstrated fell far short of the claims she had made in her recently published *Planchette's Diary.* Instead of persuasive "communications" from the beyond, the planchette produced wrong and evasive scrawls. Whittier, who had read the *Diary* and longed for proof of Kate's claims, shared her disappointment. As a remarkably empathetic way of dispelling it, Annie took Kate aside to read her "an interesting private letter" she had recently received from Dickens, in which he spoke of trying out new readings from *Oliver Twist.*[27]

Two months later, the Fieldses were on hand to cheer when Kate tried yet another route to money and fame. She mounted the lyceum platform to deliver a stirring lecture with a self-reflexive title: "Women in the Lyceum." As Jamie wrote afterward, it was the most successful debut he had seen; "Aspasia pleading the cause," Annie called it in her diary. Kate soon prepared two additional lectures, one on Dickens and the other on John Brown, and toured successfully with all three, by then such a prominent public figure that each issue of the *Woman's Journal* reported her latest activities. Meantime, she followed Annie's initiatives at the North End Mission, histrionically concluded that it was "the one charity to pursue," and planned to say so in a lecture. For her next and even more congenial initiative—producing private theatricals starring herself—she consulted Annie, who consulted Anna Cabot Lowell about how to launch her career.[28]

Yet Annie was increasingly dismayed by a self-centeredness at the core of Kate's initiatives. In April 1871, for example, Annie mused in her diary about the limited success of some women lecturers—Anna Dickinson because she was too concerned with money and clothing, and Kate Field because the Lord did not speak through her. A subsequent comment was even more acerbic: Kate had some talent "but her admiration for Kate Field interferes therewith." When Kate's mother died that June, the Fieldses attended the funeral. But they were not greatly surprised that Kate had not returned from England for it.

"Have you forgotten me?" Kate wrote from New York in the spring of 1874, then asked about coffee house alternatives to saloons: "Can you tell me about the success of your Holly Tree Inns. Can you give me any statistics . . . ? I want to agitate the subject here. The women are making such big fools of themselves in this temperance crusade that it seems a pity not to tell them how they really can help temperance."[29] Annie supplied the statistics and cautioned Kate to stress the project and not the projector.

When Kate began fund-raising for a new theater to be built in Stratford-on-Avon, the Fieldses were on her list of contributors. But in the spring of 1878 when Kate wanted to deliver a series of Shakespeare lectures in Boston, Annie discouraged her. The lecture season was nearly over, she argued, wondering also what remained to be said about Shakespeare. Nonetheless, she offered mild support by inviting Kate to Charles Street for "tea and then a reading" when she next came to town.[30] Two years later, both of the Fieldses attended the "Musical Monologue" that Kate brought to Boston, a lightweight but entertaining vehicle for self-display that included songs, dances, and humorous skits. It was perhaps the last time that they saw her. Jamie sent a note telling Kate that he and Annie enjoyed her performance, but neither of them said so in person.[31]

Over the course of two decades, both of the Fieldses were "more than kind" to Kate Field, particularly during the sixties. But they eventually perceived her as a moral lightweight. Even during the late sixties when the two women shared their obsession with Dickens and became involved in the women's club movement, they never became confidantes. As a single example, Annie knew nothing about Kate's platonic intimacy with that "soul of honesty" Anthony Trollope. Yet Kate was Trollope's model for both of the American women in his 1869 novel *He Knew He Was Right*—the radiantly independent American girl Caroline Spalding and the loud feminist Wallachia Petrie—and his lifelong tenderness for Kate is at the heart of *An Old Man's Love* (1884).[32] As Kate hopped from one venture to another, one star turn to another, and one locality to another during the seventies, Annie's interest in her simply waned.

Anna Leonowens (1831–1914)

In the summer of 1868, Laura Johnson told Annie that the Welsh-born widow Anna Leonowens had arrived in Staten Island to assume a teaching post, accompanied by her sweet fourteen-year-old daughter Avis. She had rented a house, her teaching was going well, her son was in an English boarding school, and she had read Laura some Persian poetry. She was also planning a book about her five years of teaching the children of the Siamese king. Laura introduced Annie to Anna Leonowens soon afterward, and it was hardly coincidental that three chapters of "The English Governess at the Siamese Court" appeared in the *Atlantic* in April, May, and June of 1870, or that Fields issued the entirety as a book.[33]

Leonowens's second book about her years in Siam, *The Romance of the Harem*, was published by Fields's successor Osgood in December 1872. Leonowens dedicated it "to the noble and devoted women whom I learned to know, to esteem, and to love in the city of the Nang Harm"—a unique world inaccessible to most westerners that included lowborn as well as highborn women, consorts and concubines as well as slaves, Buddhists but also Muslims, workers of all kinds, and their children. Her colorful and often melodramatic stories about the harem women bemoaned their hopeless submissiveness and (more broadly) the evils of Siamese slavery. Of particular interest to American readers was Leonowens's account of the Siamese princess who studied English with her by translating *Uncle Tom's Cabin*. Enormously moved by it, the princess freed all of her hundred and thirty slaves and added "Harriet Beecher Stowe" to her own name. Far more consequential was Leonowens's influence on her most important pupil, the young crown prince. The boy who had studied Abraham Lincoln with her succeeded his father as king in 1868 and proclaimed the end of slavery four years later.[34]

In March 1872, Annie began booking lectures for Leonowens in Boston and invited both mother and daughter to stay at Charles Street. Because their luggage was delayed, "the young beautiful Avis and her mother" had to don "odd bits of my clothes," Annie noted. Leonowens was "a woman of about forty years" with a "classic head and sweet manner of speaking not only like a lady but a linguist as one who knows the value of words." For Annie, the combination of beauty, gentility, and learning was irresistible. Leonowens evidently had no family but her children and no personal history prior to Siam. But she spoke "seven Oriental languages and seems well versed in Sanscrit and Persian literature," she told fascinating stories about Siam, and her knowledge of Buddhism and Oriental poetry made her "a pioneer among women in this field." Annie was pleased that Leonowens earned $362 for "the public reading we arranged" and $25 for a private one.

In December, the month the *Romance* appeared, Leonowens again lectured in Boston and again stayed at Charles Street. The conventional Annie's sympathy for Leonowens soared when she said she mounted the podium only to support her children: "As a woman she detests it, as a mother she performs it." When Leonowens was again scheduled to lecture in Boston the following spring, Annie again invited her to Charles Street and decided to absorb some of her expenses. Leonowens protested that the check Annie sent was too large because she had not deducted her costs, but gratefully accepted her "sweet goodness."[35]

Leonowens's lecture on Buddhism got better every time she gave it, Annie told Laura Johnson in October 1874, yet she continued to be "her own dear self in private, animated by the thought and purpose of the time, utterly self-forgetful and absorbed." Then waxing comical, Annie added that her nephews believed a bat which had invaded Leonowens's room was "part of her weird life."[36] Over the next few years, Annie continued to book lectures for Leonowens with a shrewd eye to the market. For example, in the spring of 1876 when several other Orientalists were scheduled to speak in Boston, Annie deferred booking Leonowens until the autumn.

Because Leonowens was "increasingly dear and delightful," she was one of Annie's first guests at Gambrel Cottage, the Fieldses' new summer house in Manchester, Massachusetts. Hearing her read Sanskrit poetry was an enormous pleasure, and so was walking along the Manchester shore with her. As Annie noted to herself, Leonowens's "modesty and sweetness and special refinement make her most attractive to women as well as men."

In the fall of 1878, through Annie, Harriet Beecher Stowe solicited and received Leonowens's account of the Siamese princess who had translated *Uncle Tom's Cabin* and subsequently freed her own slaves, and included it in a new introduction to the novel.[37] Leonowens moved to Nova Scotia that year, but her relationship with Annie continued. "How are you and how is your work prospering?" she inquired a few months later. "We very much need some one like you for the poor here." Among her requests over the next few years, Leonowens asked Annie to find "suitable work" for two Halifax women who were heading for Boston, to find employment for a capable Halifax nurse, and to find a suitable teacher for an art school she was starting. As another kind of reciprocity, Leonowens agreed to address the Young Ladies of the Saturday Morning Club when she stayed at Charles Street in January 1883 (perhaps on "my Russian experiences"). At least once, Leonowens became involved in a reform effort that paralleled Annie's. In 1896 when she wanted to inspect Boston's Female Prison so that she could recommend reforms in Halifax, Annie paved the way through a note to "the good matron." Meantime, Leonowens welcomed each of Annie's publications and sometimes used her as a literary intermediary, as when she considered preparing an annotated edition of Omar Khayyam's poems and asked Annie to "see Mr. Houghton and let me know whether he wished it to be done."[38]

During all those years, Leonowens's daughter Avis continued to figure in the women's friendship. In the mid-eighties, for example, Leonowens welcomed "your invitation to my dear Avis to pause a day or two under your charmed roof," then mentally revisited the Charles Street drawing room herself, "with you and dear Miss Jewett seated together, with the same feeling with which one pauses before some grand old painting." Avis treasured memories of her girlhood visits, Leonowens added, "and why should she not?" A few years later, Leonowens mourned with Annie the death of Laura Johnson, the woman of "private heroinism" through whom she and Avis had met Annie. Soon Avis's daughter Anna also entered the women's web of concern; on Annie's advice, in the spring of 1902 young Anna was about to take piano lessons from Edward MacDowell in New York. A few months later, Avis died. Annie urged Leonowens to join her in Manchester, but Leonowens was too grief-stricken to accept.[39]

From the start, Annie admired the learned woman imbued with the "spirit of the Orient" whose values matched her own, and Leonowens more than returned that admiration. Her long and lively letters reported on each new enterprise, as in the fall of 1900 when she studied Sanskrit at the University of Leipzig. After hearing about Annie's serious illness in the winter of 1902, Leonowens declared that she could only picture her "as well, bright, helpful and inspiring to all around," and said "no more glad and heroic service has ever been given by a single devoted life." Visiting Annie two years later, Leonowens rejoiced at seeing her once more "in the dear consecrated old home with dear Miss Jewett still your companion and friend, with the same deep enthusiasm for all that is truest and noblest in life." As a woman who had both evoked and shared that enthusiasm, Anna Leonowens had good reason to call Annie Fields "the beautiful inspiring friend of my new life of this side of the Atlantic."[40]

11

Sustaining Intimacy—Harriet Beecher Stowe (1811–1896)

Anyone who happened to notice Harriet Beecher Stowe and Annie Fields on a Boston street in the 1860s might have wondered about the relationship between the small middle-aged woman with bobbing sidecurls and the tall young patrician with her hair pulled back. In fact, Annie Fields was Stowe's closest personal friend.[1] It is easy to argue that Stowe used and even exploited Annie Fields while turning out manuscripts for the publishing house of James T. Fields, and equally easy to argue the reverse. Their relationship was certainly strongest during the sixties, when Stowe was the most popular woman writer in America and James T. Fields was her publisher. But their tender mutual regard continued long after Fields's retirement and ended only with Stowe's death.

None of this could have been predicted when they first met in Florence at the beginning of 1860. Stowe was then an international celebrity of the first magnitude, as she had been since the publication eight years before of *Uncle Tom's Cabin*, arguably the century's most popular and politically influential novel. She was also America's most popular woman writer, a seasoned professional with a list of publications dating back to the year before Annie was born and three years before she married a professor of biblical literature named Calvin Stowe. When Harriet Beecher Stowe and Annie Fields met in 1860, Calvin Stowe was still a professor at Andover Theological Seminary, a position he would retire from three years later, and his wife was already the family's chief breadwinner. Her second novel, *The Minister's Wooing*, set in New England, had been serialized in the *Atlantic* before appearing as a book, and one of her main motives for traveling to England in 1859 was to secure the English copyright.

Next came a vacation in Italy, shared by her twenty-three-year-old twin daughters and occasionally her twenty-year-old son Fred, while Calvin supervised their two younger children in Andover. In Florence, Stowe immediately became part of the city's lively expatriate community. Meantime, she augmented her income by writing for the New York *Independent,* an antislavery Protestant weekly.

Annie's introduction to Stowe at a large reception in an old palace on the Arno left her in despair. As she recalled years later, she felt

> a faint thrill of surprise when a voice by my side said, "There is Mrs. Stowe." In a moment she approached and I was presented to her, and after a brief pause she passed on. All this was natural enough, but a wave of intense disappointment swept over me. Why had I found no words to express or even indicate the feeling that had choked me? Was the fault mine? Oh, yes, I said to myself, for I could not conceive it to be otherwise, and I looked upon my opportunity, the gift of the gods, as utterly and forever wasted. I was depressed and sorrowing over the vanishing of a presence I might perhaps never meet again, and no glamour of light, or music or pictures or friendly voices could recall any pleasure to my heart. Meanwhile, the unconscious object of all this disturbance was strolling quietly along, leaning on the arm of a friend, hardly ever speaking, followed by a group of travelling companions, and entirely absorbed in the gay scene around her. She was a small woman; and her pretty curling hair and far-away dreaming eyes, and her way of becoming occupied in what interested her until she forgot everything else for the time, all these I first began to see and understand as I gazed after her retreating figure.[2]

Though Stowe might not have realized that she had just met the wife of the *Atlantic's* new owner, she had good reason to cultivate both Fieldses. Any manuscript that was serialized in the country's most prestigious literary magazine might also be issued in book form by the country's most prestigious literary publisher. Yet surely Stowe's professional ambition was only one reason why she greeted Annie warmly when they next met, and then took the initiative by calling on them. She spoke "charmingly" about Hawthorne's fiction, Annie noted afterward: "Like old pictures, she thinks, an uncultivated taste would hardly relish him, but once understand him and you feel that the marvels of Highest Art stand before you." Another of her pronouncements during that first visit was more consequential: Stowe "promised that she would write for the Atlantic." It was a promise she would keep, to their mutual advantage, though in her own way and on her own terms.

Meantime, the Fieldses were much struck by the range of her narrative skills. When they returned her call, "her dramatic power showed itself strikingly in a few stories she told towards the end of the evening"; in Charlotte Cushman's rooms a few days later, Stowe "told ghost stories all the evening"; and when she was the guest of honor at one of William Wetmore Story's dinner parties, her sagas about the escaped slave Sojourner Truth thrilled the entire group. By then the Fieldses were seeing her almost every day—at art galleries, at mutual friends' apartments or their own, or at a "capital little party" that Stowe herself gave. When the Fieldses left for Rome, Stowe accompanied them.

Yet their growing intimacy did not prevent Annie from sharing a "general feeling of reverence and gratitude" for the author of *Uncle Tom's Cabin.* One manifestation occurred during a visit to the Castellani brothers' celebrated art gallery, when one of the brothers gave Stowe an onyx head of an Egyptian slave, declaring, "We ourselves are but poor slaves still in Italy: you feel for us."[3] Annie felt privileged to be at Stowe's side that day, as during their last "pleasant evening" together at Stowe's lodgings when she "asked me to write to her."

A few months later, Stowe arranged to return to America with the Fieldses. "On the strength of having heard that you were going in the Europa June 16th we also have engaged passage therein for that time & hope that we shall not be disappointed," she told Annie. Then she candidly announced her twofold purpose: "Apart from pleasure I have some particular *business* to arrange with your husband—I have begun a story for the Atlantic & want to talk with him about it." Weary of traveling, she longed for "a quiet home and for *rest*"; but meanwhile she was "anticipating so much from the idea of making the voyage with you." The "you" was plural.[4]

During that voyage on the *Europa*—with the Hawthornes also on board—Annie found herself "learning to love Mrs. Stowe" while listening to her stories about New England life and her own early experiences. Because James T. Fields was often prostrated by seasickness or locked in talk with Hawthorne, the three women spent hours on their own; and Stowe became so fond of Annie that by the time the *Europa* docked, she was eager for "a quiet evening *with you* by your own fireside looking at your own household gods."[5] But she had not yet concluded her "particular *business*" with Annie's husband: securing his agreement to publish *Agnes of Sorrento,* a romance about Italy that she had already started.

Annie's delight in Stowe's reminiscences of New England, but also the success of *The Minister's Wooing* (set in the Calvinist world of Stowe's famous preacher-father), make it easy to understand why the Fieldses wanted to serialize another of Stowe's New England novels in the *Atlantic*. But Stowe had something else in mind. "To Mr & Mrs Meadows," she punningly wrote across the top of a folded sheet, then penned a tiny sketch of a flowery field below, and addressed her letter to the "Sweet Fields beyond the swelling flood." The letter itself was essentially a shrewd brief for *Agnes,* "the subject we discussed" on the *Europa*. Because New England stories by Rose Terry and Harriet Prescott had recently appeared in the *Atlantic,* Stowe argued, the Italian story she now felt compelled to write "might be desirable as a change." Only then did she admit that she had promised a "yankee story" to the *Independent*. Not only would she risk repeating herself if she tried writing another for the *Atlantic,* but her fans might complain of "overmuch at once of the same kind of thing." As she assured her "dear Friends," *Agnes* would do the *Atlantic* no discredit, and she could finish it speedily. She yielded only on a point of style: "Your ideas of conversation I concluded to take." To cinch her case, she enclosed the relatively few pages that she had completed, enough to "make about thirteen of Atlantic pages."[6]

At that point, Fields accepted an offer he could not refuse. He agreed to publish *Agnes* and offered generous terms—$200 for each installment and half the profits on book sales. Predictably, however, writing *The Pearl of Orr's Island* impeded Stowe's completion of *Agnes*. And although *Pearl* boosted circulation for the *Independent*, *Agnes* did nothing of the sort for the *Atlantic*. In 1862, however, Fields was pleased to publish both of Stowe's new novels.

Because by then Stowe had come to trust Annie as a sympathetic critic, any trip to Boston was an occasion to "say many things to her & read her now & then a scrap as I go on." Stowe also enjoyed sharing a rare tribute with Annie. After her sketch of Sojourner Truth—"The Libyan Sybil"—appeared in the 1863 *Atlantic*, she exultantly told Annie that she had "heard from Old Sojourner—she is alive—has had my article read to her & enjoyed it hugely—wondered Mrs Stowe could remember so much."[7]

By that time Stowe had come to depend on Annie for professional assistance. Sometimes she requested proofreading, most notably for her most famous wartime essay, "Reply to the Affectionate and Christian Address of the Women of England," written to celebrate the Emancipation Proclamation and to solicit English support for the antislavery cause. Stowe traveled to Washington in November 1862 to hear from "Father Abraham" that he would sign the Proclamation on New Year's Day, and she prepared her ardent "Reply" for the January *Atlantic* on the assumption that he would keep his promise. But because the issue was about to go to press, she begged a favor: she wanted the editor or his wife to "read the proof sheets and correct any mistakes."[8] Later, Stowe requested a larger favor for an *Atlantic* essay that urged Northern women not to buy imported goods in wartime. "Please let Annie look it over & if she & you think I have said too much of the Waltham watches make it right," she told Fields in the summer of 1864, then sweepingly added, "If Annie thinks of any other thing that ought to be mentioned & will put it in for me she will serve both the cause & me." A simpler request came the following November: because she wanted to make a few changes in her New Year's essay, Stowe asked Annie to speed the proof sheets to her.[9]

Such requests for assistance did not end when the war did. Probably in jest, Stowe asked Annie to contribute poems to a collection of her own work. But she could be direct and even imperious, as when she requested a bit of help for her long overdue *Oldtown Folks* in 1868. "I want a favor of you," Stowe told Annie. "I am come to a place in my story where my characters having always attended old town church are taken by Lady Lathrop in her grand coach to attend Easter Sunday in the Old North in Boston—& I want a description of that old church."[10]

At least once, Stowe enlisted Annie's help on a manuscript that she did not prepare for James T. Fields—*Men of Our Times*, sketches of contemporary statesmen that were commissioned by the Baptist periodical *Watchman and Reflector* and that the Hartford Publishing Company then issued as a subscription volume. When she visited Annie in the fall of 1867, Stowe discussed the entire project with her and requested help for her sketch of John A. Andrew, Massachusetts's wartime governor and a good friend of the Fieldses. "I shall want all I can get about the Governor next week as the book is going on rapidly," Stowe wrote; then on 21 November, three weeks after Andrew died, she asked Fields to remind Annie "of her promise to get me some taking anecdote that will help me to show how good & generous Andrew was." Evidently Annie complied. As Stowe wrote a few weeks later, "on the rule that one good turn deserves another as I have found you so good I ask again. I am writing on Governor Andrew & want his farewell speech to the Mass Legislature. *Can* you get me a copy & send it in all haste."[11]

Annie never resented such assignments. She could pride herself on being the trusted assistant of America's most important woman writer, an advocate of social ideals they both shared. She was also helping a friend who was short of both money and time.

During the sixties, Stowe also felt free to lobby the editor through his wife. She once asked Annie to transmit a poem she had especially enjoyed writing—"for the next Atlantic if your Jamie wants to put it in." And she once unsuccessfully lobbied for someone else's work—a sea-story by a Mrs. Ruggles that she wanted both Fieldses to read. It was fresh and original and she could help the author improve it, Stowe assured them. She then appealed to their sympathies: the author needed money to repay a debt contracted by her father.[12]

Such manipulations were more often on her own behalf. She offered to draw her own illustrations for her poems about Italy, for an artist to "touch up." More calculatingly, she tried to maneuver her own husband to complete his history of the Old Testament, by indirectly pressuring James T. Fields. She asked Annie to ask Jamie to announce the book in order to pressure Calvin to complete it (though in fact, he never did).[13] Occasionally Stowe even enlisted Annie as a kind of secretarial surrogate, as when she was packing for Florida in the winter of 1867 just before her *Religious Poems* appeared. Annie should make sure that copies were sent to Holmes, Longfellow, and a few other friends, Stowe wrote, "—& will you dear friend write 'from the Author' on the blank leaf."[14]

In that case as always, Stowe assumed that Annie was privy to her business arrangements with Mr. F. Thus if she expected to miss a deadline for one of her "House and Home" papers for the *Atlantic,* she often sent the news and her excuses through Annie. In July 1864, for example, she told Annie how hard it was to outfit her son Charley for sea duty while nursing her son Fred (who had been wounded at Gettysburg), then said, "As to my Sept # Mr F must allow me till the end of next week." Similarly, while struggling to cope with Fred's alcoholism four years later, Stowe told Annie she had been unable to work on *Oldtown Folks* and her publisher simply had to be patient: she needed "time to write it *when* I can write well—& without my mind distracted with something else."[15]

Annie was also a conduit for good news, as in the summer of 1867 when Stowe happily reported that her material for *Oldtown Folks* was rich and abundant. Then after the book's long delayed completion, Stowe announced through Annie that she was ready to contract for its sequel "on the terms named." *Oldtown Fireside Stories* would be a good title, she thought, with each *Atlantic* installment given a title of its own. She was not yet sure how many installments she would produce. There might be twelve or perhaps fewer, "according as they run, or as the spirits from the vasty deep hand them up"; but she wanted the book to begin with a ghost story she had already written—"The Ghost in the Cap'n Brown House." Such specificities never included finances, however: Stowe once simply told Annie that she would gladly receive any money Fields might owe her.[16]

Even after Fields retired from publishing in 1870 and attained success as a lecturer, Stowe continued to expect and receive practical assistance from both of her "dear Friends," particularly in 1872 when she agreed to make a reading tour of New England. At Fields's suggestion, a booking agent had urged Stowe to do so and offered liberal terms. She hesitated for months, fearing that her health might suffer and that she might not be able to hold a large audience. But she finally contracted for forty readings that included a late September booking in Boston's Tremont Temple. On 20 August, she invited herself to stay with the Fieldses on that occasion, wondered if late September was "too early for Boston," then wryly remarked, "I don't know as its my business—which is simply to speak my piece and take my money."[17]

"I wish much I could see you & talk over my programme," Stowe told Annie a day later, hoping for "a bit of guidance" from both of the Fieldses.[18] That opportunity came right after she gave her first reading, in Springfield. On 13 September she arrived at the Fieldses' lodgings in Manchester, confessed to stage fright, and spent the next few days recuperating. Then on 16 September, the Fieldses accompanied her to Lynn for her second reading, which Annie pronounced a success.

Stowe's long anticipated reading at the Tremont Temple would be a greater success. She arrived at Charles Street the day before, worried that her voice might be inadequate for that large hall. Her dinner conversation was nonetheless as interesting as ever, Annie marveled, though her obliviousness to a spot on her new dress seemed "wonderful and terrible," and she left a mess on the dinner table and a "tangle" in her bedroom. Even so, Annie prized Stowe's friendship as "a boon of heaven."

Over a quarter of a century later, Annie vividly recalled the day of Stowe's long-feared reading:

> She called me into her bedroom, where she stood before the mirror, with her short gray hair, which usually lay in soft curls around her brow, brushed erect and standing stiffly. "Look here, my dear," she said; "now I look exactly like my father, Dr. Lyman Beecher, when he was going to preach," and she held up her forefinger warningly. It was easy to see that the spirit of the old preacher was revived in her veins, and the afternoon would show something of his power. An hour later, when I sat with her in the anteroom waiting for the moment of her appearance to arrive, I could feel the power surging up within her. I knew she was armed for a good fight.
>
> That reading was a great success. She was alive in every fibre of her being; she was to read portions of "Uncle Tom's Cabin" to men, women, and children who could hardly understand the crisis which inspired it, and she determined to effect the difficult task of making them feel as well as hear.

Although some of her words did not reach the back of the hall, as Stowe had feared, people stood up and moved forward "gladly, that no word might be lost."[19]

Stowe returned to Charles Street afterward, and she surprised the Fieldses by returning the following week before giving another reading nearby. As she happily informed her husband, she "tumbled in" at Charles Street, settled into "her" room, and had a good nap and a good dinner. Then she set off with the Fieldses for her reading, the audience was "very jolly and appreciative," and afterward "we all jogged home."[20]

Not surprisingly, the woman who could call Charles Street "home" never had qualms about enlisting Annie's help in domestic matters. "I know you always have your hands full," Stowe once wrote, "but since you *will* go about doing good you might as well do a little for me." That "little" ranged from making appointments for her daughters with a Boston oculist to purchasing dishes for her, getting her a pound of the dandelion coffee she had enjoyed at Charles Street, and sharing the recipe "for a certain nice way of preparing fish—which used to be brought to us on a platter & look as if cooked with cream—."[21] For Stowe as for her famous older sister Catharine Beecher—with whom she wrote *The American Woman's Home* (1869)—a nicely prepared fish exemplified the domestic values that Annie obviously shared.

Stowe also kept Annie informed about her own domestic enterprises. Thus in November 1863 when her eight-gabled Hartford house neared completion, she reported that she was "busy with drains sewers sinks digging trenching—& above all with manure!—You should see the joy with which I gaze on manure heaps in which the eye of faith sees Deleware [*sic*] grapes & D'Angouleme pears & all sorts of roses & posies."[22] As she had already realized, such experiences were excellent material for *Atlantic* essays: the first of her enormously successful "House and Home Papers" had appeared in October. Then after establishing a winter home in Florida in 1868, Stowe began showering Annie with enticing letters that she also drew on for essays (albeit not for the *Atlantic*). In a typical 1872 letter to her "Dearly Beloved," Stowe fancifully offered Annie a branch from one of her own orange trees and wished she could "look into my grotto & see yourself surrounded by a frame of live oak grey moss & palmetto leaves." Her new grandson was the "little king," she was "first granny-in-waiting," her twin daughters were fine housekeepers, and she wished Annie could see them all riding in a wagon pulled by a mule named Fly, "who looks like an animated old hair trunk & the waggon & harness to match!—It is too funny."[23]

As that letter suggests, Stowe expected Annie's unqualified sympathy in all things. That was even true about her "True Story of Lady Byron's Life," which appeared in the *Atlantic* while the Fieldses happened to be abroad. During Stowe's visit to England in 1856, Lady Byron had confided the history of her husband's incest with his half-sister, a shocking tale that Stowe had advised her not to make public. In 1869, however, Byron's last mistress, Countess Guiccioli, published her

Recollections of Lord Byron, blaming his wife for their failed marriage. Stowe leaped to Lady Byron's defense by writing the "True Story" for the September *Atlantic.* But as soon as it appeared, it was attacked as scandalous and obscene in England and America, and hundreds of *Atlantic* subscriptions were canceled. At that point Stowe speedily prepared the better-argued and better-supported *Lady Byron Vindicated,* which Fields agreed to publish, and she then canceled a visit to Annie to lobby for it. "I have given up six months heart soul income life strength all for the *love* I bear her—who I love & shall love forever," Stowe poignantly declared, "& you dear Annie can understand this—that all my movements are determined by this."[24]

A few years later, when Stowe's beloved brother Henry Ward Beecher faced a legal charge of adultery with a parishioner, Stowe vented her pain to Annie and requested a favor. During the Byron furor, George Eliot had sent Stowe a sympathetic letter, and she now hoped to elicit a second such "kiss" from her "sister soul." Therefore she asked Annie to tell Eliot "how *false* all this is & that *good* people dont believe it—It will be more clear."[25] Out of loyalty to Stowe, and although many of the "good people" Annie knew seriously doubted Beecher's innocence, she made the case for him to Eliot, who then sent Stowe a "womanly, tender, and sweet" letter. Stowe's appeal through Annie Fields to the "large-souled and intelligent" George Eliot boils down to a kind of skewed syllogism: I trust my brother, you and I and Eliot trust one another, so you and Eliot should trust my brother. A third assertion was implicit: your trust validates mine.

If doing Stowe's bidding in that case (as in all others) was partly a matter of hero (or heroine) worship, it was also a form of daughterly solicitude. Yet Stowe did more for Annie than Annie did for Stowe. Having Stowe as her friend enlarged Annie's sense of importance and vastly enriched her life. Admittedly, the Fieldses rarely visited her, and Stowe's publishing deadlines and family obligations limited her opportunities to visit them. Yet Stowe frequently enjoyed playing what she called the "trump card" of an invitation from Annie, and in 1862 when Louisa May Alcott listed the celebrities she had met at Charles Street, the name of Harriet Beecher Stowe came first.[26]

For Annie, one pleasure of such visits was simply sharing her daily life with Stowe, whether they went shopping or called on friends or ate lunch together. Stowe's overnight visits were occasions for what Annie called "Harrieting"—sitting before the fire together and talking for hours. On one such evening in 1866, for example, Stowe's conversation ranged from Frederick Olmsted's frustrations in love to "her dear dead boy who came to her in her dreams a few nights ago . . . saying much that was beautiful but eludes me now," and her yearning for the consolations of spiritualism. And when Stowe arrived in the summer of 1867 after attending the funeral of two nieces who had drowned, Annie empathetically mused, "just as her son was drowned so few years ago."

Stowe's long visit to Charles Street in November 1866 was more varied than usual, partly because her husband came along. On the first day, the two women went out driving and discussed two manuscripts that Stowe was preparing—*Men of Our Times* and the yet untitled novel *Oldtown Folks,* which was her "chief delight." They also made a few calls including one to Maria Chapman, an early supporter of Garrison, who recalled the dark days when anti-abolitionists mobbed their meetings and even burned her house down—a "queenly creature," Stowe declared. That evening at Charles Street, Calvin Stowe discoursed about "his supernatural visions, old times at Natick, etc." while his wife interpolated "anecdotes he had forgotten or omitted." Perhaps for the first time, Annie realized how thoroughly Harriet Beecher Stowe had appropriated her husband's imagination—fictionalizing him as the vision-prone narrator of *Oldtown Folks* and incorporating his anecdotes into that novel, as she would do again in the *Oldtown Fireside Tales.*

The next day, Annie took the Stowes to Cambridge to visit "the Industrial School for Freed-people getting on famously under Miss Lowell's indefatigable care" (as they perhaps recalled when they tried to establish a school for their Florida neighbors a few years later). Afterward, when Oliver Wendell Holmes and a Lord and Lady Amberley joined the two couples at Charles Street, Stowe breached decorum by attacking Holmes's new novel *The Guardian Angel* (which was dedicated to Fields and published by him), largely because his depictions of New England village Calvinism and his portrayals of incompetent ministers were wholly at odds with her own nostalgic recollections. Holmes took her attack so humbly that she stopped. But good tea-talk followed; and the following day's events included lunch with the Aldriches and talk about Edwin Booth, then a visit to the Edward Everett Hales where they all deplored the death of Governor Andrew. That evening, Fields took Calvin Stowe off to his "Dante Festival," an all-male celebration to honor Longfellow's completed translation of the *Divine Comedy* and the six-hundredth anniversary of Dante's birth. The ladies sent a wreath and then settled in at Charles Street for hours of talk. Emerson and Mary Dodge came for a lively breakfast the next morning, and then the women "trotted about shopping."

Stowe's "coming was always a pleasure," Annie later wrote, "for she made holidays by her own delightful presence, and she asked nothing more than what she found in the companionship of her friends."[27] The pleasure was particularly intense one day in January 1868 when Stowe arrived early for a visit and sat down for a talk that ended only at nightfall. Two days later, Annie was still thinking about it: "There is something in her friendship more satisfactory, or I would rather say, as truly satisfactory as that of any woman I have ever known—her insight and sweetness and words, her rest in love and desire for it, her other worldliness and abstractions have a comfort for me beyond expression. They lift me up and brush me into the peace of love." Annie was still "dreaming over" Stowe's friendship and what it meant to her the following day.

A month later, another long conversation with Stowe provoked an epiphany: "It came to me how fast the sphere is opening before any woman, especially if she has talent, to help to humanize and harmonize society." For perhaps the first time, Annie could think of herself as such a woman, and in that sense as Stowe's peer. That might even explain why she now permitted herself to mention Stowe's weaknesses, including the brief lapses of consciousness that she called "going off in spirit." When Stowe came to lunch in January 1871, Annie observed that she was "more 'distraite' more undressed, and inclined to be more silent than ever." But despite Stowe's bad cold and complaints of exhaustion, she was soon expounding on women's capacities for self-advancement and noble accomplishment, moving from women's right to vote to George Eliot's career and Annie's "Holly Tree" coffee house alternatives to saloons, "which she gives too high a place in the good work of the period."

Stowe encouraged Annie's efforts "to humanize and harmonize society" even in small ways. A practical humanitarian, she accompanied Annie to inspect "benevolent work" in the Boston slums during an 1864 visit, and they brought home a dirty "street Arab." Stowe volunteered to scrub him; but he screamed all night and disappeared the next day. Then after Annie found him again and placed him in a "charitable home," Stowe indulgently commented, "you are a dear young angel just as smart & lovely as you can be, but better fitted *personally* to superintend young cherubim than young male humans . . . , but your *will* in the matter was beautiful & heroic & our good Father who is the father of all poor boys has found you the best *way* to execute it. . . . [H]e'll be better off than if you had all the trouble of him under your roof."[28]

Stowe also supported Annie's relatively impersonal benevolences, as when she painted fans for Annie to sell at a Cretan relief fair in 1868. But she was most enthusiastic about Annie's own initiatives. In February 1872, for example, she told Annie not to waste time with "illuminati" who have "a refined way of doing nothing," then declared, "Your Holly trees are worth a dozen of them"; and she praised both the project and "the good fairy who set all this agoing" in the *Christian Union*. News of Annie's Lincoln Street residence for working women made her eager "to see your girls & get acquainted with them." In March 1872, Stowe praised her "Dear little Saint" for "laboring with that stupid relief committee to get your wise plan of a girls' sewing room" instituted at the North End Mission, then whimsically exclaimed, "My dear, you ought to be lady Mayoress of Boston—there's no doubt of that—& a nice one you would be but you see we can't always make the world go as it should." And after the fire that devastated Boston's North End that November, she sent Annie a hundred dollars for the Fireman's Fund, wishing it could be more.[29]

Yet Stowe said almost nothing about Annie's publications. Perhaps referring to *Asphodel,* she told Fields she had received "Anna's book," read it, and recommended it to the *Hartford Courant,* hoping it would "sell 50000—it ought to."[30] And after receiving Annie's *Under the Olive* in 1880, Stowe said she was pleased by its enthusiastic reception but "hardly *know* enough to follow you—It is so long since I used to turn to my classical dictionary & knew all about those mythic stories."

Her priorities were clear: "I think your Holly Tree coffee rooms, your north end labors—& all your other works for humanity have a higher beauty. I heard a minister say once "there is no work of art so beautiful as a noble life"—& one wonders when your hands are so full of better things where you found time for picking all these flowers. . . . [T]he cultured ones will admire your verses but those who know you best will think *you* yourself outshine your poems."[31] Stowe also praised Annie's *Biographical Notes of James T. Fields* the following year primarily because it "enlarged my knowledge of his worth of heart & character."[32]

As that judgment suggests, issues of heart and character also weighed heavily in both women's judgments of other women writers, most notably of George Eliot. As Annie wrote years later, Eliot "greatly enlisted Mrs. Stowe's sympathies and enriched her life. Her interest in any woman who was supporting herself, and especially in any one who found a daily taskmaster in the pen, and above all when, as in this case, the woman was one possessed of great moral aspiration half paralyzed in its action by finding itself in an anomalous and (to the world in general) utterly incomprehensible position, made such a woman like a magnet to Mrs. Stowe." And, she might have added, to herself.[33]

Whenever Stowe received a letter from Eliot, she promised to show it to Annie and meantime quoted it at length. "We are all full of George Eliot," Stowe told Annie in the spring of 1869. "She is a noble true woman & if any body doesn't see it so much the worse for *them* not her." A "sweet note" from Eliot three years later prompted Stowe to ask "Can't she be got to come to America: England wears her out." And when Stowe was visiting Annie in September 1872, they discussed *Middlemarch* and wished Eliot was with them. At that point, writing from Annie's "lovely little nest," Stowe offered Eliot an unusual enticement. Something was missing in *Middlemarch* that she would find in America, Stowe argued, "namely, 'jollitude.' . . . We want to get you over here, and into this house, where, with closed doors, we sometimes make the rafters ring with fun, and say anything and everything, no matter what, and won't be any properer than we's a mind to be."[34]

Eliot declined that offer on grounds of poor health, as she would decline Annie's "hospitable friendly invitation" the following year. But she remained in touch with both women. After George Lewes died in 1879, Stowe told Annie about the "oppressively sad & desolate" letter she received from Eliot; and after Eliot herself died two years later, Stowe thought of writing an article for the *Atlantic* that would draw on letters which "show her to be so fine & noble." Hesitating on grounds of decency, Stowe wondered if either of the Fieldses knew whether "any marriage ceremony of *any* kind passed between her & Mr Lewes."[35] She never prepared that article.

But Annie would use Eliot's letters in her memoirs of both women. In the sketch of Eliot that she published in 1899, Annie dramatized their discovery that they were both friends of Stowe, then commented, "The affectionate generosity with which she poured out her unbounded admiration for Mrs. Stowe, and her love for her work, is never to be forgotten."[36] In her biography of Stowe, Annie compared both novelists to the only other woman of the period who was their professional equal—George Sand. "There was a strange similarity of character, not of likeness, between the three women of genius," Annie wrote, then managed to find a ground of likeness. Although their faces seemed "weighted with the heavier tasks of life" when they were abstracted, during animated conversation they all looked beautiful.[37]

Another woman writer who figured in Stowe's friendship with Annie was Mary Dodge ("Gail Hamilton"). In December 1866 Stowe cryptically told Annie about writing a *"thundering"* letter to Mary, "which I dare say will make her laugh at the old goose who ought to have sense enough to be a gander"; the following summer, Stowe hoped Annie would come to Hartford when Mary was there; and in August 1868 she asked "if Mary Dodge has gone or is going to Europe—or where she is now—." Mary herself put an end to such inquiries by telling Stowe about her bitter break with James T. Fields.[38]

On one occasion a decade later, Stowe's friendship with Annie included Anna Leonowens. "Can you get this note for me to Mrs Leonowens who was governess to the King of Siam"? Stowe asked Annie in the fall of 1878. "I am making out a history of Uncle Tom and have asked her for some facts of its influence there." Annie transmitted that note and then Leonowens's account of "the particular incident from one of my books which proves the influence of 'Uncle Tom's Cabin' on the Amelioration if not Abolition of Slavery in Siam"—one of the many poignant "incidents" in her *Romance of the Harem* (1872):

> Among the ladies of the harem I knew one woman who more than the rest helped to enrich my life. . . . Our daily lessons and translations from English into Siamese had become a part of her happiest hours. The first book we translated was *Uncle Tom's Cabin,* and it soon became her favorite book. She would read it over and over again, though she knew all the characters by heart and spoke of them as if she had known them all her life. On the 3d of January, 1867, she voluntarily liberated all her slaves, men, women, and children, one hundred and thirty in all, saying, "I am wishful to be good like Harriet Beecher Stowe, and never again to buy human bodies, but only to let them go free once more." Thenceforth, to express her entire sympathy and affection for the author of *Uncle Tom's Cabin,* she always signed herself Harriet Beecher Stowe; and her sweet voice trembled with love and music whenever she spoke of the lovely American lady who had taught her as even Buddha had taught kings to respect the rights of her fellow-creatures.

Stowe would include Leonowens's reply in her introduction to a new edition of *Uncle Tom's Cabin.*[39]

Stowe had probably met Sarah Orne Jewett (perhaps at the home of their mutual friend Mary Claflin) before Annie and Sarah visited her in September 1884, and perhaps she knew how deeply Sarah admired her work (The *Pearl of Orr's Island* in particular). Certainly she enjoyed seeing them. "How many delightful memories your short little visit brought back to me," she told Annie soon afterward, thanking her for bringing Miss Jewett, and passing on "love & thanks" for her "interesting & bright" new novel, *A Country Doctor,* which Calvin Stowe had also enjoyed reading. Calvin apparently undertook a curious initiative afterward. As Whittier commented, "I am not sure that Mr Stowe's attempt at match-making for Sarah is not an instance of mistaken vocation"; even if a certain "good doctor" did propose to her, Sarah would probably reject him. In 1896, Sarah attended Stowe's funeral with Annie; and Stowe's twin daughters later gave Sarah two mementos—a photograph of their mother and a stamp box she had used.[40]

The only woman writer whose career both Harriet Beecher Stowe and Annie Fields helped shape was Elizabeth Stuart Phelps Ward. "Lilly" was only seven when Calvin Stowe began teaching at Andover Theological Seminary (where her father was on the faculty), and "the greatest of American women" became her role model.[41] They remained in touch after the Stowes moved to Hartford, and one of Stowe's letters announcing a visit to Annie in the mid-sixties declared, "I should love to see you all & Lilly Phelps too." In 1868 James T. Fields followed his wife's recommendation to publish Phelps's first novel, *The Gates Ajar.* Two years later when Fields published her *Hedged In,* a novel about the problems of a poor young unwed mother, Stowe asked Annie for a copy and then confided her reactions: "To you privately I will say it has disappointed me. Lillie is too young a girl to deal with that dreadful problem & I fear for her success. The reviewers will be cruel I fear to her—however I think all *good* people will respect her object whatever they may think about her success. Dont say to any one what I say tho—I dont think Lillie *knows* enough yet of life to write edifyingly on such subjects—But her book will have a sale because her first one has created for her a clientele."[42] At the age of fifty-eight, Stowe was certain that she and the thirty-five-year-old Annie knew much more about life and the vagaries of literary success than the much younger woman who loved and admired them both. It seems appropriate that when Phelps took her first diffident steps onto the lecture platform in 1876, she spoke about the woman novelist her two mentors most deeply admired—George Eliot.

It also seems appropriate that when the *Atlantic* gave a large garden party honoring Stowe's seventy-first birthday in June 1882, Annie Fields wrote a poem for the occasion and Elizabeth Stuart Phelps was seated on the speakers' platform. Annie was then in Europe on her first trip abroad with Sarah Orne Jewett, and Phelps sent her a lively report, together with the *Boston Advertiser* "containing your poem with the whole account of the affair."[43] In that poem, Annie praised Stowe as a moral heroine whose field of action happened to be storytelling, and concluded with a tender address:

> Friend, how calm your sunset days!
> Your peaceful eyes are set on heaven,
> For peace upon the promise stays—
> Who loves much is forgiven.

This birthday party would be Stowe's last public appearance, and fourteen years of intermittent senility lay ahead, but Annie would subsequently see Stowe and exchange a few more letters with her.

When Stowe died, Annie attended the funeral and laid purple flowers on the coffin. She then assumed the task of preparing her "Days with Mrs. Stowe" for the *Atlantic,* and joined Charles Dudley Warner in a fund-raising plan to support Stowe's daughters. Within the year, Stowe's family asked her to prepare Stowe's official *Life and Letters.*

In "Days with Mrs. Stowe," Annie drew largely on her own diaries and letters to establish what Stowe "has been to her friends, to her country, and to the world." As in her birthday poem, she began by stressing Stowe's moral greatness: "Her heart was like a burning coal laid upon the altar of humanity" (159). Then she discoursed on Stowe's career, her love of her home and family, and the joys of being her friend. Only occasionally did she sound a note of criticism, as when she said *The Pearl of Orr's Island* would have been "good enough . . . to have added a lustre even to Stowe's name" if the author's judgment had not been "overridden by greedy editors and publishers" (176).

When Annie compiled the *Life and Letters of Harriet Beecher Stowe* the following year, she had much more material and much more space. Drawing on letters that Stowe's son Charles had gathered and that Houghton Mifflin sent her, she celebrated Stowe's robust good humor and her great capacity for friendship while presenting her as a remarkable writer who successfully coped with financial need, uncertain health, a sensitive social conscience, and the demands of marriage and motherhood.

The book's most revealing anecdotes include one provided by a friend who had pressed the young mother to finish an overdue magazine story. Stowe had worked on "'her sentimental tale of Ellen and her lover amidst the eggs, pork, laundry, and babies in the kitchen,'" continuing to mix "'cooking, writing, nursing, and laughing'" until the tale was complete. The episode was amusing because they both "chose to be amused," Annie commented, "but it easily has another side, when we consider Mrs. Stowe's health, and the work which lay before her" (98–101).

But Annie usually let Stowe speak for herself, as in a letter wryly informing another friend about her eye problems and about the childbirth that had confined her to bed for two months, troubles that were "but enough to keep me from loving earth too well." Calvin Stowe's letters to his wife during that period display him as a smaller figure, a self-serving if genially supportive mate who was more than willing to let his wife be the breadwinner. When Harriet declared that she needed a room of her own to write in, he readily agreed to arrangements that she had previously made, saying complacently, "God has written it in his book that you must be a literary woman, and who are we that we should contend against God?" (102, 105). But whatever Annie thought about Calvin's virtual abandonment of his academic career, she made it amply clear that Stowe relied on her husband's judgment and that they dearly loved each other.

Annie's volume concludes on the same religious note that she had sounded in "Days with Mrs. Stowe": "A great spirit has performed its mission and has been released" (393). Passing lightly over Stowe's years of dotage, she presented that mission, affirming her beloved friend's lifelong belief in the spiritual and social value of service to others and her certainty of an afterlife. In the process, Annie also affirmed her own deepest beliefs.

Annie Fields's biography of Harriet Beecher Stowe was one of her three books about women writers who had been her close friends. The one on Celia Thaxter came before, and the one on Sarah Orne Jewett would follow. As she did for Celia Thaxter, Annie first wrote a memoir for the *Atlantic,* republished it in *Authors and Friends,* then expanded it into a book. But the Stowe *Life and Letters* was her longest biography, for decades the standard one. It is diplomatic, affectionate, densely detailed, and lively.

Annie Fields and Harriet Beecher Stowe never troubled to honor each other's birthdays or anniversaries. But until she met Sarah Orne Jewett, no woman exacted more from Annie or more richly rewarded her. Without Stowe, Annie Fields might have been more the genteel lady and less the committed activist, more the serene "Peri" that Sophia Hawthorne adored and less capable of being Celia Thaxter's confidante or Sarah Orne Jewett's "Fuff," and certainly far less capable of becoming the judicious biographer of them all.

12

Sustaining Intimacy—Laura Winthrop Johnson (1825–1889)

Theodore Winthrop, a major in New York's Seventh Regiment and a resident of Staten Island, became one of the Union's first war heroes when he died in June 1861 while leading an attack in one of the earliest major engagements of the Civil War. He had just published an article on his wartime experiences in the *Atlantic,* and another was already scheduled for July—the first issue under the editorship of James T. Fields. His notes for a third such article appeared at the end of a ten-page eulogy by George William Curtis, the veteran *Atlantic* contributor who was Major Winthrop's close friend and literary executor. Curtis had by then given Fields a thick file of Major Winthrop's other manuscripts; and as his sister Laura Winthrop Johnson put it decades later, Ticknor and Fields became the "tender and enthusiastic friends and guardians of his name and fame."[1]

Within two years after Major Winthrop's death, five Ticknor and Fields books bore his name. In swift succession, Fields issued three of his novels—*Cecil Dreeme* (1861), *John Brent* (1862), and *Edwin Brothertoft* (1862); the 1862 *Atlantic* included two of his short stories, several lively travel sketches, and a poem about him; and two collections of his travel sketches appeared in 1863—*The Canoe and the Saddle* and *Life in the Open Air.* Fields's promotion of Winthrop supported the Union cause while expanding the hero's posthumous fame. Each of Winthrop's books went through numerous editions, some of them illustrated, with *John Brent* the best seller.[2]

A year after Major Winthrop's death, his sister Laura Winthrop Johnson—an otherwise unknown Staten Island housewife and minor poet—became one of Annie Fields's closest friends. Her circle and Annie's included many of the same New York literati, William Cullen Bryant, N. P. Willis, and Curtis among them. But for Laura, Annie was only incidentally the wife of the famous editor; and for Annie, Laura was not primarily a writer to be cultivated. During the summer of 1862, when Winthrop's reputation was at its height, Annie invited Laura Johnson to Charles Street. Addressing Annie as her "Dear Friend" soon afterward, Laura self-consciously asked "why should I not call you so?" and then announced her hope of perfecting their friendship.[3] Over the next twenty-seven years, primarily through letters, the two women shared their daily lives and served as each other's confidantes.

That relationship enriched both women but was central to Laura's life. "I write freely to no one else but you," she once confessed, assuring Annie that "every thing you can say is precious to me" and that "my correspondence with you takes the place of society."[4] Toward the end of the Civil War, Laura sent Annie a poem simply titled "To A.F.," which she would publish a decade later in her *Poems of Twenty Years*. "I have shed some bitter tears," the speaker confesses in the first stanza, which concludes "Thou knowest why, my friend!" The second stanza asserts her patriotic pride, and also concludes, "Thou knowest why, my friend!" But the third and last stanza end with an extraordinary tribute to A.F.: the sorrowful war years were blessed "Because upon their changeful track / They brought to me a friend!"[5] Each of Laura's visits to Annie and Annie's much rarer visits to her was stretched by anticipation and retrospect. "When I am with you, dear Annie," Laura once assured her, "I am a better and happier woman."[6]

"We were of course much interested to get Miss Winthrop to talk of her brother," Ralph Waldo Emerson's daughter Ellen told her aunt Susan after meeting Laura at Charles Street in January 1865. "I had no idea how much our, and especially Father's admiration and affection for him pleased her till she told us this story." The story was of Theodore Winthrop's joy at his first letter of acceptance from the *Atlantic*.[7]

One of Laura's first letters to Annie enclosed several poems, "some of them an intimate part of myself," and the poems she received from Annie became "dear companions in my loneliness."[8] Because Laura had an affectionate family and many friends, the word "loneliness" might seem curious; but it suggests Annie's immediate importance to her. She read and reread each poem Annie sent, feeling proprietary pride whenever she saw one in print. And at least once—in the winter of 1864—Annie admired one of Laura's poems enough to show it to her husband. Laura then made a few "improvements"; and "On Picket Duty"—the meditations of a Union soldier presented in twenty-eight terza rima stanzas— appeared in the *Atlantic* that April.

It was the only poem by Laura that Jamie published. Speaking for him, and on grounds of the high publishing costs in wartime, Annie turned down a volume of Laura's poems. Laura simply said she was not surprised, though she had better luck with a New York publisher a decade later. Her *Poems of Twenty Years* appeared in 1874, "On Picket Duty" among them, directly followed by the loving tribute "To A. F."[9]

The following year Annie played an indirect role in a more unusual publication. When Laura was planning a trip to Wyoming, Annie urged her to keep a detailed travel journal. Laura did so and then sent it to Annie, who encouraged her to publish it. Laura's account of traveling "where no white women had ever gone" before—in a group of twelve that included five other women and three children—appeared in *Lippincott's Magazine* in June and July of 1875, titled "800 Miles in an Ambulance." It still has historical as well as literary interest, particularly for its detailed descriptions of forts and Indian agencies, of Indian chiefs including Red Cloud and Sitting Bull, and of rituals including the Sun Dance. Her descriptions of sublime western landscapes are arresting, especially in her concluding account of a weeklong "picnic" on Laramie Peak.[10]

Laura's final publication was *The Life and Poems of Theodore Winthrop* (1884), which presented her brother as the quintessential Civil War hero, a spiritually aspiring individual who was destroyed in his prime, "the representative man of the hour, the representative of the promise, beauty, culture, and patriotism that were crowding to the front." His (and of course her) eminent ancestors included John Winthrop and Jonathan Edwards; President Theodore Dwight Woolsey of Yale was their uncle, and their family included six other college presidents. Reared in New Haven, they had left for Staten Island after their father died, and joined a congenial community that included George Curtis and the young painter Frederic Church. But Laura's *Life* focuses on the dozen travel-filled years between her brother's graduation from Yale and his enlistment in the army, presented primarily through his letters, journals, and poems.[11]

In his introduction to the posthumously published book version of *800 Miles in an Ambulance* (1889), George Curtis described Laura Winthrop Johnson as an ideal nineteenth-century woman—a woman with "catholic sympathies" and high intelligence who maintained a lovely home and a lovely garden, a serenely beautiful wife and mother who even at sixty retained "the aspect of her blooming prime," a woman empowered by education and taste "to appreciate the best in literature and art." Except for Annie's childlessness, Curtis might have been describing Annie Adams Fields. Despite the huge differences between her privileged life at the center of Boston's cultural world and Laura's self-described monotonous one on rural Staten Island, the two women were alike in their humanitarian concerns, domestic ideals, cultural values, and quest for self-perfection.

That each expanded the other's sense of self is clearly evident from their ongoing exchanges about contemporary literature. Though Annie had readier access to new publications, Laura was equally confident in pronouncing literary judgments. Lowell had not fulfilled his "youthful promise," she once declared; she disliked Mrs. Browning's "great egotism and pedantry"; Harriet Prescott's "Amber Gods" was "smut"; Gail Hamilton was sometimes "downright silly"; and *Pink and White Tyranny* made her conclude that Stowe's "good people are such bores." Most of her broader generalizations are at least equally provocative, as when she compared George Sand's novels to George Eliot's, or declared that James's and Howells's heroines "seem the girls of Miss Alcott and Mrs. Whitman, grown up & masculinized."[12]

Annie enjoyed agreeing with Laura, as when she exclaimed, "You are right about Thoreau! How inexhaustible and inspiring he is!" A related pleasure was sharing her insider's knowledge of writers and their writings. In that same letter, for example, Annie said the Longfellow poem Laura had enclosed struck her strangely because the celebrated ballad singer William Dempster had sung it at Charles Street and repeated the performance for Longfellow, and she then complained that Robert Browning had not even mentioned the Civil War in his new book. Aware of Laura's enthusiasm for Emerson, she also copied out a passage from Menander that he had quoted in "Domestic Life." She later sent Laura an Emerson autograph, and later still a more remarkably solicitous gift: a thirty-six-page summary of "The Natural History of Intellect," the sixteen lectures that Emerson gave at Harvard in the spring of 1870. It was her "happiness to be one of the 30" who heard them, Annie told Laura, certain she "could send you nothing in my letters (apart from home news always) which you will enjoy more than bits of these lectures."[13]

Sharing her judgments with Laura was often a way of refining them. She said about George Eliot, "I do not call her distinctively a woman of imagination—but it is a kind of wide fine intellectual ability combined with the insight of a great and suffering woman, *who has lived.*" Turning to John Ruskin, she said he "seems to be getting lost among the eccentricities his own fancy has evolved" in "Ecce Homo," and she liked him "less in the 'Wild Olives' than ever before." She also vented complaints about writers she admired, as when she said Matthew Arnold's *Literature and Dogma* was beautiful in spirit but too drawn out. More surprisingly, she read Walt Whitman "with a virile delight," astonished by the "glorious doctrine and soul-music if not body-music his lines make."[14]

Annie often recommended new books by writers they both admired. Hawthorne's "Septimius, the story of a deathless man" was "autobiographic" and serenely wise, she told Laura. If the writer was a woman, Annie's recommendations were often imperatives. "The book is an era," Annie exclaimed right after reading *Middlemarch* in 1874, urging Laura to get a copy; and when Elizabeth Stuart Phelps's second novel was published three years later, she simply inquired, "Did you read Avis?"[15]

Yet arguably Annie's greatest literary gift to Laura was vicarious participation in the lives of writers they both admired. She told Laura all about Hawthorne's last visits to Charles Street, for example, and gave a detailed account of his funeral.[16] All Laura could contribute in kind was a disconcerting bit of secondhand gossip: her neighbor Mrs. Shaw "did not like or think well of [Hawthorne] on acct of his engagement to Miss E.P. his sister in law. We will talk about this when we meet."[17] But whether Annie was reporting the good news of Edith Longfellow's engagement to Richard Henry Dana Jr. or sad news about Emerson's fading memory or Longfellow's rheumatism, she was sharing her own privileged entry into the domestic lives of New England literati.

The women's mutuality is clearest in their personal exchanges, however, Laura's in particular. In September 1864, for example, Laura told her "Dear Love" what she had often written before: "Your letters are my joy and my comfort at all times." In that same spirit, she insisted soon afterward that "You cannot write me too much of your own life—tell me everything, who & what you see, what you read, think, and do. Even the color of your bonnet is interesting to me!" Like Rebecca Harding and Harriet Beecher Stowe, Laura also requested recipes, on one occasion Annie's "recipe for chowder and also that nice fruit pudding you have sometimes made of bread and berries." She recounted dreams of being with Annie, and she once announced her desire to found a colony that would include "you two, the Shaws Dr. Holmes Mr. Emerson Tom Appleton George Curtis and a few others." All in all, Laura explained near the end of her life, she lived two very different lives through Annie, "one of external, outside social pleasure, and communication with nature and art, and one of inward life, friendship and sympathy with what is deepest and best for my soul and heart."[18]

Annie returned Laura's affection and admiration, if not as fully. She marveled that the woman who was nine years her senior seemed "all youth and life and love a little creature half veiled to this world or to herself," and nonetheless managed to be "sprightly sweet a devoted wife mother gardener housekeeper." She felt "rich, rich beyond all possibility of poverty in this world where 'Love is all in all,'" she told Laura after reading her grief-stricken poems and letters about her sister's death. "Nothing will bring us to a better comprehension of each other than such unveiling." Yet she rarely risked such unveiling herself. At one point when Laura asked to see some of her recent poems, for example, Annie simply said they were too "fragmentary."

There were other problems. When Annie sent Laura a copy of *Asphodel* without telling her who wrote it, Laura made a "provoking" comment in a letter that has not survived. But in her next letter, Laura soothingly attributed that comment to a hasty reading, promised to reread the novel many times, and assured Annie that "many things in it . . . made me think of you."[19] A greater vexation was Laura's "cumbrous" husband, who sometimes accompanied her to Charles Street, a man Annie thought had little to recommend him "but his good principles." After his death in 1869, Laura herself sometimes seemed cumbrous. During one of her visits when she was struggling with a crisis of religious faith, Annie felt entrapped in "long wasteful sessions of talk" that left her utterly depressed. Similarly, she felt trapped when Laura "asked to be asked" to Manchester in the summer of 1873 and arrived ahead of time with her emotionally disturbed daughter Bessie. Worse still, their departure was delayed by a storm. "I have made a resolution not to ask them again," Annie huffily wrote in her journal. "People who are always ready to visit, are people one seldom wishes to see." Even so, Annie admired the woman whose "devotion to her queer nervous daughter Bessie is so perfect and so wise" and reminded herself that they had all made a "cheerful circle" during the storm.

If Annie was not then or ever entirely frank with Laura, she was more so than with any other friend but Sarah Orne Jewett. When Boylston Adams was missing in action in 1864, for example, Annie told Laura how worried she was, and two years later she bragged that Louisa Beal's baby was beginning to talk. She also exulted with Laura about Lissie Adams's imminent return from Europe—"my sweet precious sister, whom you are yet to know"; and after the two women met, she reported each new development in Lissie's life. More important, to no other friend did Annie admit how helpless she felt during her mother's final illness; and to no one else did she confide her anxieties about Jamie's health or her despair after he died.

It was of course easier to celebrate other women's accomplishments. She reported to Laura that their mutual friend Anna Leonowens's lecture on Buddha improved with each delivery, and that Anne Whitney's statue of Samuel Adams was ready for exhibition and already winning high praise. "What a portrait bust that woman makes!" Annie exulted. "I know no one her superior!" Similarly, she rejoiced in Charlotte Cushman's theatrical triumphs and in the "striving restless intelligence" of the civic reformer Zena Fay Pierce. And after organizing a "small club of ladies interested in literature" who gathered at Charles Street "every Tuesday each one to read something of her own," she bragged that Elizabeth Stuart Phelps, Celia Thaxter, Harriet Beecher Stowe, and Lucy Larcom had already presented new work, "and so the ball rolls on." Proud of all such women, she compared the "wonderful circle" that included Caroline Sturgis, Anna Shaw, Margaret Fuller, and Elizabeth Peabody to "the famous Weimar women," and she said Madame Récamier's "power was so essentially womanly, so much of it the result of sweetness of character and unselfishness that I think the tale can never be too often retold."[20]

A corollary was lamenting any constraints on women, including the constraints of high fashion and the obligations of housekeeping. When a dressmaker designed underclothing without heavy stays and lacings, Annie gleefully assured Laura she would "do much to emancipate the race." When Laura felt overburdened by housework, Annie advised her to enlist her daughter's help, then philosophized, "We can never accomplish much if we allow ourselves to make our homes too nice." And as one happily married woman to another, Annie could worry that a friend who was engaged to an army officer might become repelled by his smoking and heavy drinking; she could sympathize with a new widow as a "poor lonely bird"; and she could denounce Mrs. William Morris Hunt for closing her husband out of her life.[21]

Annie could even share domestic trivia with Laura, as when she wrote with more amusement than distress that a clumsy burglar who entered her house "took nothing and was himself caught." And from the moment the Fieldses acquired the "bit of land" in Manchester where they would build Gambrel Cottage, Laura was in on the details. The owner was eager to sell during the depression of 1873 and they happened to have "a few hundreds," Annie reported, then said they would economize by building a wooden cottage instead of a brick house and by buying secondhand furniture. Occasionally she complained about her new responsibilities. "The cottage won't build itself so I must go down," she told Laura in 1875, adding, "I do not like building. I knew I should not." She later admitted to the difficulties of country hospitality, whimsically wishing someone else would "run the house—on noiseless wheels," and she once said she and Jamie were thinking of selling it, though "I fear Jamie will be sorry."[22]

She also kept Laura informed about her philanthropic enterprises. In December 1871, for example, she told Laura that five Holly Tree coffee rooms offering workers alternatives to barrooms were already under her "banner and care." The following year when her home for working women was inaugurated, Annie exulted that the residents lived comfortably for a dollar or less a week. She similarly reported her initiatives in the aftermath of Boston's devastating fire in November 1872, which included visiting unemployed sewing women "in their places of abode and judging as well as I can what to do for them, . . . and listening to doleful cases or exhorting promising ones, all day long"; and she reported opening a factory that made "women's suits, children's clothes, aprons, and useful articles" to supply "the deficient market."[23]

Perhaps not even her husband knew as much as Laura about all the philanthropic projects Annie worked on or contemplated in the seventies. As one practical reformer to another, she once asked Laura if she knew anyone "who can *think* out a laundry," and she consulted Laura about training women to work in "households which need relief."[24] She also sent news of her centennial work, her settlement house work, and such personal beneficences as housing the motherless eight-year-old Esther Albee at Charles Street for a winter and the homeless Imogen Eddy and her daughter at Manchester for a summer.

Occasionally Annie also shared purely personal frustrations. In January 1867, for example, she said she was withdrawing from a ladies' social club not because "I feel older or like people less but because I like them more and it hurts me to meet them too often on what seems to me a false basis." Sometimes she admitted to weariness, as when she decided not to attend Concord's centennial celebration in April 1875 because she felt drained by her work for "the poor hanging at our skirts," or when her efforts to restore the Old South Church made her "wish the Old South was in the Red Sea."[25]

Such bright bits of comic candor testify to easy intimacy. Her nephews thought a bat in Anna Leonowens's room "was a part of her weird life"; Charles Sumner's pictures were for sale but seemed "of the kind to be pushed out the attic window"; and she once saw "naked ballet girls who could not, for the most part, dance, expose themselves to a vulgar audience, chiefly of men." But far more surprising is Annie's wry admission to vanity on the occasion of her forty-sixth birthday: "Being the birthday time I must confess this year to becoming fully convinced as to being the 'same age as other folks.' It has taken me a long time, but the serious work and experiences of the past year and the many grey hairs break the subject clearly though tenderly."[26]

For over twenty-five years, Annie's friendship with Laura was an ongoing fact of her life. She told Laura "how sincerely and entirely I feel you to be mine" only two years after they met; and time and again she expressed gratitude for Laura's "strong untiring friendship of which I feel myself unworthy," as when she urged in 1870, "take my dearest love and constant faith dear Laura and remember sometimes when you think of me what a precious gift I consider your friendship to be." Even more explicitly pious was the conclusion of an 1874 letter: "God bless you, dear Laura. He only knows how much we all need friendship such as yours, how much we depend on its fidelity." Much more self-consciously, Annie sometimes used the rhetoric of romantic love, as when she signed herself "yours *as* ever and *for* ever" (just as Laura once called herself a "fervent & adoring lover" and feared "JTF will sometime send me a book with poisoned leaves, a la Medici"). "Because my own pleasures are in a degree pleasures of yours also," Annie regularly reported on her anniversary celebrations; and the Fieldses' twentieth anniversary was an occasion to wish "for my sake, that you lived in Boston" and to declare "What a happy thing to have had so much love as we both have and to know it is not dead."[27]

Among the women's other regular exchanges, Laura sent a "barrel of plants" to Charles Street each spring; Annie usually wrote to Laura on Sundays; and she followed an invitation to Manchester by remarking, "We like to make a point of August don't we? Every year?" Not surprisingly, each birthday was an occasion for a poem. The poem Annie composed in September 1865, simply titled "Laura's Birthday," begins with the speaker "Watching the sunset, you, in thought, with me." The following September, after regretting that her birthday verses were not decorated as the previous year's had been, Annie said Jamie thought the newer verses were better, "so I send them with my love in them and wish they were better than they are." She was evidently even prouder of the 1867 "Ode to Laura," which concludes by flattering them both:

> Were it not always morning with true love
> I would not write thus for thy festival
> Dear Laura, while these noon-day foot-steps rove
> Among dead clover and the falling fruit;
> I would be silent as noon birds are mute,
> But thou, sweet Love, hast made me musical.

By 1873, the birthday exchange had gone on so long that it seemed "ancient"; and the next year's well-turned birthday poem sounded a note of piously sentimental resignation: "You and I a year / Have gained toward the solemn shore, / Where love shall live forevermore." Still more poignant is "To L.W.J., on her birthday, September 13, 1878"—the only birthday poem Annie included in her 1895 collection *The Singing Shepherd*—, which gracefully if conventionally links Laura to the season of plenitude when "all things wear the tender light / Love wears before it vanisheth."[28]

An undated fragment of a letter to "Dear Laura" addresses an ideal other: "I believe no number of sheets would satisfy me to write to you for all my talk is but the fringe of speech I wish to have with you—And yet the meaning of all I could write would be only this, love me and hold us in your thoughts as I do you & yours. I think of your calm presence oftener than you will believe." Annie never even hinted at such painful subjects as her yearning for motherhood, however; and her New Year's Day letter in 1884 only obliquely conveys her complete sense of union with another woman: "We are sitting at home writing this evening, Miss Jewett and I, while the whole world outside melts and drips and seems to be dissolving utterly away."[29]

Five years later, a letter arrived from Staten Island on which Annie penciled a moving farewell: "My last letter from Laura! Her body was laid in Greenwood Cemetery—Jan 15. Peace! Peace to you my beloved!" As Laura tenderly wrote, "You seem dear, to have found some higher, or more spiritual life that comforts you, but I find my daily life beautiful and clear, and so do you, though it is better than mine. But we must take things as they come." That last letter expresses the sympathetic admiration and humble self-acceptance that had sustained Laura's relationship with Annie for more than twenty-five years. With no hint of envy, Laura wished Annie and "Miss Jewett" a Happy New Year, and then pronounced herself "Yours as ever with a heart full of love."[30]

Portrait of Annie Adams Fields by Richard Rothwell (c. 1854). *Courtesy of Nancy Adams Bole.*

Daguerreotype of Annie Adams Fields by Southworth and Hawes (1861). *Courtesy of the Metropolitan Museum of Art, gift of I. N. Phelps Stokes, Edward S. Hawes, Alice Mary Hawes, and Marion Augusta Hawes, 1937. (37.14.27).*

Daguerreotype of James T. Fields by Southworth and Hawes (1861). *Courtesy of the Metropolitan Museum of Art, gift of I. N. Phelps Stokes, Edward S. Hawes, Alice Mary Hawes, and Marion Augusta Hawes, 1937. (37.14.36).*

Engraving of James T. Fields, presumably based on a
photograph by Julia Margaret Cameron (1869).

Pencil drawing of Annie Adams Fields by Elizabeth Adams (c. 1866). *Courtesy of the Boston Athenaeum.*

Annie Adams Fields and Sarah Orne Jewett in the Charles Street library. *Courtesy of the Society for the Preservation of New England Antiquities.*

Annie Adams Fields on the piazza of Gambrel Cottage in Manchester, Massachusetts. *Courtesy of the Society for the Preservation of New England Antiquities.*

Photograph of Sarah Orne Jewett. As reproduced in M. A. DeWolfe Howe, *Memories of a Hostess . . .* (1922).

Portrait of Annie Adams Fields by John Singer Sargent (1890). *Courtesy of the Boston Athenaeum.*

SECTION III
Loss and Consolidation

13

The Changing Panorama

Resignation and Recovery

In the fall of 1869, soon after the Fieldses returned from their second trip abroad, Annie wrote in her journal, "Jamie very sad—he is too young for this but—." Her incomplete sentence betrays her sense of helplessness. Jamie had fallen into a depression. Despite her best efforts to cheer him by keeping their home "bright" and inviting old friends to dine, he continued to be—as she delicately told Laura Johnson—not "altogether well." "We were in trouble about our affairs," she mused a year later, "but far worse than that was the trouble I felt about my dear love who seemed breaking in spirit and energy under his afflicting load. I was filled with grief and sadly in need of occupations all my old habits having been broken up by our long tour."

The country's financial instability at that time was one cause of her husband's problems. Though money matters rarely surface in Annie's journals, in November she noted the country's financial crisis; and the following March she lamented the sharp drop in the price of gold: "No man can see the end of this sudden downfall. The business world is sadly depressed and wavering—Men know not what to do—." All she herself could do was "trim sails" by deferring household repairs and reducing her household staff.

Her brief account of that dark time in her *Biographical Notes* poignantly acknowledges her husband's physical and emotional collapse: "In the winter of 1870 Mr. Fields's health began to give way. The voyages, the excitement of travel, and his return to business responsibilities, proved too much even for his excellent constitution. His sleep was broken and his spirits suffered. He who had been the life of every feast was often silent and fatigued. His strength seemed to fade away from him, and after any little exertion or excitement he would fall asleep from utter exhaustion. That winter was like a valley of shadows which led us in June to Dickens's grave."[1]

It is hardly surprising that her own spirits suffered. Even the pleasures of "family dining" with Longfellow were contaminated by Annie's recollection of how she had missed him while they were on separate continents; and after a lively dinner party that included Emerson, Dana, and Henry James Sr., she ruefully remarked that she was grateful for "all we have and all we enjoy" but had no desire to record her famous guests' conversational "tidbits." Concerned about her own lethargy, she launched an ambitious self-improvement program that included reading Saint-Simon, Pepys, Homer, and Longfellow's Dante, but soon abandoned it. At a meeting of the new Radical Club, she heard only "vague talk and restless expression of self without any high end being furthered"; and the "high enthusiasms" at an organizational meeting of the Working Women's Club became chilled when Julia Ward Howe entered like a whirlwind spluttering egocentric complaints. By then, Annie could anticipate Christmas only because "much could be done to make it beautiful for others"; and Dickens's death the following June seemed almost unbearable.

The darkest year in the Fieldses' lives concluded when Jamie completed arrangements to sell all his interests in Fields, Osgood and Company. "J is no longer to bear the weight of this great business house on his shoulders," Annie exulted in November 1870, "and he is to occupy himself altogether with literature. He seems like a different man already from last year. And I am too happy to be able to think it over yet."[2]

Busy though she was, Annie had already consulted her "poor little diary with all its imperfection" for material Jamie could use for a new *Atlantic* essay, specifically "for notes of Hawthorne which I found very scanty." The explanation was simple: when she had "the great men and women inside my doors of whom I should best love to record, I am often too much occupied with household affairs to have even my ordinary weight into things said and done." Her family was another ongoing occupation. The Fieldses often visited Mrs. Adams and Sarah in Roxbury and more often entertained them at Charles Street, they dined with the Beals almost weekly and sometimes babysat their "two beautiful boys who are the delight of our hearts," and Boylston was "married from here" in December 1870.

By contrast, Annie rarely even mentioned George Fields and his family. They were "in a sad strait" when Jamie called on them after lecturing at Dartmouth in June 1874, "having carelessly gone on spending what money they have and making no effort to get any until they find themselves absolutely poor. For there are two sons and a husband and only the one poor little wife and mother to represent womankind and they cannot starve. . . ." Quarterly payments to "G. A. Fields" appear in James T. Fields's ledger book afterward, and Jamie's efforts to keep his brother "from despair" even included buying him a burial plot at Mount Auburn Cemetery. Annie's contemptuous 1874 entry would have no sequel. But she reaffirmed what remained central to her existence: "We are very happy to be together more more [*sic*] dear J and I. The time was very long while he was gone."

Meantime, her own schedule was remarkably full. Trying to account for a two-week gap in her journal in March 1872, she said "the most interesting events and people have been passing before me but I am so much a part of the panorama as to have no time left to stand apart and observe." During those two weeks she attended a Christine Nilsson concert, a series of lectures by her friend Robert Collyer, and two weddings. Henry James Sr. read his paper on Emerson to a "brilliant company" of thirty-three in her library a week earlier; and her houseguest Anna Leonowens delivered two public lectures that Annie herself had helped arrange. Annie also wrote a few poems including "Little Guinever" (one of Longfellow's favorites and later Willa Cather's). But at least equally important was her burgeoning identity as a philanthropic entrepreneur.[3]

During a single representative week in 1872, Annie attended a meeting at the settlement house called the North End Mission to help arrange Sunday excursions for poor children, inspected a new working women's residence that she had inaugurated, and marked the anniversary of Dickens's death by bringing flowers to workers' coffee houses. The following week she visited a "poor sick girl" who refused to be hospitalized unless her young daughter was cared for, promised to get her work after she recovered, sent her clothes, and offered to care for the child herself. She felt disappointed when the child was "kidnapped" by her father.

In many ways, Annie and Jamie grew closer after he retired. At his desk in the library, he produced lectures and essays that he tried out on his wife; at her own desk she copied out passages from her journals for him to use in those essays; and she suggested that he organize the series of lectures on literature addressed to women that eventuated in the founding of Radcliffe College. He often accompanied her to meetings of the New England Woman's Club, and sometimes he even shopped for dresses with her. He also enjoyed fussing over her birthdays. In June 1871 he presented her with a Chickering piano, and the following year he honored her with an elaborate birthday dinner that began with lamb "a la Elia."[4] Their age difference diminished as Annie moved into middle age, and they could as easily discuss financial issues, housing reforms, guest lists, and each other's manuscripts.

Philanthropic Initiatives

At the end of 1870, as James T. Fields prepared to retire from publishing, his wife initiated a new project. "I am entirely filled with my endeavor to form a coffeehouse to counteract whiskey drinking," Annie wrote in her journal on 13 November 1870, then piously added, "God knows if I shall succeed." But the woman who is still known as "a principal leader" of Boston's charity reforms was vigorous and innovative from the start.[5] Her coffee house endeavor was rooted in the temperance movement and her prior volunteer work at the North End Mission, but also in her roles as a housewife and hostess. Her plan was simple, though working out the details stretched her old skills and demanded new ones. Not only did she have to define the project but budget it, raise start-up funds, locate suitable space in a working-class neighborhood, purchase furniture and equipment, and hire a responsible manager.

Setting genteel reticence aside, Annie discussed her project with such male eminences as Emerson and Whittier and petitioned wealthier friends including Tom Appleton for contributions. Her arguments were clear and persuasive. A worker would pay a nickel for a good cup of coffee, especially in a comfortable place where he was treated with dignity; and because the coffee house would stay open late, it would offer refuge from crowded living quarters that only barrooms had provided before. Moreover, because the worker would spend very little in the coffee house and return home sober, his family would benefit.

In December 1870, Annie opened her first Holly Tree Coffee House; and when Harriet Beecher Stowe came to Charles Street on New Year's Day, she gave that venture a high place "in the good work of the period." By then Annie had promoted her plan beyond her own circles of friends; and on January 25 "the city fathers waited upon me and hope to establish coffee houses all over the city at '5 cents a cup.'"

The name was inspired by Dickens. His Boston readings at the end of 1867 had included a cheerful Christmas story about warm relationships that cross class divisions, titled "Boots at the Holly Tree Inn"; and the central image of Annie Fields's elegy for Dickens had been the beneficent holly tree at his graveside. Assured of the active cooperation of the "city fathers," Annie shrewdly negotiated arrangements that included six months rent free for one of the new coffee houses, and well-wishers contributed sums ranging from five dollars to two hundred. Five Holly Trees would be under her care within a year, each of them serving not only coffee but wholesome and inexpensive food.[6]

To mark the first anniversary of Dickens's death in June 1871, Annie cut flowers from her garden to bring to her first Holly Tree. By then a second was assured: she had already raised the money and found a suitable location, and a policeman had dropped by to say he had found a good man to run it. "You must be a very happy woman," Holmes told her after visiting the first Holly Tree, confiding that he had been moved to tears by her accomplishment. She then announced that a second coffee house, which she had been working on all week, would open in a few days.

Soon articles about the Holly Trees appeared in newspapers and magazines across the country (including an article by Annie and another by Harriet Beecher Stowe in the *Christian Union*), and inquiries from would-be emulators flooded in.[7] When the first of three Holly Trees opened in Chicago in June 1872, local newspapers praised the attractive restaurant for its good food, nonalcoholic drinks, and nominal cost, then praised Mrs. James T. Fields for originating the plan and for advising the local organizers.[8] Over the next few years, dozens of other Holly Trees opened in other cities, many of them after consultation with Annie. In April

1874, Kate Field wrote an enthusiastic article about them for the *New York Herald Tribune,* abiding by Annie's instructions to stress the project and not the projector. Gratifyingly, it "stirred a new wave of interest."

Annie intended her Holly Trees to be self-supporting, and all but one soon were. Moving swiftly and confidently into male territory, she became an efficient entrepreneur without breaching womanly propriety. Admittedly, her coffee houses did not address basic economic problems; but she had found an easy and easily imitated way to ease workers' lives.[9]

A year after her first Holly Tree opened, Annie inaugurated a more ambitious project—a residence for unmarried working women in Boston's North End that she hoped would be the model for others "in our large cities, where women *cannot afford to live honestly* on the sums they receive in the shops for work." Residents paid a dollar a week or less for comfortable lodgings, and a coffee room on the premises served good but inexpensive meals.[10] Annie hired a manager to run its day-to-day operations, but retained supervisory control until everything ran smoothly. She did even more.

The Lincoln Street Home was inaugurated during Christmas Week of 1871 with an elaborate program Annie prepared. Anna Caswell offered a prayer, Harriet Beecher Stowe read one of her stories, Lucy Larcom sang a hymn she wrote for the occasion, Sunday school children sang Christmas songs, and Mary Livermore sent a congratulatory letter that was read aloud. Trying to make the residents' lives at least somewhat approximate her own, Annie had hung pictures on the walls and decorated the place with evergreens. To her great delight, the "tradegirls" invited "the ladies to their home" the following week, most of them accepted, they all had tea in the coffee room, and everyone "had a very merry time."

By then Annie felt no anxiety about the project: "I never do about things so good and so much needed," she told Laura Johnson.[11] But because she had a few misgivings about the manager a few months later, she asked her friend Abby Diaz to move in as a kind of undercover agent, then "bestirred" herself to address the problems Diaz uncovered. She monitored room charges to make sure they were not excessive, for example, and she even prepared the menus. Determined to enrich the residents' lives, Annie also arranged concerts, lectures, and parties for them, including a sparsely attended May Day party. She had never suspected that some of the residents might have other priorities, but her mood lightened when Mrs. Claflin arrived with flowers, and Mrs. Diaz was on hand to keep the entire group cheerful.

All went well until November 1872, when the worst fire in the history of New England devastated sixty-five acres of downtown Boston, damaged the house, and threw the residents out of work. Driven by strong winds, the fire lasted for three days and left hundreds of people homeless and unemployed. Publishers were "in a bad way," Annie noted in her diary, feeling lucky that her husband had retired.

The residents of the Lincoln Street Home had managed to save it from total destruction by wetting down the roof and throwing off firebrands. But it was Annie who kept the home going. First, she had to persuade the owner of the damaged building not to convert it to a warehouse. Next came an urgent appeal to Otis Norcross, a former mayor of Boston who had been authorized by the Fire Commissioners to dispense emergency funds:

> There is immediate want of assistance for "The Working Women's Home" in Lincoln Street, an establishment for boarding and lodging poor women who go out to work and have no other home, not being able to afford any other on account of their small wages. The fire injured the house badly, and has almost broken up the establishment as many of the girls having not a cent left, and being thrown out of employment by the fire have no means even of paying the small board they have been accustomed to pay. Consequently . . . I beg you will consider the propriety of asking in our behalf an appropriation of two or three hundred dollars to keep up the plan till we can see better days.

The letter is marked "Approved for two hundred dollars."[12]

By then Annie was working within but also beyond the city's established relief organizations, and not only for the Lincoln Street Home and its residents. Because the mayor had turned out to be "a timid poor creature" unable to cope with the disaster, she felt impelled to do whatever she herself could for the fire victims. "I never wished so heartily to be two women!" she told Laura Johnson, complaining that she had been housebound by laryngitis after interviewing clients "in the cold bad air of the Relief rooms."[13] As one small but characteristic form of help, she provided a free dinner for the "poor creatures" of the North End. "I never saw anyone eat in a more determined and unending fashion," Annie wrote in her diary. "There was enough for them to carry away also."

Another effort would be more consequential. In order to feel closer to the unemployed and better assess their needs, though also to escape the discomfort of the relief rooms, Annie started visiting them at home (a procedure that would be fundamental to the Cooperative Society of Visitors which she would start in 1875). Though several of her clients did not "excite sympathy," she believed "sympathetic help" could enlarge their "capacity and experience" and change the current of their lives.[14] Her first priority was to find—and sometimes even create— appropriate work for them. "Continuous work on the Relief Committee prevents me from coming to see you," she told a friend from Maine who was visiting Boston, then gave her the names of two women who wanted to "live out" with their employer, and "would be so glad of the chance to go with you."[15]

But her most unusual initiative in the aftermath of the Great Fire was founding and investing some of her own money in a clothing factory in February 1873. Though only thirty of the many women who swarmed in could be hired, "this is better than nothing and I trust it is a beginning," Annie told Laura; "—there never was such suffering among the poor before in Boston as just now when the Relief

Committee consider their work 'drawing to a close.'" As she then explained, "We are making women's suits, children's clothes, aprons, and useful articles *for the shops,* coming into competition with nobody but simply supplying the deficient market. I found a dressmaker to undertake the work, who is an old adherent of mine and we are working on co-operative principles. She is as much interested in the girls as I am: at the same time she may herself in the end reap a benefit from this new business. In any event she cannot fail to get back what she has put in." Some of the girls seemed inept but most were "first rate," and a "lady from Salem" helped pay off some of the initial debts.[16]

A year and a half later, however, when Annie was no longer overseeing the factory, her "old adherent" Mrs. Murphy ran into financial trouble and thought Annie should bail her out. After sending a threatening letter demanding money, she showed up in Manchester when Jamie happened to be in Boston. "Imagine my agony," Annie told Laura Johnson: fearing a violent scene, she had cowered inside until Jamie returned. He then talked to Mrs. Murphy and got her to apologize, loaned her $200 to pay off her creditors, and sent her away satisfied. Enormously relieved, Annie could now sympathize with Mrs. Murphy as a woman who had led a "dreary" life" with a "hard" husband.[17] Although she felt ridiculous while hiding from Mrs. Murphy, and although her banker brother-in-law assured her that silent partnerships like hers rarely succeed, Annie Fields merits praise for conceiving and launching the clothing factory. She had moved resourcefully, sensibly, generously, and even daringly at a time of public crisis to provide useful work for dozens of women, Mrs. Murphy among them.

Moreover, all her other initiatives on behalf of the working poor continued to thrive. Shortly before Mrs. Murphy arrived on her doorstep, on her own fortieth birthday, Annie inspected a new working women's residence on Edinboro Street on the plan of the Lincoln Street Home, relieved to see that it was clean and efficiently managed by a right-minded if somewhat "nigh" woman. Although the "quiet refuge" had not yet become self-supporting by the fall, Annie had the comfort of knowing that similar establishments were already earning their way in and beyond Boston.

The following summer, with her friend Mary Lodge, Annie began planning what would be her most ambitious effort to alleviate workers' problems, through an organization they called the Cooperative Society of Visitors. Their motto was "not alms but a friend." Her visits to the homes of sewing women who were thrown out of work by the great Boston fire had convinced her that "sympathetic treatment" combined with practical help could enable most if not all of them to take charge of their own lives. Now setting her sights higher, she planned to organize a corps of visitors who would be subdivided into district committees and trained to visit the urban poor, ascertain their needs, find or even create appropriate jobs for them, and arrange for whatever instruction or other practical help they needed. Each committee would also meet regularly to pool experiences and exchange advice. The Cooperative Society worked well from the start; and Annie remained at the helm when it was consolidated into the Associated Charities of Boston four years later.[18]

Annie's many other social welfare initiatives of the seventies include an address to the New England Woman's Club which eventuated in the Cooperative Building Committee to investigate "homes for the poor," an influential committee on which she served.[19] That same imperative of service explains why Annie undertook to nurse her chambermaid Maggie when she became terminally ill in June 1871, a task her other servants feared to assume. And because her neighbor Mrs. Dorr seemed exclusively interested in dinner parties and "mere" socializing, Annie simply wrote her off as "a flea on the body of society."

Meantime she continued to move along well-worn paths of self-fulfillment as well as service. She attended all Emerson's public lectures and many of her husband's; she suggested the series of Conversations on Literature that Emerson delivered at Mechanics' Hall in April 1872 (and even the title); she studied philosophy with one woman friend and German with another; she wrote and published poems; she read challenging new books; she corresponded with scores of friends; she did a lot of traveling and a lot of entertaining. But whatever she did, her primary identity was Mrs. James T. Fields, and her husband was her closest companion.

Houses and Hospitality

In 1873 the Fieldses purchased "a bit of land" in Manchester, the seaside town north of Boston where they had boarded for years, and where Richard Henry Dana, Cyrus Bartol, and many of the Fieldses' other friends owned summer homes. The "bit" they had long admired was a five-acre parcel overlooking the harbor and "the shore we love so much," the highest point in the area. "Thunderbolt Hill!! There's a name for you!" Annie exulted to Laura Johnson soon after acquiring it, then somewhat apologetically explained their acquisition: the Panic of 1873 had left the owner short of cash and by a "stroke of luck" they had "a few hundreds to invest."[20]

By the following spring, plans for their "permanent summer home" were in place. Because brick was too expensive for their limited budget, they opted for a three-story gambrel-roofed shingled house in a "simple cottage style" with "wide hall—low rooms, rafters etc—no hangings—no carpets—but dark and simple and perhaps quaint." With a thin purse but a keen eye, Annie started buying secondhand fixtures and furnishings, two thick mantlepieces from a country tavern among them. "Will get everything for under 1000," she gloated in August. "Avenue begun this week." A few months later, the steep avenue leading to the house was finished and stone-cutters were digging the cellar. In the spring of 1875 the house neared completion. The interior woodwork was darkened to match the secondhand furniture Annie bought, and she began planting trees, shrubs, and flowers along the curving path that led from the back of the house to the foot of the hill.

In July 1875, the Fieldses moved into a spacious house whose broad piazza overlooked a ravine in the back and the ocean beyond. Seated in her "book room at Manchester for the first time at my own desk," Annie rejoiced, "We cannot recover from the wonder of it, and the beauty of it too. It is an ideal country house to look at and I shall try to make it such in reality—a place where dear 'J' should find leisure and I also for he will not be happy without this." In Boston, her "mind had been too possessed with *things* and with work of every perishable description, so occupied with the affairs of this world that I am estranged from my own country and feel like an outcast"; now she could "return to Nature my real home." Whether seated inside or out or walking along the shore, she exulted in "the glories of Nature in this perfect season."

Yet Annie soon discovered that country living had problems. The servants she brought from Boston soon quit, so disaffected by solitude that they ran "like horses from open pasture." Nor had she anticipated the heavy personal and financial costs of protracted country hospitality. "I enjoy having our friends around us immensely save for that waste of time and thought which it sometimes involves," Annie reflected, and at a particularly glum moment she thought their first summer in Gambrel Cottage might be their last. Jamie felt too burdened to write, and it seemed wrong to spend so much of themselves and their "substance" on company.

From the start, however, they felt "almost ashamed of enjoying such a Paradise by ourselves." During their interludes alone they interspersed long walks and talks with work of their own—Jamie's primarily on his lectures, Annie's on her gardening as well as her poems and essays. They would return to Manchester every summer until Jamie's death, sometimes remaining until mid-October, and Gambrel Cottage continued to be Annie Fields's "permanent summer home" throughout her long widowhood.

During the rest of the year, Annie continued to entertain old friends at Charles Street. Though there was no longer a professional imperative for such entertainments, Holmes, Longfellow, Emerson, and Lowell were among her frequent dinner guests, Whittier often dropped in for breakfast, and Harriet Beecher Stowe often stayed overnight. Annie also continued to give evening receptions, albeit smaller ones than in the sixties, usually organized around a guest of honor such as the distinguished violinist Ole Bull. Jamie encouraged such hospitality, thrived on it, collaborated on it, and once initiated it—when on 6 June 1872 he organized an elaborate champagne dinner in honor of Annie's thirty-eighth birthday.[21] But with that single exception, Annie had primary charge of their joint entertainments.

Sometimes Annie organized a series of cultural entertainments for a small group, as when she convened the "'Club' as our small eating party has named itself" on Friday evenings in the winter of 1871, a group that included the painter

William Morris Hunt and his wife, and Mr. and Mrs. Henry James Sr., and their son Henry. Emerson attended the meeting of 24 March to read passages from his journal about his encounters with De Quincey, Tennyson, and Carlyle; and on 31 March the season concluded with songs, recitations, and laughter.

The following winter, Annie invited a larger group to come to Charles Street on Fridays and again persuaded Emerson to perform. By February he had agreed to speak "if I can alight upon any thing not too grave for the occasion"; then the following month he promised to "untie the papers of Amita, & see if I dare read them on Friday."[22] On that occasion, before an audience of about forty in the Fieldses' library, Emerson delivered his now celebrated tribute to his aunt Mary Moody Emerson—his "Amita." "A humble lot, a great soul, fearlessness towards the world, fear only of the Lord, all these characteristics he brought out into fullest relief," Annie noted. As an admirer of Emerson, an admirer of great-souled women, and a conscientious hostess, she rejoiced that "the company enjoyed it to the full" and that their discussion continued for hours.

Meantime she continued to welcome one-on-one visits from women she admired, as when in April 1873 "good Mrs. Osgood [gave] me the story of her wedded life which began and indeed ended nine years ago. She was married five months when her husband died of consumption." Similarly, when Harriet Beecher Stowe shared recollections of her dead son, and when Celia Thaxter talked about her son Karl's mental illness, Annie sympathetically accepted their poignant stories as gifts of intimacy, and as proof that a "good" woman can rise above tribulation.

14

The Surging Condition of Women

"You would be much impressed I think with the surging condition of women here," Annie Fields told Laura Johnson in February 1870, when her friend was abroad, proud that Boston women were doing exciting things and facing important issues including "the approaching necessity of universal suffrage." She was one of them, doing whatever she could to expand women's options, determined to subordinate personal pleasures to noble purposes, and averse to "mere" socializing. The New England Woman's Club was now a large group with rooms in the Bureau of Charity building on Chardon Street which also housed the *Woman's Journal;* in its meeting rooms "the best speakers and all the foremost topics of the time appear"; and many women who previously "had no access to the best things which were going forward, or to a society for which they were well fitted, find much to satisfy them." As she also bragged, working women had separate "rooms and weekly meetings and a society [where] much that is strange and interesting comes up," suffrage meetings were frequent, and a horticultural school was in the offing. All in all, though some women had "narrow notions of reform to further and many of them unsex themselves and bring disgrace upon the whole," never before had there been "such a joint effort . . . to emancipate women from the needle as well as other wrongs and oppressions." She was part of that effort. Meantime, she also closely monitored other women's goals and roles.[1]

The Children of Lebanon and the World's People

In June 1871, the Fieldses spent a day at the Shaker community of Lebanon, New Hampshire, the center of the Shakers' ministry, then made a long-deferred visit to William Cullen Bryant's estate on Long Island. During each of these excursions to very different worlds, one that found virtue in self-denial and the other in self-gratification, Annie found herself fascinated by a woman whose life was utterly different from her own.

They had visited the Lebanon community three years before; and this time they were struck by a sharp decline in the group's membership. There were "fewer young people among them, and the elders with their self denials their penances, and their much labor, seem older than their years—Such a lonely loveless forlorn life!" Only Hawthorne's "Canterbury Pilgrims" approached the subject, Jamie remarked. Perhaps this prompted Annie to try doing so.

Annie's journal account of the Sunday service began with Frederick Evans, the best known and most widely published Shaker elder and "the only real power among them as to natural gifts," who forcefully informed the "world's people" that they could expect only "nonentity" after death, "while we having lived a life of the spirit shall be already among the angels." Several Shakers rose to speak after him, but only one moved Annie to tears—a pale young woman who fervently thanked God for bringing her to the Shakers and pledged to devote herself to "the strait way." "I can never be grateful enough to you for keeping me from myself," she declared; then her hands began shaking and blood suffused her face until a hymn "subdued the painful appearance of rising emotion." Then when a pale young man rose to speak and began twitching, Annie was afraid she was about to witness "one of the terrible scenes of convulsion I had heard described."

Next came a meticulous description of the Shakers' repugnantly uniform but immaculate clothing:

> The women wore muslin caps perfectly ironed and plain and shaker bonnets of straw which they took off on entering the church—white muslin kerchiefs, or the old woven white silk folded over their shoulders—these were a perfect square folded together and the folds pinned down behind at the neck. They wore under these a high white linen or cambric collar on a round neck kerchief of linen or cambric—then came the dress of pear colored stuff of cheap quality the skirts ironed into plaits and all made just alike—tight sleeves no cuffs a white handkerchief folded over their knees when they sit down, one white petticoat and odd looking shoes with small uncomfortable looking heels and broad soles, home made.

The men's clothing—like the men themselves—interested her less. Their suits were "a kind of brown home spun—the trousers evidently made by no good pattern but straight from top to bottom." But at least their shoes and straw hats seemed comfortable.

Her only real pleasure was in the tenderness between a little boy and an elder who "evidently found it the one joy of his life to educate this adopted son" (an insight that would figure—though between an eldress and a daughter—in the poem about the Shakers that she would soon write). All in all, however, the Shakers were "poor estranged ones" who led "miserable and heart rending" lives. Their misery "comes over me in this sunshine and among these hills, and over the brightness of the landscape hangs like a pall."

On a warm summer's day at Manchester only six weeks later, Annie read Jamie her new poem. "We have been on the hillside where I have read the 'Children of Lebanon' to J," she noted, without even hinting at J's response. A year later, "dear J read *The Children of Lebanon* with great pride and feeling, as a surprise to our little circle."[2] The long narrative poem had just been privately and anonymously published, presumably at Jamie's initiative. Two weeks later, Jamie sent Longfellow a copy of the "little poem which my wife has written about the Shakers," explaining that the hymns were copied from the Shaker Psalm Book, they had both visited the Shakers, "and the poem I consider a perfect picture of this strange people."[3] A few days later, Longfellow told Annie that it was a "beautiful poem" which he had already "read and re-read . . . with great pleasure." It was "simple and tender, as an Idyl should be, particularly an 'Idyl of the Shakers.'" He had "long thought that a poem could be drawn from their strange and unnatural lives of self-surrender and seclusion from the world," and Annie had now done so "with great delicacy and sympathy."[4]

Annie asked Whittier's advice about her Idyl soon afterward, then made the few changes he recommended before sending it off to London. "The suggestions have been valuable," she told Whittier, and enclosed a revised copy of "the little story."[5] It would be published in England a few weeks later by Alexander Macmillan, a former colleague of Jamie's who had become Annie's friend as well. "The Children of Lebanon"—now subtitled "An American Idyll"—appeared in *Macmillan's Magazine* in January 1873.

Despite its sentimentality yet also because of it, "the little story" has considerable literary and extraliterary interest. Like Catharine Sedgwick in *Redwood*, Hawthorne in "The Shaker Bridal" and "The Canterbury Pilgrims," and Howells in fictions he was yet to write, Annie Fields tells the story of a young Shaker couple torn between a commitment to their celibate community and a yearning to fulfill their love. Sympathetically, she presents Phoebe and Nathan "sheltered from the earth's care" during their childhood at Lebanon. They eventually announce to a disapproving conclave that they must leave together. They work apart for five years to earn "store for our marriage-day and humble home," marry, and settle into a seashore cottage.

Annie also explores the tender relationship between the orphaned Phoebe and the aging Sister Dorothy, a surrogate mother who also eventually decides to leave a community which is "Unbound, unguided, by those human cords / Of natural love, which fetter earth to heaven." Like Hawthorne and Howells, Annie makes the best case she can for the Shakers' "stern denial of man's self in holy service"; and in a long passage reminiscent of Dickens, she praises their generosity to the orphaned and the impoverished, in contrast with the "world's people," whose

> rich tables groaned with sweets,
> While hungry children lived forgot near by,
> And women gathered costly garments up
> Lest they should touch a filthy beggar's foot.

Yet the Shakers also sternly deny human love, and for this she faults them.

The last section of the poem presents Phoebe and Nathan in their cottage by the seashore, happy with each other and with a new baby, as remote from the self-denying Shakers as from the self-indulgent world's people. Because Phoebe was "strong through Love," she "gladdened many a widow's door" in the nearby village and lifts "the burdens of the rest." With the arrival of Dorothy, the poem nears narrative and emotional closure. Phoebe—who had been dreaming about Dorothy—"lifted her, and held her to her heart."

Annie's many-layered narrative celebrates the love of man and woman, of parent and child, and of one woman for another, while also celebrating humanitarian love, dedication to God's service, and the love of nature. The narrative also expresses Annie's yearning for motherhood, her commitment to philanthropy, and her affection for the Manchester shore. Through her blissful couple, Annie Fields celebrated her own domestic idyll. And as Jamie told Longfellow, her poem provides a sympathetic yet also realistic picture of the Shakers.

It might seem a stretch to connect Annie with the heroine of *The Children of Lebanon:* Phoebe is a poor orphaned Shaker girl who later becomes a loving mother and humble villager. Yet she is also her author's ego ideal. Like Hawthorne's Phoebe in *The House of the Seven Gables,* she is empowered by love to work confidently and contentedly within her own family, and to gladden the hearts of other "villagers." As wife, friend, hostess, author, and civic entrepreneur, that is just what Annie Fields tried to do.

The Fieldses' 1871 visit was informed by prior experience of Shaker communities. In 1868, accompanied by Lucy Larcom, they had visited the Enfield community, driving past miles of impoverished New Hampshire farms before arriving at the prosperous Enfield "United Society" for an overnight stay. Their dinner was sumptuous, and they were lodged in scrupulously neat bedrooms, but the celibate Shakers put Jamie in one bedroom and the women in another. The next day Annie admired the Shakers' orderliness and efficiency. But she deplored their lack of culture: they had never even heard of Ticknor and Fields, and they knew nothing at all about current literature.

Soon afterward, the Fieldses made their first visit to Lebanon, where they attended Sunday services, heard Elder Evans preach, watched the famous Shaker dance, and accepted Evans's invitation to stay for dinner and tour the community. As at Enfield, Annie enjoyed a "bountiful repast" and admired the Shakers' efficiency. And though their dancing seemed grotesque, Evans's explanations of their traditions and beliefs made her conclude that they were "really holy as far as they see the truth."

But by the time of her second visit to Lebanon, Annie had lived through the sorrows of Dickens's death and her husband's depression, and she had made her first successful efforts to improve the lives of Boston slumdwellers. That deepened familiarity with pain and poverty enabled her to sympathize with the pale young woman who thanked God for bringing her to the Shakers and fervently accepted their "strait way." But her heart lay with the heroine of her poem, who rejected the Shakers' self-denying security.

Immediately after that second visit to Lebanon came immersion in an entirely different world. The Fieldses made a two-day visit to "Mr. Bryant's beautiful home" on Long Island, traveling from Manhattan to Roslyn in a crowded train while Bryant proudly discoursed about the terrain they were passing. They spent the morning hours talking to the seventy-seven-year-old poet in his library. But they were housed in the adjacent capacious house of Bryant's son-in-law Parke Godwin; and at lunchtime they joined a group of twenty at Godwin's house—among them the celebrated twenty-seven-year-old soprano Christine Nilsson and "her French lover." Next came sightseeing on a steam-yacht with an interlude for tea, and then "more jollity than I ever saw except at Dickens's and alas! I must say it with more real lightness of heart than I ever saw at Gad's Hill."

At the high point, Godwin danced a "negro 'break-down,'" Nilsson joined in "until they were both in rivers of laughter," and other guests strummed banjos and sang slave songs. That evening, Nilsson sang "in her perfect way," the "Godwin ladies" also sang, and everybody danced to exhaustion. "How Dickens would have enjoyed the sight and sound," Annie exclaimed. "It was one of the wildest gayest scenes I ever beheld. Mr. Bryant was not present and there appeared to be absolutely no limit to the wild spirit of the company and what can be more exciting when there is such talent."

The spirit was intoxicating. At one point Christine Nilsson "burst out with a wild flood of Swedish song," displaying such "wild daring" that Annie was still too excited that night to sleep. There could have been no greater contrast to the "grotesque ecstasy" of the Lebanon Shakers than the gaiety at Roslyn, nor between the anonymous Shaker woman who thanked the community for "keeping me from myself" and the audacious Swedish soprano who had brought her lover along.

"Queen Christine" was the center of the next day's revelries. When the Fieldses returned to Godwin's house after again visiting Bryant, they saw "the company seated on the grass under the great waving trees, eating cherries." Annie was struck by the "perfect picture—Christine the queen in her sailor hat seated on a chair, with her lover on the grass nearby. . . . —all—so gay—so happy, so French." She puzzled over the character of the woman she now called Christine, "a woman of genius, a queer wayward creature, full of charm, full of *brusquerie,* and much of what our poor old forsaken Shakers would call the natural woman." Pondering such details as the singer's retentive memory for music, her use of American slang, her whims, "her lover, whom we think she will never marry," and her oscillations from frantic revelry to thoughtfulness, Annie wondered "if she did not feel a lack and desire something further."

When the proper Boston lady later asked herself why everyone at Roslyn had felt so "jovial together," she attributed it to "J's suggestion on the night of our arrival that we should call each other by our Christian names." It was a daring suggestion: as Jamie told Godwin afterward, he had startled a few Boston friends by using their Christian names. All in all, Annie told Bryant a few months later, "We look back upon your Roslyn home and our visit as we do to the thought of summer fields in winter."[6]

Though Bryant as well as Godwin had figured in their pleasure, Christine Nilsson was central to it. The previous November, after one of Nilsson's concerts in Boston, Annie had given a reception for sixty at Charles Street, and then rewarded herself with "a quiet cosy talk and sit-down" with her guest of honor. She admired Nilsson's singing, her conversation, her "light hair, deep blue eyes, full glorious eyes," and she had concluded that "her broad intellectual brow, her beautiful teeth, and strong character, belong only to the type of genius and beauty, . . . strong sweet beauty."

But after spending two days with her on Long Island, Annie reached a more complex assessment: Nilsson was a "natural woman" with a "wayward" temperament, a dazzlingly energetic woman whose fiancé was in no way her match. The genteel dictum that "nice" women should avoid the public eye was as irrelevant for Nilsson as for the Shaker woman who felt impelled to put modesty aside and rise to thank the Shakers for saving her from herself. Annie was attracted to the one and repelled by the other, but they both stirred her imagination.

Two Women Artists

Among the dozens of women who were often at Charles Street during the seventies were two unmarried artists Annie had met years before, the sculptor Anne Whitney (1821–1915) and the actress Charlotte Cushman (1816–76). In 1867, Annie had urged Anne Whitney to study in Rome. When she returned four years later, she told Annie she wanted recognition and expected to get it. One way Annie tried to help in the spring of 1872 was by buying her "noble" marble bust of Keats; and the following year when the sculptor won a competition for a statue of Samuel Adams to be exhibited in Washington, Annie helped her locate a foundry for casting it. Annie meantime served as her confidante. When Whitney won an anonymous competition for a statue of Charles Sumner in 1875, only to have the commission withdrawn when the jurors discovered she was a woman, she poignantly told Annie, "I have at last learned how to do my work, but I have only fifteen or twenty years more left to me and in the present condition of affairs it is not wanted." As it turned out, she was too pessimistic: her career flourished, and she eventually executed the Sumner statue. It still overlooks Harvard Square.

Annie admired Anne Whitney not only as a fine sculptor but as a "noble, simple, strong loving woman." "It is a privilege and an epoch in one's life such a friendship," Annie once mused. "What a handsome creature she is too—with that fine clean-cut sweet face." Among the many other things the two women had in common, Whitney was a published poet and an active supporter of women's rights. And among Annie's grounds for admiration was Anne Whitney's friendship with the painter Abby Adeline Manning. One of Annie's comments on it seems proleptic of her union with Sarah Orne Jewett: "The two women complement and repose each other."

Annie might have made exactly the same comment about Charlotte Cushman's friendship with the sculptor Emma Stebbins. But when Cushman returned from abroad in 1871, over a decade after Annie first met her, there were new grounds for admiration. "A wonderful woman with a cancer at her breast, she is preparing again for a season on the stage," Annie wrote in her journal that September. Then she continued even more melodramatically, "Twice it has been destroyed but the myriad headed serpent seems to be gnawing at her heart—Such pathos as there is in it—such power and sweetness and courage! Poor soul! The valley looks very very dark to her but she struggles on and on, making the days sunshiny for others which are often frightfully dark to herself." Because Emma Stebbins was then also unwell, Annie offered to care for her, a generous offer apparently refused.

Sitting in the Globe Theatre on 13 November 1871, raptly watching Cushman's "noble piece of acting" as Queen Katherine in *Henry VIII,* Annie felt she "spoke to every woman's heart there; by this I felt the high art and the noble sympathetic nature far above art which was in the woman and which radiates from her." Seated between her husband and Longfellow, Annie was sure that as a woman, her appreciation exceeded theirs. As Cushman portrayed her, the unjustly abased queen was an embodiment of womanly courage. Perhaps because Annie thought "much of the play beside was poor," she did not accompany Jamie backstage.[7]

Instead, she gave a dinner in Cushman's honor two weeks later, with Stebbins and Longfellow among the guests. "We have Miss Cushman here and are enjoying her very much both as an actress and a woman," Annie told Laura Johnson the following day, marvelling that the fifty-five-year-old woman still stood "quite alone on the English stage," managed to seem vigorous despite the pains of cancer, and "likes those persons she can give to and do for—it is a vocation."

A long conversation with Cushman soon afterward provoked a deeper and more complex tribute: "Her full brain was brimming over, and her rich sympathetic voice is ringing now in my ears. She does not over-estimate herself, . . . which is a part of her greatness, for the word *does* apply to her in a certain way because she grows nearer to it every day. . . . [Her] hand to hand fight with death over herself (loving life *dearly* as she does), has strengthened her hold upon her affection for life, insensibly. She grows daily wiser and nobler."[8]

Annie counted many of the period's most celebrated actors as her friends, Edwin Booth, Charles Fechter, Helena Modjeska, and Ellen Terry among them. But she admired none of them more than Charlotte Cushman. A woman of impeccable probity whose first American ancestor had arrived on the Mayflower, Cushman at first mounted the stage to support her family, and soon attained international fame. It was simply irrelevant that she shared her life with another woman and often played men's roles. Even Whittier—who never went to the theater and decried "her actress vocation"—called Charlotte Cushman "a great woman with a large heart," "one of the noblest of women," "a reformer of the better stamp," and a good "friend of all good causes."⁹

From the time she met Annie in Italy until her death sixteen years later, Charlotte Cushman enlarged Annie Fields's ideas about what a virtuous woman could do and be. Although her reading of the *Organ Ode* in 1863 was only an incidental event in a long and distinguished career, it was crucial to Annie. When Charlotte Cushman died in February 1876, both of the Fieldses attended her funeral services at King's Chapel, joined the long cortege that proceeded to Mount Auburn Cemetery, and mourned her as a great artist who was also a magnificent woman.¹⁰

Exemplars as Colleagues

One of Annie Fields's new heroines in the early seventies was Anna Caswell, a sweet-voiced but determined woman who had spent seventeen years as a missionary to Native Americans before coming to the North End Mission. Although she was "almost destitute of what we know as culture," Annie wrote in her journal, Mrs. Caswell's power "increased daily as more and more people leaned on her and loved her." Appropriately, Annie asked Mrs. Caswell to give the opening prayer when her Lincoln Street Home for working women was inaugurated in December 1871.

Annie tried to understand Anna Caswell's remarkable power in the light of Théophile Gautier's remark that "a man's chief purpose in life is to learn to play his intellectual instrument and to bring it to the farthest point of perfection." "The instrument may be tuned in various ways, and may be kept in tune in other ways than by the study of books," she concluded; and she admired the saintly Mrs. Caswell for using the abilities which constituted her "instrument . . . simply as such, and not as the poor little litterateur considers it, a superior and peculiar gift to be petted for its own sake." When Mrs. Caswell nearly died from exhaustion soon afterward, Annie thought it was a form of martyrdom. Then after her recovery, Annie collaborated with her on projects that ranged from setting up vocational courses to opening a new women's workroom.

A more celebrated exemplary figure was Mary Ashton Rice Livermore (1820–1905). A minister's wife with three grown daughters when Annie first met her, Mary Livermore was a determined woman with a talent for organization who had entered the public sphere during the Civil War with her husband's complete support. She had codirected the Sanitary Commission (the forerunner of the Red Cross), whose primary task was nursing wounded soldiers; she had organized the widely imitated 1863 Chicago Sanitary Fair; and her subsequent work included founding the Massachusetts Woman Suffrage Association, editing the *Woman's Journal,* and presiding over the Massachusetts Temperance Union as well as the Association for the Advancement of Women. Billed as the "queen of the platform," Livermore toured the country from 1870 to 1895, delivering about a hundred fifty lectures a year on such high-minded topics as woman suffrage, temperance, dress reform, and educating "our daughters" to be self-sufficient. A spirited redhead, Mary Livermore was in every sense far more visible than Annie Fields. But as founding members of the New England Woman's Club and the Women's Educational and Industrial Union, they were colleagues in reform who supported each other's initiatives. Annie invited Mary Livermore to help inaugurate the Lincoln Street Home for working women in December 1871, and her letter praising the project and regretting her absence was read out as part of the "simple services."[11]

Annie never felt closer to Mrs. Livermore than during her weekend at Manchester in the fall of 1876. She came primarily to deliver a Sunday lecture that the Fieldses had arranged. "At four came Miss Phelps, at six came Mrs. Livermore," Annie wrote in her diary that Saturday. "Ah! She is indeed a great woman— a strong arm to those who are weak, a new faith in time of trouble. She came to tea as fresh as if she had been calmly sunning herself all the week instead of speaking at a great meeting at Faneuil Hall the previous evening and taking cold in the process." An ideal guest, Livermore talked "most wittily and brilliantly, besides laughing most heartily and merrily over all dear J's absurd stories and illustrations."

More memorably, one of "J's" stories about women's limited educational opportunities prompted Livermore to recount a girlhood trauma. She and five other teenaged girls had studied in company with their brothers until the young men were admitted to Harvard. At that point all six girls went to see President Quincy, and Livermore as their spokesperson begged permission to attend classes. Quincy's reply was unequivocal: "We never allow girls at Harvard; you know, the place for girls is at home." Over thirty years later, Livermore could still repeat his words and her own enraged reply—"I wish I were God for one instant, that I might kill every woman from Eve down and let you have a masculine world all to yourselves and see how you would like that." Later, she and her friends had cried themselves "half-blind." Recording the entire anecdote in her journal, Annie felt she was "standing over the cradle of woman's emancipation and seeing it rocked by the hand of sorrow and indignation."

Sunday's highlight was Livermore's lecture in the Manchester Town Hall, a lecture she spent the morning polishing while Annie walked on the beach with her other houseguest, the novelist Elizabeth Stuart Phelps. Then after lunch, Livermore delivered a "moving sermon" to a capacity audience, its "loveliest" part boosting Annie's new project—a night school for working boys. A more private pleasure followed: Annie took both of her guests for a drive, during which their conversation ranged from *Daniel Deronda* and "the life and character of Mrs. Lewes and Mrs. Stowe" to "strange calls for assistance famous people get." On Monday, Annie was so eager to launch her boys' school project that she invited a group of local women to a planning session, and all the fund-raising was completed in a few days. Then on Friday, still energized by Mrs. Livermore's example,

Annie presided over a meeting of the Women's Union that she herself pronounced a success.

Although Mary Livermore's heavy schedule made her refuse Annie's subsequent invitations, her increasing respect for Annie's ventures underlay a casual remark she made to James T. Fields a year later: she and their reformer friend Mary Beedy had spoken so much about Annie "that I think she must have felt the warmth of our spoken love and admiration."[12] In 1887 Mrs. Livermore would invite Annie to lecture on the Associated Charities before an audience of two hundred in her own hometown.[13]

But the most notable if most disturbing woman in Annie's world was Julia Ward Howe (1819-1910). Howe cofounded the New England Woman's Club in 1868 and became president in 1871; in 1868 she also cofounded the New England Woman's Suffrage Association; in 1870 she cofounded the *Woman's Journal* and became one of its editors; and in 1881 she became president of the new Association for the Advancement of Women. The wound Howe had inflicted by blasting Annie's ode in 1863 had presumably healed by the winter of 1870 when Annie invited her to give a benefit reading (perhaps for the first Holly Tree coffee house). Howe accepted, as she would later accept other requests for help "in furtherance of your reform." Annie's addresses to Howe's Saturday Morning Club for young women were another form of collegiality. And Annie may have felt satisfied when the woman who had once attacked her ode requested "a contribution, in verse or in prose" for a publication she was editing for a suffrage bazaar.[14]

By then their overlapping personal relationships included Sarah Orne Jewett and Howe's daughter Laura as well as Laura's daughter; and because Howe's temperament had mellowed and her wit remained astute, she was often invited to Charles Street when Annie was entertaining such distinguished foreigners as the French writer Thérèse de Solms Blanc and the English novelist Mrs. Humphry Ward. Howe's death in October 1910 was "natural and sweet," Annie wrote in her journal. She then described the elaborate funeral, altogether unlike the modest one she had already planned for herself: "the singing by the blind the beautiful tributes and at last when the doors opened for the departure of the tiny white casket the trumpets blared as if the world rose to herald her advent into the new life—it was all something to lift up the hearts even of the most deeply bereaved."[15]

A closer colleague in reform and a much closer friend was Abby Morton Diaz (1821-1904), who first entered Annie's life as an *Atlantic* contributor. A cheerful and intelligent woman with one ancestor who had arrived on the Mayflower and another who was a Massachusetts supreme court justice, she had joined the utopian commune Brook Farm at the age of twenty-one. There she taught school, married a young Cuban, and bore him three sons; then after her husband deserted her and the commune disbanded, she supported herself and her sons by teaching and nursing.

In 1861, she made her *Atlantic* debut with a good-humored story about village life, and she soon placed four others in the *Atlantic* and dozens of others in juvenile magazines (including the enormously popular "William Henry" stories, which were among Theodore Roosevelt's favorites). She modestly called herself "a novice in writing" who knew "nothing of rules, or fitness," and she repeatedly urged the *Atlantic* editor to "have no hesitation in altering or amending anything of *mine*."[16] By the mid-sixties, Abby Diaz was a familiar figure at informal Charles Street gatherings though not at Annie's formal dinners, and by the early seventies Annie began enlisting her help in philanthropic initiatives including the Lincoln Street Home.

Because Mrs. Diaz shared Annie's commitment to improving other women's lives but knew much more about household management, Annie asked her to move into the Lincoln Street Home to check on the manager. Mrs. Diaz's experience and resiliency as a teacher also made her an ideal collaborator for several of Annie's ventures at the North End Mission. Thus when Annie planned a series of Sunday excursions for schoolchildren in 1874, Abby Diaz helped her organize and conduct them, not at all discomfited by the children's "strange" language or the boys' unruliness. That winter when Annie was housing the eight-year-old motherless Esther Albee and one of her self-help projects was studying philosophy with Abby Diaz, the latter's "gift for entertaining children" made it "high holiday" for Esther whenever a study session ended.[17] By then, Abby Diaz had made her "very dear gentle Annie" her confidante about such personal matters as her "unprincipled" husband and her "bad" son who had been imprisoned for theft.

One evening in the spring of 1876 when Abby Diaz was in one of the Charles Street guestrooms and Mary Lodge (with whom she had just founded the Cooperative Society of Visitors) was in the other, Annie took stock of their dissimilarities:

> What strangely interesting characters I have for friends. How little they would understand or appreciate each other. Mrs. Diaz is struggling with her desire to enlighten the world and sometimes loses her balance a trifle, I fear, yet she is dead in earnest and if her culture were equal to her endeavor she could be a power indeed. Mrs. Lodge *is* a power in the present with her ceaseless energy and determination, but she does not bring her thought steadfastly to bear on serious subjects or find her joy in them altogether. She is a charming woman of society without strong passions or iron purpose, but she is most loveable and amiable and useful. They are both of them very valuable and dear to me.

Yet Annie was fonder of the more ebullient if less refined Abby Diaz. Diaz was also more affectionate. "I thought I should soon hear from you all the week previous & had felt a sort of yearning towards you and a longing to see you," she had recently written, then moved from one topic of mutual interest to another. Kingsley's *Life* was fascinating, she was glad "Miss Phelps' book is out and is highly spoken of," and she was "mightily" interested in Jamie's *Underbrush,* particularly his "paper on *his friend's library.*" As an insider, she knew that Charles Kingsley and Elizabeth Stuart Phelps were Annie's friends, and knew the "friend" of Jamie's title was Annie.

When Annie started "a club of about ten ladies who meet here every Tuesday each one to read something of her own" in January 1877, Abby Diaz was one of them. As Annie told Laura Johnson the following year, "Mrs. Diaz reads next. It is a very agreeable club. This is my diversion. The visiting is my occupation."[18] Annie shared her "occupation" with Mary Lodge as well as with Abby Diaz, but she could also share her "diversion" with Abby Diaz. That spring both Annie and Abby Diaz helped found the Women's Educational and Industrial Union, designed to increase fellowship among women of all classes and promote the best methods for women's educational and social advancement; and they both continued to work through the New England Woman's Club to enhance working women's lives by establishing meeting rooms, libraries, and educational programs.[19]

Annie was appointed to a Harvard Medical School committee on the admission of women in the fall of 1880; and Abby Diaz responded to Annie's desire to "talk things over" by sending a twelve-page brief. Her chief argument was that because women physicians were both a necessity and an accomplished fact, it was in the public interest to give women the best possible medical education. Many women were too "delicate" to discuss their complaints with men, as she told Annie, and their mutual friend "Helen" had been remarkably successful with difficult childbirths. Next came a bit of sound advice: before making her report, Annie should "interview women doctors of Boston."[20]

Abby Diaz's many other collaborations with Annie include years of paid service as an Associated Charities visitor; she once agreed to say "something appropriate" to a meeting of working women about their right to earn more than a bare subsistence; and Annie edited at least one of Diaz's lectures on teaching and character development. Although it would be hard to say which of the two was busier, Abby Diaz always assumed it was Annie. "I know how it is with you, every moment has to be saved for some purpose and to some purpose," she wrote shortly before her death, nonetheless hoping that Annie might spare a moment to pay her a visit. For over three decades, they had worked separately and together to improve women's physical, intellectual, and spiritual lives. They were not social equals, and Diaz never entered into Annie's intimacy with Sarah Orne Jewett. But they were equals when they discussed women's education or woman suffrage or exchanged recipes for succotash or soothing syrups, and they depended on each other for "warm and ready sympathy" as well as practical help.[21]

Annie Fields's admiration of Abby Diaz's "wondrous" effect on the eight-year-old Esther Albee makes special sense in the context of her own childlessness. It also explains why she often invited Mabel Lowell to stay with her for a week, why she regretted Esther's departure, and why she invited a needy German woman—a college student—to spend an entire summer at Manchester.

Her involvement with Imogen Eddy and her daughter Nelly in the seventies was a more sustained form of vicarious mothering. In the winter of 1871, Annie invited Imogen Willey Eddy and her two-year-old daughter Nelly to Charles

Street. She had met the young woman during the sixties while boarding at the Willey farm in Campton, New Hampshire, and the news that Imogen was married to a "sot" prompted the invitation. After observing how happily Imogen played with her little daughter, Annie decided to invite them again. She also decided to buy clothes for Nelly, and the following summer she invited Imogen and Nelly to spend a week with her in Manchester. Intense sympathy for Imogen underlies a subsequent journal entry: "Divorce at last."

As she watched the child playing with other children in Manchester over the next few years, Annie feared that she was becoming selfish and vain. Yet she enjoyed having Nelly and Imogen as part of her household, and she enjoyed the consciousness of doing them good. That is particularly clear from a note to Laura Johnson of June 1877: "Imogen Willey and her child who are poor and homeless are to pass the summer with us."[22] An unpublished poem whose narrator seems based on Imogen provides a more poignant gloss on the childless Annie's empathy with her. After recalling her carefree youth, the young mother looks at her three-year-old daughter and declares, "With all my loss and all my pain / I would not change this present gain / For girlhood's vanished charm."[23]

Dress Reform

Without abandoning her belief that women should dress attractively, Annie Fields became an enthusiastic and even enterprising proponent of the dress reform movement of the 1870s. During a benefit ball for Cretan relief in the late sixties, she had felt ashamed of wearing a satin gown and expensive jewelry when Cretans were starving. From then on, her wardrobe reflected her growing distaste for conspicuous consumption and her expanding feminist consciousness.

She was hardly alone in scorning preoccupation with clothing or in rejecting elaborately cut and expensively trimmed dresses, tight corseting, and high heels. Only the foolish women in Harriet Beecher Stowe's stories worry about such matters as the right kind of lace for a new satin gown. More consequential were Elizabeth Stuart Phelps's 1873 lectures to the New England Woman's Club about the symbolic and literal "bondage" of women's clothing, in which she argued that heavy skirts and tightly corseted waistlines damage a woman's body, limit her physical activities, and even cause moral and intellectual harm. Those lectures eventuated in a four-part serial for the liberal *Independent* magazine and then a book titled *What to Wear?* Meantime, the New England Woman's Club established a dress reform committee which corresponded with similar groups around the country. They consulted Dr. Dio Lewis and other advocates of physical education for women about appropriate clothing, they recommended patterns and materials for dress-reform clothing, and they opened a store that sold such garments.

Annie took additional initiatives of her own. "Mary Dewey and I went to see a clever work-woman by the name of Flynt, a dressmaker who has invented underclothes and waterproof clothing which will be a comfort to woman-kind, I sincerely believe," she noted in her journal in June 1874. As she then more expansively told Laura Johnson, who was about to make a long camping trip, "Mrs. Flynt, a dressmaker formerly notorious for fashion & high heels, has invented the cleverest arrangement for women's underclothing I have ever seen. She has patented her work and I really think will do much to emancipate the race. Her waterproof clothing is also delightful. I wish you could have her make a travelling suit for you but I fear there will not be time before you go—" However extravagant her praise of the dressmaker might seem, Annie had long since concluded that women who dressed simply and comfortably could accomplish more than those who submitted to the tyrannies of fashion. They could move more easily, without spending the time and money that "fashion & high heels" required. Therefore Annie happily reported that Mrs. Flynt hoped "soon to have her articles everywhere. The factory will probably take the patent and pay her a royalty on each article sold."[24]

Annie's subsequent diary entries about her own wardrobe were few and often apologetic, as when she mentioned wearing a "lilac polonaise with a yellow rose," then said, "—I speak of the latter because it seemed to please W. M. Hunt to see the dash of color." Yet she never abandoned her conviction that women should be "tastefully and appropriately clothed," and Henry Wadsworth Longfellow's praise of her Venetian lace bodice seemed worth recording. "What a harmonious spectacle is a well-dressed woman," she exclaimed in the mid-seventies, then reflected that "well-dressing is not accomplished either in a moment or by the help of a dressmaker." Therefore, even while begrudging the time it took, she carefully chose and packed her clothing for the Philadelphia Centennial Exposition in 1876, and she evidently relished Joaquin Miller's extravagant praise during the opening reception.

Even so, Annie was by then committed to simple but dramatic outfits that ignored current fashion. An unusual example is the "morning costume" her friend Mary Osgood described after a visit to Charles Street in 1882: "I could only think of a monk, altho' I never heard of a woman monk. She had on a very light gray, full robe, tied about the waist with a girdle of double gray silk cord. It had a monks hood and very large drapery sleeves over tight sleeves the hood and sleeves faced with darker gray. The robe was long all round sweeping a little behind."[25] By wearing that "costume," Annie Fields showed herself to be as liberated from tight lacing as from the constraints of style, continuing what had become her practice over a decade before.

Women's Education

Throughout the seventies, women's education remained central to Annie Fields's personal program and her civic mission.[26] Education was crucial to her ideal of self-fulfillment, never more than in the seventies. One of the many long reading

lists she prepared for herself was organized as a course in philosophy, and many
of the books on her lists were in French, Italian, and German. A single book might
generate other projects, as when she translated Goethe's "Pandora," later read
that translation to her club of women writers, and subsequently published it. Attending lectures was another kind of study, with Emerson's among her favorites.
Her less personal enterprises included teaching Sunday school in the churches of
Cyrus Bartol and James Freeman Clarke and teaching French and Italian at the
North End Mission; fund-raising for Freedmen's schools, kindergartens, industrial training schools, horticultural schools, and Dr. Dio Lewis's physical training school; and working through the Women's Educational and Industrial Union
(which she helped found) "to promote individual, intellectual, aesthetic, moral,
and physical education" for all women.

In a stock-taking journal entry on New Year's Day of 1874, Annie struggled to
reconcile her commitment to self-education with her fundamentally Christian
commitment to selfless service: "I discern in myself 1st the desire to serve others
unselfishly according to the example of our dear Lord 2d the desire to cultivate
my powers in order to achieve the highest life possible to me as an individual existence by stimulating thought to its finest issues through reflection, observation,
and by profound and ceaseless study of the written thoughts of the wisest in every
age and every clime." Recasting those desires as duties, she subdivided the first:
"As a woman, and a wife my first duty lies at home; to make that beautiful; to
stimulate the lives of others by exchange of ideas, and the repose of domestic life;
to educate children and servants; 2d To be conversant with the poor; to visit their
homes; to be keenly alive to their sufferings; never allowing the thought of their
necessities to sleep in our hearts." Then she more passionately recast her desire
for self-fulfillment into a duty: "By day and night, morning and evening, in all
times and seasons when strength is left to us, to study, study, study—."

Women need to know much more than they did, Annie believed. Their knowledge was "usually as nought" compared to men's, though not because of intellectual inferiority. "To do good work with the brain, the brain must be instructed";
and few women had been adequately instructed. Therefore each woman should
"seize every opportunity" for attaining knowledge and thus "become strong to
perform our especial work for humanity." Implicit in that intellectual, moral, and
social obligation was another: to expand such opportunities for other women.

Previously, at a planning meeting for the state's first coeducational university
(Boston University), Harriet Beecher Stowe and her sister Catharine Beecher had
argued that "education in training children, sewing, gardens—in short, home
care" should be part of the curriculum. Annie thought otherwise. "We are at present full of starting a university for women in Boston," Annie wrote in her journal
in May 1872. "To this end Jamie intends having a course of free lectures on English
literature in the last trimester of this year in order to bring the audience together."
Her own immersion in literature, her Arnoldian belief in it as a civilizing force,
and her commitment to a traditional liberal arts education for women at least

partly explain why all the lectures in the "university class for women in Boston" focused on literature.

Emerson promised to "do his best for [it] next December," she noted in her diary, then happily reported a few days later, "Today appeared our prospectus for the lectures for women which are to forerun a university we hope for women in this city." According to that prospectus, a "Free Course of Lectures on English Literature for Ladies" would be given on Saturdays at three from October to December at the Technological Institute, open to "all women who wish to avail themselves of the course." The "gentlemen" who agreed to lecture included James T. Fields, George William Curtis, Ralph Waldo Emerson, Oliver Wendell Holmes, Phillips Brooks, James Freeman Clarke, Henry Ward Beecher, and Wendell Phillips. A woman was added to the list only after Phillips argued that "no matter what *some* think the women's present fitness to stand side of R.W.E. & G.W.C., the *general public* have, of late, got such an estimate of woman's platform power that (unable to draw the line between this & that) it will hold it ungracious, to say the least if, in a move to aid the sex, one of them cannot be found to represent it." Ednah Cheney was soon enlisted to deliver the inaugural lecture.[27]

Although the lecture series was not an accredited course in a degree program, it did indeed "forerun a university." Less than two years later, in 1874, women were permitted to take Harvard examinations which were graded by Harvard professors. The Harvard Annex, forerunner of Radcliffe College was incorporated eight years later, with Annie's old friend Elizabeth Agassiz—the widow of the scientist Louis Agassiz—as president.[28]

In 1873, one year after the pioneering lecture series, Annie helped launch the state's first coeducational university—Boston University, where women were admitted on the same terms as men even for doctoral study, and where professorships were open to women. Elizabeth Stuart Phelps would be the first woman to lecture there, delivering a series of four talks titled "Representative Modern Fiction" first tried out on the Fieldses. "In the evening she read us a noble lecture she has just written upon George Eliot," Annie noted. They were "fine pieces of analysis," Annie concluded, though she worked with Phelps on a few problems in their "delivery."

Annie was one of the women who met at her friend Mary Claflin's home to organize the Boston University Women's Education Association (later known as the Massachusetts Society for the University Education of Women). And it was Annie who went to the State House to incorporate it. One purpose of the association was to provide scholarships for young women at Boston University. Another was more far-sighted. Convinced that it was legally and morally wrong to deny girls the same quality of free public school education that boys enjoyed, the association appointed a committee of three to make that argument to Boston's School Board. Annie was one of the them. As a direct consequence, the Girls' Latin School was officially established in 1878 with a college preparatory curriculum and academic standards identical to those at the Boys' Latin School.[29] When its doors opened a few years later, 148 girls were enrolled.

The eminent Harvard Medical School professor Edward Clarke—Annie's own physician—argued in *Sex in Education* (1873) that college study was bad for women's health and injured the "female apparatus." Although that "apparatus" was hardly a subject for polite conversation, Clarke's book was widely discussed and disputed. Annie had anticipated a book that would "help elevate the condition of American women," and felt enormously disappointed.[30] When she visited Dartmouth College in the spring of 1873 and closely observed the professors' wives, she exulted, "New England women are the best instructed women as well as the best housekeepers on the face of the earth." But that was not good enough.

Centennial Work

From 1873 to 1876, Annie worked with one committee to recreate the original Boston Tea Party and with another to preserve the Old South Church. But her major centennial responsibility was chairing the Massachusetts Women's Centennial Executive Committee. "I hear you are to be on the great central committee of the Centennial," Harriet Beecher Stowe wrote. Given Annie's many successful interventions in the public sphere by then, the appointment does not seem surprising. It demanded administrative and fund-raising expertise as well as aesthetic discrimination and social skills. Her most substantive duties were fundraising for the Women's Pavilion of the Philadelphia Exposition and selecting the works to be sent there.

Annie had complete charge of the committee's finances; she attended every meeting of the Committee on Exhibits and the Committee on Interior Decorative Art; she processed orders for exposition medallions; she corresponded with committeewomen throughout the state; she handled applications for space at the Women's Pavilion and decided which to accept; and she arranged to collect, pack, and ship each object she accepted. By selling centennial medals, she helped fund the pavilion. By selecting and shipping women's work to be displayed there, she would bring public attention to paintings and statues that everyone agreed merited comparison with men's. She would also bring public attention to outstanding examples of such traditional "women's" crafts as weaving and china decoration, and—more surprising—to inventions women had patented. Fittingly, when the Women's Committee closed its office on Pemberton Square that May, Annie brought home its record book and financial receipts. A receipt for $1,240.32 "from the Massachusetts Ladies' Centennial Committee by the hand of Mrs. Fields" to the Old South Church Preservation Committee suggests how well she served both groups.[31]

"I am much exercised just now with the Centennial business," Annie told Laura Johnson in October 1873; getting enough help had already demanded "kicking

against the pricks." By April 1875 Annie could assure Laura that Boston was "at
last awake to Centennial work," but she herself was too busy and too tired to attend the opening celebrations.[32] When three southern army regiments subsequently arrived to help celebrate the battle of Bunker Hill—"the first real recon-
ciliation of North and South"—she felt sure the centennial would benefit the entire
country.

Meantime, her ordinary life went on. One day in February 1876 when Celia
Thaxter was her houseguest, Annie told her friend Laura that "Mrs. Winthrop
gives her receptions, the Chardon Street Charity Bureau is more overwhelmed
than ever before, there being no work for the people, Centennial meetings come
thick and fast, and so the world wags." Her own entire morning had been spent
at the centennial office working with the Committee on Exhibitions and filling
orders for "our" beautiful centennial medal, though "the studio of Miss Greene
stands gaping for me and later we dine with the Langs and have music—Such is
the day."[33]

Two months later, after chairing the statewide meeting of the Women's Centennial Committee, Annie marveled at how hard everyone had worked and
how much they had accomplished, then made a staunchly feminist statement:
"Women must certainly have a voice in government before we can get things
quite out of the corrupted condition of the present." Meantime, she sometimes
felt daunted: "what is a woman to do who is getting off the Women's work to a
Centennial Exhibition and striving to arrange to keep some poor people in work
during the Summer by selling tickets for Mendelssohn's Operetta when nobody
has money to buy them!"[34]

When the Centennial Exposition officially opened in Philadelphia on Wednesday, 10 May, Annie and her husband were on hand for the ceremonies, walking in
thick crowds through drizzling rain to the place reserved for invited guests.
Though it was impossible to hear the speakers, a thousand-voice chorus thrill-
ingly sang Whittier's "Centennial Hymn" and a cantata by Sidney Lanier. Next
came a reception for "officials and literary people" where Annie was presented to
the Empress of Brazil, and where Joaquin Miller offered her praise "fulsome
enough for Aphrodite." The following day, Lissie Adams came up from Baltimore
to attend painting exhibitions with Annie; and while Jamie was delivering a lecture on Friday, Annie went to the Women's Pavilion "to set several matters right."

In that distinctive building in the form of a Maltese cross where the arts and ar-
tifacts of American women were on display, the national chairwoman confided to
Annie that jealousy of her authority and complaints about insufficient opening
day tickets depressed her. But no one complained about the building or the exhibitions. Annie's work for the Centennial Tea Party and for preserving the Old
South Church had helped celebrate the nation's revolutionary past. But through
the Massachusetts Women's Centennial Executive Committee, she brought attention to the accomplishments of contemporary women.[35]

15

New Directions

The Lecturer's Wife

In November 1872, right after the fire that devastated downtown Boston and nearly two years after her husband retired from publishing, Annie looked up from her journal to admire "the row of beautiful books he fathered in the American world." That row now included a beautiful new book of his own—*Yesterdays with Authors,* the essays about "his" books and their authors (Hawthorne, Dickens, Thackeray, and Mary Russell Mitford among them) which had first appeared in the *Atlantic,* a volume still regarded as his major contribution to literary history.[1] Meantime he continued to produce essays and poems for the *Atlantic* and other periodicals, and he would later "father" two more books—*Underbrush* (1877), a collection of his *Atlantic* essays, and *Ballads and Other Verses* (1881). But during his final decade, Fields's cultural mission to "the American world" was primarily conducted from the lecture platform, and his wife was enormously proud of his success.

"Mr. Fields 'lectured' in Boston," Annie wrote in her diary in November 1871; "Continues to lecture; making additions and changes continually in his essays," she wrote a month later; and in January she summarily reported that he was "continually lecturing." His repertoire soon included dozens of lectures, most of them about famous writers he had known and published. Whether under an umbrella title such as "Fiction Old and New and Its Eminent Authors" or a more limited one such as "Longfellow, the Man and the Poet," Fields presented well-known writers as fascinating and exemplary individuals, and promoted interest in their work. Whatever his topic, Fields was both an advocate and an exemplar of self-help. In "Masters of the Situation," for example, he used lively anecdotes about Napoleon and Dickens to prove that success requires careful preparation, study, and hard work.[2] In 1873 Fields was invited to give the prestigious Lowell Lectures, and the next year he was appointed a lecturer in English literature at Boston University. Throughout the decade, he could as easily fill an urban auditorium or a college lecture hall as a village lyceum.

For Annie, one of the benefits of accompanying him was glimpsing lives far different from her own—those of professors' wives at Dartmouth, for example. One of her most memorable experiences as the lecturer's wife was her overnight stay under Emerson's "roof-tree."

When the Fieldses reached Concord on a cold and snowy afternoon in January 1872, Emerson had not yet returned from lecturing in Washington. Wryly amused by Lidian Emerson's ugly cap and by her complaints of a nervous disease that disrupted her sleep, Annie nonetheless admired her informed support of woman suffrage and relished her portrait of the "dear sage" as "a naughty boy at college" who "read everything he could find and let the lessons take care of themselves." Emerson arrived after supper, shortly before the Fieldses left for the lecture hall. But he promised to pause only for a cup of tea, "and before the speaker had finished his opening sentence Mr. Emerson's welcome face appeared at the door."[3]

The evening's other pleasures included the smiles of the "plain country women" who had braved the snow to hear Fields's lecture, and a wine and cheese reception at the Emersons' house afterward. Better still was waking at dawn, feeling "the influence of the great nature who was befriending us within the four walls," and looking out at the landscape "which was the source of his own inspirations." The Fieldses went downstairs at eight to find Emerson awaiting them, then sat down to a breakfast of eggs, biscuits, and apple pie (though not the beefsteak that their host also wanted his daughter Ellen to serve). But for Annie, the chief treat was listening to Emerson speak, whether about "the lack of education in English literature among our young people" or Coventry Patmore's "unreadable" new poem or Whitman's failure to "advance."[4] Soon after that overnight stay, she urged Emerson to offer a new series of lectures in Boston and even suggested the title he used: "Conversations."

Because of her many ongoing commitments as well as the rigors of travel, Annie rarely accompanied Jamie on his long lecture tours. As he had first learned through Dickens, touring was debilitating. Sometimes he burlesqued his plight in his daily letters home, as when he told Annie that everyone in Buffalo was "furred and freezing," or that there was nothing to eat between Buffalo and Pittsburgh but "the steak of wild cats and tigers." But his main refrain was longing for Annie. "We decided wisely," he wrote his "dear Birdie" from Philadelphia at the beginning of one long and arduous tour, then complained of missing her. "Everyone regrets you did not come and so do I most of all," he wrote during another lecture trip to Philadelphia, and a dancing stick figure in another letter signaled his joy at his imminent return to her.[5]

Their twentieth wedding anniversary prompted a particularly tender letter. Touched by the "dear verses" Annie had sent to mark "our day," Jamie solemnly wrote, "God bless you, dear Love, & may we be a long time yet together is my constant prayer. Our lot is a happy one, and we will try to help others just so far as we can."[6] Beneath the phrase "so far as we can" was concern about Annie's health (though also his own), which in January 1875 surfaced in an unusual plea: he asked Annie to reduce her commitments to the North End Mission. Instead of refusing outright, she simply said it was hard to hear that request. He then solemnly told his dear love, "do not let me stand in the way of your happiness, but if you think you can . . . do that work, . . . I must not interfere. It has always been my desire to see you contented and happy in your duties in life, and to help only so far as I could see wisdom in the helping. The Mission seems to be your magnet, and in God's name, I say, go on and do all the good you can, everywhere."[7] Admitting to exhaustion, however, he asked Annie to consider accompanying him on his brief tour of New York the following month. Not surprisingly, she agreed to go.

The following fall, Annie accompanied her husband on a western tour that lasted for an entire month. Traveling was arduous but "the compensations were marvelous," Annie wrote to Laura from Omaha in October 1875, delighted to be "seeing our growing country."[8] The Fieldses had reached Omaha after stops in Rochester, Niagara Falls, Chicago, and Wisconsin, and immediately after a "long night and half day" train ride through what seemed "like some noble garden, exquisite in sunset, moonlight, and morning." Omaha turned out to be dusty and windswept, a place where Annie began "to see the life Bret Harte describes." During the afternoon she saw "fine horses and stalwart men but nothing of what can be called 'gentle people.'" To her surprise and delight, however, the opera house was filled with men who "came in from the prairie in high boots to hear the lecture, leaving their horses outside."

Next came a grueling day-long trip to Iowa City, first on a jolting bus filled with "the unwashed," then in cold and rattling railroad cars. But again Jamie had a "fine audience"; and the next morning Annie enjoyed the "fine sight" of "six hundred boys and girls together" on the University of Iowa campus. Her earlier reason for opposing coeducation had been that students' "natural affinity" for one another might interfere with their studies. But after seeing the young men and women in easy conversation, she acknowledged that coeducation has its advantages.[9] Another gratification followed an exhausting day-long trip to Bloomington. The Fieldses arrived at their hotel while a reunion of the Thirty-third Illinois Regiment was in progress; Jamie was urged to speak "for Massachusetts"; and "the applause was simply terrific."

Chicago's new Palmer House Hotel—a "palace built for the entertainment of the public"—was their most elegant lodging. However wasteful its opulence seemed, Annie enjoyed having four large mirrors in her bedroom, fine bed linens, a large bathroom, and sumptuous meals. The Fieldses also attended a splendid evening party and heard one of Robert Collyer's sermons, and Annie found time to complete "a long article for Mr. Murry's paper 'Under the Golden Rule'" and a poem on Lake Michigan.

Utterly unlike the Palmer House was the next place they stayed—a sparsely furnished "queer place" in Lafayette, Indiana, where their bedroom had torn wallpaper, a soiled carpet, a broken chair, and rough sheets. Yet their bed was excellent; and despite their hostess's incongruous garb of old boots and a stylish black silk dress, she cooked delicious meals. Annie appreciated the "good people" who housed them: "Everything possible for them to do for our comfort was done." But she was amused that Jamie's audience laughed uproariously at all his jokes, then became nearly comatose.

Detroit was more to her taste, a place of "culture and repose," as Annie concluded while taking tea at Governor John Judson Bagley's mansion. She was immediately drawn to his wife, a well-bred woman with an "ideal home" and seven healthy and interesting children, who was president of the Detroit Woman's Club and had founded another in Lansing. According to Mrs. Bagley, there was more cultural "attainment in the West and less talk of culture than in the East," and Annie thought it would "do our women good to know such a person." She provided "a revelation of Western culture and home life of which we know nothing. The East can hardly compete with it." Annie was sorry to leave her but more than ready to return home, though she would undertake another long western tour the following year.

Jamie maintained a crowded schedule of lecturing for the next few years. He enjoyed the income and the applause, and his own consciousness of enriching the nation's cultural life. But lecturing drained his energy, and worse was to come: a brain hemorrhage in May 1879 followed by several others, then a heart attack in January 1880 followed by recurring angina pains, and by the attack that ended his life the following year.

As Annie neared the end of the *Biographical Notes* she began assembling a few months after his death, she presented his career as a lecturer by quoting from her own journals and from his letters to her (which typically reported "fine audience; great enthusiasm; papers all jubilant"). As more objective evidence of his "genuine public recognition," she included excerpts from newspapers. America "owes him a debt of gratitude" for sharing his knowledge of great men of letters, one reporter concluded; and another said Fields's effect on "the great public" was impossible to calculate because at each lecture "there must be at least a small number to whose minds a new world is suddenly opened." The lectures of James T. Fields would never be published, but the lecturer's wife did her best "to rescue some memory of their peculiar qualities and influence."

Three Westerners

During the early seventies, three writers became identified with the landscapes, characters, and vernacular of the American West—Joaquin Miller (1837–1913), Bret Harte (1836–1902), and Mark Twain (1835–1910). Annie's interest in all three was part of her lifelong openness to promising new writers, and she judged them aright. Her curiosity about the flamboyant Miller terminated soon after they met, she felt strongly drawn to the lively Harte for nearly four years, and her appreciation of Twain's complexity as both a man and a writer grew until the end of her life.

"We been reading the new poet Joaquin Miller. . . . We glowed with the fervor of the new poet so in harmony with the glory of the day," Annie wrote in 1871, soon after *Songs of the Sierras* appeared in England. Characteristically, she wrote him to say so—"the first American lady of culture that has written me," Miller replied, "certainly the first from Boston." Acclaimed by English critics in general and William Michael Rossetti in particular as the Bard of the Wild West, the goateed poet wearing a sombrero and high-heeled spurred boots had recently become a familiar figure in fashionable London drawing rooms. Yet after he returned to America that September, the man who had grown up in Oregon and lived among Indians claimed that he had "always shrunk from Boston" because he "feared its learned and brilliant people." Encouraged by Annie's praise, however, he announced his professional goals and felt "trustful we may be the best of friends." Predictably, Annie invited him to Charles Street. "A letter from Joaquin Miller!" she exclaimed a few weeks later. "A queer epistle enough but so friendly and hearty that we were delighted with it." As Miller had ingratiatingly written, reading Dickens's letters to the Fieldses in the *Atlantic* had made him more eager than ever to meet them, and he enclosed a photograph of himself that Mathew Brady had just taken. But it would be a year before he came himself.[10]

On 22 September 1872, Annie returned from a walk through the Public Garden to receive thirty-three-year-old "poet of the Sierras," who turned out to be a very "natural" slightly built man with long auburn hair. As he candidly told her, he had published *Songs of the Sierras* himself under a feigned publisher's name, given away copies, then received good notices and was taken up the Rossettis. But Annie said nothing else about his visit. He left her to dine with Longfellow, who liked him "much" (as he told Annie) yet found "some things about him not altogether agreeable, such as flinging a quid of tobacco out of his mouth under the table; 'but I don't mind those things; perhaps,' he added, 'perhaps I might have done the same as a youth of 20!!!'"

Miller would never again visit either of them. In 1874 he took the unusual liberty of sending Jamie the sheets of a new book, hoping he could "sell it to Osgood for a lump sum." Annie's second and probably final encounter with Miller occurred at a large reception at the Philadelphia Centennial Exposition in 1876, where he praised her effusively. After Jamie's death five years later, Miller rhapsodically recalled "that evening in Philadelphia; the President, the Emperor, the strength, and the beauty of this new world!" Equally effusive about Jamie, he said "few, if any, admired or looked up to Mr. Fields more earnestly than I"; and his "life seemed the most rounded and perfect of all men's I ever met." The widow replied with a photograph of Jamie and included Miller's tribute in her *Biographical Notes*.[11]

Five years later, when Miller was living in a two-room log cabin that he had built on the edge of Washington, D.C., in what is now Rock Creek Park, he made two requests of Annie. He wanted a photograph of his "dear beautiful friend" to place alongside her husband's on his mantle. He had already entertained many congressmen and their constituents, Miller bragged, and he hoped for a visit from the "beautiful woman who was the *first* in America to write me a kindly letter."[12] Presumably Annie sent the picture but declined his invitation. Yet surely she felt flattered by the place she had retained in Miller's memory.

Annie's initiative in sending Miller that first "kindly letter" is evidence of her remarkable hospitality to spirit and imagination. When she wrote it, many reviewers including William Dean Howells had charged Miller with prolixity, vacuity, artificiality, and sensuality. Without disagreeing, Annie was so struck by his "fervor" that she wrote him to say so. But neither his flamboyant egocentrism nor his flattery appealed to her, and his first visit exhausted her interest in the Poet of the Sierras.

Bret Harte interested her far more, and her interest lasted much longer. In January 1862, the Fieldses' friend Thomas Starr King, a Unitarian minister who had left his Boston pulpit for one in San Francisco, urged them to pay serious attention to an *Atlantic* submission by a "very bright young man who has been in literary ways for a few years." Publication in the *Atlantic* "would inspirit him, & help literature on this coast where we raise bigger trees and squashes than literati & brains." Their mutual friend Mrs. Jessie Frémont thought so well of Harte's "powers," he added, that she had arranged a clerkship for him in the Law Survey Office.[13] Over a year later, Fields accepted Harte's humorous "Legend of Monte Del Diablo" for the October 1863 *Atlantic*. During the next few years, particularly after "The Luck of Roaring Camp" appeared in the second issue of the *Overland Monthly* in 1868, Harte was hailed as an American Dickens and praised by Dickens himself. That October when Fields requested another submission, Harte said editing the *Overland* took most of his time but promised to send "something." That something turned out to be a collection of his *Overland* fiction titled *The Luck of Roaring Camp and Other Sketches;* and as Harte later told Annie, he received her first kind, considerate, and graceful letter in the same "haul" that brought the Ticknor and Fields volume.[14] By the time Harte left California for Boston in early 1871, the book had made him so famous that hordes of reporters covered his cross-country progress. He began a week as the guest of the new *Atlantic* editor William Dean Howells and as the pet of the entire *Atlantic* circle on 25 February; and he soon accepted Howells's unprecedented offer of a thousand dollars for a year's exclusive rights to magazine publication of at least twelve new sketches and poems.

Immediately after his "first appearance among the literati of our shores" at the 25 February meeting of the Saturday Club, James T. Fields brought him home for tea along with Longfellow, Holmes, and a few other club members. What Annie saw was a relatively short man with deep smallpox scars that produced redness around the eyes, but who also had "fine hazel eyes, full lips, large moustache, an

honest smile," and remarkable aplomb. More surprisingly, he seemed so unconscious of his own celebrity that Jamie likened him to the young Charles Dickens.

"Too many days full of interest have passed unrecorded," Annie wrote in her
diary after a two-week gap, then identified the major interest: "Francis Bret
Harte, who has made his first visit to the East just now, since he went to San Francisco in his early youth." He was about thirty-five, she correctly guessed, with a
mind "full of the grand landscape of the West, and filled also with sympathetic interest in the half-developed natives who are to be seen there," a point she illustrated by summarizing several of his comical stories. Better still, the man "the
world" called Bret Harte was "natural, warm-hearted, with a keen relish for fun,
disposed to give just value to the strong language of the West, which he is by no
means inclined to dispense with; at ease in every society, quick of sense and sight,"
and "lovable above all." As she and her husband also agreed, his wife and two children were worthy of him.

Annie became more aware of Harte's complexities during his overnight visit to
Manchester the following September. Alerted by Jamie's telegram, she "drove
hard" in her pony cart to collect him and Harte at the Beverly train station. Then
after calling on Susan Cabot and her sister Miss Howes where "the talk turned a
little upon Hawthorne," Annie and "the two good boys" walked along the shore
and sat up late talking. With characteristic diligence, Annie recorded Harte's
opinions about California (he liked its flowers, but complained of its cloudless-
ness and its bleak mountains); then recounted his ghost story about the house
he had rented in Newport, and summarized a few comical tales "characteristic
of California." Their wide-ranging conversations the following day produced
several surprises. Bret Harte was a "sensitive and nervous man" who "struggles
against himself all the time," Annie now realized, an absent-minded and tender
man whose favorite writers included Montaigne and Horace, yet who did not
fully understand Emerson, and an open-minded man whose "pleasant acceding
to both sides in politics, and other traits of like nature, gives him affinity with
Hawthorne." As she also realized when he quoted a particularly sly line about
Brook Farm from the *American Notebooks*—"Margaret Fuller's cow hooked the
other cows"—Harte was "a true appreciator of Hawthorne."

But by the time Harte came to Charles Street in January and said he was moving to New York because he thought Boston's "provincialisms . . . would hurt
him," Annie had formed serious reservations about his character. He had a "queer
absent-minded way of spending his time," she wrote, "letting the hours slip by as
if he had not altogether learned of their value yet. It is a miracle to us how he lives,
for he writes very little." Harte would never again match the wealth and fame he
enjoyed that year. During the Fieldses' trip to New York in February, they enjoyed
a "merry dinner" at Harte's house and then saw Booth's "Julius Caesar" with him.
But though they enjoyed his company, when Harte was in Boston to deliver a lecture the following year and a sheriff arrested him for debt, Annie ruefully concluded that he had a "screw loose."

What was probably the Fieldses' last long visit with Harte occurred in September 1875, near the end of their first season in their new Manchester cottage. Harte arrived "bubbling over with fun, full of the most natural and unexpected sallies" and comical stories, and entertained them with an affectionate anecdote about Longfellow. He also proudly presented his latest publications—*Gabriel Conroy* (his only novel) and "Two Men of Sandy Creek" (his first play)—which he mistakenly assumed would get him out of debt and increase his fame. Annie praised their "passion." But she was far more enthusiastic about the "dramatic, lovable creature with his blue silk pocket-handkerchief and red dressing slippers and his quick feelings." As she indulgently yet archly declared after he left, "I could hate the man who could help loving him—or the woman either."

The whimsical letter that arrived almost immediately afterward displays Harte at his best and most shrewdly astute:

> I know all! I know now why Fields has become a popular lecturer on authors, living and dead. He is only basely utilizing—for a puerile, personal, pecuniary purpose the faculty of elegant compliment which belongs to *you*! He—this wild Manchester Pirate and Rover of the Gloucester Shores!—is demanding from a timorous and credulous public seventy-five cents . . . for the graceful compliment and kindly and tactful appreciation which drops spontaneously from your tongue and pen. He lies in wait, apparently engaged in the preoccupation of hitching his trousers, while you and I are talking, and appropriates to his own aggrandizement the good things that your good heart and good taste dictate [and] . . . with a wicked, salty eye—apparently scanning the horizon for weeks . . . overlooks your kind pages, and—is—a Pirate still!

Beyond the comic hyperbole, he acknowledged Annie's agency as the lecturer's wife and literary partner. And if he envied their summer house, his self-dramatizing accolade to it was flatteringly precise:

> I have excited the pallid envy of countless householders—among them the mistress of my own home—by extravagant descriptions of Gambrel Cottage, and its interior. They have accepted everything but the India matting on the wainscotting of the halls. There they pause, breathless and incredulous! Then I sling in an account of the procession of heathen Deities in outline on the entablature. Then they succumb! And I stand over them, with a continuous and florid narrative of the hall window and its red cushions, and retire, with the field to myself![15]

Annie Fields's Bret Harte is a more amiable version of the writer Howells would present in *Literary Friends and Acquaintance,* the irreverent ironist who made his "progress" East like a Fairy Prince, a man liable to come late even to a dinner in his honor, a man who did not dependably meet his deadlines or pay his debts, even to his one-time collaborator Mark Twain. For the Fieldses, Harte was a colorful embodiment of the "great landscape of the West," a man who could bubble with jollity and show them an America they did not otherwise know. When Jamie was lecturing in Omaha in October 1875—a month after Harte's visit to Manchester—he and Annie could "see the life Bret Harte describes in the faces, manners, and bearing of the people." But the man who had told Annie that he might some day bring his entire "crew" to see her soon faded out of her life. He would be virtually penniless in 1877, then leave the country forever the following year.[16]

The last and by far the greatest of the three writers who brought frontier language and experience to eastern readers in general and the Fieldses in particular was Samuel L. Clemens, a man they first heard of in the fall of 1868, when the poet Henry Brownell "was full of appreciation of 'Mark Twain'" and the essayist James Parton suggested "that a writer named Mark Twain be engaged" to help make the *Atlantic Monthly* more popular. A few months later, when Twain was lecturing in the Boston area and planning to marry Olivia Langdon of Elmira, New York, he dropped into "the little office of James T. Fields, over the bookstore of Ticknor & Fields, at 124 Tremont Street, Boston," an event Howells nostalgically recalled in his autobiography decades later.[17] Annie's secondhand report of the event includes little more than Twain's whimsical reply to one of Jamie's questions: "'I don't know where I live but I find letters directed to Elmira *always* reach me; if they are sent anywhere else, they don't." Howells's praise of *Innocents Abroad* appeared in the *Atlantic* a few months later, and from then on Twain socialized with *Atlantic* writers during his trips to Boston, though he would not publish in the magazine until 1874. By then he was a husband and father, and he had moved to Hartford. But Annie did not meet him until the spring of 1876, when she accompanied Jamie on a lecture trip to Hartford.

A few weeks earlier, when Jamie first visited Twain's "brick villa" and heard "the whole story of his life," he repeated it to Annie, She set it all down in her journal, then concluded, "He and his wife have wretched health, poor things! And in spite of their beautiful house must often have rather a hard time. He is very eccentric, disturbed by every noise, and it cannot be altogether easy to take care of such a man. It is a very loving household." A few weeks later, at Twain's urging, Annie saw it for herself.

The visit was surprising from the start. The evening before Jamie's lecture, the Fieldses were met at the Hartford railroad station and whisked to the theater where Twain was giving the second of his two performances as Peter Spyle in *Loan of a Lover.* "Mr. Clemens' part was a creation," Annie enthused, certain that if he turned professional, he would match the success of the immensely popular Joseph Jefferson. After "a bit of supper" at Twain's club, they arrived at his house after midnight, where his wife awaited them with "a pretty supper table laid." Kneeling abjectly before her, Twain explained that the excitement of the play had made him forget "all her directions and injunctions." If the histrionic husband was wholly new to Annie's experience, his fragile wife was not—"a very small, sweet-looking, simple, finished creature, charming in her ways and evidently deeply beloved by him."

The following day, the Fieldses met the Clemenses' two young daughters—
"exquisite affectionate children, the very fountain of joy to their interesting parents," and Annie pursued her own interests by visiting Hartford's Union for
"home work" (where she met the "angelic" woman who ran it). But she observed
no one more intently than her host, a man with a "heavy light-colored moustache, and overhanging light eyebrows," piercing yet soft grey eyes, and "exquisite" neatness, his mass of hair "the one rugged-looking thing about him" (which
Annie "thought in the play last night . . . was a wig"). Instead of accompanying
her husband to his lecture that night, Annie stayed behind and wrote down every
word she could recall of Twain's conversations, including his arguments in favor
of weighted votes, his criticisms of the American government, and his comments
about the autobiography he had been working on in bed that morning. In response to his wife's laughing remark that she would remove all "objectionable
passages" from it, he had insisted that it would be printed exactly as he wrote it,
"told as truly as I can tell it." But he mitigated his own sternness by a wryly witty
pronouncement that now seems quintessentially his own: "Every man feels that
his experience is unlike that of anybody else and therefore he should write it
down. He finds, also, that everybody else has thought and felt on some points precisely as he has done, and therefore he should write it down."[18] Struck by Twain's
"wondrous and noble" commitment to truthfulness, and certain it would "continue to make him a daily increasing power among us," Annie found it "curious
and interesting to watch this growing man of forty—to see how he studies and
how high his aims are. His conversation is always earnest and careful, though full
of fun."

The next morning's interchanges with him complicated that judgment.
Though Twain greeted her cheerfully when she entered the drawing room after
breakfast, his comment that one of his daughters was very sick made Annie realize that both parents "were half-distracted with anxiety." Since the child did not
seem really sick to Annie, she simply concluded that "they were unnecessarily excited." After Twain sent his carriage for the doctor without knowing that the
Fieldses were about to leave in it, he asked his wife "'Why didn't you tell me of
that,' etc. etc.," apologized to the Fieldses, and then claimed that "he had spent
the larger part of his life on his knees making apologies." "He was always bringing the blood to his wife's face by his bad behavior," Annie mused, though she herself had felt embarrassed when Olivia "told him to see how well we behaved (poor
we!)." And though Twain's abjection had made them all laugh, she "could see that
it was no laughing matter to him. He is in dead earnest, with a desire for growth
and truth in life, and with such a sincere admiration for his wife's sweetness and
beauty of character that the most prejudiced and hardest heart could not fail to
fall in love with him."

Twain emerges from Annie's journal as an entertaining, volatile, yet profoundly serious man who was still growing at the age of forty, anxiety-ridden

about all his performances—whether as an actor, autobiographer, husband, father, or host. Annie's account of the author of *Tom Sawyer* who had not yet become the author of *Huckleberry Finn* testifies to her perspicacity and sensitivity. As DeWolfe Howe remarked in his *Memories of a Hostess,* that account deserves a "place in the authentic annals of an extraordinary personality."[19]

In 1887, after Twain came to Boston for a memorial tribute to Longfellow and then enjoyed "a rousing good time" at Charles Street, he told Annie that "Mrs. Clemens was speaking of the unspeakable grace and peace and loveliness of your home when I interrupted her to say you had expected her there with me and would have been glad had she come; which pleased her very much indeed."[20] Clearly, they had both enjoyed Annie's hospitality before then. And at least once Twain himself missed out on an invitation. "Mrs. Clemens has just been telling me that [Charles Dudley] Warner was your guest in Boston, and that you had invited me to dine there," he told Annie in 1889, then explained that her letter had not reached him.[21]

In April 1892, Annie enjoyed a serendipitous reunion with Twain and his wife in Italy; and his visit to Boston in January 1894 was the occasion for an unusually intimate Charles Street dinner. Though Holmes was then so frail that he seldom went out, as Twain told his wife, he "wanted to 'have a time' once more with me." Afraid of overtaxing him, Annie invited only her "family"—Sarah and Mary Jewett—to join them; and Holmes enjoyed himself so much that he was reluctant to leave.[22]

In 1901, Olivia Clemens thanked Annie for an invitation to Charles Street and her "good letter" about one of Twain's publications—presumably "To the Person Sitting in Darkness," a powerful political invective which had provoked reproaches from some friends and reviewers and silence from others. Grateful for her support, Mrs. Clemens assured Annie that "Mr. Clemens could not if he had wished—and he did not wish—to have done otherwise than he has done because his convictions were so very strong."[23]

That was no surprise to Annie, who had recognized his commitment to tell the truth as he saw it during her two nights in Hartford twenty-five years before. Without excusing his "bad behavior," she had discerned the anguish beneath his self-deprecating drollery and guessed right about his "growing power." In 1912, two years after Twain's death, she set down a few lines that suggest how important he had become to her. She had just finished Albert Paine's new biography of Twain—"the life of a man who had greatness in him"; she was reading his *Joan of Arc;* and she hoped "to wait as cheerfully as he did for the trumpet call and as usefully." Frail but resolute at the age of seventy-eight, Annie seized on Twain's cheerfulness as a moral imperative.

During the years when Joaquin Miller, Bret Harte, and Mark Twain emerged as spokesmen for the American West, Annie Fields met them, entertained them, corresponded with them, and took their measure. It did not take her long to realize that only Twain "had greatness in him," a realization that deepened over time.

Persephone

The decorous Ann West Adams Fields was rarely explicit about her affection for her decorous mother Sarah May Holland Adams. Surely it underlay her fondness for women who were also solicitous daughters—including Laura Johnson, Rebecca Harding Davis, Gail Hamilton, Kate Field, Celia Thaxter, and Sarah Orne Jewett. But it would be impossible to guess from Annie's journals that Mrs. Adams was seriously ill in September 1875 and became terminally ill a year later.

During the winter of 1876–77, Annie's nightly journal entries reported such events as Jamie's lectures, her dinners for Longfellow and other old friends, the "brilliant" meetings of her club of women writers, her Wednesday evening receptions for about twenty (including the occasion when "Mr. Graham Bell [came] with his telephone"), and her charity work.[24] Therefore an entry in early March comes as a surprise: "I cannot or do not make time to write down here some of the many interesting things which absorb our lives, but while my dear mother is so ill every extra thought and moment is directed her way if I am not by her side." On the first day of spring, Annie reported making two visits to her mother, who was "very very low." Then on 27 March came a profoundly emotional entry: "Mother died this morning at 6 A.M. at this writing (early in the afternoon) it already seems an eternity—so surely is time marked by feeling & experience and not by deeds done or moments counted."

Only to her friend Laura had Annie confided her anxieties about her mother's health. In September 1875 when Mrs. Adams was at Charles Street convalescing from a serious illness, Annie had said she was happy to have her there but could not expect or even hope that she would have many more years. When her mother's terminal illness began in December 1876, Annie anticipated spending long hours at her bedside to relieve her sister Sarah, though she soon realized that with two nurses in attendance, even she and her sister Louisa "seem to be too many for any length of time." Therefore her life went on as usual. The sewing rooms she had started were busy, and "co-operative visiting goes forward well"; Elizabeth Stuart Phelps had read a new story at the first meeting of her club of women writers; Edith Longfellow was engaged to the Danas' son—"a great pleasure to us all"; and Whittier "came to breakfast as usual," bringing a fine new ballad called "The Witch of Wenham." In February 1877, Annie told Laura that a Dr. Nelson eased her mother's "restless nights by laying hands on her," then returned to such ongoing interests as her writers' club and "a new association for funding scholarships for young women in Massachusetts Universities." A month later came the news that Mrs. Adams was dead "at last." "Endless tributes to mother's memory were sent in to us and the solemn festival was beautiful and consoling," Annie reported, and so was reading Charles Kingsley's *Life* with her family afterward—"a divine story, or as near to that as any mortal can come I think," a story of faith in Christianity and social justice "in perfect consonance with our thoughts and feelings."[25]

Within a few weeks, Annie found a more constructive way to ease her grief. After a two-week gap in her journal came a cryptic announcement: "Now and then I work upon *Demeter* and ponder it deeply." An only slightly less cryptic announcement came ten weeks later, on 25 June: "Finished 'Persephone' except two or three songs which are not yet to my mind and must wait for a clearer mood." After their mother's death, Annie's sister Sarah had spent two weeks at Manchester and then sailed for Europe, leaving Annie free to complete her own act of emotional closure. In the ambitious poetic drama whose title was no longer "Demeter" but "Persephone," the narrative focus effectively shifts from the mythic mother to the mythic daughter. In mid-August of 1877, following a four-week gap in the journal she had kept for fourteen years, Annie made a brief entry about visiting Elizabeth Stuart Phelps. Although there are torn-out pages after it, this was her final entry.[26]

The Return of Persephone: A Dramatic Sketch was privately printed at the University Press in Cambridge, Massachusetts, in the fall of 1877, its author identified as "A.F." When she inscribed a copy of the four-act blank verse "dramatic sketch" to her friend Lilian Fairchild, Annie added the dedication which the printer had "carelessly omitted" but which would appear in the second printing: "To the memory of my mother."[27] It was an apt dedication for a poem celebrating the love between a heroic mother and a heroic daughter. When she translated Goethe's "Pandora" a few months before, Annie had submerged her own identity while putting her literary and linguistic skills in the service of a much greater poet. But retelling the myth of Persephone was a more challenging and more deeply private project. While honoring her mother, she reconceived the interdependent love of mother and child at the heart of the myth.

"O sweet new days! wherein the young moon folds / The old on her bright breast, to nourish her!" Demeter exclaims near the beginning of the poem when Persephone goes off to gather flowers. That image encapsulates a revisionary theme: the mother who loves and teaches her child is also nurtured by that child. In Annie's poem as in most versions of the myth, the mother deprived of her daughter permits and even causes death. But because Annie's Persephone became vulnerable to abduction when she disobeyed her mother, she is implicated in that deprivation. The poet nonetheless affirms the girl's moral soundness. Taught by her mother to embroider images of the earth and the sky, Persephone also aspires to capture "the light in human eyes, / When joy transforms or pity bids them weep." Demeter·then tells her daughter what they both have yet to learn: "joy and grief spring from one common root."

Embodied in Annie's version of the ancient myth is a daughter's self-revealing self-justification for moving out of her mother's life and into her husband's. Persephone loves her husband and is beloved by him. He allows her to spend part of each year with Demeter and she does, because love bids it, and because she hears "my mother's longing cry." As a corollary, Demeter regains her lost beauty only when she learns from her daughter to enjoy "making others glad"; and her final statement—"my darling will return!"—signals her understanding that Persephone's separate life with her husband does not mean that her daughter is lost to her.

Annie also made the myth her own through her characters' humanitarian concerns. The philanthropist who tried to improve the lives of the poor was also the poet who composed Demeter's charge to her daughter: instead of picking the "strange purple blooms" beyond the dark stream, she should "pluck blossoms from thy path / And strew them in the places without bloom." That is only a slightly displaced version of Annie's advice to herself whenever she encountered "places without bloom," and most of *Persephone*'s characters act in that spirit: Hecate offers Demeter light, Helios offers sympathy and intervenes with Aidoneus for Persephone's return, Keleus's daughters worry about their sick brother, and Demeter herself finally enjoys "making others glad" with the bounty only she can produce.

Like many of Annie's other friends, the writer Harriet Waters Preston praised her "mastery of the antique dramatic form." Annie had retold the myth with "peculiar grace and tenderness," Preston said, and the dedication to her mother was "very sadly and tenderly fit."[28] Although Annie had previously written elegies for Hawthorne and Dickens, she had no precedent for an appropriate tribute to her beloved mother, a woman with virtually no public identity. One way was by following Mrs. Adams's specific injunctions, including a deathbed behest to love a woman named Kate Gannett; and on 11 April Annie could report feeling closer to Kate. Another was to begin work on "Demeter," a commemoration that spurred her own moral and artistic growth. "My mother's life is such a blessed memory and inspiration," she told a friend in May, then said she missed her mother yet retained her as "a living and active spirit of good."[29] In that spirit, submerging yet affirming her own identity as daughter and poet, wife and humanitarian, "A. F." appropriated an ancient myth of maternal vitality to create her own *Persephone*.

Under the Olive

In November 1880, Houghton Mifflin published a small green-bound volume called *Under the Olive* with no name on the cover or title page, though the verso announced that it was copyrighted by "Mrs. Annie Fields." The book contained nineteen original poems in classical meters on classical subjects, including *Persephone,* and four translations of Goethe including the long dramatic poem "Pandora." The poems occupy 264 pages, and they are followed by 38 pages of explanatory notes in small print. Annie had been writing and publishing poetry for nearly two decades—over a dozen during the sixties, and nearly twenty in the seventies. But except for the privately published *Persephone,* she had not displayed her engagement with Greek myths; she had only incidentally displayed her scholarship and her linguistic skills; and she had never before published a collection of her poems.

In December 1876, Annie had organized a club of women writers who held weekly meetings at Charles Street to read their new work to one another. Taking her own turn in January, she had read her translation of Goethe's "Pandora" to a group of ten women who "expressed satisfaction." Their response might well have encouraged her to write poems of her own on classical themes; and her friends' praise of *Persephone* must have been a strong incentive to write others.

In the mid-sixties, Annie had simply accepted exclusion from the all-male club which discussed Longfellow's translation of the *Divine Comedy* in the course of its composition, although she had been reading Dante since her schooldays. She passed judgment on that translation to Laura Johnson and other women friends, and she used a passage from *Purgatorio* as the epigraph for *Asphodel.* In 1865 when David Wasson was writing his long essay on *Wilhelm Meister* for the *Atlantic,* he honed his ideas by discussing them with Annie. But when *Under the Olive* appeared fifteen years later, even close friends were impressed by Annie's skillful appropriation of Greek poets, playwrights, myths, and poetic motifs, and by her familiarity with Dante, Goethe, Hegel, Fichte, and Grote.

By putting words into the mouths of the three major Greek tragedians in three successive poems—"The Last Contest of Aeschylus," "Sophocles," and "Euripides"—, Annie implicitly put herself in their league, just as she did in giving speech to the gods in "Herakles" and "Aphrodite." At least equally audacious is her domestication of legendary conflicts. In the sibling rivalry plot of "Herakles," Prometheus's selfless brother brings the jealous rebel back into Jove's fold; the elderly protagonist of "Sophocles" defends himself against his son's charge of incompetence by reading a choral ode from *Oedipus at Colonus;* and in "The Lantern of Sestos"—in classical hexameters—the passionate Hero and Leander story is tempered by Annie's sense of propriety:

> There in her arms she received her love, the voyager, wave-stained,
> Led him within, and his limbs washed and anointed with oil.
>
> Bride and bridegroom were there, but where was the feast of the bridal!
> Wedding was there, yet where, guest of the wedding, wert thou!
> Bliss of marriage was there, but absent the blessing of parents!
> Silent the halls, and the hollows of the night were grown still.

As yet another kind of personal appropriation, Annie's ode to "Theocritus," the poet "Loved by the satyr and the faun," incorporates a tribute to New England:

> . . . unto us, to us,
> The stalwart glories of the North;
> Ours is the sounding main. . . .

Her lyrical voice sometimes falters (as in "the hollows of the night were grown still"), and many images are stale (including "the sounding main"). But her tone is suitably lofty, her prosody is skillful, and she is remarkably effective at domesticating mythical situations.

Although all the poems she had published before were anonymous, pseudonymous, or signed only with her initials, Annie had already earned a reputation for excellence among literati. In 1879, for example, when the editor of the New York *Home Journal* wanted to include "all, or nearly all, the leading poets of America" in an anthology, she invited Annie to contribute.[30] But *Under the Olive* magnified her reputation and elicited respectful reviews.

Many of Annie's eminent male friends offered witty compliments. Longfellow rejoiced in Annie's "double success—the *esoteric* and the *exoteric,* as the Pythagoreans would say; the success in the book itself, and its success with the public, which is sure to follow"; and the critic Moncure Conway said he loved and reverenced Annie's work even when he found himself disagreeing with her, as about "Herakles siding with Jove, that egotist."[31] Charles Dudley Warner of the *Hartford Courant* assured Annie that he felt "as much imposed on as if I had visited the temple of Apollo, and been waited on by the priestess, who veiled her eyes and never let me know she was the priestess," then more facetiously asked if Fields might request "a divorce on the ground that he did not intend to marry a Greek." Amazed that any American had "the scholarship plus the poetry" to produce such work, he reprinted several of her poems in the *Courant.*[32]

Even Annie's neighbor Oliver Wendell Holmes confessed to surprise. Her friends "knew in some measure what they had a right to expect from your poetical nature and thoughtful cultivation" but might have "feared that you would be content with being useful, hospitable, benevolent, agreeable, tasteful, accomplished, and so at last exhale with all your music in you." Then he sounded an extravagant fanfare "in the name of my lineal ancestress Mistress Anne Bradstreet" to signal Annie's "formal entrance to the company of the singing sisterhood, which may you long adorn!"[33]

By contrast, most of Annie's women friends simply stressed their pleasure at her achievement. Only one expressed reservations, though couched as praise. "I hardly *know* enough to follow you—It is so long since I used to turn to my classical dictionary & knew all about those mythic stories," Harriet Beecher Stowe wrote, though "as to your manner of treating them nothing could be lovelier." Delighted by "the verdict of the press" and "the plaudits of all the knowing ones," Stowe nonetheless believed that Annie's "works for humanity" had a higher beauty than her poems.[34] By contrast, another old friend—the children's writer Adeline Whitney—saw a causal connection between the two kinds of work. She told Annie, "You have a right to tell us of 'Herakles,' you who also take up the labors, and have grown in the appointed day to the power of telling."[35] A loftier tribute came from a more famous and more versatile writer, the poet and essayist Helen Hunt Jackson. No American "could have written these poems except

Stedman," Jackson declared, "—and you have said things that he—being a man—couldn't have said."[36] A newer friend offered a more personal compliment: "Your *Under the Olive* is always more and more of a pleasure to me," Sarah Orne Jewett wrote, "and I read the notices of it as eagerly as possible."[37]

Uneasy about her own pleasure in "praise sweet though it may be to the spirit" while up to her ears in reform work, Annie could only hope that her poems would stand the test of time.[38] A few months later, she was a widow, so devastated by her loss that she could perform only the private work of grief.

Part Two

MRS. ANNIE FIELDS

(1881–1915)

SECTION IV

Autonomy and Independence— the Eighties

16

Widowhood

Mourning and Beyond

"My dear partner is really better," Annie assured Whittier on 16 March 1881, two months after Jamie had suffered an attack of angina pectoris.[1] But a month and a half later, he succumbed to a final attack. After visiting the Beals on the last Sunday in April, the Fieldses were sitting in their library with Celia Thaxter and a few evening callers when the sound of fire engines drew Jamie to the window. He collapsed, then was helped to a chair. To help him relax, as she had often done before, Annie picked up a book and began reading it aloud. But James T. Fields died only moments later in the library he and his wife had created, surrounded by books he had published and in the company of friends, listening to his wife read Matthew Arnold's biographical sketch of Thomas Gray. Devastated by grief, Annie retreated to the bedroom that was now hers alone.[2]

The following morning, only family members and a few close friends were admitted to the flower-filled house. After a brief private service at King's Chapel, with Cyrus Bartol officiating, James T. Fields was buried in Mount Auburn Cemetery. Meantime, local publishers and booksellers held a memorial ceremony of their own at the Old Corner Bookstore. At least one of them—Thomas Niles, a Roberts Brothers editor who had once clerked for Fields—resented the "*privacy* of his funeral." As he told his friend Louisa May Alcott, "Distinguished people only seem to have been invited. His old business associates sent to Mrs. Fields to know if a committee might have the gratification of paying a last tribute & were told they were not wanted."[3] In fact, Annie was so shrouded in grief that she wanted to see no one. It was not Annie but Celia Thaxter who telegraphed the news of Fields's death to Whittier. Stunned by the loss of his own "best friend— kind, helpful, generous, always," Whittier told the "dearest friend of the dear friend who has left us, and whose love made his life perfect and beautiful" that he wanted to stand beside her at the funeral. Then he offered the advice that other friends would reiterate: Annie should think of how blessed she had been to share so much love.[4]

"Oh my darling it is hard to be alone, [especially] when the first exaltation of grief passes," Laura Johnson wrote a month after Fields's death, then urged Annie "to take up your life as well as you can and to fulfill his." Two weeks later—on 6 June, her own forty-seventh birthday—Annie replied that she could not "write to anyone just now & I see no one." Yet even while protesting that she could not write and saw no one, she was writing to say so, and she had just invited Lucy Larcom to join her in Manchester.[5]

It is "right and good for me to be with Mrs. Fields in her bereavement, if she wants me," Lucy told Whittier that same day, explaining why she could not join him in North Conway.[6] During the next few weeks the women sometimes took walks or drives along the Manchester shore together, but Annie spent "much of her time out among the flowers, and in looking over her husband's correspondence when she is in the house."[7] Looking through that correspondence was a form of retreat, but it also prepared her to resume her life. Over the next few months, she worked diligently on a biography of her husband, occasionally consulting Aldrich and Whittier on matters of taste and Holmes about editorial procedures and even typography. "How lonely she must be; and how happy it is for her that she can devote herself to writing a life of her husband," Longfellow told Elizabeth Stuart Phelps in August, pleased "for her sake and for ours" and certain "the work could not be in better hands."[8] By then, Annie was accepting brief visits from a few close friends, Phelps and Howells among them. Though her grief was still "a vast abiding presence absorbing my life" and she still felt "rapt away from the old earth," preparing the biography was a "beneficent occupation."[9]

James T. Fields: Biographical Notes and Personal Sketches, with Unpublished Fragments and Tributes from Men and Women of Letters appeared with remarkable dispatch in November. Annie's "whole heart was in the pages" yet it was not "overwrought," her chief adviser Holmes assured her. She had produced a "beautiful memorial volume" and created a "life-like picture" which the public "had a right to." As for Annie herself, Holmes said no woman had more perfectly "fulfilled, not only every duty, but every ideal that a husband could think of." Next came a grateful acknowledgment: "Under your roof I have met more visitors to be remembered than under any other. But for your hospitality I should never have had the privilege of personal acquaintance with famous writers and artists who I can now recall as I saw them talked with them heard them in that pleasant library, that most lively and agreeable dining room."[10]

Of the many tributes to the *Biographical Notes,* none was more self-revealing than a note on a telegraph blank from Elizabeth Stuart Phelps. As she told "My dear girl,"

I write on the way to town on all the paper I can muster to tell you that I received your book yesterday evening, and that I have this moment finished the last word, reading it all; a feat of which I am very vain, as it is years since I have read much more than one half hour consecutively, or been overlong at anything. There isn't much of me left to tell you how the memorial has swept me along; but what there is shall go without an hour's delay to reach you if it may be by night.—It is a fine, strong, controlled, and beautiful thing in itself, as a work; one of the types, and one which will endure. For what it is of *him,* I hardly know how to speak, so near has it brought me to him and so deeply has it touched me. . . . [T]he gap which he has left even in my life no one else will ever fill, or can. . . . You had a "strait and narrow" task, and have performed it like yourself. . . . I closed the book, choking, when I came to your first years together.

But Annie, you have *had* it. . . . He was always my ideal of a husband.[11]

Harriet Beecher Stowe's response was more solemnly thoughtful. The memorial "has enlarged my knowledge of his worth of heart & character," she wrote, shared a few of her own recollections, said she was "prepared to go over" (that is, to die) herself, and urged Annie to visit her in Florida. But her main purpose was spiritual consolation. As she assured Annie, "you have not lost him—all that was noble just kindly upright & pure the traits developed in his earth life he carries up with him. . . . That cheery brightness, that play of humor which made him so delightful a companion will not be wanting in those higher spheres—our friend will *be himself.*"[12] Perhaps that assurance is one reason why Annie consulted a medium five months later, though by then she had found another companion for her "earth life."

Although most of Annie's friends showered praise on the *Biographical Notes,* at least one of them had serious reservations. The book was by "no means as good as it ought to be," Caroline Dall complained in her journal: "Mr. Fields was built on a far grander pattern than his wife sees," nor did she see that his "devotion— to his first love—& her sister his first wife—& his careful provision for his old mother, had much to do with his rise in general esteem."[13] Today's reader might also wish for more analyses, less eulogizing, at least some astringency, and a tighter organization. But selecting from a vast amount of material, Annie restored her husband to life within the world of letters that he had helped shape. In Whittier's words, she had created a delicate book "in which all the rare and talented of the last half century pass before the eye of the reader."[14]

That accomplishment alone made Annie a role model for many other widows, including Marie Taylor and Elizabeth Agassiz. For the widow of the writer Bayard Taylor, Annie's biography was an exemplary "monument" completed with exemplary speed. Marie Taylor had begun her own such monument soon after her husband's death in 1878, but it was far from completion when Annie's appeared. At that point, she requested copies of any letters from her husband to the Fieldses, and she asked to be asked to Manchester. Next came an effusive note of thanks followed by a curious invitation: Marie Taylor hoped Annie would stay with her when she and Sarah next came to New York, for fifteen dollars a week with an extra charge for "breakfast carried to the room," as "a business matter, of course, and something that does not concern ourselves as friend to friend."[15]

Whatever Annie thought of that offer, she was among the first to praise *The Life and Letters of Bayard Taylor* the following year. Annie's letter was "very dear to me, coming from you with your fine appreciation of my dear departed one and the works he has left behind him," Marie Taylor wrote, then poignantly added, "Ah, dear, you know as well as I, how we snatch at every straw, to make us feel a little less the burden of our loss." Then she made such a snatch, saying she hoped to spend "a few such pleasant days at Manchester as last year."[16] During the sixties, because their husbands were old friends and because Bayard Taylor was a major *Atlantic* contributor, Annie had often invited the couple to Charles Street and sent them newsy letters. But neither as a wife nor a widow did Annie ever pursue or even encourage a separate relationship with Marie Taylor.

Like Marie Taylor, Elizabeth Agassiz praised Annie's speedily completed memorial volume at a time when she had not yet completed her own. "It will lead many of us back and make the past live again," Mrs. Agassiz said, sure it would "bring a kind of peace & calmness to you as a last loving act accomplished."[17] Like both Marie Taylor and Annie Fields, Elizabeth Agassiz was the second wife of a loving husband—the distinguished scientist Louis Agassiz; and her accomplishments as a wife and widow were arguably greater than Annie's. She ran a girls' school for seven years while her children were young, enlisting her husband as a teacher; she prepared the notes on his scientific lectures which he expanded for publication under his own name; and she not only accompanied him to South America but kept the journal which grew into their coauthored *Journey to Brazil*. "What a wife that man has!" Annie once exclaimed in her journal. "The labor of his books falls chiefly upon her." Shortly after Louis Agassiz died in 1873, his wife began preparing a conventional *Life and Letters*. But she was more concerned with the work for women's higher education which eventuated in the establishment of the Harvard Annex and then Radcliffe College, with herself as president. In 1885 when she finally completed the biography she had been "putting together" for twelve years, she told Annie, "I need say nothing to you of the doubts & fears I have had and still have, about my own share in it."[18]

By then, the women had become such fast friends that Annie often invited Mrs. Agassiz to Charles Street, sometimes to meet such eminent foreigners as Alice Meynell and Mme. Blanc. She also sent Mrs. Agassiz each of her own new books and Sarah Orne Jewett's, as well as books that she had recently read and wanted to discuss. Mrs. Agassiz reciprocated with flowers, photographs, comments on the books Annie sent, and invitations of her own.[19] It was "helpful to hear of all you have been doing so quietly and efficiently," she wrote after reading one of Annie's publications (perhaps *How to Help the Poor*); then she told her that Radcliffe students were informally invited to drop in on Wednesday afternoons, and urged Annie and Sarah to "come & take a cup of tea with us." At least once afterward, Annie entertained Mrs. Agassiz and some of "our girls" at Charles Street.[20]

Another widow resembled Annie only in her devastation at the loss of a beloved husband. In September 1881, five months after her own husband's death, Annie sent Mrs. Sidney Lanier a deeply sympathetic condolence letter. Explaining that she had been prostrated by grief, Mary Lanier did not reply until April, but said she felt drawn to Annie "in a way that is quite beyond reason." By then she had read Annie's *Biographical Notes* and her other "beautiful work," and envied her ability to write. As to Annie's envy of her three "dear, dear children," Mrs. Lanier pathetically confided that her "entire failure of mind and body" extended even to them, then asked, "O, friend, will one outlive this death?"[21] Annie Fields had already answered that question for herself. But in an effort to help Mary Lanier make the same answer, Annie organized a fund for her support.

A much more famous widow who felt devastated by her loss set much greater store by Annie's sympathy. As Mrs. Matthew Arnold declared after her husband's death in June 1888, "Nobody appreciated more entirely than you did, his great intellectual gifts, his high aims and the genial loveable nature which gave him such a charm as a companion and friend—Of myself it is hard to write—*You* can feel I am sure all that must have gone out of my life with him—who was the joy and light and centre of his home." Her husband had always insisted on using time well, Mrs. Arnold confided, but she felt inert. When Annie went to see her in Surrey four years later, Frances Arnold invited her to pay obeisance in Matthew Arnold's study, which remained just as he had left it, and then to walk on his favorite paths. Mrs. Arnold felt Annie's "*absolute* sympathy," she wrote soon afterward, then recalled visiting Charles Street with her husband in 1884 and wondering at how "*you* made everything seem bright and pleasant." But for Frances Arnold, Annie's primarily importance was as a link to the cherished past.[22]

Household Companionship

Even after completing her *Biographical Notes,* Annie felt unable to resume her own life. Longing to "get to you & put my arms round you & comfort you," Celia Thaxter spoke for many of their friends when she urged Annie not to shut herself away because she had "lost the greatest love on earth." Celia realized "what twenty-six years were yours! Indeed, they were enough to unfit anyone to live in this tough world at all—a bit of heaven come down to earth—Few women ever had the like—what shelter!" The woman who had only briefly known such shelter herself urged Annie not to remain alone. Perhaps Jessie Cochrane was at Charles Street, Celia speculated on 11 November, and a few days later she felt relieved that Lily Fairchild was staying with Annie.[23]

But she was soon heartened by a change in Annie's life. "Ask the little owl if she has been asked to write a love poem for the new Illustrated Weekly in Philadelphia," Celia asked Annie in January 1882.[24] The "little owl" was Sarah Orne Jewett. According to Mark DeWolfe Howe, she had struck James T. Fields as "the ideal friend to fill the impending gap in the life of his wife." That is exactly what Sarah turned out to be.[25]

They had known each other for some years. As early as 4 December 1877, Sarah sent Annie an amiably self-revealing letter. Disheartened by a snowstorm "since snow shuts one in," she told Annie that she did not always keep to the roads when she went walking but went off to investigate deserted farms and ramble across hills and hollows. Then after asking if Annie had a good Thanksgiving, she commented on Elizabeth Stuart Phelps's latest novel—*Avis,* about a painter whose devotion to her art separates her from ordinary life. In the process she implicitly defined her own very different kind of literary heroine:

> I have been reading *Avis* and it interests me very much as Miss Phelps's books always do, but I think it wont do the good she fancied and I am afraid it will do harm—Avis is far too exceptional a character—one can hardly say that Miss Phelps's characters are untrue—but they seemed to me like what I know of Turner's pictures beyond most people's comprehension, or without their observation, at any rate—I think it is better not to take the perfect type of a class when one wishes to write such a book as that! So few girls can possibly be so devoted; as Avis was to her art—[26]

They both attended Holmes's seventieth birthday party in December 1879, Annie sitting at the head table and Sarah at another that included Elizabeth Stuart Phelps. Soon afterward, Annie invited Sarah to spend a week at Charles Street, but a flare-up of Sarah's rheumatoid arthritis prevented it.[27]

Their friendship really began with a chance meeting in July 1880. When Sarah arrived with her friend Cora Clark Rice at the Oceanic Hotel on Star Island, one of the Isles of Shoals, she found "a great many Boston people there whom I knew" including the Fieldses.[28] She and Annie then wandered about the island together, explored the deserted village of Gosport, and climbed to the belfry of its church. One consequence was Sarah's poem titled "Gosport," which ends in the belfry where the speaker "rang the knell for Gosport town." Another was Annie's invitation to spend three days at Manchester in August. This time Sarah went.

"I have been wishing to tell you how much I like to think about the days I spent with you, and how much I missed you after I came away," Sarah told "Dear Mrs. Fields" shortly afterward. Writing from Cora Rice's house in Little Compton, Rhode Island, and about to visit another friend in Newport, Sarah added, "And whether I drive or sail I am the most placid and serene of all your friends, and I forget that I ever was a girl who couldn't go to sleep at night." As the phrase "all your friends" anticipates, her intimacy with Annie would never exclude other friendships. Annie would soon see "our" Gosport poem in *Harper's,* Sarah said: "I feel that you and I are partners in those verses." On that wave of intimacy, she sent love to Annie's husband and their friend Eva von Blomberg and a greeting to the "handkerchief doll," then prophetically concluded, "I will always be your sincere and affectionate friend."[29]

"I know how many friends you have," Sarah wrote in November after receiving Annie's *Under the Olive*, "—but I take it, as I know you will let me, as a sign of something that is between us, and since we have hold of each others hands we will not let them go—." As she assured Annie, "many a line will seem as if it were spoken and not written to me, and bring back other things—that you have said and I like to remember." Then with girlish breathlessness, Sarah anticipated a "little visit" to Charles Street: "And we will play with each other whenever we have a chance, and talk about the rose tea set—and find time every day for one handkerchief doll at least."[30]

Annie invited her to come in January, but Sarah's sister Mary was away in Boston and she did not like to leave their mother alone during the winter. Nonetheless eager for a few days with Annie, she whimsically said that whenever she did get to Charles Street, they could "play that it is still January—the time when you asked me to come." As for *Under the Olive*, it was "always more and more of a pleasure to me," she read the reviews eagerly, and she wondered if Annie had seen the one in the *Christian Union*.[31]

It would be ten months before Sarah made her first visit to Charles Street. She came at the end of November, seven months after Annie was widowed, and she remained until mid-winter. During those months and for over a quarter of a century longer, Annie felt sustained by Sarah's "beautiful household companionship."[32]

Backgrounds and Foregrounds

In November 1881, Annie Fields was forty-seven, a woman who had published poetry and prose but was best known for her hospitality and philanthropy, a genteel Bostonian who for twenty-seven years had been the loving and beloved wife of the city's major publisher. Sarah Orne Jewett was an unmarried woman of thirty-two, a native of South Berwick, Maine, who was best known for her stories of rural lives. Yet despite the numerous differences between them, the women had a lot in common.

They were both reared in close-knit families that provided security but encouraged individuality, and both were doctors' daughters. They shared the dual goals of self-fulfillment and service to others, and the same ideals of friendship. They had many dear friends including some of the same ones, they were both close to their sisters, and they both enjoyed socializing. Literature was central to their lives, they had been writing since childhood, and they both enjoyed gardening. Moreover, they were both dealing with bereavement when their friendship began: Annie's mother died in 1877 and her husband four years later; Sarah's father died in 1878 and her mother's health was failing.

Although Sarah's childhood in rural South Berwick was far different from Annie's Boston childhood, they were both children of privilege. The house Sarah was born in and died in—which still stands at the head of the village square—is a gracious and even elegant Georgian hip-roofed white clapboard two-story building with flared eaves and a Doric portico; and its furnishings include Chippendale and Sheraton tables and chairs, Wedgwood and Staffordshire china, imported wallpaper, and bookcases filled with leather-bound books. When Sarah was born, the household included her great-grandfather, two grandparents, an uncle, and Irish servants, as well as her parents and her sister Mary. Shortly before her sister Carrie was born, Doctor Jewett built his family a smaller Greek Revival house next door. After he died, Sarah moved back to the older house with her mother and Mary, leaving the other for Carrie and her new husband.

Like Annie, Sarah grew up in a secure and beautiful world that was undergoing rapid economic change. During her childhood (when Annie was already married), warehouses were built along the Piscataqua River for timber to be loaded onto flat-bottomed gundalow boats and shipped downstream; and when timbering declined in the mid-sixties, textile mills provided a new source of revenue. Sarah's own pleasures from childhood on included skating and sledding in the winter, rowing and sailing in the summer, and long walks and horseback rides all year round. Like Annie, she went to a good school, though Berwick Academy was less rigorous than George B. Emerson's school, and the pains of rheumatoid arthritis often kept her from attending. Among her other kinds of education, she often accompanied her father on house calls, their discussions ranging from plants and animals to people and books; she avidly listened to the yarns of her grandfather and other retired sea captains, and she prompted her mother's friends to reminisce about their youth. Through friends and relatives in Boston and Newport, she also enjoyed such refined pleasures as concerts and lectures, balls and receptions.

When Annie and Sarah began sharing their lives, neither of them relinquished old friendships, family ties, or customary activities. Sarah had her own room at Charles Street and another at Gambrel Cottage but returned to South Berwick for weeks and months at a time. Whether or not Sarah was with her, Annie continued her charity work and housekeeping duties, gave parties, and spent part of each day writing. But each woman's separate activities became altered by the other's concern.

During their first winter together, after Jamie's death, they planned a long trip to Europe that each of them believed would benefit the other. Sarah hoped traveling would lighten Annie's spirits, and Annie was sure it would improve Sarah's health. Writing to "dear friends" in Europe that February, Annie reported, "I have let our cottage at Manchester for the summer and I am talking of passing a few months on your side of the water. I have partly promised to join my sister in Switzerland for a month, but I go with a young lady, Sarah Orne Jewett who is not strong and who needs such a journey. We have both known her for several years because her native land is the neighbourhood of Portsmouth, New Hampshire and we both liked her from the first. This winter she has been living with me and I have learned to love her and to find great comfort in caring for her health and spirits. Perhaps we may see you." As in most of her letters, she offered news about mutual friends, starting with the men: "You will like to hear that Mr. Whittier has

been here lately looking uncommonly well and that Mr. Longfellow though extremely delicate is again down stairs. Dr. Holmes is as young as ever. Aldrich is
again in his little home opposite this and is editing the 'Atlantic' which is better
than it has been for several years (I hope you see it); also Howells and Henry
James Jr. are close by—so you see the old circle retains its warm grasp even
though the ranks are thinned." As to the women, Sarah Whitman had "made a
beautiful portrait of Helen Bell," Sophie Darrah's "pictures are to be shown this
week," and Mary Lodge "grows more interesting every day, more tender, more
dependent on her friends and more capable of friendship." Then she effusively declared, "I love you tenderly and think of you as bound to me while we live."[33]

Evidently replying to a nearly identical letter in early March, the English writer
Mary Cowden Clarke exclaimed "How like everything that I have heard of you,
dear Friend, is the point you tell me of your having with you a young lady 'who
is not well and needs just the change that a summer in Europe would give her.'
May your plan for giving her this needful change and for giving your sister the de-
sired delight of seeing you, be crowned with the success it so richly deserves! And
I will trust that the 'hope' you include therein, of an exchanged 'kiss' between you
and me 'yet before this scene changes for us both,' may also be fulfilled."[34]

If Annie had barely hinted at her closeness to Sarah in those two letters, it was
old news to Celia Thaxter and John Greenleaf Whittier, who both enjoyed feeling part of it. A few weeks after Sarah returned to South Berwick in February,
for example, Celia Thaxter told her "dearest owl" that she "went to dine with
Flower. . . . She was dear. But we both want owl." And the next day, Annie told
Whittier "How glad I shall be to have you and our dear Sarah Jewett again in
Boston."[35]

But she longed much more for Sarah, just as Sarah longed for her. She was in a
"stiff and crooked . . . state" and not "getting on very well without you," Sarah
wrote from South Berwick, "and I *had* to hear from you just as often as I could."
Annie's "second little letter" made her almost feel "as if I could really put my head
in your lap and tease you as you sit at your desk—It is just like being with you
still—I believe everything of me but my boots and clothes, and the five little
stones and the rest of the things in my pocket, and the hairpin—all goes back to
Charles Street and stays with you half a day at a time." When the pussy willows
budded in March, Sarah sent some to Annie and tenderly asked, "Are you sure you
know how much I love you?" Soon afterward, she planned a surprise visit to Annie that she relinquished because her mother looked pale, then lamented, "I came
so near to seeing you today darling that I miss you all the more because I gave it
up."[36] Over the next few months, she made a few brief visits to Boston, and Annie
made one to South Berwick. Letters helped fill the gaps. Though Annie's sometimes sound a bit stuffy, to no one else but "dear J." did she ever write so lovingly,
whether addressing Sarah as a "dear child" in need of care, or (more often) as the
"darling" she longed to see.

A few days before sailing for Europe in May, Sarah told Annie's sister Louisa that she felt elevated to royal status and about to make a royal progress, then said she felt "almost as if I were 'one of the family,'" and declared, "there cannot be anyone outside it who will think of you more affectionately than I."[37] She and Annie had merged their lives, and thus their families and friends. They sailed from New York on the *Scythia* with Henry Alden waving goodbye, and Whittier marked the occasion with a sonnet wishing "Godspeed" to

> . . . her in whom
> All graces and sweet charities unite,
> The old Greek beauty set in holier light;
> And her for whom New England's byways bloom,
> Who walks among us welcome as the Spring,
> Calling up blossoms where her light feet stray.[38]

Celia Thaxter had started monitoring their journey nearly a week before they left, when she sent a letter to greet them when they docked. Then on the day they sailed, she rejoiced at their good weather and declared what she would often repeat: "Dear Flower, dear Owlet, I shall long to hear from you! . . . I kiss you both & love you & bless you."[39]

All the women's letters to their friends and families suggest that they felt virtually interchangeable, though Annie (as the stronger) did most of the writing. She told Mary Jewett about their first days at sea; then Sarah sent her mother the "disappointing" news that she had not been seasick; and soon after docking in Ireland, Annie told Whittier that they both thought of him every day, and "dear Sarah looks a great deal better already . . . [and] enjoys everything with the keenest delight."[40] A week later, Sarah told her Grandfather Perry that it was "worth crossing the sea if it were twice as wide, just to have had these ten days in Ireland, and Mrs. Fields and I have enjoyed every day and only wish we could stay longer." They would head for London the following day and hoped "to have a very good time indeed—but I cant have the delight and strangeness of this week but once."[41]

Everything in Ireland was new to them both, just as everything would be during their two weeks in Norway with Mrs. Ole Bull. But whatever country they were in, Annie made all the travel arrangements, as Jamie had done for her. In some measure, she was reliving the past: Charles Reade escorted Annie and Sarah around Oxford; and in London they visited Anne Thackeray Ritchie and Georgina Hogarth, they dined with Mary Cowden Clarke, and they called on Christina Rossetti. It was wonderful "to find my dear one tenderly remembered" by the Tennysons, Annie told Whittier, then assured him "what a comfort little Sarah is to me every day" and rejoiced that Sarah's health kept improving.[42] One of the high points for Sarah was meeting Anne Ritchie, whose *Village on the Cliff* was one of her favorite books, and another was meeting Annie's sister Sarah in Interlaken. "What a happy summer it has been for me," Sarah Jewett told Louisa Beal in mid-August.[43] By the time she and Annie returned to Boston after five months abroad, Annie had virtually recovered from her bereavement.

17

Best Friendship

Dear Partners

For Annie Fields, friendship was a personal need but also a spiritual imperative. Friendships prepare us "for our higher and diviner life," she once wrote; therefore we should offer love and help to those around us, "trying to make ourselves beloved."[1] That belief eventuated in her social welfare enterprises including the Associated Charities, whose motto was "Not alms but a friend." It also entered into her loving solicitude for her scores of personal friends. Celia Thaxter and Laura Johnson were only two of the women who considered Annie their closest friend; and her volume of essays on writers including Thaxter, Stowe, Longfellow, Holmes, and Whittier was aptly titled *Authors and Friends*. But Annie's deepest and most fulfilling friendships were with her "dear partner" James T. Fields and, after his death, with Sarah Orne Jewett.

Loving friendship was at least as central to Sarah Orne Jewett's life as to Annie's, and for her too it had a strong spiritual component. "We should give our best friendship whenever we can," she once wrote. "The deeper the friendship reaches the more secure and sweet it is," because our truest friends "know our best selves, our innermost natures," and "even our thoughts of the world to come."[2] Better still, "there is something transfiguring in the best of friendship. One remembers the story of the transfiguration in the New Testament, and sees over and over in life what the great shining hours can do."[3] Like Annie, Sarah had many close friends. But her deepest and most transfiguring friendship was with Annie Fields.

In her diaries of the early seventies, Sarah monitored her need for intimacy. When she reported an intense discussion with Georgiana Halliburton, for example, Sarah said she had not forgotten "dear darling" Kate Birkhead, "but I cannot be with her now and have her talk to me and I need someone." If she was primarily referring to her emotional neediness, one of Georgie's remarks provided a spiritual context for it: she and Sarah loved "what is good in each other, and that is God's, and is in Heaven." Sarah later sat down to list her good friends: thirty-two of them, including her sister Mary. Yet she felt drawn to some more than to others. As she once told her aunt Lucretia when Mary was away from home, "I 'want to see her' in the same fashion that I do Kate or Grace—only more so."[4]

In her first published book, *Deephaven* (1877), the best friend of the semiautobiographical narrator is a composite of several of Sarah's good friends, Georgie and Kate among them. None of those friends could be described as "literary." But shortly after *Deephaven* appeared, Sarah requested "honest criticism" from Harriet Waters Preston, an older woman she had recently met and immediately loved, a writer and translator who had often published in the *Atlantic*. "I love you so much and I cant get over that dear feeling that I belong to you," Sarah told her, then humbly asked, "wont you talk to me and teach me and tell me where I am wrong?" But, for whatever reason, Preston severed their friendship after two or three years.[5]

"When a girl is growing up, she has one friend after another to whom she tells everything," Sarah once wrote, comparing such "violent fallings in love" to "the playthings of one's childhood" put aside when outgrown. But when a "young lover" becomes infatuated with an "older woman with a strong personality and a loving heart joined to a desire to be helpful to her," she will "wear the colors and adopt the opinions of her friend" as long as their relationship lasts.[6] Harriet Preston was such a woman. But Annie Fields had all the attributes that Sarah had loved in Preston, and many more. Annie turned out to be someone to whom Sarah could tell everything but never outgrow. An "older woman with a strong personality and a loving heart joined to a desire to be helpful to her," she was also someone who needed Sarah as much as Sarah needed her.[7]

Sarah's brief undated fragment titled "The Story 'A Friendship of Women'" is a unique act of homage:[8]

> Almost every one of the truly majestic women that I have seen were short and heavily built—but she was at least five foot seven and looked a head taller than most women. There was something severe and even hard in her face that gave a look of great power, but children always ran to her like an old friend as we walked in the village. We never thought of kissing each other in those first weeks nor did we kiss without thinking as most women do, but she always give [sic] me her hand when we met and before we parted she would sometimes keep it in hers in a half conscious affectionate way and once she put her arm about my shoulders as we stood looking down at the sea.
>
> But there was beside her strength of character, her iron resolve when she saw that some service [was] needed for her beloved Boston[.]

Next, Sarah praised her "exquisite early beauty and charm" and the "autumnal beauty and distinction that made her the beloved and chosen companion and kinswoman in spirit here and in England of many of the greatest men and women of her time." Irving and Thackeray were among her guests, Sarah added. Then this fragment of a story breaks off in mid-sentence.

Annie Fields was surely a model for the regal woman who resolutely served her "beloved Boston" and who attracted, offered, and deserved love. But what Sarah's fragment primarily conveys is her tender admiration of a marvelous "other."

That feeling was mutual. From the late sixties on, the childless Annie enjoyed nurturing younger women; and from her girlhood on, Sarah sought out older women as confidantes and enjoyed playing the little girl. When Henry James said Sarah Orne Jewett came to Annie Fields "as an adoptive daughter, both a sharer and a sustainer," he was essentially right; but he was entirely right in saying that "their reach together was of the firmest and easiest."[9] They complemented each other, whether as playmate, confidante, consoler, traveling companion, or literary adviser; and Willa Cather was only one of many young writers who looked to them both for sympathetic counsel. For over twenty-five years, Annie had been the loving and beloved companion of a man seventeen years her senior who nurtured her personal and professional growth. For even longer, she was the loving and beloved companion of a woman fifteen years her junior who also offered personal and professional nurturance. That nurturance was reciprocal. What each woman discovered in the other, though not only in the other, can be summed up in a phrase from Annie's *Letters of Sarah Orne Jewett:* "the power that lies in friendship to sustain the giver as well as the receiver."[10]

Their friendship was not only sanctioned but welcomed by their friends and families. Yet it resists pigeonholing. It was certainly a "union" and an "absorbing affectional intimacy," to use Mark DeWolfe Howe's words. When they were apart, the two women yearned for each other and exchanged declarations of love and recollections of hugs and kisses. But such romantic and even passionate expressions between women were well within the bounds of nineteenth-century propriety. Moreover, neither of the two women nor anyone in their circles saw anything deviant in their relationship. Quite the reverse.[11]

Thus in February 1882 after returning to South Berwick from Boston, Sarah had no compunction about telling Whittier that she longed to hear Annie's voice, to hold her hand, and to "be close beside her"; certainly he knew "how well worth the best love in the world she is." Her next declaration was more explicitly platonic: "I could not love her any better now, but I shall by and by, as fast as I grow better myself"; and she might eventually offer "the best love in the world." Sarah concluded by assuring Whittier that Annie often spoke of him "in the most loving and tender way," then signed off "yours most lovingly."[12]

As they all understood, however, the women's love for each other was even more tender. When Annie was preparing the *Letters of Sarah Orne Jewett,* she took Mark DeWolfe Howe's advice to expurgate expressions of affection from Sarah's letters to her that might be misconstrued. But neither she nor Sarah ever thought their intimacy was aberrant.

In fact, they both believed it was authorized and even blessed from beyond the

grave by the two men they had most dearly loved—James T. Fields and Sarah's father, Dr. Theodore Jewett. In the spring of 1882, after completing arrangements
for their five months abroad, first Annie and then Sarah consulted a medium in
Boston. "Don't say anything to anyone about it please," Sarah told Whittier after
her own visit, "for nobody is to know but you and Mrs. Fields." Grief-stricken by
Longfellow's recent death and still mourning for her husband, Annie had visited
the medium and felt solaced by her assurances that the two men were enjoying
the afterlife together. Sarah then consulted that same medium and exulted over
what she had learned.

The European journey "was even going to be pleasanter than I thought," she
told Whittier. The medium had spoken "about Mrs. Fields and our going together, . . . said 'James' wished to speak to me, and described Mr. Fields perfectly,"
and also said "he and my companion for the journey were very near each other
'like one person.'" Next came "wonderful things about my father" and "capital
advice" from both him and Mr. Fields—"perfect 'sailing orders' you know!"
When Sarah asked whether they knew each other, they had laughingly replied
that they had paid her a visit together "soon after Mr. Fields died, which was the
truth, for the Sunday I went to hear Dr. Bartol's funeral sermon last spring I had
a sudden consciousness of their being in the pew too, in a great state of merriment." Sarah was now certain that "they had made all the plans for Mrs. Fields and
me and helped us carry it out," because they knew "we needed each other and
could help each other." She had been "given a dear and welcome charge and care
over Mrs. Fields" by both her father and Annie's husband, Sarah believed, "and I
think this has been a great blessing to her, and a great comfort."[13] It was also a
great comfort to her.

Women of Letters

During the sixties, whenever Annie showed a manuscript poem to Jamie or Whittier, she anticipated praise and tactful criticism. But she could never abide having
her talent impugned, as when Julia Ward Howe lambasted her anonymous *Ode
on Great Organ* or when Jamie doubted that she would ever write anything that
surpassed it. Nor could she risk showing a work in progress to even such devoted
admirers as Laura Johnson and Lucy Larcom. But she could easily solicit criticism
from Sarah Orne Jewett, as she did with her 1883 poem titled "Chrysalides." As
Annie told "My darling, . . . It was so strange and good that you should have felt
as you did about the latter lines in the first half. . . . I too had my suspicions in that
direction . . . , so I believe I shall cut the passage quite out. Whatever can be
spared in a poem certainly, should be omitted. But wasn't it interesting that you
and I had thought it together." She felt relieved that Sarah had "found something
in the verses," and she planned to rework them; then "when I have done all I can
to them we will talk them over." Professional pride nonetheless surfaced in her instruction to destroy the uncorrected lines "or else they will turn up some day in-

stead of the better ones." She wished "they would drown my old verses" though "I have a tenderness towards them," and she reiterated an old complaint: "I *cannot* get that repose physical and mental which I need both for good health and good writing."[14]

Yet heartened by Sarah's perceptive criticism, Annie continued to produce and publish poetry throughout the decade. In addition to "Chrysalides," which appeared in the 1883 *Atlantic,* nineteen of her poems appeared in major periodicals—ten in *Harper's,* five in *Scribner's,* two in *Century,* and two in the *Atlantic.* Two occasional poems also appeared during the eighties: the "Prelude" to a composite narrative titled *A Week Away from Time* (1887), and a tribute to Harriet Beecher Stowe.

The chief interest of Annie's eight-line introductory poem to the anonymous *A Week Away from Time* is its very existence as part of a collaborative venture conceived during a weeklong houseparty at Mary Lodge's summer cottage in Fairhaven, Massachusetts—a loosely organized narrative about a pleasure party similar to their own. But Annie's brief poem elevated the entire project by identifying her friends as an "enchanted circle" comparable to Boccaccio's, "Who in their own Fair Harbor dream, and tell / The matter of their dreaming."[15]

The much loftier, longer, and more heartfelt poem "To Harriet Beecher Stowe. June 14th 1882" was composed for a major cultural event: the large garden party Stowe's publishers gave to celebrate her seventy-first birthday. Though Annie was then abroad with Sarah, friends assured her that the eight-quatrain poem was read beautifully; and the *Boston Advertiser* published it the next day. The very existence of several manuscripts of the poem proves that Annie herself thought it was worth preserving.[16] Celebrating Stowe as a seer who had raised the "Torch of love" on behalf of "sad humanity" and won "Dearest laurels," Annie wrote as one friend to another, one servant of "sad humanity" to another, and one woman of letters to another.

Perhaps with Stowe in mind, Annie repeatedly put her own pen in the service of sad humanity during the decade. It was not a new form of service: she had published six essays advocating social reforms during the seventies, including two in *Harper's* and one in the *Atlantic.* Her ongoing advocacy in the eighties includes two papers composed for the *Nation* ("Monster Asylums" in 1884 and "Work for Paupers and Convicts" in 1886) and three prepared for her friend Edward Everett Hale's new social welfare periodical, *Lend a Hand.* Her "Lend a Hand, for 'Pain is Not the Fruit of Pain'" was the "short sketch, piquant and dramatic" that Hale had solicited as the lead piece for his first issue of January 1886. Her two other *Lend a Hand* essays also conjoined report and advocacy: "Three Real Cases" (1886) and "Special Work of Associated Charities" (1887).[17]

Meantime, Annie also promoted social activism from the podium, primarily to women's civic and cultural groups. In her lecture "Choice of an Occupation" in January 1883, she urged the young ladies of the Saturday Morning Club to expand their minds not only through education but by working for the Associated Charities. And in a lecture to that same group on "Prisons and how to keep them from being filled" six years later, she more forcefully declared that women must try to improve their world or expect it to sink.[18]

But Annie Fields's most sustained and most influential statements about institutionalized reform appear in her *How to Help the Poor,* which Houghton Mifflin published in 1883 and frequently reprinted. Drawing on her years of experience as an organizer and fieldworker, Annie produced a book of interest to the general reader which could also serve as a manual for charity workers and an efficient organizational plan that other cities could emulate. Over 22,000 copies were sold. The book was widely reviewed and strongly praised, though no response was more fervent than John Greenleaf Whittier's. As he assured Annie, he "would rather have been its writer than that of any book, however informed with genius, where act & imagination have no place for Christian charity and tender consideration of human needs."[19]

Annie begins by modestly stating her purposes—"to give a few suggestions to visitors among the poor," to encourage them "to attend the conferences which are now held weekly in almost every district of our larger cities" and so share each others' experiences, and to recruit qualified visitors, both men and women. Even more modestly, and taking no personal credit, she then explains how and why the Associated Charities began. Next, she offers practical advice about administration and about coping with particular difficulties, often citing the experience of an autobiographical "Mrs. X." There are better ways to help the poor than by giving alms, Annie insists, forcefully arguing that most people who ask for help really need "a chance to learn how to work, and sufficient protection, in the meantime, from the evils of idleness, drunkenness, and vice." Making education a central issue, she says that both children and adults require appropriate training if they are to find work, save money, and help others.

Among her other recommendations, Annie singled out her own first reform initiative, arguing that coffee houses provide healthy alternatives to barrooms. She also pragmatically argued that men rather than women should serve as charity visitors to families where drunkenness was a problem. "The book itself has not enough sledge-hammer quality," she told Laura Johnson, "but I did what I could not being much of a sledge-hammer myself and seeing a need for something." Even more modestly, she said it was loyal of George W. Curtis "to write such a notice of my small book in Harper! Loyal to the cause I mean, for he always does what is possible for his friends, but in this case it was pure 'charity-work' and I was delighted with the care and sweetness he put into it."[20]

Both as a practical manual and as a statement of principles, the book was an important and influential work by one of the Associated Charities' most active and creative directors. Annie had not only engaged in every aspect of Associated Charities work but had established principles and procedures that were adopted across the nation. One of her main points in *How to Help the Poor* drew on her expertise as a hostess as well as a charity worker: she insisted on the direct involvement of one individual with another, in this case the Visitor and the Visited.[21]

Annie's efforts to implement charity reforms included urging men in power to take action. But she was always decorous in doing so. In March 1884, for example, she advised the Associated Charities president, Robert Treat Paine, to make radical alterations (such as reapportioning districts) in the interests of efficiency. A petition to Governor John D. Long in the winter of 1881 is more typical in its deferential assertiveness: "If I were not as ignorant and could guess what wires to pull in heaven above or on the earth beneath to have our Police Commissioners appointed by the State I could willingly try for that and nothing else for a long time to come. . . . Our work for the poor in Boston is almost neutralized by the absence of help from the very source where we should look for it." As she modestly concluded, "This note requires no answer but if you see the way open at any time for one woman to do anything I shall hope to be at the right place."[22] Her radical suggestion to Long was itself a way of doing something.

Meantime, she found other ways of connecting her philanthropic activism with her other activities and interests. She enlisted Howells and Higginson as charity visitors, for example, and it is easy to understand why Higginson asked her "to join a proposed society of 40 members, to be called 'The Round Table', whose object is to meet at private houses once a month for the consideration of social, educational & philanthropic questions."[23] As a more personal kind of philanthropy, she stretched what she herself could contribute by fund-raising for Sidney Lanier's widow and children, for the British novelist George Macdonald's family, and for the poet Louise Imogen Guiney's hospital bills, and she anonymously contributed to the support of needy writers including her old friend Lucy Larcom but also Walt Whitman. And Julia Ward Howe knew she could count on Annie for "a contribution, in verse or in prose, for the paper which is to be published at the Woman Suffrage Bazar . . . 'pro bono publico.'"[24]

The essays Annie addressed to girls and young women during the eighties were also a form of pro bono work. In a brief autobiographical narrative titled "The Poet Who Told the Truth," for example, Annie implicitly presented herself as a role model by recalling the occasion in her girlhood when she resolved to take morally committed individuals as role models. "The little paper in *Wide awake* is very sweet," Sarah Orne Jewett told her "Dear Mouse" soon after it appeared in 1886, urging her to prepare others including the one on clothing that she had virtually promised.[25]

She did so. In "About Clothes" (January 1888), Annie told her young readers that there is beauty in simple clothing and that neatness is essential, then advised them to settle on styles that suited them and use their favorite old clothes as patterns. She had already offered loftier advice in "Noble-Born" (April 1887), based on Walter Besant's story of two girls who were raised together, one of noble and the other of humble birth. The girl born to privilege proves her true nobility (as

Annie herself had done) by not being "afraid to look misery in the face, nor to do hard work." Another *Wide awake* essay, "A Helping Hand" (August 1888), makes a more specific recommendation: privileged young women should enrich the lives of poor working girls by establishing schools and clubs for them.[26]

But for today's readers as well as her contemporaries, Annie's most notable publications during the eighties were her memoirs of English and American friends who had recently died. Drawing on her own diaries and letters, she had the "peculiar satisfaction" of providing her readers with intimate glimpses of important writers. "Mr. Emerson in the Lecture Room" appeared in the *Atlantic Monthly* in 1883 and "Glimpses of Emerson" in *Harper's* in 1884. Two *Century* essays were later collected in *Authors and Friends:* "Acquaintance with Charles Reade" in 1884 and "Glimpses of Longfellow in Social Life" in 1886. And two *Scribner's* papers were later included in *A Shelf of Old Books:* "Leigh Hunt" and "Edinburgh."[27]

While preparing the Longfellow "Glimpses," Annie had the special satisfaction of his family's approval. "You saw so much of my brother during his best years that I am sure your notes & your memory will hold much of value," Samuel Longfellow told Annie. He later thanked her for the essay that filled in many gaps in his brother's life and reminded him of the many ties between Craigie House and Charles Street. As Alice Longfellow put it, "We have so much to remember together."[28]

During the eighties, Sarah Orne Jewett was also writing more than before and drawing more widely on her own experiences. Her collection of sketches titled *Country By-Ways* (1881) was followed by a volume of children's stories called *Katy's Birthday* (1883), then the collection of short stories dedicated to Annie Fields titled *The Mate of the Daylight, and Friends Ashore* (1884); her first novel, *A Country Doctor* (1884); a second novel, *A Marsh Island* (1885); and two additional short story collections—*White Heron and Other Stories* (1886) and *The King of Folly Island and Other People* (1888). Meantime, each of the women took enormous pride in the other's accomplishments.

18

Overlapping Circles

John Greenleaf Whittier (1807–1892)

Delighted by Annie Fields's intimacy with Sarah Orne Jewett, John Greenleaf Whittier often wondered "how I have deserved such friends," and even whether he had any real "claim upon the love and friendship which have made my life in its late autumn beautiful as its spring time." The delight was mutual. Perhaps the clearest and most unusual expression of Annie's love and friendship for Whittier came in October 1885, when she invited her then seventy-eight-year-old friend to move in with her. The invitation made him happy, but he had ample reasons for refusing. Boston's excitements were hard to bear, and his deafness made him feel confused in the presence of strangers, he told Annie, and he then burlesqued his deeper concerns about being burdensome. The crowds who wanted to see him would make her miserable, and not even Sarah's dog could drive them away: "It would be like having a waif from Barnum's Museum shut up in your library, and people coming to see what it looks like. You would have to get out a writ of eject-ment and set me and my carpet-bag into the street."[1]

Whittier nonetheless continued to ring Annie's doorbell whenever he came to Boston from Amesbury and felt frustrated if she happened to be out. One such disappointment generated a self-revealing poem:

> I stood within the vestibule
>   Whose granite steps I knew so well,
>   While through the empty rooms the bell
> Responded to my eager pull.
>
> I listened while the bell once more
>   Rang through the void, deserted hall;
>   I heard no voice, nor light foot-fall,
> And turned me sadly from the door.

> Though fair was Autumn's dreamy day
> And fair the wood-paths carpeted
> With fallen leaves of gold and red,
> I missed a dearer sight than they.
>
> I missed the love-transfigured face,
> The glad, sweet smile so dear to me,
> The clasp of greeting warm and free.
> What had the round world in their place?
> O friend! whose generous love has made
> My last days best, my good intent
> Accept, and let the call I meant
> Be with your coming doubly paid![2]

Yet he never complained about the relative infrequency of Annie's visits. She was "the busiest woman in Boston," he once said, perhaps even the busiest woman in the whole country.

His loving respect for Annie included respect for her writings. The Ideal Reader of her published memoirs, he enjoyed her delicate, beautiful, and "most lifelike" sketch of Emerson, and said her Longfellow essay provided "a better, lovelier idea of him than his biography does, which is indeed good, but somehow fails to give us the sweetness, tenderness and charm of his social life." He was also an Ideal Critic of her poetry, as when he returned one of her manuscripts for "improvement" in the summer of 1884 but said its concepts and expression were fine. Annie had good reason to thank him "for the verse you straightened out for me, and to which you gave the master's touch." Equally welcome were the master's tributes to Annie's published verses, including a "strong and noble" sonnet in the *Atlantic* that he had read to relatives and friends who pronounced it "inspired."[3]

His praise of Sarah's work was also enthusiastic. *A Country Doctor* was "better than 'Deephaven' even," he told Annie, then exclaimed, "What a lovely picture she has given of the quaint old Idyllic life of New England, & how admirable is her character of the Doctor & his ward! The style is well nigh perfect." And after hearing that the Irish liked "The Luck of the Bogans," he bragged about being among the first to "discover" Sarah.[4]

Meantime, Whittier's ties to Annie continued to include other mutual friends, Celia Thaxter and Elizabeth Stuart Phelps among them. In March 1885 when Celia Thaxter was on Appledore Island, for example, Whittier hoped that "on that lonesome, windy coast where she can only look upon the desolate, winter-bitten pasture-land and the cold grey sea" she would warm herself with "memories of her Italian travels."[5] And in October 1888 when Annie breached a confidence to report "that before the sun sets Elizabeth Phelps will have married her young friend Mr. Ward," Whittier exclaimed with shock and delight, "Was there ever so droll a thing!" Yet the young groom seemed sensible and cultivated and maybe it was all for the best. At any rate, love had evidently "cured" their high-strung friend.[6]

One of their many shared beliefs was that if they liked a book they would like its author. Therefore when Annie invited Edith Thomas to Charles Street in the spring of 1885, Whittier was eager to meet the young poet with "a divine gift" whose first book was "more than a promise—an assurance."[7] Yet because his growing deafness made him reluctant to make new acquaintances, he was probably not greatly disappointed when Thomas had to leave Boston before they could meet.

That same reluctance might explain why Whittier refused Annie's invitation to meet Matthew Arnold at Charles Street when he lectured in Boston in the fall of 1883. "I feel *sure* you will like each other for he is very simple and manly and gives one a sense of goodness," Annie assured Whittier. Because Arnold planned to read one of Whittier's poems during his lecture on Emerson, "he really needs to see you to understand both Emerson and yourself better. . . . for I think the New England type and character should be as intelligently treated as possible by this man who is to live and teach many years yet, so far as poor human eyes can tell." Annie later reported that Arnold had delivered a noble lecture on Emerson to a full house, and had hoped Whittier might attend. Arnold called on Whittier soon afterward. But in June 1886 when Arnold was her houseguest during his final American tour, Whittier again resisted Annie's invitation. Arnold "inquired for you very earnestly," Annie told Whittier. "He was full of boyish spirits and we enjoyed him better than ever. He read the 'Scholar Gipsy' aloud one evening and we could seem to see the upland field the tree and the whole summer scene." Whittier later called Arnold "one of the foremost men of our time, a true poet, a wise critic, and a brave, upright man to whom all English-speaking people owe a debt of gratitude." And after Arnold's death two years later, Whittier mourned the "terrible loss" and condoled with Annie: "Thee knew him well, he was a friend of thine, and I am sure you must feel it deeply."[8]

Until Whittier's own death in 1892, he continued to share Annie's life primarily through copious letters. When Annie was bedridden by pneumonia in February 1888 and reported that Lowell had just read her his latest "verses," Whittier whimsically figured the scene as a tableau: "A convalescent princess with her minstrel in attendance!"[9] In spirit, he was another such minstrel. One of Annie's typical letters of the late eighties began with news of Ethel Arnold's stay at Charles Street, moved on to her own charity work, said Sarah was keeping house in South Berwick while her mother and sisters went traveling, promised to send Motley's "manly" letters, said she had visited Celia Thaxter in Portsmouth and found her "very anxious," then reported seeing Lowell "fresh from the Saturday Club" and thinking he would remain vigorous "as long as he and Holmes go on talking like the two inspired grigs they are, for the benefit of the human race," and ended with news of Holmes's "touchingly beautiful" reading during a meeting about authors' copyrights.[10] As usual, Annie had addressed Whittier as a concerned and loving peer, though her attitudes toward him ranged from daughterly solicitude to profound reverence. As she once solemnly assured the frail poet, "Your love and your faith, dear friend, uphold me."[11]

New and Deepening Relationships

Throughout the eighties, Annie often cultivated the acquaintance of newly acclaimed women writers, as in the spring of 1885 when she invited a young poet from Ohio to Charles Street. By doing so, she was acting on her commitment to help other women. But it was also a way of remaining a literary insider.

Soon after *A New Year's Masque and Other Poems* appeared to spectacular reviews in 1885, Edith M. Thomas (1854–1925) received a telegram from Annie Fields that urged an immediate visit to Charles Street. Thomas accepted, saying Annie Fields and Sarah Orne Jewett were chief among "those whom one woman's imagination has elected as its friends," women who led where she wanted to go. She expected to stay for a week. But she was still recuperating from a serious illness when she arrived at Charles Street, and she left after only three days—a wise decision, her doctor said. "How sorry I was to miss seeing Edith Thomas!" Lucy Larcom lamented, and Whittier was among the many other Charles Street regulars who felt the same way.[12]

Soon after reaching home, Edith Thomas told Annie that she had been rereading *Under the Olive* and enjoying old favorites—"Beautiful things!"—but wished she could "hear them read by the one who gave them being." Then she signed her letter "Ever devoutly yours." A few days later, grateful for the "doctor's stuff" Sarah sent her, Thomas lamented the poor health that had made her leave "the beautiful chamber overlooking the Charles," and hoped Annie could exorcise the "imps of Insomnia" from it. Yet she had the comfort of knowing that her "three red-letter days" in Boston were "fast and safe forever." Only four days later, Thomas sent a box of medicine that she hoped might help Sarah, asked "My dear Lady Under the Olive (Pallas Athene)" to "salute for me the masters in 'My Friend's Library,'" regretted missing Charles Craddock's visit and a call on the Aldriches, and concluded with "grateful love."[13]

But Thomas's plan for a second visit to her "dear Lady" never materialized. She got as far as New York in February 1886 but felt too weak to travel further, and yielded to Annie's old friend Anne Botta's insistence on a "prolonged stay." A writer whose celebrity as a literary hostess matched Annie's, Mrs. Botta would not be refused. After her mother died in 1887, Thomas and her sister moved to New York and supported themselves largely through hack work. Meantime, she continued to write and publish poetry and sent Annie copies of her new books; she once reported dreaming about Sarah; and Annie's invitation to Manchester in August 1887 prompted her to rejoice that "our sweet New England annalist and yourself are still leading your lives together." As she observed, "A sort of pensive happiness (have I hit it rightly—or very crudely?) seems the atmosphere in which you twain dwell." Still "mindful of you and your delicate housemate" the following spring, Thomas wondered what they were reading, said the last thing she had read to her dying mother was one of Sarah's stories, and reported that she and her sister were toiling away on the *Century Dictionary*. Memories of Charles Street were among her bonds to Mrs. Botta, Henry Alden, Mrs. Ole Bull, and many other New Yorkers. But Thomas would become increasingly withdrawn during the following decades, and she would never again visit her "dear Lady Under the Olive."[14]

Among the writers Annie invited to meet Edith Thomas in the spring of 1885 was another out-of-towner she had just met—Mary Noailles Murfree (1850–1922), a Tennessee native who wrote stories about Tennessee mountaineers under the name of Charles Egbert Craddock. Those stories had been appearing since 1878, and Houghton Mifflin had recently issued her first collection. The freshness and strength of *In the Tennessee Mountains* (1884) had moved Sarah Orne Jewett to write a fan letter, assuming that she was addressing a Tennessee mountain man. There was no reason to think otherwise. Then in March 1885, the revelation that Craddock was a woman produced a surge of national publicity and a brief entry into the lives of Annie and Sarah.

That revelation occurred in the offices of the *Atlantic.* Four of Craddock's stories had appeared when Howells was editor, and his successor Thomas Bailey Aldrich had published three others. He had also arranged for the publication of *In the Tennessee Mountains* and commissioned a serial novel. But only when the author came to Boston and entered his office did he discover that Charles Egbert Craddock was the pseudonym of an engaging (though lame) young woman. Only a few hours later, Lilian Aldrich called at the hotel where Mary Murfree was staying with her sister Fanny and their father and invited them all to a dinner in Craddock's honor the following night. It was in a sense a surprise party. As Craddock's biographer writes,

> The guests were Oliver Wendell Holmes, Lawrence Barrett, and Mrs. James T. Fields. Miss Jewett was ill, and Edwin Booth sent regrets. . . . W. D. Howells came in, although . . . he could not stay for dinner. As the guests were successively introduced to "Mr. Craddock," whom they had all been invited to meet, their surprise was extreme—most of all that of Mrs. Fields. She was rather late, and when she joined the party the first effect of the announcement had worn off. The continual addressing of a strange lady as Mr. Craddock, however, she considered a joke, and rather a poor joke, she said, having deduced the theory that Craddock had for some reason given his hosts the slip, and the party was carrying off his dereliction as pluckily as they might.[15]

Immediately after discovering who the "strange lady" was, Annie invited her to Charles Street, promising an introduction to Edith Thomas that the poet's early departure would preclude. Mary and Fanny Murfree were soon thanking Annie for theater tickets and a volume of Edward Hale's stories. Though they even made time to visit Celia Thaxter on the Isles of Shoals, they were by then so homesick that they headed straight back to Tennessee. Mary nonetheless assured Annie, "I am glad to have known you."[16]

The Misses Murfree returned to Boston two years later, this time to arrange *Atlantic* publication for the younger sister's novel. They stayed with the Aldriches.

But their visit to Annie's Manchester cottage turned out to be a highlight of their trip. Writing from Intervale House in New Hampshire a few days later, Mary regretted leaving "you and that splendid ocean view," then nostalgically recalled "the sound of your voice reading aloud. That story of Tolstoi's, and the spirited measure of your poet's singing from 'the king's seat,' linger in my memory with the sight and sound of the sea and the peace of that perfect sunshiny weather." At that point she was interrupted by a "very pleasant call from Miss Jewett, who desires me to send you her love," and she fancifully deducted "a small portion of affection by way of taking toll."[17] Immediately, afterward, however, the sisters learned that their mother was ill and left for home. From then on, Annie and Sarah followed their fortunes only by monitoring the thick stream of books that Craddock continued to produce.

In December 1870, soon after James T. Fields published Helen Hunt's first volume of poems on a half-profits contract, Annie noted in her journal that Emerson had met her in Newburyport and admired the woman and her *Verses*. The daughter of an Amherst professor and a childhood friend of Emily Dickinson, Helen Hunt Jackson (1830–85) had started writing poetry in 1865, as an outlet after the sudden death of her second son, but also to earn money. Her husband had died a year and a half earlier, and her first son had died in infancy. She soon moved to Newburyport, submitted herself to Higginson's mentorship, and began publishing widely. Neither Whittier nor Jamie particularly liked her "poetically or personally" at first, and Jamie ridiculed her for paying him a $520 subvention to publish a "silly pinch of poetry" which would never repay the investment. The success of her verses proved him wrong, however, and her admirers soon included Whittier and Stowe as well as Higginson and Emerson.

Helen Hunt moved to Colorado in 1873, married a businessman named Jackson two years later, occasionally returned to New England, and continued to produce poetry as well as fiction and travel literature (including two highly paid and highly regarded articles about the West that appeared in the *Atlantic*). She and Annie were both seated at the head table when the magazine's publishers celebrated Holmes's birthday in 1879; and Annie's gift of *Under the Olive* the following year prompted Jackson to declare that it "laid us all under obligations of gratitude and pride."[18] By then Jackson had become a champion of Indian rights. In *A Century of ·Dishonor* (1881), she exposed the government's mistreatment of Native Americans, as she would again do in her enormously popular novel *Ramona* (1884). When Annie and Sarah were about to visit Florence in the summer of 1882, Whittier not only knew that Jackson was there but assumed they would see her.[19]

When Jackson was in Boston in January 1883, she told Annie she knew almost no one else "in whose literary taste and judgment I have any confidence," and therefore wanted to read her the report on the Mission Indians that she planned to submit to Washington. Her report failed to persuade the Congress to assist those Indians. But Jackson's invitation to Annie in the spring of 1884 suggests that their friendship had by then gone well beyond sisterly professionalism: she urged Annie to join her in Colorado and bring Sarah along so she could show them "our mountains." That never happened. In August 1885, Annie heard that Jackson was alone and seriously ill in San Francisco; and she died of cancer a few months later.[20]

During Jackson's final years, the women's links included their enthusiasm for Edith Thomas and their long-standing friendships with Higginson, Whittier, Stowe, Charles Dudley Warner, and Sarah Woolsey. Moreover, they both published in the same prestigious magazines and they both pressured editors for fair pay. Another kind of commonality was their social activism. And although they never became intimate, the women's mutual respect kept pace with their expanding personal and professional identities.

Rose Terry Cooke (1827–92) was one of the many writers who entered Annie's outer orbit of friendship when James T. Fields began editing the *Atlantic,* and she remained in that orbit until the end of her life. Although Cooke rarely came into Boston from rural Hartford, the women monitored each other's careers and felt concerned about each other's welfare. Cooke had started producing lively local color stories in the 1850s and become an important *Atlantic* contributor from the time of its first issue; and two of her poems and three of her stories (including the quietly humorous "Dely's Cow") appeared under Fields's editorship.[21]

After 1873, when she married an improvident young widower with two daughters, Cooke concentrated on supporting them all by producing children's stories and other pot-boilers. Yet a note she sent Annie in January 1880 suggests that she managed to remain wryly good-humored. It also illuminates the women's ease with each other. Responding to Annie's invitation to give a reading at Charles Street, Mrs. Cooke said she had not intended to visit Boston that winter and felt doubts about "reading before such critics, but I think I could hold my own as to chaffing!" More poignantly, she hoped Annie might "come see me in my queer old house and look up at the stars through the big fireplace." James T. Fields's death shortly afterward prompted an affectionate letter of sympathy, and the women's relationship deepened when Sarah Orne Jewett became part of it. From then on, Rose Cooke's letters to Annie always included affectionate messages to Sarah; and until her own death in 1892, she tried to see them both whenever she came to Boston.[22]

Sarah Chauncey Woolsey (1835–1905), who entered Annie's life soon after Jamie's death, was a resident of Newport, Rhode Island, whose good friends included Helen Hunt Jackson, Sarah Whitman, and Sarah Orne Jewett's childhood friend Minnie Pratt. Under the name of Susan Coolidge, Woolsey drew on her own large and close-knit family for her high-spirited fiction about spunky girls, achieving national popularity for stories published in the *St. Nicholas* and the five Katy books that began with *What Katy Did* (1872). "It will be such a help to every girl who reads it," Sarah Orne Jewett told Annie after reading one of them. "I don't know a better book to give a child or growing girl."[23]

Meanwhile, Sarah Woolsey read and admired Annie's work. As she wrote in October 1883, she loved *Under the Olive,* and she was sure that *How to Help the Poor* would "rectify the popular conception of benevolence." Wondering if Annie had by then returned to "what Minnie Pratt used to call 'Charley St,'" Woolsey hoped to come there during her next visit to Boston. But she also fondly recalled "my dear Manchester visit and all the good it did me," and a later letter anticipated returning to "that dear delightful rock-perch."[24] She occasionally entertained Annie and Sarah in Newport; and in 1891 when Mrs. Jewett's final illness prevented Sarah from reviewing Helen Hunt Jackson's posthumous *Calendar of Sonnets* for the *The Book Buyer,* she advised the editor to give Woolsey the assignment. But perhaps the high point of the women's relationship came two years later, when Woolsey attended the Chicago Columbian Exposition with Annie, Sarah, and their French visitor Mme. Thérèse de Solms Blanc.[25]

When Louise Imogen Guiney (1861–1920) was first invited to Charles Street in 1884, the twenty-three-year-old woman had already established a modest reputation as a fastidious poet and a dependable literary scholar.[26] Her first collection of poems, *Songs at the Start,* had just been published; and her first collection of essays—*Goose-Quill Papers,* dedicated to Oliver Wendell Holmes—would appear the following year. A bright and determined young woman who was the only child of Irish Catholic immigrants, she had left her convent school at the age of sixteen to support herself and her widowed mother, primarily as a hack writer. But she continued to study the great English poets, wrote about them, and produced poems that echoed them.

"I never go by your own House Beautiful save with reverent feet," Guiney told Annie soon after her first visit, "and I hope, at some not far day, to venture in once more, and find that this gentle good-will of yours is still mine." Modestly responding to Annie's praise of her essay on Leigh Hunt, which had just appeared in the *Atlantic,* Guiney said Mrs. Fields was among "the very few for whose pleasure I mainly cared and worked."[27] She soon received the invitation she solicited, she became a frequent guest at the House Beautiful, and she accepted Annie's invitations to Manchester whenever she could. What she offered in return included fruit from her mother's orchard and effusive gratitude.

Each of Guiney's news-filled letters to Annie is an act of homage, whether announcing her eagerness to set her "happy eye" on Annie's "'magic casement opening on the foam,'" or praising Annie's latest poem in *Scribner's,* or enclosing a "spring posy" to adorn Severn's portrait of Keats, or signing off as "Your friend and vassal." A typically effusive letter thanks her "Donna Adorata" for an "Arcadian visit . . . and your kindness and dear Miss Jewett's, and the 'sleep till break of day in the chamber whose name is Peace,' and the long evening before it, which slipped away in a sort of enchantment." Then she assured Annie, "I care for your approbation beyond most." Grateful for Annie's invitation to read her latest "little sketch" at Charles Street before it appeared in the *Atlantic,* Guiney humbly said she was a "shabby reader" and could not get in from Auburndale until after eight, but she planned to begin without preliminaries and try to avoid seeming shy. Annie's solicitousness extended to the loan of her Athenaeum library card; and when

Guiney sailed for England in 1889, she carried Annie's letters of introduction to Georgina Hogarth and Mary Cowden Clarke.[28]

If Annie saw anything of her younger self in Guiney, it was a self who had to earn her own way. Guiney's drudgeries during the nineties included serving as the Auburndale Post-mistress and then as a cataloger for the Boston Public Library (a job Annie helped her get). Meantime, she became a central figure in Boston's aesthetic movement and a familiar figure at Isabella Stewart Gardner's receptions; she produced her third and fourth volumes of poetry as well as scholarly editions of Matthew Arnold and other eminent poets; and she composed chatty essays for Boston periodicals, including one on Annie for the *Critic*.[29] The energetic young woman also helped found the Women's Rest Tour Association, at one point inviting Annie and Sarah to attend an organizational meeting and "allow various happy people to be presented to you." And as a devotee of Keats, Guiney was one of the literati who solicited funds for Anne Whitney's bust of the poet, which would be presented to the Hampstead Parish Church. Predictably, Annie was one of the contributors.[30]

Writing from shipboard on her way to England in 1895, Guiney thanked Annie for "one of the most beautiful surprises that ever happened to me." Whatever that surprise was, Guiney protested that Annie was "altogether too good and providing," never tired of "experimenting on me to see how much pleasure the human organism can endure." Therefore she felt free to invite herself to Charles Street. A few years later, she said she would be "happy as a King" if she could stay overnight following a Women's Rest Tour meeting, calling herself Annie's "lover and beggar."[31]

That definition would never be more appropriate than in the winter of 1910, when Guiney suffered a "nervous weakness" and spent a week and a half under Annie's roof. "Of all the sweet things ever done for me by my many sweet friends, your taking me in and coddling me for those blessed eleven days was the very sweetest!" Guiney told Annie. A patient in St. Elizabeth's Hospital at that point, she had just received the "wonderful assurance" that Annie had arranged to cover her hospital expenses. The following month came another act of "super-Samaritan charity": Annie's invitation to convalesce at Charles Street. Instead, Guiney opted to remain on her own. But Annie continued to coddle her with flowers, meals, and dinner invitations; she dispatched her manservant to do Guiney's errands; and she even hired a seamstress to do Guiney's mending.[32]

Though such ministrations ended with Guiney's final departure for England soon afterward, by then their friendship included Willa Cather—a long-time admirer of Guiney's poetry and at that point an editor for *McClure's*. An unusual gloss on their interconnections is Guiney's reply to Annie's advice against sending editors manuscripts they might not want (which followed Guiney's own complaint that the *Atlantic* had rejected her essay on Vaughan). When she approached "our dear Willa" about a story she had written and was told it was "unMcClure-able," that was a "fair and square" verdict, Guiney said. But that was wholly unlike "being solicited by a purely literary magazine, and then having your purely literary wares fired back at your unoffending head."[33]

Cather also figured in Guiney's response to the "darling" *Letters of Sarah Orne Jewett*. It was "fragrant and humane and serene, just like *her,* and like you, too," Guiney assured Annie; and one of Sarah's letters to Willa was so similar to one she herself had received "that it quite brought the tears to my horny eyes." As Guiney acknowledged, "How grateful one is, especially when young, for such sun-like and dew-like strong encouragements!"[34]

Cather's fiction was yet another topic for discussion. "My own feeling about her Bohemian Girl was much like yours," Guiney told Annie in January 1913. "There is a true literary gift and much humanity in dear W.S.C.; but I am sorry she likes so much the note of revolt and rebellion *per se.* . . ." Meantime, dear W.S.C. told Guiney about each of her visits to Charles Street. Her account of staying there in June 1911 was "almost as good as running down the hill to sup at 148," Guiney wistfully wrote; and many of her other letters performed the same office. "The last news I heard of you was through Willa enviable girl!" Guiney wrote in December 1913. "Wasn't it good of her to send it, knowing how much I cared!"[35] Annie bequeathed her two Keats portraits to Willa Cather. But she left four thousand dollars to the thin-pursed poet-scholar Louise Imogen Guiney, whose "Donna Adorata" she had been for over thirty years.

Many other women writers courted Annie and basked in her encouragement; but in 1887 Annie offered help to one poet who had little interest in it. Annie had called on Christina Rossetti when she and Sarah were in London five years earlier, and she now offered to pave the poet's way to Scribner's. "It is pleasant to be remembered, as I hope you and Miss Jewett will agree with me, accepting my return-remembrances," Christina Rossetti politely responded. But she had no need "to enlarge my field of possible work, as I do not half fill that already open to me." Acknowledging Annie's praise of her poem "Fluttered Wings," she ruefully added, "I fancy I have already produced the bulk of what is mine to produce." But at least Annie had tried to be of help.[36]

Running Away

Most of the trips Annie and Sarah took during the eighties were relatively brief, ranging from day trips to see Whittier and other old friends to weeklong seashore vacations. Occasionally they were more venturesome, traveling to Quebec on one occasion and to a Moravian settlement in Pennsylvania on another. "Sarah and I have run away!" Annie exultantly wrote Whittier from New York in the spring of 1884, then said they wanted to see Richmond, Virginia, "before the forces of the North breathe a new life in its veins."[37] And when "Mrs. James T. Fields, accompanied by Miss Sarah Orne Jewett" took a "loitering journey" up the Connecticut River in October 1886, at least one newspaper reported that fact, noting that their many friends delighted in their close friendship.[38]

But many of their trips were primarily efforts to relieve Sarah's arthritis and rheumatism, as when they traveled to Richfield Springs in upstate New York in the summer of 1886. "Sarah's daughterly dependence upon me is a great happiness and occupation," Annie told Barrett Wendell before they left.[39] A few weeks later, she told Whittier that Sarah was feeling better, warned him against kneeling in the wet grass to gather nuts, and suggested that they should all go to Richfield Springs together the following year. Sarah's "White Heron" was beautiful and her *Story of the Normans* "reads delightfully," Annie said, but "she is not to be allowed to do any more work for a long time."[40]

The roles of patient and caregiver were reversed in the winter of 1888, when Annie was so prostrated by pneumonia and convalesced so slowly that (under doctor's orders) she and Sarah traveled south. When they reached St. Augustine, Florida, they took rooms at the Ponce de Leon, the palatial new Spanish Renaissance–style hotel that Henry Flagler had built to accommodate passengers on his new Florida East Coast Railway, a hotel whose many splendors included campaniles, domes, arcades, fountains, Roman baths, lush gardens, stained glass windows, and interiors designed by Louis Comfort Tiffany. "A singular fortune has befallen this little half decayed Spanish town," Annie told one of her Boston friends. "One of the richest oil kings of this wonderful country of ours has taken a fancy to the place and has built a palace here for a hotel as huge and glorious as the Spanish palaces of old." One of her pleasures was conversing with the oil king.[41] But as usual, she and Sarah constituted a community of two, each ministering to the other's needs and sharing her enjoyments.

When they returned to Florida in the winter of 1890, a writer for a New York weekly devoted to literature and the arts breezily informed his readers that "Mrs. James T. Fields and Miss Sarah O. Jewett are, I was about to say, summering at Saint Augustine, Fla., not simply because the weather there suggests the butterfly season, but because wherever these close literary friends are they diffuse a genial social warmth." As he then explained, "Miss Jewett, whose home is in South Berwick, Me., amid the scenes which she has invested with such picturesque interest, is in the habit of visiting Mrs. Fields during the winter in Boston, and they enjoy taking trips together wherever their fancy leads them." But it was Sarah's arthritic pains rather than fancy that had again brought them to the Ponce de Leon.[42]

SECTION V
High Water

19

Abroad

Europe, 1892

On 27 February, 1892, Annie Fields and Sarah Orne Jewett boarded a North German Lloyd Company steamer then making its first crossing from New York to the Mediterranean, traveling for pleasure but also in the hope of improving Sarah's health. In addition to arthritic pains, Sarah was still feeling the strains of tending her mother, who had died a few months before.

"Annie Fields came at once from Manchester and was the best of comforts," Sarah told her friend Loulie Dresel in October 1891. "I don't know what we should have done without her."[1] After the funeral, Annie took Sarah back to Boston and managed to convince her that a second long trip to Europe would do them both good. She then booked passage on the *Werra* and began planning an even longer trip than the one they had taken a decade earlier.

Many "agreeable persons of social prominence" were on board, the *Century* editor Robert Underwood Johnson recalled years later, the publisher Charles Scribner and the Baltimore philanthropist Mary Elizabeth Garrett among them, "and their afternoon meetings on the promenade deck were much like a five o'clock tea in a New York or Boston drawing-room." Not surprisingly, Annie Fields was "full of reminiscences of the authors she had known in Boston or in England," and the "more downright" Sarah Orne Jewett "was the best of company."[2]

Yet the trip did not begin well. Sarah suffered a "frightful fall" and a painful blow on her head on their first night out, and she had not fully recovered by the time they docked in Genoa and called on Mary Cowden Clarke. In Rome, where Sarah was bedridden by tonsillitis (leaving Annie to sightsee with Mary Garrett), she soon suffered a heavier blow: she learned that her brother-in-law Theodore Eastman had died. Although Sarah at first felt impelled to return home immediately, her sisters' protests as well as Annie's dissuaded her, and she seized on

Annie's suggestion that her sisters would enjoy receiving copious travel letters. That left Annie to take on more than her usual share of correspondence with old friends, including Holmes (who protested that "Boston is hardly itself without you two") and Whittier (who quipped that as their invisible fellow traveler, he risked being charged full fare).[3]

Sarah was soon well enough to enjoy the sights of Rome and the company of friends, including Mark Twain, who later reminded Annie of an amusing incident:

> Many's the time Mrs. Clemens recurs with evil delight to that time in the Sistine Chapel when you were silently adoring Michel Angelo's riot in heaven & hell & I kept breaking into your meditations with ignorant criticisms of those lubberly saints & angels till Mrs. Clemens lost her patience & shattered me with a dynamite rebuke, & Sarah Orne Jewett finished up the incident with the admiring remark, "Now you're spoke to!" Remember it?[4]

By the time she and Annie reached Venice, Sarah could assure Whittier that "Nobody had ever had such a good time in this world." Annie the early riser slept late after an especially late night on the Grand Canal; and she had thrown peach pits into the canal from their splendid hotel room as if she were throwing flowers to her subjects.[5] A richer "good time" followed another serendipitous encounter with Mark Twain and his wife "in front of one of the restaurants in the Piazza of his patron saint." As Robert Johnson recalled years later, "the great humorist did most of the talking"—about "occult things," "second-sight," and a premonitory dream about his brother's death—, while Annie and Sarah inserted "a few words now and then by way of keeping him going"; and they were all invited to hear him give "readings from Browning" that night.[6]

Annie and Sarah were in France by early June. They spent Annie's birthday driving from Martigny to Chamonix, reveling in vistas of mountain peaks and flower-filled valleys with shepherds in the foreground, and admiring Mont Blanc by moonlight. Next came a concerted effort to improve Sarah's health—a month of therapeutic baths at Aix-les-Bains (where, in Sarah's words, crowned heads mingled with "persons from Berwick"). Then they headed for Paris.[7]

A minor episode that Johnson preserved in his *Remembered Yesterdays* centers on Annie's desire to hear a popular Parisian chanteuse. Excited by the Johnsons' account of Yvette Guilbert's brilliant performance at a middlebrow "café chantant" in the Champs Elysées, Annie persuaded them to accompany her the following night. They arrived early to get front row seats, Annie intently followed each song, and a particularly plaintive one in a nearly incomprehensible *argot* made her lift "her handkerchief to her eyes." But as Johnson later discovered, the lyrics were among "the most objectionable sung at that time in Paris!"[8] While mocking the genteel Annie's sentimental response to an off-color song, he nevertheless displayed her endearing eagerness for new experience.

Annie's most consequential new experience in Paris was meeting the eminent critic and novelist Marie Thérèse de Solms Blanc, who had been corresponding with Sarah for the past eight years. Mme. Blanc had introduced Sarah to her countrymen by reviewing *A Country Doctor* in the *Revue des Deux Mondes;* and Sarah's note of thanks to the presumably male writer "Th. Bentzon" had initiated an increasingly warm correspondence. Standing with Annie before the door of Mme. Blanc's mansion, Sarah feared that seeing her might jeopardize their intimacy; but as Annie later recalled, "her companion, being of a more daring mind in such matters, rang the bell, and the trial moment was soon most happily over."[9]

Mme. Blanc then introduced them into elite circles otherwise closed to them. A member of the old aristocracy (the daughter of one count, the stepdaughter of another, and a woman who had lived in the palace at Fontainebleau), she took them to call on such august friends as "a comtesse of the old school, in the Place Vendôme, whose self and house together were like a story-book." She also introduced them to the *Revue* editor Ferdinand Brunetière and other literary notables. A protégée of George Sand, she was then steadily writing fiction, essays, and reviews for the *Revue,* she had already translated Thomas Bailey Aldrich and Bret Harte as well as Sarah Orne Jewett, and she would eventually produce over forty books (five of them about America). The women grew closer while spending a few days in a quaint stone cottage near Fontainebleau, in an area that Millet had made famous. After doing "literary work" each morning, they "met at table in the open air," Annie recalled, and then walked into the great Barbizon forest. "Mme. Blanc apparently knew every inch of the way . . . , and from noon until dark we would walk and rest under the great trees, and walk again, while she peopled the forest with histories connected with that romantic region, or read to us from her enchanting store of George Sand's unpublished letters. My companion and I used sometimes to confess fatigue the following morning after these endless tramps; but Mme. Blanc was always perfectly fresh the next day, and eager to continue her walks and talks; and continue we did, most gratefully and delightedly."[10]

Their three-way friendship would end only with Mme. Blanc's death in 1907. She would stay at Charles Street in the fall of 1893 and visit both Annie and Sarah four years later, they both helped her gather material for her books and helped her place essays in American periodicals, and they would visit her on both of their later visits to France.[11]

In mid-July Annie and Sarah left France for England, and a richer mix of old and new experiences, including a walk on the Yorkshire moors near the Brontës' home with Annie's old friend Robert Collyer, the Chicago minister who had been born nearby. "The only bright thing was to remember how brief the lives were of the women who were forced to live there among the graves," Annie remarked, though she found something brighter to tell Whittier. Looking at the "noble hills" of the Brontë country and the heather budding on the moors, she could sense "how much joy their young poetic minds found after all in the sense of divine life which is borne in by such vast solitudes in the great air."[12]

As another kind of literary homage, Annie and Sarah visited Mrs. Matthew

Arnold in Cobham, Surrey, and then the Tennysons' "high court of poetry" at Aldworth in Surrey. "The one thing which made me feel most anxious to have you get to England this summer was to make sure of your seeing him again," Sarah told Annie after Tennyson's death shortly afterward. "None of the great gifts I have ever had out of loving and being with you seems to me so great as having seen Tennyson."[13]

Utterly unlike their acts of fealty to literary patriarchs was their visit to Matthew Arnold's niece Mrs. Humphry Ward (1851–1920), a woman whose literary career had only recently begun. After reading *Robert Elsmere* (1888), the popular but controversial story of a clergyman who leaves the church to work for the underprivileged, Annie and Sarah were eager to meet its author. Although Mrs. Ward was convalescing from a serious illness when they arrived, she struck Annie as young and girlish, sweet-natured and even shy, but also "brilliant and full of charm." Better still, she shared Annie's belief that women could and should effect social change without abandoning the domestic hearth. Impressed by Mrs. Ward's devotion to her lively family, her literary ambitions, and her social activism (which included founding a settlement house), Annie was convinced that all her projects would succeed unless her health was impaired. From then on, all three women exchanged letters, Mr. Ward stayed at Charles Street during his American lecture tour in 1895, and Mrs. Ward and her daughter Dorothy visited Annie in 1908. Despite ideological differences that included Mrs. Ward's opposition to woman suffrage, she and Annie saw their best selves in each other: as womanly women, successful writers, and effective reformers.

There would be one last encounter with a popular novelist before Annie and Sarah left England. Visiting the picturesque town of Digby was partly an act of homage to an old friend who had recently died, James Russell Lowell, who had often vacationed there during the 1880s. But their main purpose was to meet George du Maurier, a friend of Lowell's and a cartoonist for *Punch,* whose *Peter Ibbetson* had won wide acclaim the previous year when it appeared serially in *Harper's* and then as a book. While walking through the old town with them, du Maurier sang them all the old songs he had included in his novel, "with their right tunes"; and despite his failing eyesight, he brought them to his house and showed them his drawings, "with all the simplicity of a boy with a slate, and all the feeling of a great artist."[14]

But after seven months abroad, Annie and Sarah were eager for home; and on 21 September they sailed for New York on the *Cephalonia.* "I never shall forget the beauty of that first evening on Charles Street as we sat looking out over the river, and being so glad to be off the steamer," Sarah told Lilian Aldrich; "and next day, when I came here to the dear old house and home, it all seemed to put its arms round me."[15]

"Going to the Tropics," 1896

The women's most unusual trip was a Caribbean cruise—their only visit to that part of the world, their only trip on a private yacht, and the only time they spent two whole months with another couple. In January 1896, just when *The Country of the Pointed Firs* started appearing serially in the *Atlantic,* Annie and Sarah headed for Georgia to board the *Hermione,* anticipating a good rest, warm weather, and exotic sights.

The summer before, they had visited the Aldriches in Tenants Harbor, Maine, and then had rented a cottage in nearby Martinsville for a month of writing and correcting proofs; and their heavy work schedules had continued into the fall. At that point, Aldrich invited them to make the cruise as guests of their mutual friend Henry L. Pierce, a former mayor of Boston. Pierce had "bought the 'Hermione' a little while ago, one of the finest steam yachts afloat," Annie told Charles Dudley Warner on New Year's Day, and their own small group would have "the whole ship to ourselves." "I thought I had told you!" she exuberantly exclaimed, "but I suppose this 'going to the Tropics' fell on us just after you left."[16]

Perhaps because it was both her first cruise and her first trip to the Caribbean, Annie resumed regular journal-keeping after a gap of nearly twenty years. She carefully cataloged "characteristics and remarkables," as Hawthorne had called them, meticulously describing each island's flora, fauna, geography, and inhabitants. Like her earlier travel diaries, the "Diary of a Caribbean trip 1896" is largely impersonal in tone and objective in detail, whether she was describing a cave of coral, a "phosphoric" lake, or a pelican. But her own character and values nonetheless emerge, most obviously in her account of visiting a school in Brunswick, Georgia, before boarding the *Hermione.* Delighted by the children's liveliness but dismayed by their rote learning, she reached a startlingly bitter conclusion: her own academic triumphs as a girl had been essentially triumphs of memory. Therefore she accepted an invitation to address the children, and urged them to develop their minds instead of their memories.

That same moral earnestness often colors her comments on Caribbean people and places. The hunting resort of Jekell Island was merely a "luxurious hermitage"; the "Orientals" she saw in Port au Prince made her wonder about future race relations; in a Kingston church, she felt pleased by the very fact of its multiracial congregation; and aesthetics again took second place to moral judgments when she admired Nassau's trees and flowers and its inhabitants' complexions but contrasted Caribbeans who turned their faces to the sun with Bostonians who turned theirs to action. Yet when she observed Caribbean women carrying heavy baskets on their heads and hitching up their skirts to wash clothes in the river, the committed social activist responded primarily as a connoisseur of the picturesque.

Such pleasures were multiplied by sharing them. "I who write you have seen cocoanuts a-growing," Sarah told Sarah Whitman, then exulted that "as we drove along the bushy roads, A.F. did so squeak aloud for joy at every new bush and tree and tame flower a-growing wild."[17] Aldrich continued to be a lively if intellectually lightweight companion. But there was at least one mind-stretching conversation on board—when the president of Haiti came to dine and spoke about Cuba's imminent liberation from Spain.

On the downside, Sarah was often seasick and sleepless, a yellow fever quarantine in St. Thomas prevented them from landing, and Annie ended the voyage so satiated with the tropics that she longed for a "nice little fringe of New England winter." Worst of all, Sarah was weaker at the end of the journey than when it began; as Annie told Robert Johnson in April, "We were in New York for a few days upon our return from the West Indies but Miss Jewett was too unwell to allow us to see our friends."[18]

Europe, 1898

In the spring and summer of 1898, Annie and Sarah made their third long trip to England and the Continent, for much of the time accompanied by Sarah's sister Mary and their nephew Theodore Eastman. Annie and Sarah sailed for England in April, Mary and Theodore joined them in France in July, and they all returned to America in September on the "good ship New England." Whenever they were a party of four, Annie counseled herself to patience and renewed her determination "to make the others enjoy themselves if possible." Though Mary's "ideals and interests are not ours" and it was "rather uphill work," one of Annie's rewards was the heightened pleasure of her private time with "Dear S.O.J."[19]

The voyage began inauspiciously with the discomfort of high seas. "I am afraid you have been as ill as I," Frances Hodgson Burnett (the author of The Secret Garden) commiserated in a penciled scrawl, and hoped she might eventually totter out to see Annie. At best, the crossing to Plymouth was gray, and even Paris was cold and wet.[20] Therefore Annie and Sarah soon headed for the warmth and color of Provence. But the highlight was their visit to the region's greatest poet, Frédéric Mistral, whose Mireio Annie had first read in Harriet Preston's translation over two decades before. Identifying with Mistral and his wife, who were childless but "exceedingly happy together," Annie admired their flourishing garden and their collections of Provençal art and literature, proof that they "love their country and their surroundings and endeavor to ennoble them and make the most of them."

The women celebrated Annie's birthday by traveling to Mme. Blanc's ancestral home—La Ferté, near the old walled town of Jouarre and not far from Paris—and then spent almost a month in her company, saturating themselves in the area and taking "occasional flights to Paris and to Rheims and so on." When they visited the chateau of Mme. de Sévigné, the perspicacious aristocrat whose hundreds of letters about public and private life under Louis XIV had set a standard for literary correspondence, Annie felt close to the woman herself as she strolled through her gardens and stood near the desk where she wrote to her beloved daughter. But she felt even more like an insider during their visit to Paris when Mme. Blanc took her to one of the weekly dinner parties given by the writer, editor, and bibliophile M. Dezant. Seated in the place of honor at the dinner table, she enjoyed lively conversation in a room filled with fine books and beautiful works of art, perhaps recalling similar parties at Charles Street. Yet Annie did not identify with her hostess, a devoted mother who never published any of her manuscripts, "wasted" herself in good deeds, and affected a nunlike dress. Next came a few crowded weeks of touring under the guidance of Mme. Blanc, who knew all of France "in a most extraordinary way."

In England, Annie and Sarah again rendezvoused with Robert Collyer in Yorkshire and made another pilgrimage to Brontë country, the "dreadfully sad old village" of Haworth,[21] then traveled up to Scotland and down to London. Among their many acts of literary homage, they visited Hallam Tennyson and recalled conversing with his parents six years before; they called on Rose Kingsley and visited her parents' graves; they knocked on Georgina Hogarth's door in Chelsea and then strolled past the houses of the Rossettis, George Eliot, and the Carlyles; and they called on Mrs. Gaskell's daughters in Manchester.

Though Annie's social conscience was essentially on hold, it occasionally erupted. She stayed in "overly elaborate" hotel rooms that a friend had prepaid, but would have preferred "less luxury" and an opportunity to put the difference in cost to "some good end"; and after taking tea in an ABC shop where the weary waitresses were never permitted to sit, she determined "to see Lady Henry Somerset to ask if something may not be done."

Her chief pleasures came from seeing old friends. She visited Mrs. Humphry Ward, Rudyard Kipling, and her expatriate friend John Singer Sargent, and spent a day with another expatriate. On the second Sunday in September, Annie and Sarah took a train to Rye "to pass the day with Mr. Henry James," who had urged them to stay overnight. The day before, James had exuberantly declared "with what pride & joy I expect you tomorrow & how extravagantly kind I shall find it of you to make so ample a pilgrimage to so meagre a shrine," promising that "the shrine will do its very best."[22] He was "intent on the largest hospitality," Annie noted; Lamb House was "large enough for elegance, and simple enough to suit the severe taste of a scholar and private gentleman"; and his secretary had "a bump of reverence and appreciates his position and opportunity." Clearly, James enjoyed "having a home of his own to which he might ask us," and the women enjoyed his praise of *The Country of the Pointed Firs*: the language was "'so absolutely true—not a word overdone—such elegance and exactness.' 'And Mrs. Dennet—how admirable she is,' he said again, not waiting for a reply."

They took a carriage ride along the coast to Winchelsea and past Ellen Terry's summer cottage—"a true home for an artist"; and Annie was sorry to miss seeing her but "happy to see the place which she described to us with so great satisfaction." Then taking James's aged terrier along, they all boarded the train for

Hastings, drove along the esplanade, replaced the dog's lost muzzle, stopped for tea, and "enjoyed more talk under new conditions" before parting. James had displayed what he knew his guests would admire, including his admiration of them. He would visit them in Boston, and celebrate them both in his memoir of "Mr. and Mrs. Fields."

Europe, 1900

In 1900, Sarah and Annie took their last trip abroad together. That February Annie gleefully told Charles Dudley Warner that she and Sarah were about to "leave for Athens by invitation of Miss Garrett"—Mary Elizabeth Garrett, the wealthy Baltimore philanthropist and ardent suffragist whom they had met on the *Werra* eight years before.[23]

Their crossing was difficult, Naples was unusually cold, and their itinerary was demanding. After a day at Paestum and a few hours at Pompeii, the three women left for Brindisi and the next day took a steamer to Corfu. Then they sailed to the Greek mainland and spent a day "in the trains going along the southern shore of the Gulf of Corinth, and at sunset we saw the light on the Acropolis and all the great pillars of the Parthenon high against the sky." Athens seemed almost unbearably beautiful. They spent whole mornings in museums and afternoons on the Acropolis, rejoicing in the marvelous statues, the "spring landscape and the wintry sky." Then they headed west across Arcadia "with dragomen and cooks, and all our bags and shawl-straps to be taken out of the carriage and opened at night, and rolled up and shut again and loaded in the mornings, with a huge new-old stone theatre to see in a hill-side, and the snow mountains looking over the tops of the purple ones," all the while admiring "the handsome sturdy people and the clear-eyed children." They were in Megalopolis on Palm Sunday, about to board a steamer for Olympia and then visit Delphi before returning to Athens. Next, they headed east to spend a week in Constantinople and make "the Arabian Nights come true."[24] As spring drew to an end, they paid a brief visit to Mme. Blanc and then sailed for home. Annie and Sarah would take other trips together, but never abroad, never for so long, and never again to such exotic places.

20

Connoisseur, Cynosure, and Advocate

Leading Ladies

During the 1890s, when Boston's cultural life flowered and two splendid McKim, Mead and White buildings arose—the Boston Public Library and Symphony Hall—Annie kept pace with the times. She regularly attended Symphony Hall concerts, for example, and she tried to assist several of the artists who sought commissions to adorn the Public Library. By then she herself had become a cultural icon, attracting as much attention as John Singer Sargent's portraits when she poured tea at his first Boston exhibition.

Conversation continued to be the main cultural fare Annie offered at Charles Street, whether to a dozen dinner guests or a single caller. Occasionally, as in the old days, she also offered music. Jessie Cochrane might play the piano, Mary Cabot Wheelwright might sing, and the composer Ethelbert Nevin once accompanied Miss Wheelwright and then played his "In Arcady" as Annie had suggested. But whenever such great performers as Mme. Modjeska and Ellen Terry came to Boston, they specifically anticipated one-on-one talks with Annie.[1]

The Polish-born Shakespearean actress Helena Modjeska (1840–1909) first came to Charles Street in 1869, during her first triumphal American tour. Struck by Annie's "sweet pensive face" and her "divine harmony of heart and mind," she requested her photograph, and subsequently sought her company and her "judgment on my art" whenever she played in Boston. Although Modjeska's performances were always sold out, she always reserved seats for Annie. "Superior minds like yours ready to appreciate my work" were rare, she once explained. After one of her performances in the early nineties, Modjeska said "if there were a few new expressions in my part last night, they were due to the fact that you were looking at me"; and a new play by Hermann Sudermann ("the writer of the future—as you said—") provided the "opportunity of appearing in a new light before you."[2]

The great English actress Ellen Terry (1848?–1928) was a more intimate friend, as one of her many notes of the period suggests: "May I come in for a little while and sit in the garden with you?" No doubt they discussed mutual friends such as John Singer Sargent, who painted a magnificent portrait of Terry as Lady Macbeth, and Terry's neighbor Henry James. A surprising bit of news in the summer of 1895 was that Terry had just commissioned James to write a one-act play in which "I am an American Lady!!" In her autobiography, Terry said Annie Fields reminded her "of Lady Tennyson, Mrs. Tom Taylor, and Miss Hogarth," and insisted that at Charles Street "the culture of Boston seems no fad to make a joke about, but a rare and delicate reality." Isabella Stewart Gardner "represents the private worship of beauty in Boston," Terry said, while "Mrs. Fields represents its former worship of literary men."[3]

Terry's pairing was astute. Isabella Stewart Gardner (1840–1924)—a New Yorker who moved to Beacon Hill after marrying the wealthy John Gardner in 1860, and entertained far more lavishly than Annie Fields—expressed her "worship of beauty" through a collection of art vastly larger than Annie's. With the Harvard-educated connoisseur Bernard Berenson as her adviser, she started buying European paintings and statues long before inheriting her father's millions in 1891; and by the time Jack Gardner died in 1898, she had already bought land for the palatial building on Boston's Fenway that would house her collection. On 24 December 1901 it was ready for display to her friends, Annie among them, and she opened it to the public two years later. Her forte was carefully controlled display, including self-display, as evident from the collection still exhibited as she herself stipulated in what is now called the Isabella Stewart Gardner Museum—still one of the country's most remarkable private museums.

John Singer Sargent's portraits of Isabella Stewart Gardner and Annie Fields convey two very different personalities. In the full-length portrait that Mrs. Gardner commissioned in 1888, she looks straight at the viewer, wearing a tightly fitted low-cut black evening gown, while her hands—clasped halfway between her shawl-tied hips and her pearl-roped waist—exaggerate the curves of her figure; and her head seems haloed by the wallpaper behind. Doubly an embodiment of what Ellen Terry called "the private worship of beauty in Boston," Mrs. Gardner seems to invite such worship of herself. Utterly different is the half-length portrait of Annie Fields that Sargent painted in 1890. Wearing a high-necked long-sleeved white blouse fastened with a brooch at the neck, the sitter looks meditatively to her right, a dignified private individual who can accept the public approval she does not court.

Appropriately, Sargent's portrait of Mrs. Gardner was included in his first Boston exhibition, at the exclusive St. Botolph's Club. It then went on permanent display in Mrs. Gardner's museum, in the prominent position she herself chose. Also appropriately, the portrait of Annie Fields was Sargent's gift to his sitter. At her death it went to her sister Louisa Beal, and then descended through the family. It is now owned and displayed by the Boston Athenaeum. Despite the striking

contrasts between the women embodied in those two Sargent portraits—the plu-
tocratic aesthete and the serene Boston Lady—they moved in the same orbit, admired one another's dignified individuality, and became friends.

Mrs. Gardner's boldly scrawled notes make it easy to trace their relationship
from the nineties on. One acknowledges Annie's condolence on the death of her
husband; and others thank her for such modest gifts as a newspaper clipping, a
photograph, "wonderful yellow flowers," or a book. After reading one especially
"precious book" (probably the *Letters of Sarah Orne Jewett*), Mrs. Gardner felt particularly moved because "this book comes from you." Many other notes concern
visits to or from Annie, usually when one or the other was entertaining a cultural
celebrity. When Mrs. Humphry Ward and her daughter were ending their visit at
Charles Street in the spring of 1908, for example, Mrs. Gardner was coping with
"the grippe" yet expected to "see the dear ladies & say au revoir." When Annie
was herself recovering from an illness, Mrs. Gardner made a flattering yet considerate proposal: "Mr. & Mrs. Bernard Berenson are here, & naturally care more
to see you than anyone—I know I can't induce you to come here for luncheon or
dinner to meet them! So will you forgive what I am about to suggest? Could I
bring them to supper with you on Sunday . . . ? It seems to me that would be the
quietest and simplest way for you to see these delightful people and for them to
enjoy an unforgettable pleasure—" Then the affluent woman concluded with a
characteristic flourish: "These orchids take to you my love—."[4]

At least once, in the fall of 1902, Mrs. Gardner played a more intimate role in
Annie's life, and two solicitous letters to Sarah Orne Jewett convey the circumstances. "I have just come from spending the night in your room at 148 Charles
Street!" she wrote, then explained why: "Mrs. Fields was bad and wicked, overworked 'doing Boston' with Lady Henry Somerset, Miss Cameron, and Miss
Saunders, and topped off last night by the symphony concert, where the heat was
intense! The combination was too much for her, and she had a fainting spell. She
was sitting in Mrs. Whitman's seat, directly behind me, so that when she went
out, I went too. When she was in bed at 148 Charles Street, with Dr. Williams and
a nurse in attendance, I thought the servants might get rattled, so I calmly walked
into your room and spent the night." After urging Sarah to forgive Annie, "not a
young girl although she acts like one," Mrs. Gardner reassuringly said she "looked
so pretty in bed this morning, with her soft hair about her face. I told her I would
write to you." Then on the envelope flap, she tried to allay any possible concern
that she had intruded on Sarah's privacy: "I nearly stole your story which I saw on
your table. But really I did *not touch.*" The next day, she sent another letter to Sarah
from Charles Street and mentioned a "second scolding to Mrs. Fields." But its
main purpose was to assure Sarah that Annie was "an obedient dear, and does as
she is told. Chicken soup and squab seem the chief of her diet. She is all but recovered urging her friends to see the wonderful embroideries of Miss Cameron."[5]

That same night, Annie's sister Louisa told Sarah's sister Mary about Mrs.
Gardner's solicitude, and explained that what they had agreed to call a fainting

spell was in fact a slight stroke. A month earlier when Sarah suffered a concussion in a carriage accident, Annie "worried very much over your Sarah's illness and altogether it has been too much for her," Louisa said, but Mary should tell Sarah "only what you think best of this." And as Louisa remarked the next day, "How singular it is that Sarah should be at South Berwick and Annie here when at any other time in their close friendship, they would go to each other if needed."[6]

The entire episode displays Annie's cultural status. In a sense, she had fallen in the line of duty, after "doing Boston" with an English aristocrat and a needlecraft expert, and while attending the symphony, where she occupied the seat of her artist friend Sarah Whitman. The great patron of the arts Mrs. Gardner was concerned enough to accompany Annie back home and intimate enough to remain overnight; and although Annie remained confined to her bed the following day, that did not keep her from urging friends to see another woman's "wonderful embroideries."

Artists and Friends

During the nineties, Annie invited many artists she admired to Charles Street, and offered various forms of patronage. She sent John Singer Sargent a pair of theater tickets, for example, and she loaned Elihu Vedder an illustrated book that she thought might inspire him. She also commissioned a small stained glass window from Sarah Whitman, and she bought a bust of Keats from Anne Whitney. But writing an essay about stained glass to promote Whitman's career was her most solicitous act of patronage.

Sarah Wyman Whitman (1842–1904) was a close friend of Annie Fields and even closer to Sarah Orne Jewett. An ebullient Baltimore-born woman who had married a Boston wool merchant, she had studied painting with Thomas Couture in Paris and with William Morris Hunt in Boston, then exhibited widely in Boston and New York and at such distinguished venues as the Columbian Exposition and the Pan American Exposition. Among her civic and cultural activities, she helped found Radcliffe College and the Boston Museum of Fine Arts, and she taught a popular Bible class at Trinity Church and ran its annual fairs. Her many specific involvements with Annie included collaborating on the houseparty narrative *A Week Away from Time*.

But Whitman was primarily an artist whose many productions included vibrant landscapes, still lifes, and portraits, innovative art nouveau book covers for Houghton Mifflin, and boldly colored stained glass windows. Her Houghton Mifflin assignments included the covers for four of Sarah Orne Jewett's books—*The King of Folly Island, Betty Leicester, The Queen's Twin*, and *Strangers and Wayfarers*—, and *Strangers and Wayfarers* was dedicated "To S.W., Painter of New England Men and Women, New England fields and shores." S.W.'s stained glass commissions included two from Sarah Orne Jewett—one for Berwick Academy and the other for Bowdoin College. More professionally significant are the stained glass windows that Whitman made for Harvard's Memorial Hall, Trinity Church, Radcliffe College, and other prominent Boston institutions.

Despite Annie's intervention, however, Whitman did not design any windows for the Boston Public Library. When Annie wrote to Charles McKim on Whitman's behalf in 1891, he promised to pass her recommendation to the trustees but made his own choice amply clear: John La Farge "who has taken much interest in this work from the start should if possible receive the votes of the trustees."[7] Predictably, La Farge received those votes.

Eight years later, after Whitman produced her stained glass window for Harvard's Memorial Hall, Annie wrote an essay on stained glass that discusses both La Farge and Whitman but concludes by praising the color and design of the Harvard window. Although the *Atlantic* editor Walter Page advised her to end the essay with La Farge because he was more famous, Annie refused, insisting that her own sequence provided "unity and sweetness." But obviously, her primary concern was promoting the reputation of a beloved friend.[8]

Annie's friendship with John Singer Sargent (1852–1925) began sometime before the spring of 1882, when she arrived in London and found a note from him saying, "A line from you will evoke me with a suddenness that may give you a shock."[9] But their intimacy began when he made his first working visit to Boston in 1887 and became part of her circle. By then a celebrated and highly paid portrait painter, he had already completed several commissions in New York. His first solo exhibition at the St. Botolph's Club in January 1888 put twenty portraits on display, Isabella Stewart Gardner's among them, with Annie (as well as Sarah) on hand to pour tea.

Two years later, Sargent returned to Boston to paint a series of murals titled "The History of Religion" for the new Public Library. Though the commission would occupy most of his time for the next few years, he also resumed painting portraits of the city's social and cultural elite, Annie's among them.

Sargent had long since become a familiar guest at Charles Street and Manchester. "Indeed I will come—and if it had not been that up to today I have been from morning till night on the scaffolding of the library, you would have had my visit before this," one of his undated notes reads. Another thanks Annie for a pair of theater tickets, says he will probably take "a Fairchild," and asks if she could spare a copy of the "exquisite photograph" of her that Mrs. Fairchild showed him. What Sargent sent in return included tickets for private viewings of his work.[10] But surely his greatest gift was his portrait of Annie Adams Fields.

Another artist who figured in Annie's life in the nineties was Elihu Vedder (1836–1923), the New York–born painter and illustrator who had often visited Charles Street during the sixties and who (though Annie never knew it) was then romantically involved with Kate Field. When he briefly returned to Boston in the early nineties after years of working abroad, hoping to secure mural commissions for the Boston Public Library and other new buildings, he enjoyed Annie's hospitality, her comments about his work, and her practical advice. After a "never to be forgotten visit" to Charles Street in October 1894, Vedder told Annie that a group of his sketches and paintings was about to go on display at Doll de Richards's Boston gallery, and he would "like very much to be there when you see them." The following month, he had good reason for saying "You are always my good friend." She had suggested that he write to potential patrons in New York and Boston, he had already heard from George Vanderbilt and anticipated meeting him, and he had secured an appointment with "the formidable Mrs. Huntington," whose bare walls seemed to ache "for the same kind of decoration I put on the ceiling—and who knows what may happen." In December, he reported progress "in the Library matter," promised to return the wonderfully illustrated *Pilgrim's Progress* that Annie had loaned him, and said he now thought of doing a book "of my own ideas if I ever get time to do it."[11] Although Annie never had a major impact on Vedder's career, she had earned his gratitude and trust.

"The Opportunity Opens"

During the nineties as before and after, Annie interacted with many of the period's most influential women reformers. Frances Willard, founder of the Woman's Christian Temperance Union and a strong suffragist, called herself "a weary worker who has loved you long"; and Jane Addams, the pioneering social worker who in 1899 founded the influential settlement house called Hull House, tried to see Annie whenever she came to Boston.[12] Annie also interacted with old and new friends who shared her commitment to expand women's education.

Her support for women's education included entertaining English lecturers who came to Boston on tour, and occasionally getting them bookings. More important, she supported Radcliffe and Wellesley not only through gifts of books and money but also through her friendships with college administrators, particularly with President Elizabeth Agassiz of Radcliffe and Agnes Irwin (the first dean). A typical letter from Agnes Irwin acknowledges a financial contribution, another asks permission to bring Dean Smith of Barnard College to Charles Street, and still another invites "you and Miss Jewett, the Ladies of the Charles," to join a group of Radcliffe students for dinner.[13] Though Annie was never as close to the administrators of Wellesley, her relationships with them were otherwise much the same.

As she had done since the sixties, Annie sometimes assumed the role of educator herself. One year she convened a group of primary school teachers at Charles Street for discussions that ranged from pedagogy to the importance of literature; and at least once, she invited a high school teacher to bring all her students to Charles Street. She also served as an educator whenever she mounted the podium to recommend initiatives to other women—on one occasion urging the young ladies of the Saturday Morning Club to volunteer for charity visiting as a two-way educational opportunity, and on another urging them to make practical use of their educations by working for prison reform.

More important were her efforts to expand women's access to college and professional schools, medical schools in particular. After being appointed to a committee on women's admission to Harvard Medical School in the eighties, Annie amassed forceful arguments yet failed to persuade the administrators. Then in 1890, she participated in a Baltimore-based women's initiative to raise enough money to establish "a first rate Medical School in connection with the famous Johns Hopkins Hospital and University." The gift was contingent on women being admitted. "The opportunity opens for a school good enough to make a sojourn in Europe no longer a necessity for every well-educated woman doctor," she told Whittier, then sardonically added, "I hope we can get the dirty dollars."[14]

The "we" included the Baltimore philanthropist Mary Elizabeth Garrett, a founder of the Women's Medical Fund Committee. With four other Baltimore women, Garrett had earlier established the Bryn Mawr School for Girls and Bryn Mawr College. Now, in a national effort, the Women's Medical Fund Committee raised the $500,000 the Hopkins trustees had stipulated, Mary Garrett herself contributing half of it.[15] By chance Garrett sailed for Europe on the same ship that carried Annie and Sarah in February 1892, but by choice the three women traveled together on the Continent, and returned to America together. By the time they returned, the Hopkins trustees had accepted the Women's Medical Fund gift with its proviso.

Underlying that proviso was the conviction that educational and vocational opportunities should not be limited by gender or social status. It informed the three women's shipboard friendship and their later relationship—when Garrett came to Manchester, when Sarah visited Garrett's cottage in Maine, and when the three women spent a week in the Adirondacks together in September 1894 (the year Sarah's book for girls titled *Betty Leicester's English Xmas* was published by the Bryn Mawr School and dedicated to M.E.G.). In 1900, when the much wealthier Garrett invited Annie and Sarah to join her for a four-month journey abroad, it was yet another instance of enterprising women using their unique resources to expand women's lives, including one another's.

21

Editors and Friends

James T. Fields was Annie Fields's first and most important editor. During the sixties, he published nineteen of her lyrics in the *Atlantic,* he had her *Ode* privately printed after presumably getting her the commission to write it, and he published her one and only novel. Like the two long poems whose publication he later arranged—*The Children of Lebanon* and *The Return of Persephone*—they all appeared anonymously or pseudonymously. We can only guess what editorial changes he may have made or suggested, whether he rejected any of Annie's *Atlantic* submissions, or what (if any) payment she received.

But Annie Fields's poetry and prose appeared in the *Atlantic* and in other important periodicals as well, and as books, after James T. Fields's retirement and after his death. Three of the period's major editors succeeded him as Annie's publishers, advisers, and supporters—William Dean Howells and Thomas Bailey Aldrich of the *Atlantic Monthly* and Henry Mills Alden of *Harper's Monthly.* They all owed both of the Fieldses debts of gratitude. But none of them lowered their standards to accept Annie's submissions, they sometimes refused them, and they were not the only distinguished editors who accepted and sometimes solicited her work.

Even during her widowhood, Annie did not have to support herself by publishing. But she was not wealthy. The small nest egg that Jamie had amassed by arduous lecturing was subject to the vagaries of the stock market; at one point when she considered mortgaging her summer home, Sarah offered instead to lend her money; Annie always needed to weigh her expenditures carefully; and several bequests of specific sums in her will could not be paid. Rich though she was in culture and friendships, her ego as well as her budget required that she be paid well for her writing. From the seventies on, she moved shrewdly yet decorously through a rapidly changing literary marketplace, demanding fair payment—as she saw it—even from friends.

William Dean Howells (1837–1920)

In 1860 when William Dean Howells first met Annie Fields, she struck him as the ideal embodiment of the genteel world of letters he yearned to enter. The day before, the twenty-three-year-old Ohioan had made his first visit to the Old Corner Bookstore, proofread a poem that would soon appear in the *Atlantic,* and collected his payment for it. Afterward, he had dined at the Parker House with Lowell, Holmes, and Fields and proposed himself as Fields's assistant. Instead, Fields invited him to breakfast at Charles Street the next morning.

Four decades later, when he and Annie were both in their sixties, Howells nostalgically recalled that entire morning, beginning with the moment when the Fieldses' door opened and he began breathing "an odor and an air of books such as I fancied might belong to the famous literary houses of London." Soon he was relishing his first taste of blueberry cake in a room "whose windows looked out through leaves and flowers upon the river's coming and going tides, and whose walls were covered with the faces and the autographs of all the contemporary poets and novelists." Better still, after James T. Fields left for the Bookstore, Annie spoke about her recent visits to Tennyson, Dickens, and other literary eminences. Then she showed him the library's treasures, and "dazzled me with the sight of authors' copies, and volumes invaluable with the autographs and the pencilled notes of the men whose names were dear to me from my love of their work. Everywhere was some souvenir of the living celebrities my hosts had met." Long since a literary celebrity himself, Howells marveled in 1900 that it was "still there, that friendly home of lettered refinement, [and] that gracious spirit who knew how to welcome me, and make the least of my shyness and strangeness, and the most of the little else there was in me." When Annie died in 1915, Howells mourned her for herself and as "the last of the world I came into at Boston." He also told his daughter Winifred something Lowell had said: "It was to Mrs. Fields liking me . . . that I owed my place on the *Atlantic.*"[1]

He was offered that place in January 1866, over five years after he requested it. Meantime, he had married, produced the first of three children, served as the American consul in Venice, published a book titled *Venetian Life,* and moved to New York to become assistant editor of the *Nation.* Many Bostonians were surprised that Fields hired a young midwesterner as his own assistant. But when Fields stepped down as editor of the *Atlantic* five years later, no one was surprised that Howells succeeded him. He retained that position for a decade.

Howells's move to Boston brought immediate entry into the Fieldses' extensive social and cultural networks. Jamie took him to the Saturday Club and the Longfellow-centered Dante Club, where his fluency in Italian made him especially welcome, and Annie invited him to her entire range of entertainments. His children "fondly remember every party which you've given heretofore," Howells told Annie in 1875 when her mother's illness made her cancel her usual Christmas party. Annie never felt drawn to Howells's wife, the "pallid, wide-eyed" Elinor, who seemed sweet and pure though "a nervous little creature at best." But she soon invited both of the Howellses to share such casual pleasures as a "long stroll over the beach and through the woods"; and Howells told Annie after a "little visit" to Manchester in the seventies that it "lacked nothing but a trifle of perpetuity to make it perfect. . . . We have done nothing but celebrate its loveliness since we came home." Annie's "constant kindness" continued even after he moved to New York: in 1886, for example, he thanked Annie for a book she sent for his sister and also "for the dear and lovely friendship, so true to us . . . for so many years."[2]

Howells's tender solicitude for Annie after her husband's death is thus hardly surprising. He went to Manchester in August 1881 as soon as he heard she was ready for visitors; and though illness prevented him from reviewing her *Biographical Notes* for the *Atlantic* that fall, he sent a penciled tribute to her "beautiful and interesting book" from his sickbed.[3] But their professional relationship was thickest during the seventies, when Howells edited the *Atlantic.* Annie submitted at least six manuscripts to him. He published five.

Only once did Annie presume on Howells's friendship during those years, and then only on behalf of someone else: in January 1872, she asked him to treat Celia Thaxter with special editorial kindness.[4] Perhaps he recalled that request two years later while returning one of Annie's submissions: "I have behaved very badly about those verses, which I long ago meant to have put in type, and then sent to you for modification. When I first read them last summer I felt the simple charm that was in them, and I feel it still; but I am still puzzled in following your intention throughout the piece, and the final meaning or moral seems extorted from it. Could you not with some word or phrase thrown into the preceding stanza, make it end with the ninth? I think the eighth stanza particularly lovely." Though Howells claimed to be "very much ashamed" of himself, the shame was merely for his delay.[5] But three of her poems had already met Howells's high standards, he published her essay titled "Three Typical Workingmen" in 1878, and her long poem titled "Defiance" appeared in the *Atlantic* the next year.

Howells's professional interest in Annie's work continued after he left the *Atlantic.* When *Under the Olive* appeared in 1880, he admired her mastery of Greek meters and singled out "Theocritus" as especially "beautiful—well-thought, keenly felt, and admirably said." Then after agreeing to coedit *Cosmopolitan* twelve years later, he urged her to "try some poetry on me." "You know I like it, when I get it good," he told her, and his next letter prodded her to "send *all* the children, and let *me* make the choice." He left *Cosmopolitan* soon after joining it, and evidently none of Annie's poems appeared in that magazine. But Howells continued to monitor her literary career at least as late as the fall of 1900, when he said *Orpheus* had raised him "as far above this workaday world as the sunset I looked at from your porch in Manchester," then exclaimed, "What vitality there still is in the old allegories when a poet's hand touches them!"[6]

At least as early as 1878 when he published her essay on self-help reforms titled

"Three Typical Workingmen," Howells not only admired but supported Annie's social projects. In fact, none of her other friends more actively or more variously supported her work for the Associated Charities. Howells served as a volunteer visitor, he sent Annie money for "the Charioteers," and he participated in at least one of the conferences she organized. As a unique form of support, the first installment of *The Rise of Silas Lapham* in the November 1884 *Century* included a newspaper profile that identified Silas as a liberal contributor to the Associated Charities.[7] More surprisingly, in the winter of 1890 Howells told Annie that he went to the Charity Building "meaning to offer myself [but] came away shyly" and wondered how he could "be of use in the organization." And when the 1892 "Charities Directory" arrived on Howells's desk during his brief tenure as *Cosmopolitan* editor, his immediate concern was "how to have it mentioned."[8]

The following year, Annie's "lovely and like-you" essay on Whittier inaugurated a new stage in her relationship with Howells. Reading it "brought back my earlier acquaintance with you and dear Mr. Fields, whose sweetness to me in the past I can never forget," Howells told Annie in January 1893. "You were both present to me as I read, and as if you were both living." Perhaps as a consequence, Howells soon began setting down reminiscences of his own; and in November 1894, he sent Annie proofs of a few pages about her husband and herself that he hoped would "please and not vex" her.[9]

Two years later when *Authors and Friends* appeared—the book that solidly established Annie as a celebrant of their shared literary past—Howells reported reading it "with wet eyes, for the lost Cambridge and Boston, which it made me see in these years of hopeless exile" in New York. While thinking about the dignified and serene lives "on which you lift the veil," he imagined Annie's pleasure in writing the book. "No one who has not been part of those great and happy times, could know how true and fine your record is," he remarked, "but all can somewhat feel its loveliness."[10]

Years later, at Annie's request, Howells participated in tributes to two men who had shared those great and happy times, Longfellow and Holmes. Though he was too ill to attend the Longfellow commemoration in 1907, Howells sent an address for someone else to read which Annie assured him was "not disgraceful"; and when she asked him to participate in a tribute to Holmes that she was organizing in 1913, Howells whimsically said he was "proud and glad to be on any committee (that required no work) with you."[11] Howells followed where Annie led.

In the fall of 1867, Annie was not simply being modest when she said he "should be congratulated by abler critics than myself" for his *Italian Journeys*. But he valued and even sought her praise. When *The Rise of Silas Lapham* neared completion in the 1885 *Century*, for example, he said "I am glad S. Lapham pleases you still, and I hope for your favor to the end, in which resides whatever lesson I meant to teach."[12]

But none of Howells's works moved Annie more than the long memoir titled *Literary Friends and Acquaintance*. It was so "wonderfully fresh and fair, and so "entirely true" that "we must believe it will rejoice the hearts of a large reading society," Annie wrote soon after it appeared in 1900. As she then confided, Howells had made her "look back in a way I seldom dare to do for myself into a past full of inspirations." Better still, that past now seemed not only "a 'great good place' into which we may sometimes go and shut the door" but "a tender confirmation of a future which we know by faith."[13] If Howells indeed owed his place on the *Atlantic* to Annie Fields, she must have considered herself amply repaid.

Thomas Bailey Aldrich (1836–1907)

When James T. Fields first met Thomas Bailey Aldrich in New York in the mid-1850s, he might well have seen something of himself in the ambitious young poet and editor who had also left Portsmouth as a teenager. Over the next decade, whenever Aldrich reviewed a Ticknor and Fields book for the *Evening Mirror* or the *Home Journal*, he sent a copy of his review to Fields. He also submitted a volume of poems that Fields refused but a New York publisher accepted. Then in 1865, the year that Aldrich married, Ticknor and Fields published his second volume of poems and Fields invited him to edit his new eclectic magazine *Every Saturday*. Aldrich accepted immediately. He edited the magazine's first issue, dated January 1866, and continued to edit it for the next eight years. Meantime, he also produced manuscripts for the *Atlantic,* and in 1881 he would succeed Howells as its editor.[14]

As soon as Lilian and Thomas Bailey Aldrich moved to Boston, they were embraced by the Fieldses' friends. Longfellow often dropped by at their picturesque little house on Pinckney Street, a house Fields took Charles Dickens to visit, and Annie often invited the young couple to Charles Street. They found "a warm place at your hearthside," Aldrich nostalgically recalled on his own fiftieth birthday, two decades after they met, "and after all these years we know of no fire-light that falls with such tenderness on our hearts. I never approach or leave the doorstep of the house in Charles Street without thinking and thinking and thinking."[15]

Though Annie never thought Aldrich had more than a small "spark" of wit, she was fond of him from the start. But his wife Lilian improved with age. A woman who at first struck Annie as irresponsibly frivolous, she turned out to be an admirable wife and mother, a fine housekeeper, a clever individual, and a loyal friend. During Annie's long widowhood, both Aldriches were part of a small nicknamed group that included Sarah Orne Jewett: Aldrich was "T.B.A." or "Linnet," Lilian was "Lily," together they were "the Duke and Duchess of Ponkapog," and their own nickname for Sarah was "Sadie Martinot."

Although Aldrich is now virtually unread, his contemporaries ranked him with Longfellow, Lowell, and Whittier as a poet; his autobiographical *Story of a Bad Boy* brought him enormous popularity in 1869; and in 1873 his sentimental love story "Margery Daw" established him as an important regional writer. He would continue to publish poems, short stories, essays, travel books, novels, and plays throughout his lifetime; and by the time he began his nine-year stint as editor of the *Atlantic* in 1881, he was considered one of the country's most important men of letters.[16]

He was among the select few who knew that Annie was the author of *Asphodel* and among the many who trusted her as a critic. One evening in 1873 after the Fieldses dined with the Aldriches at Lowell's house, which the Aldriches were renting while Lowell was abroad, T.B.A. took Annie into the downstairs study for some shop talk. He wanted her response to a few of his new poems, and he wanted to discuss a story he had recently published and complain about critics' responses to it. He also wanted her to know that he had found Lowell's copy of *Asphodel* "all worn to pieces, read and reread in the upstairs study."

When Annie's *Under the Olive* appeared in 1880, Aldrich's professional respect for her soared. It was "the most remarkable volume of verse ever printed by an American woman," he told his friend Edmund Stedman, a volume that he placed on a par with Landor's *Hellenics*. "Here's a New England woman blowing with sweet breath through Pandean pipes!" he marveled. "What unexpected antique music to come up from Manchester-by-the-Sea!" Yet, he astutely added, the volume "represented only her intellect and its training; I don't find her personality anywhere."[17]

The following year when Aldrich succeeded Howells as editor of the *Atlantic,* his professional relationship with Annie thickened. Whenever he entertained a new contributor, as when "C. E. Craddock" (Mary Murfree) came to Boston in 1884, Annie was part of that entertainment. More important, he published six of her poems as well as her "Mr. Emerson in the Lecture Room" during his nine years as editor. During those years his professional correspondence with Annie always included some mention of Sarah Orne Jewett, as when in July 1883 he accepted one of Annie's poems and asked if "Sadie" was with her, since "I don't know these days where to send proof to her." And though he rejected some of Annie's submissions and suggested revisions on others, he painstakingly sweetened each letter that said so. Thus in October 1884 he told Annie he was returning two poems only "because I like other things of yours better," then self-disparagingly invited her to "try my bad taste again." For whatever reason, it would be nearly six years before her next poem appeared in the *Atlantic*. "I greatly like the poem with the motto from Theocritus, and will print it, if you'll kindly give the verses a title," Aldrich told Annie in March 1890. "The Pathless Way" appeared in the June 1890 *Atlantic* and two others that same year, Aldrich's last year as editor.[18]

But one unpleasantness occurred during Aldrich's incumbency. In April 1884, Aldrich told Annie he would welcome an essay she proposed to write on Charles Reade. But by the time she submitted it four months later, he had left on vacation and Horace Scudder was in charge. Indignant when Scudder requested revisions and balked at her price, Annie reclaimed the manuscript. Aldrich tried to make peace when he returned, assuring Annie that the revisions Scudder requested were merely suggestions, and that all would have been "sweetness and light" if he had been in town when her manuscript arrived. But by then, Annie had sold it to the *Century*.[19]

The year before, Aldrich had advised Annie to make *Harper's* "pay handsomely" for a paper on Carlyle;[20] and he continued to offer marketing advice and criticism after he retired from the *Atlantic*. Thus in 1900 he told her that her manuscript of "Orpheus: A Masque" was charming, effectively dramatized, and finely lyrical, though a few lines might be more "musical." But placing it would be a problem. He thought a public "clogged up with Cockney concert-hall poetry" might not appreciate her "chaste, spiritual little work of art," and it was probably too long for the *Atlantic*. Yet he believed it "would make a lovely little book—and you may tell anybody that I say so!" Just as he had anticipated, Bliss Perry, who was then editing the *Atlantic*, said "Orpheus" was too long for the magazine. But whether or not Aldrich's praise had anything to do with it, Houghton Mifflin published *Orpheus: A Masque* later that same year.[21]

Annie meantime remained close to both of the Aldriches, as when she bought some inexpensive rugs in New York and offered Lilian two, or sent over a tin of biscuits supposedly good for seasickness, or welcomed Lilian's gift of a three-legged stool. One of Aldrich's ongoing roles was sharing intimate gossip, as when he said of Mark Twain in March 1895, "In his business failure I am inclined to think that he lost almost everything except his vivacity and eccentricity."[22] T.B.A.'s own vivacity continued to seem as inexhaustible as his store of anecdotes even when they spent two whole months in the Caribbean together in 1896: his "wit and pleasant company never fail," Annie noted. Then she dryly added, he is "a most careful reader and a true reporter upon the few good books of which he is cognizant." Predictably, Annie invited the Aldriches to join her small social and cultural "Home Club" in 1905, and T.B.A.'s death two years later struck her as a deep personal loss.

Henry Mills Alden (1836–1919)

"You sat by me at dinner, & I vividly remember your almost girlish face & talk & laughter, & the cheer dear Mr. Fields brought into my life," the distinguished *Harper's Monthly* editor Henry Alden nostalgically told Annie Fields in 1897. The year was 1862, the place was New York, and their hostess was Mrs. Anne Botta.[23] Alden was then a schoolteacher struggling to repay his student loans, but eager for a full-time career in the world of letters.

He had taken his first steps toward it three years before. While studying for the ministry at Andover Theological Seminary, he wrote a penetrating essay on the Eleusinian mysteries that he showed to Harriet Beecher Stowe, the wife of one of his professors. She liked it and sent it to Lowell, who accepted it for the *Atlantic*.[24] Then in 1862, shortly before meeting the Fieldses, Alden submitted an erudite essay on Hellenic art and literature to the *Atlantic*, an essay that both the editor and his wife admired.

During their first meeting, James T. Fields formally accepted the essay, handed Alden $300 in cash for it, and made an irresistible offer. Authorized by Lowell, Emerson, and Wendell Phillips, who had also read Alden's new essay, Fields invited him to give the prestigious (and well-paid) Lowell Institute Lectures in 1863. On the crest of that success came another: Alden became managing editor of *Harper's Weekly* that same year. Then in 1869 he became editor of *Harper's Monthly,* a position that he filled with outstanding success until his death fifty years later.[25]

When Alden first sat beside Annie in Mrs. Botta's dining room, he was so impressed by her familiarity with English literary celebrities that he consulted her about an essay on De Quincey that he was planning. Both of the Fieldses offered a few anecdotes, and Annie then culled her letters and diaries for more material. It was the first time her letters and diaries served such a purpose, and the only time she would mine them for anyone other than her husband or herself. When Alden's "Thomas De Quincey" appeared in the September 1863 *Atlantic,* it acknowledged indebtedness to "F-" and an unnamed "American friend."

Predictably, Annie invited Alden to stay at Charles Street when he delivered the Lowell lectures that same year, and he and his wife often returned. He talked with relaxed brilliance at Charles Street "as nowhere else," Mrs. Alden once told Annie. In an unusual tribute, the Aldens named their firstborn child after Annie, a daughter who died in infancy, and then also named their second daughter Annie Fields Alden.

In February 1875, when Alden thanked Annie for hospitality to her namesake, he also urged her to contribute poems and essays to *Harper's Monthly.* A long-time admirer of her *Ode on the Great Organ,* he requested any poems she thought might be suitable for *Harper's.* Annie sent fourteen, and he soon sent $200 for twelve of them, returning two as "not especially adapted to my needs."[26] In March 1882, after all twelve had appeared, Annie sent Alden four more and soon received a check for $100. By the end of the eighties, twenty of her poems had appeared in *Harper's,* and eight more appeared in the nineties.

By the fall of 1890, Annie was setting a price on each poem she submitted. When she sent two poems and requested $25 apiece in November, Alden sent her $25 for "Silence and Solitude" but returned the other, explaining that he was "tempted by its brevity and your name," and it seemed absurd to calculate payment by length, but "it wasn't worth more than $15 to the magazine." He also said he welcomed her frankness and hoped it would continue.[27] Presumably he paid the price she set for the five poems he later published.

For one of them, which Scudder had rejected for the *Atlantic* on grounds of price, Alden suggested a few revisions. After Annie made them, Alden declared that she had improved "the most heavenly uplifting poem I have ever read." "The Singing Shepherd" appeared in *Harper's* in December 1891, its importance signaled by a full-page illustration on the opposite page.[28] Four years later, it would become the title poem of Annie's second collection of poems.

When Alden first solicited Annie's poems in 1875, he also asked her to "contribute on Organizations of Charity—not short articles but comprehensive." As he flatteringly explained, "You have been so intimately connected with this new order, which inspires self-respect & self-help, that I can confidently commit this subject to your hands." The articles would be "beautifully illustrated," he promised, and they could be published anonymously. Annie agreed, though she was too busy to prepare them immediately. "A Beautiful Charity" appeared in July 1877, and "A Glimpse at Some of Our Charities" in February and March 1878. Meantime, Alden consulted Annie about appropriate illustrations for someone else's essay on reform; and fifteen years later he deferentially promised to remove a sentence "which grieved you" from the next edition of his own book on reform.[29]

Annie never took Alden up on a third request he made in 1875—for "some genial & interesting reminiscences of authors' wives" in a single article (since "a series is always more or less formidable").[30] But perhaps that request spurred her to contemplate writing about Hawthorne's wife Sophia, who died in 1871; and she later submitted four other articles. "Saint Cecilia" appeared in the 1880 Harper's, followed by three essays about famous authors she had known: "Glimpses of Emerson" in 1884, and memoirs of Tennyson and Whittier in 1893. After Alden accepted her proposal for "Whittier: Notes of His Life and of His Friendship," Annie asked him how long an essay he wanted and what the introduction should contain. Her twenty-one-page essay appeared in the February 1893 Harper's and was published separately in the Harper's Black and White series of biographies.[31] Like "Glimpses of Emerson" and "Tennyson," it would be reprinted in Authors and Friends.

A year later, however, Alden turned down Annie's offer to write an essay on their mutual friend Celia Thaxter. He wistfully recalled visiting Celia the month before and regretted not attending her funeral, but said Harper's could not publish anything about her "this year," and next year might be too late. He also turned down Annie's proposal for a collection of Thaxter's letters; Harper's "would not care to publish such a book," he said, though Houghton Mifflin might.[32] Only a few months afterward, Annie's "Celia Thaxter" appeared in the Atlantic, and Houghton Mifflin published the Letters of Celia Thaxter.

Many other writers figured in Annie's relationship with Alden, including two who were Alden's friends before they were Annie's—Harriet Beecher Stowe and Elizabeth Stuart Phelps, who both lived in Andover during Alden's student days. Another mutual friendship was with William Dean Howells, who became a contributing editor to Harper's in 1885 and coedited numerous collections of essays with Alden. But during Annie's widowhood, her strongest literary link with Henry Alden was Sarah Orne Jewett, whose work had appeared in Harper's since the 1870s.

From 1881 on, a recurrent theme in Alden's letters to Annie is admiration of Sarah's publications as well as hers. It was not simply out of courtesy that his letters to Annie always included a "message of love to my dear friend, Miss Jewett."

After Annie sent him *The Country of the Pointed Firs* as a Christmas gift in 1896, Alden told Sarah that the book immediately took its place with the many others "associated with dear remembrances of you & of her."[33]

A more intimate link with Annie was his daughter Annie Fields Alden. Annie Fields frequently sent Annie Alden gifts, often invited her to Boston, and included the young woman in her will. Annie Alden's affection for Annie Fields irradiates her condolence letter following the death of Sarah Orne Jewett: "You have been a light bearer always and we love and honor you," Annie Alden wrote. Because "you have always shown such a dear and sweet interest in what I looked forward to doing," she also sent Annie three *Harper's Bazaars*—one with an essay by her father, one with an essay by herself, and the third with her own first illustrations.[34] By then the young woman was terminally ill with cancer; and when she died two years later, Henry Alden told Annie he found consolation in the way his daughter had "always naturally turned to you in her joys and sorrows, and you were always so kind and loving to her."[35]

"You and I live in haunted houses, my dear friend," Alden wrote Annie in 1897, right after Harriet Beecher Stowe died and two years after the death of his wife.[36] But his most nostalgic tribute to Annie came a decade later, when she was unable to attend his seventieth birthday party. As he assured her, "you were present, in an illuminated chamber of memory, and he, your dear husband, to whom I owe everything. How vividly I recalled the evening at Miss Botta's when I first met you both!. . . . God bless you, my dear friend of many years. To me you are always young."[37]

Horace Elisha Scudder (1838–1902)

Horace Elisha Scudder edited the *Atlantic* from 1890 to 1898, following occasional stints as Aldrich's acting editor. From 1885 to 1902, he was also Houghton Mifflin's chief editor. But unlike the two *Atlantic* editors who preceded him, the two who followed him, and his college roommate Henry Alden, Scudder was never invited to Charles Street. His dealings with Annie were at best coolly professional until the fall of 1894, and he was the only editor who had what he himself called a "row" with her.

The row occurred in the summer of 1884 when he offered Annie ten dollars a page for her essay on Charles Reade instead of the thirteen she wanted, and asked her to revise some of her "intemperate and ungrammatical expressions regarding International Copyright." With "suppressed anger and freezing scorn," as Scudder later told Aldrich, Annie refused his request and retrieved her manuscript, which she then sent to the *Century*. Her price was not unreasonable. It was the rate Sarah Orne Jewett then received, albeit for fiction, and Sarah herself had advised Annie to set terms in advance. Whatever the *Century* paid, "An Acquaintance with Charles Reade" appeared there in November.[38]

A second dispute with Scudder occurred in 1891, when he refused to pay Annie's price for "The Singing Shepherd." Once again, she reclaimed her manuscript and submitted it elsewhere—this time to *Harper's,* where it appeared a few months later. A more complete vindication came in 1895, when Houghton Mifflin under Scudder's editorship published *The Singing Shepherd and Other Poems.*

Sarah Orne Jewett's own relationship with Scudder dated back to 1869, when he accepted one of her stories for the *Riverside Magazine for Young People* and began offering her "kind and helpful" advice. She never broke with him. But for over a year after the "Singing Shepherd" dispute she sent him nothing for the *Atlantic,* and he was the target of one of her rare sarcastic remarks, accompanied by an appropriate zigzag hand gesture: "What a strange world this is, . . . full of scudders and things."[39]

Then after Scudder accepted Annie's memoir of Celia Thaxter for the *Atlantic* in the fall of 1894, both women went out of their way to be nice to him. He soon received a cordial letter from Annie followed by a visit from Sarah and another from Annie. "I am afraid that in bringing about this change . . . I have been laying a trap for myself," he exclaimed in his diary. "Too much good will on her part!"[40] That good will continued. From then on, Annie's name recurred in Sarah's frequent letters to Scudder, as when in 1897 she said Annie was unwell or "She would send you her very kind regards—I am sure—with mine."[41]

In 1895, under Scudder's editorship, Annie's "Celia Thaxter" appeared in the *Atlantic,* and Houghton Mifflin published her *Letters of Celia Thaxter* and *The Singing Shepherd and Other Poems;* and the following year Annie's "Days with Mrs. Stowe" appeared in the *Atlantic* and Houghton Mifflin published her *Authors and Friends.* She herself proposed the Thaxter volume to Henry Houghton, telling him that "the family would like to have me undertake the labor," and urging a speedy decision "because it is important to make the announcement in season to prevent anything else being attempted."[42] When the Stowe family asked her to undertake a similar task, Scudder was eager to have her do so. He offered her the firm's file of Stowe letters and clippings, the proofsheets of Charles Stowe's biography, and Houghton Mifflin's new edition of Stowe's works, hoping his own introductions might supply a "hint now and then."[43] Annie's *Life and Letters of Harriet Beecher Stowe* appeared in 1897. By that time, *Authors and Friends* was selling so well that Annie's royalty had been raised from 10 to 15 percent.

Over the next few years, Scudder's exchanges with Annie continued to be cordial. In England in the summer of 1897, for example, he reported meeting a woman who as a girl had met Annie "and remembers you with great pleasure."[44] The following January, Scudder accepted Annie's "Round the Far Rocks" for the *Atlantic,* her last publication in the magazine where she had made her professional debut; and in 1900 he accepted her *Orpheus* for Houghton Mifflin. That same year, when Houghton Mifflin was preparing a new edition of Hawthorne's work, Scudder requested a bit of help on the Miscellany volume and offered a confidence: he had been asked to step in after Walter Page's retirement from the *Atlantic,* and felt "fortunate in having so sane an editor as Perry." Then he politely hoped Annie was enjoying the seashore, sent regards to Sarah, and conveyed his wife's friendly greetings. But their friendship would go no further.[45]

Walter Hines Page (1855–1918) and Bliss Perry (1860–1954)

Walter Hines Page edited the *Atlantic* from July 1898 until July 1899 following three years as Scudder's associate editor, the first southerner to hold those positions. During that entire period, he was a regular visitor to Charles Street.

In June 1896, when the *Atlantic* was planning a new department to be called "The Humanities"—brief articles "written only by persons who have fairly won a place in our Literature"—Page sent the first invitations to Annie, Aldrich, and Howells, since "If the Department can be begun with something from you three, it will start with great distinction." He also enclosed a typed copy of Annie's Stowe manuscript with suggestions for cuts, urging her to return it quickly because the *Century* had also scheduled a Stowe essay "and we do not wish the Atlantic to seem behindhand." "Days with Mrs. Stowe" was the lead article in the August issue.[46]

When Annie later requested the return of some poems she had submitted, Page said he was retaining a typed copy of her sonnet "The Poet" for publication; in addition, he promised to read two articles she recommended, and thanked her for suggesting that Mrs. Owen Wister might be induced to write about her husband. During his single year as editor, Page accepted Annie's "Notes on Glass Decoration" (which the *Century* editors had refused). At his request, she changed the title and reduced the beginning. But she refused to move the last section praising her friend Sarah Whitman, saying she would rather reclaim the article: "I fear you would not then find any unity or sweetness left."[47]

Annie had a longer and closer relationship with Bliss Perry, who succeeded Page as *Atlantic* editor in 1899 and held that position for a decade. He then became a professor of English at Harvard. During his years as editor, he was even more gracious than Page in dealing with Annie, even when he returned a manuscript. He thanked her for sending "Orpheus" in February 1900, regretting that it was too long for the *Atlantic;* and he was delighted that it would become "a little book."[48] Yet he would publish only one of her manuscripts—"Saint Teresa," in March 1903—and he showed no interest in her proposal for a similar essay on Saint Catherine two years later.[49]

In December 1904, Perry agreed to join Annie's Home Club, a group of people "interested in letters who will find it an advantage to be better acquainted" during a series of dinners at Charles Street, saying he and his wife would gladly "sit at your table as often as possible." Such intimacy never entailed professional compromise, however, as evident in Perry's response to a proposal Annie sent him in October 1907. He would be glad to publish the welcome address she planned for a "Whittier gathering," Perry wrote, but the *Atlantic* was publishing its own "bow to Whittier" before then, and he doubted that she wanted her address published before she delivered it. "If you do so want," he nonetheless added, she should let him see it within a week.[50]

Richard Watson Gilder (1844–1909) and
Robert Underwood Johnson (1853–1937)

Richard Watson Gilder was a poet and reformer who edited New York's *Century Illustrated Monthly Magazine* from its inception in 1881 until his death in 1909. Though he and Annie had occasionally met during her trips to New York in the seventies, when he was assistant editor of *Scribner's Monthly,* their professional relationship began after Annie reclaimed "An Acquaintance with Charles Reade" from the *Atlantic* in 1884 and submitted it to the *Century.* Like the other five essays Gilder would accept over the next two decades, the Reade essay offered "hitherto unpublished letters" intermixed with Annie's reminiscences of the writer and assessments of his career and character. "Glimpses of Longfellow in Social Life" appeared in 1886, "Oliver Wendell Holmes: Personal Recollections and Unpublished Letters" in 1895, and essays on the Cowden Clarkes and on George Eliot in 1899. For "Two Lovers of Literature and Art: Charles and Mary Cowden Clarke" (a title Gilder supplied), Annie provided the illustrations. Although Gilder had no interest in "Notes on Glass Decoration," the "brief paper" Annie offered him in 1899, he later commissioned her essay on Mme. Blanc. It was Annie's only study of a living celebrity, and she made a modest request: she wanted her name to appear as "simply 'Mrs. Fields,' a form lately adopted by others and one which strikes me as far more *suitable* and *dignified* than any other."[51]

By then, Gilder had also published four of Annie's poems. "I take the liberty of sending you 'a batch of verses,'" Annie told him in July 1886, soon after her "Glimpses of Longfellow" appeared, stipulating that if they seemed "worth printing I shall be glad to have you do so at twenty-five dollars each."[52] Gilder rejected the whole batch. But Annie fared better in the fall of 1887, when she submitted "a little poem which has grown out of a hint in the 'Epic Songs'" and requested its speedy return if it seemed unsuitable.[53] That poem appeared in December, a second the following June, and two more in 1892.

That same year, Annie's relationship with Gilder's associate editor Robert Johnson and his wife Katherine developed into an intimacy that soon included the Gilders and even their sons. "Miss Jewett and I crossed the ocean in the same steamer with Mr. & Mrs. Johnson and we have the pleasure of seeing Mr. & Mrs. Gilder whenever we go to New York and now and then in Boston," Annie told "two 'noble scions' bearing the names of Johnson and Gilder" in April 1894, when they were attending boarding school in nearby Milton. She invited the boys to spend a weekend with her, then urged Katherine and Robert Johnson to join them.[54]

Two years later when Houghton Mifflin was about to publish *Authors and Friends,* Annie asked Johnson's permission to include her Longfellow and Holmes essays in it "although the agreement was really made in the first contract." As she explained, "it will be pleasant to know that you feel I am no transgressor in asking to use these papers elsewhere."[55]

Only one of the essays posed any problems. In the spring of 1898 after Gilder accepted her essay on Mary Cowden Clarke, Annie submitted a list of illustrations she could send to accompany the article, subsequently shipped photographs of some of these and originals of others, then telegraphed "Pray keep photographs." The essay appeared a year later. Soon afterward, Annie wryly fielded Johnson's report that a reader had questioned the date of Mary Cowden Clarke's death. "I am much obliged to the gentleman for calling my attention to the subject which he can easily settle for himself," she wrote, promised to check the date herself, then commented, "I suppose you would not especially care to correct the *magazine!*" She had in fact wrongly given the death date as 1897 rather than 1898. But she took the high ground when she asked Johnson to return the many illustrations she had submitted: "It is more than a year since I sent them to you!!"[56]

A clearer index of the comfortable high ground she had long since occupied with the *Century* editors is Annie's note to Gilder about the 1897 Christmas issue. It was "the very idea of what a magazine ought to be," Annie declared, then undercut her compliment by saying it was "the only Century magazine I really feel so about."[57] Annie's fondness for Gilder and respect for his work continued until his death, as evident from a letter of March 1909. After wistfully wishing that Gilder lived nearby, Annie reported on Sarah's gallantry during her final illness and told him that "At Christmas Miss Jewett gave me your volume of collected poems which I keep on the small table by the evening lamp where I can (and do) dip into it from day to day."[58]

Charles Scribner (1854–1930) and Edward L. Burlingame (1848–1922)

Scribner's Magazine entered the field as a competitor to the *Atlantic, Harper's,* and *Century* in January 1887, with Charles Scribner as publisher and Edward L. Burlingame as editor. Annie made her debut in the magazine with a poem in September 1887 and published an essay in it six months later. Within less than a decade, *Scribner's* would publish a dozen more of her poems and three additional essays.

Burlingame's desire for well-illustrated essays on literary subjects made him welcome Annie's essay "A Shelf of Old Books: Leigh Hunt" (published in March 1888) and her "Second Shelf of Old Books" (published in April 1889), both illustrated from her own collections. Burlingame also accepted her 1892 essay titled "Guérin's 'Centaur,'" a biographical essay on the French poet that accompanied her own translation of his best-known poem. Then two years later, at the request of Charles Scribner himself, Annie wrote what would be her last essay for *Scribner's.*

In "A Shelf of Old Books: Leigh Hunt" as in all of her literary memoirs, Annie gracefully if loosely interwove personal reminiscences of the writer with cogent assessments of his career and character. This time, books served as her organizing principle, books that Hunt had once owned and now belonged to her; and she enclosed a few photographs of her own library shelves that displayed some of them. When Burlingame sent her a check and requested a tighter beginning, Annie agreed to consider that suggestion but also asked for more money. "I have known of no payment as large as you suggest, for any paper of this character," he replied in December 1887. She nonetheless insisted. He then agreed to "increase the payment in accordance with your wish," but urged her to reduce a demand which "would involve injustice to others" and "consider" a payment of $150 above what she had already received. Whatever bargain they finally struck, the essay appeared in March 1888.[59]

There was no such hassle about Annie's second "Shelf," which focused on John Brown and other Edinburgh writers and again included illustrations that Annie provided. This time Burlingame's only requests concerned two picture captions. He agreed to include a watercolor portrait of Marjorie Fleming—"in many ways the gem"—although it had already appeared in the children's magazine *Wide awake;* but he wanted Annie to name both the artist and the owner. He also wanted her Burns portrait to be identified as "from a daguerreotype in the possession of Mrs. Fields—after a miniature."[60]

The third and last "Shelf" resulted from Annie's initiative but also Charles Scribner's. In the spring of 1894, Annie wanted to bring out the first two essays as a book, and asked him to quote a price for the printing plates. She could not have hoped for a more flattering reply. He would rather have his own firm do the book, Scribner said, then asked her to provide a third essay to thicken the volume, and to provide it quickly for prior magazine publication. "Perhaps it is too soon to 'name terms,'" he wrote, "but it can do no harm to add that our usual arrangement for such books, where we furnish a considerable number of illustrations, is ten per cent on the retail price and I presume that will be satisfactory to you."[61]

"From Milton to Thackeray" appeared in the September *Scribner's,* and once again included illustrations Annie provided. Her special interest in woman writers emerges in two subsections: a four-page tribute to Barry Cornwall's wife Anna Proctor ("one of the most brilliant women in London society" and clearly one of Annie's role models), and a longer commentary on the seventeenth-century poet Katherine Phillips, the "Matchless Orinda" whose poems Keats had loved "for their womanly, as well as their poetic, qualities," as did Annie herself. She concluded with something more explicitly personal: a touching account of Thackeray's kindness to her when she was a young bride.

The opulently produced three-essay volume appeared that same year in both America and England, with the title and "Mrs James T. Fields" goldstamped on the beige cloth cover and spine. Printed on glossy paper, with a picture of the Fieldses' library as the frontispiece and nearly five dozen other full page illustrations, *A Shelf of Old Books* was well and widely reviewed and sold well. Charles Scribner had made a shrewd investment.

Charles Dudley Warner (1829–1900)

For forty years, Charles Dudley Warner edited the influential *Hartford Courant*. A neighbor of Harriet Beecher Stowe and Mark Twain (with whom he wrote *The Gilded Age*), he was also a contributing editor of *Harper's Monthly* and editor of the thirty-one-volume *Library of the World's Best Literature;* he succeeded James T. Fields as editor of the American Men of Letters biographies; and his own literary productions included travel books, biographies, and novels. Fields published his first collection of essays, *My Summer in a Garden*, in 1870. Annie's separate relationship with Warner began in 1880 after he praised *Under the Olive,* then reviewed it in the *Courant* and reprinted some of its poems.[62] Over the next twenty years, they exchanged lively letters; and Warner and his wife Susan—a central figure in Hartford's cultural life—were often Annie's guests.

Both Warner and Annie were committed to "practical benevolence" (Annie's term), projects that help individuals to help themselves. Warner's principal advocacy took the form of pamphlets and magazine articles about a prison program in Elmira, New York, that offered early parole to inmates who completed vocational training courses. Annie's support included asking Warner to determine whether a Massachusetts prisoner might be transferred to Elmira, then arguing for the Elmira program during "a kind of prison-reform-revival" in Boston in 1894. She had not gotten "much help on the Reformatory question," she complained in 1900, shortly before Warner's death, but four years later she would reraise the question in *Charles Dudley Warner,* the last biography she published.[63] Another of Warner's projects was improving educational opportunities for Negroes, a project she supported by circulating his essay "The Education of the Negro" to friends. Her own related efforts included corresponding with Booker T. Washington about Tuskegee Institute, sending him money, and inviting him to Charles Street. As an incidental form of support, she sent Warner "a bit of Mr. Chestnutt's [sic] newspaper writing," telling him that Charles Waddell Chesnutt had "done some good stories" and was "one of the dark race himself."[64]

Annie was more firmly linked to Warner through literary friendships, with Twain and Stowe in particular. In July 1896 they both attended Stowe's funeral; Annie wrote "Days with Mrs. Stowe" soon afterward and Warner praised it; and in January, Annie told him she had promised to talk with Stowe's unmarried twin daughters Eliza and Hattie to draw them out about their mother for her *Life and Letters of Harriet Beecher Stowe.*[65] But Stowe's estate was still in probate in early September, the Forest Street house in Hartford where the twins still lived was up for sale, and the trust fund Stowe had left them seemed inadequate for their support.

At that point Warner sent Annie an assurance and a proposal. The twins "have *entire* confidence in you and me, and anything that we agree should be done they will assent to," Warner said. He suggested raising funds for a memorial to Stowe, the twins to have the income while they lived.[66] Though Annie worried that Stowe's "mad, bad" half-sister Isabella Hooker—who had lived with her husband before they were married—would want to be on their committee, she began fund-raising. "Mrs. Cabot gives five hundred dollars," she wrote two weeks later. "Mrs. Dexter is busy 'organizing' for Chicago and wants your name dear C—to go with mine from New England. Mrs. Longworth will give me names in Cincinatti." She also got the name of the real estate agent who was handling the Forest Street house and asked Warner to "get the refusal." But the agent gave them only a week, and by Christmas the house was sold. The proceeds were added to Stowe's estate and shared equally by the twins and their brother Charles, and the twins then accepted Charles's invitation to live with him and his family in nearby Simsbury. We cannot know what happened to the money Annie had raised for a Stowe Memorial and the twins' support. "In any event," Annie told one of the many contributors to the Stowe Memorial Fund, "we give up the plan."[67]

Meantime, another link between Annie and Warner was their interest in each other's writings. In the summer of 1899, for example, Annie thanked Warner for his new novel and praised it, then told him about the life of Hawthorne that she was preparing. When the biography was published a few months later, Warner told her, "I took it up after dinner to merely look at how it began and I kept right on to the end," and he regretted not asking her to do the Holmes volume for the American Men of Letters series.[68] Perhaps his enthusiasm for Annie's *Nathaniel Hawthorne* figured in her commission to prepare Warner's biography.

In that brief biography, which McClure, Phillips published in its Contemporary Men of Letters series in 1904, Annie stressed Warner's commitment to literature as a civilizing force. As a corollary, she praised the characters and ideas in his three novels of the early nineties but said he was essentially an essayist. Warner emerges as a kind-hearted and generous man who tried to make the world a saner and more wholesome place. It nonetheless seems strange that Annie devoted almost a fifth of the book to Warner's advocacy of the Elmira prison reform plan, and hoped everyone "who cared for his life and work" would support it.[69]

Mark DeWolfe Howe (1864–1960)

Mark Antony DeWolfe Howe looms large in any study of Annie Fields if only because Annie made him custodian of her personal papers, and because he later wrote *Memories of a Hostess: A Chronicle of Eminent Friendships Drawn Chiefly from the Diaries of Mrs. James T. Fields* (1922). An assistant editor of the *Youth's Companion* from 1888 to 1893, he found at Charles Street (as his daughter said) "that rarest and most precious gift a writer can come upon—the spark of genuine interest and belief in his work for its own sake." Because Annie knew "the magazine world of Boston and New York quite as well as any living being," he trusted her advice. When Scudder asked him to join the *Atlantic* in 1893, he consulted her before accepting. Two years later, when eye problems forced him to leave the magazine— and for a few years to leave Boston itself—she offered solicitous cosseting, as when she invited him to a dinner "in memory of Keats" and then to stay on for "as many days as you like." After his marriage in 1899, Annie's friendship extended to his wife and then his two children. If it is hard to imagine both Annie and Sarah romping with the children, it is still more surprising that young Quincy Howe once spent an entire autumn at Charles Street while the rest of the family remained on Cape Cod.[70]

Meantime, Mark DeWolfe Howe served Annie as a literary confidant. She declared to him that she felt diffident about writing a Stowe biography: "It is indeed true that I have been rash enough to promise her daughters, who felt very strongly on the subject that I would do it; whether I shall be able to carry out this rash undertaking I may confess to you, seems to me 'rather doubtful.'" Having promised to do it, however, "I shall try. If it proves the distinguished failure of the age, the New England fire-place still remains a refuge for disappointed authors; in which resort I sometimes wish we more frequently took refuge."[71] But when Howe was about to review *Authors and Friends* for the *Bookman*, Annie decorously exerted control. He could "print anything which seems to you in good taste . . . (except my own picture!)," Annie said, then told him to "say that there is much new material in the book, incorporated into the papers which have already been published; as well as a very brief sketch of Lady Tennyson written since her death." When his highly favorable review appeared, she called it "a tribute to your own gift for friendship," then admitted, "Such things are very agreeable to hear but they are something to live up to, after all."[72]

In the summer of 1899, as editor of Small and Maynard's Beacon Series of "Brief Biographies of Eminent Americans," small volumes that ran to about twenty thousand words, Howe persuaded Annie to do the Hawthorne volume. When he requested a preface, however, Annie said it was unnecessary. "My taste revolts at the idea," she told him. "I think the little book ought to be taken as it is or left alone." As for the bibliography and chronology he requested, Annie said she was not good at either but she would list her sources. Payment was another vexed issue. The 15 percent royalty that she had received from Houghton Mifflin was her price, Annie said, but she would accept Small and Maynard's lower terms as a favor to Howe. She then worked with such remarkable dispatch that only ten days later she thanked Howe for carefully reading her proofs and asked him if he liked the cut she had made at the beginning: if not, she would try again.[73]

Fuller proof of Annie's trust in Howe's judgment came after Sarah's death. She planned to publish "a sort of continuous group of her letters" which "make quite a perfect diary and possess a character of their own without any striving for cleverness but simply showing her own bright humanity," Annie told him.[74] He encouraged her but also offered thoughtful advice "regarding the nicknames—especially where an assumed childish diction is coupled with them. An occasional 'Pinny,' I should think might be left," though more might lead to "all sorts of people *reading them wrong*."[75]

"Pinny" had always been "Miss Jewett" to Howe (as Annie was always "Mrs. Fields"). He called their relationship a "union—there is no truer word for it," and they both befriended his children. When his daughter Helen was born, Sarah sent two of her own books inscribed "from one of her oldest friends." Many years later, Helen herself recalled visiting Charles Street with her brother Quincy and seeing "two old ladies, letting loose for our benefit some balloons which floated airily beneath the high ceiling."[76]

As one of the members of Annie's Home Club in 1905, Mark DeWolfe Howe performed the task of escorting Julia Ward Howe to and from a lively meeting that Henry James also attended. What most amused him was "the utterance of Mrs. Howe as she slumped into her seat for the homeward drive. Diminished as she was in stature by her nearly ninety years, she declared with an air of finality 'Annie Fields has shrunk.'" When Annie Fields died ten years later, Howe's daughter heard him say with unprecedented sadness, "I have lost one of my best friends."[77]

Annie stipulated in her will that Mark DeWolfe Howe was to be her literary executor. She left her "letters and scribblings in your hands knowing that you will use nothing publicly which is not worth while," and instructed him to "destroy everything which is of no public value." She then disingenuously added, *"that I think* will mean *everything."*[78]

Annie had often told Howe that her own life should not be documented except "for some reason not altogether connected with myself." The reason he found was her connection with her famous friends as "a central animating presence, a focus of sympathy and understanding, which seemed to make a single phenomenon out of a long series and wide variety of friendships and hospitalities."[79] He presents that "phenomenon" mostly through long quotations from Annie Fields's journals, loosely focused on a single figure (as in the chapter called "Dr. Holmes, the Friend and Neighbor") or group (as in "Stage Folk and Others"), introduced by modest explanatory comments.

His book is in the grand tradition of the Victorian "Journals, Letters, and Remains," usually published soon after a celebrated public figure died, intended to provide glimpses of that person's sensibility and opinions as preserved in private papers. Many of Annie's anecdotes and ruminations about well-known writers and other cultural figures are included, somewhat randomly—there is much about Dickens though nothing about Howells, for example. Howe included none of her own private thoughts, feelings, or aspirations, and nearly nothing about her women friends or associates apart from Sarah Orne Jewett. Jewett is the supposed subject of a final chapter that includes the women's encounters with Mistral, Henry James, and the president of Haiti, and briefly mentions Annie's publications and philanthropic work. The "Grecian spirit" of her poems is represented by a single sonnet from *The Singing Shepherd* that "came to her complete . . . in about fifteen minutes."

Most of the book is drawn from the journals Annie kept from 1863 to 1877, supplemented by extracts from letters that she or her husband received from famous men. In his conclusion, Howe bade farewell to the serene and gracious past that

Annie both recorded and represented: "We would not wish them back, those Victorians of ours. They were the product of their own day, and would be hardly at ease—poor things—in our twentieth-century Zion. Even some of us who inhabit it gain a sense of rest in reentering their quiet, decorous dwelling-places. As we emerge again from one of them, may it be with a renewed allegiance to those lasting 'things that are more excellent,' which belong to every generation of civilized men and women."[80] He gave us the Annie Fields we have known ever since. She would have been pleased.

She had told Ferris Greenslet of Houghton Mifflin that she expected Howe to use her letters and journals to compile a book Houghton Mifflin would publish. But Howe did not get to that task until 1921, when he had become a vice president of the Atlantic Monthly Company. Although Greenslet protested that Howe had violated a clear understanding with Houghton Mifflin, the Atlantic Monthly Press issued the book in 1922. Howe contended that Annie Fields had authorized him to use her papers for his own best advantage; and evidently he thought his best advantage lay with his own company.[81]

As a woman who had learned to negotiate the terms of her own publications, and a woman whose husband had achieved fame as a shrewd publisher, Annie Fields would have understood her executor's decision. She might have been pleased by his determination, and also pleased to have the name "Atlantic Monthly" again associated with the name of Fields. But as a matter of loyalty though also of vanity, she would surely have preferred having *Memories of a Hostess: A Chronicle of Eminent Friendships Drawn Chiefly from the Diaries of Mrs. James T. Fields* issued by Houghton Mifflin—the successor to her husband's firm, the firm that had published most of her books, the most prestigious publisher in Boston.

22

Authority and Celebrity

The nineties turned out to be Annie's most productive decade as a woman of letters, partly because many of her celebrated friends died and she took on the charge of memorializing them. Her memoirs of Tennyson and Whittier appeared in *Harper's;* memoirs of Thaxter, Holmes, the Cowden Clarkes, and George Eliot appeared in the *Century;* and the *Atlantic* published her essay on Stowe. Six of her seven books of the nineties also celebrated writers she had known and loved: *Whittier: Notes of His Life and Friendships* (1893), *A Shelf of Old Books* (1894), the *Letters of Celia Thaxter* (1895), *Authors and Friends* (1896), the *Life and Letters of Harriet Beecher Stowe* (1897), and *Nathaniel Hawthorne* (1899). Annie also published twenty-two poems in major periodicals during the nineties, and her second and last collection, *The Singing Shepherd and Other Poems,* appeared in 1895. Sarah Orne Jewett was also remarkably productive during the decade. In addition to the *Country of the Pointed Firs* (1896), her own personal favorite, four collections of her short stories appeared as well as a volume of sketches and two novellas for girls.[1]

All of Annie's prose works of the nineties celebrate individual achievement, though two are otherwise hard to classify—"Guérin's 'Centaur'" (1892) and "Notes on Glass Decoration" (1899). After the French poet Maurice de Guérin died in 1840, George Sand had his "Centaur" published in the *Revue des Deux Mondes* and wrote a biographical sketch to accompany it. Following in Sand's footsteps half a century later, Annie published her own translation of the "Centaur" accompanied by a brief biography of Guérin.[2]

"Notes on Glass Decoration" was primarily intended to celebrate and promote the work of her friend Sarah Wyman Whitman. After a brief history of stained glass, Annie discussed recent developments of the art in America as part of a "new religion of spirit," citing the work of two outstanding artists—the widely celebrated John La Farge and the moderately celebrated Whitman. Then she cannily concluded by praising the color and design of Whitman's latest work, a window honoring the Civil War dead in Harvard's Memorial Hall. "Nobody has said a word yet about her achievement," Annie told Robert Underwood Johnson of the *Century* when sending him the essay; then unfazed by his rejection, she successfully submitted it to the *Atlantic*.[3]

By then, Annie had become famous enough to warrant two profiles in periodicals—one in the "Famous People at Home" series in *Time and the Hour* (1897), and another in the "Authors at Home" series in *The Critic* (1898).[4] The anonymous *Time and the Hour* author ushers the reader into the famous library, introduces "the votaress of this sacred shrine," and praises her work for the Associated Charities: "Mrs. Fields may be said to be the heart of the great movement." After identifying Sarah Orne Jewett as Annie's companion and "the Berwick girl whose idyls of New England are our best local literature," the author praises Annie's literary work (singling out *Under the Olive* and *A Shelf of Old Books*). Next comes an overarching tribute that anticipates Cather's: "Gentle, quiet, and reserved, as are the motions of her daily life, there is no power to-day in Boston like that of Annie Fields."

The longer *Critic* profile, written by Annie's friend and protégée Louise Imogen Guiney, presents 148 Charles Street as a "literary shrine" filled with "memories of men of genius," particularly the famous drawing room with its beautiful views, its "nave of books," and its portraits of famous writers, then enters the adjoining "homelike convent cell" where Annie wrote "calm Virgilian verse" and "harmoniously-proportioned biographies, which no one else does so well outside of France." As an insider, Guiney moved from praise of Annie's good humor and good taste to her hairstyle—"the loose, low-drawn coiffure of gentlewomen in the years of her youth"—then declared that Annie bypassed fashion yet exerted "a shy but positive influence in behalf of simplicity, self-knowledge, and repose." Guiney's most fervent praise applies equally well to herself: Annie Fields's "pleasure, her strict enthusiasm, is, of course, literature," and her "work in letters is impersonal, as only a strong personality dares to make it." Next, she praised Annie for producing the "honey of pure literature . . . in the heart of the town, though also in a sort of abbatial solitude, among her plants, her books, her memories, and the faces of affectionately-cared-for guests." Then topping even that layered tribute, Guiney said Annie ran a "perfectly ordered household" yet also actively supported "what is best in the spirit of the community which so much admires her."

The Singing Shepherd

Twenty-two poems by "Annie Fields" appeared in the *Atlantic, Harper's, Scribner's,* and the *Century* during the nineties, and Annie entered the new century with *Orpheus: A Masque* (with her name given as "Mrs. Fields"). But her major bid for poetic fame came when Houghton Mifflin published *The Singing Shepherd and Other Poems* in 1895, with the name "Annie Fields" on its title page. The small green-covered volume contained ninety-one original poems and one translation, rang-

ing in length from half a page to three and a half, for a total of 155 pages. They
sample a lifetime of writing poetry, some of the poems appearing for the first
time. They include moralizing lyrics, birthday celebrations, memorials to friends,
versified narratives, and (as in *Under the Olive*) ambitious appropriations of classical material.

"'Song, to the Gods, is Sweetest Sacrifice'" opens with a sneering question
from Criton (Plato's *Crito*), "Who reads the poets now?" and ends with a yearning counterquestion:

> Where are the singers, with their hearts aflame,
> To tell again what those of old let fall,—
> How to decaying worlds fresh promise came,
> And how our angels in the night-time sing.

In that sonnet, as in her title poem and many others in the volume, Annie
affirmed the poet's timeless moral ministry. She gave no endnotes for this poem
or for any others in the volume, though a few have epigraphs from such major
poets as Theocritus, Shakespeare, and Milton. She was staking a claim for recognition as a serious poet.

The volume's title poem, "The Singing Shepherd," implicitly proclaims that
lofty ambition. Dedicated "To a Poet's Memory," it ends with its speaker committed to follow the dead singer's path, aware that "thou, dear shepherd, still art
shepherding thy flock." The next poem, "The Comforter," also mourns a beloved
poet but ends more solemnly when a voice "Deeper than thought" declares, "I am
the presence at the dark, low door." The next eight poems address Civil War issues with tight tonal control—whether explicitly, as in two tributes to bereaved
mothers, or implicitly, as in Annie's first *Atlantic* publication, the 1861 "Wild Endive" (now retitled "Blue Succory").[5]

The poet's moralizing mission to affirm life in the face of death continues in
"Ros Solis" and the many other poems that can be loosely categorized as nature
poems. The speaker addresses the "lowly herb" and humbly declares

> The lesson thou canst teach my heart would learn,
> For the road is hot,
> The centre of my being a dry spot!

The book's final poem, "Death, Who Art Thou?"—like most of the others in the
collection—moves from doubt to acceptance. It sweeps exaltedly from ancients
"who watched the Aegean Sea / Stretch up white arms to drag the diver down"
to the time of Jesus, and ends with a bereaved speaker who ultimately concludes
that "Death will show that Love and he are one."

When Mark DeWolfe Howe reviewed the volume for the *Atlantic,* he particularly praised "the poems which seem to have sprung most directly from human
intercourse" (presumably including Annie's pensive tributes to Laura Johnson,
Tennyson, and Celia Thaxter). "C. T." begins with a sad apostrophe to Celia,
whose letters to Annie were often signed "Sandpiper":

> Beloved, on the shore of this gray world
> Thy little bird, the sandpiper, and I
> Now stand alone. . . .

The poem then wistfully concludes that the bird's "song leads on," a trope similar to that of "The Singing Shepherd" but more explicitly personal. Another poem that sprang "directly from human intercourse" expresses deeper affection; and it was almost certainly addressed to Sarah Orne Jewett. "To———, Sleeping" begins with the speaker observing "the tender curving of thy mouth, / That cheek, our home of kisses, the soft hair," and concludes with a trope of mutual consolation:

> And yet, dear love, how oft thou leav'st thy flowers,
> Here in the rain to walk with me and grieve!

A more poignant consolation emerges from the denser and more ambitious love lyric "Winter Lilacs," addressed to "G. D. H.," a poem that begins with

> A bunch of lilacs there by the door;
>   That and no more!
> Delicate, lily-white, like the new snow
>   Falling below.

Those flowers that "Into my darkness brought their own light" evoke happy memories of an "old, old love, and the summer hush / And the lilac bush."[6]

Most of the poems display skilled craftsmanship and offer spiritual consolation to both the speaker and the reader. But prosody occasionally dominates, as in the insistent meters of the epigrammatic "Compensation" (the second of Annie's *Atlantic* publications):

> In the strength of the endeavor,
> In the temper of the giver,
> In the loving of the lover,
>   Lies the hidden recompense.
>
> In the sowing of the sower,
> In the fleeting of the flower,
> In the fading of each hour,
>   Lurks eternal recompense.

More surprising is Annie's occasional wink at moral propriety, as when in "Little Guinever" she presents Guinever's intimate play with Launcelot as harmless. In the words of the smiling handmaidens,

> "All we see we need not say,
> For Guinever is but a child."

"The Bee and the Rose" is more representative in its use of conventional symbols to fuse self-reliance with obligation. Annie uses the simile of a brier rose for a Thoreauvian affirmation:

There is an ecstasy that I have known
Among the shadows of green arching things
That I could breathe, if I had only grown
In fragrant beauty like this brier rose,
Which lowly lives and wholly unpraised blows,—
Cheering the bright air where the robin sings,
And only this one simple duty knows!

Although DeWolfe Howe's *Atlantic* review offered only qualified praise of *The Singing Shepherd*, other writers were gratifyingly laudatory. The New Orleans author Grace King, for example, told Annie how pleased she was to rediscover "verses that I have often wanted to read again that I knew in the magazine before I knew you,—and the many others that I am glad to know, now knowing you." And the eminent critic Edmund Stedman was amazed by the wealth of poetry that Annie had produced since *Under the Olive*. Paying tribute to her skilled hand and classical touch, Stedman said he knew of no other woman "who instinctively and ably has sustained herself in poetry of the 'objective' type."[7]

Authors and Friends

Each time Annie wrote about a well-known author who had been her friend— whether commissioned by publishers, urged by the writer's family, or on her own initiative—she drew on her own journals and letters to create a beguiling portrait. That she gave readers what they wanted is suggested by the success of *Authors and Friends*, which Houghton Mifflin published in 1896. Though seven of the eight essays had been published before, over five thousand copies were sold within a few months, reviews were uniformly enthusiastic, five editions appeared during the next few years, and the book was reprinted as late as 1924.

In 1894, Charles Scribner had published Annie's first collection of literary essays—*A Shelf of Old Books*, three loosely structured yet densely detailed essays that had already appeared in *Scribner's*, primarily though not exclusively about English writers she knew. Her second collection is more consistently an insider's report. *Authors and Friends* is an affection-drenched volume designed to acquaint readers with literary celebrities who had recently died and had been her friends for decades.

Keeping herself virtually invisible, Annie served as a cultural showman, a literary professional with a rare treasure at her disposal. Like most of her contemporaries, she believed that an author's life and literature illuminate each other. Therefore as the heir and survivor of a great literary tradition, she garnered lively and revealing passages from her journals and letters to share with her readers. Though she resorted to such loose connectives as "I find the following brief record of the occasion" or "at another time he wrote," she created vibrant portraits. Five of her essays are about men and three about women; six are about Americans and two are about English notables; seven are about writers and one about a writer's wife. Annie's epigraphs from Chaucer define her project as inherently noble and even timeless—honoring "great knights and champions, the constant lovers and pure women of past and present times," and in the process "Keping beautie fresh and greene." As another deferential yet implicitly self-affirming statement of purpose, Annie dedicated her volume to a woman of enormous charm, wit, and social power who was reputedly the most brilliant talker in Boston—her old friend Helen Choate Bell, "*O Comes musica et praeclara.*"[8]

Annie's lead essay, "Longfellow: 1807–1882," conveys her love of the poet and his poetry. Though she did not say so, she had treasured his poems since her childhood, and he was the first of Jamie's friends that she met. She began with his fondness for lilacs, revealing him as "a seer of beauty in common things and a singer to the universal heart," then described him as a scholar and poet who was also a loving father, a generous friend, and an ideal host. Developing that last tribute, she anticipated what her own friends would say about her: "one was always sure of being taken at one's best" in his book-filled house. As usual, she included humanizing details (such as his occasional "mental lapses") within a loosely chronological structure, casually linking passages from her own diary to excerpts from his letters with a simple "again." Her memoir presents America's most celebrated poet as an endearing individual whose comforting words were "repeated upon the air" at his funeral.

If Longfellow was the poet she loved best, Emerson was the philosopher she most respected. She began her "Glimpses of Emerson" with a quasi-Emersonian generalization of her own: "The perfect consistency of a truly great life, where inconsistencies of speech become at once harmonized by the beauty of the whole nature, gives even to a slight incident the value of a bit of mosaic which, if omitted, would leave a gap in the picture." As her title suggests, she was not writing a "Life" but presenting some of her own observations of the great man—as he bounced balls of wit off the "elastic wall" of his audience while lecturing on Brook Farm, for example; as he read his Amita lecture at Charles Street with "a kind of squirrel-like shyness and swiftness," aware of "his own wit as reflected back from the faces of his listeners"; as he read his poems to a hushed audience eager "to catch his voice"; or as "he wore an expectant look upon his face in company, as if waiting for some new word from the last comer."

Hoping his admirers' "joy in their teacher" would be enhanced by her glimpses of "the righteousness and beauty of his personal behavior," Annie praised Emerson's generosity to young writers who asked for help, and his spirited tribute at the funeral of Henry David Thoreau. But since her main purpose was bringing the Great Man "nearer to our daily lives," she also included unflattering glimpses—of Emerson's apprehensions before delivering his lectures, for example, when he seemed "detained by his own dissatisfaction with his work," and of his discomfiture at one of Dickens's readings when he laughed "as if he might crumble into pieces, his face wearing an expression of absolute pain." But in her essay as in her diary entries after such encounters, Annie Fields wrote as Emerson's votary.

Her essay about Oliver Wendell Holmes stresses his "social nature" and his geniality and wit, whether as the "king of the dinner-table" at the Saturday Club or as a guest at "the long series of early morning breakfasts at his publisher's house"—that is, at Charles Street. Surprisingly, Annie shot a few barbs that she then partly deflected, as when she said "he loved himself, and made himself his prime study—but as a member of the human race." More comically, she said he warmed to conversation at a small party "like an old war-horse" responding to the battle cry; and when admirers called, "He entered into their curiosity regarding himself with . . . charming sympathy." Even more slyly, she quoted only Holmes himself about his writings. Many out-of-towners accepted her breakfast invitations primarily to hear his conversation, she said (complacently noting that "There were few men, except Poe, famous in American or English literature of that era who did not appear at least once"); and she quoted examples of Holmes's wit that she had preserved in her journals.[9] He was a faithful friend who knew his own limits, she wrote with loving irony, and more ironically declared that his wife "absorbed her life in his, and mounted guard to make sure that interruption was impossible." She also tenderly sketched him as a doughty survivor after his wife and daughter died; when he read his poem "The Last Leaf" at the Longfellow memorial meeting in his "late October," his hearers for the first time understood its self-referentiality. Yet Annie's praise of Holmes fell short of her tributes to her other eminent friends. In fact, the chief tribute she offered him was for something ephemeral—his table talk.

The fourth and fifth sections of *Authors and Friends*—"Days with Mrs. Stowe" and "Celia Thaxter"—are the only accounts of women writers in the book. The Stowe piece is framed and informed by fervent praise of a "great spirit," a woman whose "heart was like a burning coal upon the altar of humanity." As to her personal appearance, Annie said Stowe received "no mercy at the hands of the photographer" though during animated conversation she looked beautiful. More solemnly, Annie commented on Stowe's serious absent-mindedness, saying "no one could be prepared for these vanishings, not even herself," particularly near the end of her life. Best of all, Annie vividly dramatized scenes from Stowe's life, repeatedly stressing the domestic burdens which made the "high average value" of Stowe's literary work a surprising achievement. The writer emerges from Annie's pages as a complex but sensible woman with a "heroic nature" and a "delightful power of knowing what she wanted," and an intimate friend whose visits to Charles Street were marked by "long croonings over the fire far into the night."

The Celia Thaxter essay is a more conventionally eulogizing obituary for a woman who was neither as famous nor as important as Stowe, though an even more loving, needy, and (perhaps therefore) more beloved friend. To frame her account, Annie invoked the Isles of Shoals where Thaxter spent her childhood and her last years, stressing her close observations of those islands in her poems and prose pieces, though also her "beneficent soul." A reader who knew nothing of Thaxter's strained marriage, her mentally unstable son, or her straitened finances would miss Annie's veiled allusions to them—to a life "overclouded with difficulties and sorrow." But no one could miss the tenderness of Annie's tribute to an exuberant woman "whose life was divorced from worldliness, while it was instinct with the keenest enjoyment of life and of God's world."

Annie's memoir of Whittier encapsulated their four decades of deeply affectionate friendship and conveyed her profound respect for the modest "Quaker poet." Solemnly, she portrayed him as a unique individual whose life was shaped by humanitarian concern and lofty spirituality, a man with a "burning eye" and sharp wit but staid Quaker habits. As his intimate friend, she recreated some of the conversations they had on mornings when he arrived at her doorstep when no "lions" were around, looking ill but high-spirited and eager to talk about literature and such social issues as woman suffrage or the welfare of Negroes and Indians. As an insider, she also reported on his close friendships with other writers including Lydia Maria Child and Bayard Taylor, and included some of his speculations about spiritualism. Then she summed him up as a holy man whose "spirit animated the air," a man who survived in his poetry. He also survives in Annie's essay.

The relatively brief essay on Tennyson written soon after his death is informed by reverence for his poetry, which transformed English literature and became "part of the air we breathe." After a personal anecdote about her enthrallment by his poems during her childhood, she celebrated him as the quintessential poet who attuned readers' hearts and taught them about "the affinities and symbolisms of nature." Granting that he had remained remote from ordinary life and worldly affairs, she diplomatically concluded that he was hospitable only to those "who really wanted what he could give." Clearly, she was one of them. She dramatized her dreamlike ramble with him on the downs during her first visit to Farringford, which made her realize how fully poetry was "the business of his life." Her final reverent vignette depicted him enthroned on a couch overlooking the green valley and "his own trees," and (as she recalled in language not unlike his) "Again we heard the voice; again we felt the uplift of his presence."

Perhaps the brevity of the Tennyson essay she had placed in the January 1893 *Harper's* was one reason why she wrote a few pages on "Lady Tennyson" while compiling *Authors and Friends* three years later. Moreover, Emily Tennyson had died in the interim, and (as Annie pointed out to her publisher) advertisements for *Authors and Friends* could announce that the book included new material. Annie Fields's Emily Tennyson is an ideal woman devoted to her children and her husband, a gracious and delicate yet self-abnegating semi-invalid in a long gray dress: "her poet's life was her life, and his necessity was her great opportunity." She was the "living inspiration at the heart of the poet's every-day life," with no life apart from her husband's.

When Annie contrasted Emily Tennyson's "lofty serenity" and her husband's "great talk" with "the fatuous talk at dinner-tables where I had sometimes met Browning," she was writing off Browning and exalting the Tennysons. In 1860, when Elizabeth Barrett Browning remarked that Tennyson's wife "does not criticise enough" Annie had turned that negative into a positive: Emily Tennyson knew her husband needed "worshipping affection and devotion," and knew his delicate imagination "was not to be carelessly touched." Decades later Emily Tennyson's remark that Browning did not visit them because "we are too quiet" increased Annie's disdain for the worldly widower. By ending *Authors and Friends* with the figure of Emily Tennyson, defined as a vision of "heavenliness," Annie elevated an already high-minded book. She described Tennyson's wife as a "lady who held the traditions of high womanhood safe above the possible deteriorations of human existence," as Annie Fields herself had always tried to do.

Celebrating Women

Annie Fields had good reason to cherish her relationships with three nineteenth-century women writers, two of them now virtually unknown and the other even then world famous. In 1899, three years after the publication of *Authors and Friends,* the *Century* published Annie's two essays about two Englishwomen—Mary Cowden Clark (1809–98) and George Eliot (1810–80). Following her usual practice, she fleshed out biographical detail with personal reminiscence and quotations from private letters. Her established reputation as a biographer—though also America's nostalgia as the century was ending, and its entrenched Anglophilia—made those essays particularly appropriate for a magazine noted for well-illustrated sketches of public figures. Like the essay on the Frenchwoman Mme. Blanc that she wrote for the *Century* four years later, they are as interesting for what they reveal about their author as for what they say about their subjects.

"Two Lovers of Literature and Art: Charles and Mary Cowden Clarke" pays tribute to a widely admired English literary couple who in many ways resembled two other "lovers of literature and art," Mr. and Mrs. James T. Fields. They were "appreciators and disseminators of the best things in literature" but not "great originators," Annie informed her readers, then declared that the appreciation of genius is "almost as valuable as the creative power itself." Reiterating that point in her conclusion, she praised the couple's "tender reverence" for and service to the "best things" in literature and art.

But the essay centers on Mary Cowden Clarke, who had recently died. At the age of nineteen, she had (like Annie) married a much older man whom she would outlive. An accomplished actress, she was also a professional writer who was best known for her concordance to Shakespeare. Leigh Hunt and Charles Dickens were among the couple's close friends, and (like James T. Fields) Charles Cowden Clarke had delivered popular lectures on literature. The illustrations Annie provided included bust portraits of both husband and wife and a sketch of Mary Cowden Clarke as Mistress Quickly in "Dickens's amateur company in 1848." Annie's summary assessment of Mary Cowden Clarke seems proleptic: she was a vivacious and kindhearted woman with a remarkable memory and "power of enjoyment" whose death severed one of the last links with the great writers of a previous age, a woman who not only maintained old literary relationships during her widowhood but "with the zest of a girl" took on new ones, Sarah Orne Jewett and Louise Guiney among them.[10]

After James T. Fields died, Mary Cowden Clarke had told Annie she knew what a "helpful occupation" it was to write about "the noble life so long one with your own," then singled out a "golden sentence" from Annie's *Biographical Notes:* "'I hold that husband and wife should be *lovers* all their days.'" She and Annie soon had something else in common. Mrs. Cowden Clarke, who had suffered a similar loss and was by then sharing her life with her sister Sabilla, was delighted that Annie was coming to England with "a young lady 'who is not well and needs just the change that a summer in Europe would give her.'" A year later, she rejoiced "that you have the permanent companionship of so extremely attractive a woman as admirable Miss Jewett," then said it was yet "another instance of what Sabilla and I maintain to be a truth . . . ,—that a friendship between two women is not only quite possible, but is often fervent and strong, besides being a source of intense mutual happiness." An added pleasure was hearing about Celia Thaxter, another "choice-spirited" woman she had met through Annie; and during Sarah's frequent illnesses, Mrs. Cowden Clarke sympathized with Annie's pain and felt sure she found "assuagement" in "loving tendance."[11]

In the winter of 1889, reading Sarah's *Marsh Island* provoked a delighted exclamation: "What a pleasure it is for us women-writers to have the privilege of looking into each others' hearts & minds thus through our books,— 'Under the Olives [sic],' 'A Marsh Island,' 'The White Heron,' 'A Country Doctor,' 'The Isles of Shoals,' 'Driftwood'—how they let me see the fine brains & noble opinions of their Authors! And how they enable me to commune in spirit with these high-thoughted sisters of the pen! How often, across the wide Atlantic, do my thanks & praises silently, but currently, float over the 'moving miles' to them." At that point she was awaiting Annie's first "Shelf of Old Books" and asked if she happened to know Louise Imogen Guiney, who had introduced herself by sending copies of "her clever Goose-Quill Papers" and a volume of her poems.[12]

But most of Cowden Clark's remarks about women's friendships are rooted in her own union with her sister Sabilla. A typical letter sent regards "to *your Sarah* ('My Sarah,' as I rejoice to see you call her!)" and hoped "*you two* are enjoying your togetherism this summer as much as *we two* here." In another, she asked Annie to tell Sarah that she and Sabilla "often speak of the pleasure we had . . . of seeing her with your loved & admired self together," then exclaimed, "How nobly does her and your friendship—as well as that of several other similarly-attached woman-couples we know—refute the vulgar fallacy of the impossibility of female friendship!"[13] For both Mary Cowden Clarke and her sister, Annie and Sarah were (like themselves) a nobly attached "woman-couple" who moved within an extended network of female friendship. In yet another similarity, their overlapping circles of friendship continued to include men and married couples (Charles Dudley Warner and his wife among them).

A briefer essay about a far more important English woman writer appeared in the *Century* a few months later—a sympathetic study of "the very extraordinary and interesting woman known to the world as George Eliot." Focusing on Eliot's character rather than her career, Annie presented her as a loving, loyal, and profoundly conscientious individual whose letters "contain an almost unrivaled record of mental activity and energy in the pursuit of knowledge," a woman who had endured "overwork and solitude of the heart" after "her home circle was gradually dissolved by death," then met George H. Lewes and bravely helped support his dependents by "incessant drudgery of the pen." Eliot also emerges as a woman who generously befriended other women and commanded their affection. After a brief biographical sketch and a paragraph about Eliot's devoted women friends including Harriet Beecher Stowe, Annie loosely organized her essay around her recollections of meeting Eliot and a group of letters "now printed for the first time"—three to herself and one to her husband, each displaying the affectionate and kindly nature which was "a moving spring in all her greatness."[14]

The liveliest section of the essay dramatizes Annie's first call on Eliot one Sunday afternoon in 1869. A few days after Lewes called at the Fieldses' London hotel, spoke about Eliot, and invited them to meet her, they entered a pleasant tree-shaded house with "plenty of books inside" where a small group was engaged in conversation. As Annie clearly enjoyed recalling, Eliot soon "disengaged herself from the general talk" and sat down beside her "for a more intimate acquaintance." Then after discovering that Stowe was a mutual friend, Eliot poured out her "unbounded" love and admiration for both the woman and her work. Conjoining her memories of that first visit with later ones, Annie praised Eliot's beautiful voice as well as the vibrant discourse that revealed "her unusual qualities both of mind and heart." This section concludes as Annie's first visit did—by following Lewes into his "private room" to see his wife's portrait and the bound manuscripts of her books which contained "touching dedications" to him. "She was his chief topic of conversation, the pride and joy of his life," Annie fervently declared, "and it was quite evident that she returned his ardent devotion with a true love."

"I trust you and your husband are well and happy," Eliot poignantly wrote after Lewes's death a decade later. "That is the best that is left to me—to know that others are leading a life of loving union." Eliot herself would soon enter into another. As to the young man that Eliot married, Annie said he knew her "perfectly and loved her as he knew her." She also praised J. W. Cross for letting Eliot "write her own life" through her letters, adding only "slight additions and explanations," Annie's own usual practice as a biographer.

At the end of her essay, Annie modestly justified her own contribution to the biographical record: she was gratifying a universal interest in "little runnels of information about every-day things which appear to link the lives of those who have attained supremacy with those of ordinary mortals" and in "discovering how great spirits deal with difficulties that even they cannot avoid." Sidestepping the question of whether Eliot and Lewes were legally married, she said only that "the universal wish to know all there is to know about prominent persons has at times degenerated into low curiosity."

Four years later, Annie wrote about another woman writer for the *Century*, a woman she knew much better. In "Notable Women: Mme. Blanc ('Th. Bentzon')," Annie presented Thérèse de Solms Blanc as a talented, hardworking, and perspicacious woman with a special interest in Americans, a woman committed to her career who was not limited by genteel conventions of womanly behavior, an important member of France's literary elite, and an advocate of women's rights.

Annie wooed her *Century* audience by saying it was natural for Americans to be interested in a woman who had assiduously tried to understand them, and who had described "the labors and achievements of our women to their sisters in France." She then offered a lively account of Mme. Blanc's childhood, her growth to maturity, and her emergence as a writer. Her sheltered childhood as the only daughter of the Comtesse de Solms and the only granddaughter of the Marquis and Marquise de Vitry had ended when at sixteen she married her father's friend Alexander Blanc, who (though Annie only hinted it) turned out to be improvident and neglectful. Her father died soon after, she had a son the next year, and she began writing professionally to support herself. Though Annie did not even mention it, Mme. Blanc won a divorce when she was nineteen. Her life opened out when her mother married an equerry of Napoleon III who provided entrée to the royal court. Through him the budding writer met George Sand, then at the height of her popularity, who (as Annie said) offered "counsels and encouragement." Annie then turned to Mme. Blanc's phenomenal industry and "pronounced success" in producing stories, reviews, and translations for the country's major literary periodical, *Revue des Deux Mondes*, while also writing dozens of novels.

At that point, Annie recalled her own "happy fortune" in spending time with Mme. Blanc in a cottage near Fontainebleau, hearing her read George Sand's letters, and taking long walks through the forest which she "peopled" with stories. She had first encountered Mme. Blanc through her perceptive essay on Sarah Orne Jewett, Annie said, then recreated the moment before the three women met when Sarah hesitated "on the staircase of an old mansion in the ancient part of the city," before Annie rang Mme. Blanc's bell.

In the last third of her essay, saying nothing about herself, Annie discussed Mme. Blanc's trips to America and the books she wrote about them afterward. Mme. Blanc "had many friends and readers, and could not feel herself a stranger" when she arrived in this country in 1893. But she had "a distinct purpose to observe and record" and traveled as far west as Chicago, then wrote *Les Américaines Chez Elles* (published in America as *The Condition of Woman in the United States*). In that book, Annie said, Mme. Blanc celebrated the independence, cultural activities, education, and social benevolence of American women and gave "a charming account of Boston." But she did not mention her own centrality to that account.[15]

In the section of Mme. Blanc's book titled "Mrs. J. T. Fields.—Drawing-Rooms and Interiors," she said the Charles Street library resembled "the drawing-rooms of France at its best" yet was also unique—"a registry office for wits of the most refined originality" and a place where everything seemed "dedicated to literature." As Mme. Blanc told her readers, Annie was "the widow of the well-known publisher, James T. Fields, who was the friend of the most famous writers of his time in France and England, and who left behind him precious proofs of his intimacy with them all" in the form of books, portraits, and autographs. But Annie herself was the "Athenian of Boston," a beautiful woman with literary talent who told interesting stories about her literary friends. As proof, Mme. Blanc recounted some of Annie's stories about Dickens, Emerson, and other celebrated writers. She also had high praise for many of Annie's other roles. Although she made a few complaints about American cooking, the meals she enjoyed at Charles Street provoked the curious generalization that in Boston "the pursuit of outward elegance in no way impairs the excellence of the substantial part." More important, she named Annie as one of the handful of women central to the city's "culture, pedagogy, poetry and philanthropy," and the philanthropy she especially praised was Annie's major one, the Associated Charities.[16]

Annie's comments on *The Condition of Woman in the United States* in her *Century* profile centered on Mme. Blanc's realization that American individualism was not limited to men and that women could also exercise power. Even more self-revealingly, Annie singled out Mme. Blanc's astonishment at American women's dedication to "the service of others outside their homes as well as inside."

As Annie also reported, Mme. Blanc made her second visit to the United States in March 1897 in the company of the *Revue des Deux Mondes* editor Ferdinand Brunetière, who had come to lecture at Johns Hopkins and Harvard. Though she did not say so, she and Sarah were on hand to greet them when they arrived in Baltimore.[17] After the Brunetières sailed for home that May, Mme. Blanc stayed with Annie in Manchester and then with Sarah in South Berwick, a visit that included an overnight stay at the Shaker colony in Alfred. Impressed by the Shakers' industry and tranquility, she engaged in long discussions with them and came away with a Shaker cloak and ample material for the essay she would publish in the November *Revue*, titled "Le Communisme en Amérique." It was reprinted the following year in *Choses et Gens d'Amérique* and translated as *People and Things in America*.[18]

Her friendship with Mme. Blanc was Annie's only intimate relationship with a French writer and her only literary friendship that originated with Sarah Orne Jewett. Their three-way friendship easily accommodated separate pairings, it involved professional assistance to one another, and it expanded to include other friends. The Aldriches and the Johnsons sent news of Mme. Blanc whenever they were in France; Mme. Blanc regularly asked Annie about Elizabeth Agassiz, Jessie

Cochrane, and other women she had met at Charles Street; and she mourned the deaths of Sarah Whitman and Sarah Chauncey Woolsey.[19]

Mme. Blanc emerges from Annie's essay as a dutiful daughter and a devoted mother, a perceptive social and literary critic, a skillful and remarkably productive author and translator, and an open-minded woman with a lively conscience and an activist agenda. As one discerning woman writing about another, Annie repeatedly focused on Mme. Blanc's relationships with other women—including her mother, her grandmother, her English governess, George Sand, and Sarah Orne Jewett. After noting that she lived alone after her mother died and her son moved away, Annie permitted herself a personal aside: "Of course her life was a very busy one, but when did 'affairs' in a woman's life ever fill the place of the affections and the cares of a home!" As Annie then assured her readers, Mme. Blanc was a woman of grace, wit, and kindness who "eagerly embraced the opportunities which have presented themselves to enlarge the scope of her interests"; but she concluded by praising "above all, the noble character and determination with which she stands for what she believes."[20]

Orpheus: A Masque

Annie's last major poetic work and one of her longest, *Orpheus: A Masque,* embodies values and attitudes that underlay most of her prior publications and most of her philanthropic work. The imperatives of love and service to others weave through the entire forty-one-page poem. It is not surprising that she relied on Greek myth but modified it, that she affirmed the poet's social mission, or even that she did so through a male protagonist.

The poem was well dramatized and "finely lyrical," Aldrich told her when she sent him the manuscript in January 1900, but he thought it was probably too chaste and spiritual for the general public and too long for the *Atlantic.* He nonetheless thought it "would make a lovely little book." The following month when she offered the manuscript to the *Atlantic* editor Bliss Perry, he agreed with Aldrich. But by then Houghton Mifflin had agreed to publish *Orpheus: A Masque,* and Perry felt sure it would "please everybody whom you would wish to reach."[21]

The poem is preceded by an argument that sums up Annie's moralistic variant of the familiar Greek myth. Orpheus mourns for the death of Eurydice without accepting what life still offers him. When the Gods allow him to enter the underworld, he feels so moved by the shapes of human woe he encounters that he tries to comfort them with his lyre. He then sees Eurydice and forgets them. But "she, having passed into higher conditions, is now only moved by the love which allies itself to the highest good." Orpheus tries to win her back but she wants to help "the woeful" and leaves him, and he is then seduced by pleasure seekers who destroy him. But like the bereaved poet of Annie's novel *Asphodel,* he ultimately attains spiritual purification and deepened poetic powers. Through him, Annie defined her own aspirations as a poet and reformer.

The poem vivifies Annie's argument, as when Eurydice movingly urges Orpheus to soothe the wretched and lonely with his songs and resists his pleas to return home with him, then disappears. "She strove to lead me to my finer self," he mourns, then sinks to his lower self by joining the Bacchantes. When Orpheus hears the hermit thrush's song of pain, he again yearns for Eurydice (perhaps an unusual homage to Walt Whitman's "When Lilacs Last in the Dooryard Bloom'd"). Furious at Orpheus for poisoning their pleasure, the Bacchantes tear him apart and break his lyre. The masque ends when the Muses bear him to Mount Olympos and his lyre is restored:

> Now the chords responsive ring!
>   Behold them lead, in steadfast joy and real,
>   The immortal chorus, chorus hymeneal.

At the heart of *Orpheus* is the artist's responsibility to ease other people's pain. More broadly, it is about everyone's responsibility to do so. Annie's Orpheus errs when he ignores the claims of suffering humanity, and her Eurydice returns to the underworld because she wants to alleviate suffering and not because Orpheus turned back to look at her. Annie identified with Orpheus, though also with Eurydice and the hermit thrush. In her masque, she affirms the sweetness of earth and the lover's desire for union with the beloved, but also the higher importance of confronting and soothing sorrow. She had already done so in many of her lyrics as well as in *Persephone* and *Asphodel,* implicitly defining her own goals as a reformer. And as in *Under the Olive,* she had confidently appropriated Greek classical materials, speaking as easily through a man's voice as in a woman's. But possibly recalling Harriet Beecher Stowe's remark that her "works for humanity" had a higher beauty than *Under the Olive,* Annie had also insisted that poetry can serve humanitarian imperatives.

Orpheus raised him "as far above this workaday world as the sunset I looked at from your porch in Manchester," Howells told Annie.[22] Years later, Harriet Spofford praised *Orpheus* as a wonderful reinterpretation of a familiar myth, a dramatic poem that celebrates beauty, music, grace, and ideality. But as she also said, Annie Fields's "life work among the poor and suffering suggested of course the motive of the Masque."[23]

SECTION VI
Final Years

23

Hospitality and Enterprise

The Home Club

In the winter of 1905, Annie Fields invited a small group of "persons interested in letters who will find it an advantage to be better acquainted" to attend six bi-weekly dinners at Charles Street, a group she called the "Home Club." As in the past, most of Annie's guests in the new century were people whose achievements she admired, ranging from Booker T. Washington to Helen Keller and Owen Wister (the Boston-born author of the classical frontier novel *The Virginian*). Occasionally, she also invited young people to stay with her, as when Julia Ward Howe's granddaughter Julie Richards spent a month at Charles Street in the winter of 1901—one of the happiest times of Julie's life, her mother Laura Richards assured Annie.[1] But the Home Club, like the season-long clubs the Fieldses had occasionally organized during the seventies, was designed to promote mind-stretching conviviality among a select group of the literary elite. Although Annie did not keep a regular journal that winter, she made records of each meeting that include her guests' names and some of their "sparkling conversation."[2]

Four couples assembled for the initial dinner meeting: the Aldriches, the Mark DeWolfe Howes, and two Boston novelists and their wives—the Grants and the Sullivans. Another writer was late. Aldrich set the tone for the evening by telling "immensely amusing" literary anecdotes, including one about Edith Wharton at an Authors' Club meeting: when someone talked about reviving his "black cat," Wharton had not realized he was talking about a magazine. As if on cue, Gelett Burgess arrived amid the general laughter, which Annie fanned by announcing that "The Purple Cow is now Upstairs."[3] Whatever disappointment she might have felt when "there was no great champion for Henry James' work," she recorded her guests' quips about it, including Aldrich's claim to know someone who had read James "in the original."

The next three meetings went smoothly. At the second, whose "members" included Sarah and Mr. and Mrs. Bliss Perry, Annie herself championed the work of Henry James. When Bliss Perry said he had rejected one of James's submissions to the *Atlantic* and quoted a few phrases to explain why, she staunchly declared "that was hardly ground on which to condemn a really great author." The table talk was less "general" than at the first meeting, Annie noted, but only "because Miss Jewett engaged her end of the table delightfully." During the third Home Club dinner, Thomas R. Sullivan's lecture on Tomasso Salvini's house and family in Orvieto stimulated "interesting talk about books and men";[4] and the fourth meeting produced the tepid consensus that Mrs. Humphry Ward's novels could be appreciated even in monthly installments.

Henry James and Julia Ward Howe made the fifth meeting more memorable. To Annie's delight, James was "witty and friendly and altogether delightful. Most helpful too in drawing out Mrs. Howe who is now too deaf to make it easy to keep her 'au courant.'" James prompted Mrs. Howe to reminisce about Fanny Kemble and about Mr. and Mrs. Longfellow, after which Annie urged her "to repeat her Army Hymn—so at the last she rose and did so very gracefully and impressively too." The group then left the dining room for the library, where Annie enjoyed a private talk with James; and when the general conversation turned to Charles Eliot Norton's beautiful new edition of Ruskin, James "fell into a flood of laughter at the melting of this queer pernickety genius by so mild a fire." That evening, Annie's only regret was that "There is only one more dinner and so will end a series which has given me much pleasure."

The recollections two of her guests preserved of that evening were utterly different. Mark DeWolfe Howe vividly recalled what Julia Ward Howe said as they began their ride home: "Annie Fields has shrunk."[5] And as "the very last word" of Henry James's eulogy for Annie Fields in 1915, he recalled "a haunted little feast as of ghosts, if not skeletons, at the banquet, with the image of that immemorial and inextinguishable lady Mrs. Julia Ward Howe, the most evidential and most eminent presence of them all, as she rises in her place, under the extremity of appeal, to declaim a little quaveringly, but ever so gallantly, that 'Battle Hymn of the Republic,' which she had caused to be chanted half a century before and still could accompany with a real breadth of gesture, her great clap of hands and indication of the complementary step, on the triumphant line, ' . . . be jubilant my feet!'"[6]

"On the whole I think 'The Club' has been a marked success," Annie complacently wrote after the final dinner on 30 March, glad "dear S. O. J. could come for they all sincerely wished to see her," and admitting to a moment of anxiety when talk did not flow. As in the old days, she had arranged to use "leisure for pleasures that enrich life and bring true pleasures." Yet the bits of conversations she considered sparkling hardly seem so today. And whether or not Annie had indeed markedly shrunk, what had certainly shrunk was the scope, scale, and cultural reverberations of her entertainments.

English Visitors

Five otherwise very different English women of letters who lectured in Boston in the 1900s gladly accepted Annie's invitation to stay at Charles Street. If each invitation was an act of generosity, it was also a mode of self-enrichment.

The first of those houseguests was a poet Annie had previously known only through her publications. In the fall of 1901, as soon as she heard that Alice Meynell planned an American lecture tour, Annie invited her to Charles Street and even offered to arrange a few lectures in Boston. The women had a lot in common. Meynell's friends included Tennyson and Dickens; she had helped her beloved husband edit a magazine; and she had produced volumes of fastidious poetry as well as a biography of her friend Ruskin. Because both Annie and Sarah admired "the thoughtfulness and beauty, and . . . the reticence and restraint, of her poems and brief essays," Annie set the earliest available date for Meynell's visit.[7]

Soon after she arrived, Mrs. Meynell told her family that "Mrs. Fields is indeed a rare creature, with some reminiscence of Lady Taylor," and reported on a dinner in her own honor "to which came Professor Norton, Ruskin's old friend, and Mrs. Gardner who has that almost miraculous Venetian palace." During her week at Charles Street, Meynell delivered four lectures and formed firm friendships with Annie and Sarah. Americans had been kind to her, she told Annie, but "this undeserved kindness of yours has been the most precious and dear."[8] From then on, the women frequently exchanged letters, publications, and gifts, including such unusually personal gifts as a pin that Annie herself had worn.

After Sarah suffered a carriage accident in 1902, she entered into an even deeper friendship with Meynell than Annie's. Forbidden to read or write, she longed for Meynell's poems "and almost cried as I said so." Her nurse then produced a copy and read a few poems aloud; and as Sarah confided two years later, "I never knew how I loved you, either in your work or out of it, before that summer brought me a long way further into the country of our friendship."[9] Annie included that letter to "My very dear friend" in her edition of Sarah's letters, although Mrs. Meynell had hesitated to send it because it seemed "too much about me and not enough about her."

Annie then invited Meynell to write an introduction to that edition. "Should it not accompany yours?" Meynell modestly asked, and she felt relieved when Henry James accepted the task. The introduction that Annie herself eventually wrote incorporates a few lines of tribute from Meynell. After Annie sent her the book, Meynell said she had never read more exquisite letters; and Annie's next gift—a photograph of Sarah—made her recall "the face that was almost instantly dear to me and grew dearer, from the hour she met me at the station until the goodbye which was to be final in this world."[10]

A far more celebrated English writer spent a few days at Charles Street in 1908—Mrs. Humphry Ward. The friendship that began when Annie and Sarah visited Mrs. Ward in England in 1892 had continued through correspondence and deepened during their second visit in 1900. In 1899, Mrs. Ward had praised Annie's "charming little book on Hawthorne" and made a "bold request" that drew them closer. She wanted to send pre-publication proofs of her novel *Eleanor,* which included a New England girl named Lucy Foster, hoping that Annie would "suggest in Lucy's talk here or there, the distinctive American shades, that I find it so difficult to give. Half a dozen phrases or passages, suggested in pencil on the margin would be quite enough." Presumably Annie sent them. Then a few years later, while preparing a play version of *Eleanor* and completing *Lady Rose's Daughter,* Mrs. Ward whimsically exclaimed, "How I wish I could fly across and drop into your drawing room one evening in the firelight! How much there would be to talk about!"[11]

That opportunity came when Mrs. Ward made an American tour in the spring of 1908, accompanied by her daughter Dorothy. They spent three days at Charles Street, and Annie gave both a lunch and a dinner in their honor on the day they arrived.[12] "A 'luncheon with Mrs. Humphry Ward at Annie Fields,'" Julia Ward Howe reported in her journal afterward; "very pleasant. Edward Emerson there, easy and delightful."[13] Because the eighty-nine-year-old Howe "could not negotiate the stairs," lunch was served in the ground floor reception room; and because Howe was hard of hearing, Emerson was the only additional guest. "Mrs. Howe arrived looking just like a Fairy Godmother. She was greeted like a queen by the ladies," Annie noted in her journal, and conversation soon turned to early New York. Though Mrs. Ward's staunch opposition to woman suffrage kept Annie from raising that subject, she regretted not hearing Mrs. Howe speak "of her faith and its causes." That evening, at a dinner attended by Helen Bell, Mrs. Parkman, and Alice Longfellow, a high point was Mrs. Ward's "dear story" about a whimsical note her uncle Matthew Arnold had sent his brother (her father) after Thomas's conversion to Catholicism.

Mrs. Ward's activities during the next two days included a visit to Isabella Gardner and a benefit lecture for her London Play Centers (forerunners of modern day care centers), titled "The Peasant in English Literature." Mrs. Ward feared the lecture was too "classic" in the beginning, but Annie assured her that everyone liked it (although she complained in her journal that Mrs. Ward had not spoken loudly enough). By then Mrs. Ward trusted Annie enough to show her the manuscript of *The Testing of Diana Mallory,* explaining that it needed two more weeks of hard work because she had lost scale a bit and had to move some material into the background. Feeling privileged by that invitation to follow "the careful processes of an author who is so frank and so determined," Annie concluded that *Diana* was "one of her best."[14] After Mrs. Ward and her daughter left Charles Street, Annie felt completely drained. Yet she regretted that "our happy visit" was over, and declared, "They are most loving friends and have made themselves a part of our life of the spirit henceforth."

Sarah Orne Jewett wrote Mrs. Ward from Manchester soon afterward to say "how happy you made our dear A. F. and me." She also assured them that A. F.'s health was improving, then added, "the air here is always just the right thing, and I love to see her in her little pale grey dress sitting on the piazza looking seaward over the green tree-tops." Sarah later reported that everyone was "talking about 'Diana'" and finding it hard to wait for the book, and said she planned to see the dramatization of Mrs. Ward's novel *Lady Rose's Daughter* in Boston.[15] In 1909, after the cerebral hemorrhage that would end Sarah's life, Mrs. Ward wrote Annie to commiserate, "That it should have happened to her of all people,—the darkening of so bright and clear a mental life!—And what a strain of grief on you!" After Sarah died, Mrs. Ward sent Annie typed copies of Sarah's letters for eventual publication, though some seemed too "intime" to publish. After the volume appeared, she praised it for revealing Sarah's "schöne seele" and marveled at how "tactfully and wisely" Annie had performed her task.[16]

At that point Mrs. Ward's *The Case of Richard Meynell* was receiving mixed reviews in England, and she worried about its American reception, because "America does not yet seem to have forgiven me *Daphne*." In that novel—initially titled *Marriage à la Mode*—the American-born heroine is criticized for divorcing her English husband. Mrs. Ward had told Annie soon after completing her "moral tale" that it evolved from "what was impressed upon me in America,—the levity with which divorce is sought, & the ease with which it can be got."[17] To Mrs. Ward's disappointment, American readers found the central character disagreeable and resented the novel's attack on lenient divorce laws.[18] Soon afterward, Annie sent her an article about divorce, Mrs. Ward thanked her for it, reported meeting with suffragists to discuss possible legislative changes, and then remarked, "Divorce I imagine will come in."[19]

For the rest of Annie's life, she and Mrs. Ward exchanged news about their many civic and literary ventures. In January 1913, for example, Mrs. Ward said she was busy with the suffrage crisis and her play centers; she had just completed a novel about English country life and was starting another that *Harper's* would begin serializing in April; she had told Doubleday to send Annie *The Mating of Lydia;* and her son Arnold was prospering in Parliament. The following year, she reported critical enthusiasm for *The Coryston Family,* then assured Annie that her new novel *Delia Blanchflower* was "not in any sense an attack on the *suffrage* movement—but on the association of women with violence."[20]

Meanwhile, Annie maintained a separate friendship with Mrs. Ward's sister Ethel Arnold, an essayist and lecturer who first came to Charles Street in the eighties and returned whenever she was booked in Boston. "How deeply I have prized my days with you this year," Ethel Arnold wrote in the spring of 1910; "how much intellectual and spiritual contact with such a woman as yourself has helped and stimulated a groping, wandering, wavering soul." Therefore she treasured each memory of "that dear house on Charles Street full as it is not only with hallowed memories of the past but of a living personality which can only bring rest and refreshment to all such wayfarers as myself." Similarly, she told Annie the following year that she had felt "stupidly over-tired and cotton woolly" when she arrived at Charles Street but left "feeling refreshed and fortified in mind and body—only sorry to say goodbye even for a time!" Then she rhapsodically declared, "you are so *wonderful,* dear Mrs. Fields—such a lesson to us all in courage—cheerfulness and thought for others—and in your presence I feel ashamed of my own cowardice and shirking. Yet—thank you, dearest, from my heart, for all you've done and been to me—which is more than you know or than I could ever tell."[21]

When a Boston lecture fell through the following month, Ethel Arnold told Annie she could not return to Charles Street because she could not afford the trip without the engagement. Her agent had failed her, which was especially disappointing because she had never before done such good work. In fact, some of her friends were so impressed by the suffrage lecture she had just delivered at the Hudson Theatre that they planned to hire Carnegie Hall so she could repeat it.[22]

But Annie's report that she had lined up a Boston engagement provoked a surprising reply. Annie had gotten the "wrong impression," Arnold said. She did not want friends to line up work for her, she knew she would have money soon, and she now had four Boston engagements. Moreover, her "school lectures" were going well, she would soon address a group of suffrage societies in Chicago under the auspices of Jane Addams, and she was anticipating "my big suffrage meeting at Carnegie Hall." If Annie had indeed gotten the "wrong impression," it is easy to understand why. She had answered what seemed to be a call for help from a noted English woman of letters (an Arnold at that, albeit one subject to mood swings) who was lecturing on topics close to Annie's heart.[23]

"Last week William Morris's daughter, May, passed the week with me staying over Christmas Day," and enjoyed "a very happy little Christmas dinner," Annie complacently noted on 30 December 1909. "She is an excellent and admirable woman. I should soon learn to love her. I hope she will return presently."[24] May Morris was then on tour giving lectures and embroidery lessons, and she never would manage a second visit to Charles Street. But she was grateful for admission to Annie's world. Perhaps the best thing Annie did for May Morris that week was encouraging her to memorialize her father. The following September, May wrote that she was planning a collected edition of her father's work, and also hoped to prepare "the little talk about my Father that you and I discussed," and deliver it in America.[25]

In July 1911, May was still hoping to return to America and lecture on her father, which would "justify the journey to my conscience." But in December, after thanking Annie for the *Letters of Sarah Orne Jewett* and promising to "read and love the book for your sake," she sadly reported that work on her "big edition" still prevented her return. Not until the fall of 1914, when she was mourning the death of her mother and trying to cope with a "public calamity," the outbreak of war, did May Morris near completion of what had become a twenty-four-volume edition of her father's work. Another visit to Charles Street at last seemed imminent. But by the time *The Collected Works of William Morris, with Introductions by May Morris* was finished, Annie Fields was dead.[26]

In the fall of 1905, when the young English novelist May Sinclair's *The Divine Fire* was winning strong critical praise, Annie invited her to Charles Street. From then on, Sinclair solicited Annie's criticism of each novel she wrote. In September 1908, for example, she said many critics disliked her *Kitty Tailleur,* which was unlike anything else she had written, then wondered what Annie would think of it. Annie's discriminating praise provoked a flattering reply: "You *always* understand just what I mean in everything I've written, and you can't think how dear your approval is to me." Sinclair then spoke of her pleasure in meeting a few of Annie's friends in London, including Edith Wharton; and a few years later she exulted that Henry James "came out to see me in my funny flat."[27]

After Sarah Orne Jewett's death, Sinclair recalled her "sweetness and kindness to me when I was with you"; and she later called her first visit to Charles Street "the happiest and most *living* thing that happened to me in America," particularly because of Annie herself: "I loved you from the minute when you asked me (*you* won't remember, but *I* do!) to give you my arm when you went across the room; and I can feel yours now, as it touched mine—very light and very gentle. Somehow I knew that you wouldn't have taken my arm if you hadn't liked me a little." Then as one writer to another but primarily as one friend to another, Sinclair confessed that writing and reading proofs had left little time for reading during the past year, but "I am looking forward now to living with you again in your book." Neither woman played a significant role in the other's life. But their relationship was evidently as gratifying to the prolific young novelist as to the older woman who had taken her arm.[28]

24

Willa Sibert Cather
(1873–1947)

Willa Sibert Cather offered Annie Fields what turned out to be her final opportunity to nurture a talented woman writer. From the time of her first visit to Charles Street in March 1908, Cather regarded Annie Fields as an embodiment of America's great cultural past, though also as a salient feature of its cultural present. Therefore she humbly courted an intimacy that included Sarah Orne Jewett and enriched all three women.

Years later, Cather began her essay titled "148 Charles Street" with herself as an outsider about to enjoy the privilege of entrance:

> Mrs. Louis Brandeis conducted me along a noisy street in Boston and rang at a door hitherto unknown to me. Sometimes entering a new door can make a great change in one's life. That afternoon I had set out . . . to make a call on Mrs. Brandeis. When I reached her house in Otis Place she told me that we would go farther: she thought I would enjoy meeting a very charming old lady who was a near neighbor of hers, the widow of James T. Fields, of the publishing firm of Ticknor and Fields. . . . In my father's bookcase there were little volumes of Longfellow and Hawthorne with that imprint. I wondered how the widow of one of the partners could still be living.[1]

In her mid-thirties when she first stood outside Annie Fields's door, Cather had already published a volume of poems and another of short stories, and she had spent over five years teaching high school and seven as an editor in Pittsburgh before moving to New York to join *McClure's* as a staff writer in 1906. In 1907, S. S. McClure sent her to Boston to correct and amplify a biography of Mary Baker Eddy that he had already started publishing, an arduous assignment that would occupy most of that year and part of the next. Cather had not yet published a novel, or begun to mine her Nebraska childhood for the fiction that would make her famous. But she took a step in that direction on a winter day hinting at spring when she entered the drawing room where Annie Fields and Sarah Orne Jewett were seated at tea.[2]

From the moment she saw Annie Fields "reclining on a green sofa, directly under the youthful portrait of Charles Dickens," Cather felt she had entered a shrine where "the past lived on—where it was protected and cherished, had sanctuary from the noisy push of the present." Better still, when her hostess began reminiscing about Dickens, Emerson, Hawthorne, and other literary giants who had sat in that very same room, Cather felt those "great shades" come to life. The woman who had extended hospitality to "the aristocracy of letters and art" for over half a century was now extending it to an "American of the Apache period" and inviting her to inspect "some of the treasures of the house." The chief treasure she inspected was Mrs. Fields herself, a "flower-like" woman with clear eyes, a fine complexion, a mobile mouth, and a musical laugh "with countless shades of relish and appreciation and kindness in it," a seventy-four-year-old woman wearing a scarf of Venetian lace who "did not seem old to me." Amazed by her vitality, Cather admired Mrs. Fields's "little triumphs over colour-destroying age and its infirmities, as at the play one rejoices in the escape of the beautiful and frail from the pursuit of things powerful and evil."

During the next six years, Cather increasingly admired Annie Fields as the producer and director of her own drama, a woman with a "great power to control and organize" who had created "an atmosphere in which one seemed absolutely safe from everything ugly." Offering "unruffled" hospitality in a narrow four-story building with a basement kitchen must have "cost the hostess something—cost her a great deal," Cather realized. Annie had once laughingly complained that she was doomed to escape nothing, "'not even free verse or the Cubists.'" Yet all her judgments were "generous and just," Cather believed, and she "rose to meet a fine performance, always—to the end." Cather's were among them.

Soon after their first meeting, Cather sought another, telephoning so often that she risked seeming "importunate." Her explanation was flattering: she had wanted to meet both Annie Fields and Sarah Orne Jewett for so long that she could not bear to leave Boston without seeing them again. A later note combines courtliness with intimacy. Cather bade Mrs. Fields good morning, hoped she was "herself" again, described her visit to Mrs. Gardner's museum, then humbly concluded that Mrs. Fields and Miss Jewett were somehow her reward for "servitude" to Mary Baker Eddy. About to leave Boston for the summer, she anticipated seeing them in the fall, begged permission to write, then signed off "Faithfully."[3]

Cather received more than permission to write. In mid-August, Sarah told Cather as the newly appointed *McClure's* editor that she had sent in a poem she had found among her papers—"The Gloucester Mother"—but still hoped to produce a new story "for you who gave me a 'Hand up' in the spring." Then assuring Cather that "Mrs. Fields bids me say this," Sarah invited her to Manchester "for more than a night, or as long as you could stay."[4]

Though she was delighted by the invitation, S. S. McClure had gone abroad and left Cather tied to the office. But as she also told Annie on 29 August, she would get to Boston within the next three weeks and telephone as soon as she arrived. She concluded with gratitude and affection.[5]

Those emotions intensified during her September visit to Manchester, the only time she would be there with both Annie and Sarah. During those days of perfect weather, she enjoyed leisurely meals that "liberated recollection" (primarily Annie's), listened to Annie read aloud, observed her friends' mutual concern, and entered into one-on-one conversations with each of them. During a particularly poignant moment of intimacy, Sarah confided her anxieties about Annie's health, a concern that seemed amply warranted when Annie fell ill just before Cather left. Warmed by her inclusion in their friendship, the young woman offered a few confidences of her own, complaining about the pressures of her magazine work and announcing that she and her friend Edith Lewis would soon move in together. When she looked back on that period of domestic intimacy in "148 Charles Street," Cather gave it a wry spin by declaring that whenever she "went a-calling with Mrs. Fields and left her card with Thunderbolt Hill engraved in the corner," she felt like a nonentity "paying calls with the lady Juno herself."[6] But her interactions with Annie then and immediately thereafter clearly suggest that she thrived on and in Annie's presence.

Thus she both telephoned and wrote to inquire about Annie's health right after leaving Manchester for Boston, and she sent a long and newsy letter right after returning to New York. Their mutual friend Ferris Greenslet had been very helpful during her days in Boston, she told Annie, but his new biography of Aldrich had disappointed her; and Annie's questions about her new apartment prompted complaints about its wallpaper and furniture. More important, Cather confided that recalling her days at Manchester enabled her to survive the bleak discouragements of life at *McClure's*. More pragmatically, Cather reached out to Annie as one woman of letters to another by saying she had not yet read the first two chapters of *Marriage à la Mode*, a new novel by Mrs. Humphry Ward that McClure had contracted to serialize in *McClure's*, but she had been perturbed by colleagues' comments that they were melodramatic yet uninteresting. Therefore, she planned to read them herself and then send page proofs to Annie. Then she signed off "Lovingly."[7]

When she mailed Annie the page proofs, Cather instructed her to show them only to Sarah and then destroy them. Presumably unaware that Mrs. Ward was a friend of Annie's who had stayed at Charles Street that very spring, Cather sadly reported that they struck her as tedious and commonplace. But she was soon "mightily" cheered by the news that both Sarah and Annie had found "vitality" in the chapters, and in a letter to Sarah, Cather promised to send them Mrs. Ward's outline of the rest.[8]

In that letter to Sarah, Cather went on to condole with her and Annie on the death of their friend Charles Eliot Norton, then offered a remarkable double tribute to Annie. Annie Fields was now the only one left to evoke a nobler time now vanished, Cather declared, then marveled at how well she evoked it. Next came resounding praise for Annie's *Singing Shepherd,* a gift from Sarah that was evidently Cather's introduction to Annie's poetry. She rejoiced in "The River Charles," a celebration of the river she had watched from Annie's windows during her visits to Charles Street, then specifically praised other poems by name. "Blue Succory" was one, the strong four-stanza lyric which finds symbolic meaning in a humble wildflower that is "Only a weed to the passer-by, / Growing among the rest." "The Bee and the Rose" was another, one that might easily be mistaken for an Emily Dickinson lyric: the bee "goes booming toward the sea, / Making the most of summer, gone so soon." Better still, the editor who was also a poet declared that "Little Guinever"—in which the queen is a willful child who dismisses grave Prince Arthur and summons Launcelot to feast on milk and honey—was a perfect Elizabethan song. "'Still in thy Love I Trust'" evoked even more sweeping praise. It was perhaps Annie's most beautiful poem, Cather wrote, a complete thing that was completely satisfying.

Her own domestic news was that she and Edith Lewis were enjoying their apartment and doing most of the cooking and housekeeping themselves—not only as a matter of economy, she wanted Annie to know, but as a distraction from office problems. But the heart of the letter was a plea for Sarah's judgment of two new stories. Cather worried that Sarah might not like the one whose proofs she enclosed—"On the Gull's Road"—and wondered what she thought of another that she preferred but McClure disliked—"The Enchanted Bluff," a tale rooted in her Nebraska childhood.[9]

A month later, eager for the reply she had not yet received, Cather went up to South Berwick, but found Sarah too ill for serious discussion. Instead, Sarah sent a letter that admixed generous praise with earnest advice. Urging Cather to try writing from a woman's perspective, she argued from deep personal experience that one woman could love another as protectively as the narrator of "On the Gull's Road" loved its heroine.[10] Then after returning to Charles Street a few weeks later, Sarah offered more thoughtful assessments and recommendations. Cather could not mature as a writer until she left *McClure's,* Sarah argued. Only after becoming surer of her "own background" including her "Nebraska life" could Cather find her "own quiet centre of life," and only then could she successfully address "the human heart, the great consciousness that all humanity goes to make up." Next, Sarah insisted on the Arnoldian imperative that she and Annie shared: "We must be ourselves, but we must be our best selves."[11]

Cather could not immediately act on that advice because she could not yet afford to leave *McClure's.* Nonetheless longing to see Annie and Sarah, she wished she could spend Christmas with them, promised to think of them often that day, and pledged to visit them as soon as she could.[12] But before Cather could arrange that visit, Sarah suffered the stroke from which she would never fully recover. "Willa Cather came from New York on purpose to ask after dear S. O. J. and to see me," Annie wrote in her diary in March 1909. But "dear Willa" would never again see "dear S. O. J."

When the news of Sarah's death reached her in London that June, Cather shared her grief with Annie. Numbed and inert yet hoping to ease Annie's loneliness, Cather said she could not tell even herself how dear Mrs. Fields and Miss Jewett were to her.[13] Two weeks later, she took comfort from a letter that Annie had written her from Manchester soon after Sarah died. It evoked recollections of seeing the two of them at Thunderbolt Hill together, Cather told Annie, then offered an intimate confidence. She often dreamed they were there together, and perhaps they really were.[14]

Nearly two years later, Willa Cather brought a New Englander in her twenties to 148 Charles Street—Elizabeth Shepley Sergeant, a McClure's colleague who had recently graduated from Bryn Mawr and "preferred Amy Lowell to James Russell." The young woman who "did not bow to the ancient and honorable idols" of the world of letters was amazed at her stalwart editor's "tender homage" to an "exquisite survivor of the Golden Age of American Literature" who treated Cather "as a sort of Midwest grandchild, a creature of zestful surprises who still needed a little toning down." Cather "stepped right out of her dominant personality and melted." Yet instead of answering Annie's questions about Thomas Hardy and other English writers she had recently seen in London, Cather redirected her hostess's attention to "the manuscripts, the portraits and photographs that crowded the walls and tables." Finally, "as the atmosphere thickened with ghostly presences, murmuring their wit and wisdom, Willa was happy and things were as they should be." Clearly, Cather felt intimidated yet privileged and sustained by the cultural tradition that Annie personified. But what Sergeant especially relished was her editor's subservient manipulation of the exquisite survivor.[15]

When Cather spent a week at Charles Street in May 1911—during which she learned to operate the elevator that had just been installed as a concession to her hostess's failing health—Annie was at the South Street station to meet her, social schedule in hand. Still resolutely determined to introduce talented and hardworking individuals to one another, she had already invited the poet and biographer George E. Woodberry to come to lunch a few days later, describing Cather to him as a "fine fresh creature" who was an editor of McClure's. Because she knew that they shared an interest in Keats, Annie had also arranged for them to visit Amy Lowell and inspect her Keats manuscripts—to look but not touch, as it turned out.[16] Woodberry enjoyed meeting Cather and found her "a charming companion," he told Annie; and she later reported that McClure's rarely included poetry but Cather hoped to publish some of his.[17]

"Willa has been here poorly," Annie noted on 11 February 1912, three years after Sarah's final illness began, then added, "She is better & has now gone homewards." Surely with both Cather and Sarah in mind, she next set down a quotation from Robert Louis Stevenson: "'we are indispensable, and no one is useless while he has a friend.'"

Cather returned to Nebraska that June, at last following Sarah's advice to seek the formative center of her life in order to address the human heart. *McClure's* was now behind her, and she had just published her first novel, the moderately successful *Alexander's Bridge*, drawing on 148 Charles Street for some of her settings and characters. Invigorated by her return to the world of her childhood, she described it to Annie in language that would recur in *O Pioneers!*, the novel she would dedicate to Sarah Orne Jewett.

Cather's first letter to her "dearest Lady" from Nebraska at the end of June 1912 vividly evokes the terrain that continued to nurture her, where the fields seemed to glow and the ripe wheat smelled like bread baking. Already planning a short trip through the nearby French and Bohemian territory to see the wheat harvest and the subsequent merry-making, Cather quoted Wagner's statement that whenever he felt dull, he sought rejuvenation in Bohemian soil. As she also told Annie, her visit to Arizona had enabled her to understand Balzac's remark that "In the desert there is everything and nothing—God without mankind." She did not mention the handsome young Mexican she had met in Arizona, though she whimsically told Sergeant how lovely Julio would look at Charles Street.[18]

The following month, Cather sent Annie detailed descriptions of the Bohemians' wheat harvest, their enormous wheatfields, and the big church of St. Anne that anticipate passages in *O Pioneers!*. As one cosmopolitan to another, she also shared her pleasure in the beautiful service she had heard at St. Anne's—in French, and with excellent music. She declined her Dear Lady's invitation to visit her in Manchester because she felt committed to devote the next three months to her novel, but said she thought of her lovingly.[19] As she would later say, she tried to tell her story "as truthfully and simply as if I were telling it to [Sarah Orne Jewett] by word of mouth."[20] Meantime, on the verge of writing a novel about her prairie world that centered on a remarkable woman, Cather felt sustained by Annie's sympathy and encouragement, and signed her letters "Devotedly" or "Lovingly."

Annie welcomed all those letters and thoughtfully prepared for each of Cather's visits. Each was also an occasion to see other literati who were Annie's friends, as when Cather called on the novelist Margaret Deland during her New Year's visit to Annie in 1913. Another mutual friend was Ferris Greenslet, Cather's editor at Houghton Mifflin.[21] But none of the Bostonians more fully or more tenderly shared Cather's affection for Annie than Louise Imogen Guiney.

In the spring of 1910 when Guiney was living in Oxford, for example, she told Annie she was reading about 148 Charles Street in a McClure's publication, Ellen Terry's *Story of My Life*, which "That Dear Thing Willa Cather" had just sent her.[22] Terry's accolades accorded with Guiney's and Cather's: all three regarded Annie as a "great American lady whom to know is a liberal education," and admired her home as a place filled with "relics of the past," a place "where the culture of Boston seems . . . a rare and delicate reality."[23] A long letter from dear Willa, much of it about Annie, "was almost as good as running down the Hill to sup at 148"; and one of Guiney's last letters to Annie sounds a familiar note: "The last news I heard of you was through Willa enviable girl! Wasn't it good of her to send it, knowing how much I cared?"[24]

Annie Fields willed four thousand dollars to Louise Imogen Guiney, whose income was always small, but she bequeathed "to my dear Willa Sibert Cather the bust of Keats, the original marble of which is in the Hampstead church in Hampstead, England, and the copy of Severn's full length portrait which hangs on the bookcase next the street." It was a legacy that conveyed a custodial obligation. Prominently displayed in Cather's Bank Street apartment, the Keats portraits invited cultural communion with the cherished past—with Keats and Severn but also with Annie Fields—and an expanded sense of self rooted in devotion to literary excellence.[25]

Writing "148 Charles Street" was another way that Cather fulfilled her custodial obligation to the cherished past. In December 1936, soon after its publication in *Not Under Forty*, Willa Cather told Annie's nephew Boylston Beal how glad she was that the essay rang true to him, entirely agreeing with him about Annie's remarkable ability to connect the present with the past.[26]

Cather had sounded a different note five years earlier, however, when she instructed Mark DeWolfe Howe to burn her letters to Annie Fields instead of sending them to the Huntington Library. Insisting that they would be of no help to any future researcher because they were artificial, she dismissed them as a series of long and meaningless sentences that she had written out of a sense of duty, because she knew Annie liked opening the morning mail. But even the most obsequious of the relatively few letters that have survived is self-revealing, as is Cather's claim that she always tried to avoid saying anything that might disturb Mrs. Fields.[27]

If "148 Charles Street" gently mocks Annie Fields as the Juno of Thunderbolt Hill, that very mockery is a form of praise. More important, the essay honors Annie Fields as the keeper of the Charles Street shrine, a woman of indomitable spirit who kept up with the present but carried the past with her, a generous woman who despite Cather's ambivalences helped her grow into her "best self."

Although Cather prepared separate essays on Annie and Sarah for *Not Under Forty*, she usually thought of them as a couple. They helped her understand how women can be defined and sustained by their affection for one another. Moreover, both Annie and Sarah respected Cather's talent and did their best to foster it; when she returned to Nebraska, she was following Annie's advice as well as Sarah's to find her own center as a writer. By precept and example, they both taught Cather that a writer requires solitude but also "needs the widest outlook upon the world." That outlook included the views from Charles Street and Thunderbolt Hill.

25

Endings

No sorrow in Annie Fields's life except the death of her husband matched the sorrow of Sarah Orne Jewett's final illness and her death. "My dear S. O. J. was stricken down early Sunday morning a small blood vessel giving way in the brain," Annie solemnly wrote on 4 February 1909.[1] Six days later, Sarah still lay half-conscious in her Charles Street bedroom, attended by nurses, while those who loved her "can know and do nothing." Friends came and went, Willa Cather among them. A month later, Sarah was "still in a low state though reviving a little from time to time." Though she could speak a bit and even joke with the nurses, she was virtually helpless. Then on 21 April, "she was carried to her South Berwick home from her Charles Street home. We did not speak again together after the morning. She needed all her steadiness and so did I. She understood and wrote me afterward that she loved it so." The "it" was their silent farewell. "I could not speak for crying," Sarah wrote from South Berwick the next morning; and for the last two months of her life she continued to send Annie brief, scrawling, love-filled letters.[2] At the top of one, Annie noted that it was written "3 months & 3 days after she was stricken down," and wrote on the back, "My courage and hope ended with this note." And she copied into her diary what may have been the last of them: "Goodbye darling with my heart's love your Pinny."

On 24 June (the day of Sarah's death, though Annie did not yet know it), she told Lilian Aldrich, "She no longer suffers, no longer hears any echoes from this, our world. I went to see her last week and stayed two days. She is quiet and beautiful and does not suffer. She knew me and told me the few last things she had in mind and seemed to love to have me there. She soon relapsed into sleep—a sleep from which she will not entirely waken."[3] It would be a week before Annie could report in her diary that "her spirit finally took its flight." From then on, she repeatedly reminded herself that Sarah had been released from pain, but continued to mourn the "dear beautiful helpful generous self who will not come back, no, no, no!"

Yet Annie's life went on. She was easily fatigued, and she mourned the deaths of other old friends including Ellen Emerson and Oliver Wendell Holmes. But not even eyestrain kept her from reading widely—including Rabelais and Bergson. "Friends have been so kind that I am seldom alone," she noted soon after Sarah's death, a statement she would often reiterate. Jessie Cochrane spent long stretches of time with her in Boston and Manchester, and her old friend Helen Bell came once or twice a week, bringing the stimulus of her "swift mind and heart longing to serve friends." Only a month after Sarah's death, Annie invited Alice Longfellow, Agnes Irwin, and Mabel Boordmore (the head of the Red Cross) to have lunch with her at Manchester and was struck by Boordmore's "energy and concern for others' suffering." At that point, as often thereafter, she felt consoled that Sarah was no longer suffering.

That October while preparing to return "to Boston and our home there without her," Annie recalled leaving Manchester with Sarah exactly a year earlier: "I had been very ill for a month and she had nursed and companioned me until life seemed like a rose which had opened into full beauty in this exquisite place." Sarah was also on ongoing part of her present. "The season spins on apace— without her!" Annie wrote in November. "And yet her sweet presence her loving care are not really absent."

By then she had decided to prepare a collection of "Dear SOJ's letters" and started gathering them. They were "getting into shape steadily" by the first anniversary of Sarah's death; and when Henry James came to call in December 1910 "in one of the 'let-ups' of his long illness and sadness," he offered to "write a few words in tribute." But he never would. "Have just given dear Sarah's Letters to the printer though the book will not appear until mid-summer," Annie noted in March 1911. "Henry James is still unfit to write."

The *Letters of Sarah Orne Jewett*, published by Houghton Mifflin in October 1911, was the last book Annie assembled. She gathered and edited all the letters, omitting most of the deeply personal passages from the over seventy letters addressed to her. The collection begins with a letter addressed to "Dear Mrs. Fields" at the beginning of their friendship, for example, but does not include Sarah's intensely personal final goodbye to her "darling" Annie. The dozens of letters to Annie at the start of the book are in rough chronological order, as are those to other friends as well as Annie that follow. As Annie told Mark DeWolfe Howe while preparing it, the "continuous group of her letters make quite a perfect diary and possess a character of their own without any striving for cleverness but simply showing her own bright humanity."[4]

Like the *Biographical Notes* of her husband that Annie had prepared thirty years before, the book is a testament of love, a mode of emotional closure, and a significant contribution to literary history. It would be the standard collection of

Sarah's letters for decades. Its lofty epigraph from Spenser's "Hymn in Honour of Beauty" seems equally applicable to Sarah and herself:

> For Lovers' eyes more sharply-sighted be
> Than other men's, and in dear Love's delight
> See more than any other eyes can see.

Annie's nine-page introduction begins with Sarah's death in South Berwick, where she had grown up "with hills and waters and a large open country [that] . . . she knew and loved well, as her books show." Her father's death in 1877 was "her first sorrow," Annie said, "and soon after began the correspondence contained in this volume." Subordinating her own identity and skirting a gender issue, Annie compared Sarah's *Letters* to Swift's journal to Stella, which uses the same "little language" and expresses "the same joy and repose in friendship."[5] That comparison was an unusual way of addressing Mark DeWolfe Howe's concern that childish nicknames, "especially where an assumed childish diction is coupled with them," might lead to "all sorts of people *reading them wrong*."[6] But as Howe had advised, Annie also excised most of the pet names and childish diction from Sarah's letters to her, retaining only a few iterations of love and longing.

The *Letters of Sarah Orne Jewett* displays Sarah as "a true lover of nature" and of her many close friends, a wise and witty woman with a "sweet dignity of character" despite "trammelings of ill health," a woman whose literary interests ranged from Pliny to Dorothy Wordsworth, Balzac, Tolstoy, and Willa Cather, and whose "*métier* was, to lay open, for other eyes to see, those qualities in human nature which ennoble their possessors." Her unique character emerges through such lines as "I am bewitched with a story, though I have nothing to say to you about it yet," through her seminal advice to Willa Cather, and through her accounts of wandering through a glen or along a tree-lined riverbank. The book's penultimate sentence presents the dying Sarah's plaintive cry, "'I do not know what to do with me!'" Annie's own last sentence soars: "Then she was borne away from these human trammels and her young soul was free to move in the atmosphere of Divine Love."[7]

Next came the task of sending the *Letters* to dozens of friends, and the double reward of their tributes to the book and to Sarah. Even while wondering when she might "join again those I love," Annie reminded herself of the "many still here who are very dear and I can still thank God and pray for strength to wait until *His* will says this too is finished."

Feeling "stronger and better than before," Annie continued to entertain old and new friends, Helen Keller and President Taft among them. She continued to give lunches and supper parties, and sometimes she had houseguests. Sometimes she joined friends for dinner, on one occasion a dinner where the main topic of discussion was Mrs. George Widener's gift to Harvard of a million dollars for a library. She also continued to mark anniversaries of her life with Sarah including the day of her "deliverance"; and after reading a biography of Mark Twain and beginning his *Joan of Arc* in the summer of 1912, she declared, "I hope to wait as cheerfully as he did for the trumpet call and as usefully." A typical bit of stock-taking came soon afterward: "I have had no severe illness and a good season of much content but the great messenger still delays. Perhaps there will be another season." As it turned out, she had over two more years to live.

Her correspondence remained as lively as her social life, and her efforts to stay useful included a few final publications. In October 1912, the Boston Athenaeum printed "'A Letter from Mrs. Fields' to the Arabella Club, 'A Friendly Circle of Girls,'" which urged the moral benefits of reading poetry. An equally typical but more ambitious bit of advocacy titled "Nurses and Nursing" appeared in the *Boston Transcript* of 22 May 1914. Beginning with Florence Nightingale's death and her legacy, Annie argued that nurses should receive excellent professional training that includes training in morality and discipline. Only a few months before her death, "Recollections of Old Boston, from a Conversation with a Boston Lady of the Period" appeared in a collection titled *Days and Ways of Old Boston*. Annie had argued that it was too fragmentary to publish and insisted on withholding her name, but the editor, William Rossiter, presumably contrived to have her identity revealed in the *Transcript*.

On 5 January 1915, halfway through her eightieth year, Annie died at Charles Street of myocarditis and arteriosclerosis. At her own request, friends gathered at sundown for a modest funeral ceremony that included music but no singing. What happened next seems remarkably appropriate. As she had stipulated in her will, her body was cremated, and her ashes were placed in an urn and buried in Mount Auburn Cemetery at the foot of her husband's coffin.

Annie Fields had exerted a remarkable degree of control over her life, and she left a complex legacy that included many bequests (the largest of them to the Associated Charities), many publications, and strong moral imperatives. While remaining a Boston Lady, she stretched the definition of that term. "Mrs. J. T. Fields Dies at Her Home; Widow of Former Boston Publisher," the *Boston Evening Transcript* announced. The headline was as Annie would have wished. So was the long list of Annie's own accomplishments which followed.

Annie Adams Fields was an exemplary woman of her time, in all senses of the word. Her seeming subordination to her husband was an aspect of their larger mutual commitment to the loftiest ideals of their age. Her marriage provided the means for her own self-fulfillment and opportunities for her to help others toward theirs, as did her subsequent union with Sarah Orne Jewett. Most of the writers and the scores of others whose lives entwined with Annie's thrived on their relationship with her. Whether writing a letter or a journal entry or a poem at her desk, entertaining friends, or interviewing clients of the Associated Charities, she prompted people to become their own best selves—as George B. Emerson had put it, to "strive . . . to surpass yourselves." Through her letters and journals, she admits us to her world and theirs. The woman who read Longfellow as a child and Bergson near the end of her life absorbed and yet also challenged the sometimes conflicting values of her own time, place, gender, and class. Whether as a hostess or a social activist, a biographer or a poet, a nurturer or a catalyst, deferential or assertive, she demonstrated women's power to take charge of their own lives.[8] Along with her husband, she helped create "the high-literary establishment of the later nineteenth century." Her accomplishments and influence extend from the genteel world of mid-nineteenth-century America to the transformed sensibility of our own age.

ABBREVIATIONS USED IN THE NOTES

ARCHIVES:

Berg, NYPL	Berg Collection, New York Public Library
BPL	Boston Public Library
HL	Huntington Library
Ho	Houghton Library, Harvard University
MHS	Massachusetts Historical Society
NYPL	Manuscripts Division, New York Public Library

CORRESPONDENTS:

TBA	Thomas Bailey Aldrich
WSC	Willa Sibert Cather
CD	Charles Dickens
RHD	Rebecca Harding Davis
AF	Annie Fields
JTF	James T. Fields

LG	Louise Imogen Guiney
NH	Nathaniel Hawthorne
SH	Sophia Hawthorne
MDH	Mark DeWolfe Howe
OWH	Oliver Wendell Holmes
WDH	William Dean Howells
LWJ	Laura Winthrop Johnson
SOJ	Sarah Orne Jewett
LL	Lucy Larcom
HWL	Henry Wadsworth Longfellow
HBS	Harriet Beecher Stowe
HPS	Harriet Prescott Spofford
CT	Celia Thaxter
JGW	John Greenleaf Whittier

NOTES

INTRODUCTION

1. "Mrs. J. T. Fields Dies at Her Home: Widow of Former Boston Publisher Had Lived at 148 Charles Street for Sixty Years," *Boston Evening Transcript*, 5 January 1915, 1.

2. Helen J. Winslow, *Literary Boston of To-Day* (Boston: L. C. Page, 1902), 60.

3. William S. Rossiter, ed., *Days and Ways in Old Boston* (Boston: R. H. Stearns, 1915), 39–44. The newspaper disclosure of Annie's authorship may well have been planted by Rossiter.

4. After a fire burned the ropewalks between Pearl and Atkinson Streets in 1794, a large tract was opened for residential use, and Pearl Street was soon lined with fashionable houses. Most of the original owners were gone by the end of the forties, replaced by businessmen and Irish immigrants. See Walter Muir Whitehill, *Boston: A Topographical History* (Cambridge: Harvard University Press, 1959), 55–58, 114–18, 174; and William H. Pease and Jane H. Pease, *The Web of Progress: Private Values and Public Styles in Boston and Charleston, 1828–1842* (New York: Oxford University Press, 1985), 2–4. Annie spent her teenage years and the first year and a half of her marriage in her parents' house on Boylston Street.

5. Henry Cabot Lodge, *Early Memories* (New York: Scribner's, 1913), 14–24.

6. "Famous People at Home. IX. Mrs. James T. Fields," *Time and the Hour* 5 (17 April 1897): 6–7.

7. The selling price was $14,000. James T. Fields paid an annual rent of $1,100 to Ticknor and Fields, which officially purchased the property and later the lot behind (William S. Tryon, *Parnassus Corner: The Life of James T. Fields* (Boston: Houghton Mifflin, 1963), 213. The property was entirely Fields's after Ticknor's death, and he willed it to Annie. According to her will, the house was to be destroyed if her heir—her nephew Boylston Adams—did not want to occupy it, but the garden was to be held in common by owners of surrounding property. Boylston Adams, who wanted the Manchester house but not the one on Charles Street, abided by her wishes. What was once a secluded riverside garden is now a private playground separated from the river by Embankment Road and the embankment itself. Annie Fields's will (including many codicils) is at the Houghton Library.

8. Willa Cather, "148 Charles Street," in *Not Under Forty* (New York: Knopf, 1936), 54.

9. Her pseudonymous poems were signed "Ann West" (her first and middle names), "A. West," or "A.W."; but she signed five of her last volumes and many late poems and essays "Annie Fields."

10. William S. Rossiter to AF, 19, 21, and 27 November [1914?], HL. "Much against my will and under great pressure they use the talk with me," she wrote at the top of his letter of 19 November.

11. Mark DeWolfe Howe, *Memories of a Hostess* (Boston: Atlantic Monthly Press, 1922), 3. Howe assembles passages from Annie Fields's journals to present her social relationships with celebrities of a "vanished society," most of them men. But he does not assess the woman herself or her relationships

with other women, her own contributions to her husband's work as editor and author, or her reform initiatives; he gives only two pages to her publications; and her decades of widowhood get short shrift in a brief final chapter titled "Sarah Orne Jewett."

12. Henry James, "Mr. and Mrs. James T. Fields," *Atlantic Monthly* 116 (July 1915): 21–31.

13. The first scholarly study of Annie Fields was Barbara Ruth Rotundo's readable and reliable "Mrs. James T. Fields, Hostess and Biographer" (Ph.D. diss., Syracuse University, 1968), whose subtitle defines its scope. In the first published book about her—*Annie Adams Fields: The Spirit of Charles Street* (Bloomington: Indiana University Press, 1990)—Judith A. Roman goes well beyond Rotundo, discussing some of Annie's other activities, including her charity work. Two doctoral dissertations on Annie Fields appeared in 1996—Carol L. Nigro's "Annie Adams Fields: Female Voice in a Male Chorus" (Georgia State University, 1996) and Norma Haft Mandel's "Annie Adams Fields and the Gift of Sympathy" (City University of New York). Nigro rightly says that Annie Fields met her period's expectations for "elite" poetry and prose fiction, but wrongly argues that she did not adequately develop her talents because neither her husband nor male friends like Longfellow and Whittier offered sufficient encouragement. Mandel offers the unassailable argument that Fields's "gift of sympathy" is crucial to her attainments as a wife, hostess, friend, and philanthropist. Other studies of Annie Fields include George Curry, "Charles Dickens and Annie Fields," *Huntington Library Quarterly* 51 (Winter 1988), and Josephine Donovan's "Annie Adams Fields and Her Network of Influence" in her *New England Local Colorists: A Women's Tradition* (New York: Ungar, 1983). My own writing on her includes the recent *American National Biography* essay; "Annie Fields's Nathaniel Hawthorne," in *Hawthorne and Women: Engendering and Expanding the Hawthorne Tradition,* ed. John Idol and Melinda Ponder (Amherst: University of Massachusetts Press, 1999); "Subordinated Power: Mrs. and Mr. James T. Fields," in *Patrons and Protegees,* ed. Shirley Marchalonis (New Brunswick, N.J.: Rutgers University Press, 1988), 141–60 and 236; "'Pegasus in the Pound': The Editor, the Author, Their Wives, and the *Atlantic Monthly*," *Essex Institute Historical Collections* 125 (1989): 104–22; "Annie Fields: Living in a World without Dickens," *Huntington Library Quarterly,* 52 (1989): 409–14, "Annie Adams Fields (1834–1915)," *Legacy* 4 (1987): 27–36; and "Annie Fields's Nathaniel Hawthorne: 'Grand as Ever,'" *Postscript* 4 (1987): 9–30.

CHAPTER 1

1. JTF to Mary Russell Mitford, 27 October 1854, HL. During his visits to England in 1847 and 1851, Fields had endeared himself to Mitford (1787–1855), best known for the collection of sketches of rural life and character titled *Our Village* (1819). The sixth and last section of his *Yesterdays with Authors* is devoted to Mitford, and the December 1900 issue of the *Critic* includes a brief tribute to her by Annie Fields.

Eliza Adams Willard, the mother of Mary and Eliza Willard, was the sister of Annie's father.

2. Mary Russell Mitford to JTF, 9 and 22 November 1854, and JTF to Mitford, 8 December 1854, HL.

3. JTF to Bayard Taylor, 10 November 1854, and JTF to HWL, 10 November [1854] and "Monday morning," [6 November 1854,] HL.

4. Washington Irving and William Cullen Bryant were among the eminent New York writers eager to meet the "elect lady" during the Fieldses' wedding trip; and when bad weather made Fields cancel a visit to Sunnyside, Irving urged him to reschedule it. Washington Irving to JTF, 25 November 1854, HL.

5. Gannett had been William Ellery Channing's assistant at the Federal Street Church until Channing retired in 1842. King's Chapel, Unitarian since 1787, was built in 1750 at Tremont and School Streets to replace the 1688 edifice which was Boston's first Anglican church. Fields's mother had died six years before he married Annie. His brother George was then a junior partner in the firm of Benjamin Bradley, the bookbinders used by Ticknor and Fields. He would soon leave to form his own firm, Lemon, Fields and Company, which Ticknor and Fields then began patronizing. William S. Tryon, *Parnassus Corner: A Life of James T. Fields* (Boston: Houghton Mifflin, 1963), 176; and John William Pye, *James T. Fields: Literary Publisher* (Portland, Me.: Baxter Society, 1987), 17, 18, 26. Pye thinks Ticknor and Fields's acanthus-stamped brown cloth binding was probably designed by George Fields, perhaps in collaboration with his brother, and also thinks they collaborated in designing the

equally famous blue and gold binding. James and Annie rarely visited George and his family and perhaps never entertained them, but remained concerned about their welfare and contributed to their support after the financial panic of 1873.

6. His funeral service was at the Federal Street Church, conducted by Dr. Gannett. According to the obituary titled "The Good Physician" in the *Boston Daily Evening Transcript* for 26 January 1855, Dr. Adams had never "lost a day by sickness" and had earned "the esteem and friendship of our most intelligent citizens." As one expression of Annie's regard for her father, his portrait hung above her desk in the Charles Street library. For further details about the Adams family, see Andrew N. Adams. *A Genealogical History of Henry Adams of Braintree Massachusetts and his Descendants* (Rutland, Vt.: Tuttle, 1898), 460.

7. Charles Newton Peabody, *ZAB: Brevet Major Zabdiel Boylston Adams, 1829–1902, Physician of Boston and Framingham* (Boston: Francis A. Countway Library of Medicine, 1984), distributed by the University Press of Virginia, 7.

8. AF to LWJ, 2 February 1878, HL. Sarah kept track of her activities in a travel diary Annie gave her, now at the Houghton Library. That July, Annie told her friend Laura Johnson that Sarah was about to attend a musical festival at Erfurt with friends who "know Liszt as well as she and Von Bulow also and they will have the best of everything. She has been gone a year the whole time crowded with satisfaction and pleasure." AF to LWJ, 10 July 1878, HL.

9. All five volumes were published in Boston: Grimm's *Life and Times of Goethe* (Boston: Little, Brown, 1880), *The Destruction of Rome* (Boston: Cupples, Upham, 1886), *Literary Essays* (Boston: Cupples and Upham, 1886), and *The Life of Raphael* (Boston: Cupples and Hurd, 1888); and a popular novella by Conrad F. Meyer titled *The Monk's Wedding* (Boston: Cupples and Hurd, 1887).

10. Sarah Adams died in 1916 at the age of ninety-three. A note on a family copy of her photograph gives her address as the Hotel Ludlow. After visiting her there in 1898, Louise Imogen Guiney told Annie, "She was sweeter and kinder than I can say, leaning a good deal on my shoulder in going about to show me her treasures, and smiling at me very often because, she said, she looked for a much older person. We had a charming time." LG to AF, 4 August 1898, HL. In *Boston Days* (Boston: Little, Brown, 1902), 441–43, Lilian Whiting reproduces that photograph and calls Sarah Adams "one of the most interesting figures in cosmopolitan society," a woman of "exquisite culture," "intellectual grasp, imaginative power, sympathy," and charm, whose "picture and book-lined rooms" overlooking Copley Square are "a social centre of the finest Boston life" and "always brilliant with flowers sent by her myriad friends." The sisters corresponded regularly while Sarah was abroad, spent time together in Switzerland in 1881, and shared a number of friends including Longfellow and the Emersons. Writing in October 1879 to his friend Cornelia Lucretia Boardman—a medical student who had been unable to complete her studies in America and was then in Dresden—Longfellow said he hoped "Miss Adams is still with you. Mrs. Fields has told me something of her translation of Grimm's Lectures on Goethe," and he urged, "Encourage her to go on; and trust to the future for a publisher." Longfellow thanked Sarah Adams for her "valuable and interesting work" in March 1881, then reported on the activities of a few friends and on James T. Fields's illness. In Andrew Hilen, ed., *The Letters of Henry Wadsworth Longfellow*, 6 vols. (Cambridge: Harvard University Press, 1967–82), 6:526 and 693. As evidence of Sarah Adams's friendship with the Emersons, on 2 June 1880 Gisela von Arnim Grimm told Ellen Tucker Emerson that the "very amiable Miss Adams" had spent the winter in Berlin, that she had "translated my husband's *Goethe* into English and was very diligent here, a refined, high-minded person," and that she had spoken lovingly of the Emersons. Sarah Adams's 1902 obituary of Grimm includes a lively account of his first meeting with Emerson. Luther S. Luedtke and Winfried Schleiner, "New Letters from the Grimm-Emerson Correspondence," *Harvard Library Bulletin* 25 (October 1977): 454.

11. JTF to AF, 24 November 1875, HL.

12. Quotations are from Richard Burton, *A Life Sketch* (Baltimore: Priv. Ptd., 1899). Photographs of her studio were in the collection of Mrs. Nancy Bole, the granddaughter of Zabdiel Boylston Adams, when I saw them. As Boylston told his mother in December 1861, Lissie's greatest problem was her own diffidence, and he hoped she would "stop studying books and only study pictures and nature and trust her own fancy" (Zabdiel Boylston Adams to Mrs. Sarah Adams, 15 December 1861, Count-

way Library, Harvard Medical School). Perhaps her eventual professional success came from doing so. In terms that apply equally well to Annie, her biographer Burton praised Elizabeth Adams's "sweetness, dignity and strength," her character, breeding, charm, idealism, and sense of humor, and her "benignant tolerance toward others [which] expresses itself practically in good works."

13. Peabody, 25, 207.

14. Zabdiel Boylston Adams to Louisa Beal, [?] May 1865, Countway Library.

15. Peabody quotes this sentence from Frances Kidder Adams's signed but undated will, 173.

16. Peabody, 203–4.

17. Thomas P. Beal, a founder and president of the Second National Bank of Boston, was an important figure in Boston financial circles until his death in 1923. See Peabody, 9, and *Fifty Years of Boston: A Memorial Volume Issued in Commemoration of the Tercentenary of 1930*, ed. Elisabeth M. Herlihy (Boston: Subcommittee on Memorial History, 1932), 233.

18. The will and its various codicils are at the Houghton Library.

19. The artist was presumably the Irish-born portrait painter Richard Rothwell (1800–68), who exhibited at London's Royal Academy from 1830 on. His 1840 portrait of Mary Shelley is one of several Rothwells owned by the National Portrait Gallery. It seems a good guess that he painted Annie Fields during the second of his two visits to Boston in the 1850s, shortly after her wedding and before he settled in Leamington Spa in 1858. He died in Rome and was buried next to John Keats by their mutual friend Joseph Severn.

20. AF to HWL, 14 January 1864, HL.

21. AF, "The Poet Who Told the Truth," *Wide awake* (December 1886): 87–88.

22. Annie Fields, *Authors and Friends* (Boston: Houghton Mifflin, 1895), 337–38. Beneath the layered frustration and self-vindication in both of these shaped memories is an emerging self-definition consistent with Carol Gilligan's conclusions about women's moral development in *In a Different Voice* (Cambridge: Harvard University Press, 1982). As Gilligan puts it, a girl's "ethic of responsibility" can shift from a simple desire to please and "become a self-chosen anchor of personal integrity and strength" (171).

23. Thomas Woody, *A History of Women's Education in the United States* (New York: The Science Press, 1929), 1:348; R. C. Waterston, *George B. Emerson: His Life and Times* (Cambridge, Mass.: John Wilson, 1884), 8; and George B. Emerson, *Reminiscences of an Old Teacher* (Boston: Alfred Mudge, 1878).

24. Emerson, *Reminiscences*, 66.

25. Ibid., 66–69.

26. Ibid., 140–45.

27. The quotation is in an unpublished and undated thirty-page address to charity workers, now at the Huntington Library.

28. [Annie Fields,] *James T. Fields: Biographical Notes and Personal Sketches* (Boston: Houghton Mifflin, 1881), 52.

29. Annie fits Nancy Chodorow's profile of the girl raised in a nurturing family. She experienced warm acceptance if not deep understanding, respected the individuality of others, pursued divergent personal interests without profound inner conflict, yet assumed her social status was essentially defined by her relationship to men. See Chodorow's "Family Structure and Feminine Personality," in *Woman, Culture, and Society*, ed. Michele Zimbalist Rosaldo and Louise Lamphere (Stanford: Stanford University Press, 1974), 43–46; and Chodorow's fuller study, *The Reproduction of Mothering: Psychoanalysis and the Sociology of Gender* (Berkeley: University of California Press, 1978).

30. Rufus Griswold to JTF [? November 1854], HL. See William Charvat, "James T. Fields and the Beginnings of Book Promotion, 1840–1955," in *The Profession of Authorship in America, 1800–1870*, ed. Matthew J. Bruccoli (Columbus: Ohio State University Press, 1968), 172–77: The "ubiquitous and versatile Mr. Griswold" produced anthologies and book reviews and "functioned in various business capacities for at least thirteen book publishers, twelve magazines, eight newspapers, and seven authors." In 1852, he asked Fields to be the best man at his third wedding.

31. *Biographical Notes*, 2–8. The following year, his brother George began an apprenticeship in the Boston bookbinding firm of Benjamin Bradley. As Charvat points out in "James T. Fields and the Be-

ginnings of Book Promotion," 169–71, at that time most publishers were principally booksellers, and most of them published primarily for the local trade. Carter and Hendee was one such firm. For fuller information about Fields's career, see James C. Austin, *Fields of the Atlantic Monthly* (San Marino, Calif. Huntington Library, 1953), Tryon, and Pye.

32. *Biographical Notes*, 52; [Curtis,] "Editor's Easy Chair," *Harper's* 63 (July 1881): 305; and Tryon, 224. In September 1865, a year and a half after Ticknor's death, Fields moved from the Old Corner Bookstore to larger quarters on nearby Tremont Street. Within two years, he was publishing four periodicals there in addition to the *Atlantic Monthly*—the *North American Review, Our Young Folks, Every Saturday*, and the annual *Atlantic Almanac*, all edited by his friends.

33. Martin Green, *The Problem of Boston: Some Readings in Cultural History* (New York: Norton, 1966), 78.

34. Most of Susan Coultrap-McQuin's generalizations about the Gentleman Publisher in *Doing Literary Business* (Chapel Hill: University of North Carolina Press), 1990, esp. 32–40, apply to Fields: he was a benevolent man who cultivated loyalty and trust in "his" authors, he often paid their bills and advanced them money, he read and selected book manuscripts, and his office was a congenial gathering place.

35. JTF to Mary Russell Mitford, 8 December 1854, HL; Harriet Spofford, *A Little Book of Friends* (Boston: Little, Brown, 1916), 4; and Helen Howe, *The Gentle Americans, 1864–1960* (New York: Harper and Row, 1965), 74.

36. Lindsay Swift, *Literary Landmarks of Boston* (Boston: Houghton Mifflin, 1903), 17–19. Evidently those "worthies" did not particularly want "striking" features.

37. "Mrs. James T. Fields," *Time and the Hour* 5 (17 April 1897): 6–7.

38. Spofford, 16–17.

39. William Dean Howells, *Literary Friends and Acquaintance* ([1900,] Bloomington: Indiana University Press, 1968), 40–41. Howells also fondly recalled Annie Fields's account of visiting Tennyson "and how he said, when he asked her to go with him to the tower of his house, 'Come up and see the sad English sunset!' which had an instant value to me such as some rich verse of his might have had"; and he "breathed in that atmosphere as if in the return from life-long exile." When Annie Fields died, Howells told his daughter "she was the last of the world I came into at Boston." *Life in Letters of William Dean Howells*, ed. Mildred Howells, 2 vols. (Garden City, N.Y.: Doubleday Doran, 1928), 2:348.

40. Henry James, *The American Scene* (Boston: Houghton Mifflin, 1907), 236.

41. Willa Cather, "148 Charles Street," in *Not Under Forty* (New York: Knopf, 1936), 52–76.

42. E. H. Clement, "The Personal and Social Side of Mrs. Fields," *Boston Evening Transcript*, 6 January 1915, 18.

43. Spofford, 17.

CHAPTER 2

1. [Annie Fields,] *James T. Fields: Biographical Notes and Personal Sketches* (Boston: Houghton Mifflin, 1881), 60.

2. Julia Ward Howe to JTF, n.d., HL.

3. Catharine Sedgwick to AF, 15 June and 8 September 1858, Ho. Sedgwick, who had recently published the last of her six novels, would later send Fields two stories and two essays for the *Atlantic*. Urging Annie to visit her again, she explained that she was covetous of what enriched her final years. The two women continued to correspond and exchange gifts until Sedgwick's death in 1873, and tried to see each other whenever Sedgwick came to Boston. After one such occasion in the winter of 1867, Annie expressed admiration for at Sedgwick's wit and wisdom and said she had "never known a more lovely and spirited talker." A few of Mary Kelley's conclusions in *The Power of Her Sympathy: The Autobiography and Journal of Catharine Maria Sedgwick* (Boston: Massachusetts Historical Society, 1993), 34–41, apply equally well to Annie Fields: they both believed women "had a claim on individual fulfillment," and they both "made connection and choice complementary imperatives for both sexes."

4. *Biographical Notes*, 60, and AF to Sarah May Adams, [June 1859], Annie Fields Papers, MHS.

5. AF to Elizabeth Adams, 15 June 1859, MHS. Annie Fields's 1859–60 travel diary, like the other journals she kept between 1863 and 1877 and intermittently during the following decades, is at the Mass-

achusetts Historical Society. Undocumented quotations from Annie Fields in this book are from her journals.

6. JTF to Zabdiel Boylston Adams, 4 August 1859, MHS.

7. It would be published the following year—in England under the title of *Transformation*.

8. AF to Louisa Adams, 26 June 1859, MHS.

9. AF to Sarah Holland Adams, 8 July 1859, MHS.

10. AF to Elizabeth Adams, 19 July 1859, and AF to Zabdiel Boylston Adams, 19 July 1859, MHS. In her memoir of Tennyson, Annie Fields praised his "natural sublimity" but also his "capacity for friendship" (*Authors and Friends* [Boston: Houghton Mifflin, 1895], 341).

11. JTF to Zabdiel Boylston Adams, 4 August 1859, MHS. Evidently Mr. Robertson felt equally drawn to both Fieldses. "I know not two persons who on so short an acquaintance my heart has so clung to," he told Annie soon afterward, and the following year he declared that his last heartbeat would pulse with love for the Fieldses. Frederick Robertson to AF, 15 August 1860, and 12 December 1861, HL.

12. Annie's admiration of Mrs. Greene (and of other "gracefully and carefully" dressed women) is consistent with Valerie Steele's argument in *Fashion and Eroticism: Ideals of Feminine Beauty from the Victorian Era to the Jazz Age* (New York: Oxford University Press, 1985), 4–5, that Victorian fashion did not signal "the social and sexual repression of women." Although Victorian women were socialized to be "pleasing and attractive to men," their ideal of beauty offered wide latitude for personal choice "within the changing limits of the socially acceptable." Yet by linking graceful dress to moral duty, Annie implicitly affirmed the period's idealization of domesticity.

13. *Biographical Notes*, 74.

14. HBS to AF, 28 May 1860, HL.

15. AF to "Dearest Folkses," 4 April 1860, MHS.

16. AF to Sarah May Adams, 14 May 1860, MHS.

17. Ibid.

CHAPTER 3

1. Willa Cather, *Not Under Forty* (New York: Knopf, 1936), 58.

2. Fields's large memorandum and account book in the Fields Collection at the Huntington Library includes lists of disbursements between 1864 and 1867 and from 1877 to 1881, in addition to such other entries as "tickets wanted for Dickens readings," lists of books in preparation, on hand, and under consideration for Ticknor and Fields's blue and gold series, and tables of contents for issues of the *Atlantic*.

3. *Letters of Ellen Tucker Emerson*, ed. Edith E. W. Gregg, 2 vols. (Kent, Ohio: Kent State University Press, 1982), 1:659. Ellen's letter to her aunt Edith is dated 25 April 1872. According to a note on a photograph of the Charles Street library inherited by Annie's grandniece Nancy Bole, the eight Duke of Ormond chairs—two with arms—were purchased for the Fieldses by Dickens at an auction of the Duke's estate. At some point, one was given to Isabella Stewart Gardner, who displayed it in the music room of Fenway Court.

4. Charlotte Cushman and Christine Nilsson appear in the chapter entitled "Stage Folk and Others," and Sarah Orne Jewett has a chapter of her own.

5. [Annie Fields,] *James T. Fields: Biographical Notes and Personal Sketches* (Boston: Houghton Mifflin, 1881), 83. According to Caroline Ticknor, *Hawthorne and His Publisher* (Boston: Houghton Mifflin, 1913), 289–90, Fields opposed the purchase. See also Frank Luther Mott, *History of American Magazines, 1850–1865* (Cambridge: Harvard University Press, 1957), 502–3.

6. These phrases come from the chapter on the *Atlantic Monthly* in *A Catalogue of Authors Whose Works are Published by Houghton, Mifflin and Company. Prefaced by a Sketch of the Firm, and Followed by Lists of the Several Libraries, Series, and Periodicals. With Some Account of the Origin and Character of These Literary Enterprises* (Cambridge, Mass.: Riverside Press, 1901).

7. The practice of anonymity continued during the sixties, though some poems and articles were signed or pseudonymous; subsequently, most of them were signed. Most of the anonymous and

pseudonymous authors (including Annie Fields) were identified in the first general index (published in 1877) and in the second (published in 1889).

8. Thomas Starr King to JTF, 26 June 1863, HL. King, an abolitionist minister who had left Boston for San Francisco, would die the following year.

9. RHD [to JTF and AF], 20 August 1862, HL.

10. JGW to AF, [?] September 1867, HL; JGW to AF, [mid-sixties,] Ho; JGW to JTF and AF, November 1863, HL; and HBS to JTF, 19 December 1865, HL.

11. Anna Waterston to AF, 29 October 1862, HBS to AF, 26 July 1864, and Julia Ward Howe to AF, 3 March [1862], HL; and LWJ to AF, 24 and 26 February [1864], Laura Winthrop Johnson Papers, NYPL.

12. The complainant was probably the distinguished historian John Gorham Palfrey, whose "The New England Revolution of the Seventeenth Century" appeared in the March 1864 *Atlantic*.

13. With characteristic humility, Diaz had previously urged Fields to "have no hesitation in altering or amending anything of *mine*, for I am a novice in writing, and know nothing of rules, or fitness." Abby Morton Diaz to AF, 15 March [1869?], and Diaz to JTF and W. D. Ticknor, [c. 1863,] HL.

14. Clark's two-part "Hospital Memories" appeared in August and September 1867.

15. Louisa May Alcott to AF, 24 June [1863], HL; in *The Selected Letters of Louisa May Alcott*, ed. Joel Myerson, Daniel Shealy, and Madeleine B. Stern (Boston: Little, Brown, 1987), 84. Alcott modestly yet wittily added, "If my little ship is to be launched in the Atlantic I must attend to her build & rigging & see that she does not founder for want of proper ballast as an honorable flag is flying at the mast head." But she never considered poetry her forte, and she told Cousin Annie that "the lines were never meant to go beyond my scrap book"; they had "jingled" into her brain one night when she was on nursing duty in Washington and "were forgotten till father found them among my papers." Annie Fields and Louisa May Alcott were related through their mothers, both members of the May family. Louisa lived with the Fieldses from January to April 1862, while running a kindergarten nearby. As she told her friend Alfred Whitman, "I visited about at J. T. Fields the great publishers where I saw Mrs. Stowe, Fanny Kemble, Holmes, Longfellow, & all the fine folks besides living in style in a very smart house with very clever people who have filled it with books, pictures, statues & beautiful things picked up in their travels." Louisa May Alcott to Alfred Whitman, 6 April [1862], *Letters*, 144.

16. JGW to AF, 18 August 1867, HL.

17. HBS to JTF, 3 June 1864, HL. The "cause" was promoting American manufactured goods to help the wartime economy.

18. David Atwood Wasson to JTF, 20 March 1865, HL. Wasson is one of fourteen authors who rates a chapter to himself in James C. Austin's *Fields of the Atlantic Monthly* (San Marino, Calif.: Huntington Library, 1953), 249–65. "Wilhelm Meister's Apprenticeship," the Unitarian minister's most comprehensive work of criticism, appeared in the *Atlantic* in September and October 1865.

19. Anna Waterston to AF, 29 October 1862 and 13 June 1863, HL. The Austen essay appeared in March 1863, and Waterston subsequently prepared three other essays for the *Atlantic*. Anna Cabot Lowell Quincy Waterston (1812–99), the fourth daughter of President Josiah Quincy of Harvard, and the wife of the esteemed minister Robert Waterston, had long been part of Annie's extended network of friendship. In 1860, after the death of her seventeen-year-old daughter Ruthven—whom Annie had befriended in Italy—Mrs. Waterston sent Annie a copy of the memoir her husband had written. Among the women's many other connections, they belonged to the same social club; they were both poets; and Mrs. Waterston's publications included a biography of Adelaide Phillips, the famous singer who was one of Annie's friends. The women's friendship evidently peaked around 1863, but they continued to exchange visits, news, and gifts. Responding to Annie's gift of *Persephone* in 1878, for example, Mrs. Waterston praised its "taste, grace, & beauty," and two years later she thanked Annie for *Under the Olive*, an "honorably finished" proof of Annie's "poetic gift." Anna Waterston to AF, 3 January 1878 and 23 November 1880, HL.

20. Anna Waterston to AF, 12 June 1863, HL. Whether or not Annie shared that opinion, several of Chesebro's stories appeared in the *Atlantic* during the next few years.

21. Marjorie Drake Ross, *The Book of Boston: The Victorian Period, 1837–1901* (New York: Hastings

House, 1964), 65. The organ built by the firm of Walcker in Ludwigsburg at a cost of $60,000 was installed in an elaborately carved case designed by Hammatt Billings.

22. To thank Cushman for the benefit performances she gave between 12 September and 22 October, a group of her admirers assembled a thick album containing "about fifty paintings in oil and water colors, which were contributed by some of the leading artists of New York, Boston, and Philadelphia . . . those cities in which she had acted for the cause." *Charlotte Cushman: Her Letters and Memories of her Life,* ed. Emma Stebbins (Boston: Houghton Osgood, 1878), 185–88. All Stebbins said about the inauguration of the great organ was that Cushman looked beautiful and "the organ and everything else seemed small beside her, as she stood on the platform, so simple and so grand in her black silk dress, which she was so fond of."

23. JGW to AF, 8 November 1863, HL.

24. SH to AF, 8 November 1863, BPL. Sophia's strong-minded sister Elizabeth Peabody also praised Annie's ode and said she had read it aloud to herself several times. Elizabeth Palmer Peabody to AF, 24 December 1863, BPL.

25. Edward Everett Hale to AF, 18 December 1863, HL.

26. Anna Waterston to AF, [14? November 1863,] HL. The first stanza of Mrs. Waterston's eulogy of Shaw is carved on the base of Saint-Gaudens's bas relief in Boston which depicts the colonel leading his soldiers into battle.

27. [Julia Ward Howe,] "How to Regard the Great Organ," *Commonwealth,* 13 November 1863. Howe's husband Samuel Gridley Howe edited the abolitionist paper and supervised "the political department." Julia Ward Howe, *Reminiscences 1819–1899* (Boston: Houghton Mifflin, 1899), 252–53.

28. JTF to SH, 17 November 1863, Berg Collection, NYPL.

29. Annie later crossed out the entire entry.

30. JGW to JTF, 25 December 1863, HL.

31. Samuel Gridley Howe, who had returned to America in 1831 after fighting for Greek independence, subsequently established the Perkins Institute for the Blind in Boston.

32. Whittier, Holmes, and Lowell were among Howe's advisers. I am grateful to Joel Myerson for a copy of *The Boatswain's Whistle.*

33. Julia Ward Howe to AF, 9 January 1870, HL.

34. Howe, *Reminiscences,* 372. Though Annie never said so explicitly, she also shared Howe's belief that woman is "a free agent, fully sharing with man every human right and every responsibility." After the *Reminiscences* appeared, Annie Fields paid tribute to Julia Ward Howe in a speech now preserved at the Huntington Library (though without any indication of its date or occasion).

35. Anna Waterston to AF, [7 December?] and 10 December 1863, HL.

36. JGW to AF, 2 January 1864, and Elizabeth Whittier to AF, 13 March 1864, HL. After Elizabeth died a few months later, Whittier told Annie, "We were friends before thee knew my dear Sister, but now all who loved her and who loved in turn are nearer and dearer to me." JGW to AF, 14 September 1864, in *The Letters of John Greenleaf Whittier,* ed. John B. Pickard, 3 vols. (Cambridge: Harvard University Press, 1975), 3:78.

37. SH to AF, 2 and 25 January 1864, BPL.

38. Harold Francis Pfister, *Facing the Light: Historic American Portrait Daguerreotypes* (Washington, D.C.: Smithsonian Institution Press, 1978), 160–61. Mark DeWolfe Howe reproduced Rowse's portrait of Annie Fields in *Memories of a Hostess,* but for his frontispiece he used a copy of a Southworth and Howes daguerreotype that he identified simply as "From an early photograph." It is copied from one of three similar "sixth plates" produced at the same sitting. When Longfellow thanked Fields for his wife's "charming likeness" in September 1862, he was presumably referring to one such copy (HWL to JTF, 30 September 1862, HL). But the sitting might well have occurred in 1861, the year the partnership of Southworth and Howes ended. Pfister reproduces all three—a full-page copy of one and small copies of the other two. As he says of the first, reproduced from a copy at the Metropolitan Museum of Art, "the well-known beauty of Mrs. Fields and the masterful artistry of the Southworth and Howes studio produced one of the loveliest daguerreotype portraits ever made." This book includes the same image. The one DeWolfe Howe used is identified as a 1941 gift of Boylston Beal (Annie's nephew, who presumably inherited it). Fields's satisfaction with Rowse's work led him

to commission a posthumous crayon portrait of Hawthorne based on a photograph, and Fields's subsequent memoir of Hawthorne is framed by glances at that "exquisite" and "truthful" portrait (adjectives he might well have used for Rowse's portrait of his wife). Predictably, Sophia admired Rowse's portrait of her husband yet found fault with some of the details.

39. Ednah D. Cheney, "The Women of Boston," in *The Memorial History of Boston*, ed. Justin Winsor, 4 vols. (Boston: Ticknor and Company, 1881) 4:331–32.

Chapter 4

1. See Debra Gold Hansen, *Strained Sisterhood: Gender and Class in the Boston Female Anti-Slavery Society* (Amherst: University of Massachusetts Press, 1993), esp. 4 and 106; and Lori D. Ginzberg, *Women and the Work of Benevolence: Morality, Politics, and Class in the Nineteenth-Century United States* (New Haven: Yale University Press, 1990), esp. 63–65.

2. A typed copy of these extracts from Annie Fields's diary entries of 2 March and 4 November 1867 is at the Houghton Library.

3. AF to LWJ, 5 January 1867, HL. "A Soldier's Mother" is in Annie Fields, *The Singing Shepherd* (Boston: Houghton Mifflin, 1895), 19.

4. Anna Waterston to AF, 18 November 1863, and AF to LWJ, 27 December 1866, HL.

5. Pioneering studies of the ideology and actualities of women's lives during this period include Nancy Cott, *The Bonds of Womanhood: Woman's Sphere in New England, 1780–1835* (New Haven: Yale University Press, 1977); Carl N. Degler, *At Odds: Women and the Family in America from the Revolution to the Present* (New York: Oxford University Press, 1980); Karen J. Blair, *The Clubwoman as Feminist: True Womanhood Redefined, 1868–1911* (New York: Holmes and Meier, 1980); Dolores Hayden, *The Grand Domestic Revolution: A History of Feminist Designs for American Homes, Neighborhoods, and Cities* (Boston: MIT Press 1981); and Susan Phinney Conrad, *Perish the Thought: Intellectual Women in Romantic America, 1830–1860* (New York: Oxford University Press, 1976).

6. Zabdiel Boylston Adams to Sarah May Adams, 15 December 1861, Countway Library, Harvard Medical School.

7. Manuscripts of "Alice of the Hills" and "The Lady Ursula" are at the Huntington Library; and the copy of "In the Palace, Florence 1530" that Annie made for Sophia Hawthorne is in the Berg Collection of the New York Public Library.

8. What James C. Austin (*Fields of the Atlantic Monthly* [San Marino, Calif.: Huntington Library, 1953], 176, says of *Atlantic* poetry is true of Annie Fields's. It is marked by "austere ethics," "passion for beauty," "belief in progress," and "humaneness," and its major subjects included war, death, and illustration of a moral principle.

9. In her provocative and perceptive discussion of this poem in "Not Just Filler and Not Just Sentimental: Women's Poetry in American Victorian Periodicals, 1860–1900" (*Periodical Literature in Nineteenth-Century America*, ed. Kenneth M. Price and Susan Belasco Smith [Charlottesville: University Press of Virginia, 1995], 202–19), Paula Bennett says it "may at first seem . . . unprepossessing," but its economy "astonishes," it is "striking" in its "specificity," and (especially by comparison to a "fervently patriotic" poem by Oliver Wendell Holmes in the same issue of the *Atlantic*) it can be seen as a powerfully "ironic, antiheroic war poem." Using "one of nature's most despised forms, roadside weeds," Annie anticipated William Carlos Williams's "Spring and All." Paula Bennett includes two poems by Annie Fields in her *Nineteenth-Century American Women Poets: An Anthology* (Malden, Mass: Blackwell, 1998),— "The Wild Endive" and "Comatas."

10. LWJ to AF, 10 June 1866, Laura Winthrop Johnson Papers, NYPL.

11. SH to AF, 1 October 1866, BPL.

Chapter 5

1. In his *Memories of a Hostess* (Boston: Atlantic Monthly Press, 1922), Mark DeWolfe Howe copied long excerpts about Hawthorne from Annie's journal, and James T. Fields had already incorporated some of them in his own memoir of Hawthorne; but they were both selective, neither drew on Annie's scrapbooks, and they made little use of her correspondence.

2. Scrapbook of "Fragrant Memories," HL. The July 1862 entry reverently concludes, "White lilies

were in bloom in the garden but better, those eternal white lilies of love which never fade out of the bosom of this family." The entry of 28 July 1863 accompanies a clover that Annie had found on her dressing table when she arrived, a token of her "loving reception from the Hawthornes."

3. Rose Hawthorne Lathrop, *Memories of Hawthorne* (Boston: Riverside, 1897), 424. "Heart's-Ease" was a nickname used by the Hawthornes and several of the Fieldses' other close friends.

4. She later crossed out the phrase "and as true" and the word "either." Fields would place those pages of the "Dolliver Romance" on Hawthorne's coffin, but then retrieve them for publication in the July 1864 *Atlantic*.

5. *Dealings with the Dead,* a two-volume collection of a hundred sixty essays by Lucius M. Sargent (identified only as "A Sexton of the Old School") was published by Ticknor and Fields in conjunction with Dutton and Wentworth in 1856. It ends with a dedication titled "Dust to Dust," preceded by the explanation that it seemed "meet and right, that the corpse should go before":

> READER—if you can lay your hand upon your heart, and honestly say, that you have read these pages, or any considerable portion of them, with pleasure—that they have afforded you instruction, or amusement—I dedicate this volume—with your permission, of course—most respectfully, to you; having conceived the most exalted opinion of your taste and judgment.

Presumably Hawthorne regarded Sargent's wry attitude toward his reader as a variant of his own.

6. Other members of the Saturday Club (which met at the Parker House on the last Saturday of each month) included Emerson, Longfellow, Lowell, and Fields (whom Hawthorne had proposed for membership in June 1862).

7. Annie Fields, *Nathaniel Hawthorne* (Boston: Small and Maynard, 1899), 124.

8. AF to LWJ, [April 1864,] HL.

9. AF to LWJ, [24 May 1864,] HL. Lucy Larcom responded to Annie's account of the funeral by saying other friends had told her "how sad and how beautiful it was" and also reported that his sister Elizabeth "does not yet realize it as death. . . . It seems to her impossible." LL to AF, 9 June 1864, Daniel Dulaney Addison Papers, MHS.

10. This item is reproduced by permission of the Huntington Library, San Marino, California. The poem is written in ink in a notebook containing manuscript poems dated between 1864 and 1873, preserved in Box 2 of the Fields Collection at the Huntington Library. Another notebook in the same box contains poems written between 1857 and 1864, among them a poem of five six-line stanzas titled "Loss and Gain" which is dated 16 June 1864, "After Hawthorne's death." Struggling to cope with "unforgotten pain," the speaker says, "We count our loss and still the river flows / And still we drink the fragrance of the rose," then receives spiritual consolation from "the light of Love whose gleam is permanent."

11. T. W. Higginson to AF, 24 June 1888, and Moncure Conway to AF, 14 December 1889, HL.

12. Scudder to AF, 21 August 1900, Ho. The request seems curious because her husband had restored the dropped passages about Lincoln in his "Hawthorne" (published in the *Atlantic* in 1871 and in *Yesterdays with Authors* a year later), and those same passages appear in the 1883 Riverside Edition of Hawthorne. If Scudder was pursuing a hunch that the original manuscript differed, he was right. But that manuscript (which Fields had long since given to his friend Robert Collyer) contains no crucial differences: a slightly different footnote explaining the Lincoln omission, an additional footnote, and a few phrases sympathetic to the southerners. The entirety is published in *Miscellaneous Prose and Verse,* vol. 23 of *The Centenary Edition of the Works of Nathaniel Hawthorne* (Columbus: Ohio State University Press, 1994), 403–42. Other inquiries about Hawthorne were addressed to Annie at least as late as 1908, when the Harvard professor Barrett Wendell asked if Hawthorne might have written a story about old time Boston that he had recently read. Though it was possible, she said, "Miss Jewett and I feel the only way to tell is through style." AF to Barrett Wendell, 24 July 1908, Ho.

13. Although Howe asked her to prepare a preface, Annie replied that she thought it unnecessary, then followed up with a postcard saying "My taste revolts at the idea of such a preface! I think the little book ought to be taken as it is or left alone." The next day she agreed to accept Small and Maynard's offer of a 10 percent royalty only because Howe had asked her to, setting 15 percent as her price in the future. AF to MDH, 29 and 30 August 1899, Ho.

14. Annie Fields's nineteen-page manuscript is in the James T. Fields Collection, Box 1 (2) at the Huntington Library. Quotations are reproduced by permission of the Huntington Library, San Marino, California.

CHAPTER 6

1. For further information about Dickens's American tour, see George Curry, "Charles Dickens and Annie Fields," *Huntington Library Quarterly* 51 (Winter 1988); George Dolby, *Dickens as I Knew Him: The Story of the Reading Tours in Great Britain and America (1866–1876)* (London: Fisher Unwin, 1885); Edward F. Payne, *Dickens Days in Boston: A Record of Daily Events* (Boston: Houghton Mifflin, 1927); Edgar Johnson, *Charles Dickens, His Tragedy and His Triumph,* vol. 2 (New York: Simon and Schuster, 1952); and Max Adrian, *Georgina Hogarth and the Dickens Circle* (New York: Oxford University Press, 1957).

2. James T. Fields, *Yesterdays With Authors* (Boston: Osgood, 1872), 166. The Parker House was and still is a famous Boston hotel.

3. Dolby, 148–50. Although tickets were not cheap at two dollars for general admission and four dollars for reserved seats, the demand was so great that speculators could later get twenty-six dollars apiece.

4. AF to HWL, 20 November 1867, and HBS to JTF, 21 November [1867], HL.

5. The portrait remained in the Charles Street library until Annie Fields's death, and was then bequeathed to the Boston Museum of Fine Arts as part of the James T. Fields collection.

6. Dolby, 177.

7. HWL to Charles Sumner, 8 December 1867, *The Letters of Henry Wadsworth Longfellow,* ed. Andrew Hilen, 6 vols. (Boston: Harvard University Press, 1967–82), 5: 191.

8. Urging her friend Laura Johnson to come in from Staten Island to hear Dickens, Annie assured her "there is nothing like it and nobody like him." AF to LWJ, 10 December 1867, HL.

9. Stephanie Seacord, *A Pocket History of the Omni Parker House* (Boston: Omni Parker House, 1993) gets the facts comically wrong: "At Christmas 1858, [Dickens] wrote to his sister-in-law about Mrs. Fields, the housekeeper, who with her staff had decorated his rooms with moss and holly" (6).

10. CD to Georgina Hogarth, 22 December 1867; quoted by Curry, 12.

11. James Parton's article on the recently developed sewing machine had appeared in the May 1867 *Atlantic,* and sewing machines were heavily advertised in the magazine.

12. CD to JTF, 3 February 1868, HL.

13. HWL to JTF, 19 February 1868.

14. See Curry, 50, and Adrian, 114.

15. Payne, 227.

16. AF to Mrs. Andrew White, 4 March 1868, Cornell University Libraries.

17. Lowell was so grateful for Fields's offer to take Mabel along that he volunteered to take on "a kind of militia-generalship of the A.M." in his absence. James Russell Lowell to JTF, 19 January 1869, HL.

18. CD to JTF, 15 February 1869, HL.

19. AF to Louisa Beal, 15 May 1869, Annie Fields Papers, MHS.

20. Ibid.

21. Annie Fields, "George Eliot," *Century* 58 (July 1899): 442–46.

22. Annie Fields, *Authors and Friends* (Boston: Houghton Mifflin, 1896), 354.

23. After Taylor's visit a few months before, he sent the poet Edmund Stedman a letter about it, and Stedman showed it to another friend, who sent it to a newspaper. Tennyson felt his hospitality had been betrayed. When Fields was preparing a lecture on Tennyson in 1872, the poet agreed to some mention of his readings "& that these were grateful to yourself & Mrs. Fields," trusting that Fields would "respect the sanctity of home." See James C. Austin, *Fields of the Atlantic Monthly* (San Marino, Calif.: Huntington Library, 1953), 398–99.

24. [Annie Fields,] *James T. Fields: Biographical Notes and Personal Sketches* (Boston: Houghton Mifflin, 1881), 174–75. Cameron's sepia photograph of James T. Fields is one of the best and best-known of his portraits. The portrait she took of Mabel Lowell that same day is reproduced in Mark DeWolfe Howe's *New Letters of James Russell Lowell* (New York: Harper, 1932), 138.

25. The women's relationship centered on their devotion to Dickens and resulted in an increasingly intimate if sporadic correspondence. They exchanged letters on Dickens's birthday, on the anniversary of his death, and at Christmas, and Annie visited Georgina in 1882 and 1898. As Adrian observes, Georgina cherished the memory of the Fieldses' visits to Gad's Hill as long as she lived (126).

26. JGW to AF, 13 June 1870, HL.

27. Two slightly different manuscripts of the poem are at the Huntington Library.

CHAPTER 7

1. Although Lowell was then still nominally the *Atlantic* editor, it was Fields who accepted the story and offered a hundred dollar advance for a new one. Flattered though she was, Harding declined, saying she might otherwise feel constrained to produce only a hundred dollars' worth. RHD to JTF, 26 January [1861] and 15 March 1861, University of Virginia Library.

2. Nearly a hundred and fifty letters from Rebecca Harding Davis to Mr. and Mrs. James T. Fields are in the Richard Harding Davis Collection (#6109), Clifton Waller Barrett Library, The Albert H. Small Special Collections Library, at the University of Virginia Library, but evidently she did not preserve their letters to her. In her letter to Fields of 11 April 1861, Harding said his "candor and kindness" had emboldened her to question him closely. RHD to JTF, 11 April [1861], University of Virginia; RHD to JTF, 10 May [1861], HL; and RHD to AF, 20 May [1861], University of Virginia.

3. RHD to AF, 18 June [1861], and RHD to JTF, 30 July and 9 and 17 August [1861], University of Virginia.

4. In the afterword to her edition of *Margret Howth* (New York: Feminist Press, 1990), Jean Fagan Yellin contends that "the leading member of the white male literary establishment demanded that a nineteenth-century writer 'feminize' her text"; and in *Rebecca Harding Davis and American Realism* (Philadelphia: University of Pennsylvania Press, 1991), 69, Sharon M. Harris compares Fields to Rebecca's Dr. Knowles, who wielded "an almost demonic 'kingly power'" over Margret." Yet Fields's complaint about "gloom" was not a demand, and the author said she had originally intended a sunshiny ending. In *Parlor Radical* (Pittsburgh: University of Pittsburgh Press, 1996), 58, Jean Pfaelzer seems right on the mark when she says that "the tension between realism and sentiment in the novel marks Davis's definition of social responsibility as active participation in a sympathetic community."

5. RHD to AF, [7 May 1862], 15 May [1862], and 10 January [1863], University of Virginia.

6. Sophia Hawthorne's notes on the first few days of Harding's Boston visit and her subsequent stay in Concord are in her 1862 pocket diary (Morgan Library), published as "With Hawthorne in Wartime Concord: Sophia Hawthorne's 1862 Diary," ed. Thomas Woodson et al., *Studies in the American Renaissance 1988* (Charlottesville: University Press of Virginia), 281–359, esp. 303–4.

7. Rebecca Harding Davis, *Bits of Gossip* (Boston: Houghton Mifflin, 1904), 30–64, and RHD to AF, 27 June [1864], University of Virginia Library. As Harding recalled in *Bits of Gossip*, she had once spent a whole day in a tree devouring an unsigned collection of "moral tales," unaware of the author's name until she encountered a volume of *Twice-told Tales* early in 1862. She wrote Hawthorne saying so shortly before his trip to Washington, and he promised to pay a visit that Confederate activity in the area made impossible. In Harding's account of her two days in Concord (which implies that she stayed much longer), she sarcastically sketched Alcott as a would-be seer who chanted "paeans to the war" while the real seer Emerson listened "with profound submissive attention" and "Hawthorne's sagacious eyes watch[ed] us, full of mockery." The Fieldses sent the Davises a portrait of Emerson and a seven-volume set of his works as a wedding gift, unaware of Rebecca's distaste for the seer's "blanched wife and her ghastly eyes" and his "unhomelike library." But she would always revere Hawthorne, and she regarded his death as "a people's loss." RHD to AF, 8 March [1863] and 27 June [1864], University of Virginia. Although Sophia later told Annie that she and her husband disliked the flabby style and narrative "squalor" of "the gifted Rebecca," Annie diplomatically ignored those remarks.

8. RHD [to AF and JTF], 21 August 1862, HL. Elizabeth Peabody had sent Rebecca a packet of letters from Dr. and Mrs. William Ellery Channing as appropriate material for a story, but Rebecca told Annie how vexed she felt at such indecorous violation of the Channings' privacy, urging her to tell no one about it.

9. RHD to AF, 25 October 1862, University of Virginia.

10. RHD to AF, 10 January [1863] and "Monday evening" [1863], University of Virginia. Tillie Olsen quotes liberally from Rebecca Harding Davis's letters to "dear *dear* Annie" in her "Biographical Interpretation" in *Life in the Iron Mills* (Old Westbury, N.Y.: Feminist Press, 1972), 69–174, and rightly remarks that that Rebecca never had a more supportive literary friendship. Gerald Langford in *The Rebecca Harding Davis Years* (New York: Holt, Rinehart, 1961), Helen Woodword Sheaffer in "Rebecca Harding Davis: Pioneer Realist" (Diss., University of Pennsylvania, 1947), Sharon Harris, and Jean Pfaelzer also draw heavily on the women's correspondence, though without using Annie's journals and with only an incidental interest in the women's friendship.

11. Carroll Smith-Rosenberg, "The Female World of Love and Ritual: Relations between Women in Nineteenth-Century America," *Signs* 1 (Autumn 1975): 22. The poem dated 3 March 1863 is in the scrapbook called "Fragrant Memories" and a second copy is in an early manuscript album at the Huntington Library.

12. RHD to AF [November 1863], University of Virginia.

13. RHD to AF, "Wednesday" [April 1863], University of Virginia.

14. RHD to AF, 6 May and 3 June [1863], University of Virginia.

15. "Monday," University of Virginia. The doctor who forbade her to read or write was S. Weir Mitchell, who imposed the same proscriptions on other women writers including Charlotte Perkins Gilman and Edith Wharton. Rebecca's later confidences included the news that her abolitionist husband had decided to avoid army service by paying $300 for a substitute.

16. RHD to JTF, 26 November [1866], University of Virginia. The letter began by apologizing for the length of her "Christmas story" "George Bedellion's Knight," which Fields would serialize in February and March 1867. Fields would accept three more of her submissions and several of her husband's essays; Clarke Davis's "A Modern Lettre de Cachet" would appear in the May 1868 *Atlantic*. Meanwhile, Rebecca's work also appeared in other periodicals including *Galaxy* and *Lippincott's* as well as *Peterson's*.

17. RHD to AF, 22 December [1870], [1871], and [1873], University of Virginia.

18. After Fields lectured on "Cheerfulness" in Philadelphia in May 1872, Rebecca told Annie she was glad to see him for his own sake and "to bring you nearer," and said he had often been quoted in sermons and editorials. When Fields was again lecturing in Philadelphia in November 1874, he told Annie he had called on Rebecca and reported that Clarke Davis was "devoted to me & my lectures." RHD to AF, 3 May [1872], University of Virginia, and JTF to AF, "Friday morning" [November 1874], HL.

19. Fields had offered the story to Dickens at Rebecca's suggestion. See James C. Austin, *Fields of the Atlantic Monthly* (San Marino, Calif.: Huntington Library, 1953), 380. After Dickens's death, both of the Davises warmly praised James T. Fields's "noble tribute" to him in the *Atlantic*, without even suspecting that Annie had a large hand in it. RHD to AF, 19 July [1870], University of Virginia.

20. RHD to AF, 21 April [1863], University of Virginia. As she also said, her husband was glad that her critical allusion to "your demigod" General Butler was deleted.

21. Harriet Prescott Spofford, "Biographical Sketch," in *Gail Hamilton's Life in Letters*, ed. Augusta Dodge, 2 vols. (Boston: Lee and Shepard, 1901), 1:ix–xiv. Although the correspondence between Annie and Mary has disappeared, Annie made similar pronouncements in her journals and in a letter to Laura Johnson.

22. Whittier later told Mary, "I want to tell thee how much I like thy article upon the painter Blake. . . . The man was a marvel." JGW to Mary Dodge, [April 1864,] in *The Letters of John Greenleaf Whittier*, ed. John B. Pickard, 3 vols. (Cambridge: Harvard University Press, 1975), 3:67. In "Annie Adams Fields: Female Voice in a Male Chorus" (Diss., Georgia State University, 1996), 157, Carol L. Nigro assumes without proof that Fields asked his wife to write the review and then "withdrew her article to make space for an article by a woman, Annie's friend Gail Hamilton." Still more untenable are Nigro's central assertions that for Annie as a writer, the disadvantages of being married to James T. Fields outweighed the advantages, and that she could not be "too visible as a writer or she would present competition for [his] other Atlantic contributors and Ticknor and Fields writers" (152–55).

23. Mary's letter of 16 February 1863 to her sister Augusta is in *Gail Hamilton's Life*, 1:338.

24. AF to LWJ, 16 April 1867, HL.

25. As the arbiters had suggested, Fields paid the difference between the royalties Gail Hamilton had received and the 10 percent he had paid many other Ticknor and Fields writers. In 1862, Fields had offered to pay fifteen cents a volume for *Country Living and Country Thinking,* which then sold for $1.50, making for a 10 percent royalty. But he continued to pay fifteen cents a volume after the book's price went up. See Randall Stewart, "'Pestiferous Gail Hamilton,' James T. Fields, and the Hawthornes," *New England Quarterly* 17 (1944): 418–22, and Austin, 312–13.

26. JGW to JTF, [1870,] HL. In *A Battle of the Books* (Cambridge: Riverside, 1870), 260, Gail Hamilton had self-defensively declared, "If, after two years of clapper-clawing among a quartette of cats, a mouse is still unskilled in feline ways, in what state of helplessness must be those unadventurous little things who have never left their holes?"

27. JGW to Gail Hamilton, 29 May 1865, in Pickard 3:92. Mary's break with the Fieldses did not lead her to break with any of their friends.

CHAPTER 8

1. AF to Sarah Adams, 8 July 1859, Annie Fields Papers, MHS, written after spending an afternoon with the "pure and lovely" sixteen-year-old Una.

2. Annie Fields, *Life and Letters of Harriet Beecher Stowe* (Boston: Houghton Mifflin, 1897), 282.

3. The remark is in Annie Fields's unpublished memoir of Sophia Hawthorne, at the Boston Public Library.

4. Sophia Hawthorne's letters to Annie Fields are quoted from manuscripts in the Rare Books Department at the Boston Public Library, by courtesy of the Trustees. The excerpts above are from letters of 12 May and 4 August, 1861; 21 January, 13 July, and 3 November 1862; 13 June 1863; 24 September 1864; and 25 April 1866. Sophia's pocket diaries for 1861 and 1862 (now at the Morgan Library) list her letters to and from Annie Fields, the Fieldses' visits to the Wayside, and her own visits to Charles Street. The 1862 diary is published in *Studies in the American Renaissance 1988,* ed. Joel Myerson (Charlottesville: University Press of Virginia, 1988), 281–359. See also Edwin Haviland Miller, "A Calendar of the Letters of Sophia Peabody Hawthorne," *Studies in the American Renaissance 1986* (Charlottesville: University Press of Virginia, 1986), 199–282.

5. SH to AF, 24 February 1865 and 2 August 1863, BPL.

6. SH to AF, 16 March 1865, BPL. The women's pleasure in Annie's "beautiful attire" transcends the Victorian readings of costume as indexes of class, fashion-consciousness, sexuality, and morality, as Valerie Steele discusses them in her chapter on Victorian fashion in *Fashion and Eroticism* ([New York: Oxford University Press, 1985], 51–84). But both of the hats Sophia described substantiate Steele's statement that by the 1870s women's hats were charmingly "decorated with feathers, lace, and flowers, and worn titled coquettishly forward or back" (64). Annie's fur-trimmed black velvet sack was presumably more in the regally simple style she usually chose, though she would soon espouse what Steele calls the "neo-feminist" belief that "fashion is bad because it is sexually exploitive and . . . a waste of time" (243).

7. SH to AF, [29 May] and 14 December 1862, BPL.

8. SH to NH, 25 September 1862, Morgan Library. As Rose Hawthorne Lathrop recalled in her *Memories of Hawthorne* (Boston: Riverside, 1897), 423–24, "An oasis bloomed at remote seasons, when we went to visit Mr. and Mrs. Fields in Boston. My mother writes of my reviving, and even becoming radiant, as soon as a visit of this fragrant nature breathed upon me"; and she quoted some of her mother's reports to her father about the pleasures of Charles Street, including a jovial teaparty during which Annie wore "a scarlet coronet that made her look enchanting, and Mr. Fields declared she was Moses in the burning bush."

9. SH to AF, [4 August 1861,] 7 May [1862], and [c. 7 May 1862], BPL. As Sophia noted in her pocket diary on 9 May 1862, the Fieldses came to Concord for Thoreau's funeral: "They came first to see us and then dined and took tea at Mr. Emerson's," and she "went to see Annie at the Emersons."

10. SH to AF, 17 March 1863, BPL.

11. SH to AF, [29 May 1862,] BPL.

12. SH to AF, 14 June [1862], BPL.

13. SH to AF, 20 February 1863, BPL. Una returned with "Louisa Alcott in her arms, as it were," Sophia wrote, without mentioning that Bronson Alcott was on the same train.

14. Soon afterward, Annie sent Louisa a few suggestions for change which resulted in a revision of the final couplet—from "Spring came to us in guise forlorn / The Genius of the wood is gone" to "Spring mourns as for untimely frost, / The genius of the wood is lost." Sophia regretted losing the first of those lines and wished Louisa had simply improved the second, yet dared not say so because "She is far too petardy." SH to AF, 7 July [1863], BPL.

15. SH to AF, 11 April 1862, BPL.

16. SH to JTF, 13 July 1862, BPL.

17. SH to AF, 29 July 1863, BPL.

18. SH to AF, [July] and 11 October [1863], BPL.

19. SH to AF, 29 November 1863 and [c. 6 December 1863] BPL.

20. SH to AF, 31 March and 11, 13, and 18 April [1864], BPL.

21. SH to AF, [29 April 1864] and 5 May 1864, BPL.

22. SH to AF, 20 May [1864], BPL.

23. SH to AF, 25 May [1864], BPL.

24. SH to AF, 19 January and 26 May 1865 and 28 May 1866, BPL.

25. SH to AF [June 1864], BPL.

26. SH to AF, 3 November 1862 and 3 May 1863, BPL. Sophia would later tell Annie about her many letters and visits from "Miss Dodge."

27. SH to AF, 25 April and 1 October 1866, BPL.

28. SH to AF, 8 November 1863 and [October 1864], and 25 April 1866, BPL.

29. SH to AF, 1 October 1866, BPL.

30. SH to AF, 7 October and 24 November 1866, BPL.

31. SH to AF, 16 October 1867, BPL.

32. SH to AF, [July 1864] and 2 August 1864, BPL.

33. SH to JTF, 3 June 1864, private collection of Mrs. Nancy Adams Bole.

34. SH to AF, 9, 16, and 30 March 1865, BPL. The owners of the Old Manse had given the chair to their daughter, Sophia Ripley, when she married.

35. SH to AF, 16 October and 4 December 1867, BPL.

36. SH to AF, 24 May 1868, BPL.

37. JTF to NH, 12 July 1862, HL.

38. Though Annie wanted to buy the vases, Sophia had already promised them to their mutual friend Mrs. Mary Hemenway.

39. [Annie Fields,] *James T. Fields: Biographical Notes and Personal Sketches* (Boston: Houghton Mifflin, 1881), 91.

40. The Scrapbook is at the Huntington Library.

41. The single sheet—with ink corrections and the date and place in pencil—is at the Huntington Library. A letter to Rose dated 15 August 1873 is less conflicted. Inviting her to make an overnight visit to Manchester with her husband George Lathrop, Annie said she did not know if it would be "a pleasure or a pain for you to see my handwriting after so long a time, but I feel it would be *my* fault not to write to you now when I remember your new life and your nearness and dearness to us." I am grateful to Sister Mary Joseph, O.P., for sending me a copy of this letter, the only one from Annie Fields in the archives of the Rosary Hill Home which Rose founded in Hawthorne, New York, and grateful to Patricia Valenti for informing me of its existence.

42. The thirty-one-page manuscript of Annie's memoir, a pastiche of clippings from Sophia's letters connected by an introduction and bridging commentaries, is at the Boston Public Library. It was published (though not in a reliable transcription) as "Letters of Mrs. Hawthorne to Mrs. Fields," ed. Ellen M. Oldham, *Boston Public Library Quarterly* 9 (July 1957): 143–53. Although the manuscript is undated, the fact that Annie showed it to Sarah Orne Jewett proves it was compiled well after their intimacy began. "Every word you say about the S.H. paper is true," Annie ruefully replied to her response, "but I wish you had liked it, or rather that it had been worth liking a little just a little better. But I am sure it needs quiet thought and the kind of work I can perhaps do at Manchester and I was

in a 'driving hurry' to get the material together for that I knew I could not get in the country—that you think I am on the way to something more is a great deal" (AF to SOJ, n.d., Ho).

CHAPTER 9

1. The letter and the poem dated 4 April 1861 are in the Daniel Dulany Addison Collection at the Massachusetts Historical Society (as are all letters to and from Larcom cited as MHS), and appear in Daniel Dulany Addison, *Lucy Larcom: Life, Letters, and Diary* (Boston: Houghton Mifflin, 1894), 148–50. For a fuller and more reliable account of Lucy Larcom's relationship with the Fieldses, see Shirley Marchalonis, *The Worlds of Lucy Larcom, 1824–1893* (Athens: University of Georgia Press, 1989).

2. Annie's statement is from her three-and-a-half-page unpublished account of Lucy Larcom's career now at the Houghton Library, easily dated by the statement that *American Life* (1886) was published "last year." Lucy's autobiographical "Among Lowell Mill-Girls" was commissioned for the 1881 *Atlantic*, and her *New England Girlhood* was published by Houghton Mifflin in 1889. Her friendship with Whittier dated back to the mid-forties, when he heard her read one of her poems at a millgirls' club. Whittier unsuccessfully urged Fields to publish a volume of Lucy Larcom's work during the mid-fifties; and when Lucy herself submitted a volume of poems in 1860, Fields refused it on the grounds that his list was "over-loaded." JTF to LL, 10 October 1860, MHS. "The Rose" appeared in the June 1861 *Atlantic*, the last issue Lowell edited. As Shirley Marchalonis observes (139), the ambitious poem that many readers initially attributed to Lowell or Emerson established Larcom as "a true poet and a legitimate part of the literary world."

3. JGW to LL, 27 April 1861.

4. LL to AF, 18 December 1862, MHS. Lucy was then in Connecticut, taking a break from the rigors of teaching but feeling "childishly homesick" for Boston.

5. JGW to LL, 17 June 1863, in *The Letters of John Greenleaf Whittier*, ed. John B. Pickard, 3 vols. (Cambridge: Harvard University Press, 1975), 3:43.

6. LL to JTF, 15 June 1863, MHS. Taken aback by her own whimsy, Lucy was surprised that she could "jest about one of my bitterest losses."

7. LL to AF, 11 September and 12 November 1863, MHS. The poem "was immediately appreciated as a strong statement of true womanly nobility and patriotic feeling" (Marchalonis, 148). Larcom's September letter to Annie enclosing the poem appears in "A Model for Mentors? Lucy Larcom and John Greenleaf Whittier," *Patrons and Protégées: Gender, Friendship, and Writing in Nineteenth-Century America*, ed. Shirley Marchalonis (New Brunswick, N.J.: Rutgers University Press, 1988), 105.

8. LL to AF, 12 November and 4 December 1863, MHS.

9. LL to AF, 22 October and 12 December 1863, MHS; and AF to LL, 3 December 1863, NYPL.

10. Marchalonis assumes she was rejected (151), though Lucy might have declined an offer on the grounds of her own poor health or her widowed sister's desire for companionship or doubts about her fitness for the task.

11. William S. Tryon, *Parnassus Corner: A Life of James T. Fields* (Boston: Houghton Mifflin, 1963), 290, and Marchalonis, 154–56 and 182. Of the other two editors, Gail Hamilton left the magazine after her row with Fields, and John C. Trowbridge was essentially an absentee editor until he became editor-in-chief in the spring of 1870. Lucy remained with the magazine until Osgood sold it at the end of 1873.

12. Whittier wrote an introduction to the volume, which Lucy had dedicated to his sister Elizabeth.

13. LL to AF, 14 May 1864 and 26 May and 21 June 1866, MHS, and 24 December 1871, HL.

14. LL to AF, [November 1863] and 26 February 1864, and LL to JTF, 23 December 1864, MHS. Lucy asked Fields to give the "bauble" to Annie during her Christmas party "when the rest of the children are peeping into their Xmas stockings," humbly called it "'a poor thing but mine own'" and wished "it were a thousand times prettier, for her sake."

15. JGW to LL, 7 February and March 1866, and JGW to Gail Hamilton, 30 June 1866, in Pickard, 3:118–19. Lucy copied out the poem for Annie.

16. LL to AF, 21 June 1866, MHS. Lucy was presumably reading Margaret Fuller's translation of the correspondence between Elizabeth von Arnim ("Bettine") and her poet friend Karoline Günderode,

which became enormously popular among the Boston literati after Elizabeth Peabody published it in 1842. Perhaps Lucy compared herself to the sensitive, introspective, and deeply religious Günderode (1780–1806), whose poems had been likened to Keats's (and who committed suicide after a disappointment in love), and perhaps she saw something of Annie in Bettine (1785–1859), the ardent and intellectually accomplished woman who in 1840 had organized their correspondence into the epistolary narrative titled *Die Günderode.* Whether or not Annie had *Die Günderode* in mind while creating the strong "woman-friendship" in *Asphodel,* Bettine bears comparison to the warm-hearted happily married Alice, and Günderode has a lot in common with the sensitive unmarried Erminia, whose disappointment in love drives her to suicide.

17. LL to AF, 24 September 1866, MHS.

18. AF to LL, 11 February [1867?] and [September 1867?], MHS.

19. LL to AF, 2 May 1868, MHS. "Woman's League" was the original name of the New England Woman's Club.

20. AF to LWJ, 11 January 1872, HL. As further evidence of Lucy Larcom's lifelong concern about women's self-fulfillment, each of the five poems she wrote for the *Atlantic* between 1871 and 1874 concerns a woman who insists upon or sadly surrenders her integrity. See Marchalonis, 181–83. Yet like Annie's, Lucy's hierarchy of writers and thinkers was topheavy with men, as is evident in a letter reporting her pleasure in hearing Emerson read his "noble paper on 'Immortality'" at Professor Thayer's house in Cambridge, and then discussing it with Longfellow (who reported he was including "Hannah Binding Shoes" in his new anthology). LL to AF, December 1865, MHS; in Addison, 178–79.

21. LL to AF, 15 January 1872 and 22 November 1880, HL.

22. LL to AF, 1 September 1863, MHS.

23. LL to AF, 10 November 1871, HL.

24. LL to AF, [1874,] HL.

25. LL to JGW, 6 June 1881, MHS.

26. AF to JGW, 19 September 1883, HL. Annie Fields sent Whittier $500 and contributions from other women friends, telling him not to let Lucy know: she would find out in the next world. Acknowledging Annie's "liberal response" and also thanking "the good ladies who add their contribution," Whittier said $1,100 would produce $100 a year, but ascertaining Lucy's exact age would require skillful diplomacy (a point he later reiterated). JGW to AF, 22 September 1883 and 22 December 1886, HL.

27. AF to JGW, 22 December 1886, HL. Asking Howells to forward a copy to his sister, Annie said "Miss Larcom has brooded over it and has felt the helpfulness of every word herself before she has admitted it into her inner temple." AF to WDH, [December 1886,] HL.

28. The manuscript is at the Houghton Library.

29. Nathaniel Hawthorne, *American Notebooks,* ed. William Charvat et al. (Columbus: Ohio State University Press, 1972), 511–37. Her marriage was the first on the island since the Revolution, Celia told Hawthorne during his 1852 visit, "and her little Karl (now three months old) the first-born child in all those eighty years" (543). See Jane E. Vallier, *Poet on Demand: The Life, Letters, and Works of Celia Thaxter* (Camden, Me.: Down East Books, 1982); Susan Faxon, *A Stern and Lovely Scene: A Visual History of the Isles of Shoals* (Durham: University of New Hampshire Press, 1978); Lyman V. Rutledge, *The Isles of Shoals in Lore and Legend* (Boston: Star Island Corp., 1971); Frank Preston Stearns, *Sketches from Concord and Appledore* (New York: Putnam, 1895); and Celia Thaxter, *Among the Isles of Shoals* (Boston: Osgood, 1873), as well as Annie Fields's memoir of Thaxter and her editions of the *Letters of Celia Thaxter* (Boston: Houghton Mifflin, 1895) and *The Poems of Celia Thaxter* (Boston: Houghton Mifflin, 1896).

30. CT to AF, 1 September 1873, BPL, 22 March 1876, HL, and 11 January 1878, BPL. Celia did not even know the *Atlantic* had her poem until she received Fields's note of acceptance and a check for ten dollars. Presumably submitted by her brother Cedric, to whom Celia had sent a copy in May 1860, the poem had remained in Lowell's files until Fields replaced him.

31. Thomas Wentworth Higginson to AF, 30 January 1895, HL.

32. The seabird metaphor is from a diary entry of 12 October 1863. The description of Celia appears in Annie Fields, *Authors and Friends* (Boston: Houghton Mifflin, 1895), 236.

33. CT to JTF, 23 September 1861, HL. Vallier exaggerates when she says that "James and Annie Fields were virtually to control Celia's literary life" and that she "absorbed many of the literary standards that made her popular" from them (22).

34. Annie entered the statement on the first page of her new scrapbook of "Fragrant Memories," next to a blueberry blossom.

35. CT to AF, September [1862] and 23 October [1862], and CT to JTF, 25 October [1862], HL.

36. As Hawthorne had noted in 1852, the hotel was about 120 feet wide and had a long piazza in front, and "a covered verandah, thirty or forty feet square, so situated that the breeze draws across it, from the sea on one side of the island to the sea on the other" (512). Celia's father later enlarged the dining room and added additional bedrooms, a dance hall, a billiard room, and a bowling alley.

37. In 1877, Osgood issued it as a fifty cent guidebook to the Shoals, and other editions still sell well in New Hampshire bookstores and on excursion boats to the Shoals.

38. Pickard, 3:127 and JGW to AF, 24 July 1872 and 18 July 1875, HL.

39. Whittier had been delayed by illness but eventually kept their "tryst." AF to LWJ, 15 July 1874, HL.

40. AF to LWJ, 15 July 1873, HL. As a "dutiful son" of Portsmouth, James T. Fields had remained there to attend the city's centennial celebration instead of going to Appledore.

41. In a note refusing the concert tickets Annie offered in the winter of 1871 because getting to Boston would be difficult, Celia said she was "charmed to hear of my spouse & Mr. Hunt partaking of your famous toddy the other night— . . . would I had been there!" CT to AF, 5 February 1871, HL.

42. CT to AF, 4 December 1870, HL, and 24 February 1869 and [December?] 1872, BPL. Perhaps out of gratitude for Celia's ministrations when he was recuperating from a serious illness, Levi had "offered advice about the selections and sequence" of her *Poems* (1872).

43. During Annie's next visit to Appledore, she realized that Karl was "full of poetry" but also perceived that his eyes were dull, his wits wandered, and he was wholly undependable. Annie would encourage Karl's later interest in photography by sitting for him (as Sarah also did). She knew relatively little about Celia's other two sons, however, except that Roland became a Harvard professor and himself produced two sons.

44. CT to AF, 20 November 1873, HL.

45. Pickard, 3:261.

46. CT to AF, 22 and 28 April 1873 and 10 October 1877, BPL.

47. CT to AF, 7 February 1872, BPL, and AF to WDH, 11 January 1872, HL.

48. CT to AF, 1 November 1873, 14 March 1876, October 1872, and 5 December 1872, BPL.

49. CT to AF, 1 September 1873 and 19 May 1881.

50. CT to AF, 11 January 1878, BPL.

51. The quotation is from one of Annie's letters to her friend Laura Johnson. AF to LWJ, 6 December 1869, HL.

52. CT to AF, 12 February 1877, BPL. Annie sent Celia crackers, cordials, and other delicacies not readily available on Appledore. Soon another bond between Annie and Celia was mourning their mothers' deaths.

53. CT to AF, [September 1879,] BPL. Celia initially concluded that Hunt's despondency over his estrangement from his wife had driven him to suicide, but later thought he might have fallen accidentally. The Fieldses shared Celia's affection for Hunt, owned several of his drawings and paintings, and were sympathetically aware of his marital problems.

54. CT to AF, 5 January 1873, HL, and 3 October 1872, 21 February 1873, and 7 January 1877, BPL.

55. CT to AF, [March 1881], HL. However Levi might have demonstrated that "genius," he had recently completed a successful series of Browning readings, his first public performances, which perhaps quelled his jealousy of his wife. He would give another series of readings the following year, two years before his death. One of Helen Bell's undated notes to Annie said Levi would read in her parlor on Monday, but also said Annie should not buy a ticket simply out of charity "since I can make up our number easily." Helen Bell to AF "Thursday" [1881 or 1882], HL.

56. CT to AF, 23 and 25 October 1881, "Friday" and 30 October 1881, BPL. In "Love Shall Save Us

All," presumably addressed to Annie, the poem's speaker advises the "Pilgrim" not to let "the dark thy heart appall."

57. CT to AF, 27 December 1881, HL, and 3 January 1882, BPL. Celia's 1872 poem "The Sandpiper," in which the speaker identifies with the bird, immediately became her most popular lyric.

58. The medium Celia consulted in the winter of 1882, Rose Darrah, is presumably the same one that Annie visited twice and Sarah once before their first trip abroad. While they were abroad, Celia's letters repeatedly included messages that she believed James T. Fields had transmitted during seances, and her interest in spiritualism remained intense for the next few years. Annie and Sarah were sufficiently interested to attend a few more of Darrah's seances, including one at Charles Street.

59. CT to AF, 18 May [1882], CT to SOJ, 17 April 1889, and CT to AF, 30 November 1889, BPL. When Annie and Sarah sailed from New York on May 24, Annie's old friend Henry Alden saw them off.

60. *Letters of Celia Thaxter*, 218–19. Torrey responded to a notice Annie placed in *The Critic* by sending some letters Thaxter sent "me—who had never seen her," which expressed her "passion for nature" and thoughts "about the mysteries of human existence." Bradford Torrey to AF, 5 October 1894, HL.

61. In a series of letters to Oscar Laighton between November 1894 and March 1895, now at the Huntington Library, Annie asked him for letters and pictures and for the date of a wreck Celia had mentioned. Rose Lamb, who helped Annie edit the letters, was a Boston painter who had studied with William Morris Hunt. She lived near Annie in Boston and became close to Celia while vacationing on the Shoals. A year after Celia's letters were published, Annie assembled *The Poems of Celia Thaxter* with Rose's assistance, and Sarah wrote the introduction. Perhaps with that book in mind, Annie had pasted dozens of Celia manuscripts into an album, and copied out the one titled "Modjeska," written in March 1878 "in memory of the delightful day" when Otto Dresel played Chopin for the great actress and the Fieldses' other guests—Edward Booth and his wife, Elizabeth Stuart Phelps, Mrs. Dresel, and Celia herself. While preparing the Thaxter books, Annie became so fond of Rose that she gave her a copy of her Stowe book and a picture that Rose "framed and shall hang in Sisters Parlor." As further evidence of the friendship that included Sarah Orne Jewett, although Sarah was not well enough to spend Annie's sixty-ninth birthday with her, she was happy to hear from Rose that Annie looked lovely—"like the blessed damosel" (Rose Lamb to AF, 4 March [c. 1897], and [1900], HL; and SOJ to AF, June 1903, HL).

62. AF to Henry Oscar Houghton, 8 September 1894, Ho; *Letters of Celia Thaxter*, 193. Samuel T. Pickard, who had just compiled his *Life and Letters of John Greenleaf Whittier* (1894) sent Annie more of Celia's letters than she could use: as she explained, Celia's "own taste would have prescribed simplicity of treatment." AF to Pickard, October 1894 and April 1895, HL.

63. *Letters of Celia Thaxter*, 221.

CHAPTER 10

1. The novel is part of the Fields collection at the Huntington Library.

2. Thomas Wentworth Higginson, *Cheerful Yesterdays* (Boston: Houghton Mifflin, 1894), 130. In 1851 Higginson was nearing the end of his ministry in Newburyport—a seashore town thirty-five miles northeast of Boston where many New England literati vacationed.

3. Elizabeth K. Halbeisen, *Harriet Prescott Spofford: A Romantic Survival* (Philadelphia: University of Pennsylvania Press, 1935), 50. See also Alfred Bendixen's introduction to Spofford's *The Amber Gods and Other Stories* (New Brunswick, N.J.: Rutgers University Press, 1989).

4. Rose Terry Cooke, "Harriet Prescott Spofford," *Our Famous Women* (Hartford, Conn.: Worthington, 1884), 531. The story's punning title indicates where a stolen diamond is concealed (in a salt cellar).

5. William Dean Howells, *Literary Friends and Acquaintance* ([Boston: Houghton Mifflin, 1900] Bloomington: Indiana University Press, 1968), 15. Perhaps Howells had also read Hally's melodramatic first novel—*Sir Rohan's Ghost* (Boston: Tilton, 1860)—which centers on an artist's discovery that he is in love with his own illegitimate daughter.

6. Harriet Prescott Spofford, *Little Book of Friends* (Boston: Little, Brown, 1916), 5.

7. That statement appears in Annie's unpublished and undated essay on Harriet Prescott Spofford, which is in the Fields collection at the Massachusetts Historical Society. Her *Biographical Notes* in-

cludes a long letter from Sheppard's closest friend which praises the subtlety and power of Hally's criticism, but without mentioning her name (62–64). Hally would draw on her own essay over thirty years later for her introduction to the American edition of Sheppard's novel *Rumour* (1893).

8. AF to JGW, 13 July 1885. Ho. Deer Island was connected by bridges to both Newburyport and Amesbury.

9. SOJ to Harriet Prescott Spofford, 9 June 1897, in *Sarah Orne Jewett Letters,* ed. Richard Cary (Waterville, Me: Colby College Press, 1967), 83–84.

10. Annie mistakenly assumed that Hally would be remembered as a poet, and she could never have guessed that in 1920 Harriet Prescott Spofford would reach a new generation of readers with a volume of local color stories titled *The Elder's People.*

11. *Little Book of Friends,* 1–20.

12. Kate also told her Aunt Corda that Fields had told her what price she should ask for her newspaper work and when she could raise it. Quoted in Lilian Whiting, *Kate Field: A Record* (Boston: Little, Brown, 1900), 99.

13. AF to Kate Field, 14 February 1866, BPL. The book was Isabella Blagden's *Agnes Tremone.*

14. Whiting, 186.

15. AF to Kate Field, 30 December 1866, BPL. Kate Field had covered Ristori's New York, Philadelphia, and Boston performances for local newspapers in each city (Whiting, 165–67). For whatever reason, the idea of a benefit reading never materialized. The Ristori autograph is in one of Annie's autograph albums at the Houghton Library.

16. Whiting, 173–75.

17. AF to Kate Field, 10 January 1868, BPL.

18. Whiting, 177, 179.

19. Ibid., 180, 170.

20. Ibid., 181–82.

21. Ibid., 181. The New England Woman's Club had been meeting informally since mid-February.

22. See Jane C. Croly, *The History of the Woman's Club Movement in America* (New York: Henry C. Allen, 1898), 13–20; and Karen Blair, "Sorosis and the New England Woman's Club," *The Clubwoman as Feminist: True Womanhood Redefined, 1868–1911* (New York: Holmes & Meier, 1980), 33–125. Blair mistakenly gives 13 April as the date of the first Sorosis meeting at Delmonico's and thinks the name was fixed by then, and her comments on Kate Field also contain minor factual errors. Yet like Croly, Blair facilitates assessment of Annie as a clubwoman—of her period and class in her initial interest in "Sorosis," a secular organization that promoted "agreeable and useful relations among women of literary and artistic tastes," and more so in her ongoing commitment to the broader-based New England Woman's Club (which promoted social reforms as well as cultural activities and did not exclude men). But true to her genteel self, Annie was repelled by egocentrism and self-display, whether in a clubwoman (like Kate Field or Julia Ward Howe) or in anyone else.

23. Croly, 20.

24. AF to Kate Field, 8 May 1868, BPL.

25. AF to Kate Field, 8 and 18 May 1868, BPL.

26. Whiting, 187–88. When Jamie subsequently rejected Kate's essay "Luminara of Pisa," saying it was "capital, but not important enough for the 'Atlantic,'" Kate pragmatically noted that she had anticipated that comment and then successfully placed the essay with Lippincott (ibid., 198–99).

27. Journal entry of 1 January 1869 in ibid., 196–98. On the cover of *Planchette's Diary* (New York: Redfield, 1868), Kate Field identified herself as its editor.

28. Anna Cabot Lowell to AF, 2 February 1870, HL. Mrs. Lowell suggested that Kate might give one performance for friends and another for "tickets."

29. Kate Field to AF, 2 April 1874, HL.

30. AF to Kate Field, 14 April 1878, BPL, and Whiting, 363–66.

31. According to a *New York Tribune* reviewer, the two-hour "Monologue" that Kate performed in New York and Boston that spring was engaging but thin and unambitious. Both the *Tribune* review and Jamie's letter to Kate of 28 March 1880 are in Whiting, 386–87.

32. Trollope corresponded with Kate and saw her whenever he was in America or she was in En-

gland. A letter of July 1868 sent her "a kiss that shall be semi-paternal, one third brotherly, and as regards the small remainder, as loving as you please," and his autobiography identifies her as his "most chosen friend." See *The Letters of Anthony Trollope*, ed. Bradford Allen Booth (London: Oxford University Press, 1951), esp. 222–25 and 362–63; James Pope Hennessy, *Anthony Trollope* (Boston: Little, Brown, 1971), 214–21; Bradford Booth, *Anthony Trollope: Aspects of His Life and Art* (Bloomington: Indiana University Press, 1958), esp. 127; and Michael Sadleir, *Anthony Trollope: A Commentary* (Boston: Houghton Mifflin, 1927), 210–29 and 275–87.

33. LWJ to AF, 16 August 1868, NYPL. When Leonowens read some of Saadi's poems to Laura, some of the lines sounded familiar because (as her daughter Bessie recognized) Swinburne had appropriated them. Leonowens had arrived in Staten Island after spending over five years at the Siamese court—from March 1862 until July 1867. The indefatigable British widow's experiences during her five years of teaching in Bangkok entered our own popular culture through Margaret Landon's *Anna and the King of Siam* (New York: John Day, 1943) and the 1946 film based on it, the Rodgers and Hammerstein musical of the same title, its 1956 film version, and a nonmusical 1999 film titled *Anna and the King*.

34. In her densely detailed introduction to *The Romance of the Harem* (Charlottesville: University Press of Virginia, 1991), Susan Morgan points out the admixture of fiction and fact in Leonowens's autobiographical statements (e.g., she claimed to have be on born in India rather than Wales and lied about her birthdate, her parentage, and her husband's name and occupation) but rightly celebrates the book itself. It is certainly not "factual history." But Leonowens effectively dramatized the harem women's blighted lives and the "greatness of their response" to their "state of oppression" (xxxvi–xxxvii). Morgan attributes the attention Leonowens received in America to "the friendship of Stowe and Annie and James Fields" (xxiii).

35. Anna Leonowens to AF, 21 May 1873, HL.

36. AF to LWJ, 26 October 1874, HL.

37. HBS to AF, 3 October [1878]; and Anna Leonowens to AF, 15 October 1878, HL.

38. Anna Leonowens to AF, 12 May 1879, 17 July 1879, 14 January 1883, 9 October 1896, and 17 May 1884, HL.

39. Anna Leonowens to AF, 20 January 1885, 10 December 1889, 3 February 1902, and 21 May 1902, HL.

40. Anna Leonowens to AF, 28 December 1902, 10 January 1904, and 17 May 1908, HL. Annie followed the lives of Leonowens's grandchildren but felt closest to her grandson James, who often visited Annie during his years at Harvard and subsequently became a doctor, first in Canada and then in Siam.

CHAPTER II

1. In his *Crusader in Crinoline* (Philadelphia: Lippincott, 1941), Forrest Wilson draws heavily on Stowe's letters to Annie and concludes that she was Stowe's "most intimate friend" (451). Joan D. Hedrick's more densely contextualized *Harriet Beecher Stowe: A Life* (New York: Oxford University Press, 1994) makes even fuller use of that correspondence. But neither biography draws on Annie's journals or explores the women's relationship. My own study uses the journals, her "Days with Mrs. Stowe" (in *Authors and Friends* [Boston: Houghton Mifflin, 1895], 157–226), her *Life and Letters of Harriet Beecher Stowe* (Boston: Houghton Mifflin, 1898), and the 132 letters from Stowe in the Fields Collection at the Huntington Library. Undocumented quotations are from Annie's journals. I refer to Stowe by her last name because she signed her letters to Annie "HBS" or "HBStowe" and because Annie's journal entries identify her as "HBS" or "Mrs. Stowe." Consistent with period proprieties, Annie customarily identified even close friends that way or by their first and last names.

2. "Days," 164–65.

3. Ibid., 172.

4. HBS to AF, 28 May [1860], HL. The "we" included her twin daughters. Stowe's anonymous allegorical tale "The Mourning Veil" had appeared in the first number of the *Atlantic* and her signed essay "New England's Ministers" in the third, followed by her serialized novel *The Minister's Wooing*, whose last two installments appeared after Ticknor and Fields purchased the magazine.

5. HBS to AF, "Saturday morning" [c. 1861], HL.

6. HBS to JTF and AF [c. February 1861], HL.

7. HBS to JTF, December [1866], and HBS to AF and JTF, 10 March [1863], HL.

8. HBS to JTF, 27 November [1862], HL. Presumably Stowe considered her essay too important to trust to an ordinary proofreader.

9. HBS to JTF, 3 June 1864, and HBS to AF, 29 November [1864], HL. Stowe wanted to amend what she had said about the sisters of charity movement.

10. HBS to AF, [1866] and [1868], HL. Although Stowe had refused to let Fields serialize the novel, he regularly sent her large cash advances while she was completing it. *Oldtown Folks* finally appeared in the spring of 1869.

11. HBS to AF, 21 October [1867], HBS to JTF, 21 November [1867], and HBS to AF [December 1867], HL. When Andrew's brother complained about inaccuracies in Stowe's sketch, she told Fields she had done her best with the information Annie sent and the few anecdotes she had picked up on her own, but now planned to ask Whipple (Andrew's official biographer) what corrections she should make before *Men of Our Times* appeared as a book. HBS to JTF, [February 1868,] HL.

12. HBS to AF [1866], and HBS to JTF, 19 December 1865, HL.

13. HBS to AF [1866], HL. See Hedrick, 327.

14. HBS to AF, 26 February 1867, HL. Stowe also requested a copy of her own that she could carry down to Florida.

15. HBS to AF, 26 July 1864 and 27 July 1868, HL. In April 1861, at Stowe's request, Annie had successfully petitioned her brother Boylston—who was then a surgeon in the First Massachusetts Regiment—to get Fred Stowe chosen as a hospital steward (Hedrick, 299). Evidently Stowe then formed a separate relationship with Boylston. Writing to Annie from Framingham on 25 December 1872, she said "Your good brother has been a God send to us," and she had enjoyed staying under his roof (HL). And early in 1875, Stowe acknowledged the birth of Boylston's son Zabdiel, thanked him for his "recipe" for quinine pills, and invited him to Florida (HBS to Zabdiel Boylston Adams, 15 March 1875 and 17 May [1875]. I am grateful to Mitchell Adams for providing me with photocopies of these unpublished letters.)

16. HBS to AF, 16 August 1867, 21 March 1870, and 1 May [1864], HL. That Annie had some knowledge of what Stowe received is evident from an uncharacteristically resentful comment in her diary: her husband was subsidizing Stowe by paying in advance for her yet unfinished *Oldtown Folks*.

17. HBS to AF, 6 February and 20 August 1872, HL.

18. HBS to AF, 21 August 1872, HL.

19. "Days," 220–21.

20. *Life*, 347.

21. HBS to AF, 17 February [1869], and HBS to JTF, 9 November [1864], HL.

22. HBS to JTF, 3 November 1863, HL.

23. HBS to AF, 6 February 1872, HL. Stowe would soon begin writing the enticing sketches about Florida titled "Palmetto Leaves," which first appeared in the *Christian Union* and then as a book published by Fields's successor Osgood.

24. HBS to AF [c. December 1869], HL. Without passing judgment on the facts or the narrative, Annie sympathetically noted that Stowe had "braved the world for her friend's sake" (*Life*, 322).

25. HBS to AF, 1 August [1873], HL.

26. "I saw Mrs. Stowe, Fanny Kemble, Longfellow, & all the fine folks," Alcott told Alfred Whitman. *The Selected Letters of Louisa May Alcott*, ed. Joel Myerson, Daniel Shealy, and Madeleine B. Stern (Boston: Little, Brown, 1987), 73.

27. "Days," 205.

28. Ibid., 181–83, and HBS to AF [July 1864?], HL.

29. HBS to AF, 6 February, 2 and 16 March, and 28 November 1872, HL. While preparing her Stowe memoir years later, Annie penciled a notation on top of the November letter: "Boston fire will show how alive she was to the needs of the period."

30. HBS to JTF, [c. July 1868], HL.

31. HBS to AF, 2 December 1880, HL. Forrest Wilson oversimplifies when he concludes that Stowe

disliked "Annie's verse, which was much too subtle and shaded and indefinite for an elderly lady who preferred beefsteak and potatoes in her literary ration" (697). But Stowe's limited praise may well have wounded Annie, as Wilson assumes.

32. HBS to AF, 31 November [1881], HL.

33. *Life,* 368.

34. HBS to AF, 9 May [1869], 30 April [1872], and 2 September [1872], HL, and *Life,* 340–41.

35. HBS to AF, 24 September 1873 and 28 April 1879; HBS to JTF, 1 January [1881], HL. "We Americans are perfectly willing to accept if there was—even though the laws of England would not," Stowe added. She also wondered if Eliot's husband, J. W. Cross, would return her own letters to Eliot. When Annie asked Cross for them fifteen years later while preparing her life of Stowe, he promised to see what he could find. Stowe's 1872 letter to Eliot, which Annie included in her biography, was presumably one of the results.

36. Annie Fields, "George Eliot," *Century* 58 (July 1899): 444–45. Eliot's mournful reply to Annie's letter of condolence about the death of Lewes, included in that sketch, asked her to thank Stowe for her "generous and kind-hearted sympathy."

37. *Life,* 206. Annie made a similar point at the beginning of her article on Eliot, though without invoking Stowe or Sand: "Affection irradiated the heavy lines of her strong countenance and made it beautiful to those who loved her" (442).

38. HBS to AF, 6 December [1866], HBS to JTF, 8 August [1867], and HBS to AF, 17 August [1868], HL.

39. HBS to AF, [October 1878,] and Anna Leonowens to AF, 15 October 1878, HL; *Uncle Tom's Cabin* (Boston: Houghton Mifflin, 1878), lxxviii–lxxix.

40. HBS to AF, 24 September [1884], and JGW to AF, 31 October 1884, HL; Hedrick, 398.

41. See Elizabeth Stuart Phelps, *Chapters from a Life* (Boston: Houghton Mifflin, 1896).

42. HBS to AF, 7 November [1865] and 9 March 1870, HL.

43. The *Atlantic* had celebrated Whittier's seventieth birthday with an all-male dinner in December 1877 and Holmes's seventieth with a breakfast two years later, and now it was Stowe's turn (although on her seventy-first birthday). "Except for those who must be missed, there was no sadness in the affair," Phelps told Annie, saying she had felt "for a week before as if I were going to be married or buried or some other good fortune were to befall me." Elizabeth Phelps Ward to AF, [June 1882,] HL. Annie's account of that party in her Stowe biography (380–81) drew on Phelps's long letter.

CHAPTER 12

1. Laura Winthrop Johnson, *The Life and Poems of Theodore Winthrop* (New York: Henry Holt, 1884), 283. He died at Big Bethel, Virginia.

2. Fields published sixteen editions of *John Brent* within three years, and other publishers also issued it—most recently in 1979.

3. LWJ to AF, 23 July [1862], Laura Winthrop Johnson Papers, NYPL. Over three hundred of Laura Winthrop Johnson's letters to Annie Fields are at the New York Public Library, and over a hundred thirty of Annie's letters to Laura are at the Huntington Library. As "Mrs. Emily Hare," Laura had published a children's Christmas book titled *Little Blossom Reward* (New York: Phillips Sampson, 1854).

4. LWJ to AF, 29 January [1863?], NYPL. However hyperbolic that statement seems, it is substantiated by Anna Leonowens's comment to Annie soon after Laura's death: "in you she found her secret spring and outlet" (Anna Leonowens to AF, 10 December 1889, HL).

5. Laura Winthrop Johnson, *Poems of Twenty Years* (New York: De W.C. Lent, 1874), 140.

6. LWJ to AF, 11 April 1867, NYPL.

7. Edith E. W. Gregg, ed., *The Letters of Ellen Tucker Emerson,* 2 vols. (Kent, Ohio: Kent State University Press, 1988), 1:322. Ellen's letter of 5 January 1865 to her aunt Susan Emerson got Laura's last name and marital status wrong.

8. LWJ to AF, 11 August [1862?], NYPL.

9. LWJ to JTF, 21 May 1864, and LWJ to AF, 30 May 1864, NYPL. Presumably Laura wrote at least one book review for the *Atlantic.* When Horace Scudder requested Annie's help in identifying anony-

mous authors for the magazine's first general index, she said she thought Laura had written the unsigned review of Thomas Bailey Aldrich's fiction. AF to Horace Scudder, 23 December 1876, Boston Athenaeum.

10. Riding in ambulances that were accompanied by three wagons "containing all the comforts necessary" for several weeks of camping, Laura and her group left Cheyenne "under the care of a paymaster of the U.S.A., to visit with him some of the forts and Indian agencies of Wyoming Territory and beyond." When they reached Indian territory, they were joined by a thirty-wagon supply train and an escort of fifty men. A sales catalog for *800 Miles in an Ambulance* (New York: Lippincott, 1889) includes the subtitle "Journal of a Trip through the Forts and Indian Agencies of Wyoming from Cheyenne to the borders of the Territory and beyond," identifies the author as Theodore Winthrop's sister, and praises her for capturing the little-recorded period when "it was still possible for a lady to tour the frontier, with an Army Officer as escort, and see . . . the real Wyoming Indian," on territory "never before trodden by a white woman." A copy of the catalog is at the Houghton Library.

11. Among her specific tributes to her brother, Laura said his critique of Church's "Heart of the Andes" (included in *Life in the Open Air*) proved "his knowledge of mountains and their architecture was equal to that of the painter." *Life and Poems*, 2, 260.

12. LWJ to AF, 7 July and 24 September 1864, 4 August 1871, 22 February 1876, and May or June 1877, NYPL.

13. AF to LWJ, 27 December 1866, HL, and AF to LWJ, 28 April 1870, Ho. Annie wrote the summary from memory, because Emerson objected to note-taking during his lectures. Ronald A. Bosco's definitively edited transcription of Annie's remarkable letter to Laura is at the heart of "His Lectures Were Poetry, His Teaching the Music of the Spheres: Annie Adams Fields and Francis Greenwood Peabody on Emerson's 'Natural History of the Intellect' University Lectures at Harvard in 1870," *Harvard Library Bulletin* 8 (Summer 1997): 1–79. Because no manuscripts of those lectures survive, as Bosco states, Annie's long letter and Francis Peabody's brief notes document "the otherwise unstudied close of Emerson's long career as a lecturer and intellectual presence in America," and his last "formal accounting of 'mind'" (8). After Emerson's death in 1882, Annie wrote abbreviated "memory-pictures" of those thirty-minute lectures for the June 1883 *Atlantic*—"Mr. Emerson in the Lecture Room" (818–32).

14. AF to LWJ, 4 September 1866, 10 May 1873, and 20 July 1876, HL.

15. AF to LWJ, 5 August 1871, 17 May 1874, and 27 December 1877, HL.

16. AF to LWJ, 24 May 1864, HL.

17. LWJ to AF, 7 July 1864, NYPL. That rumor passed on by Curtis's mother-in-law Sarah Sturgis Shaw probably originated with her friend Elizabeth Peabody, who may have misinterpreted Hawthorne's interest in her during his secret courtship of Sophia.

18. LWJ to AF, 13 September 1864, [December 1864?], 16 July 1865, and [summer 1887], NYPL.

19. LWJ to AF, 10 June 1866, NYPL.

20. AF to LWJ, 26 October 1874, 26 January 1877, and 7 October 1875, HL.

21. AF to LWJ, 6 June 1874, 20 October 1878, and 15 November 1866, HL.

22. AF to LWJ, 30 December 1874, 23 October 1873, 6 June 1874, 18 April 1875, and 20 July 1876, HL.

23. AF to LWJ, 2 December 1871, 11 January and 1 December 1872, and 9 February 1873, HL.

24. Meetings of the New England Woman's Club included discussions of cooperative laundries and job training and placement services for domestic workers. See Dolores Hayden, *The Grand Domestic Revolution: A History of Feminist Designs for American Homes, Neighborhoods, and Cities* (Cambridge: MIT Press, 1981), esp. chap. 4: "Housewives in Harvard Square."

25. AF to LWJ, 5 January 1867, 18 April 1875, and 3 June 1877, HL.

26. AF to LWJ, 26 October and 14 December 1874, 10 December 1868, and 16 June 1880, HL.

27. AF to LWJ, [May 1864], 10 February 1870, 15 November 1866, and 15 November 1874, HL.

28. AF to LWJ, 24 August 1876 and 4 September 1866, HL. Manuscripts of Annie's poems to Laura are at the Huntington Library. The 1864 birthday poem, included in an 1864–73 notebook and corrected in pencil and ink, imagines Nature clasping "in shining arms / A blossoming circle of my Laura's life."

29. AF to LWJ, [n.d.] and 1 January 1884, HL.

30. LWJ to AF, 29 December 1888, NYPL. A scrawled note from Laura's daughter Bessie reported that Laura had died from a cerebral hemorrhage.

CHAPTER 13

1. *Biographical Notes and Personal Sketches* (Boston: Houghton Mifflin, 1881), 180.

2. The firm of James R. Osgood & Company came into existence on 2 January 1871. Fields received a large initial payment, the remainder to be paid in installments. William S. Tryon, *Parnassus Corner: A Life of James T. Fields* (Boston: Houghton Mifflin, 1963), 360.

3. Her expanded identity is best understood in the larger context of how genteel American women moved beyond their traditional roles as nurturers during the post–Civil War years. For useful explorations of how middle-class women extended their domestic endeavors into such precincts as schools and settlement houses, see Nancy Cott, *The Bonds of Womanhood: Woman's Sphere in New England, 1780–1835* (New Haven: Yale University Press, 1977); Carl N. Degler, *At Odds: Women and the Family in America from the Revolution to the Present* (New York: Oxford University Press, 1980); and Gerda Lerner, *The Majority Finds Its Past* (New York: Oxford University Press, 1979). Although almost none of the women Annie knew had direct access to political or economic power, many attained it by joining forces with other women (as Annie did at the North End Mission) and through individual pressure tactics (as Annie did when she established her coffee houses and petitioned for funds to sustain her fire-damaged women's residence).

4. Among the Fieldses' friends who put the Chickering to good use was their neighbor Otto Dresel, a celebrated concert performer, who in March 1878 "played Chopin to the lovely creature we call Modjeska" and an audience that also included Celia Thaxter and Elizabeth Stuart Phelps; and the distinguished teacher and solo performer Jessie Cochrane regularly played for such gatherings during her visits to Charles Street.

5. Nathan Irvin Huggins, *Protestants against Poverty: Boston's Charities, 1870–1900* (Westport, Conn.: Greenwood, 1971), 58–60.

6. The Annie Adams Fields papers at Simmons College include financial records in her hand, correspondence including requests for information about the Holly Trees, and managers' reports, newspaper clippings, and advertisements.

7. A note from the *Christian Union*'s managing editor George S. Merriman to Annie Fields dated 6 March 1872 enclosed a check for fifteen dollars, reported Henry Ward Beecher's pleasure in her article, and invited further contributions. Simmons College Archive.

8. The Simmons Archive contains three similar clippings and a series of letters to Annie from the Unitarian minister Charles W. Wendtke requesting detailed advice about the Holly Trees, explaining their special importance to laborers in Chicago's burnt-out district, and thanking her for a seventy-five-dollar contribution as well as practical guidance.

9. Huggins misjudges Annie when he says she "would devise schemes for the elimination of some evil and throw herself into its promotion, at least until it bored her," as when she wanted to cease her connection with the Holly Trees after two years (173). Her initial involvement in each Holly Tree included such tasks as buying coffee pots and coffee, and her plan included giving managers autonomy. She severed connections with a particular Holly Tree only when it was running smoothly; and she counseled philanthropists who planned similar establishments at least as late as 1878.

10. AF to LWJ, 11 January 1872, HL.

11. Ibid.

12. AF to Otis Norcross, 26 November 1872, Otis Norcross Diaries and Papers, MHS. Norcross had been mayor in 1866–67. A merchant esteemed for efficiency and high ethical standards, he had also been an alderman, director of the Boston School committee, president of the Water Board, and treasurer of the Overseers of the Poor.

13. AF to LWJ, [November 1872,] HL.

14. AF to LWJ, 1 December 1872, HL.

15. AF to Mary Usher Osgood, 5 December 1872, Society for the Preservation of New England Antiquities.

16. AF to LWJ, 9 and 24 February 1873, HL.

17. According to Huggins (174–76), Annie had "discovered that selflessness could be harmful; one had to be discriminating in the giving of self as well as goods." He is correct in writing that Annie was "ripe for the instruction of Octavia Hill [an English reformer] and the charity organization philosophy" and soon afterward became "one of America's leading advocates of charity organization principles." But he posits a false binary in saying that she worked "in organizations rather than for people."

18. The women drew heavily on the theories of Octavia Hill, "who, in 1864, under the tutlage of John Ruskin, managed an experiment in housing for the poor in East London slums" that relied on "personal visitors, rather than rent collectors." Huggins, 59. Annie had read Hill's pamphlets, corresponded with her, and met her in England. In *In the Shadow of the Poorhouse: A Social History of Welfare in America* (New York: Basic Books, 1986), Michael B. Katz acknowledges Annie's leadership in establishing Boston's Associated Charities and points to its success in "persuading large numbers of women to serve as friendly visitors," but notes the ultimate failure of such organizations to "reduce dependence in American cities" (80–81).

19. Jane C. Croly, *The History of the Woman's Movement in America* (New York: Henry C. Allen, 1898), 39.

20. AF to LWJ, 23 October 1873, HL.

21. I am grateful to Joel Myerson for sending me a copy of the handwritten Birthday Menu, now in the Americana and English literature collections of the Rosenbach Museum & Library in Philadelphia, which was published in *The Rosenbach Newsletter* 14 (September 1989).

22. RWE to AF, 24 February and 19 March 1872, HL, included in *The Letters of Ralph Waldo Emerson*, ed. Ralph L. Rusk, 6 vols. (New York: Columbia University Press, 1939), 6:205–207. Three years before, Emerson had delivered an earlier version of "Amita" to the New England Woman's Club, to an audience of over a hundred that included Annie Fields.

CHAPTER 14

1. AF to LWJ, 10 February 1870, HL. The weekly *Woman's Journal,* edited by Mary Livermore, Julia Ward Howe, Lucy Stone, William Garrison, and Thomas Wentworth Higginson, was the official organ of the new American Woman Suffrage Association.

2. The very fact that Annie included that journal entry in the *Biographical Notes* reflects her pride in the event, though in neither her journal nor the biography did she mention her own authorship. [Annie Fields,] *James T. Fields: Biographical Notes and Personal Sketches* (Boston: Houghton Mifflin, 1881), 194.

3. JTF to HWL, 28 August 1872, Ho, tipped into Longfellow's copy of *The Children of Lebanon.*

4. HWL to AF, 3 September 1872, Ho.

5. AF to JGW, 1 December 1872; in *The Letters of John Greenleaf Whittier,* ed. John B. Pickard, 3 vols. (Cambridge: Harvard University Press, 1975), 3:291.

6. JTF to Parke Godwin, 5 July 1871, and AF to William Cullen Bryant, 2 November 1871, Bryant-Godwin Papers, NYPL. Annie's letter to Bryant was primarily a thank-you note for his new translation of the *Odyssey.*

7. According to Emma Stebbins, in *Charlotte Cushman: Her Life, Letters, and Memories* (Boston: Houghton Mifflin, 1878), 215, Katherine was Cushman's favorite role.

8. AF to LWJ, 2 December 1871, HL. Annie's longer tribute to Cushman is on a separate sheet at the Huntington Library.

9. Pickard, 2:471, 476.

10. See Joseph Leach, *Bright Particular Star: The Life & Times of Charlotte Cushman* (New Haven: Yale University Press, 1970).

11. AF to LWJ, 11 January 1872, HL. In her *Biographical Notes,* Annie included Livermore's tribute to James T. Fields as a "friend of women" who supported woman suffrage and organized the 1872 literary lecture series for women which included women lecturers (190–93). Evidently Livermore was unaware of Annie's role in that project and in his other efforts for "women's advancement."

12. Mary A. Livermore to JTF, 10 October 1877, HL. Mrs. Beedy had been Annie's houseguest in January after addressing the New England Woman's Club.

13. As Livermore later sadly reported, her own tight schedule might keep her from returning in time to hear Annie. Mary A. Livermore to AF, 19 April and 4 November 1887, HL.

14. J. W. Howe to AF, 9 January [1870], 28 February 1877, and 12 November 1886, HL. In May 1897, Howe enlisted Annie to help fund-raise at the Woman's Meeting of Aid and Support to Greece.

15. Annie made this entry in her commonplace book (now at the Massachusetts Historical Society) soon after the "noble" memorial service for Howe at Boston Symphony Hall in January 1911, saying she had probably not mentioned the funeral earlier because she had written so many letters about it.

16. Abby Diaz to JTF [c. 1863], HL.

17. AF to LWJ, 29 January 1874, HL.

18. AF to LWJ, 26 February 1877 and 2 February 1878, HL. Annie's journal remark that Diaz sometimes lost her balance presumably referred to her predilection for controversial arguments—for example, that teaching Bible stories in Sunday schools could cause brutality.

19. The WEIU began in May 1877 with forty-two members but soon grew to four hundred, outnumbering the New England Woman's Club. Mrs. Diaz would serve as president from 1881 to 1892, administering facilities that soon included a job bureau, a lunchroom, a salesroom for handicrafts and baked goods, and a health clinic. In *A Domestic Problem: Work and Culture in the Household* (1875), *Only a Flock of Women* (1893), and many other publications, Diaz articulated the principles of domestic feminism, particularly her conviction that women could rear their children properly, enjoy companionate marriages, and pursue self-fulfillment only if they were emancipated from household drudgery and male domination. She also thought wealthy women should abandon idle luxury and perform useful work, beliefs Annie shared. See Frances E. Willard and Mary A. Livermore, *A Woman of the Century* (Buffalo: Moulton, 1893), a 1903 *Woman's Journal* essay titled "The Life Work of Abby Morton Diaz," and Karen Blair, *The Clubwoman as Feminist: True Womanhood Redefined, 1868–1911* (New York: Holmes and Meier, 1980), 45–49 and 75–77.

20. Abby Diaz to AF, 13 September 1880, HL.

21. Abby Diaz to AF, [c. 1880], [c. 1882], and [c. 1904], HL.

22. AF to LWJ, 16 June 1877, HL.

23. The manuscript is at the Huntington Library.

24. AF to LWJ, 6 June 1874, HL.

25. Mary Usher Osgood to her sister Rebecca, "Friday" [1882], Society for the Preservation of New England Antiquities.

26. Barbara Miller Solomon's study of how social, economic, and cultural circumstances expanded American women's access to education, *In the Company of Educated Women* (New Haven: Yale University Press, 1985), provides a good context for understanding Annie Fields as a representative mid-nineteenth-century woman who tried to combine her own commitment to liberal study with women's duties as defined by the code of true womanhood. But though Solomon rightly links women's push for higher education to the burgeoning women's club movement, she is not concerned about several related issues in which Annie was also involved, including women's admission to medical school and women's increasing roles as college administrators and lecturers. In *Perish the Thought: Intellectual Women in Romantic America, 1830–1860,* (New York: Oxford University Press, 1976), Susan Phinney Conrad presents the mid-century woman of letters in her various roles as translator, historian, teacher, recorder, memoirist, philosopher, critic, lecturer, editor, and writer of fiction and poetry. Elizabeth Peabody is her chief example. But Annie Fields also fits Conrad's definition of the woman intellectual as a romantic with a broad social vision who was deeply concerned about morality, and who believed that art could be redemptive and regenerative. She likewise bears out Conrad's generalization that intellectual women were usually daughters of professionals who were raised with high intellectual ideals but realized that most women were excluded from the mid-century's expanding professional opportunities.

27. Wendell Phillips to JTF, [1872], HL. Phillips assured Fields that Curtis would support his position. A printed prospectus for the series and Annie's penciled draft of it are at the Huntington Library. According to a newspaper clipping preserved in an album owned by Annie's great-niece Mrs. Nancy Bole, the hall could seat nine hundred, all the lectures were such as had "hitherto been given in col-

leges," and the course was "designed by Mr. Fields to be the forerunner of a school of instruction for women which shall give them the advantages so long accorded only to their brothers." In her *Biographical Notes*, 187–88, Annie quoted an article titled "Good News for Women" which her husband prepared for local newspapers, and an advertisement for the course which lists E. D. Cheney as the first of twelve lecturers.

28. The Harvard Annex, which was not empowered to grant degrees, was incorporated in 1882; Radcliffe College was established as a degree-granting college two years later.

29. Justin S. Winsor, ed., *Memorial History of Boston* 4 vols. (Boston: Ticknor, 1881) 4:253–54.

30. AF to LWJ, 6 October 1873, HL.

31. Both the receipt and the record book (which runs from 3 January through 19 May 1876) are at the Huntington Library. Ledger entries include records of medallion sales, applications for space in the Women's Pavilion, and bills for advertising and shipping. Annie's correspondence with Massachusetts women on centennial business as well as the records of the Old South Church Preservation Commission (which received the unexpended funds of the Women's Centennial Committee) is at the Boston Public Library.

32. AF to LWJ, 23 October 1873 and 18 April 1875, HL. As Annie noted in her diary, centennial celebrations were scheduled on the evening of 18 April 1875 in both Concord and Lexington, the president had stopped in Boston on his way to participate in them, and two lanterns would hang that night in Boston's North Church steeple.

33. AF to LWJ, 9 February 1876, HL.

34. AF to LWJ, 9 April 1876, HL.

35. The Women's Pavilion was a "neat and tasteful edifice . . . 208 feet by 208 feet," officially opened by the national chairwoman and the Empress of Brazil. In addition to women's arts, crafts, and inventions, the building contained looms operated by skilled weavers and "run by a six-horse power Baxter engine" which the Empress set in motion. J. S. Ingram, *The Centennial Exposition* (Philadelphia: Hubbard, 1876), 116, 97–98.

CHAPTER 15

1. The book went through twenty editions during the decade before his death. As James C. Austin (*Fields of the Atlantic Monthly* [San Marino, Calif.: Huntington Library, 1953], 436) remarks, with *Yesterdays with Authors* Fields became "not only the foremost publisher of good literature in mid-nineteenth-century America, and one of the greatest magazine editors of the period, but also one who belongs in the first rank as a writer of reminiscences."

2. When the lecture was first announced in July 1873, Annie proudly noted that it was anticipated as "one of the best intellectual treats ever enjoyed by our citizens." "Masters of the Situation" is the only complete lecture by Fields preserved at the Huntington Library, along with outlines of a few others and such miscellaneous items as a memo of February 1874 stating "I will lecture for $100 in any place so near Boston that I can return the same evening," but anything more than a four-hour train ride away required special terms and "Western applications I must look over with the Bureau before a decision is made." Fields's repertoire included lectures on over two dozen writers including Milton, Pope, and Goldsmith, the most celebrated English romantics, and Americans including Bryant and Rufus Choate as well as Hawthorne and Longfellow. His umbrella titles include "Reading," "Biography and Autobiography," "The English Stage," and "A Plea for Cheerfulness." Of the thirty separate lectures he gave at Boston University, the one titled "Representative Men" assumed such ritual importance that classes were dismissed whenever it was scheduled. William S. Tryon, *Parnassus Corner: A Life of James T. Fields* (Boston: Houghton Mifflin, 1963), 369.

3. Annie Fields, *Authors and Friends* (Boston: Houghton Mifflin, 1895), 103–5.

4. When compiling her "Glimpses of Emerson" twelve years later, Annie used her journal account selectively, saying nothing about Lidian Emerson, Jamie's audience, or the breakfast menu.

5. JTF to AF, [1875], 21 January 1875, "Wednesday" [1874], and [1874], HL.

6. JTF to AF, 15 November [1874], HL.

7. JTF to AF, 25 January 1875, HL.

8. AF to LWJ, 17 October 1875, HL.

9. Colleges restricted to women continued to open, including Wellesley and Smith in 1875 and Bryn Mawr in 1884.

10. Joaquin Miller to AF, 9 and 25 September 1871, HL. See M. M. Marberry, *Splendid Poseur: Joaquin Miller—American Poet* (New York: Crowell, 1953), and Martin Severin Peterson, *Joaquin Miller: Literary Frontiersman* (Stanford: Stanford University Press, 1937).

11. [Annie Fields] *James T. Fields: Biographical Notes and Personal Sketches* (Boston: Houghton Mifflin, 1881), 267.

12. Joaquin Miller to AF, 24 September 1885, HL. The cabin Miller occupied between 1883 and 1886 (which included a bed covered with animal skins) had not only made him a tourist attraction but prompted invitations from Washington hostesses and even the White House (Peterson, 87–89). In 1886 he built the hut in Oakland, California, which he would occupy until his death in 1913.

13. Thomas Starr King to JTF, 31 January 1862, HL. Although Austin says Jessie Frémont brought Harte to Fields's attention on 3 October 1862 (369), Starr King had already done so.

14. Bret Harte to AF, 27 September 1875, HL.

15. Ibid.

16. Harte served as a United States consul in Germany from 1878 to 1880, spent the next five years as a consul in Glasgow, then resided in England until his death in 1902.

17. William Dean Howells, *Literary Friends and Acquaintance* ([Boston: Houghton Mifflin, 1900] Bloomington: Indiana University Press, 1968), 256.

18. Robert Underwood Johnson used these lines as the epigraph to his *Remembered Yesterdays* and said Annie Fields had recorded them in the September 1912 *Atlantic,* but I have found no such record.

19. Mark DeWolfe Howe, *Memories of a Hostess* (Boston: Atlantic Monthly Press, 1922), 244.

20. Mark Twain to AF, 1 April 1887, HL.

21. Mark Twain to AF, 12 March 1889, HL.

22. Albert Bigelow Paine, *Mark Twain: A Biography,* 4 vols. (New York: Harper, 1912), 3:980–81, and Albert Bigelow Paine, ed., *Mark Twain's Letters,* 2 vols. (New York: Harper, 1917), 2:602 (25 January 1894). Annie had refused Aldrich's plea for an invitation. Holmes died later that year.

23. Olivia Clemens to AF, 19 February 1901, HL. Speaking for her husband, Mrs. Clemens said he could not then spare time for the visit but hoped to come when his work was further along. Though I find no evidence of such a visit, Annie continued to hear about Twain from mutual friends including Robert Collyer, who in September 1906 assumed that she had already read the first installment of his autobiography and in December reported being invited to Andrew Carnegie's dinner in Twain's honor (17 September and 9 December 1906, HL).

24. The invention was then brand new. The Scottish-born Alexander Graham Bell (1847–1922)— who had come to Boston in 1872 as a professor of vocal psychology in the School of Oratory of Boston University, and to work with children at the Boston City School for the Deaf—had first demonstrated his new invention in 1876, first for the American Academy of Arts and Sciences at the Boston Athenaeum, and then at the Philadelphia Centennial Exposition.

25. A few weeks later, Annie proudly sent Laura an obituary notice "more fitting than anything more descriptive or personal . . . by my aunt Miss Holland of Cambridge, no common woman as you will see by this." AF to LWJ, 13 September 1875, 30 December 1876, and 26 January, 26 February, 31 March, and 23 April 1877, HL.

26. In *Biographical Notes,* 217, Annie later said she had stopped keeping a journal in December 1876 when other commitments absorbed her "and personal interests gave way to other claims." But she did not abandon the journal until the following summer, when she had completed *Persephone* and was preparing it for publication.

27. The volume is at the Houghton Library.

28. Harriet Waters Preston to AF, 31 October 1877, HL. Other friends who sent high tributes include Longfellow, Whittier, and Laura Johnson.

29. AF to Frances Osgood, 26 May 1877, Society for the Preservation of New England Antiquities. According to Annie, her sister Sarah had gone abroad because it was "less sad for her than to remain in the old ways just now."

30. Sallie Brock Putnam to AF, 27 May 1879, HL. Putnam wanted "to give women more promi-

nence than they had yet received in anthologies, and she hoped Annie would let her name be associated with her husband's "and with your many sisters in song, in the proposed volume." We can only guess what Annie replied, and I have located no such anthology under the name of Sallie Brock Putnam (though she had previously edited an anthology of war poetry).

31. HWL to AF, 18 November 1880, HL; and Moncure Conway to AF, 27 December 1880, HL.

32. C. D. Warner to AF, 29 November 1880, HL.

33. OWH to AF, 23 November 1880, HL. Her mentor Whittier's praise was high but qualified: there were "occasional defects," he told Annie, but "a genuine poetic feeling pervades all." JGW to AF, 19 November 1880, HL.

34. HBS to AF, 2 December 1880, HL.

35. Adeline Whitney to AF, 25 November 1880, HL. Whitney, ten years Annie's senior, had attended George B. Emerson's school from 1837 to 1841.

36. Helen Hunt Jackson to AF, 15 June 1881, HL.

37. SOJ to AF, 12 January 1881, Ho.

38. AF to LWJ, 5 December 1880, HL.

CHAPTER 16

1. AF to JGW, 16 March 1881, Ho.

2. As Annie wrote in her *Biographical Notes* (Boston: Houghton Mifflin, 1881), 26, "the last words he heard on earth were from Mr. Matthew Arnold's beautiful sketch of Gray's life, published in Ward's English Poets." "The ringing of the fire bells took him to the window at a little quicker pace than usual & the strangulation of the heart began—," The author and reformer Caroline Dall learned during a visit to Baltimore. As she wrote in her journal on 27 April, she had called on Lissie Adams and found her "with a pile of obituaries just received, which I read aloud," mourned with her "about the beautiful home life which has just ended," and learned that "Annie is stunned—went at once to her room, would see no one, & does not want her sister to come to her now." I am grateful to Helen Deese for sending me these passages from Caroline Dall's journals, which are at the Massachusetts Historical Society.

3. Thomas Niles to Louisa May Alcott, 28 April 1881, Ho. I am grateful to Daniel Shealy for calling my attention to this letter. Niles also told Alcott that Fields's "best friends among his *ordinary* associates would say of him 'Jimmy is a clever fellow but he has no heart.' He never offended them but his friendship was an out of door friendship. The social intercourse of the house was extended to more distinguished people."

4. JGW to AF, 25 April 1881, HL. Illness prevented Whittier from attending the funeral.

5. LWJ to AF, 24 May 1881, Laura Winthrop Johnson Papers, NYPL, and AF to LWJ, 6 June 1881, HL.

6. LL to JGW, 6 June 1881, Daniel Dulany Addison Collection, MHS.

7. LL to Ada Elsie Locke, 28 June 1881, BPL. I am grateful to Shirley Marchalonis for calling my attention to this letter.

8. HWL to Elizabeth Stuart Phelps, in *The Letters of Henry Wadsworth, Longfellow*, ed. Andrew Hilen, 6 vols. (Cambridge: Harvard University Press, 1967–82), 6:728, 21 August 1881. When the book came out three months later, Longfellow told George Greene that it was "very interesting, and written with good taste and judgment. A difficult task, well done." HWL to G. W. Greene, 28 November 1881, in *Letters*, 6:750.

9. AF to Edmund C. Stedman, 9 September 1881, HL.

10. OWH to AF, 16 November and "Christmas" 1881, HL. Holmes urged Annie to think about how much she had done for "the public weal" and how much she had contributed "to the best social life of the wide circle around you."

11. Elizabeth Stuart Phelps, to AF, 30 November 1881, HL.

12. HBS to AF, 30 November 1881, HL.

13. I am grateful to Helen Deese for sending me this entry dated 23 November 1881.

14. JGW to AF, 20 November 1881, HL. Whittier also expressed his relief that Annie was now back in Boston "engaged in thy old labor of love for the poor & suffering."

15. Marie Taylor to AF, 27 November 1881, and 15 August, 30 September, and 8 October 1883, HL. Bayard Taylor—the New York poet, translator, fiction writer, travel writer, and amateur painter who became minister to Germany in 1878 (the year of his death)—had often visited Charles Street with his German-born wife.

16. Marie Taylor to AF, 21 November 1884, HL. The two-volume *Life and Letters of Bayard Taylor,* ed. Marie Hansen-Taylor and Horace E. Scudder (Boston: Houghton Mifflin, 1884), includes dozens of letters from Taylor to Fields, five to Annie, and seven of Fields's letters to Taylor. Annie's letters to the Taylors (now at Cornell University) include literary gossip, invitations to Charles Street, and acknowledgments of Bayard Taylor's gifts of poems and paintings.

17. Elizabeth Agassiz to AF, 21 November [1881], HL.

18. Elizabeth Agassiz to AF, 8 October [1885], HL.

19. In a typical letter addressed to "My well beloved friends" and signed "Your loving old friend," Mrs. Agassiz delightedly recalled "the glimpse of Sarah and yourself in dear South Berwick," then reminisced about Radcliffe's "small beginnings—without buildings or books" and marveled that she had "anchored against the whole teaching force of Harvard." Elizabeth Agassiz to AF, 1 April [?], HL.

20. Elizabeth Agassiz to AF, 14 March [?], Special Collections, Colby College, and 14 April [1904?], HL. The April letter thanks Annie for "the pleasure you gave our girls last night."

21. Mary Lanier to AF, 27 April 1882, HL. Mrs. Lanier also said her near-blindness precluded editing her husband's papers.

22. Frances Arnold to AF, 21 June 1888, 24 October 1884, and 21 January 1893, HL.

23. CT to AF, 23 and 25 October, "Friday," 30 October, and 12 and 16 November 1881, BPL. As Richard Cary notes in his edition of the *Sarah Orne Jewett Letters* (Waterville, Me.: Colby College Press, 1967), 149, "Jessie Cochrane was a gifted amateur pianist from Louisville, Kentucky, who became something of a protégée of Mrs. Fields," took "long and frequent trips to Europe," and made long visits to Annie both before and after them.

24. CT to AF, 3 January 1882, BPL.

25. Howe, *Memories of a Hostess* (Boston: Atlantic Monthly Press, 1922), 283. Paula Blanchard, who shares Howe's belief, perceptively discusses the women's loving and mutually sustaining relationship in a biography rooted in social history—*Sarah Orne Jewett: Her World and Her Work* (Reading, Mass.: Addison Wesley, 1994).

26. SOJ to AF, 4 December 1877, Ho. Phelps's title character is a talented painter who is tormented by the claims of marriage and motherhood. Blanchard plausibly suggests that Annie and Sarah "met through James Fields's connections in Portsmouth where he had grown up" (113). It is also possible that they met through Howells, who accepted "The Shore House" for the 1873 *Atlantic* and then encouraged Sarah to develop it into the book that established her reputation—*Deephaven* (1877).

27. See Blanchard, 114 and 123.

28. The phrase is from a letter to Lilian Munger of 8 August 1880, quoted by Blanchard, 123. Celia Thaxter's brothers had bought the Oceanic Hotel a few years before.

29. SOJ to AF, 8 September 1880, Ho. Annie began her *Letters of Sarah Orne Jewett* with this letter. On the inside back page of one of four bluebooks of manuscript poems titled "Manchester 1880" now at the Huntington Library, Annie jotted down the names of the guests she had entertained that summer, listing "Miss Jewett" for one night and "Miss Jewett & Mrs. Clarke" for two.

30. SOJ to AF, 23 November 1880, Morgan Library.

31. SOJ to AF, 12 January 1881, Ho.

32. The phrase is from a letter to an unidentified correspondent dated "August 21," Ho.

33. Annie to "My dear friends," 20 February 1882, Schlesinger Library, Radcliffe Institute, Harvard University.

34. Mary Cowden Clarke to AF, 3 March 1882, HL.

35. CT to SOJ, 23 February 1882, and AF to JGW, 24 February 1882, Ho. In the women's roster of pet names, Annie was Flower and sometimes Mouse or Fuffy; Sarah was Owl, Pinny, or Pinny Lawson; Celia Thaxter was Sandpiper; and the young poet Louise Imogen Guiney was Linnet.

36. SOJ to AF, "tenth of February" [1881], "Thursday" [March 1882?], and "Saturday" [March 1882?], Ho.

37. SOJ to Louisa Beal, 20 May 1882, Ho.

38. The manuscript is in one of Annie's scrapbooks at the Huntington Library and is quoted by Howe, 289.

39. CT to AF, 18 and 24 May 1882, BPL.

40. AF to Mary Jewett, ? May [1882]; SOJ to Mary Jewett, 1 June [1882]; and AF to JGW, 9 June [1882,] Ho.

41. Included in Cary, 48.

42. AF to JGW, 28 June 1882, Ho. Whittier said he shared their pleasures by proxy, advised Sarah to get more rest, and told Annie he understood "what the comfort and joy of her presence must be to thee, and what perfect satisfaction she has in thy company." JGW to AF, 14 July and 15 August 1882, HL.

43. SOJ to Louisa Beal, 18 August 1882, Ho. As Annie told Whittier, Sarah Adams was enjoying herself so much in Europe that she was not eager to return to America.

CHAPTER 17

1. The statements are in an undated draft for a speech at the Huntington Library.

2. The statements are from manuscript fragments in folders dated 1889–91 at the Houghton Library.

3. SOJ to Sara Norton, [3 September 1897,] Ho.

4. Diary 1871–79, Ho, and SOJ to Lucretia Perry, 4 January 1872, Colby College.

5. SOJ to Harriet Preston, incomplete draft of an 1877 letter, Ho. In *Sarah Orne Jewett* (Kittery Point, Me.: The Gundalow Club, 1960), John Frost says a misunderstanding terminated the friendship (53–54), and Paula Blanchard thinks Preston became "offended at something Sarah said or did" after two or three years of friendship (*Sarah Orne Jewett: Her World and Her Work* [Reading, Mass.: Addison Wesley, 1994], 109). In September 1877, after thanking her long-time mentor Theophilus Parsons for his literary advice, Sarah reported her happiness at being with Preston. SOJ to Theophilus Parsons, 17 September 1877, Special Collections, Colby College. Preston, who had recently translated the Provençal writer Frédéric Mistral's *Mireio,* belonged to the club of women writers that Annie convened in the winters of 1877 and 1878. That Sarah harbored no resentment of Preston is suggested by an 1886 letter in which she urged Annie to "read Miss Preston's paper about Pliny the younger in the 'Atlantic'" and by an 1889 letter saying Preston's *Atlantic* article on Russian novels looked interesting. *Letters of Sarah Orne Jewett,* ed. Annie Fields (Boston: Houghton Mifflin, 1911), 29, 42–43.

6. The three-page incomplete and undated manuscript titled "Old and New Friends" is at the Houghton Library.

7. Among Sarah Orne Jewett's many unpublished love poems in the Houghton Library is one dated 23 August 1880 which Josephine Donovan believes is addressed to Annie Fields and "indicates the beginning of their relationship." But it seems far more likely that it was addressed to an earlier friend or (as Donovan also suggests) to a fictive or composite "darling." "The Unpublished Love Poems of Sarah Orne Jewett," *Frontiers* 4 (Fall 1979): 28. The poem begins by asking,

> Do you remember, darling
> A year ago today
> When we gave ourselves to each other
> Before you went away
> At the end of that pleasant summer weather
> Which we had spent by the sea together?

The anniversary prompts a solemn recommitment:

> And so again, my darling
> I give myself to you,
> With graver thought than a year ago
> With love that is deep and true.

The thirty-six-year-old happily married Annie Fields seems an unlikely prototype for the "girl" who "went away" the year before and whose ring the speaker now wears. In August 1880, Annie was still

"Mrs. Fields" to Sarah. Yet the poem certainly expresses the poet's prior experience of emotional growth through the reciprocated love of another woman.

8. The manuscript at the Houghton Library consists of a long paragraph that fills one small sheet and the top half of a second, and an incomplete paragraph that begins midway on a third sheet and breaks off after a few lines on a fourth.

9. Henry James, "Mr. and Mrs. James T. Fields," *Atlantic Monthly* 116 (July 1915): 30.

10. *Letters of SOJ*, 11.

11. The English writer Mary Cowden Clarke used the term "woman-couple" for Annie's "noble" relationship to Sarah, and Howe's daughter Helen is among those who call it a "Boston marriage"— that is, a loving relationship between two unmarried women who share their lives. In *Surpassing the Love of Men: Romantic Friendship and Love between Women from the Renaissance to the Present* (New York: Morrow, 1981), Lilian Faderman calls Annie and Sarah "lesbian," though her definition seems too broad. She acknowledges that women's socially condoned passionate relationships with other women during the nineteenth century did not necessarily include genitality, but she applies the term "lesbian" to any "relationship in which two women's strongest emotions and affections are directed toward each other" (17–18). In "'Women Alone Stir My Imagination': Lesbianism and the Cultural Tradition," *Signs: Journal of Women in Culture and Society* 4 (1979): 718–39, Blanche Wiesen Cook offers a broader definition that avoids virtually all questions of genital sexuality, self-definition, and cultural conceptions of deviance: "women who love women, who choose women to nurture and to create a loving environment in which to work creatively and independently" should be called "lesbians." Certainly Annie Fields and Sarah Orne Jewett loved and nurtured each other, and certainly they hugged and kissed. Yet that does not make them "lesbian" as that term is now generally understood. And it seems worth pointing out that whether in each other's houses or during their travels, they occupied separate bedrooms.

Because Faderman is often cited as an authority on the women's relationship, it also seems worth pointing out that she is sometimes misleading (as in her reference to Sarah's "self-imposed prison in South Berwick"), or simply wrong (as in her statement that "the two women had a support group of three other couples who were engaged in 'Boston marriages'" including Willa Cather and Edith Lewis [201]). Annie's circles of friendship both before and after meeting Sarah included many woman couples: Charlotte Cushman and Emma Stebbins, for example, as well as Anne Whitney and Abby Manning, Alice James and Katharine Loring, and Annie's sister Lissie and Frances Burnap. I find no evidence that any of them relied on "support groups."

In her groundbreaking essay "The Female World of Love and Ritual: Relations between Women in Nineteenth-Century America" (*Signs* 1 [Autumn 1975]: 1–29; included in *Disorderly Conduct: Visions of Gender in Victorian America* [New York: Oxford University Press, 1985]), 53–76, Carroll Smith-Rosenberg convincingly concludes from an extensive analysis of letters and diaries that deep affection between pairs of nineteenth-century women was "socially acceptable and fully compatible with heterosexual marriage," that such pairs "did not form isolated dyads but were normally part of highly integrated networks," and that their relationships were "close, often frolicsome, and surprisingly long lasting and devoted," often marked by "an undeniably romantic and even sensual note." She might have drawn those same conclusions from the diaries and letters of Annie and Sarah. Judith Fryer pursues this argument in "What Goes On in the Ladies Room? Sarah Orne Jewett, Annie Fields and Their Community of Women," *Massachusetts Review* 30 (1989): 610–28.

12. SOJ to JGW, 21 February 1882, included in "'Yours Always Lovingly': Sarah Orne Jewett to John Greenleaf Whittier," ed. Richard Cary, *Essex Institute Historical Collections* 107 (October 1971): 418–19, and SOJ to JGW, 24 February 1882, Ho.

13. SOJ to JGW, 4 April [1882], included in "'Yours Always Lovingly,'" 424–27. Sarah also told Whittier that she would not visit the medium again because having the future too precisely defined might compromise her freedom of choice.

14. AF to SOJ, [1883,] Ho.

15. *A Week Away from Time* (Boston: Roberts Brothers), 1887. Annie's collaborator in reform Mary Lodge wrote the preface, her artist friend Sarah Whitman wrote the conclusion, and the young novelist Owen Wister (the son of Annie's actress friend Fanny Kemble) wrote one of the chapters.

16. Copies are at the Boston Public Library, the Houghton Library, and the Huntington Library.

17. E. E. Hale to AF, 12 August 1885, HL. At Hale's urging, Annie allowed him to publish her name.

18. Records of the Saturday Morning Club, II: 5 (6 January 1883) and II: 7 (19 January 1889), Schlesinger Library, Radcliffe Institute, Harvard University.

19. JGW to AF, 13 October 1883, HL.

20. AF to LWJ, 6 December 1883, HL.

21. Nathan Irvin Huggins, *Protestants against Poverty: Boston's Charities, 1870–1900* (Westport, Conn.: Greenwood, 1971), 57–79. When the Cooperative Society of Visitors was succeeded by the Associated Charities in 1879, Annie began fifteen years of service as a director, followed by twelve years as vice president.

22. AF to Robert Treat Paine, 20 March 1884, Robert Treat Paine Papers, MHS; and AF to John D. Long, 21 February 1881, John Davis Long Papers, MHS, marked "Private."

23. T. W. Higginson to AF, 14 January 1883, HL. The group was an outgrowth of the Social Science Association, he explained, and Clara Barton would talk about the Red Cross at the first meeting.

24. Julia Ward Howe to AF, 12 November 1886, HL.

25. *Wide awake* 25 (December 1886): 87–88, and SOJ to AF, [1886?], Ho. The magazine was edited by Annie's old friend Minnie Pratt.

26. See *Wide awake* 26 (January 1888): 85–87; 25 (April 1887): 342; and 26 (August 1888): 43–49.

27. *Atlantic Monthly* 1883, 818–32; *Harper's* 1884, 457–67; *Century* 1884, 67–79, and 1886, 884–93; and *A Shelf of Old Books* (New York: Scribner's, 1894), 285–305 and 453–76.

28. Samuel Longfellow to AF, 29 September and 9 December 1883 and 12 March [1887]; and Alice Longfellow to AF, 23 August [1884], HL.

Chapter 18

1. JGW to AF, 20 July 1883, and 29 July and 2 October 1885, HL.

2. JGW to AF, 12 October 1886, Ho. The *Letters of John Greenleaf Whittier*, ed. John B. Pickard, 3 vols. (Cambridge: Harvard University Press, 1975), 3:529–30, and in Annie's memoirs of Whittier.

3. JGW to AF, 24 January 1884, 2 April 1886, 23 August 1884, and 10 January [1890], HL; and AF to JGW, 7 September 1884, Ho.

4. JGW to AF, 11 June 1884 and 21 January 1889, HL. In October 1884 after hearing the curious news that Calvin Stowe had tried matchmaking for Sarah, Whittier doubted whether the candidate—a doctor—was "the paragon who is worthy of her"; and the following month he called Sarah "fresh, natural, loveable," praised her "rare intellectual gifts," and said "She is always a pleasant surprise to me. It pleases me to think of you together." JGW to AF, 31 October and ? November 1884, HL.

5. JGW to AF, 24 March 1885, HL.

6. AF to JGW, 19 October 1888, Ho, and JGW to AF, 29 October 1888, HL.

7. JGW to AF, 24 March 1885, HL.

8. AF to JGW, "Friday" [1883?], 2 December 1883, and 22 June 1886, Ho; and JGW to AF, 4 September 1886 and 30 April 1888, HL. According to Pickard, 3:527, Arnold visited Whittier in 1883.

9. JGW to AF, 9 February 1888, HL. Lowell's new poem—on Ruskin—would soon appear in the *Atlantic*.

10. AF to JGW, 2 April [1889?], Ho.

11. AF to JGW, 8 July 1889, Ho.

12. Edith Thomas to AF, 21 March and 1 April 1885; and LL to AF, 10 April 1885, HL. Lucy had already exchanged a few letters with Thomas, and "of course enjoy her vigorous writing very much."

13. Thomas to AF, 1 April 1885; Thomas to SOJ, 4 April 1885; and Thomas to AF, 8 April 1885, HL.

14. During Thomas's first trip to New York in 1881, everyone she met at Mrs. Botta's salon had been struck by her beauty and charm, and her vigorous lyrics soon began appearing in major periodicals. Thomas to AF, 3 February 1886; Thomas to SOJ, 8 June 1886; and Thomas to AF, 18 January and 8 August 1887 and 23 April 1888, HL. Helen Hunt Jackson, Parke Godwin, Edwin Booth, and Elihu Vedder were among the women's many other mutual friends.

15. Edd Winfield Parks, *Charles Egbert Craddock* (Chapel Hill: University of North Carolina Press, 1941), 121–31.

16. Mary Murfree to SOJ, [March 1885,] and Mary Murfree to AF, [March 1885,] HL.

17. Mary Murfree to AF, 5 October 1887, HL.

18. Helen Hunt Jackson to AF, 15 January 1881, HL.

19. JGW to AF, 15 August 1882, HL.

20. Helen Hunt Jackson to AF, 5 January 1883 and 25 May 1884, HL; and AF to JGW, 13 July 1885, Ho.

21. Thirty of Cooke's stories eventually appeared in the *Atlantic,* in addition to thirty in *Harper's* and over forty more in other magazines.

22. Rose Terry Cooke to AF, 10 January 1880 and 21 November 1881, HL. A letter of 21 September 1884 regretted that she had not been home when Annie and Sarah called, declared that she would have waited if she had known they were coming, and urged them to return. In an equally characteristic letter of 1 October 1889—when Cooke was living in Pittsfield but staying in a Boston boarding house—she urged Annie to visit and bring Sarah along, and in the meantime to give Sarah her love.

23. SOJ to AF, n.d., Ho.

24. Sarah Chauncey Woolsey to AF, 16 October 1883 and 21 June 1885, HL.

25. *Sarah Orne Jewett Letters,* ed. Richard Cary (Waterville, Me.: Colby College Press, 1967), 77, and John Frost, *Sarah Orne Jewett* (Kittery Point, Me.: The Gundalow Club, 1960), 99. The group also included Sarah's recently bereaved sister Caroline Eastman and her son Theodore.

26. In *Fifty Years of Boston: A Memorial Volume, Issued in Commemoration of the Tercentenary of 1930,* ed. Elisabeth M. Herlihy (Boston: Subcommittee on Memorial History, 1932), 307, Guiney is identified as a "postmistress in Auburndale, literary hack in Boston, research scholar in Oxford, England, and always a poet." In *Nineteenth Century American Women Poets: An Anthology* (Malden, Mass.: Blackwell's, 1998), 317, Paula Bernat Bennett places her "among the most significant women poets of the *fin de siècle,* and one of the few to whom early modernists acknowledge a debt." She would publish five volumes of poems.

27. LG to AF, 30 September 1884, HL.

28. LG to AF, 9 and 23 February 1886, 27 February 1888, and 7 and 26 January 1889, HL. One hundred twenty-six letters from Guiney to Annie Fields are at the Huntington Library, in addition to scores of others in other repositories.

29. [Louise Quiney,] "Authors at Home: Mrs. James T. Fields in Boston," *The Critic* 29 (4 June 1898): 367–69.

30. LG to AF, February and 30 April 1892, HL. The fund-raisers included Charles Eliot Norton, Harvard's first professor of art history, who was Annie's old friend and the father of Sarah Orne Jewett's friend Sara. Annie's bust of Keats was a copy of the original.

31. LG to AF, [?] 1895, and 15 February 1898, HL.

32. LG to AF, 16 January, 21 February, and 3 March 1910, HL.

33. LG to AF, 29 February 1911, HL. As Sharon O'Brien points out in *Willa Cather: The Emerging Voice* (New York: Oxford University Press, 1987), 150, Cather's 1902 essay "Poets of Our Younger Generation" commended Guiney's "commitment to will, action, and force, . . . frequently expressed in hymns to a chivalric past."

34. LG to AF, 25 October 1911, HL.

35. LG to AF, 7 January 1913, 15 June 1911, and 16 December 1913, HL.

36. Christina Rossetti to AF, 12 January 1887, HL.

37. AF to JGW, 12 April 1884, Ho.

38. Edmund Stedman sent Annie the clipping from a New York newspaper, and further ingratiated himself by saying Sarah was one of the few women writers "whose every page I have read from the first. No one paints our New England *life* with such purity, with so exquisite a *reserve,* with so easy a precision & delicacy, as well as strength of outline. Within her range she is a most perfect artist." Edmund C. Stedman to AF, 28 October 1886, HL.

39. AF to Barrett Wendell, 31 August 1886, Ho.

40. AF to JGW, 29 September 1886, Ho.

41. AF to "Dear Friend," 20 April 1888, University of New Hampshire Library. The palatial hotel designed by the celebrated architects John Carrere and Thomas Hastings—the first major poured-concrete building in the country—had been under construction from 1885 to 1887 (with Italian crafts-

men imported to do the tile and mosaic work), and it would soon attract such notables as John Jacob Astor and Theodore Roosevelt.

42. The item in the *Critic* was presumably written by Charles E. L. Wingate, the paper's Boston correspondent; quoted in Cary, 63. Annie and Sarah would again return to the Ponce de Leon after their trip to the West Indies eight years later.

CHAPTER 19

1. SOJ to Louisa Dresel, 28 October 1891, Special Collections, Colby College.

2. Quotations are from Robert Underwood Johnson, *Remembered Yesterdays* (1923: Boston: Little, Brown, 1929), 392. Of Johnson's twenty-six sections on "Men and Women of Distinction" only the one titled "Mrs. Fields, Sarah Jewett and Madame Blanc" (392–95) is devoted to women. The Johnsons spent a lot of time with Annie and Sarah on the Continent, they all exchanged visits after returning home, and four of Annie's biographical sketches would appear in the *Century*.

3. OWH to AF, 30 June 1892, and JGW to AF, 30 April 1892, HL.

4. Mark Twain to AF, 16 July 1903. I am grateful to Mitchell Adams for providing me with a photocopy of this unpublished letter.

5. SOJ to JGW, [April 1892,] Ho.

6. *Remembered Yesterdays*, 320–21.

7. SOJ to JGW, 9 July 1892, Ho, and SOJ to Alice Howe, in *Letters of Sarah Orne Jewett*, ed. Annie Fields (Boston: Houghton Mifflin, 1911), 97–100.

8. *Remembered Yesterdays*, 394–95.

9. Mrs. Fields, "Notable Women: Mme. Blanc ('Th. Bentzon')," *Century* 66 (May 1903): 134–39. See also Richard Cary, "Miss Jewett and Madame Blanc," *Colby Library Quarterly* 11 (1967): 467–88, and *Letters of SOJ*, 91–92.

10. *Letters of SOJ*, 91–92, and "Mme. Blanc," 137.

11. Mme. Blanc's account of *Things and People in America* (1898) includes admiring references to Annie and Sarah, and Annie's essay on Mme. Blanc in the *Century* was a form of reciprocation. Mme. Blanc continued to publish translations of Sarah's work, Sarah helped translate Mme. Blanc's "Family Life in America" for the *Forum* of March 1896, and that same year both Sarah and Annie arranged to have other essays by Mme. Blanc published in *Scribner's* and the *Century*.

12. AF to JGW, 1 August 1892, Ho.

13. *Letters of SOJ*, 101–02.

14. Two years later, du Maurier's *Trilby* (which he himself illustrated) was spectacularly successful. He died in 1896.

15. *Letters of SOJ*, 89–90.

16. AF to C. D. Warner, 1 January 1896, Watkinson Library, Trinity College, Hartford, Conn.

17. *Letters of SOJ*, 161–62. Although Annie tried to arrange Sarah's letters in chronological order, she sometimes erred, as when she dated this 1896 letter "1899," which led Josephine Donovan among others to assume that the women took a second Caribbean trip. Donovan, *New England Local Colorists: A Woman's Tradition* (New York: Ungar, 1983).

18. AF to Robert Johnson, 13 April 1896, Robert Underwood Johnson Papers, Rare Book and Manuscript Library, Columbia University.

19. Mary became Theodore's guardian after Caroline Eastman's death in April 1897, and she and Sarah thought he would benefit from a trip abroad before entering Harvard in the fall. Annie's unusually sketchy travel record divides the journey into four parts: 1. Before going to France; 2. Provence; 3. La Ferté and Bretagne; and 4. England and return.

20. Frances Hodgson Burnett to AF [April 1898,] HL.

21. *Letters of SOJ*, 156–58.

22. Henry James to AF, 20 August [1898], 5 September [1898], and [12 September 1898], HL.

23. AF to C. D. Warner, 20 February 1900, Watkinson Library, Trinity College, Hartford, Conn.

24. Quotations are from the *Letters of SOJ*—to Sarah Whitman from Athens on 27 March 1900, 171–73; and to Whitman from Megalopolis on 15 April 1900, 173–76.

CHAPTER 20

1. Ethelbert Nevin to AF, 24 July [1899?], HL. Nevin—on whom Willa Cather based Adriance Hilgarde in "A Death in the Desert" and Valentine Ramsey in "Uncle Valentine"—would die in 1901 at the age of thirty-nine. The pianist Jessie Cochrane often spent weeks at a time at Charles Street and Manchester en route to and from Europe; and Mary Cabot Wheelwright was an old friend and neighbor who would later move to New Mexico, where she founded the museum that bears her name. "Our friend Miss Cochrane is here and her music is a true delight," Sarah Orne Jewett once wrote from Manchester to Wheelwright's sister Sarah, saying if the two Wheelwrights could come, Mary could sing when Jessie stopped playing, "*and vice versa!!*" SOJ to Sarah Wheelwright, "Thursday," Special Collections, Colby College, Waterville, Me.

2. Touched by Annie's *Whittier* and a few other books inscribed to "her friend," Modjeska called them "precious tokens of one . . . whose sweet face and words are engraved in my heart forever." Helena Modjeska to AF, 22 May 1879, 5 April 1889, [c. 1894], 20 February 1894, [c. 1895], and 2 March 1898, HL.

3. Ellen Terry to AF, [c. 1890?] and [c. August 1895], HL. Terry had asked James to write the play in February 1895, and he had it ready when she left for America that July. But she never staged it; and two years later James turned the script into a story titled "Summersoft." See Leon Edel, *Henry James, The Treacherous Years: 1895–1901* (New York: Avon, 1969), 107 and 141–42, and Ellen Terry, *Story of My Life* (New York: McClure, 1908), 313–14.

4. I quote from the nine letters from Isabella Gardner to Annie Fields at the Huntington Library, which often give the day and the month but never the year. The note about the Berensons was written sometime before 12 January 1914, since Berenson's letter to Annie of that date (also at the Huntington Library) reported that Mrs. Gardner's gift of *Authors and Friends* would "remind us of the too charming evening we spent with you." In *The Art of Scandal: The Life and Times of Isabella Stewart Gardner* (New York: HarperCollins, 1997), Douglass Shand-Tucci briefly discusses Gardner's friendship with Annie, Sarah, and Louise Imogen Guiney, unequivocally asserts that Sarah and Guiney were lesbians, and identifies Guiney as Gardner's link to the "Boston intelligentsia" (73, 84, 131–32).

5. Isabella Gardner to SOJ, [25 October 1902] and [26 October, 1902,] SPNEA.

6. Louisa Beal to Mary Jewett, [26 October 1902] and [27 October 1902,] SPNEA.

7. Charles McKim to AF, 1 March 1891, HL.

8. AF to Walter H. Page, [1899], Ho. Whitman's best known works include the Brooks Memorial Window at Trinity Church, the Harvard window, and the many paintings of the early eighties which she bequeathed to the Boston Museum of Fine Arts. Paula Blanchard notes that "there were small Whitman windows in both Annie's house and the Jewett house in Berwick" (*Sarah Orne Jewett: Her World and Her Work* [Cambridge, Mass.: Addison-Wesley, 1994], 218). Sarah Orne Jewett prepared a loving preface for the *Letters of Sarah Wyman Whitman* (1907), and Annie's *Letters of Sarah Orne Jewett* include fifteen to "Dearest S.W."

9. John Singer Sargent to AF, 10 May 1882, HL.

10. Quotations are from Sargent's undated notes of the nineties to Annie Fields at the Huntington Library.

11. Elihu Vedder to AF, 10 April 1880, and 9 October, 23 November, and 14 December 1894, HL.

12. Frances Willard to AF, 4 June 1897, and Jane Addams to AF, 13 February 1899 and November 1911, HL. In her letter of February 1899, Addams anticipated telling Annie about a conference she had just attended, and praised an essay of Annie's she had just read. The women had become closer friends by November 1911, when Addams thanked Annie for the Jewett *Letters* and a "dear letter" which pleased her "even more than Col Roosevelt's," then anticipated seeing her in Boston.

13. Agnes Irwin to AF, 25 March 1895, 19 November 1894, and 8 March 1898, HL.

14. AF to JGW, 24 April [1890], Ho. She also mentioned that Sarah was so weakened by tonsillitis that she could barely sit up, which perhaps heightened both women's interest in facilitating women's access to excellent medical training.

15. See *The Making of a Feminist: Early Journals and Letters of M. Carey Thomas*, ed. Marjorie Housepian Dopkin (Kent, Ohio: Kent State University Press, 1979). Mary Garrett was the daughter of John Work Garrett, a president of the Baltimore and Ohio Railroad, and the intimate friend of M. Carey

Thomas, who became president of Bryn Mawr College. In 1904 Garrett moved into the Bryn Mawr deanery with Thomas, who inherited her considerable estate eleven years later.

Chapter 21

1. William Dean Howells, *Literary Friends and Acquaintance* ([Boston: Houghton Mifflin, 1900] Bloomington: Indiana University Press, 1968), 40–41, and *Life in Letters of William Dean Howells,* ed. Mildred Howells, 2 vols. (Garden City, N.Y.: Doubleday Doran, 1928) 2:348–49. After telling Winifred how glad he was to have seen Annie the summer before she died, Howells wished he "had gone oftener to see her in Boston" but consoled himself by saying "we cannot treat people as if we expected them to die."

2. WDH to AF, 19 December 1875, 16 August 1866, [August?] 1878, and 15 December 1886, HL.

3. WDH to AF, 10 December 1881, HL.

4. AF to WDH, 11 January 1872, Ho. Perhaps influenced by Annie's request, Howells quickly accepted the poem that Thaxter had just submitted.

5. WDH to AF, 1 April 1874, HL.

6. WDH to AF, 25 November 1880, 9 and 31 January 1892, and 25 November 1900, HL; and AF to WDH, 26 November 1900, Ho.

7. Howells's best-known novel centers on a nouveau-riche paint manufacturer who ends up choosing moral integrity over financial success and social prestige. His contributions to the Associated Charities define him as a man with a social conscience.

8. WDH to AF, 1 March 1886, 14 June and 4 February 1890, and 9 January 1892, HL. According to William Alexander in *William Dean Howells: The Realist as Humanist* (New York: Burt Franklin, 1981), 31–32, it is impossible to fix the precise years when Howells was an official Associated Charities visitor and a financial donor.

9. WDH to AF, 21 January 1893 and 25 November 1894, HL.

10. WDH to AF, 13 December 1896, HL. Another bond during Annie's widowhood was Howells's admiration for Sarah Orne Jewett, as when in 1890 he wished she would keep writing "till the crack of doom. Though . . . why should doom crack, anyway?" WDH to AF, 4 February 1890, HL.

11. WDH to AF, 21 February and, 4 March 1907 and 3 May 1913, HL.

12. AF to WDH, 26 November 1867, Ho; and WDH to AF, 19 July 1885, HL.

13. AF to WDH, 26 November 1900, Ho.

14. See Charles E. Samuels, *Thomas Bailey Aldrich* (New York: Twayne, 1965); Ferris Greenslet, *The Life of Thomas Bailey Aldrich* (Boston: Houghton Mifflin, 1908); Lilian W. Aldrich, *Crowding Memories* (Boston: Houghton Mifflin, 1920); and Ellen B. Ballou, *The Building of the House: Houghton Mifflin's Formative Years* (Boston: Houghton Mifflin, 1970), 172–74, 353–80.

15. TBA to AF, 12 November 1886, HL.

16. Although as *Atlantic* editor Aldrich was sometimes criticized for indolence, for insufficient interest in the new, and for excessive concern with style, most of his judgments were discerning, including his decisions to publish such important new writers as Thomas Hardy.

17. TBA to Edmund C. Stedman, 20 November 1880, quoted in Greenslet, 139.

18. TBA to AF, 16 July 1883, 10 October 1884, and 11 March 1890, HL.

19. Ballou, 377–79; and TBA to AF, 24 April and 3 August 1884, HL.

20. TBA to AF, 5 October 1883, HL. I have found no evidence that Annie ever wrote such a paper or even proposed it to Alden.

21. TBA to AF, 27 January 1900; and Bliss Perry to AF, 13 February 1900, HL.

22. TBA to AF, 30 March 1895, HL.

23. Nine years later, he again fondly recalled "the evening at Mrs. Botta's." HA to AF, 23 December 1897 and 15 November 1906, HL. Annie's five-page unpublished biographical sketch of Mrs. Botta at the Huntington Library pays tribute to a woman who was in many ways like herself, a woman who wrote professionally, held "her gentle way in perfect womanliness," worked unselfishly for others throughout her long life, and whose "ready hospitality" was a "key to her greatness." Annie probably began the sketch after Mrs. Botta's death in 1891 but never completed it.

24. The first part of "The Eleusinia" appeared in September 1859 and the second in August 1860.

25. James C. Austin, *Fields of the Atlantic Monthly* (San Marino, Calif.: Huntington Library, 1953), 363–64, and J. Henry Harper, *The House of Harper* (New York: Harper, 1912), 220–22. Alden's reiterated recollection of first meeting Annie at Mrs. Botta's seems to contradict his statement to Harper that the Fieldses looked him up when they got to New York and invited him to dinner that night, though perhaps they simply took him along to Mrs. Botta's. In *The House of Harper* (New York: Harper, 1967), 79, Eugene Exman describes Alden as a "gentle man with deep-set eyes and a brown beard, a man of sound literary judgment and of sympathy and understanding." He helped many authors with revisions and, by 1885, won a wider readership for *Harper's Monthly* than any similar magazine enjoyed.

26. Alden to AF, 6 and 15 February 1875, HL.

27. Alden to AF, 12 November 1890, HL.

28. Alden to AF, 31 August 1891, HL. Although Alden had doubts about the subtitle "To a Poet," he left the decision to her. "The Singing Shepherd" appeared without a subtitle in *Harper's,* but Annie included a slightly revised dedication—"To a Poet's Memory"—in her book. Possibly she intended the poem as a tribute to Otto Dresel (1826–90), the eminent German-born concert pianist and composer who was her good friend and neighbor, though it seems more likely that she had Longfellow in mind. The speaker celebrates the shepherd who sang while he climbed ever higher and longs to follow him, then concludes by saying the singer has departed but continues to shepherd his flock. In the *Harper's* illustration, a shepherd stands in a craggy Arcadian landscape looking off into the distant clouds.

29. Alden to AF, 6 February and 27 April 1875 and 24 April 1890, HL.

30. Alden to AF, 15 February 1875, HL.

31. AF to Alden, 28 October 1892, Morgan Library.

32. Alden to AF, 5 September 1894, HL.

33. Alden to AF, 19 March 1909, and to SOJ, 26 December 1896, HL.

34. Annie Alden to AF, 24 February 1910, HL.

35. Alden to AF, 19 April 1912, HL.

36. Alden to AF, 23 December 1897, HL.

37. Alden to AF, 15 March 1906, HL.

38. Although Ballou faults Annie Fields for requesting the same page rate for her prose that Sarah Orne Jewett received, Sarah had bargained for an increased rate for a poem by saying "AF had 30 for last one in the Atlantic—At least I think she did" (377–79).

39. Robert Underwood Johnson, *Remembered Yesterdays* (Boston: Little, Brown, 1923), 392. Ballou exceeds her evidence when she says "Houghton, Mifflin would have but the smallest regret in parting with Mrs. Fields. Losing Miss Jewett would be a very different matter," and when she attributes criticisms of Scudder expressed by Aldrich, Mark DeWolfe Howe, and Ellery Sedgwick to "the malice of Charles Street" (377–79, 436). And though she also says Sarah and Annie ignored Scudder's requests for manuscripts until 1894, Sarah submitted her account of Phillips Brooks's funeral in January 1893 and it appeared anonymously in "The Contributors' Club" that April. *Sarah Orne Jewett Letters,* ed. Richard Cary (Waterville, Me.: Colby College Press, 1967), 80–81.

40. Ballou, 436.

41. Cary, 104.

42. AF to Henry Oscar Houghton, 8 September 1894, Ho. She did not mention that Rose Lamb would coedit the volume. Her letters to George Mifflin as well as those to Houghton usually include such personal matters as invitations to Manchester and reports on Sarah's health.

43. As another "possible resource," he had asked a Mr. Howard who had some Stowe letters to send them to Annie. Scudder to AF, 11 December 1896, HL.

44. Scudder to AF, 18 July 1897, HL.

45. Scudder to AF, 21 August 1900, HL. He asked whether Annie had the manuscript of "Chiefly About War Matters" and, if so, whether she would allow him to restore the passages Fields had persuaded Hawthorne to drop.

46. Page to AF, 22 June 1896, HL. "The Author of 'Uncle Tom's Cabin'" by Richard Burton appeared in the August *Century* (698–704). While the *Century* associate editor Robert Johnson was visiting Sarah earlier that summer, he said, as she wrote to Annie, that the Burton essay was "*very*

poor—He was simply destroyed when I told him about yours, but he might have known." SOJ to AF, "Friday morning," [1896,] Ho.

47. Page to AF, 9 July 1897, HL, and AF to Page, [1899,] Ho. After resigning from the *Atlantic,* Page moved to New York and became a partner in the new publishing house of Doubleday, Page.

48. Perry to AF, 13 February 1900, HL.

49. Perry to AF, January 1905, Ho. Surely Annie saw something of herself in Saint Teresa—a clever, witty, busy, and enterprising woman who established her own convent, enjoyed strong friendships with other women, respected the needs of the body, and disliked public exposure.

50. Perry to AF, 20 December 1904 and 17 October 1907, Ho.

51. He did as she asked. AF to Gilder [1901], Richard Watson Gilder Papers, NYPL. Annie received the commission only after Sarah refused it and told Robert Johnson that "Mrs. Fields does such things better than I ever could, should you care to ask her, and I would lend a hand if my hand were needed." SOJ to Johnson, 5 December [1901], in Cary, 146. Johnson became editor of the *Century* after Gilder's death in 1909, a position he retained for four years.

52. AF to Gilder, 8 July 1886, NYPL.

53. AF to Gilder, 20 September 1887, NYPL.

54. AF to Robert Underwood Johnson Jr., and Richard Watson Gilder Jr., 25 April 1894, and AF to Katherine McMahon Johnson, 30 April 1894, Robert Underwood Johnson Papers, Rare Book and Manuscript Library, Columbia University.

55. AF to Johnson, 13 April 1896, Columbia University.

56. AF to Gilder, 25 and 30 March 1898, NYPL, and AF to Johnson, 9 April 1898 and 11 May 1899, Columbia University.

57. AF to Gilder, "Christmas 1897," NYPL.

58. AF to Gilder, 22 March [1909], NYPL.

59. E. L. Burlingame to AF, 29 December 1887 and 5 January 1888, HL.

60. Burlingame to AF, 4 February 1889, HL.

61. Sounding a personal note, Scribner also recalled "our voyage to Gibraltar" and sent regards to Sarah. Charles Scribner to AF, 9 May 1894, HL.

62. Warner to AF, 29 November 1880, HL.

63. AF to Warner, 4 February 1886, HL, and 24 March [1894] and 23 August 1900, Watkinson Library, Trinity College, Hartford, Conn.

64. Sarah Adams to AF, "Monday," and AF to Warner, 23 August 1900, Watkinson Library.

65. Warner to AF, 25 July 1896, HL; and AF to Warner, 6 January 1897, Watkinson Library.

66. Warner to AF, 5 September 1897, HL.

67. AF to Warner, 6, 16, and 19 September 1897, Watkinson Library; and AF to Gilder, "Christmas" [1897], NYPL.

68. AF to Warner, 4 July 1899, Watkinson Library; and Warner to AF, 26 November 1899, HL.

69. Annie Fields, *Charles Dudley Warner* (New York: McClure, Phillips, 1904), 152.

70. Helen Howe, "The Little World of Boston Letters," *The Gentle Americans 1864–1960: Biography of a Breed* (New York: Harper, 1965), 73–94, and AF to Mark DeWolfe Howe, 21 October 1895, Ho. Quincy Howe would later become a well-known journalist.

71. AF to Howe, 11 October 1896, Ho.

72. AF to Howe, 15 September 1896, Ho. The following year she enlisted his help on the Stowe Memorial Fund.

73. AF to Howe, 29 and 30 August and 9 September 1899, Ho. She also cooperated by requesting Houghton Mifflin's permission to quote from Hawthorne books they had published. She had agreed to do the biography for Small and Maynard "knowing that you would not care for such a thing," she told George Mifflin, then amplified the point by saying she would have done the work for him "if you needed it, which you do not!" AF to George Mifflin, 31 August 1899, Ho.

74. AF to MDH, "Wednesday" [1910?] Ho.

75. Letter of 12 April 1911, quoted by Helen Howe, 84 and Judith A. Roman, *Annie Adams Fields: The Spirit of Charles Street* (Bloomington: Indiana University Press, 1990), 162.

76. Helen Howe, 75.

77. Ibid., 90–94, 74.

78. The papers about Annie Fields's estate are at the Houghton Library. She wrote the note about destroying what was of no public value in February 1910, and her revised statement of September 1911 reiterated that Howe was her literary executor and that she wanted most of her own letters destroyed.

79. Howe, *Memories of a Hostess* (Boston: Atlantic Monthly Press, 1922), 3.

80. Ibid., 285–86, 305.

81. Ballou, 577–79. Although Ballou says Houghton Mifflin published all of Annie's books after 1878, Harper's published her *Whittier* in 1893, Scribner's published *A Shelf of Old Books* in 1894, and McClure, Phillips published her *Charles Dudley Warner* in 1904.

CHAPTER 22

1. *Tales of New England, Betty Leicester: A Story for Girls,* and *Strangers and Wayfarers* all appeared in 1890, followed by *A Native of Winby and Other Tales* (1893), *Betty Leicester's English Xmas* (1894), *The Life of Nancy* (1895), and *The Queen's Twin and Other Stories* (1899).

2. Two full-page illustrations accompanied Annie's translation. Her admiration for Guérin dated back to 1867, when she and Jamie read a collection of Eugénie Guérin's letters to her beloved brother Maurice.

3. AF to Robert Underwood Johnson, 13 June 1899, Century Company Records, NYPL.

4. "Mrs. James T. Fields," *Time and the Hour,* 5 (17 April 1897): 6–7; and "Mrs. James T. Fields in Boston," *The Critic* 29 (4 June 1898): 367–69.

5. Since both "wild endive" and "succory" designate the blue-flowered chicory *cithorium intybus,* the change was not for botanical accuracy. Perhaps Annie simply preferred the more staccato sound of "Blue Succory," but she might have been punning on the word "succor" while also anticipating her reference in the poem to "heaven's blue."

6. Although Judith A. Roman (*Annie Adams Fields: The Spirit of Charles Street* [Bloomington: Indiana University Press, 1990]), thinks the poem "seems to be about the Fieldses' friendship with Dickens and the subsequent friendship between Annie and Georgina" Hogarth (130), the grieving speaker's "old, old love" is probably her husband or Sarah Orne Jewett. The poem recalls a radiantly happy summer day when her beloved looked up from a book to share its pleasures.

7. Grace King to AF, 19 November 1895, and Edmund C. Stedman to AF, 17 November 1895, HL. "Objective" during the period usually referred to narrative or dramatic poems, as against "subjective" or lyrical poems.

8. As Cleveland Amory puts it in *The Proper Bostonians* (New York: Dutton, 1947), 126–29, Helen Choate Bell (a daughter of the distinguished lawyer Rufus Choate) was "the most famous Society wit in the city's history," and "often called the Complete Boston Woman."

9. For example, "Speaking of dining at Taft's, . . . Dr. Holmes said: 'The host himself is worth seeing. He is the one good *uncooked* thing at his table.'"

10. *Century* 58 (May 1899): 122–31. The Fields Collection at the Huntington Library includes 61 letters from the Cowden Clarkes to the Fieldses between 1860 and 1896—those after 1877 from Mary Cowden Clarke alone and after 1881 to Annie alone. Mary Cowden Clarke's publications include a biography of her beloved father titled *Sketches of Writers* (written in collaboration with her husband), tales of *The Girlhood of Shakespeare's Heroines,* and an autobiography titled *My Long Life.* See Richard D. Altick, *The Cowden Clarkes* (New York: Oxford University Press, 1948).

11. Mary Cowden Clarke to AF, 2 January and 3 March 1882, 5 February and 23 October 1883, 14 January and 24 March 1885, and 31 December 1886, HL.

12. Mary Cowden Clarke to AF, 9 February 1889, HL.

13. Mary Cowden Clarke to AF, 27 August 1889 and 21 November 1894, HL.

14. *Century* 58 (July 1899): 442–46. Annie quotes from a letter "M. E. Lewes" sent James T. Fields dated 16 April 1871, and from the three letters addressed to her on 16 May 1872, 5 June 1874, and 19 February 1879.

15. An early letter from Mme. Blanc to "Chère Mrs. Fields" consults her and Sarah "ci-jointe" about the proper response to a Sadakichi Hartmann, whose book included an unauthorized printed rec-

ommendation by "Th. Bentzon, critique pour la littérature americaine à la Revue des Deux Mondes!!!!" Mme. Blanc to AF, 19 May [1892?], HL. Soon afterward, Annie became "Chère Annie." Thomas Wentworth Higginson so admired Annie's paper on Mme. Blanc that he requested permission to use it as a preface to a new edition of his own book about her. T. W. Higginson to AF, 7 December 1907, HL.

16. *The Condition of Woman in the United States,* tr. Abby Langdon Alger (Boston: Roberts, 1895), 122–31, 142–44.

17. A week later, Annie sent a Baltimore editor "a paragraph about M. Brunetière which I think you may like to find a place for in 'The Herald,'" and said "His lectures are really admirable." AF to Mr. Holmes, 29 March 1897, Collection of John William Pye. I am grateful to Mr. Pye for sending me a copy of this letter.

18. *Choses et Gens d'Amérique* (Paris: Calmann Lévy, 1898).

19. Vernon Paget, Isabella Stewart Gardner, and Mary Garrett are among the many other women who figure in Annie's and Sarah's correspondence with Mme. Blanc. Annie's professional assistance to Mme. Blanc included answering her questions about such matters as copyright law and acting as her intermediary with a few publishers. Prodding Charles Dudley Warner on Mme. Blanc's behalf, Annie wrote, "by your instigation she has written for some New York paper 'The World's Best Literature' and she hears nothing of a portrait she has sent over and nothing about the work. Her own paper is finished but she can use it elsewhere if the picture and autograph will come back—but what to do about the other authors, Heredia, Brunetiere and the rest." AF to C. D. Warner, 23 November 1896, Watkinson Library, Trinity College, Hartford, Conn. As Robert Johnson gratefully recalled in his *Remembered Yesterdays* (Boston: Little, Brown, 1923), he and his wife "owed to Mrs. Fields our introduction to Madame Blanc, who was one of the most refined and intellectual women I have ever known" (393–94).

20. At Henry Alden's request, Annie Fields gave the southern novelist Grace King an introduction to Mme. Blanc. King visited Mme. Blanc twice and entertained her once, and the two women published essays on each other. See Robert Bush, *Grace King: A Southern Destiny* (Baton Rouge: Louisiana State University Press, 1983), 118–20, 179–82, 237–40.

21. TBA to AF, 27 January 1900; and Bliss Perry to AF, 13 February 1900, HL.

22. WDH to AF, 25 November 1900, Ho.

23. Harriet Prescott Spofford, *A Little Book of Friends* (Boston: Little, Brown, 1915), 15.

CHAPTER 23

1. Laura Richards to AF, 5 February 1901, HL.

2. AF to Bliss Perry, 20 December 1904, Ho. The commonplace book is at the Massachusetts Historical Society.

3. Burgess (1866–1951) was famous for his four-line quipping rhyme on Henri Bergson's then-popular philosophy of empathic perception which begins "I never saw a purple cow" and ends "I'd rather see than be one."

4. Tomasso Salvini was an enormously successful Italian actor who played Othello to Edward Booth's Iago during his American tour in 1886, retired four years later, and published an autobiographical memoir in 1893.

5. Mark DeWolfe Howe's recollection is quoted by his daughter Helen in *The Gentle Americans, 1864–1960: Biography of a Breed* (New York: Harper, 1965), 91, a slight expansion of his statement in *Memories of a Hostess* (Boston: Atlantic Monthly Press, 1922), 10.

6. Henry James, "Mr. and Mrs. James T. Fields," *Atlantic Monthly* 116 (July 1915): 31.

7. Alice Meynell to AF, 14 November [1901] and 18 February [1902], HL; and SOJ to Sarah Norton, 20 March 1902, in *Letters of Sarah Orne Jewett,* ed. Annie Fields (Boston: Houghton Mifflin, 1911), 181.

8. Alice Meynell to "My darling Dimpling," in Viola Meynell, *Alice Meynell, A Memoir* (London: Jonathan Cape, 1929), 192; and Alice Meynell to AF, 11 April [1902], HL.

9. SOJ to Alice Meynell, 14 December 1904, in *Letters of SOJ,* 199–200.

10. Alice Meynell to AF, 7 December [1909], 24 March [1910], 11 November [1910], 2 November

[1911], and 12 January [1912], HL. Meynell's January letter also reported meeting Annie's friend Eva von Blomberg.

11. Mrs. Humphry Ward to AF, [1899] and 28 February 1902, HL.

12. Annie's report follows her account of the Home Club. See note 2.

13. *Julia Ward Howe 1819–1910*, ed. Laura E. Richards and Maud Howe Elliott, 2 vols. (Boston: Houghton Mifflin, 1925), 2:422.

14. According to John Sutherland, *Mrs. Humphry Ward: Eminent Victorian, Preeminent Edwardian* (New York: Oxford University Press, 1991), 288, Mrs. Ward had sent the manuscript to her English publisher in February 1908, before sailing for America. The opening chapters had already appeared serially in *Harper's* when Annie saw the yet unfinished final chapter.

15. *Letters of SOJ*, 233, 236–37.

16. Mary Augusta Ward to AF, 24 February 1909 and 27 October 1911, HL. The *Letters of SOJ* includes two letters to Mrs. Ward, two to her daughter, and one to them both.

17. Mary Augusta Ward to AF, 27 August 1910 and 24 February 1909, HL. Mrs. Ward evidently did not know that Willa Cather had sent Annie Fields the opening chapters of *Daphne* the summer before, saying they were scheduled for publication in *McClure's* though she considered them dull and stupid.

18. Janet Penrose Trevelyan, *The Life of Mrs. Humphry Ward* (New York: Dodd, Mead, 1923), 222–23.

19. Mary Augusta Ward to AF, 25 January 1911, HL.

20. Mary Augusta Ward to AF, 28 January 1913 and 2 January 1914, HL. As Sutherland points out, the portrait of a feminist fanatic based on the suffrage leader Christabel Pankhurst was the prime attraction of the poorly reviewed, "shrill and polemical" novel (332–33).

21. Ethel Arnold to AF, 28 April 1910 and 12 December 1911, HL. Arnold's protestations of cowardice and weariness are consistent with Sutherland's characterization of her as a prickly, sickly, and neurotic dilettante who traded on her relationship to her famous sister (169–70). Similar expressions of gratitude came from other English visitors including the poet and essayist Margaret L. Woods— a good friend of Ethel Arnold and her whole family—who in the fall of 1911 thanked Annie for trying to arrange lectures for her at area colleges and said she would be delighted to "rest at your house," certain Annie would agree that education is "a thing one breathes in rather than has rubbed in." Margaret L. Woods to AF, 26 September, 13 October, and 12 November 1911, HL.

22. Ethel Arnold to AF, 20 January 1912, HL.

23. Ethel Arnold to AF, 3 February 1912, HL.

24. The notation is in a diary and commonplace book at the Massachusetts Historical Society.

25. May Morris to AF, 25 September 1910, HL.

26. May Morris to AF, [25 December] 1911 and 22 October 1914, HL.

27. May Sinclair to AF, 19 September 1908, 9 January 1909, and 16 July 1912, HL.

28. May Sinclair to AF, 14 December 1909 and 3 August 1910, HL.

CHAPTER 24

1. "148 Charles Street," in Cather, *Not Under Forty* (New York: Knopf, 1936), 52–75. Though her opening pages were new, the rest of the essay had first appeared in 1922 as a review of *Memories of a Hostess* for *The Literary World*. Mrs. Brandeis, the wife of the future Supreme Court justice, was a sister of Cather's friend Pauline Goldmark, a New York social reformer.

2. For further discussion of this first meeting, see Sharon O'Brien, *Willa Cather: The Emerging Voice* (New York: Oxford University Press, 1987), 291 and 314–22; James Woodress, *Willa Cather: Her Life and Art* (New York: Pegasus, 1970), 126; and Phyllis C. Robinson, *Willa: The Life of Willa Cather* (New York: Doubleday, 1983), 141.

3. WSC to AF, "Wednesday" [1908] and "Monday" [1908], HL.

4. SOJ to WSC, 17 August 1908, included in *Letters of Sarah Orne Jewett*, ed. Annie Fields (Boston: Houghton Mifflin, 1911), 234–35.

5. WSC to AF, 29 August [1908]. I am grateful to Mitchell Adams for providing me with a photocopy of this unpublished letter.

6. "148 Charles Street," 69. That witty statement reveals Cather (in O'Brien's words) as "the dutiful and docile daughter seeking to please a matriarch whom she both loves and fears by modifying and modulating her voice and self" (314).

7. WSC to AF, [September ? 1908]. I am grateful to Mitchell Adams for providing me with a photocopy of this unpublished letter.

8. WSC to AF, "Tuesday" [1908], HL, and WSC to SOJ, 24 October 1908, Ho. The novel—later published as *Daphne*—was serialized from January to June 1909.

9. WSC to SOJ, 24 October 1908, Ho. "On the Gull's Road" appeared in the December *McClure's* and "The Enchanted Bluff" appeared in *Harper's* a few months later.

10. SOJ to WSC, 27 November 1908, in *Letters of SOJ*, 245–47.

11. SOJ to WSC, 13 December 1908, in *Letters of SOJ*, 247–48. Sharon O'Brien rightly reads this letter as "the sign of the first mentoring relationship between two major American women writers" (344).

12. WSC to SOJ, 17 December 1908, Ho.

13. WSC to AF, 27 June 1909, Ho.

14. WSC to AF, 13 July 1909, Ho. As Cather told Annie's niece Frances Wallace in 1935, many of her fondest memories centered on Thunderbolt Hill. WSC to Frances Wallace, 2 August 1935. I am grateful to Mitchell Adams for providing me with a photocopy of this unpublished letter.

15. Elizabeth Shepley Sergeant, *Willa Cather: A Memoir* (Philadelphia: Lippincott, 1953), 40, 64–65.

16. Amy Lowell kept her guests waiting, but eventually appeared and took her Keats manuscripts out of the safe to show them. When Woodberry lifted one up, however, Lowell declared that only she could touch them. Cather had carefully edited her account of the episode for fear of distressing Annie, but Annie was distressed nonetheless. See Woodress, 239.

17. AF to George Woodberry, [?1911] and 12 August 1911, Ho; and George Woodberry to AF, 24 May 1911, HL.

18. WSC to AF, 27 June 1912, HL. Cather quoted the Balzac line and expatiated on her new understanding of it in letters to Sergeant and Guiney, but confided her erotic interest in Julio only to Sergeant. See Sergeant, 84, and O'Brien, 427.

19. WSC to AF, 24 July 1912, HL.

20. "Willa Cather Talks of Work," *Philadelphia Record*, 9 August 1913, in *The Kingdom of Art: Willa Cather's First Principles and Critical Statements 1893–1896*, ed. Bernice Slote (Lincoln: University of Nebraska Press, 1966), 446–49.

21. In his autobiography *Under the Bridge* (New York: Literary Classics, 1942), 78, Greenslet at once mocked and celebrated Annie and Sarah as two "great ladies with childlike hearts" who were "ready to giggle girlishly at any slightly malicious anecdote of the Boston great, or to expound their joint philosophy of the happy life, which consisted quite simply of taking short views," then distinguished between them by saying Annie Fields carried "the torch of an older tradition" while Sarah Orne Jewett refuted the proposition "that an artist cannot be a lady, or a lady an artist."

22. LG to AF, [1 May 1910?] HL.

23. Ellen Terry, *Story of My Life* (New York: McClure's, 1908), 313–14.

24. LG to AF, 15 June 1911 and 16 December 1913, HL.

25. When Cather moved to Park Avenue, the Keats bust again had a place of honor on the mantle. Woodress, 243.

26. WSC to Boylston Beal, 16 December 1936, tipped into his copy of *Not Under Forty* at the Boston Athenaeum. Cather told Beal she recalled hearing his aunt talk about him, recalled the first time they met, and recalled receiving the Keats bust from him.

27. WSC to Mark DeWolfe Howe, 11 November 1931, Ho. Four letters from Cather to Annie Fields that were inherited by Annie's grandniece Nancy Bole were given to the Huntington Library in 1986. At least three others remain in family hands.

CHAPTER 25

1. This quotation, like all others that follow and are not otherwise documented, is from the diary and commonplace book that Annie intermittently kept from August 1907 until "the year after dear

Sarahs going 1909" and then kept more sporadically for several more years, now part of the Fields papers at the Massachusetts Historical Society.

2. Many of those letters are at the Houghton Library.

3. AF to Lilian Aldrich, 24 June 1909, Ho.

4. AF to MDH, "Wednesday" [1910?], Ho.

5. *Letters of Sarah Orne Jewett*, ed. Annie Fields (Boston: Houghton Mifflin, 1911), 3–5.

6. Letter of 12 April 1911, quoted by Helen Howe, *The Gentle Americans, 1864–1960: Biography of a Breed* (New York: Harper, 1965), 84, and by Judith A. Roman, *Annie Adams Fields: The Spirit of Charles Street* (Bloomington: Indiana University Press, 1990), 162.

7. *Letters of SOJ*, 6, 9, 41, 252–53.

8. The phrase is Richard H. Brodhead's in *Cultures of Letters: Scenes of Reading and Writing in Nineteenth-Century America* (Chicago: University of Chicago Press, 1993), 153.

INDEX

Note: References to illustrations in the gallery following page 158 are given as *illus.*

Rita K. Gollin was born in Brooklyn, New York, and educated at Queens College and the University of Minnesota, from which she received her Ph.D. in English and American Literature in 1961. She has been awarded fellowships from the National Endowment for the Humanities, the Huntington Library, and the American Association of University Women, among others, and has served as president of the Nathaniel Hawthorne Society and the Northeast Modern Language Association. Among Professor Gollin's publications are *Prophetic Pictures: Hawthorne's Knowledge and Uses of the Visual Arts* (1991), *Portraits of Nathaniel Hawthorne: An Iconography* (1983), and *Nathaniel Hawthorne and the Truth of Dreams* (1979), as well as numerous scholarly editions, essays, and papers on nineteenth-century American literature. She is currently Distinguished Professor of English at the State University of New York College at Geneseo and lives in Rochester, New York, and Mashpee, Massachusetts, with her husband Richard. They have three children and six grandchildren.